MEDICAL MISTAKES

Key Medical Issues in Clinical Negligence Cases

Published by:
Claerhout Publishing
6 Woodstock Avenue
London W13 9UG
United Kingdom

ISBN 978 1 905895 00 7

British Library Cataloguing in Publication Date
A catalogue record of this book is available from the British Library

Cover design by Metaphors Ltd., United Kingdom
Printed and bound in Great Britain by Antony Rowe

MEDICAL MISTAKES

Key Medical Issues in Clinical Negligence Cases

Editor

CHARLES FOSTER

CLAERHOUT PUBLISHING

CONTENTS

EDITOR

Charles Foster, MA (Cantab), Vet MB, MRCVS, of the Inner Temple, Barrister, Outer Temple Chambers, London

CONTRIBUTORS

Professor Alan R Aitkenhead, BSc MB ChB MD FRCA, Professor of Anaesthesia, University of Nottingham and Honorary Consultant Anaesthetist, University Hospital, Queen's Medical Centre, Nottingham

Dr. Caroline Berry, MB BS, PhD, FRCP, formerly Consultant Clinical Geneticist, Guy's Hospital, London

Dr. Roger Blackwood, FRCP, Consultant Cardiologist, Thames Valley Nuffield Hospital, Wexham

Dr. Sarah Burnett, MB, BS, MRCP, FRCR, Consultant Radiologist, Hospital of St. John and St. Elizabeth, London

Alex Chalk, BA (Oxon), of the Middle Temple, Barrister, 6 King's Bench Walk, London

John R. Cherry, MB, BS, FRCS, Honorary Consultant Otolaryngologist, East Lancashire Hospitals NHS Trust, Royal Blackburn Hospital, Blackburn

Dr. John Cotterill, BSc, MD, FRCP, formerly Consultant Dermatologist , Leeds General Infirmary.

Dr. W.J. Ken Cumming, BSc, MD, FRCPI, FRCP, FAE, MEWI, CUEW, Consultant Neurologist, Neuroscience Unit, Alexandra Hospital, Cheadle, Cheshire

Dr Roger Evans, FRCP, Consultant in Emergency Medicine, The Emergency Unit, University Hospital of Wales, Cardiff

Stephen Evans, Partner, Hempsons Solicitors

Mr. Anthony Johnson, MD, FRCOG, Consultant Obstetrician and Gynaecologist, Jessop Hospital for Women, Sheffield

Stephen Kennedy, MA (Oxon), MD, MRCOG, Clinical Reader, Nuffield Department of Obstetrics & Gynaecology, University of Oxford and Honorary Consultant Gynaecologist, The Women's Centre, John Radcliffe Hospital, Oxford

Mr. R.S.C.K. Kerr, BSc, MS, FRCS, Consultant Neurosurgeon, Oxford Radcliffe Hospitals, Radcliffe Infirmary, Oxford

Miss R. Jane Leitch, FRCS, FRCOphth, Consultant Ophthalmic Surgeon, Epsom and St Helier NHS Trust and Great Ormond Street Hospital for Children.

Dr. Pamela Loughna, MB BS, MD, FRCOG, MRCGP, Senior Lecturer in Obstetrics and Honorary Consultant Obstetrician, School of Human Development, Academic Division of Obstetrics and Gynaecology, City Hospital, Nottingham

Dr. Elisabeth Macdonald, FRCR, MA, formerly Consultant Oncologist, Guys Hospital and Cromwell Hospital, London, and Harley Street Oncology Unit

Dr Martin A. Mansell, MD FRCP, Consultant Nephrologist, Royal Free and University College Hospitals, London

Mr. Stephen Norris, MD, FRCS, Consultant Orthopaedic Surgeon, Northern General Hospital, Sheffield and Honorary Senior Lecturer in Orthopaedics and Trauma, University of Sheffield

Bernard Riley, MBE BSc MB BS FRCA, Consultant in Adult Critical Care, University Hospital, Queen's Medical Centre, Nottingham

Dr. Stephen J. Rose, MA, MB, BChir, FRCPCH, FRCP, MD, Consultant Paediatrician, Department of Paediatrics, Birmingham Heartlands Hospital, Birmingham

Dr. Michael F Smith, MB, BS, FRCP, FRCPCH, Consultant Paediatrician, Neonatal Unit, Jessop Wing, Royal Hallamshire Hospital, Tree Root Walk, Sheffield

James R.H. Scurr, BSc MB BS MRCS, Research Fellow, Royal Liverpool University Hospital, Liverpool

John H. Scurr, BSc MB BS FRCS, Consultant Surgeon, The Lister Hospital, London

Dr. Trevor Turner, MD, FRCPsych, Consultant Psychiatrist, Department of Psychological Medicine, St. Bartholomew's Hospital, London and The City and Hackney Centre for Mental Health, Homerton Hospital, London

Mr. C. M. Ward, BSc, MA, FRCS, Honorary Consultant in Plastic Surgery, The Radcliffe Infirmary, Oxford

Mr. P.H. L. Worth, FRCS, Consultant Urologist, Institute of Urology, University College London Hospitals, London

Dr. Gavin Young, MA(Oxon), MB BS, DRCOG, FRCGP, The Surgery, Penrith.

INTRODUCTION

Charles Foster

WHAT THIS BOOK DOES

Every clinical negligence case involves expert evidence. The reports of the experts, and their evidence at trial, necessarily involve some technical language and concepts. This book is intended to tell laymen enough about medicine and surgery to make the reports and the evidence comprehensible.

There has been, and there will be, litigation which requires detailed knowledge of some very arcane corners of medicine. For those cases there is no short cut: you have to go to the specialist textbooks. But 90 per cent of clinical negligence litigation is about 1 per cent of medicine. This book focuses on that 1 per cent. Each of the contributors has a lot of medico-legal experience. Each was asked to write about the problems which occupy most of their medico-legal time. The specialties which generate the most financially significant claims, notably obstetrics and anaesthesia, were given more space.

That focus means that the book should be useful to risk managers too. The medicine in this book is the medicine that goes wrong and causes huge cheques to be written. Clinicians, too, have something to learn from the lessons here: Everyone should learn from the mistakes of their peers.

There is inevitably some repetition. Sub-arachnoid haemorrhage, for instance, is dealt with in the chapters on general practice, accident and emergency medicine, neurosurgery and neurology. It is important that it is, and the different perspectives are interesting and significant.

Many of the authors mention "recognised complications". One has to be careful about the legal significance of this. I have edited out anything which suggested that the mere fact that the damage which has occurred was a recognised complication means that there was no negligence. Some recognised complications are negligently caused; some are non-negligently caused. Of course there are often serious difficulties in proving negligence where the complication is a recognised one, but that is a different matter.

Many medical mistakes occur because the left hand does not know what the right hand is doing, or because of inadequate resources or incompetent allocation of adequate resources. For that reason the book begins with a chapter on the organisation of the medical profession.

The book was potentially infinitely long. The editorial choices are a result of my own experience of practice. They can be criticised. General physicians, for instance, do not have a chapter of their own: nor do pathologists. I took the view that other specialities covered the ground sufficiently well. Perhaps I was wrong.

WHAT THIS BOOK DOES NOT DO

It is not intended to turn lawyers into doctors, or to excuse barristers from immersing themselves in the original papers that the experts have used to justify their positions. Nor is it intended to allow lawyers to dispense with experts. Any lawyer who decides that a doctor has or has not been negligent on the basis of this or any other book is a fool.

It is not a law book. There are plenty of those. I indicate below the (very few) instances where changes in the law have affected litigation involving particular clinical specialties, but it would be ridiculous to pretend that there are legal reasons for approaching a case involving specialty X in any different way from the way one should approach specialty Y. Whether you have a case about cerebral palsy or a case about removing moles, the principles are identical. In the introductions to most chapters I have made some comments about how interesting or uninteresting the relevant specialty is to the lawyers, and something about the circumstances in which clinicians in that specialty are likely to find themselves in court.

It would have been pointless to cite all the cases concerning a particular clinical problem that have come before the courts. No two cases are the same, and that approach might have implied that a finding by a court that practice A was negligent in the circumstances considered there, amounted to a finding that practice A was negligent per se. The law of clinical negligence does not work like that. Experienced practitioners, faced with a case about practice A, will not bother to look for cases in which practice A has been judicially examined. They will simply remind themselves of *Bolitho*, read all the literature on that practice that they can get their hands on, and see what the experts say about it.

EVIDENCE-BASED MEDICINE AND RESPONSIBLE CLINICAL PRACTICE

Bolitho v City and Hackney Health Authority [1998] AC 232 put in italics the word "responsible" which had always been part of the *Bolam* test. Practitioners and judges, reminded that this was part of the test for breach of duty, started to look more critically at expert evidence than they had previously done. A lot of the abuses of the *Bolam* test stopped. All this came at a time when the evidence-based medicine revolution was gathering momentum. This revolution has obvious implications for clinical negligence litigation. If there is an objectively correct clinical answer (as embodied, for instance, in an authoritative set of clinical guidelines), can it be said with a straight face that failure to adopt that approach is responsible, even if many practitioners in fact fail to adopt that approach? Evidence-based medicine is not stridently unequivocal about the right clinical answer in all areas of medicine: nor is it likely to be, at least for a long time. But it does mean that expert reports, to be *Bolitho*-credible, have to bristle with references to the literature that support each proposition asserted, and also that clinical guidelines are increasingly determinative of good medical practice, and therefore of litigation. For that reason there are many references in this book to relevant guidelines.

The guideline-revolution has affected particularly the law relating to the proper obtaining of consent. The GMC, following the Senate of Surgery, has decreed that practitioners must adopt the procedure laid down in its guidelines when counselling patients before procedures. The details do not matter for present purposes. The point is that these non-statutory guidelines may have the effect of sidelining *Sidaway v Board of Governors of the Bethlem Royal Hospital* [1985] AC 871 - elbowing the *Bolam* test out of the law of consent. If the GMC says that patients have to be consented in such-and-such a way, so importing the full-blooded doctrine of informed consent into the UK, how can a doctor who does not comply say that he has not been negligent? As a result of all this, the law of consent is in spasm. The practical effect for this book is that I have edited into bland generalities the practitioners' assertions about how consent should be taken and what information should be given.

THE EFFECT OF THE LAW ON PARTICULAR SPECIALTIES

As noted above, the law takes an identical approach to negligence in each specialty. But there have been two fairly recent changes in the law which have affected certain specialties particularly.

The first is *Wells v Wells* [1999] 1 AC 345. This reduced the discount rate used to ascertain the multiplier which is used to calculate future loss. The details do not matter. Its practical effect was to increase very significantly the value of awards for future financial loss. All types of claim can be affected, but the effect is (obviously), particularly significant where the claimant is young. Its effect on the value of cerebral palsy and other claims arising from negligent obstetric care has been huge.

The second is *MacFarlane v Tayside Health Board* [2000] 2 AC 59. This reduced, almost to nothing, the value of claims for so-called 'wrongful life' – claims brought by a parent in respect of the birth of a child when the birth was caused by a doctor's negligence. Far and away the biggest part of these claims was damages for the cost of bringing up the child. That, said the House of Lords in *MacFarlane*, was irrecoverable. Subsequent cases have said that there are exceptions where a disabled child is born – damages for the additional costs of upbringing associated with the disability are recoverable: see *Parkinson v St. James' and Seacroft University Hospitals NHS Trust* [2002] QB 266. But the wrongful life industry has been devastated. Urologists who do vasectomies negligently, and gynaecologists who perform female sterilisations negligently, and clinicians from both disciplines who fail to warn their patients about the risk of reversal, can breathe more easily.

THE ORGANISATION OF THE MEDICAL PROFESSION IN ENGLAND AND WALES

Stephen Evans and Alex Chalk

INTRODUCTION

The total amount spent on healthcare in the UK in 2005 is estimated to be £101bn – 8.3% of GDP. Government spending on health is running at approximately 17% of total government expenditure.[1] Yet despite the enormous sums involved the structure of healthcare provision, particularly as regards the NHS, can be unclear – even to the million-plus staff working within it.

The picture is further complicated by the fact that, since devolution, arrangements for public health care differ in each part of the UK. This chapter focuses on England and Wales, and seeks to provide an overview of the structures in place. It then explores the arrangements for responding to clinical negligence claims, which cost the NHS in England £560m in 2005/6[2].

THE STRUCTURE OF THE NHS

Recent changes

> *'The sound of every dropped bedpan will reverberate round Whitehall'*
>
> *Nye Bevan, 1948*
>
> *'The 1948 model is simply inadequate for today's needs. We are on a journey - begun with the NHS Plan – which represents nothing less than the replacement of an outdated system. We believe it is time to move beyond the 1940s monolithic top down centralised NHS towards a devolved health service...'*
>
> *Alan Milburn, 2002*[3]

[1] Office of National Statistics, www.statistics.gov.uk/healthaccounts and www.hm-treasury.gov.uk
[2] www.nhsla.com
[3] Department of Health, *Press Release – 2002/0192*, 18 April 2002

Since the mid-1980s there has been a radical shift in philosophy regarding public healthcare provision in Britain. The 1940s/1950s dogma of centralised state control has given way to a cross-party drive for devolution. The origins of that change can be traced to the 1989 White Paper *Working for Patients* which paved the way for two major changes: first, the establishment of hospital trusts; and second, the introduction of GP fund-holding which gave GPs their own budgets and power to commission services on behalf of patients.

Since then the devolution process has accelerated, and has been accompanied by a marked shift in the allocation of government funds. By April 2003, as part of the Labour Government's programme, *Shifting the Balance of Power,* primary care organisations in England and Wales controlled 75% of the NHS budget compared with just 15% in 1997. The process continued with the introduction of Foundation Trusts in 2004[4]. This devolution has been accompanied by the introduction of an element of competition with a drive to provide patient choice and initiatives to increase flexibility in the delivery of services, for example, the significant widening of the categories of people who can prescribe drugs[5].

Consequently, any description of the current structure of healthcare provision in England and Wales can never be anything more than a snap-shot, at least so far as the NHS is concerned. The picture is constantly changing.[6]

---

[4] Health and Social Care (Community Health and Standards) Act 2003

[5] From Spring 2006 qualified Extended Formulary nurse-prescribers and pharmacist independent prescribers have been able to prescribe any licensed medicine for any medical condition, with the exception of controlled drugs.

[6] As of 1 March 2007 legislation relating to the structure of the NHS has itself been consolidated in the NHS Act 2006. However, within this chapter references to legislation are to the original statute.

The NHS in England today

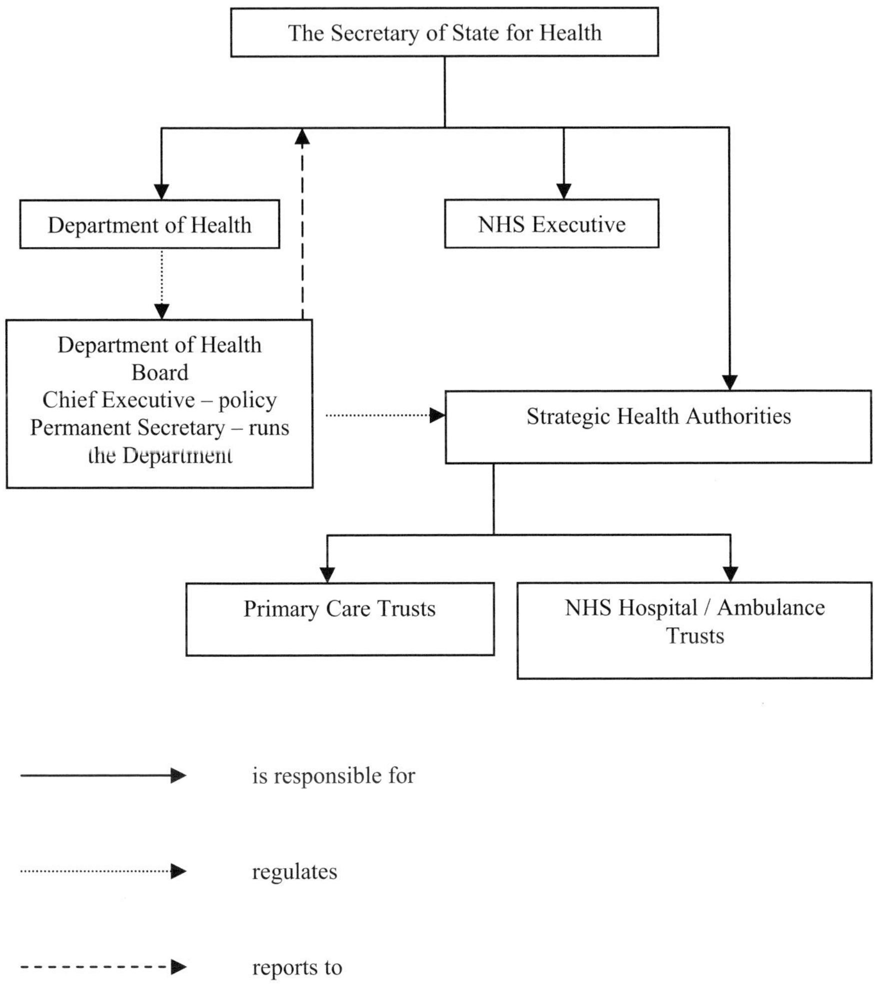

The Secretary of State

The head of the National Health Service in England is the Secretary of State for Health. The Secretary of State has overall strategic responsibility for the NHS. The Secretary is a member of the cabinet and is accountable to Parliament.

The Department of Health Board

The Board is made up of directors and senior officials responsible for different aspects of the Department's work. The Board supports the NHS Chief Executive and Permanent Secretary. The Chief Executive has day to day responsibility for ensuring the Department delivers on its strategic role in relation to health and social care. The Permanent Secretary is responsible for the way the Department is run. At times both roles have been held by the same person but they are currently split.

The Board itself is supported by the Chief Professional Officers, led by the Chief Medical Officer, and a number of National Clinical Directors for specific policy areas.

A number of "Arms Length Bodies" also play specific roles within the NHS to regulate the system, improve standards, protect public welfare and support local services[7]

Strategic Health Authorities (SHAs)

The 100 Health Authorities that used to exist in England were initially replaced by 28 Strategic Health Authorities, consolidated into 10 from July 2006. These SHAs are not involved in commissioning services, but oversee the performance management of NHS Trusts and Primary Care Trusts, ensuring they adhere to annual 'Accountability Agreements' between the parties. It is also intended that they should integrate national priority plans into plans for the local health service. The Chief Executives of the SHAs take part in NHS franchising, under which they bid to manage services of other Trusts. The idea is that the best take on and turn around under-performing organisations.

NHS Trusts

The majority of NHS Trusts in England are hospital trusts with responsibility for providing acute and specialised hospital services[8]. Whilst they have ceded control of the majority of the NHS budget, trusts remain responsible for employing the majority of the NHS workforce from doctors and midwives to porters and security staff. Their 'trust' epithet derives from the 1989 White Paper, *Working for Patients.* They are not trusts, however, in any legal sense. Rather, that term was substituted for the phrase 'self-governing hospital' which was felt not to have a sufficiently civic flavour. They are run by their own board of directors who are

---

[7] www.dh.gov.uk/AboutUs

[8] The remainder are Ambulance trusts and Mental Health trusts

free to manage their resources as they see fit, and are even able to retain surpluses and borrow money – albeit within strict limits. Although it is possible for a trust to go bankrupt, in fact its liabilities will be met by the taxpayer under the terms of the NHS (Residual Liabilities) Act 1996.

In the past NHS Trusts received the largest portion (73%) of the NHS budget,[9] but now primary care gets the lion's share as the government carries out its stated aim of devolving more power to the frontline. Trusts are accountable both to their local SHA and the PCTs with which they have service agreements. They are also subject to the Healthcare Commission, an arms length body that assesses the performance of healthcare bodies.

Foundation Trusts

Foundation Trusts are established under a new form of public ownership as independent Public Benefit Corporations. They are said not to be subject to direction from the centre and are not performance managed by SHAs, but they remain subject to NHS standards, performance ratings and systems of inspection. They also have their own independent regulator, Monitor[10]. Foundation Trusts have greater financial and operational freedoms but their liabilities will not be met under the NHS (Residual Liabilities) Act 1996. There are currently 52 Foundation Trusts but all NHS Trusts are being encouraged to change status.

Primary Care Trusts (PCTs)

The establishment of Primary Care Trusts (PCTs) represents one of the most significant departures in the provision of healthcare in the history of the NHS. Implemented under the Health Act 1999[11], they mark the final stage in a journey that began with the abolition of GP fund holding on 1 October 1999[12], and passed through the intermediate stage of Primary Care Groups.

There were 303 PCTs in England but this was reduced to 152 in October 2006. Their stated aim is to make sure there are enough services for people within their area and that these services are accessible. They must also make sure that all other health services are provided, including hospitals, dentists, opticians, mental health services, NHS Walk-In Centres, NHS Direct, patient transport (including Accident & Emergency), population screening, and pharmacies. They are also responsible for getting health and social care systems working together to the benefit of patients[13].

---

[9] Secretary of State for Health. *The New NHS: modern, dependable (CM 3807)*, London, The Stationery Office, 1997

[10] www.monitor-nhsft.gov.uk

[11] s.2 of the Health Act 1999 inserted ss16A-B and Sch 5A into the National Health Service Act 1977

[12] s.1 of the Health Act 1999 was brought into force by the Health Act (Commencement No 3) Order 1999, SI 1999/2540

[13] www.nhs.uk

PCTs both commission and provide services, but it appears Government policy favours PCTs becoming purely commissioning bodies over the next few years.

By April 2003 these primary care organisations were in charge of £46 bn a year – 75% of the total NHS budget in England – with freedom to purchase care from their choice of provider, whether public, private, voluntary or not for profit.[14]

PCTs are at the centre of the drive to provide patient choice. Since April 2005 patients have been offered a choice of at least 4 providers for their treatment including local Trusts, Foundation Trusts, Independent Sector Treatment Centres and specialist GPs.

Treatment Centres

Treatment Centres focus on the delivery of specific treatments. The principle is that the provision of dedicated and streamlined services will reduce waiting times and increase competition, thereby driving up productivity across the board.

Treatment Centres may be run by the NHS, but many are provided by the independent health sector (Independent Sector treatment Centres – ISTCs). As at February 2006 there were 21 ISTC schemes open with 11 more due to open over the next 18 months. Expressions of interest in further schemes were invited[15]. Patients treated under ISTC schemes remain NHS patients.

The NHS in Wales today

Responsibility for setting strategic policies and overseeing the funding of health in Wales now lies with Welsh Assembly.

Health authorities

Prior to April 2003 there were five health authorities in Wales:

- Bro Taf
- Dyfed Powys
- Gwent
- Lechyd Morgannwg
- North Wales

Their role was to form a bridge between the Assembly's national strategic role and the Local Health Groups and NHS Trusts. They bought services from primary care professionals (such as GPs and dentists) and from NHS Trusts providing secondary care.

---

[14] Alan Milburn - speech to the National Association for Primary Care, 5.3.03

[15] *Independent Sector Treatment Centres*, a Report from Ken Anderson, Commercial Director, Department of Health, 16/02/06

As part of the programme *Improving Health in Wales* (February 2001), health authorities were abolished in April 2003, with their functions distributed between Local Health Boards (see below) and the Assembly itself.

Trusts

Trusts are the main providers of secondary care commissioned by Local Health Boards. There are 15 NHS Trusts in Wales including one all-Wales Ambulance Trust. Between them the Trusts manage 135 hospitals. Following the 1999 changes public health provision will be located in Trusts but planned on an all-Wales basis with officers accountable to the Chief Medical Officer. The effectiveness of Trusts is measured by their contribution to improving health and service provision.

Local Health Boards

Local Health Boards (LHBs) have evolved from Local Health Groups (LHGs), which in turn previously existed as sub-committees of health authorities. There are 22 LHBs in Wales, and have the same geographical boundaries as the 22 local authorities (county councils). They include GPs and other health professionals, representatives of local authorities, as well as the voluntary sector and members of the public.

Like PCTs, LHBs have been given increased control over commissioning and delivering healthcare at various levels. They also have a duty to address health and access inequalities in their communities.

Regional Bodies

In 2004 the Health and Social Care Department was created with responsibility for general policy, performance, quality standards and safety improvement. The day to day management of performance by the Trusts and LHBs is carried out through three regional offices.

Another important regional body is the Health Commission Wales (Specialist Services), which provides dedicated support and advice on the commissioning of specialised or regional services.

Community Health Councils

Community Health Councils (CHCs) are the statutory bodies representing the interests of patients and the public in the NHS. There are 20 CHCs in Wales, based roughly on local authority or historic county areas. They act as a bridge between the public and local health providers, taking up a wide range of health issues on behalf of the public. Moreover, Health Authorities are under a legal obligation to consult local Community Health Councils if they propose substantial changes in the pattern of services.

Unlike in England, where they are to be abolished, CHCs are being retained in Wales although their functions and membership may be changed.

COMPENSATION FOR CLINICAL MISTAKES

Clinical mistakes cost the NHS in England £560m in 2005-2006 – an increase of £57m from the previous year. The total value of known or anticipated claims for clinical negligence as at March 2005 was estimated at £6.89bn, but this includes provision for actions that will, in fact, be abandoned without any payment being made.[16]

England

The National Health Service Litigation Authority (NHSLA)

Since its establishment in November 1995, the National Health Service Litigation Authority has become the single most important body dealing with clinical negligence claims in England[17]. It was established in response to two important developments in the early 1990s:

- The introduction of NHS Indemnity in January 1990[18]
- The creation of 'First Wave Trusts' in April 1991

Under NHS Indemnity the NHS itself assumed financial responsibility from Medical Protection and Defence Organisations (MPDOs) for defending and compensating medical negligence claims against NHS staff. This was a response to a growing tide of claims that was placing intolerable pressure on the MPDOs.

Because the 'First Wave Trusts' were prohibited from insuring commercially against medical negligence claims, they soon found themselves exposed to potentially massive liabilities which had to be met entirely from their own budgets. In addition it was extremely difficult to predict the volume and value of claims for any one year, which compounded budgeting difficulties. The Working Group set up in March 1993 to consider these problems recommended the establishment of a Special Health Authority to administer a NHS-wide scheme, intended to introduce greater consistency and predictability to this area.

---

[16] *NHSLA Business Plan 2006/07*

[17] The NHSLA does not operate in Wales

[18] *Health Circular HC (89)34 (1989)*, Department of Health, London

The NHSLA currently administers the following schemes[19]:

- The Clinical Negligence Scheme for Trusts (CNST)
- The Existing Liabilities Scheme (ELS)
- The Liability to Third Parties Scheme (LTPS)
- The Property Expenses Scheme (PES)

The NHSLA also runs an information service for the NHS on the impact of the Human Rights Act 1998 and the functions of the Family Health Services Appeal Authority, and provides advice about and assistance with litigation on equal pay claims in the NHS.

(a) The Clinical Negligence Scheme for Trusts (CNST)

The Clinical Negligence Scheme for Trusts is a pooling arrangement which allows each individual trust (hospital trust or PCT) to be indemnified against clinical negligence liabilities by the NHSLA in return for an annual financial contribution, paid in advance.

The full text of the arrangements can be found in the National Health Service (Clinical Negligence Scheme) Regulations 1996[20]. The most important features are as follows. The CNST only covers claims from incidents occurring on or after 1 April 1995, or whenever the relevant trust joined. Membership is open to all trusts, but remains voluntary; in fact all trusts, PCTs and Foundation Trusts are members. If, for reasons beyond the Authority's control, expenditure on the CNST exceeds the funds available, it may borrow from scheme members, strategic health authorities or the Department of Health[21].

Contributions to the Scheme are based on a range of factors including the type of trust, the nature of its clinical work, its claims history, and its compliance with prescribed risk management benchmarks.

(b) The Existing Liabilities Scheme (ELS)

This scheme, which came into effect on 1 April 1996, covers incidents occurring *prior* to 1 April 1995. Initially the scheme's expenditure dwarfed that of the CNST[22], but, predictably, the position has reversed in the subsequent eleven years.

---

[19] The task of the Authority is to administer *any* schemes that are set up under s.21 of the National Health Service and Community Care Act 1990. Paragraph 1.4 indicates that '*in due course the Authority may wish to consider the feasibility of devising similar schemes to cover other forms of third party liability, and to advise the Secretary of State accordingly*'

[20] SI 1996/251

[21] *NHSLA Framework Document*, para 6.3

[22] Expenditure on the ELS in 1996-7 was £80m as against £6m for the CNST – *NHSLA Framework Document*

There are two further important distinctions. First, payment of existing liabilities under the scheme is met out of central funding, and not by the NHSLA. Second, ELS is a *discretionary* scheme, and financial assistance will only be provided if certain criteria are met. There must be minimum standards of claims handling, including *inter alia,* access to a claims manager and a well documented procedure for handling claims[23].

The Liabilities to Third Parties Scheme (LTPS) and Property Expenses Scheme (PES) cover non-clinical risk, and fall outside the scope of this chapter. For further details on either of these schemes, a copy of the 'Rules' governing their operation can be found in the 'Documents' section of the NHSLA's web-site.[24]

Which practitioners are covered by the schemes?

The CNST guideline indicates as follows:

> *'NHS Indemnity covers the actions of staff <u>in the course of their NHS employment</u>. It also covers people in certain other categories whenever the NHS body owes a duty of care to the person harmed, including, for example, locums, medical academic staff with honorary contracts, students, those conducting clinical trials, charitable volunteers and people undergoing further professional education, training and examinations. This includes staff working on income generation projects. GPs or dentists who are directly employed [by Health Authorities], e.g. as Public Health doctors...are covered'*
>
> [emphasis added]

Conversely:

> *'NHS Indemnity does not apply to general medical and dental practitioners <u>working under contracts for services</u>. General practitioners, including GP fundholders, are responsible for making their own indemnity arrangements, as are other self-employed health care professionals such as independent midwives. Neither does NHS Indemnity apply to employees of general practices, whether fund holding or not, or to employees of private hospitals (even when treating NHS patients) local education authorities or voluntary agencies.'*
>
> [emphasis added]

It is clear that the acid test for determining whether or not an individual is covered under NHS Indemnity is employment status. The general question to ask is: at the material time was the practitioner working under a contract of service

[23] *NHS Circular EL (96) 11*
[24] www.nhsla.com

with the Trust/PCT or a contract for services? Put another way: was he an employee of the Trust/PCT? If so, under CNST he will be indemnified for any negligent harm, loss or damage caused in the course of his duties.

The issue of whether an individual is an employee or an independent contractor is a factual one, and falls to be determined on the individual circumstances. The courts will consider a variety of factors including (but not limited to) self-description, the degree of control and integration, mutuality of obligation, and the economic reality. It should be noted, however, that an individual who is found to be an independent contractor for the purposes of an unfair dismissal claim may nonetheless be an employee for the purpose of vicarious liability in a clinical negligence claim.[25]

The practitioner must have been 'acting in the course of his NHS employment'. A detailed analysis of what this phrase means is beyond the scope of this chapter. For these purposes it is sufficient to say that only the most extreme behaviour, such as a porter physically attacking a patient, could exempt the trust from liability.[26]

Some specific examples:

GPs

From the references above to now-defunct GP fund holding it will be clear that the CNST guideline pre-dates the introduction of PCTs. However, the same principles apply. Cover is only available where the individual is working as an employee or a direct agent of the PCT. Therefore GPs will be covered if they are employed by the PCT, whether under a contract of employment or for a fee reimbursable to the GP practice. The key criterion is whether at the time of the negligence the GP was subject to the managerial control of the PCT. If he was, he will most likely have been operating under a de facto contract of service, and will therefore fall under the NHS indemnity scheme.

Local authority staff

PCTs are increasingly working together with social services departments to provide integrated health and social care. These relationships are governed by individual partnership/management agreements, and issues of liability and indemnity will be determined by reference to the wording of that agreement. However, the general rule seems to be (according to Department of Health guidance on s.31 Partnership Arrangements) that where local authority staff are working under the direction and control of the PCT, liability will rest with the PCT. Conversely, where PCT employees are for the time being working the

---

[25] *Clark v Oxfordshire Health Authority* [1998] IRLR 125. A bank nurse was held not to have a global contract of employment with the health authority for the purposes of an unfair dismissal claim. However the Court of Appeal was not prepared to rule that no contract of employment subsisted for the duration of each separate hiring and remitted the issue to the industrial tribunal.

[26] *Keppel Bus Co v Ahmad* [1974] 1 WLR 1082

direction and control of the local authority, they will fall to be indemnified under the authority's own insurance arrangements.

Medical students

Indemnity extends to cover medical students, but only if they are carrying out work under the supervision of a Trust employee.

Practitioners treating patients in their own homes

Indemnity under CNST extends to Trust/PCT employees so long as they are there on Trust/PCT business.

Independent Sector Treatment Centres

ISTC providers cannot be members of the CNST scheme. However, special arrangements have been made to allow ISTC providers treating NHS patients to benefit from the referring PCT's CNST membership. This arrangement only covers claims in respect of clinical negligence[27].

Wales

The equivalent of the CNST in Wales is the 'Welsh Risk Pool'. This is a mutual self-insurance arrangement covering most risks associated with NHS activities. During 2003-2004 the Welsh Risk Pool paid out £25m to NHS Trusts and health authorities to cover clinical negligence claims[28]. A fuller discussion of this scheme is beyond the scope of this chapter.

The Medical Protection and Defence Organisations (MPDOs)

Notwithstanding the wide scope of NHS Indemnity, many medical practitioners fall outside the statutory insurance scheme. Most obviously, doctors in private practice need to look elsewhere for indemnity cover. For them, and others in the same position (importantly, most GPs), the MPDOs are the principal source of protection.

MPDOs are discretionary mutual funds wholly owned and operated by their members. The first to be established was the Medical Defence Union in 1885, following an outcry in the medical community over the case of Dr David Bradley – a doctor wrongly convicted of a charge of assaulting a woman in his surgery. In 1892 the Medical Protection Society (MPS) was founded, and over the next twenty years a number of similar organisations took shape all over the world, particularly in British overseas territories. Today the MPS has over 200,000 members in more than 40 different countries worldwide.

---

[27] NHSLA Factsheet – *Independent Sector Treatment Centres and The CNST*
[28] *The Finances of the NHS Wales 2005*, Report by the National Audit Office Wales

MPDOs can provide help with:

- Clinical negligence claims
- Complaints
- Medical Council enquiries
- Disciplinary procedures
- Inquests
- Police investigations

Assistance with some of the above (most notably with inquests) will not be provided under the NHS Indemnity scheme. For that reason many NHS practitioners feel it prudent to take out the additional layer of protection that membership of an MPDO affords.

Crucially MPDOs are not insurance companies[29]. Rather, they are *discretionary* mutual funds, whereby applications for assistance are considered on a case-by-case basis. There is no guarantee that cover will be provided. As a rule of thumb, the issue must arise from the member's professional practice, or have wider implications for the membership at large. The MPS, for example, have indicated that they would *not* normally provide help with:

- business matters that arise from running a practice or clinic
- employment and disciplinary problems that involve personal misconduct
- discrimination claims[30].

Who should be named as the defendant in a clinical negligence claim?

Allegations against GPs

As indicated above, where the GP is directly employed by the PCT he will now be covered by NHS Indemnity. The correct defendant will therefore be the relevant PCT under the ordinary principles of vicarious liability[31]. In determining whether or not the GP is an employee, the key criterion is control – was the doctor under the managerial control of the PCT at the time of the alleged negligence? The same considerations will apply to GP practice nurses or receptionists.

Where the negligence occurred *prior* to the GP's employment by the PCT, he will be regarded as an independent contractor and not as an employee of the Health Authorities which existed at the time. Where the GP was working in a partnership, then by virtue of the Partnership Act 1980 each of the GP partners will be jointly and severally liable for his negligence.[32]

---

[29] *Medical Defence Union Ltd v Department of Trade* [1980] Ch 82, [1979] 2 All ER 421, Ch D
[30] www.medicalprotection.org , 7 March 2003
[31] *Gold v Essex CC* [1942] 2 KB 293. Although this case concerned a hospital's liability, it was the first to recognise the principle of vicarious liability in a general medical context.
[32] s.12

If the GP is in private practice, or otherwise outside the scope of NHS Indemnity, he will be sued in his own name. This is by far the commonest way in which GPs are sued.

Allegations against NHS hospital practitioners or staff

So long as the practitioner was an employee, and was acting in the course of his employment he will be covered by NHS Indemnity. The NHS body should therefore be named as the defendant.

Should the NHSLA be named as a defendant in a clinical negligence claim?

No. Although the NHSLA has responsibility for management of all claims in England the trust will remain the legal defendant.

Claims against trusts that have been dissolved should be made against the successor trust or PCT. If services have split up the new bodies will be required to confirm liabilities in writing.

Allegations against practitioners and staff in private hospitals

Where a practitioner negligently treats a patient in a private hospital, the issue of whom to sue will turn on the contractual arrangement between the practitioner and the hospital. Where the practitioner is an employee, the hospital will be named as the defendant in the usual way under the ordinary principles of vicarious liability. More often, however, the agreement will grant the practitioner access to hospital facilities and nursing staff, but stipulate that he is an independent contractor for the purposes of any negligent acts or omission. In those circumstances the practitioner is solely liable, and should be named as the defendant.

The New South Wales Court of Appeal considered this issue in the case of *Ellis v Wallsend District Hospital*[33]. There C, a neurosurgeon, had an agreement with the hospital under which he undertook to provide certain services in return for use of the operating theatres for treatment of his own patients. Following surgery the claimant developed tetraplegia. Because the practitioner was clearly carrying out his own business when the claimant suffered her injuries, the hospital was not vicariously liable for his acts or omissions.

[33] (1990) 2 Med LR 103

CLINICAL GENETICS

Caroline Berry

INTRODUCTION

Clinical genetics is currently a relatively rare source of medico-legal cases. The number of clinical geneticists is small, and they frequently come from academic backgrounds and find the constant need for education and update an enjoyable challenge rather than an irritating burden.

As the field expands this may well change. Genetic information is increasingly important in all medical specialties, and many claims are likely to flow from the genetic-medical failures of non-genetic specialists. With the mapping of the human genome, clinical genetics is a fast developing field, and although the internet can provide useful updates, the non-specialist faced with a complex genetic issue is well advised to communicate with the relevant Genetics Centre, which is usually based in the nearest major teaching hospital or University.

Many of the confidentiality and consent issues raised in this chapter are legally complex and contentious as well as medically agonising.

THE GENETIC CONSULTATION

General

The genetic consultation has certain features which are different from other consultations. The person attending the clinic may be entirely well. If so, he or she is known as 'the consultand'. The affected person is known as 'the proband'.

As with other medical consultations, a correct diagnosis is crucial. But this may not be a diagnosis in the person enquiring, but in a close or less close relative who may be alive or dead. It may be necessary to obtain medical records from these family members, and this raises important issues of confidentiality.

When the diagnosis is made, the mode of inheritance and the impact this has on the consultand need to be determined. Tests may help: their implications, scope and reliability all need to be discussed with the consultand. Steps must be taken to make sure the points discussed are fully understood. Problems can arise within the laboratory. These are sometimes because of the limitations of current techniques, although of course true human and technical errors can also occur.

Finally, when the consultand has been given all the necessary information and its implications considered, future management has to be discussed. The relevant management is not only that of the consultand, but also that of other relatives for whom the test results may have equally important implications. In all these key areas clinically important mistakes may occur: these are discussed in more detail below. When an error does occur it may be very serious, resulting in the birth of one or even several seriously disabled children, or in serious but avoidable adult disability.

Correct diagnosis

Accurate genetic information is entirely dependent on an accurate diagnosis. A general term such as 'muscular dystrophy' can cover a number of very different disorders with different modes of inheritance. There needs to be good liaison between the clinical geneticist and colleagues in other specialties - in particular neurology and ophthalmology where diagnostic confusion can readily arise. While an increasing number of diagnoses can be established by molecular tests, it is still necessary to know which test is most likely to provide useful results. Cancer genetics is a rapidly expanding field, warranting close co-operation between oncologist and geneticist.

Syndrome diagnosis is an area where the clinical geneticist may have greater diagnostic experience than other colleagues. Genetic syndromes are individually rare. Cleft lip and palate is a common disorder with a moderate (4%) risk of reoccurring in another child of the same parents. However if cleft palate occurs together with other features such as microcephaly, a syndrome such as Smith Lemli Opitz may be the underlying cause. This diagnosis has serious implications for the child's mental development and has a high (25%) chance of occurring in a future child of the same parents. Thus careful examination for the less obvious features is essential.

Errors of diagnosis are therefore an important potential source of legally important mistakes. But an error of diagnosis does not necessarily connote negligence. Many syndromes are rare, and new ones arise with new genetic mutations.

Clinical photographs are useful tools in syndrome identification. These can be shown to other specialists and compared with published reports. It is essential that proper written parental consent is obtained when photographs are taken, and even greater care must be taken if they are to be published. Failure to do this would be a legally important mistake, but probably not a vastly expensive one.

The correct inheritance pattern

The risk that an individual or their child will be affected by the condition about which they are concerned will depend on the inheritance pattern known to be associated with that condition. The issue may not be straightforward: some disorders have more than one inheritance pattern and some may have both genetic and non-genetic forms. Many common disorders arise as the result of both genetic and environmental factors. Risk figures are usually based on data collected by surveys, but the figures may be modified with increasing understanding of the underlying genetic mechanisms. For families at risk of cancer there are formulae which can be used to calculate an individual's risk. These formulae are based on the family pattern, the age of onset etc. Although it might be thought that inaccurate reassurance was the only legally important mistake, this is not true. Being given a high risk for either personal health or for abnormality in offspring causes major anxiety and might cause a couple unnecessarily to avoid having children.

The different inheritance patterns have different medico-legal consequences. Recessive inheritance is the most straightforward. Here, missing the correct diagnosis of a rare disorder is the major stumbling block.

X-linked conditions affect males, and the mutated gene may be carried by females. If a woman is a carrier, on average half her sons will be affected. The genetic mutation may have started in the X chromosome of the egg giving rise to the affected boy. In this case the mother would not be a carrier, and can be re-assured about future pregnancies. When it became possible to identify the mutations in affected boys and their mothers, it seemed likely that mothers not showing the mutation could be reassured. However, while data was being gathered, it became clear that a significant number of such mothers did in fact have further affected sons. It is now realized that there may be multiple mutated egg cells (or sperm cells in other disorders). Thus a risk of recurrence remains, and its magnitude is hard to quantify. This phenomenon is known as germinal mosaicism[1] and failure to take it into account could lead to important mistakes.

Dominant inheritance gives geneticists their biggest headache and is a trap for the unwary non-specialist. Dominant inherited disorders are passed through the generations from parent to child. If a child does not inherit the gene then they will not pass it on to their offspring. The problem is that the gene may have been inherited, but for reasons not yet understood it may barely manifest itself in certain individuals. The condition appears to 'skip a generation' though in fact it is only the *features* that do: the mutated gene itself is present but does not manifest itself. Thus a person may appear not to have inherited the gene, be reassured, and go on to have an affected child who may show all the features of the condition. This phenomenon is known as 'incomplete penetrance'. If a

[1] Van Essen, AJ, Kneppers, ALJ *et al*, The clinical and molecular genetic approach to Duchenne and Becker muscular dystrophy: An updated protocol, *Journal of Medical Genetics*, 1997; 34: 805-812

molecular test is available, this provides definitive information, but there remains the proviso of germinal mosaicism (outlined above) where the parent of an affected child is being considered and no other cases are known in the family.

Different disorders are recognized as having differing degrees of penetrance. Tuberous sclerosis is notoriously difficult, and potential gene carriers need meticulous examination[2]. Fortunately molecular tests are becoming more generally available, but casual reassurance because no obvious disease features are present is a well recognised and important mistake. Incomplete penetrance also makes it difficult to give those at risk of developing the condition or of having an affected child, accurate information on the degree of severity to be expected. A risk of 10% for serious disability is very different from the 100% risk associated with fully penetrant disorders.

Discussion of the options

Genetics is a fast moving field and the options available to those facing various genetic problems are constantly changing. New diagnostic or confirmatory tests may be available, and pre-natal tests need to be evaluated for safety and reliability. Information about rare disorders may not be readily available, and may require searching of data bases or various personal communications. Failure to provide up-to date information would be a serious error.

Although most pre-natal tests give straightforward results it is sometimes extremely difficult to predict the significance for the fetus of an unusual finding in a prenatal test will have on the fetus. Careful literature searches, and in some cases further tests, may help to resolve the problem but the options available in these circumstances are limited: they are to accept the predicted risk of abnormality and continue the pregnancy, or to have an abortion. Whichever decision is made it is essential that it is based on information which is as accurate as possible.

Taking account of laboratory investigations

Failure to note and act upon an abnormal result received from the laboratory is a serious error in all areas of medicine. It is all too easy for the report to be filed without being acted upon. Checking systems need to be in place to ensure that no report is filed without the signature of the person requesting the test. It is also useful to have a system for automatically recalling the notes at a date after the date when the report is due. This gives an opportunity to chase up an overdue report and to discuss possible difficulties of interpretation with the laboratory.

---

[2] Webb, DW and Osbourne, JP, Non-penetrance in tuberous sclerosis, *Journal of Medical Genetics*, 1991; 28: 417-419.

Surveillance arrangements

Very often a single visit to the genetic clinic is all that is required, and provided the patient understands what has been discussed (see below) no further follow-up is necessary. For others, such as those with conditions such as neurofibromatosis who are at risk of developing complications, regular surveillance is essential. The same applies to those found to have mutations predisposing them to the development of malignant disease. It is important to establish clearly whether this surveillance is to be undertaken by the geneticist, by a specialist such as an oncologist or neurologist, or by the general practitioner. The arrangements will depend on the individual geneticist (as some have particular expertise with certain conditions) but failure to ensure that appropriate arrangements are set up can be significant.

Informing consultands of new developments

As new information emerges and tests multiply, the information given to an enquirer may be out of date five years later. It is difficult to say whether or not the geneticist is responsible for providing regular update information. For many clinics seeing several hundred people each year, this is not practicable except in the case of major breakthroughs. Those who request regular review can be included in a follow-up system, while others may join the appropriate support group (i.e. a semi-informal group of those affected with the same condition who share news, support one another, raise funds and often sponsor important research) and receive its regular newsletter. For others the question of responsibility for providing information on new developments remains unresolved[3].

Communication and understanding

Genetic concepts are complicated, and the person attending the genetic clinic may be extremely anxious about what they are going to hear. In these circumstances misunderstandings readily arise. A person may appear to have understood the points being made, but subsequent questioning shows that little has been retained. Realising this, many geneticists provide written information. This may take the form of leaflets given at the time of the appointment, but more often a letter is written outlining the points discussed and their implications. Sometimes a copy of the letter sent to the general practitioner can be used. As there may be just one genetic clinic appointment, it may be necessary to ask the general practitioner or other health professional who knows the person to ensure that he or she understands what was said and its implications. Alternatively, follow up visits may be arranged at home by one of the clinic staff. Important decisions may have to be made, and the geneticist has a responsibility to ensure that these are made with full understanding, and any tests undertaken only with appropriately

[3] Pelias, MZ, Duty to disclose in medical genetics: a legal perspective, *American Journal of Medical Genetics*, 1991; 39: 347-54

informed consent. Discussions on the phone or by e-mail need to be carefully recorded.

Errors associated with communication are always serious in medicine, but this is particularly so in genetics, where so much of the consultation is to do with the discussion of options. If the patient has features suggesting acute appendicitis there needs to be little discussion about the right course of action. Where the question at issue is whether or not to have a test for Huntington's disease or early onset Alzheimer's disease, the situation is very different. To provide the test without giving adequate information on its pros and cons would be a serious error. Such errors are rare at present, since tests are currently provided only by genetic clinics where fairly rigorous guidelines are followed, but may become more common if genetic tests become more readily accessible. Over-the-counter testing is an area of concern: the Human Genetic Commission's working party reported its findings in April 2003[4]. Whether this will lead to legislation remains to be seen.

Consent for pre-natal testing is usually undertaken in the ante-natal clinic, but Preimplantation genetic tests are classically the province of the geneticist. This is discussed below.

CONFIDENTIALITY AND PRIVACY

The strong presumption against disclosing medical information without the patient's consent creates major difficulties for geneticists because they tend to work with families rather than with individuals, or with an individual in the context of their family. This raises issues such as 'to whom does genetic information belong'? We receive our genes from our parents, share them with our sibs and pass them to our children. Is their information therefore ours? Must it be kept private, or should it be shared with relevant family members? Clearly there is a difference between divulging information for the benefit of a relative and divulging it to an insurance company or employer. Discussions about genetic confidentiality have tended to focus on the latter.

The great majority of families are willing to assist one another by permitting access to medical records and the results of 'genetic' tests. There are some exceptions. Some ensuing potential 'errors' are outlined below:

Obtaining a specimen

Refusal

In order to give the healthy family member fully accurate information on their carrier status and risk to themselves or their offspring, it is often essential to have

---

[4] Human Genetics Commission, *Gene Direct. Ensuring the effective oversight of genetic tests supplied directly to the public*, HMSO 2003

a sample for molecular analysis from the affected person. Blood is usually used but it may be possible to use a mouthwash or hair roots. If the affected person refuses to co-operate, it would clearly be wrong to coerce him/her into providing the sample, or to obtain a sample by stealth (eg implying the sample was being taken for some quite different reason). Under the Human Tissue Act 2004 this would now be unlawful as consent is required for taking of samples from both adults and children.

Death

It is not only downright refusal that causes difficulty. Where the affected person has died it may be possible to obtain molecular information from some source from within the family, such as a child's milk tooth but, particularly with cancer genetics, the most useful sample source may be the slivers of tissue taken from the tumour in order to make the original diagnosis. These may be stored for many years in hospital pathology departments. Following events such as those that occurred at the Alder Hey Hospital during the 1990s, the Human Tissue Act was passed in 2004. This makes detailed stipulations about the taking, storing and using of tissue from both the living and the dead. There are separate stipulations referring to DNA analysis. Initial drafts of the bill were modified in the light of the concerns raised by those working in clinical genetics and epidemiology, but it remains to be seen whether the law fulfills its purpose without adding to the geneticist's burden.

Failure to store a sample

Although attention is usually focused on the unconsented storage of samples, the reverse error – failure to store a sample – is very serious too. A sample may be obtained with considerable difficulty, may be tested at the time and the remainder frozen for storage. Alternatively the sample may all be frozen to await the development of a relevant or improved test. In either case, discarding such a sample is a serious error, particularly if the donor has died. Freezer failure, with the loss of large numbers of samples is a further hazard: there should be back up procedures to prevent it.

"Double confidentiality"

This is the situation where there is no reason to doubt that the affected person would give consent, but the consent can only be obtained by breaking the confidentiality of the person requesting information. For example: a young woman who has a brother with an X linked form of muscular dystrophy is pregnant. She comes to the clinic wanting to know whether she is a carrier or not and, if she is, whether prenatal detection is possible. When asked to contact her brother in order to identify his particular mutation, she demurs, saying that she would prefer him not to know that she is so concerned about the possibility of having a child affected by his condition. If no sample is available from him the advice the geneticist can give will be less reliable. The decision about what to do must be hers. The geneticist cannot properly approach the brother directly since this would involve a breach of the sister's clinical confidentiality.

Privacy of 'genetic' test results

It may be that the brother has already been tested and his molecular result is held in the laboratory records either in the centre the sister is attending, or in one of the small number of such laboratories in the UK. At present it is unclear whether, assuming there is no evidence that he would refuse consent if asked, his result may be disclosed to determine which test to use to establish his sister's carrier status. It could be argued that such sharing of information within the professional field is no different from the sharing of information between members of the healthcare team in other situations.

The HGC in its Report 'Inside Information: balancing interests in the use of personal genetic data' notes that there may be occasions when the benefit of disclosure substantially outweighs the patient's claim to confidentiality[5].

Confidentiality of medical records

As mentioned above, an accurate diagnosis of the condition in the affected person is essential for accurate risk predictions for the consultand. While taking the family history, the geneticist can make enquiries about the clinical features and course of the disease and with conditions that have very specific features this may provide a reasonably accurate diagnosis, although confirmation from medical records is always the ideal. It is in the rapidly expanding field of cancer genetics where this process becomes more complicated. To the family member it may appear that several family members have died from 'cancer of the brain' or 'cancer of the liver'. Many cancers metastasise to the brain or to the liver, and so the labels given give no clue as to whether the affected individuals had or have the same cancer, (perhaps with serious genetic implications), or quite different ones which have arisen randomly.

Important errors can be therefore be made by failure to obtain accurate diagnoses from medical records. But medical records are confidential, and obtaining or providing them without the consent of the person to whom they refer is ethically culpable. When relatives are readily available and willing to help, obtaining signed consent is time-consuming but possible: every effort should be made to obtain this. If consent is refused, this must be respected. Where relatives are hard to contact, or have died, the importance of the information they would contribute must be assessed.

There may be cases where the information is so crucial that obtaining the information, even though that involves a breach of confidence, can be justified.

---

[5] Human Genetics Commission, *Inside Information. Balancing interests in the use of personal genetic data*, 3.68 HMSO 2002

Individual confidentiality versus wider responsibility

When a diagnosis is made in one family member it may have important implications for other family members. For example: a woman may be found to be a carrier of a mutation which puts her at high risk of having sons with a severe form of muscular dystrophy. She can, if she wishes, avoid this in a future pregnancy by having prenatal or preimplantation testing. She may have sisters who are in the same situation. Another example: A man may be found to have a genetic form of bowel cancer which develops at a young age. It is curable if recognized early, but there is rapid progression to death if it is unrecognised. He may have brothers and sisters who also have this genetic make-up, and a similar risk. Clearly these relatives stand to gain by being warned of the condition in the family.

Usually individuals are keen to contact family members and inform them of the problem and what action to take. Others may need gentle persuasion. Occasionally individuals are adamant that they do not want other family members to know their diagnosis and are unconcerned about the fate of their relatives. What should the geneticist do?

The issue has been much discussed. The Genetic Interest Group (the umbrella group covering many patient support groups) concluded that in some such circumstances a breach of confidentiality would be justifiable[6]. This is in line with the GMC's guidelines on Confidentiality, which broadly indicate that a confidence can be broken if the breach would be likely to avoid death or serious injury. See too the Human Genetics Commission report, mentioned above[7].

Seeing the notes

A more mundane problem arises from the fact that genetic centres have notes for 'the family' rather than the individual. Although there may be separate sections for different individuals or family groups, there is important basic shared information such as that shown in the pedigree. A person may ask to see their records from the medical genetics department. These records, however, contain information on other members of their family which they should not see. Attempts to 'doctor' the notes to excise parts relevant to other family members can bring charges of cover-up.

---

[6] *Confidentiality and Medical Genetics, Report of a Working Party of the Genetics Interest Group*, Genetics Interest Group, 1998
[7] See above footnote 5

RESPONSIBILITY FOR GIVING INFORMATION

Within the family

As mentioned above, geneticists see themselves as having a responsibility to the family as well as to the individual. Whether there is a legal responsibility to the family is a very difficult question, outside the scope of this book. When some genetic error is identified in one family member they see it as their responsibility to encourage those in whom it has been found to inform other family members. The procedure for this has to be worked out. Relatives' addresses have to be obtained and this may take time. It is generally preferable for the clinic patient to make the first approach and suggest to their relative how to make contact with the appropriate genetic centre or other agency. Many clinics provide letters for their patients to give to relatives, which can be passed on to the relatives' general practitioner. Important mistakes can happen. If, for example, a letter containing crucial information does not arrive, or is not acted on, children may be born with serious disability may be born, or adults may die from potentially preventable diseases. The issue of legal responsibility for mistakes like this can be very complex.

The right not to know

The reverse of information giving is more difficult. The phase 'The right not to know' is used too glibly. It usually refers to the right to choose not to have a test to discover more about one's genetic make up. It is well established that a high proportion of those at risk of Huntington's disease do not wish to discover whether they have inherited the gene. But it is the step before this which has major implications. It is not uncommon for a parent who has been found to have the Huntington's 'mutation' to say that they do not want to burden their children with the knowledge of their 50% risk of having inherited it. Parents naturally want to protect their children, and may feel tremendous guilt that they have imposed this terrible genetic burden on them. But many 'children' who attend the clinic are angry that their parents have withheld the information from them. The parent may claim that they do not want to 'ruin their children's lives'. They have a point: simply knowing that they are at risk can have major implications for their spouse, their children, and their insurance prospects, let alone worries about their own health. Once they have been informed of the family history they know and can never 'not know'. In general, geneticists favour disclosure but there is the opportunity for misjudgement in either direction.

Genetic tests for minors

While some parents are keen to protect their children from genetic knowledge, others are keen to have them tested as early as possible. Parents argue that they have a right to know about their child's genetic make-up, so that if there is some genetic risk they can bring the child up with this knowledge rather than leave the child to come to terms with it at adolescence or in early adulthood. How far such parental rights are established in law is a moot point. If tested in the UK courts the classic test under the Children Act 1989 – the welfare of the child – would be determinative. The situation may be different in the USA[8].

Geneticists tend to prefer testing to be postponed until adolescence or at least until the child is aware of the implications[9]. (Of course this does not apply to conditions such as the childhood eye tumour retinoblastoma, which need attention during infancy or childhood).

With a condition such as Huntington's disease, where a high proportion of those at risk decline testing, it would be an error to test a child who is then precluded from choosing not to have the test. There is an internationally agreed code of conduct for Huntington's which precludes testing of those under 18[10]. There has been some discussion as to whether this should be amended to an age of '*Gillick* competence'[11] but it would be wrong to submit to parental pressure for testing in infancy. It has to be said, though, that pre-natal testing, (particularly where the mother chooses to continue a pregnancy despite the fetus being shown to be affected), provides an unavoidable exception.

With less serious disorders there must be careful discussion between parent and geneticist. Too rigid a stance on the part of the geneticist can alienate the parent. The geneticist should ensure that the parent understands that the child might be better served by not having knowledge of its condition forced on it.

A slightly different scenario arises when a child is being considered for adoption.[12] it is understandable that prospective parents and adoption agencies might wish to know whether the child has inherited a condition known to be present in the family. For a late onset condition such as Huntington's, the arguments given above must still apply. Childhood onset disorders are more difficult. Parents might not wish to commit themselves to caring for a child with a disability. On the other hand, to perform the test is not really in the child's interest. As a natural born child is accepted unconditionally, should not the same apply to an adopted one?

---

[8] See above footnote 3

[9] *The Genetic Testing of Children, Report of a Working Party of the Clinical Genetics Society*, 1994

[10] Guidelines for the molecular genetics predictive test in Huntington's disease, *Journal of Medical Genetics*, 1994; 31: 555-559

[11] Binedell, J, Soldan, JR, Scourfield, J and Harper, PS, Huntington's disease predictive testing: the case for an assessment approach to requests from adolescents, *Journal of Medical Genetics*, 1996; 33: 912-918

[12] Turnpenny, PD, Simpson, SA and McWhinnie, AM, Adoption, genetic disease, and DNA, *Archives of Diseases of Childhood*, 1993; 69: 411-413

PRE-IMPLANTATION TESTING

At the moment, most genetically determined disorders are untreatable. For parents at risk of having an affected child, the only way of avoiding this is to discover the fetal genetic make-up before birth. Once a pregnancy has started, abortion is the only way of avoiding the birth of an affected child. Samples for genetic analysis are obtained by chorionic villus sampling, amniocentesis and fetal blood sampling.

A new development is pre-implantation testing which is currently available in only four centres in the UK. It is extremely demanding and involves very close liaison between the in-vitro fertilization (IVF) team and the geneticists.

Using standard IVF techniques, several ova are fertilised and allowed to develop to the 8 cell stage or slightly further. A single cell is removed from each of these balls of cells and is analysed for the genetic condition for which the couple are at risk. Two fertilised eggs unaffected by the condition are inserted into the mother's uterus, and further management is as for any other IVF pregnancy. The testing procedure is very difficult (the sample consists of a single cell) and has an error rate (see below), so further testing by chorion villus sampling or amniocentesis is usually offered as back-up. This may be declined because of the small associated miscarriage risk to a very precious pregnancy. Use of this technique essentially avoids the need for termination of affected pregnancies, and so is the method of choice for many couples. However it is not to be undertaken lightly, and detailed discussion of possible outcomes is essential for consent to be meaningful.

As the procedure involves embryos it is regulated by the Human Fertilisation and Embryology Authority under the terms of the Human Fertilisation and Embryology Act 1990. Licensing procedures must be adhered to and the specific test approved.

LABORATORY PROBLEMS

Chromosome analysis

The most serious mistakes arise from straightforward human error. As with any laboratory work, meticulous labelling is essential. Cytogenetic examination for a full chromosome analysis depends on initial culture of the cells in the sample, as standard chromosome analysis is done on dividing cells. Then each chromosome is examined with minute attention to detail. Automated systems have been devised but have not as yet proved fully satisfactory. Even when these systems are used, the final examination is done by human eye.

Errors of interpretation are the cytogeneticist's chief concern. A small section of some chromosome may not look normal, but it can be very difficult to work out exactly what this represents and its significance. Errors here may or may not be negligent. Peer review is a useful tool for deciding whether or not the mistake is one that reasonably competent cytogeneticists might have made.

Less detailed information can be obtained more rapidly by using molecular probes which show their presence under the microscope by fluorescing when suitably treated, but the advantage of a speedy result has to be weighed against the higher error rate of these techniques. Other probes and systems can be used in certain circumstances to provide information at a resolution beyond that of the human eye. Deciding which technique to use in which case is a matter of judgment, as the probes are expensive and their use time consuming. Laboratories generally strive to provide a state of the art service within the constraints of the budget, without compromising the more mundane work. There are complex legal arguments about the culpability of failures which result from the non-availability in a particular laboratory of the most up to date methods.

Molecular analysis

This is becoming more automated, but again both meticulous adherence to the required test protocol, and informed personal judgments are essential. Human error is again the most worrying problem but, particularly with new tests in the early years of their use, there may be non-negligent difficulties in interpreting the findings. It is important for patients to be made aware of any known limitations on reliability.

Laboratory accreditation

Various professional bodies set standards. The Association of Clinical Cytogeneticists has a Professional Standards Committee, and the Clinical Molecular Genetics Society is developing best practice guidelines. The Royal College of Pathologists organizes a stringent laboratory accreditation scheme.

Errors with pre-natal diagnostic tests

These can have major medico-legal consequences. Human errors, as outlined above, are fortunately rare, but will always remain possible.

'Wrong sex' prediction

This is the commonest error with a pre-natal test, but with revision of laboratory procedures should now be vanishingly rare.

When a full chromosome analysis is done, the aim is to look for abnormalities, but the sex chromosomes are always noted (XX for a girl, XY for a boy). This information is included in the laboratory report and may be given to the parents if they request it. (Some laboratories withhold this part of the result, because (a) it is unrelated to the reason for which the test was done, and (b) out of concern that a female fetus might be aborted – as happens commonly in some communities).

Despite checking by a second cytogeneticist, the 'XX' or 'XY' which appears on the result form is occasionally the opposite of what was seen under the microscope. This is almost always due to the clerical error of incorrect transcription of the information from the analysis sheet to the computer-generated report. A girl (or boy) is predicted and a boy (or girl) is delivered. Such errors must be taken very seriously by the laboratory since they may indicate sloppy practice. Parents are likely to be confused and upset, but since they are generally thankful for a healthy baby the error is not usually of great legal importance.

It is important that the laboratory is contacted in the first instance to check the original analysis. In some cases it may be necessary to analyse the infant's chromosomes, as very occasionally a girl may be born with an XY chromosome make up but remain entirely unmasculinized as she has the X linked condition 'androgen insensitivity'. Parents should be warned of this remote possibility before agreeing to have a sample taken from the baby for analysis.

Maternal contamination

When an amniotic fluid or chorionic villus sample is obtained, there is always the possibility that maternal cells as well as fetal cells are present. Usually this is of no consequence as the fetal cells grow faster and so provide the cells on which the result is based. A male result provides reassurance that the fetus has indeed been tested. However it is possible for maternal cells to be the ones finally examined. They will give a normal but spurious result, the fetus remaining untested. This problem is most likely to arise if the sample is contaminated with maternal blood, or if the cells grow poorly and provide only few cells for analysis. Some laboratories now carry out a rapid molecular test (see below) on all their pre-natal samples to identify the presence of Down's syndrome in the fetus. This test will also identify the presence of a second genotype in the sample, and this should be used to inform the cytogeneticist of the possibility of growth of maternal cells in the cultures. If the cytogeneticist is concerned that there is a real risk that the result obtained is from maternal cells, this must be included in the report and a suggestion made that the test is repeated. The situation must be explained to the parents so that they can decide whether to repeat the procedure or accept the chance of an erroneous result.

'Apparent' errors

There are other occasions when it may appear that an error has occurred but it is not a culpable one.

For example:

(a) As new techniques are developed the amount of detail that can be detected when the chromosomes are examined increases. These newer techniques, however, are expensive and time consuming, and so they are used only when there is a high index of suspicion that the result might be positive. Pre-natal tests offered routinely are chiefly to detect Down's Syndrome and other major chromosome abnormalities - particularly those associated with increasing maternal age. Thus the depth of analysis appropriate for pre-natal screening of large numbers of amniotic fluids is less than that which might be used for the examination of a child with 'dysmorphic' features and learning difficulty which might well be secondary to a very subtle but still detectable chromosome abnormality. An amniocentesis might therefore be reported as 'normal' despite a subtle abnormality being present. This might come to light many years later when the child was re-examined because of his/her learning difficulty. By wording the report as 'no abnormality detected' using the relevant technique, misunderstandings should be avoided, but paediatricians need to be aware of the need for further investigation if indicated, even though there has been a normal amniocentesis result[13].

(b) One of the problems associated with pre-natal tests is the inevitable anxiety as the parents wait for the result which, for even a routine chromosome analysis, will take one to two weeks. In order to provide a speedier pre-natal result it is possible to use molecular or molecular cytogenetic techniques to identify the copy number of a few crucial chromosomes. FISH (Fluorescent In Situ Hybridization), using fluorescently-labelled "probes" can be used on cells that are not dividing, so the time which is usually required to grow the cells is saved. Each of the specified chromosomes appears as a different coloured fluorescent dot in the cell nuclei on the microscope slide, and the number of appropriately coloured dots per nucleus indicates the number of copies of that chromosome present. Trisomies (the presence of three copies of the chromosome instead of the normal two) for chromosomes 21, (Down's Syndrome), 18 and 13 are of chief importance, so it is possible to exclude these three trisomies and give a rapid result which means that the parents can be given some important information without waiting for a full chromosome analysis. Quantitative Fluorescence-PCR (QF-PCR) is a much more efficient and high-throughput molecular technique for establishing the copy number of important chromosomes, and has replaced FISH as the method of choice for rapid testing in laboratories processing medium to high numbers of prenatal samples. However, both these techniques fail to identify other important abnormalities that would be detected if a full analysis were done. Whether a rapid trisomy scan is adequate is a point of debate, but most laboratories do perform the full analysis whether or not they use a rapid result technique. (The situation might be different if parents were paying for each test and opted for only the rapid result one.) What is important from the medico-legal viewpoint is that the parents are fully informed about the type of test(s) to be used and their degree of reliability.

---

[13] Berry, AC, Docherty, Z and Bobrow, M, Abnormal chromosome complement after normal amniocentesis result, *Lancet*, 1992; 340: 1361

(c) Some tests are known to have an inherent error rate. Such tests are not ideal, and would not be offered unless the error rate was less than 5% or of that order. A couple might have to decide whether to undergo a preimplantation test knowing that this degree of error remained. They would be able to have, as back-up, a more reliable test during the pregnancy but might decline this for fear of the risk of miscarriage. However much the risk of error is explained and accepted there is inevitably shock and hand wringing when it actually occurs. 1 chance in 25 seems a low risk, but even with this error rate, a misdiagnosis must be expected from time to time.[14] Such an error should not be of medico-legal importance provided the risks have been carefully explained and weighed up beforehand. Careful documentation of the explanation given is important here.

CONCLUSIONS

Although there are many situations in clinical genetics where a mistake is clearly legally significant there are still a number of scenarios in which the boundaries of legally acceptable practice are as yet undefined. These boundaries are likely to become clearer over the coming decade.

---

[14] Ogilvie, CM, Uses of error: Laboratory diagnosis, *Lancet*, 2003; 361: 160

FETAL MEDICINE

Pam Loughna

INTRODUCTION

Fetal medicine is a relatively new specialty. It has, to date, been a relatively unsued one. That is likely to change. It has the potential to cause and to avoid disabilities which have lifelong and very financially significant consequences. A disabled child cannot sue saying: It would have been better if I had never been born: but he can sue saying: I have a disability which could have been eliminated by you, or which was caused by you. Parents can recover the additional costs associated with bringing up a disabled child.

Fetal medicine includes all aspects of pre-natal diagnosis and the management of pregnancies affected by fetal anomalies, including structural, genetic and growth disorders. Whilst ultrasound is the linchpin of modern pre-natal diagnosis, biochemical and haematological investigations are also involved, with cytogenetics providing diagnostic information on chromosomal and genetic conditions. There are also several interventions which may be performed. Most of these are diagnostic tests (including amniocentesis, chorion villus sampling (CVS) etc.) although some are therapeutic, eg intrauterine transfusion.

Ultrasound permits safe examination of the uterus and its contents during pregnancy. The Royal College of Obstetricians and Gynaecologists recommends that all pregnant women in the United Kingdom are offered at least one scan during the pregnancy, which should combine accurate dating of the pregnancy and examination of fetal anatomy.[1] These two factors can be satisfactorily combined in the so-called routine anomaly scan, performed between 18 and 22 weeks. Not all obstetric units offer an anomaly scan, instead offering a dating scan only, which is usually performed between 10 and 14 weeks. Across the United Kingdom, therefore, the level of prenatal screening offered to pregnant women varies.

Using ultrasound, it is possible to identify how many fetuses are present and to demonstrate the presence of a beating fetal heart confirming that the pregnancy is ongoing. Various biometric measurements may be made which, in early pregnancy, confirm the gestational age and later may be used to monitor the rate of fetal growth. Most aspects of fetal anatomy may be seen in detail, making it

---

[1] *RCOG Ultrasound Screening Working Party Report*, July 2000

possible to diagnose many structural malformations which occur. However, it is not possible to identify all structural abnormalities in this way. The placenta can be examined for location and texture, and in multiple pregnancies it is possible to identify the chorionicity i.e. whether or not twins share a placenta. Amniotic fluid volume can be assessed, and fetal wellbeing can be examined using both B mode (imaging) and Doppler ultrasound (which permits examination of blood flow).

Structural abnormalities may be external evidence of underlying chromosomal anomalies such as Down's syndrome (trisomy 21). Whilst ultrasound scanning is used both for screening and diagnosis of structural malformations, information concerning the genetic make-up of the fetus can only be obtained by invasive testing of the pregnancy which carries with it a risk of pregnancy loss of 1 in 100. All invasive tests should employ continuous ultrasound guidance.[2] To examine fetal chromosomes or DNA, it is necessary to obtain cells of fetal origin. Chorion villus sampling (performed from 11 weeks gestation) permits the sampling of placental tissue using ultrasound by either transcervical or transabdominal routes. Fetal fibroblasts (cells which have been shed from the fetal skin) can be obtained by amniocentesis which is performed from 15 weeks gestation. Aspiration of fetal blood either from the vessels in the umbilical cord or the intrahepatic portion of the umbilical vein (fetal blood sampling or cordocentesis) can be performed from 18-20 weeks gestation. Fetal blood can be tested in the same way as postnatal blood for haematological, biochemical, endocrine, microbiological and genetic tests.

Fetal therapy is not commonly indicated or performed. The oldest and most established example is intrauterine transfusion for fetal anaemia, usually but not exclusively secondary to Rhesus immunisation. Other fetal therapies include the insertion of small drains or shunts into an obstructed bladder or fluid collection in the chest (pleural effusion), relief of obstructed heart valves by balloon valvoplasty, and open surgical treatment of malformations such as congenital diaphragmatic hernia and spina bifida. The role of most fetal therapy remains controversial with poorly defined criteria for intervention and uncertain benefit. All such interventions carry a risk of pregnancy loss.

When an abnormality is found, or if a woman is deemed to be at high risk of her pregnancy being affected by a genetic or congenital abnormality, management may be within her local hospital or, more commonly, she will be referred to the regional fetal medicine unit. Once a diagnosis has been reached, decisions regarding the subsequent management of the pregnancy need to made, and these may include the option of termination of pregnancy. Whilst every effort must be made to confirm diagnosis as soon as possible, there are many occasions when the pregnancy is well advanced before the possibility of termination becomes apparent.[3] After 14 weeks of gestation, the commonest mode of pregnancy termination is by induction of labour. In order to remove the risk of a live birth, it

[2] *RCOG Green Top Guideline No: 8: Amniocentesis and Chorion Villus Sampling*, 2005
[3] *RCOG Report of the RCOG Ethics Committee: A Consideration of the Law and Ethics in Relation to Late Termination of Pregnancy for Fetal Abnormality*, March 1998

is recommended that feticide be performed when termination of pregnancy is indicated after 21 completed weeks of pregnancy (i.e. gestations greater than 21+6 weeks)[4]. Feticide involves the ultrasound guided injection of strong potassium chloride, local anaesthetic or air directly into the fetal circulation, usually the heart, to achieve asystole.

Fetal medicine is a multi-disciplinary specialty involving obstetricians, midwives, radiologists, ultrasonographers, neonatologists, paediatric surgeons, cardiologists and neurologists, and clinical geneticists. The multi-disciplinary team has an important role in counselling so that parents can make well-informed decisions about the pregnancy and postnatal care. In some instances, pre-pregnancy counselling may be an important component of clinical management and this will usually include discussion with clinical geneticists.

Mistakes and untoward events can occur in any of these areas of fetal medicine. In litigation terms, the most serious are those which lead to the birth of a handicapped child either following perceived failure to detect a serious abnormality and the subsequent denial of the possibility of therapeutic termination of pregnancy, or more rarely following an intervention which is believed to have caused or contributed to the handicap.

ROUTINE ULTRASOUND SCANS

Basics

There are two commonly performed routine scans in pregnancy: the booking or dating scan (usually performed between 10 and 14 weeks gestation) and the fetal anomaly scan (usually performed between 18 and 22 weeks). Not all women will be offered both scans; it depends on local practice. Several units still do not offer routine anomaly scans.

The dating scan (level 1 scan)

This scan is performed to assess the following:

(i) viability
(ii) number of fetuses
(iii) gestational age
(iv) chorionicity if multiple pregnancy
(v) anatomy of uterus and adnexae (ovaries and tubes)

Problems can arise with any of these aspects of the scan. The Royal College of Radiologists and RCOG have drawn up joint guidelines intended to minimise the

---

4 *RCOG Termination of Pregnancy for Fetal Abnormality in England Wales and Scotland Working Party Report*, January 1996

risk of problems arising. These address the issue of viability in particular. It is recommended that two sonographers independently perform a scan to confirm that a first trimester pregnancy is non-viable. Mistakes in this area can lead either to the evacuation of a uterus which had contained a wanted on-going pregnancy (a mistake which is rarely discovered) or disruption of a viable pregnancy which miscarries at a later date. The guidelines also make recommendations concerning the ultrasound equipment to be used. Unless scan machines are capable of being up-graded, they should be replaced every five years. Adherence to guidelines in this area reduces the risk of mistakes.

Failure to identify a multiple pregnancy at booking scan is rare, and is unlikely to have adverse consequences other than parental (and sonographer!) surprise if a later anomaly scan is performed and twins are the identified. However, the presence of a multiple gestation renders biochemical screening for Down's syndrome inaccurate, so failure to identify twins before biochemical screening will render the test useless. More serious consequences arise from the failure to identify monochorionic twins i.e. identical or monozygotic twins who share a placenta. Twin pregnancies where there are two placentas do not have a significantly higher rate of major complication other than slightly premature birth when compared with singletons. Monochorionic diamniotic twin pregnancies, on the other hand, have a significant risk of twin twin transfusion syndrome which carries a high overall loss rate and an increased risk of cerebral palsy in survivors. Twin twin transfusion syndrome can be treated and there is evidence that treatment improves outcome. However, early detection of the problem gives the best chances of success and monochorionic diamniotic twin pregnancies should be followed up with scans every two weeks from the early second trimester.

The routine scan (level 2 scan) (The anomaly scan)

This scan is performed between 18 and 22 weeks. The objectives include:

(i) reassurance that the baby is apparently normal
(ii) identification of non-viable abnormalities
(iii) identification of abnormalities associated with high morbidity and long-term handicap
(iv) identification of fetal conditions with the potential for intra-uterine therapy
(v) identification of fetal conditions which will require postnatal investigation and/or treatment
(vi) parental preparation.

In addition, the anomaly scan provides an opportunity to confirm gestational age, assess liquor volume and identify the placental site. The provision of routine anomaly scans varies across the country with only 82% of obstetric units providing the service in 1996. There is considerable variation in the degree of detail of the examination. Obstetric ultrasound units should have a protocol which defines what measurements should be taken, and which anatomical structures are to be examined and in what detail. The protocol will take into account the expertise of the sonographers, the quality of the ultrasound equipment and the time available for each scan appointment.

A good protocol will define exactly what views of each organ are to be obtained to complete the examination e.g. for the spine, transverse, sagittal and coronal views of the length of the spine. It will also provide guidance on what the sonographer is to do if certain views are not obtained. For example, examination of the fetal lips to exclude cleft lip forms part of many examinations, but if it is impossible to obtain clear views because of fetal lie etc., few units would bring a woman back for a second scan. However, the report should state what was and was not seen and the reasons why.

Sonographers in an obstetric ultrasound unit have the expertise to recognise abnormal findings but are not necessarily expected to make a final diagnosis. For example, they may recognise that a structure such as the heart is not normal but may not be able to give an exact diagnosis. Their role is to identify cases in which there is an abnormality or suspicion of abnormality which can then be referred on for a second opinion.

The detection rate of different abnormalities varies considerably from unit to unit and depending on the organ system examined. The overall detection rate varies from 13% to 85%[5]. However, for different organ systems the detection rate varies from 98% for anencephaly to 23% for major heart malformations. The difference in detection rates for different anomalies can be explained in part by the ease of recognition of abnormalities e.g. in anencephaly, the absence of the cranium renders appearances of the head abnormal in all views whereas tetralogy of Fallot, a major cardiac defect, will only be detected if the major arteries leaving the heart are examined as well as the standard screening view of the four cardiac chambers. Some abnormalities cannot be seen on prenatal ultrasound and are only suspected if there is an abnormality of, for example, liquor volume (e.g. tracheo-oesophageal fistula) and others are not apparent for developmental reasons until after 22 weeks e.g. bowel atresias.

The majority of anomaly scans are performed on women who are at low risk of having a baby with a structural malformation. This can lead to a low index of suspicion on the part of the sonographer which at times contributes to poor detection rates.

The main areas for complaint by patients are when a serious malformation has not been identified. This will usually lead to a claim on behalf of the mother, who would otherwise have sought to have the pregnancy terminated. Less commonly, a claim is brought on behalf of the child who, with possible intervention, could have avoided serious sequelae of a congenital malformation.

---

[5] Levi, S *et al*, *Ultrasound Obstet Gynecol* 1991: 1; 102-10; Luck, C, *BMJ*, 1992: 304; 1474-8

Miscarriage following a procedure

All invasive procedures carry a risk of miscarriage, ranging from 1 in 100 for CVS and amniocentesis to as high 1 in 4 for fetal blood sampling in the presence of a very sick fetus. Therapeutic interventions also carry a risk of miscarriage which varies with the nature of the intervention. When procedures are performed after 23-24 weeks, the principal risk is of premature labour with the risk of fetal demise being present but less.

All women must be counselled about the risks of the procedure being performed, and allowed to make her own risk:benefit analysis. In cases where the risk of an abnormal result is much higher than the risk of miscarriage e.g. an autosomal recessive condition, most parents who would seek termination of an affected pregnancy will be happy to proceed with an invasive test. However, a 40 year old woman in her first ongoing pregnancy after three miscarriages with a risk assessment of Down's syndrome of 1 in 50 may feel that the 1% risk of miscarriage from a test is too great.

To prove breach of duty there needs to be evidence that the procedure was performed in an inappropriate manner or by someone without appropriate training and/or supervision.

Fetal damage

The use of continuous ultrasound guidance in invasive procedures minimises the risks of fetal damage. There have been cases where brain damage has been caused by the needle used for amniocentesis being inserted into the fetal skull. Ocular and skin damage has also been reported. If continuous ultrasound guidance is correctly employed, inadvertent puncture of the fetal body will not occur. Damage may also arise during therapeutic procedures e.g. shunt insertion, laser treatment etc. If procedures are performed by suitably experienced individuals with an appropriate level of expertise under continuous ultrasound guidance, the risks of fetal damage are minimal. Most problems arise from poor technique or lack of expertise, although unexpected fetal movement may contribute. Great care must be exercised to avoid damage during procedures, which are often technically difficult and time-consuming. Expertise needs to be centralised as all procedures are performed infrequently. The RCOG has provided guidance on the number of diagnostic procedures which are probably required to be performed on an annual basis to maintain expertise[10] but it is more difficult to assess such a figure for rarely performed procedures.

Failed feticide

When feticide is performed, it is essential to ensure that the fetus has died before the labour is induced. Direct injection of potassium chloride or air into the fetal

[10] *RCOG Greentop Guidelines No: 8, Amniocentesis*, 2000

The main reason why anomalies are missed, however, is that the ultrasound examination was not performed to an adequate standard. This may be a failure on behalf of the sonographer, in which case it is probable that it represents a breach of duty of care, or may be due to difficulties experienced during the scan rendering adequate examination impossible e.g. maternal adiposity. Any such difficulties encountered must be recorded and a decision made as to whether or not a further scan should be performed. The mother must also be informed of any such difficulties and she should be aware of the reasons for the difficulties encountered.

Some units will keep hard copies or digital copies of various still images representing standard views of fetal anatomy. Whilst it is sometimes difficult to interpret still images (particularly of moving structures such as the heart), if the image does not represent the accepted view of the anatomical structure being examined, the still view may indicate that that part of the examination was not performed to an adequate standard. Problems of adequate storage of hard copies, which are usually produced on a thermal printer and which fade in time particularly if exposed to light, mean that it is not possible for every unit to adopt such a strategy. The capability of most modern ultrasound machines to store digital images will almost certainly lead to storage of images becoming universal practice in the future.

There are few structural malformations for which obstetric management needs be altered to enhance outcome for the baby, although some will benefit from delivery in a unit capable of supplying neonatal intensive care e.g. duct dependent cardiac lesions. However, this aspect of pre-natal diagnosis rarely gives cause for complaint. Lesions which might benefit from early delivery or intrauterine treatment are rare,

INVASIVE TESTS

Basics

There are three commonly performed invasive tests employed in pre-natal diagnosis. All tests are performed under continuous ultrasound guidance, with amniocentesis being available in district general hospitals and chorion villus sampling and fetal blood sampling generally limited to regional fetal medicine units. Traditionally, results from these tests have required culture of the cells obtained until sufficient are available for analysis of the chromosomes. This can take up to three weeks for amniocentesis and chorion villus sampling, although a result from blood can usually be obtained within 72 hours. Modern techniques of fluorescent in situ hydridisation (FISH) and polymerase chain reaction (PCR) have permitted preliminary results for certain chromosomes to be available within 24 hours of amniocentesis and chorion villus sampling. These techniques are not universally available and require confirmation from standard culture and cytogenetic techniques which examine all the chromosomes and can identify smaller chromosomal abnormalities such as translocations which may have severe consequences for the affected individual.

All the techniques may fail. The failure may be a failure to obtain a sample or a failed culture in the laboratory. Such failures occur uncommonly (approximately 1 in 200) but may mean a second test is necessary.

Chorion villus sampling (CVS)

This involves taking a small sample of placenta from which the fetal chromosomes and DNA may be isolated. This type of sample is also suitable for certain enzyme assays involved in the pre-natal diagnosis of inherited metabolic disorders. CVS may be performed from 11 weeks gestation. Although technically possible at earlier gestations, CVS before 10 weeks is associated with an increased risk of limb reduction deformities, and is therefore no longer performed at early gestations. CVS may be performed transabdominally, when a needle is passed through the mother's abdominal wall into the uterus and directly into the placenta (not penetrating the amniotic sac), or transcervically, when a catheter or forceps is inserted through the cervical canal directly into the placenta. When performed by skilled personnel, the risk of pregnancy loss following CVS is approximately 1 in 100 above the background risk.

CVS has the advantage of providing diagnostic information early in the pregnancy, often by 12 weeks gestation. This enables decisions to be made about the continuance or otherwise of the pregnancy to be made before the parents have made the pregnancy known to family and friends, allowing more privacy. Termination of pregnancy, if appropriate, may be performed surgically under anaesthetic, which many women find preferable to medical induction of termination.

The disadvantages of CVS include the possibility of placental mosaicism, where the chromosomes of the placenta (which are of the same origin as the fetus) may be different from those of the fetus, or may show a mixed karyotype, some cells being normal and some abnormal. Although mosaicism can occur in amniotic fluid samples and even blood, it is more common in the placenta. The discovery of possible mosaicism will usually lead to a further invasive test being necessary to confirm the fetal karyotype which carries a further 1 in 100 risk of miscarriage and delay in getting a final result as well as further anxiety for the mother. Maternal cell contamination is also possible, the placental villi being in close approximation to the decidua (lining of the womb) which is maternal in origin. It is therefore essential that the sample obtained is checked by the laboratory under a microscope to ensure that only placental villi are examined cytogenetically.

The main causes of claims arising from CVS relate to laboratory problems, including failure to exclude maternal cell contamination.

Amniocentesis

This is the commonest diagnostic test performed. Amniotic fluid is aspirated from the amniotic sac through a needle inserted through the maternal abdominal wall directly into the amniotic sac. The test is performed from 15 weeks gestation. Although it is possible to perform amniocentesis earlier, there is an increased risk of miscarriage and failed laboratory culture.

Traditionally, amniocentesis was performed blind i.e. without ultrasound guidance. This lead to a number of failed aspirations (known as dry taps), blood stained samples and fetal damage[6]. With the advent of real time ultrasound, the technique has been refined and now should always be performed under continuous ultrasound guidance[7]. The placenta should be avoided if possible, particularly if the mother is Rhesus negative, when placental puncture increases the risk of feto-maternal haemorrhage which can lead to Rhesus isoimmunisation. Using continuous ultrasound guidance, keeping the tip of the needle in sight at all times, removes the risk of fetal damage. Blood staining may be from maternal or fetal blood, and may limit the ability of the laboratory to culture the fetal fibroblast cells. Maternal cell contamination can also occur as the needle passes through the maternal tissues. This can be avoided by using a needle with a stillete which is removed when the tip of the needle is in the amniotic fluid, and by discarding the first 1-2 ml of the liquor aspirated.

Claims arising from amniocentesis generally relate to fetal damage believed to be caused by the procedure. Given that there are recommendations from the RCOG that all procedures are performed under continuous ultrasound guidance, fetal damage should not occur. Cases involving penetration of the fetal brain by the needle are likely to be settled.

Fetal blood sampling

This technique involves aspiration of fetal blood from the umbilical cord or intrahepatic vein, and is only performed in fetal medicine units. If the placental insertion of the umbilical cord is used, it is possible to obtain maternal blood and therefore samples must be checked in the haematology laboratory to confirm that they are pure fetal blood.

FETAL THERAPEUTIC INTERVENTIONS

There are a number of interventions available in fetal life to correct or ameliorate a congenital condition with the aim of preventing damage which may occur as pregnancy progresses. Fetal anaemia can be corrected by transfusion and the risks of pulmonary hyoplasia secondary to absent amniotic fluid volume when the bladder outflow tract is obstructed may be minimised by inserting a shunt

---

[6] Romero, R, *et al.*, *Obstet Gynecol*, 1985: 65; 426-30

[7] *RCOG Greentop Guideline No 8: Amniocentesis and Chorion Villus Sampling*, 2005

between the fetal bladder and amniotic sac (a vesico-amniotic shunt). Fetal therapies are only available in fetal medicine units.

The indications, safely and efficacy of fetal interventions, with the exception of transfusion, are unclear and parents must be counselled accordingly. Even with widespread experience of vesico-amniotic shunting, the true benefits remain unclear.

Claims arising from fetal therapy are few, and relate to fetal damage secondary to the procedure.

SCREENING FOR DOWN'S SYNDROME

As with ultrasound scans, practice in relation to screening for Down's syndrome, the commonest chromosomal abnormality, varies across the country. National guidelines have now been published (National Down's Syndrome Screening Programme. Antenatal screening - working standards. 2004) but will not come into effect until 2007. Traditionally, screening for Down's syndrome was based on maternal age, an individual's risk of having a baby with Down's syndrome increasing with her age. However, a woman of any age can have a baby with Down's syndrome, and therefore alternative screening modalities have been introduced.

The commonest screening test for Down's syndrome is maternal serum screening in which a blood test is taken from the mother between 14 and 20 weeks gestation and two or three hormones measured in the blood. A risk estimate is then provided. An alternative test is the nuchal translucency measurement, when the thickness of a small collection of fluid at the back of the fetal neck (present in all fetuses) is measured on an ultrasound scan performed between 11 and 14 weeks.

As screening tests, they are not diagnostic and only give an estimate of risk. Some cases will be false positive i.e. estimated to be in the high risk category (usually 1:250 or greater) when the fetus is normal. There will also be false negatives i.e. when the risk estimate was low (less than 1:250) but the fetus is affected. The detection rate of these tests i.e. the number of affected individuals identified as high risk varies from 60 – 80% overall, but serum screening detection rate is age dependent i.e. the detection rate is higher in older women[8].

Claims in relation to screening for Down's syndrome usually arise from a failure to offer screening when it is generally available, or a failure to explain the nature of the tests particularly in relation to the possibility of false negatives. Failure to offer a test when it is available will often lead to settlement, although there may be causation problems, e.g. in relation to serum screening in women under the age of 30 in whom the detection rate is less than 50%.

---

[8] Crossley, JA, *et al.*, *Prenat Diag*, 1991: 11; 83-101

WHAT HAPPENS WHEN AN ABNORMALITY IS FOUND?

Women usually attend for routine scans anticipating reassurance of normality, and some may even be unaware that the scan may detect an abnormality. If an abnormality is found, the amount of information provided by the sonographer will vary according to local practice, but an appointment will usually be made for the woman to discuss the problem with the consultant obstetrician or one of his team either on the day of the scan or within 24 hours. Problems obviously arise at weekends when delays inevitably occur.

If the sonographer is confident of the diagnosis e.g. spina bifida, a further scan may not be indicated and the obstetrician will provide counselling about the condition and discuss the options which will usually include termination of pregnancy. If the parents choose this option, arrangements are made for appropriate admission as soon as possible, usually within 48 hours. Most units will use mifepristone, an anti-progesterone, which is given in tablet form 36 hours before labour is induced. The woman remains at home during this time. Once admitted, labour is induced using pessaries or tablets and usually takes up to 24 hours. Once the baby is delivered, discussion regarding postmortem examination and disposal arrangements are made although these will have been discussed beforehand.

Thus, with a straightforward diagnosis, there need be little delay between diagnosis and management decisions.

If an abnormality is suspected, again the mother will be counselled by one of the obstetric team or specialist midwife and a level 3 scan arranged, This may be within the local hospital or, more commonly, at the regional fetal medicine unit. Most fetal medicine units will offer an appointment within 24 hours or 48 at most, again with further delays inevitable if a weekend intervenes.

In many cases, further investigations are indicated, such as karyotyping. This will be offered and usually performed on the same day as the level 3 scan, with preliminary results usually being available within 48 hours using modern techniques. Further counselling may then be necessary, but decisions regarding management may be possible within seven days of the initial scan. If rapid karyotyping is not available, then it may be three weeks before results are available. In such cases, management decisions may not be possible until four weeks after initial diagnosis.

In cases of fetal abnormality diagnosed in the first trimester, surgical termination may be available. This has the advantage of the mother having an anaesthetic and therefore being unaware of the procedure, but the disadvantage that postmortem information may not be available.

Mid-trimester termination of pregnancy involves induction of labour in the vast majority of cases, few units offering surgical termination after 14 weeks gestation. The process is usually conducted on the labour ward of the hospital, although it may take place on the gynaecology ward depending on gestation and local practice. If the pregnancy has exceeded 21+6 weeks gestation, it is recommended that feticide be performed prior to the induction of labour to ensure that the fetus cannot be born alive. This has to be performed within the setting of a fetal medicine unit, and it is essential that the operator ensure that the fetus is dead before labour is induced. Failure to achieve fetal demise can result in the birth of a live baby.

Any birth after 24 weeks gestation must be registered, even if the birth is the result of a termination. This must be made clear to the parents during counselling to avoid distress after delivery.

Section 1(1)(d) of the Abortion Act 1967 permits termination without gestational age limit in cases where there is a "substantiated" risk of serious handicap. However, late terminations cause considerable distress to parents and health care staff and therefore every effort must be made to ensure that pre-natal diagnosis is not delayed[9]. There is considerable debate about which cases fulfil the requirements for termination under Section 1(1)(d). The discovery of a fetal abnormality will not always lead to discussion regarding termination, as many obstetricians would not personally support termination of pregnancy for relatively mild and correctable abnormalities. Therefore, cases in which a woman seeks recourse to law either because of failure to detect a correctable defect, or failure to offer termination of pregnancy thus denying her the option to avoid the birth of her affected child may fail if the court is persuaded that termination of pregnancy would not have been available. Similarly, if feticide is indicated but the practitioners who would perform it do not support the termination request, the termination cannot continue. It is essential that, in cases where termination may be controversial, discussion regarding this take place in a multi-disciplinary setting and agreement from all medical personnel involved achieved prior to making an offer to the parents.

CONSENT ISSUES

Traditionally, ultrasound scans and screening tests were performed without formal consent. However, cases have arisen where women have complained because an abnormality was found when they did not want the scan to look for anomalies or where screening tests have been performed without adequate information leading to confusion and distress. There is also an issue regarding the options available to the mothers when problems are discovered. Pre-natal diagnosis is an information gathering exercise, not a seek and destroy mission. Parents must not feel pressurised to proceed with either diagnostic tests or

---

[9] *RCOG Report of the RCOG Ethics Committee, A Consideration of the Law and Ethics in relation to Late Termination of Pregnancy for Fetal Abnormality*, March 1998

termination of pregnancy unless it is their own decision. Diagnostic tests must not be denied those women who feel that they would not act on the results but who would like the benefit of foreknowledge. Each step in pre-natal diagnosis must be both seen and presented as an option rather than a predetermined conveyor belt process.

In order to ensure that women do understand what the tests they are offered can detect, many units now obtain written consent for screening tests and scans. Invasive procedures have been accompanied by written consent for some years now. The information given prior to obtaining consent may be written and should include a brief description of what may happen if certain results are obtained. The difference between screening and diagnostic tests must be explained, with mention of the possibility of false positives and false negatives.

IMPORTANT MISTAKES

Failure to offer a test

If any test or scan is routinely available but not offered to a woman who has an affected pregnancy leading to the birth of a handicapped child, litigation is possible. The failure may be on the part of the general practitioner, midwife or obstetrician. It is essential that all those involved in ante-natal care, both in the hospital and the community, are aware of what is available to whom and how to organise tests. The discussion and offering of tests should be documented as having taken place.

If the test would, on the balance of probabilities, have confirmed the presence of the abnormality or enabled the abnormality to be detected there will be liability. This causes difficulty in relation to serum screening where, although the overall detection rate exceeds 50%, the actual detection rate is age dependent with women under 30 having a detection rate below 50%.

If the test is not routinely available, or if there is no clinical indication to offer it (e.g. invasive tests usually limited to recognised high risk groups), then there is no liability on behalf of the health care professionals.

Delay in offering/performing a test

Pre-natal diagnosis is possible at any stage of pregnancy, whether by ultrasound or invasive procedure. CVS, amniocentesis and fetal blood sampling can be performed up to term. However, the options available if a result is abnormal may be limited if the diagnosis is not made before 24 weeks gestation as not all abnormalities for which termination would be offered before 24 weeks are deemed to fit the criteria for termination after 24 weeks. In addition, some women cannot contemplate feticide, finding the deliberate act of causing fetal demise (rather than it dying during an induced labour) impossible to contemplate. If the delay arises through negligence there may be liability. However, in many cases the causes of delay are multifactorial and the delay is not negligent.

Counselling issues

Poor counselling results in many complaints but rarely leads to litigation unless the counselling misinformed the mother and effectively denied her an option that she would otherwise have accepted. Examples include emphasising or exaggerating the risks of diagnostic tests, or underestimating the value of screening tests. This may lead a woman to refuse a test which, given accurate information, she would have accepted. Uniformity of information can be achieved with written information provided to all women, and with good training and updating of those involved at all stages of the counselling process. The mother must be aware that she has options at all stages, and acceptance of one test does not commit her to anything e.g. amniocentesis must not be denied those women who feel that they would not terminate an affected pregnancy but would like to know if their baby is affected. Counselling needs to be recorded in some way to ensure that a record exist of what was said.

Misinterpretation or failure to act on results

This particularly applies to results of maternal serum screening. There are two possible areas for misinterpretation: a) inaccuracy in gestational age and b) the levels of alphafetoprotein or AFP (one of the hormones measured). The levels of the hormones change with gestation and if the gestational age is either inaccurately recorded or miscalculated, the test result will be inaccurate. It is therefore essential that gestational age is confirmed by ultrasound scans and accurately recorded on the laboratory request form. If the gestational age is over-estimated, the risk estimate may be inappropriately high whereas an under-estimate of the gestation can give an inappropriately low risk.

Serum levels of AFP may be elevated in cases of certain structural abnormality e.g. spina bifida or in relation to bleeding in pregnancy. If a raised AFP is detected, ultrasound should be performed to exclude neural tube defects.

Each unit must have a system to ensure that women receive results of tests performed whether normal or abnormal. The practice of “no news is good news” is inappropriate and all results must be passed on to the mother. This ensures that all high risk or abnormal results are seen and acted upon. Most women will assume that if they do not receive notification of the result of e.g. serum screening that they are at low risk, and they will not necessarily pursue the result. This also applies to other blood tests performed routinely in pregnancy which have an effect on the fetus or subsequent pregnancies e.g. evidence of recent rubella infection, the presence of red cell antibodies etc.

Missed diagnosis

This problem principally relates to failure to detect structural malformations by ultrasound, but may arise if structural abnormalities associated with aneuploidy are diagnosed but karyotyping is not offered. In order to assess if a diagnosis has been missed because of negligence it is necessary to consider a number of factors:

(i) Is the malformation detectable by ultrasound performed at the relevant gestational age?
(ii) Was the organ system affected routinely examined according to the local protocol?
(iii) Does the examination on the protocol allow the detection of the specific abnormality?
(iv) Is the diagnosis one which the person who performed the scan would reasonably be expected to make?
(v) Was the equipment used appropriate for the level of scan?
(vi) Was the sonographer adequately trained and/or supervised?
(vii) Were there factors recorded which mitigated against accurate imaging e.g patient obesity etc?

Not all major malformations are detected; cardiac defects in particular are often missed. In order to detect an anomaly, the organ system involved must be examined in sufficient detail to permit identification of the abnormality. For example, not all scan protocols demand that the long bones of the limbs be examined and confirmed to be present and normal. Thus, if the long bones are not examined, abnormalities of them (including absence of them) will not be detected.

Incorrect diagnosis

The most serious consequence of incorrect diagnosis would be the termination of a normal pregnancy. Referral for a second opinion helps reduce this risk, as does getting a colleague to check abnormal findings – a practice which is quite common in obstetric ultrasound units. It is very important that pre-natal diagnostic units audit their performance in this regard and take steps to remedy problems identified. However, if no post-mortem examination is made, mistakes may not always be discovered.

It is always possible that samples e.g. amniocentesis samples can be mixed up or mis labelled. The labelling of such genetic samples should be checked with the patient so that she is happy that her sample is accurately identified to minimise such risks.

Miscarriage following a procedure

All invasive procedures carry a risk of miscarriage, ranging from 1 in 100 for CVS and amniocentesis to as high 1 in 4 for fetal blood sampling in the presence of a very sick fetus. Therapeutic interventions also carry a risk of miscarriage which varies with the nature of the intervention. When procedures are performed after 23-24 weeks, the principal risk is of premature labour with the risk of fetal demise being present but less.

All women must be counselled about the risks of the procedure being performed, and allowed to make her own risk:benefit analysis. In cases where the risk of an abnormal result is much higher than the risk of miscarriage e.g. an autosomal recessive condition, most parents who would seek termination of an affected pregnancy will be happy to proceed with an invasive test. However, a 40 year old woman in her first ongoing pregnancy after three miscarriages with a risk assessment of Down's syndrome of 1 in 50 may feel that the 1% risk of miscarriage from a test is too great.

Unless there is evidence that the procedure was performed in an inappropriate manner or by someone without appropriate training and/or supervision, it is extremely unlikely that a miscarriage will occur as a result of a negligent act.

Fetal damage

The use of continuous ultrasound guidance in invasive procedures minimises the risks of fetal damage. There have been cases where brain damage has been caused by the needle used for amniocentesis being inserted into the fetal skull. Ocular and skin damage has also been reported. If continuous ultrasound guidance is correctly employed, inadvertent puncture of the fetal body will not occur. Damage may also arise during therapeutic procedures e.g. shunt insertion, laser treatment etc. If procedures are performed by suitably experienced individuals with an appropriate level of expertise under continuous ultrasound guidance, the risks of fetal damage are minimal. Most problems arise from poor technique or lack of expertise, although unexpected fetal movement may contribute. Great care must be exercised to avoid damage during procedures, which are often technically difficult and time-consuming. Expertise needs to be centralised as all procedures are performed infrequently. The RCOG has provided guidance on the number of diagnostic procedures which are probably required to be performed on an annual basis to maintain expertise[10] but it is more difficult to assess such a figure for rarely performed procedures.

Failed feticide

When feticide is performed, it is essential to ensure that the fetus has died before the labour is induced. Direct injection of potassium chloride or air into the fetal

---

[10] *RCOG Greentop Guidelines No: 8, Amniocentesis*, 2000

heart is currently the preferred method. Asystole occurs rapidly but must be confirmed for a period of at least two minutes to ensure that fetal demise has occurred. Problems arise if the injection is not directly into the heart, when a prolonged severe bradycardia may occur but recover after a minute or so, or if insufficient potassium chloride is injected. If cardiac activity recommences, a further injection must be performed.

OBSTETRIC INJURIES OTHER THAN CEREBRAL PALSY

Anthony Johnson

The serious obstetric accidents other than cerebral palsy which commonly result in litigation are:-

- Shoulder dystocia resulting in obstetric brachial plexus injury (OBPP)
- Anal sphincter injury and perineal damage
- Uterine rupture
- Caesarean section
- Post partum haemorrhage resulting in hysterectomy
- Uterine inversion
- Placenta accreta
- Failure to diagnose congenital abnormalities in the fetus

OBSTETRIC BRACHIAL PLEXUS PALSY (OBPP)

Obstetric brachial plexus palsy (Erb's palsy, Erb-Duchenne palsy, Klumpke paralysis) refers to weakness or total paralysis of the muscles innervated by the nerve roots which form the brachial plexus (C5/C6/C7/C8 and T1). The incidence of obstetric brachial plexus palsy (OBPP) in England and Wales ranges from 0.2 to 2% of vaginal cephalic deliveries[1]. Evans-Jones[2] *et al* in a large series from the UK and the Republic of Ireland report an incidence of 1 per 2300 live births. There are four types of injury ranging from neuropraxia (where the nerve has been damaged but has not been torn), through neuroma (where there is fibrosis of the nerve), to rupture and finally to avulsion of the nerve from the spinal cord. The pattern of injury is classified by the scheme devised by Gilbert and reported by Birch[3]:

- Group 1: C5 and C6 have been damaged, the child is born with paralysis of the shoulder muscles and the elbow flexors.

---

[1] O'Leary, JA, *Shoulder Dystocia and Birth Injury, Prevention and Treatment*, 1992, New York, McGraw-Hill Inc.

[2] Evans-Jones, G, Kay, SP, Weindling, AM, Cranny, G, Ward, A, Bradshaw, A and Hernon, C, Congenital brachial plexus palsy: incidence, causes and outcome in the United Kingdom and Republic of Ireland, *Arch Dis Child Fetal Neonatal Ed*, 2003; 88; 185-0

[3] Birch, R, Obstetric brachial plexus palsy, *Clinical Risk*, 1995, 1:2, 71-73

- Group 2: C5 C6 and C7 have been damaged. The child is born with paralysis of shoulder, elbow and wrist extensors.
- Group 3: The whole plexus has been damaged. The child is born with complete paralysis of the arm.
- Group 4: The child is born with complete paralysis of the arm and there is a Horner syndrome.

The injury is more common on the right side than the left side. Total plexus palsy involving both the upper and lower roots is less common than damage to the upper roots alone. Damage to the lower roots alone is unusual.

OBPP is almost always caused during the delivery of the baby and results from stretching of the brachial plexus by excess traction. This occurs when the anterior shoulder is impacted above the symphysis pubis and excess traction and lateral flexion of the neck is used to deliver the anterior shoulder. The upper roots are most vulnerable, but with very excessive traction all the roots may be affected and total paralysis results. The damage is almost always in the plexus on the side of the anterior shoulder. Traction injury may also occur in vaginal breech delivery (which is not usually carried out in the present era) and during difficult Caesarean sections usually involving the delivery of a very small pre-term baby.

In most deliveries the baby's head is born occipito-anterior (OA). This means that the back of the baby's head is at the mother's front. Thus if the mother is lying on her back, the baby is facing down towards the delivery table. The head then restitutes (a movement to correct the "twist" of the neck which has resulted from internal rotation). The head then rotates (external rotation) as the shoulders turn in the birth canal to lie in the OA diameter; the baby then faces the maternal thigh. The delivery is completed by the obstetrician exerting gentle traction on the head in a downward direction. The anterior shoulder slips under the pubic arch and the trunk of the baby is then born by lateral flexion around the symphysis pubis.

In cases of shoulder dystocia the normal traction on the head (the "diagnostic traction") will not free the anterior shoulder. If excess traction is used then the brachial plexus may be damaged causing an OBPP.

Allen *et* al found that on average 47 Newtons (N) of force is applied for routine deliveries, 69N for difficult deliveries and 100N for deliveries that are complicated by shoulder dystocia[4]. Furthermore these authors suggested that the faster the force is applied the more vulnerable the brachial plexus is to injury. In a further paper by Gonick et al.[5] it was confirmed that clinicians double the amount of force they apply in shoulder dystocia deliveries.

[4] Allen, R, Sorab, J and Gonik, B, Risk Factors for Shoulder Dystocia, An Engineering Study of Clinician Applied Forces, *Obstet Gynecol*, 1991, 77; 325-5

[5] Gonick, B, Allen, R and Sorab, J, Objective Evaluation of the Shoulder Dystocia Phenomenon, Effect of Pelvic Orientation on Force Reduction, *Obstetrics and Gynaecology*, 1980, Volume 74, No 1, pages 44-48

When carrying out a medicolegal analysis of a case of OBPP four questions have to be addressed:

- Was there shoulder dystocia?
- Was the shoulder dystocia foreseeable in the antenatal period?
- Was the shoulder dystocia foreseeable in the intrapartum period?
- Were the correct manoeuvres undertaken in the correct sequence when the shoulder dystocia was discovered?

Was there shoulder dystocia?

It is common to find that there is no mention of shoulder dystocia, or even "difficulty in delivering the shoulders" in the notes made at the time. Sandmire and DeMott[6] report that only 50% of cases of OBPP are associated with shoulder dystocia. (It would have been more accurate to say that in 50% of cases of OBPP shoulder dystocia was not reported). Evans-Jones et al[2] in their study of 20,633 deliveries found 430 cases of OBPP: they concluded that "most cases are due to trauma at delivery which is not necessarily excessive or inappropriate". They did however note that there were 19 cases (5.9%) in which there was no obvious explanation for the injury and they thought that this raised the possibility of non traumatic causes.

The foreseeable features in the antenatal period:

- Previous history of shoulder dystocia.
- Recognised fetal macrosomia.
- Maternal diabetes
- Maternal obesity

Previous History of Shoulder Dystocia

In patients who have had a previous history of shoulder dystocia the risk of shoulder dystocia in the index confinement is 9.8% - 17 times the background population risk of 0.58%[7]. It follows that when an obstetrician is discussing the route of delivery with a mother who has a previous history of shoulder dystocia (with or without OBPP), the obstetrician has a duty to discuss the risk benefit analysis of elective Caesarean section versus attempted vaginal delivery.

Fetal Macrosomia

The incidence of shoulder dystocia is proportional to birth weight and ranges from 0.3% in infants less than 4000g to over 20% in infants over 5000g[8]. Roberts

[6] Sandmire, HF and DeMott, RK, Erb's palsy: concepts of causation, *Obstet Gynecol*, 2000, 95: 941-2

[7] Smith, RB, Lane, L and Pearson, JF, Shoulder dystocia: What happens at the next delivery?, *BJOG*, 1994, 101; 713-715

[8] Basket and Allen, Perinatal implications of Shoulder Dystocia, *Obstetrics & Gynaecology*, 1995, Volume 86 No 1, pages 14-17

(1994)[9] pointed out that the risk of shoulder dystocia in a diabetic mother with a fetus of 4500g or greater is 50% compared with 22.6% in a non-diabetic woman. It follows that in a pregnancy where the fetus is recognised to be large during the antenatal period, and especially so when the mother is diabetic, attempts should be made to ascertain the fetal weight. Estimated fetal weight (EFW) is derived from ultrasound scan (USS) measurements of abdominal circumference, head circumference, femur length and biparietal diameter - either singly or in combination. The fetal weight is estimated by measuring the chosen parameters and comparing them with standard charts for weight. There is an error in estimating fetal weight by ultrasound scan of +/- 10%[10]. However this technique has been criticised by Hall[11] who says that clinical examination is as good as ultrasound scanning in detecting a large baby. Despite the 10% error in EFW by USS, it must be remembered that although the confidence limits of estimated fetal weight deteriorate beyond 4000 G the primary error is an underestimate of fetal weight[12].

Maternal Diabetes

In diabetic patients where the EFW is >4000g and in the non-diabetic patient with an EFW of >4500g delivery by elective Caesarean section should be considered and discussed with the patient[13,14,15].

In a case of suspected fetal macrosomia a warning should be flagged in the notes to indicate, "Big baby; Beware shoulder dystocia"[16].

Maternal obesity

Maternal obesity (other than when it is associated with diabetes) and prolonged pregnancy is associated with an increased incidence of shoulder dystocia but this is of low predictive value.

The obstetrician should be prepared to agree to elective Caesarean section at thirty nine weeks gestation in those cases where a mother, after due consideration of the risk benefit analysis, elects for delivery by Caesarean section in order to

---

[9] Roberts, L, Progress, *Obstetrics and Gynaecology*, Vol 11, Chapter 12, pages 201-218
[10] Bisset, Khan, Thomas and McHugo, *Differential Diagnosis in Obstetric and Gynaecologic Ultrasound*, 1997, WB Saunders Co Ltd, page 20
[11] Hall, MH, Guessing the weight of the baby, *BJOG*, 1996, 103: 734-6
[12] Manning, F, Menticoglou, S and Harman, C, Fetal assessment by biophysical method: ultrasound, *in* Turnbull, A and Chamberlain, G (editors), *Obstetrics*, 1989, London, Churchill Livingstone
[13] Landon and Gabbe, Diabetes in Pregnancy, *in High Risk Pregnancy Management Options,* 2nd edition, 1999, WB Saunders, page 680
[14] Chua and Arulkumaran, Poor progress in labour, *in High Risk Pregnancy Management Options*, 2nd edition, 1999, W BSaunders, page 1114
[15] Enkin, M, Keirse, M, Neilson, J, Crowther, C, Duley, L, Hodnett, E, and Hofmeyr, J, *A Guide to Effective Care in Pregnancy and Childbirth*, 3rd edition, 2000, Oxford University Press, page 187
[16] Gibb, D, *in* Clements, R (editor) *Safe Practice in Obstetrics and Gynaecology*, 1994, Churchill Livingstone, 233

avoid the risk of shoulder dystocia. If the obstetrician declines to carry out caesarean section at maternal request then he should refer the patient for a second opinion.

Maternal risk of elective caesarean section:
There is probably no increased maternal mortality associated with elective caesarean section in a fit young woman with no intercurrent disease.
There is an increased risk of maternal morbidity. This risk involves thrombo-embolic phenomena and relatively trivial complications such as wound infection. Both of these complications are minimised by the routine use of prophylactic antibiotics and routine anti-thrombotic measures to cover the caesarean section. The mother will have to stay in hospital for two to four days post partum.

Maternal benefit of elective caesarean section:
The mother will avoid the risk of damage to her pelvic floor and the risk of anal sphincter injury.

Fetal risk of elective caesarean section:
There is no significant risk to the fetus in being born by elective caesarean section at 39 weeks.

Fetal benefit of elective caesarean section:
The baby will probably be born intact. There have been case reports of babies being born with OBPP but the incidence is rare; when it occurs it may be associated with difficult caesarean delivery, usually by an inexperienced surgeon.

Maternal risk of vaginal delivery:
There is an increased risk of damage to the pelvic floor (including anal sphincter injury) resulting from the vaginal delivery of a macrosomic baby.

Maternal benefit from vaginal delivery:
If the delivery is uncomplicated the mother is able to go home in 24 hours or less. Many mothers derive satisfaction from having given birth normally.

Fetal risk from vaginal delivery:
There is an increased risk of difficulty and delay in delivering the macrosomic fetus, which may lead to anoxic brain injury or OBPP.

Fetal benefit from vaginal delivery:
There is no significant benefit to the baby in being born vaginally.

The Intrapartum features associated with shoulder dystocia

- Delay in cervical dilatation, typically between 6 and 10 cms.
- Prolonged second stage of labour.
- Mid cavity assisted vaginal delivery

Any of these factors, and especially a combination of them, will forewarn an astute obstetrician of the risk of shoulder dystocia.

The manoeuvres used when shoulder dystocia is encountered:

In 1990 it was unusual for an obstetric unit to have protocols for the management of shoulder dystocia in place. In 2000 all units have protocols in place. A typical protocol is one based on the mnemonic "HELPERR" which is commonly taught to midwives:-

H	Call for help
E	(Evaluate for) Episiotomy
L	Legs (change of maternal position: the McRoberts position is preferred)
P	Pressure (suprapubic)
E	Enter (Woods screw)
R	Remove the posterior shoulder
R	Roll the patient to her hands and knees

In addition all maternity units should now have regular training sessions in shoulder dystocia management for the midwives and junior staff. These improvements in risk management and hence patient care have largely come about as a result of litigation.

The principles are these:

(i) Do not exert further traction until the anterior shoulder has been released from behind the symphysis; gentle, normal (i.e. non damaging traction) is permitted in association with the following manoeuvres. Shoulder dystocia is diagnosed either by the "turtle" sign (in which the head attempts to retreat back into the vagina) or more commonly, when the first "diagnostic" traction fails to deliver the anterior shoulder. The large majority of cases of OBPP result from excessive prolonged or repeated tractions.

(ii) **(H)** Summon experienced help: Most cases of shoulder dystocia will happen unexpectedly when a midwife is delivering the patient. When this circumstance arises the midwife should ask for experienced obstetric help as a matter of urgency. In most cases the midwife will have overcome the shoulder dystocia herself by the time experienced help arrives. However in cases where she has not been able to overcome the shoulder dystocia time is of the essence. Asking for experienced help as soon as the shoulder dystocia is diagnosed will minimise the time that the fetus is at risk of anoxic brain damage.

(iii) **(E)** Cut a large episiotomy: There are three reasons for an episiotomy:

- It reduces soft tissue constriction on the neck, thus reducing venous congestion in the baby's head.
- It removes soft tissue obstruction and thus encourages the posterior shoulder to fall into the sacral hollow.

- Most importantly, it allows the obstetrician room to get his hand into the vagina posteriorly to rotate the shoulder girdle should this be necessary.

(iv) **(L)** Change the maternal position: The McRoberts position is the preferred option. It has the effect of elevating the anterior shoulder of the fetus, which carries the fetus anteriorly and flexes the fetal spine. The lifting and flexion tends to push the fetal posterior shoulder over the sacrum and through the inlet. The manoeuvre changes the plane of the inlet to approach a right angle to the maternal expulsive forces. Other recommended position changes are to the all-fours position or the left lateral position. The disadvantage of the all-fours and the left lateral position is that it is difficult to apply suprapubic pressure.

(v) **(P)** Exert suprapubic pressure: Suprapubic pressure is applied laterally behind the anterior shoulder and downwards in the axis of the birth canal. This manoeuvre both compresses the shoulder diameter and rotates the shoulder to a more favourable diameter of the pelvic inlet.

In the majority of cases of shoulder dystocia the above manoeuvres will achieve delivery without causing an OBPP.

If these manoeuvres fail then invasive manoeuvres are necessary:

(vi) **(E)** Wood's screw manoeuvre: here the obstetrician's hand is introduced into the vagina and the posterior shoulder is rotated through 180°. Alternatively, delivery of the posterior arm will usually be possible.

Any healthy baby will withstand 10 minutes of acute total asphyxia before there is any probability of permanent brain damage. It follows that any obstetrician has seven to eight minutes to use the correct manoeuvres in the correct sequence to overcome shoulder dystocia before the situation becomes critical. If at the end of 7 to 8 minutes an obstetrician has not succeeded in overcoming the shoulder then he is entitled to pull hard and risk damaging the brachial plexus in an attempt to save the baby from cerebral palsy.

In the past decade there has been a succession of papers in the American literature suggesting alternative causes for OBPP:

- The positional injury
- The propulsion injury
- The posterior shoulder injury

The Positional Injury

Dunn and Engle[17] reported the first documented case of OBPP which had occurred entirely within the uterus. This was apparently a chronic long-term

[17] Dunn, DW and Engle, WA, Brachial Plexus Palsy: Intrauterine Onset, 1; *Paediatric Neurology*, 1985, 367-69

pressure injury with changes involving muscle and bone. Jennet et al (1997)[18] believe that intrauterine maladaption is responsible for some cases of OBPP.

The Propulsion Theory (the endogenous forces of labour)

Gherman et al[19] referred to uterine contractions and maternal expulsive effort subjecting the anterior brachial plexus to excessive stretch. Sandmire and DeMott[20] say "The overwhelming evidence indicts the propulsive nature of the stretching of the involved nerves over which the birth attendant has no control". Stirrat and Taylor[21], Johnson[22] and Clements[23] have criticised the American literature and rebut these conclusions. There is no empirical scientific evidence to support the endogenous forces of labour as a cause of OBPP, other than a paper by Gonik et al[24] which was subsequently discredited by Allen and Edelberg[25].

The Posterior Shoulder Injury.

Ouzounian et al[26] describe four cases of OBPP which occurred in the posterior arm of babies who had anterior shoulder dystocia. They hypothesised that the injury was not a product of traction applied at delivery but rather preceded expulsion of the fetal head and was caused by impaction of the posterior shoulder on the sacral promontory. This is an attractive theory which remains unproven. An alternative and more logical explanation is that the common obstetric manoeuvre of applying upward traction on the fetal head to facilitate delivery in a difficult case may also cause this injury. The same analysis as in an anterior shoulder injury must then be undertaken.

The contention that there was a posterior shoulder injury is becoming an increasingly common defence. It is usually based upon a recording of the position of the fetus ascertained by abdominal palpation (Leopold's manoeuvre), in early labour. It is standard practice for the midwife to record which side of the mother the fetal back is lying, e.g. ROL (right occipito-lateral). If there is an OBPP to the

---

18 Jennett, RJ, Tarby TJ, Brachial Plexus Palsy: An Old Problem Revisited Again, *American Journal of Obstetrics & Gynaecology*, 1997; 176, 1354-1357

19 Gherman, RB, Ouzounian, JG, Miller, DA, Kwok, L and Murphy Goodwin, T, Spontaneous Vaginal Delivery: A Risk Factor for Erb's Palsy, *American Journal of Obstetrics & Gynaecology*, 1998; 178 423-427

20 Sandmire, HF, and DeMott, RK, Erb's Palsy: Concepts of Causation, *Obstetrics & Gynaecology*, 2000, 95 941-942

21 Stirrat, GM and Taylor, RW, Mechanisms of Obstetric Brachial Plexus Palsy: A Critical Analysis, *Clinical Risk*, 2002, 8, 218-222

22 Johnson, A, Obstetric brachial plexus palsy: the medico-legal view, *The Obstetrician and Gynaecologist*, 2005; 7: 259-265

23 Clements, R, Obstetric brachial plexus injury, *Clinical Risk*, 2006. 12: 3-11

24 Gonik, B, Walker, A, and Grimm, M, Mathematic modelling of forces associated with shoulder dystocia: a comparison of endogenous and exogenous sources, *Am J Obstet Gynecol*, 2000, 182.689-91

25 Allen, RH and Edelberg, SC, A problematic model to predict intrauterine forces during shoulder dystocia, *Am J Obstet Gynecol*, 2001, 184. 524-5

26 Ouzounian, JG, Korst, LM and Phelan, JP, Permanent Erb's Palsy: A Traction Related Injury, *Obstetrics & Gynaecology*, 1997, 89; 131-141

right brachial plexus in such a case, this may be regarded as evidence that this is a posterior shoulder injury. The position of the fetus in early labour as defined by abdominal examination is uncertain and mistakes are commonly made. The position of the fetus is more reliably (but not infallibly) ascertained by vaginal examination in labour. "Posterior shoulder" OBPP probably does occur but it is not common.

Conclusion

Defendants commonly rely on the fact that there have been reported cases of brachial plexus injury where no recorded shoulder dystocia was encountered. They often assert that there is no way to measure "excess traction", or that the imperative o urgent delivery justified the traction that was applied. All of the literature on shoulder dystocia and brachial plexus palsy refers to the fact that there is underreporting of shoulder dystocia in up to 50% of cases. It is obviously important to look at each case individually to determine if shoulder dystocia could have been foreseen and whether the mother should have been delivered by elective Caesarean section. It is also important to analyse the degree of injury and relate this to the size of the baby and to the use (or non use) of the correct manoeuvres. The propulsion and the posterior shoulder defences have succeeded in the courts but in these cases the judge was not shown the bioengineering literature.

PERINEAL DAMAGE

Perineal damage during childbirth following extension of an episiotomy or by spontaneous tearing is commonplace. Perineal tears are classified in four degrees:

(a) A first degree tear involves the skin of the vagina and the perineum.
(b) A second degree tear includes the skin and the muscle of the vagina and the perineum.
(c) A third degree tear also involves the anal sphincter either as a full thickness or as a partial thickness tear.
(d) A fourth degree tear further involves the anal and/or rectal mucosa.

A surgical repair of an episiotomy or tear is carried out at the time of childbirth (within half an hour or so of the completion of the third stage). The repair is usually carried out either by a junior obstetric doctor (SHO) or a midwife. It is no longer acceptable for medical students to carry out these repairs. The surgical technique of the repair involves careful apposition of the damaged structure usually in three layers: a) the vaginal mucosa, b) the perineal muscle, c) the perineal skin. The purpose of the repair is to oppose the tissues and achieve haemostasis without devitalisation of the tissues. The repair is carried out using polyglycolic acid (Dexon or Vicryl). In most cases such a repair will lead to no more than transient discomfort over a few days and the end result is perfectly satisfactory.

The one suture material which should not be used to affect a repair is glycerol impregnated catgut ("Softgut"). This material has been found to lead to a high incidence of dyspareunia which persists for some months. There are however still occasional cases in which a claim is made for dyspareunia and in which Softgut has been used. It is not possible to defend such cases.

Properly repaired tears almost always heal up satisfactorily despite the fact that they are often bathed in blood, liquor (amniotic fluid), and faeces. The blood supply to the perineum is so good that infection is rare. When it does occur it usually does so because too many sutures have been inserted and tied too tightly so that the tissues are devitalised.

The common causes for litigation following perineal injury and repair are:

- Dyspareunia
- Narrow introitus
- Foreign bodies in the vagina
- Utero-vaginal prolapse/Urinary stress incontinence
- Anal sphincter damage leading to anal incontinence

Dyspareunia

Dyspareunia is pain on intercourse; following repair of the perineum at childbirth, it is usually caused by a painful scar or a tight introitus. Pain in a well healed episiotomy scar is unusual but it does occur and it is an inherent risk of childbirth. In most cases no negligence can be attributed to the way in which the tear has been repaired (other than when Softgut has been used; see above). In cases where such a problem occurs it is usually cured by a simple operation to enlarge the introitus (Fenton's operation).

Narrow introitus

Superficial dyspareunia following a tear which has been repaired is almost always due to the fact that the introitus has been narrowed, i.e. it has been sewn up too tightly to allow intercourse to occur with comfort. At the conclusion of the repair the surgeon should insert two fingers into the vagina. If two fingers can be inserted easily then the repair is judged to be satisfactory and intercourse should take place without any difficulty. If two fingers cannot be inserted easily then the repair should be taken down and a re-repair carried out. Most cases of superficial dyspareunia will resolve with time; if there is no resolution and if it is thought that the dyspareunia has resulted from narrowing (and not from psychological causes) then a Fenton's operation may be necessary.

Foreign bodies in the vagina

When carrying out a repair it is common to put a tampon in the vagina to keep the operative field clear of blood coming down from the uterus. If the tampon is not removed at the end of the repair it will lead to a foul vaginal discharge and pain on intercourse. Claims resulting from such a misadventure are indefensible.

Utero-vaginal prolapse/Urinary genuine stress incontinence

These conditions are commonplace in multiparous women. Most cases present at the age of the menopause. Occasionally a case may present soon after childbirth. The conditions are due to tearing of the levator plate and/or also damage to the pudendal nerve. They are rare in nulliparous women or in women who have been delivered by Caesarean section. There is no association between genuine stress incontinence and perineal tears and their repair.

Anal sphincter damage leading to anal incontinence

Full thickness tears of the anal sphincter which are not recognised and not repaired will give rise to anal incontinence and will often result in a claim. Third degree tears occur in approximately 1 in 200 vaginal deliveries. They may occur after spontaneous vaginal delivery. They are more common after assisted vaginal delivery and it is said that forceps give rise to greater incidence of third degree tears than the Ventouse. Such tears to the anal sphincter are rarely caused by substandard technique during delivery. It is difficult to defend a case where there has been a failure to recognise a third or fourth degree tear. In order to prevent the patient suffering from faecal incontinence, it is essential that the damage is recognised and repaired at the time of childbirth. Proper recognition of the damage entails recognition of the possibility of sphincter damage. This should be looked for after all secondary degree tears or episiotomies. Where there is any doubt the patient must be put into the lithotomy position and the perineum inspected under a good light. Two fingers introduced into the vaginal introitus and gently stretching it will demonstrate the apex of the tear in the vagina and also the depth of the tear in the perineal muscles. Such an examination may be all that is required if it is apparent that the tear only extends through the vaginal skin, the perineal skin and a short way into the perineal muscles. If there is any doubt, however, a finger should be introduced into the rectum at the same time as two fingers are in the vagina and the perineum stretched. Using such a technique a full thickness tear of the external sphincter will be readily apparent. A full thickness tear of the anal sphincter is shown by a loose end of the sphincter (usually on the patient's left side) and a "pit" in the perineum on her right side. Exploration of this pit with tissue holding forceps will find the torn and retracted end of the sphincter.

When a complete disruption of the anal sphincter is diagnosed (and as indicated above it should always be diagnosed) it should be repaired by an experienced obstetrician. The repair must be carried out in general theatres with competent assistance. The repair must also be carried out under anaesthetic (either general anaesthetic or conduction anaesthetic). Under anaesthetic the external anal sphincter is relaxed and it is easy to pick up the two ends of the divided sphincter and oppose them using figure of 8 polyglycolic acid sutures. It is not possible to repair the internal anal sphincter and if it is damaged the patient may be incontinent of flatus. Any tears in the anal or rectal mucosa are sutured. The rest of the perineal damage is then repaired.

Properly carried out repairs to the anal sphincter give good results. 66% of patients are fully continent, 25% of patients are left with some incontinence of flatus and only 9% of patients are left with incontinence of stool[27].

When a full thickness tear of the anal sphincter is not recognised and therefore not sutured at the time of delivery anal incontinence will result and the patient will require a delayed repair (usually carried out three months or more postpartum). Such delayed repairs are carried out by colorectal surgeons using an overlap repair of the external anal sphincter. Such delayed repairs are often protected by a colostomy. Over 45% of patients having a delayed repair of the anal sphincter are subsequently continent of flatus and stool, and 20% remain incontinent of solid stool.

Any patient who has had a complete disruption of the anal sphincter during childbirth should be advised to have an elective Caesarean section in any future pregnancy.

In recent years there has been an increasing number of women requesting elective Caesarean section on the basis that they wish to protect their pelvic floor. A recent survey of female obstetricians found that 31% preferred delivery by elective Caesarean section rather than vaginal delivery; 80% of these doctors cited fear of perineal damage as their main reason[28].

Elective Caesarean section in a fit young woman who has no intercurrent illness is a safe procedure. Any woman requesting an elective Caesarean section because she wishes to protect her pelvic floor should be treated sympathetically. A full risk benefit analysis should be discussed with her and if she still wishes to have a section her request should be complied with.

VAGINAL BIRTH AFTER CAESAREAN SECTION (VBAC)

Vaginal birth after Caesarean section (VBAC) was previously known as “trial of scar”. In pre-Second World War times most Caesarean sections were the classical operation involving a vertical incision in the upper segment of the uterus. In subsequent pregnancies there was a high risk of ruptured uterus and because of this the aphorism "once a Caesarean always a Caesarean" came into being.

In the present era most Caesarean sections are carried out by the lower segment operation and the risk of subsequent scar rupture is small. The incidence of scar

[27] Schofield and Grace, Faecal Incontinence after childbirth, *Clinical Risk*, 1990, Vol 5. No 6. pages 201-204

[28] Al-Mufti, R, McCarthy, A and Fisk, NM. Survey of obstetrician’s personal preference and discretionary practice, *Eur J Obstet Gynecol Reprod Biol*, 1997; 73: 1-4

dehiscence or uterine rupture in labour in a pregnancy following a previous Caesarean section is less than 2%. When such a risk materialises, however, the consequences can be severe both to mother and to fetus. It is essential that the obstetrician gives a patient who is contemplating VBAC a risk benefit analysis, comparing elective Caesarean section and VBAC. This risk benefit analysis should be given to her in clearly comprehensible terms. When such a risk benefit analysis is given to a woman her informed choice should be the major deciding factor. Enkin *et al* state that when given the option from 30 to 50% of women chose to undergo repeat Caesarean delivery[29].

In claims arising from VBAC involving serious damage or death to the fetus and/or serious haemorrhage to the mother, there is often no indication in the notes that any risk benefit analysis was given to the patient prior to her making a decision as to how she wanted to be delivered. This leaves the defendant forensically vulnerable.

When uterine rupture occurs with consequent significant maternal and fetal morbidity, subsequent expert analysis of the management of the labour usually points to significant substandard care. This substandard care usually involves failure to conduct the labour under obstetric rather than purely midwifery supervision, the injudicious use of oxytocic drugs and failure to timeously recognise arrest disorders in the first stage of labour.

SYNTOCINON

Syntocinon is the synthetic form of oxytocin which is a naturally occurring hormone released from the posterior pituitary gland. It causes the uterus to contract and is commonly used to induce or to augment labour. Syntocinon is a powerful and hence a dangerous drug and must be used with circumspection. When it is used in the induction of labour, or to augment labour, it is given by dilute intravenous infusion (a "drip"). It is started in low dose and the infusion is increased at half hourly intervals until the uterine response is adequate. The uterus in strong labour should contract up to 4 times every 10 minutes and each contraction should last 45 to 55 seconds. In modern obstetric practice it is unusual to have an intrauterine pressure transducer in situ and it is difficult to measure the strength of contractions. Midwives commonly use the terms "fair", "moderate" or "strong" to describe the strength of contractions. They estimate this by palpating the maternal abdomen. Where the contractions exceed 4-5:10 or when they last longer than 55 seconds there is a danger of fetal compromise (see the Chapter on Cerebral Palsy), or of uterine rupture.

It is important to use Syntocinon carefully in all cases and particularly where there is a scar in the uterus from a previous Caesarean section. If too much

---

[29] Enkin, M, Keirse, M, Neilson, J, Crowther, C, Duley, L, Hodnett, E, and Hofmeyr, J, *A Guide to Effective Care in Pregnancy and Childbirth*, 3rd edition, 2000, Oxford University Press, page 363

Syntocinon is used then there is a real danger of causing uterine hyperstimulation (too frequent and/or too strong contractions), which can lead to uterine rupture. When analysing claims relating to uterine rupture it is often found that Syntocinon has been continually increased after a normal contraction rate has been achieved, instead of then keeping the infusion rate constant or turning it down. It is not usually possible to defend such claims.

It is less common to cause a rupture of a uterus, which has not been subject to a previous Caesarean section, but it is possible to do so and such cases occasionally occur. The usual reason is that Syntocinon has been used inappropriately in the presence of disproportion (a large baby and a small pelvic outlet).

CAESAREAN SECTION

It is routine practice to use prophylactic antibiotics and to anti-coagulate with low molecular weight heparin and other anti thrombotic measures in conjunction with Caesarean section. Claims sometimes arise because there has been post-operative infection or thrombo-embolic disease, where routine antibiotics or routine anti thrombotic measures have not been employed. It is difficult to defend such allegations of breach of duty, although causation may remain a live issue.

In cases of Caesarean section where there has been damage to adjacent viscera (bladder, ureters or bowel) claims will often arise. It will only exceptionally be possible to defend claims based on such damage.

POST-PARTUM HAEMORRHAGE

Post-partum haemorrhage is defined as the loss of 500 mls of blood or more from the second stage of labour to the end of the puerperium (six weeks). Primary post-partum haemorrhage occurs in the first 24 hours; secondary post-partum haemorrhage occurs in the rest of the puerperium.

The causes of primary post-partum haemorrhage are:

- Retained placenta
- Lacerations of the birth canal
- Atonic uterus
- Placenta accreta
- Uterine inversion

Claims relating to post-partum haemorrhage usually arise because major surgery has been carried out to deal with the haemorrhage. Such surgery involves a laparotomy with a B-Lynch suture, or a hysterectomy (either total or subtotal) or ligation of the internal iliac arteries.

Retained placenta

Retained placenta is usually treated by manual removal of the placenta under either general or conduction anaesthesia. Such a procedure is relatively straightforward and uncomplicated and there are rarely any claims arising from it.

Genital lacerations

Lower genital tract: Significant lacerations to the lower genital tract involving major haemorrhage can be difficult to deal with. Repair of such lacerations can give rise to subsequent dyspareunia. Claims arising from this have to be judged on their individual merits.

Upper genital tract: Lacerations of the cervix and the uterus sometimes extending into the broad ligament and involving the uterine vessels can cause torrential haemorrhage. Such lacerations are unusual but when they do occur they are usually the result of an inadequately repaired Caesarean section operation. Commonly there will be extension of the lower segment scar which is not recognised. The uterus is repaired and the patient is returned to the ward only to subsequently haemorrhage. The subsequent operation is then difficult, to control the haemorrhage it may be necessary to ligate the internal iliac arteries and/or to carry out a hysterectomy. Such cases will often give rise to claims which are difficult to resist.

Atonic uterus

Atonic uterus following childbirth is an unusual but well documented cause of primary post-partum haemorrhage. Such cases arise in grand multipara or in patients who have had prolonged labour. They may arise for no apparent reason. Occasionally an atonic uterus giving rise to massive post-partum haemorrhage will be resistant to the usual measures to make the uterus contract, i.e. "rubbing up" a contraction, the use of intravenous oxytocics or the use of intra-myometrial Haemobate; surgery (as above) may be necessary.

Placenta accreta

This is an unusual condition where the placenta is morbidly adherent to the myometrium. It is sometimes found in women who have been delivered by Caesarean section on three or more occasions. Where a placenta accreta has been diagnosed prior to labour the advice is to not attempt to remove the placenta but rather leave it in situ to regress. Where it is encountered after delivery of the baby it commonly causes massive post-partem haemorrhage. The treatment is by interventional radiology or by radical surgery (either total abdominal hysterectomy or ligation of the internal iliac arteries. Often gauze abdominal packs have to be left in situ to control the venous ooze and these are removed 24 to 38 hours later). Such operations are difficult and should only be carried out by the most experienced obstetric surgeons.

The usual rule of thumb in dealing with massive primary post-partum haemorrhage is that the patient should be in theatre and anaesthetised by the time she has lost 10 units of blood and the haemorrhage must be stopped, either by interventional radiology or by surgical methods (B-Lynch suture, ligation of the internal iliac arteries or by hysterectomy), before she has lost 20 units of blood. The usual cause of maternal death from post-partum haemorrhage is because the decision to carry out surgery has been made too late, and sometimes because the surgery is inadequate due to the inexperience of the operator.

Uterine inversion

Uterine inversion causes shock and sometimes post partum haemorrhage. Uterine inversion is usually caused by mismanagement of the third stage of labour. The midwife has used traction on the umbilical cord before a uterine contraction has occurred and in cases where the placenta is inserted into the fundus of the uterus then there is a real risk that the uterus will be inverted such that it is "delivered" outside the introitus. Complex obstetric manoeuvres are required to replace the uterus and the resulting distress to the patient will commonly lead her to make a claim. Such claims are usually successful.

ANTENATAL DIAGNOSIS

It is routine to screen for fetal defects in the antenatal period. Such attempts are made by ultrasound scan (USS), by biochemical testing and sometimes by invasive testing.

USS

All mothers are offered an anomaly ultrasound scan at 18 – 20 weeks. The purpose of such testing is:-

- To confirm the expected date of delivery
- To exclude multiple pregnancy
- To exclude major structural defects:
    - Neural tube defects (e.g. spina bifida).
    - Major skeletal defects (e.g. Amelia)
    - Major cardiovascular defects (e.g. hypoplasia of the left ventricle)
    - Major gastro intestinal defects (e.g. gastroschisis)

Failure to diagnose a major structural abnormality (e.g. an absent leg) is usually regarded as substandard care. Failure to diagnose a relatively minor abnormality (e.g. an accessory digit) is not necessarily substandard care.

Chromosomal abnormalities

Ultrasound scanning will reveal the markers for some of the most common chromosomal anomalies e.g. increased nuchal thickness in Down's syndrome and, in conjunction with biochemical tests, is useful as a screening tool. However, the only way to diagnose chromosomal abnormalities of the fetus accurately in the ante-natal period is by carrying out a chorion villus sample or an amniocentesis. Both of these are invasive tests and have inherent risks. They should be reserved for cases where the patient has already given birth to a chromosomally abnormal baby, or to cases where the mother after appropriate discussion, has elected to run the risk of invasive testing because she requires an accurate diagnosis.

Biochemical screening tests are routinely offered to all pregnant women. They are based on the assay of maternal serum alpha feto-protein (MSAFP) and Human chorionic gonadotrophin (β-HCG), the "Double test". These tests are only screening tests and in older women will only be positive in about 66% of cases where the fetus is affected. In younger women the pick-up rate is substantially less. In claims arising following the birth of a baby with an unexpected chromosome abnormality (of which Down's syndrome is the most common), the patient will usually say that she thought that she was told that the test was a diagnostic test, not just a screening test. The standard of information given to pregnant women by midwives in respect of the "Double test" is variable and this aspect of care is one which has not (as yet) been widely addressed by risk management in maternity units.

CEREBRAL PALSY

Anthony Johnson and Michael Smith

INTRODUCTION

In 1861 William James Little, a surgeon, read a paper to the Obstetrical Society of London concerning "... the influence of abnormal parturition, difficult labour, premature birth and asphyxia neonatorum on the mental and physical condition of the child, especially in relation to deformities"[1]. It was the culmination of 20 years observation of children with deformities. Little drew attention to the association between difficult birth and later neurological impairment. From the outset he recognised that this association may only be an occasional occurrence. His colleagues, the accoucheurs present, were, however, of a different view. While thanking him for his contribution, several eminent practitioners in the audience disagreed with his views. One notable comment is recorded from a Dr Tyler Smith, who thought "dentition ... the great source of paraplegia and hemiplegia in young children"! So began a controversy over the relationship between birth and later disabilities in children which continues to this day.

The focus of this chapter is cerebral palsy. Where relevant, some other developmental disorders in children will be considered. Cerebral palsy exacts a terrible human and financial cost. In the NHSLA annual report (2006)[2], the value of reported CNST claims by medical speciality showed that for obstetrics and gynaecology the total value of reported CNST claims was £1,970,561, which approximates the total value of all other sub-specialities combined.

WHAT IS CEREBRAL PALSY, AND HOW COMMON IS IT?

Cerebral palsy is defined as a group of non progressive but often changing motor impairment syndromes secondary to lesions or anomalies of the brain arising in the early stages of its development[3]. The term encompasses a wide variety of clinical syndromes and causes. In the discussion of individual cases it is useful to refer to the specific sub-type of cerebral palsy. The overall prevalence of cerebral palsy varies from region to region, but is in the order of 1.7-2.5 cases per 1000

[1] Little, WJ, *Transactions of the Obstetrical Society of London*, 3: 243-344, 1861
[2] *NHSLA Factsheet 3: Information on Claims*, July 2006.
[3] Stanley, F, Blair, E and Alberman, E, *Cerebral Palsies: Epidemiology and Causal Pathways*, 2000, McKeith Press, Cambridge University Press, p 8

live births[4]. This figure has been relatively stable over the past several decades, although there is now good evidence that the number of cases of cerebral palsy amongst the very low birth weight population (less than 1.5 kg at birth) is increasing[5].

In England and Wales there are approximately 718,000 births every year. This means that about 14,300 children are born each year who suffer from cerebral palsy. It has been suggested that fewer than 13% of all children with cerebral palsy have signs of intrapartum stress[6]. Thus there are about 1900 cases of cerebral palsy each year which are associated with birth asphyxia and whose cases are likely to be the subject of a medico-legal investigation. Every case of cerebral palsy is a tragedy for the child and for the parents. Every child with cerebral palsy due to birth asphyxia which could and should have been prevented is a tragedy for the obstetricians and the midwives who had responsibility for the maternal care.

POTENTIALLY PREVENTABLE TYPES OF CEREBRAL PALSY: OUTLINE

This chapter discusses first the obstetric aspects of those cases of cerebral palsy which are potentially preventable, and which therefore may result in litigation, under the following three headings;

- Cerebral palsy associated with preterm delivery
- Cerebral palsy in the term baby
- Miscellaneous (amniocentesis, hyperbilirubinaemia etc)

Preterm babies are those born before 36 completed weeks of pregnancy and mature ("term") babies as those born after 36 completed weeks. We will discuss potential areas where breach of duty may occur.

In the second section of this chapter the paediatric aspects of causation and liability are discussed in relation to the cerebral palsy type.

CEREBRAL PALSY ASSOCIATED WITH PRETERM BIRTH

Preterm birth and the sequelae arising from it are major problems for both the obstetrician and the neonatologist. In cases of cerebral palsy associated with prematurity, failure to treat the causes of premature labour, failure to diagnose

---

[4] Stanley, F, Blair, E and Alberman, E, *Cerebral Palsies: Epidemiology and Causal Pathways*, 2000, McKeith Press, Cambridge University Press, p 28

[5] Pharoah, P, Platt, M and Cooke, T, The changing epidemiology of Cerebral Palsy, *Archives of Disease in Childhood*, 1996; 75; F169-F173

[6] Nelson, KB, What proportion of cerebral palsy is related to birth asphyxia?, *J Pediatr*, 1988, 12:572-4

premature labour and mismanagement of premature labour are likely to result in litigation.

The causes of premature labour are:

- Cervical incompetence
- Chorioamnionitis
- Intra uterine contraceptive device (IUCD)
- Trauma (Road Traffic Accidents: Domestic violence)
- Severe infections e.g. pyelonephritis
- Pregnancy dating errors

Cervical incompetence

Cervical incompetence is caused by stretching or tearing of the circular muscle fibres of the cervix. The damage may result from over vigorous dilatation of the cervix during termination of pregnancy, or during a D&C (dilatation and curettage) carried out in the non-pregnant woman. It may occasionally result from cervical trauma during childbirth.

The typical history of such a case is that the woman gives birth prematurely and that in each succeeding pregnancy the gestation is shorter. In most cases the diagnosis is made on the history of sudden premature rupture of the membranes (with no history of contractions) and on examination the cervix is found to be 6 centimetres or more dilated. The presenting part will be well down the birth canal. Investigations to confirm cervical incompetence are not completely satisfactory. Prior to a succeeding pregnancy the cervix may be investigated by examination. The easy passage of a Hegar 6 dilator suggests cervical incompetence. The cervix can also be investigated by Hystero-salpingography (HSG) using a suction cap on the cervix. In the pregnant woman where cervical incompetence is suspected on clinical grounds, the cervix may be assessed by sequential ultrasound scans with a view to inserting a cervical suture if there is progressive shortening and dilatation of the cervix.

A cervical suture (Shirodkar, McDonald lash or abdominal suture) is inserted in cases where cervical incompetence is suspected. Such a suture inserted at about 14 weeks of pregnancy is reasonably satisfactory in preventing premature labour. Sutures inserted later in pregnancy in cases where the cervix is already dilating are less satisfactory in preventing premature delivery. Failure to insert a cervical suture in such cases may be negligent, but these cases are difficult and there is often conflict of expert opinion as to whether or not a cervical suture was necessary.

Chorioamnionitis

Chorioamnionitis (inflammation of the membranes) is a major factor in premature labour. The inflammation of the membranes arising from ascending infection may affect the structural integrity of the membranes, causing premature spontaneous rupture of the membranes (PSROM), or ascending infection may cause the onset of uterine contractions. Prolonged rupture of the membranes is associated with a high incidence of chorioamnionitis and may result in neonatal sepsis. The diagnosis of chorioamnionitis is proven by histological examination of the placenta and membranes. The clinical diagnosis is made where there is bacteriological proven infection on vaginal swabs, or where there is an elevated white cell count, or an increase in C-reactive protein.

There are many organisms which are associated with chorioamnionitis which include[7]:

- Neisseria gonorrhoea
- Streptococcus Group B
- Chlamydia trachomatis
- Mycoplasma hominis
- Ureoplasma ureolyticum
- Gardnerella vaginalis
- Bacteroides species
- Haemophilus species

In cases where the mother is known to have a vaginal infection, treatment is indicated. In patients infected with sexually transmitted diseases, there should be referral to the genitourinary physicians so that contact tracing and treatment of her sexual partners can be carried out.

Streptococcus Group B (GBS)

Patients known to be carriers for GBS (including GBS bacteriuria) should be treated with antibiotics in labour. Screening all pregnant patients for GBS is not routinely carried out (as yet) in England. GBS can be recovered from the vagina or cervix in 6-30% of pregnant women at some point during gestation. GBS has been associated with PSROM and it can also cause serious neurological damage to the fetus as a result of direct infection to the fetal brain as well as damage as a result of prematurity. Serious neonatal disease occurs in approximately 1-2/1000 births in the UK, mortality and long term morbidity in such infants is significant.

Intra uterine contraceptive devices

When a woman becomes pregnant with an intra uterine contraceptive device (IUCD) still in situ she is at risk of miscarrying or of delivering prematurely[8]. If after conception the IUCD is spontaneously expelled or is removed, the risk of subsequent miscarriage is significantly reduced. Alvior (1973)[9] reported that of

---

[7] Walkinshaw, S, in *Turnbull's Obstetrics*, 2nd Edition, 1995, p 611

[8] Newton, Contraceptive Update, *Clinics in Obstetrics and Gynaecology*, Vol 11 No 3, 1984

[9] Alvior, GT, Pregnancy outcome with removal of intrauterine device, *Obstetrics and Gynaecology*, 1973, 41, 894

201 women conceiving with an IUCD in place the abortion rate was 48.3% if the device was not removed and only 29.6% if it was removed.

It is essential that the obstetrician talks at length to the woman in language that she can understand about the risks of continuing pregnancy with an IUCD in situ. She should understand that removal of the device offers the best chance of the pregnancy continuing, but she should also understand that removal of the IUCD may provoke a miscarriage. It is necessary to examine the woman and to carry out an ultrasound scan to confirm the presence of the IUCD and also to determine the position of the IUCD. In cases where the thread of the device is still visible through the cervix, the IUCD should be removed. If the thread is not visible then there should be no attempt made to explore the cervical canal with instruments in an attempt to retrieve the thread.

Failure to advise, examine and investigate the patient along the lines indicated above is substandard care. Failure to remove the IUCD in cases where it is possible to do so is substandard care. It is not possible to defend cases where, as a result of this substandard care, the baby is damaged as a result of premature birth.

Trauma

Serious trauma to the maternal abdomen (eg from a road traffic accident, domestic violence) may result in premature labour and/or fetal death as a result of placental abruption.

Serious intercurrent infection

A pregnant woman who has a severe intercurrent infection associated with significant pyrexia *e.g.* from pyelonephritis is at risk of miscarriage/premature labour. Such cases are often treated by the general practitioner or in the medical wards of hospitals. Failure to appreciate that the women is at risk of premature labour and to observe the signs of premature labour and to treat it may result in the baby being born prematurely. Such cases may be difficult to defend.

Pregnancy Dating Errors

The expected date of delivery (EDD) is calculated from the date of the last menstrual period (LMP) either by using a gestation calculator (an obstetric "wheel") or by Naegele's rule, in which the date is calculated by adding 7 days and subtracting three months. Every woman should have a "Dating" USS in early pregnancy at around 12 to 16 weeks. Such scans are accurate to within +/- 7 days. Occasionally midwives or obstetricians make a simple mistake in calculating the expected date of delivery from either the maternal dates or from the scan dates. These errors sometimes result in labour being induced for "postmaturity" or for obstetric reasons when such induction of labour would not be carried out if the correct dates had been calculated and if it was realised that in fact the pregnancy was premature. Dating errors resulting from miscalculation of the dates are indefensible.

The Diagnosis and Management of Premature Spontaneous Rupture of the Membranes (PSROM)

More than 80% of patients who have PSROM will deliver within a week of membrane rupture. Pregnant women commonly suffer episodes of transient urinary incontinence and the diagnosis depends upon a vaginal examination per speculum to ascertain whether or not there is liquor draining through the cervix and to test the liquor with an "Amnistix".

There is little or no chance of survival if the fetus is born prior to 24 weeks. The chance of intact survival at 28 weeks is 80-85%. After 28 weeks the outlook for the baby improves considerably and by 36 weeks it is virtually the same as at term.

In cases where there is PSROM from mid gestation the fetus is at risk of developing lung hypoplasia and fixed limb deformities because of the diminished liquor volume.

The management plan consists of careful maternal and fetal surveillance. The elements of a typical plan are as follows:

- Monitoring for infection: The mother will be on a six hourly TPR chart. A high vaginal swab will be taken on a daily basis. The maternal white cell count and C reactive protein should be checked daily. Any sign of infection is taken seriously and antibiotics prescribed.
- The mother will usually be given steroids (Dexamethasone or Betamethasone) to mature the fetal lungs and hence avoid or at least minimise the risk of hyaline membrane disease in the premature baby. The use of steroids also protects against intraventricular haemorrhage (IVH) in the neonate.
- Fetal well being should be checked by a daily cardiotocograph and where necessary by a bio-physical profile (BPP) and Doppler studies of the umbilical artery.

The point at which it becomes safer to deliver the baby rather than to continue to try to prolong the pregnancy is often difficult and requires careful thought and judgement. Any case of PSROM should be under the direct supervision of a consultant obstetrician.

The Diagnosis and Management of Premature Labour

Mothers in premature labour commonly have little in the way of recognisable uterine contractions. They may only have vague abdominal aches. The diagnosis depends upon the midwife having a high index of suspicion and carrying out a vaginal examination to check for cervical dilatation. The vaginal examination may need repeating at intervals. It is better to over-diagnose rather than under-diagnose premature labour. The management involves a careful search for any of the recognised causes of premature labour - especially suspected chorioamnionitis or overt infection. Steroids will be given in most cases in an attempt to minimise hyaline membrane disease in the neonate. Tocolytic drugs e.g. Ritodrine are given to try and suppress uterine contractions and hence premature delivery. The use of tocolytic therapy is particularly advantageous because there is a good chance that such therapy will at least postpone premature delivery and hence will give more time for the steroids to act in maturing the fetal lungs. The major disadvantage of tocolytic therapy is that the drugs cause maternal tachycardia and hypotension and these side effects sometimes limit the amount of drug that can be safely used.

Cases of premature labour are difficult and the management depends upon the active involvement of the consultant obstetrician who, in consultation with his neonatal colleague, has to make the difficult decision as to whether it is safer to try and prolong the pregnancy or whether it is safer to deliver the baby.

It is difficult to defend cases of premature delivery resulting in a baby with cerebral palsy when the management has been carried out by junior and inexperienced obstetricians (or midwives) and where inappropriate decisions have been made.

The types of cerebral palsy associated with the premature infant are discussed later in this chapter.

CEREBRAL PALSY IN THE MATURE BABY BEFORE LABOUR

The causes of cerebral palsy in the mature infant before labour which commonly result in litigation and which may be keenly contested are perinatal asphyxia and birth trauma.

The causes of fetal asphyxia are:

- Placenta failure
- Abruptio placenta
- Umbilical cord prolapse
- Umbilical cord compression
- Ruptured uterus
- Uterine hyperstimulation
- Trauma to the fetus

These causes may arise prior to or during labour.

Failure of the placenta

The healthy human placenta has reserves far in excess of that which are required to nurture a fetus in pregnancy and labour. Occasionally, however, the placenta may fail.

The causes of placenta failure are:

- Heavy maternal smoking
- Alcohol abuse
- Drug abuse
- Chronic infections e.g. Syphilis
- Maternal hypertensive disorders

Placenta failure in pregnancy leads to poor growth in the fetus and results in a fetus suffering from intrauterine growth restriction - IUGR. A placenta which fails from early pregnancy causes symmetrical IUGR. The more common form of IUGR is asymmetrical IUGR caused by placenta failure in the third trimester of pregnancy. In asymmetrical IUGR the growth of the fetal head is "spared" as the physiological mechanisms divert more blood to the brain. The growth of the fetal abdomen falls off as the glycogen reserves in the liver are consumed and not replaced.

The diagnosis of IUGR is made on USS and preferably on sequential USS. It is not routine to carry out scans in the third trimester for fetal growth. The diagnosis therefore depends on the midwife or obstetrician recognising on clinical examination that the fetal growth is lagging behind that which is expected. Midwives and obstetricians are not particularly good at recognising small babies. The examination of the maternal abdomen should include a tape measurement of the symphysial/fundal height. The height in centimetres is roughly equivalent to the weeks of pregnancy. All obstetricians allow +/- 3 cm. in this measurement and it is only in cases where the measurement is outside these parameters on two or more occasions that objective measurement by USS is requested.

In cases where IUGR is diagnosed or is strongly suspected, the management of the rest of the pregnancy should be under direct consultant supervision. The object is to prolong the pregnancy beyond any risk of prematurity and to deliver the baby before there is any risk of neurological damage caused by hypoxia.

Maternal hypertension is treated and the fetal condition is monitored by repeated cardiotocographs (CTG), by biophysical profiling and by Doppler studies. A consultant obstetrician should interpret the tests of fetal well being. These important decisions should not be left to an unsupervised registrar. The Claimant in these cases commonly argues that there was a failure to make the diagnosis of IUGR and this argument is often difficult to pursue. An alternative argument put forward by the Claimant is that there was a failure to monitor fetal well being or to take appropriate notice of deterioration in the fetal condition. These arguments often succeed.

Abruptio Placenta before labour

Placenta abruption can occur at any stage of pregnancy but is most common in the third trimester. It occurs as a sudden and unforeseeable event. Often the fetus will die within a few minutes of the abruption and nothing can be done.
Occasionally claims arise because the baby is born alive but brain damaged and the allegation is made that the obstetrician did not act quickly enough to deliver the baby before it suffered brain damage. The timings are usually tight and each case has to be carefully analysed on its merits.

Occasionally abruptio placenta arises in labour. This is considered in more detail below. In such an unusual case there is sometimes evidence of substandard care (e.g. prolonged labour, injudicious use of Syntocinon) which makes the abruption a foreseeable possibility, and hence gives rises to a strong claim.

Cord compression before labour

Cord compression causing fetal damage rarely occurs prior to labour. It may be due to cord entanglement, which is not foreseeable. There may be intermittent cord compression which, if severe and long lasting, or if repeated, may lead to brain damage or fetal death. It would be unusual for the Claimant to prove breach of duty of care in such a case.

CEREBRAL PALSY FROM PROBLEMS IN LABOUR

Hypoxic brain damage occurring in labour represents a small percentage of the cases of cerebral palsy but a large portion of the CNST claims each year. Of the obstetric cases involving substandard intrapartum care and subsequent neurodevelopmental disability around 70% are based on abnormalities or interpretation of CTG traces.

The causes of hypoxia in labour which may lead to brain damage in the baby are:

- Cord Prolapse
- Cord compression
- Abruptio placenta
- Rupture of vasa previa
- Ruptured uterus
- Uterine hyperstimulation

Brain damage resulting from these causes is often foreseeable and preventable. The use and interpretation of the CTG trace is important in the management of these cases both in the clinical setting and in any subsequent medico-legal analysis. It is important that junior obstetricians and midwives are trained in the interpretation of CTG traces.

The normal CTG

There are two parts to a CTG. The upper trace is the cardiograph and shows the fetal heart. It may be obtained from an external Doppler ultrasound transducer, or from a fetal scalp electrode (FSE). The lower trace is a reflection of the uterine contractions and is derived from an external pressure transducer or rarely from an internal transducer.

The normal fetal heart baseline rate is 110 - 160 beats per minute (bpm). Unfortunately different authorities give slightly different values, e.g. FIGO values are 110 - 150 bpm[10]. The Guidelines from the Royal College of Obstetricians and Gynaecologists state that the normal range is 110 - 160 bpm[11]. Traditional teaching gives a normal range of 120 - 160 bpm. Accelerations are a sign of fetal well being. Normal short term variability (beat to beat variation - btbv) is 5-15 bpm.

Contractions in strong labour should occur up to one contraction every two to three minutes (usually written as the number of contractions in ten minutes e.g. 3-4:10). A contraction should last about 50 seconds. Contractions are usually assessed subjectively by the midwives as weak, moderate, or strong. Objective measurement of contractions can only be obtained by the use of an internal transducer, but internal transducers are only rarely used in the present era. A normal CTG is shown in Fig 1.

Cord Prolapse

When the umbilical cord prolapses into the vagina it will go into spasm, thus causing the circulation in the cord and hence gas exchange in the fetus to be compromised. Cord prolapse is uncommon when the head of the fetus is engaged. It becomes progressively more common when the head of the fetus is not engaged or is high or in cases of malpresentation or unstable lie.

In cases where there is spontaneous rupture of the membranes and cord prolapse when the patient is at home, the outlook for the baby is poor. In most cases there is insufficient time for the patient to be admitted to hospital and for the obstetricians to deliver the baby before it is either dead or damaged.

---

[10] FIGO 1987, Guidelines for the use of fetal heart monitoring, *Int. J. Gynecol. Obstet.*, 1987, 25 1159-1167

[11] *The use of electronic fetal monitoring. Evidence Based Clinical Guideline No. 8 2001*, RCOG, London

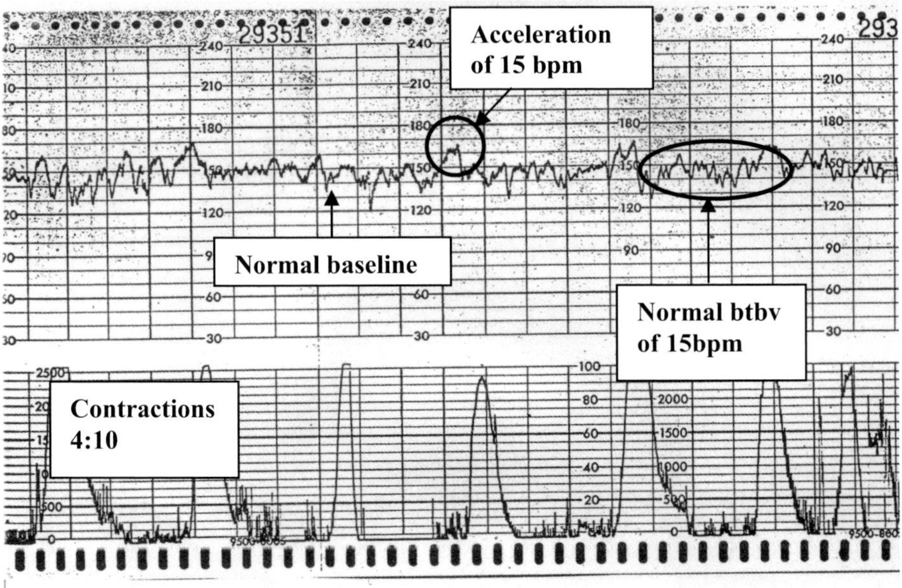

FIG 1. A NORMAL CTG

Cases of cord prolapse arise when the patient is in labour in the hospital labour ward and in these cases the outcome for the baby is better[12]. Artificial rupture of the membranes is commonly carried out as a means of inducing labour, or when the patient is in labour, as a means of speeding up the labour and gaining access to the fetus and the amniotic liquor. The membranes should not be artificially ruptured when the head is high without the most careful thought and only then when the midwife knows that the caesarean section theatre is free and obstetricians are readily available to carry out a crash caesarean section. Failure to observe these simple precautions makes it difficult to defend a subsequent case of cord prolapse resulting in brain damage.

Cord Compression

Cord compression is a common cause of fetal compromise in labour. The cord may be around the fetal neck (the nuchal cord), it may be entangled around the fetal body or it may be compressed between the fetal head and the bony pelvis or even the uterine wall. In the common case when there is a nuchal cord, the cord will tighten as the fetus descends through the birth canal. In most cases the maximum descent of the fetus is in the second stage of labour, and the fetus is at most risk of hypoxic/anoxic brain damage at this time. In cases of fetal distress leading to anoxic brain damage the fetal distress does not come "out of the blue"

[12] Murphy, DJ and MacKenzie, IZ, The Mortality and Morbidity associated with umbilical cord prolapse, *British Journal of Obstetrics and Gynaecology*, 1995. Vol 102, 826-830

but evolves over a period of time. Initially the fetal heart (FH) will increase to become a tachycardia (Fig 2) which is the normal response of the intact fetus to stress. There will then be variable decelerations which will become atypical (Fig 2) and which are pathognomic of cord compression. There will then be late decelerations (Fig 3) and finally there will be a terminal bradycardia (Fig 4). The obstetrician must be alert to developing changes in the CTG and should act to rescue the fetus from hypoxic intrauterine stress before the fetus is damaged. In many cases where babies suffer brain damage, retrospective medico-legal analysis of the CTG shows that the changes in the CTG have been ignored until the terminal bradycardia develops. It may then be too late to deliver the baby intact.

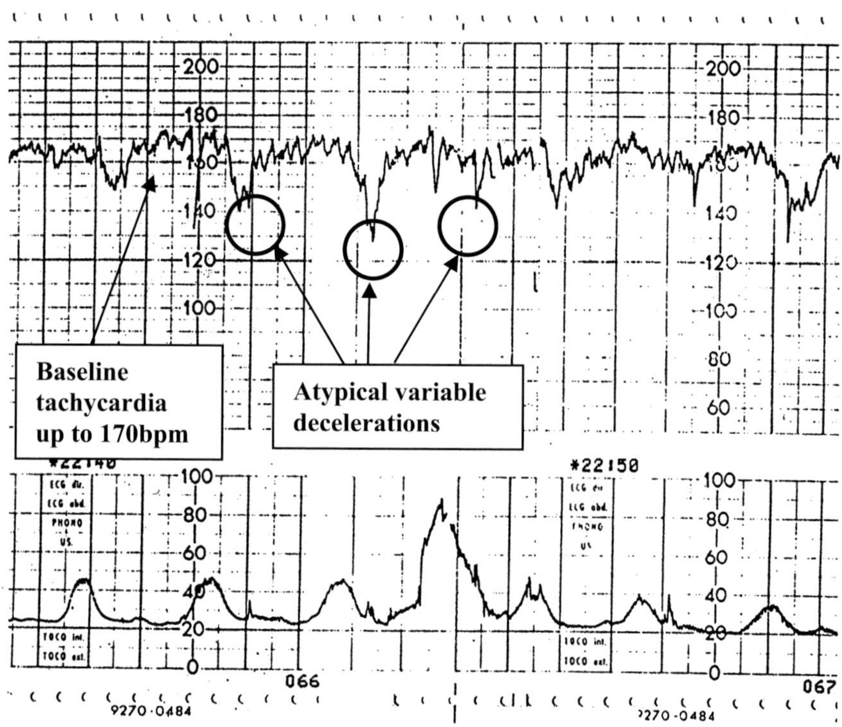

FIG 2.

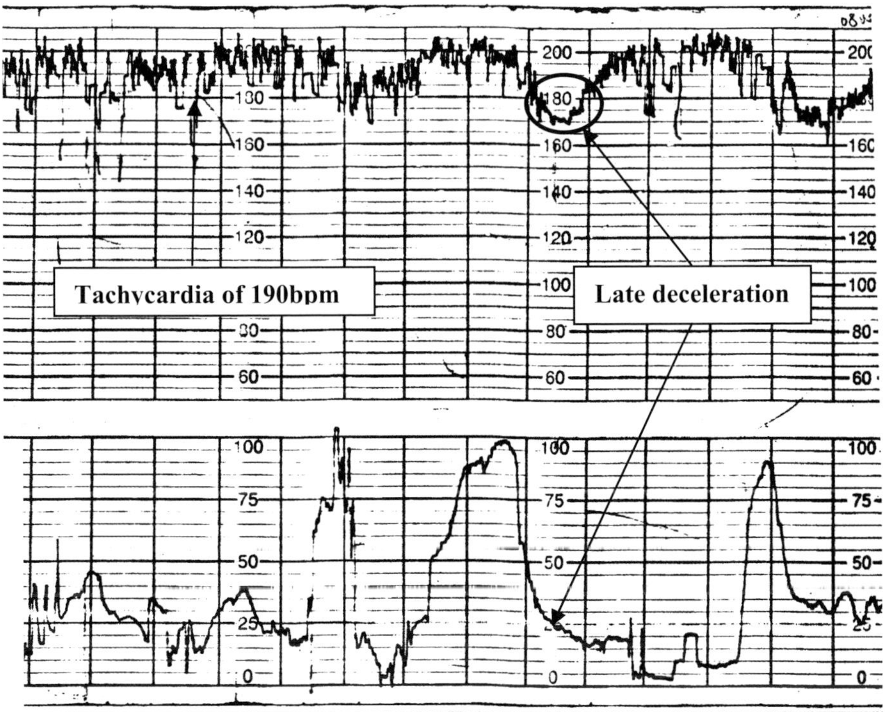

FIG 3.

Fig 4 shows a “picket fence” anomaly due to poor contact of the fetal heart transducer. Careful observation of the cardiograph through the "picket fencing", however, clearly shows that there are late decelerations. The tocograph had been disconnected but the midwives have marked the trace to indicate uterine contractions. In this case the cord was around the neck and it gradually tightened as labour progressed. The CTG changes were ignored until there was a terminal bradycardia. It was then too late to deliver the baby intact. The baby suffered a brain injury which gave rise to choreoathetoid cerebral palsy. The subsequent claim could not be defended.

Abruptio placenta

Abruptio placenta is unusual in patients in established labour. It is sometimes associated with the sudden release of excess amniotic liquor (hydramnios) when the membranes rupture. It can also be associated with uterine hyperstimulation caused by excess Syntocinon or Prostaglandin administration.

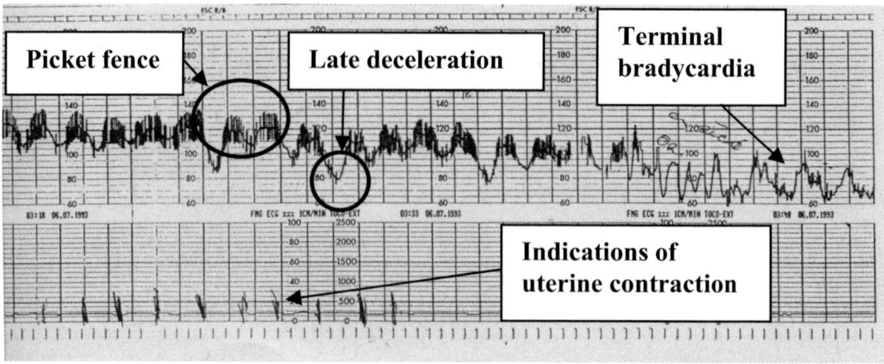

FIG 4.

Vasa Praevia

In this condition there is a leash of vessels from the umbilical cord which pass in front of the fetal head and which become torn in labour in which case fetal bleeding will ensue. Such bleeding is usually sudden and severe, and there is little or no time to act in order to save the baby from brain damage or death. In rare cases the bleeding may be chronic and can be diagnosed by a simple blood test to ascertain that it is fetal blood, in which case there may be time to deliver the baby before it is damaged by blood loss.

Uterine Rupture

Rupture of the intact uterus is rare. When it does occur it is almost always as a result of neglect in labour in allowing a patient to have a prolonged labour when there is evidence of cephalo-pelvic disproportion.

Uterine rupture in labour is most commonly seen in cases of Vaginal Birth after Previous Caesarean Section (VBAC) - formerly known as Trial of Scar (TOS). Before the Second World War most caesarean sections were the classical, or upper segment, operations. The vertical scar in the upper segment is weak and the incidence of scar rupture in subsequent labour was unacceptably high, and this gave rise to the aphorism "once a caesar always a caesar". Since the war the vast majority of caesarean sections have been and are carried out through the lower segment. The lower segment scar is stronger and much less vascular than the upper segment scar, and the incidence of rupture in subsequent labours is only of the order of 1% or less. Up until the mid to late 1990's it was thought that there was an increased maternal mortality and an increased maternal morbidity associated with caesarean section. It is now known that there is probably no increase in maternal mortality in elective caesarean sections in patients who do not have any significant intercurrent disease. The serious maternal morbidity from caesarean section is comparable to the serious morbidity from vaginal delivery.

In order for a patient to give valid consent to an attempt at VBAC it is necessary for the obstetrician to inform her in language she can understand of the risk/benefit analysis of VBAC versus elective caesarean section. The most important information that the patient needs to know is that the risk of scar rupture is low at around 1%, but if that risk materialises then the risk to the baby of death or brain damage is very high. Evidence based guidelines[13] suggest that if a woman is appraised of this risk some 50% of patients will elect for delivery by elective caesarean section.

It may be difficult to defend cases where patients have been listed for VBAC without valid consent having been obtained.

In the minority of cases where patients are prepared to accept the risks of VBAC and who have given valid consent for this procedure, it is necessary for the greatest care to be given to the woman in labour. Cases of VBAC are high risk and should be under direct and experienced obstetric supervision during pregnancy and especially in labour. These are not cases to be left to midwives or to junior doctors to look after on their own.

The obstetrician will wish to check in late pregnancy, and again on admission in labour, that the fetus is not excessively large. He will need to be certain that there is a cephalic presentation and that the head is engaged. Such high risk cases need a continuous CTG throughout labour and the obstetrician will need to carry out all or most of the vaginal examinations in labour himself. In cases where the obstetrician feels it is necessary to use Oxytocinon ("Syntocinon") to augment labour, he will prescribe this himself after careful evaluation of the case and he will personally supervise any increase in infusion rate. The patient will be prepared in case emergency caesarean section becomes necessary. Any delay in cervical dilatation velocity or in descent of the presenting part will lead the obstetrician to advise that the attempt at VBAC be abandoned and that a caesarean section will be necessary.

Lawyers and experts with experience of investigating cases of VBAC leading to ruptured uterus and brain damaged babies will appreciate that it is rare for all or even most of the criteria above to have been met and that consequently such cases are often difficult to defend.

Fig 5 shows the CTG from a case of VBAC. There was delay in labour which was not correctly evaluated. The staff used excess Syntocinon which caused uterine hyperstimulation and led to uterine rupture and the death of the baby.

Uterine hyperstimulation

The frequency of uterine contractions in strong labour should be three to four contractions every ten minutes, which is commonly expressed in the clinical notes

[13] Enkin, *A Guide to Effective Care in Pregnancy and Childbirth,* Oxford Medical Publications, p 359

made at the time as 3-4:10. A contraction frequency greater than this is uterine hypercontractility. Where an unacceptably high frequency of uterine contractions have been caused by Oxytocin the term uterine hyperstimulation is used.

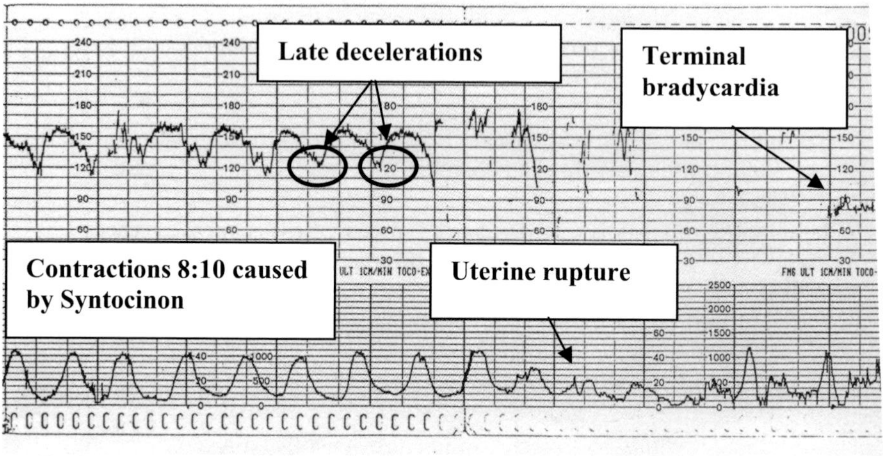

FIG 5.

The resting pressure of the uterus at term is about 5 mm Hg. The strength of uterine contractions should not exceed about 80 mm Hg. Uterine contractions should last 45 - 55 seconds. Labour that fulfils these criteria allows the placenta to fill with oxygenated blood from the maternal circulation which will keep the fetus well oxygenated. Hyperfrequent or too strong (hypertonic) uterine contractions will not allow the placenta to fill with oxygenated blood. Unless steps are taken to reduce the frequency and strength of uterine contractions the fetus will become increasingly and inexorably hypoxic.

Syntocinon is the synthetic form of Oxytocin - a hormone secreted by the posterior part of the pituitary gland. Syntocinon is used to increase the strength and frequency of uterine contractions. It is an effective, and therefore a potentially dangerous drug. If it is used injudiciously it will cause uterine hyperstimulation and or uterine hypertonia. In practice the infusion rate of Syntocinon is doubled every 1/2 hour until the uterus is contracting 3-4:10 and then concentration is not then further increased. If uterine contractions more frequent than this occur then the Syntocinon must be turned down. In cases where fetal tachycardia or decelerations of the fetal heart occur then Syntocinon must be turned off.

Objective measurements of uterine pressure can only be satisfactorily recorded by the use of an intrauterine pressure transducer. Today, with the increasing emphasis on non interventional obstetrics, the use of intrauterine pressure transducers is uncommon. Measurements of the strength of uterine contractions is subjectively measured by midwives who record their findings as "weak" "moderate" or "strong" contractions.

Additional information can be gained from the tocograph derived (as it is in the majority of cases) from an external pressure transducer. Too-frequent contractions can be easily seen (see Fig 5). "Coupling" of contractions or a sustained contraction for longer than one minute, or a failure of the recording to fall to the baseline all suggest that the contractions are too frequent and/or too strong. (see fig 6).

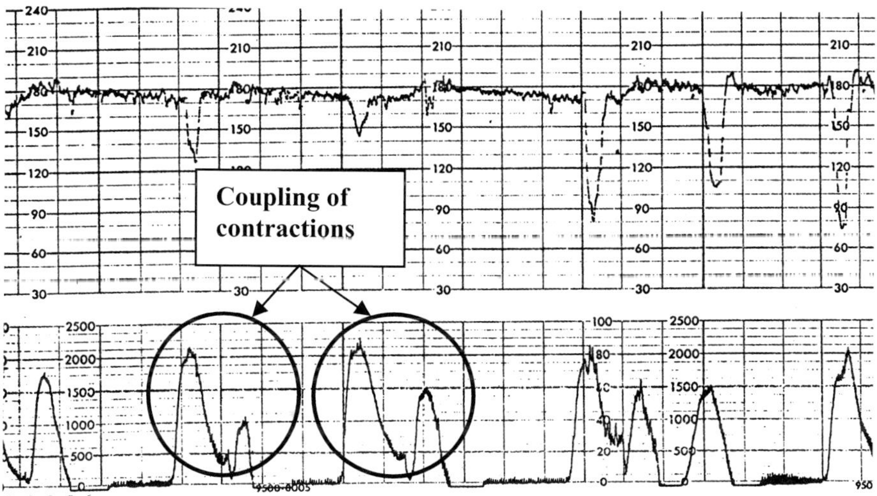

FIG 6.

Trauma

In the past, when caesarean section was thought to be a relatively dangerous operation, there was great emphasis placed on vaginal delivery. This led to obstetricians embarking on high and difficult forceps deliveries, on vaginal breech deliveries and on complex vaginal manipulations. This led to what would (by present day standards) be an unacceptably high incidence of cerebral palsy caused from trauma.

Today, when it is known that caesarean sections are relatively safe, there is much more concern about fetal well being. Difficult vaginal delivery is embarked on much less readily, and consequently cerebral palsy from trauma is now uncommon.

Cases are occasionally seen of intracranial bleeding (IVH, subdural haemorrhage intracerebellar haemorrhage and primary subarachnoid haemorrhage). Such haemorrhage may lead to death of the neonate or may cause cerebral palsy. The pathogenesis of these lesions is most commonly traumatic and the trauma is commonly associated with the difficult delivery of the breech (especially when breech extraction is involved) with the delivery of face or brow presentations, with difficult forceps or vacuum extractions. There may be skull fracture (linear, depressed "ping pong" fractures or occipital osteodiastasis) associated with intracranial bleeding.

Common findings in the history of such cases involve excessive force used with the forceps, forceps attempted when the head is above the ischial spines, and difficult rotation of the fetal head with Kielland's forceps or vacuum extraction. It is difficult to defend most cases of traumatic skull fracture associated with intracranial bleeding which has led to death of the fetus or to cerebral palsy.

MISCELLANEOUS CAUSES OF CEREBRAL PALSY

These include amniocentesis and hyperbilirubinaemia

Amniocentesis carried out in the late first or second trimester for diagnostic reasons should be carried out under ultra sound control. Failure to use ultrasound i.e. a "blind" amniocentesis may lead to the obstetrician perforating the fetal brain with the amniocentesis needle. This will cause a brain injury and it is not possible to defend such cases. Hyperbilirubinaemia is discussed below.

CEREBRAL PALSY: THE PAEDIATRIC NEUROLOGIST'S PERSPECTIVE

Definitions

Cerebral palsy is defined as a central motor deficit which is non-progressive and which is present from early life[14]. Of itself, the term cerebral palsy is unhelpful and when discussing individual children or adults it is more useful to refer to the specific sub-type of cerebral palsy.

The commonly utilised classification of cerebral palsies is shown in Table 1.

TABLE 1 – CLASSIFICATION OF CEREBRAL PALSIES

Spastic	includes hemiplegia, diplegia, tetraplegia
Dyskinetic	may be predominantly choreo athetoid or predominantly dystonic
Ataxic and Hypotonic forms	
Mixed	

[14] Stanley, F, Blair, E and Alberman, E, *Cerebral Palsies: Epidemiology and Causal Pathways*, 2000, McKeith Press, Cambridge University Press, p 8

This classification describes the predominant clinical symptomatology and physical signs in each group. It is important to realise, however, that the clinical signs may arise from lesions at different levels in the central nervous system, and the lesions themselves will have different causes. Each of the clinical syndromes may follow a term or a preterm delivery, and so in this section the clinical syndromes will be discussed in turn and considerations which relate to gestation will be discussed within that framework

Clinical syndromes

Spastic Hemiplegia

Spastic hemiplegia occurs in about 0.8 cases per 1000 live births. About 33% of the total number of children with cerebral palsy have spastic hemiplegia[15]. Spastic hemiplegia means spasticity affecting one side of the body, resulting in difficulties in fine motor control in the upper limb, and stiffness and awkwardness in the lower limb of the same side, resulting in an abnormal gait. Hemiplegia is frequently complicated by learning difficulties and behavioural problems (in up to 40% of children). These problems may be evident from early on, but in some children only emerge during the school years. Epilepsy, commonly of the complex partial type, is present in approximately 25% of children with hemiplegia, and is often associated with learning difficulties.

The causes of spastic hemiplegia are listed in Table 2

TABLE 2 – CAUSES OF SPASTIC HEMIPLEGIA

Cerebral malformation	20%
Pre-term intracerebral infarction	40%
Late pregnancy ischaemic infarction	35%
Normal scan, cause unknown	5%

Malformations of the brain resulting in spastic hemiplegia represent approximately 20% of the total of children with hemiplegia. These abnormalities arise in early pregnancy and are due to abnormalities in formation of the cerebral cortex and/or white matter. Because motor and sensory fibres from and to the cerebral cortex cross over in the lower part of the brain, disorders of, for example, the right hemisphere, may result in hemiplegia affecting the left side of the body. In the case illustrated in fig. 7, there is an abnormal section of cerebral cortex (black arrow), surrounding a cleft which penetrates from the surface of the brain but does not quite reach the cerebral ventricle (open arrow). This is cortical dysplasia around a schizencephalic cleft. The consequence of this lesion is malfunction of the brain, hemiplegia and epilepsy. These lesions are probably due to subtle genetic disturbance in the formation of the hemisphere in early

[15] Hagberg, B and Hagberg, G, The Origins of Cerebral Palsy, in David, T (ed), *Recent Advances in Pediatrics*, Vol 11, 1993, p 67-83

pregnancy, but may also arise due to vascular disturbances in mid-trimester, and occasionally due to maternal trauma or infection with cytomegalovirus.

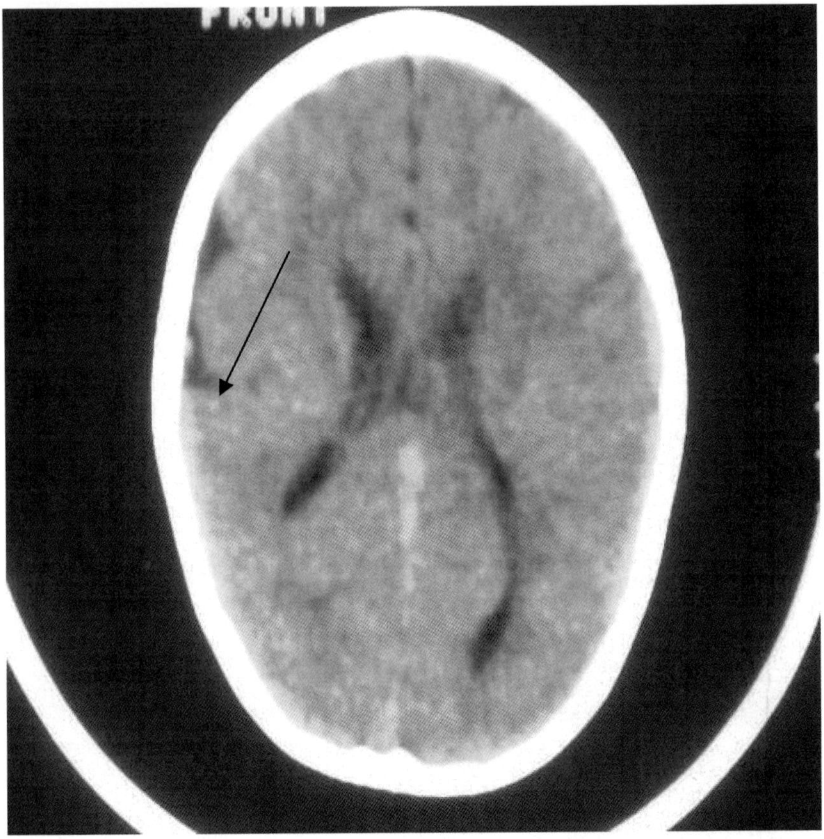

FIGURE 7 – CHILD WITH SPASTIC HEMIPLEGIA, CT BRAIN SCAN SHOWING THICKENED CORTEX ON LEFT WITH SCHIZENCEPHALIC CLEFT PENETRATING TOWARDS VENTRICLE.

The second category of spastic hemiplegia is brain damage caused by pre-term intra-cerebral infarction. In these cases there is often a porencephalic cyst in which an old intra-cerebral infarction has led to breakdown of cerebral tissue and coalescence of the degenerative cyst with the cerebral ventricle. The damage includes the descending cortico-spinal tracts from the motor and pre motor cortex of the affected hemisphere, resulting in spasticity in the limbs of the contralateral side. This lesion may arise due to intraventricular haemorrhage (IVH) in a pre-term baby. This disorder may come about as a result of haemodynamic disturbance, or trauma during delivery, or during neonatal intensive care (for example, during ventilatory management of pulmonary insufficiency). The majority of these lesions (IVH) appear in the neonatal period in preterm infants, during the first 72 hours after birth and the parenchymal haemorrhagic infarction usually develops during the 24 hours or so after the development of the intraventricular haemorrhage. In rare cases this lesion may develop in utero and be fully mature by the time of a term delivery.

The third group, late pregnancy ischaemic infarction (35%), usually involves an arterial distribution infarction in the region of supply of the middle cerebral artery. The artery may be obstructed in the main trunk by embolus arising possibly from the placental circulation in the immediate pre-natal period. Possibly such lesions may develop post-natally. The disorder may be clinically apparent because the baby develops focal seizures in the neonatal period. The seizures usually take the form of clonic jerking of the contra-lateral side to the lesion; the lesion is revealed by detailed ultrasound scanning of the brain and blood vessels during evaluation of the seizure disorder. Magnetic resonance imaging will usually confirm the nature of the lesion (Fig 8).

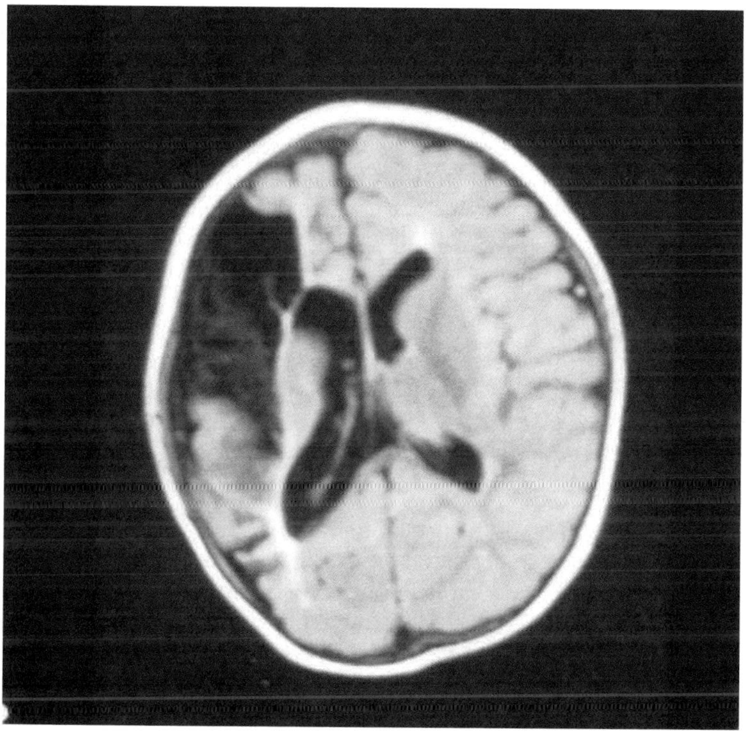

FIGURE 8 – MIDDLE CEREBRAL ARTERY DISTRIBUTION TERRITORY INFARCTION. TERM INFANT, HEMIPLEGIA, PRESENTED WITH NEONATAL SEIZURES. T1 MRI SCAN.

It is theoretically possible that middle cerebral artery obstruction may occur during perinatal asphyxia (digital subtraction angiography showing multi-focal arterial territory obstruction)[16]. Critically reduced flow may allow the development of intravascular thrombosis and middle cerebral obstruction. Quite

[16] Mannino and Trauner, Stroke in Neonates, *J Ped*, 1983, 102, 605-610

commonly, however, evidence for intrapartum hypoxic ischaemia is scant. Cord arterial and venous blood gases are usually unremarkable and evidence of hypoxic ischaemic encephalopathy and multi organ asphyxial injury in most cases is not present in most cases[17].

The formation of emboli in the fetal or neonatal circulation could occur if there were a predisposition in the subject. Studies reporting the presence of abnormalities in coagulation systems in babies with perinatal stroke show mixed results. In 1999 Harun et al[18] reported the finding of Factor V Leiden (fVL) homozygosity in association with cerebral palsy. Mercuri et al[19], studying a group of 24 infants presenting with neonatal stroke (perinatal infarction) in a tertiary level NICU found that 10 (42%) had at least one pro thrombotic risk factor, 6 with high factor Vlllc concentrations and 5 were heterozygous for the factor V Leiden mutation. The problem in assessing the relevance of the fVL mutation is the prevalence of this mutation is high - estimated at 3.4% in the UK and 2-15% worldwide. Smith et al[20], in a regional study of children with hemiplegia found 38 cases, of which 27 consented to be studied. Of these children fVL heterozygosity was present in 2, or 7.7%. Factor Vlllc elevation was present in 3 cases or 11.5%. Given the possible distribution of pathological types in a group selected on the basis of the presence of hemiplegia, a definite conclusion cannot yet be reached in this matter and further studies of specific conditions such as perinatal stroke where there is good anatomical definition of the abnormality or hemiplegia of the arterial occlusive type are needed.

The origin of the hemiplegia in children who have normal MRI scans (5%) remains obscure.

Spastic Diplegia

The term spastic diplegia covers a broad group of conditions, varying in clinical severity from that of a child of normal intelligence with good upper limb function and minimal lower limb spasticity, through to a child with severe tetraparesis, learning difficulties, and sometimes epilepsy. In all cases there is an emphasis of spasticity in the lower limbs: that is to say, the legs are more profoundly affected than the arms and hands. About 80% of children with spastic diplegia gain independent walking. There is a high incidence of specific learning difficulties in these children: moderate to severe learning difficulties are present in approximately 30%[21]. The severity of diplegia is related to the learning

---

[17] Govaert, P *et al*, Perinatal cortical infarction within middle cerebral artery trunks, *Archives Disease in Childhood*, 2000, 82(1); F59-63

[18] Harum, K *et al*, Homozygous Factor V mutation as a genetic cause of perinatal thrombosis and cerebral palsy, *Developmental Medicine and Child Neurology*, 1999, 41(11): 777-780

[19] Mercuri, E *et al*, Prothrombotic disorders and abnormal neurodevelopmental outcome in infants with neonatal; cerebral infarction, *Pediatrics*, 2001, 107(6): 1400-1404

[20] Smith, RA *et al*, Is thrombophilia a factor in the development of hemiplegic cerebral palsy?, *Developmental Medicine and Child Neurology*, 2001, 43: 724-730

[21] Hagberg, B, Hagberg, G and Olow, I, The changing panorama of cerebral palsy in Sweden 1954-1970, *Act Paed Scan*, 1975 64: 193-200

difficulties: the greater the hand/arm difficulties the greater the learning impairment. 16-27% of children with diplegia have epilepsy[22].

In the great majority of children with spastic diplegia, MRI brain studies reveal the presence of periventricular leucomalacia (PVL)[23] (Fig 9). The majority of children with spastic diplegia are born pre-term[24]. However, some infants with diplegia are born at term. Even where the infant is born at term, the predominant lesion type is PVL.

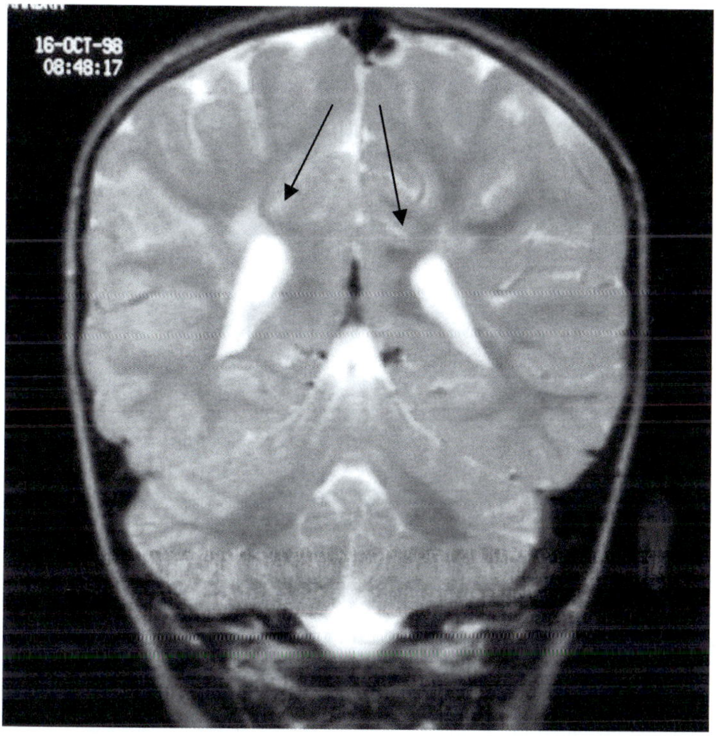

FIGURE 9 – MRI T2 WEIGHTING, PRETERM INFANT, PERIVENTRICULAR LEUCOMALACIA, SPASTIC DIPLEGIA.

PVL appears pathologically as an ischaemic lesion with ischaemic, frequently haemorrhagic, infarction in the white matter. From the pathological data it has been assumed that PVL comes about as a consequence of critical under-perfusion of the cerebral white matter, resulting in neuronal and oligo dendroglial cell necrosis. This is certainly true in many cases. Associations of PVL with hypoxic

[22] Veelken, N *et al*, Diplegic cerebral palsy in Swedish term and preterm children – differences in reduced optimality, relations to neurology and pathogenetic factors, *Neuropediatrics*, 1983, 14: 20-28; Hadjipanayis, A, Hadjichristodoulou, C and Youroukos, S, Epilepsy in patients with cerebral palsy, *Developmental Medicine and Child Neurology*, 1997, 39: 659 663

[23] Okomura, A *et al*, MRI findings in patients with spastic cerebral palsy. 11: Correlation with type of cerebral palsy, *Developmental Medicine and Child Neurology*, 1997, 39: 369-372

[24] *Ibid.*

ischaemia, blood pressure variability, hypotension and hypocarbia, all lend support to this view. However, there are also a significant number of infants with PVL who do not have documented postnatal episodes of critical hypo-perfusion of cerebral tissue. As a consequence of these observations, further investigation is continuing into the possible other causative factors involved in the generation of PVL. This research has illustrated the complex nature and origin of these lesions. Of particular importance has been the discovery of strong associations between the development of PVL and both maternal and neonatal infection[25].

A number of studies have shown that there are significant associations between the later development of PVL and the presence of infection, either in the mother prior to the birth, or in the infant after the birth. These studies raise the possibility that periventricular injury may occur not as a result of direct bacterial invasion of the brain, but through mechanisms associated with the fetal response and neonatal response to infection - that is, through the release of inflammatory cytokines which in turn may injure maturational processes within the white matter, or cause direct cellular injury.

Nelson et al[26] showed that amongst a group of infants with diplegia there was a uniform elevation of a variety of cytokine concentrations in neonatal dried blood spots compared to a control group of normal children. Clinical studies have shown the increased risk of CP and PVL in infants exposed to chorio amnionitis or neonatal sepsis[27]. The potential neurotoxicity of cytokines released in response to sepsis or low grade sub clinical infection is established. Whether these chemicals are produced and cause damage in response to infection in human infants remains to be seen. The cause-effect relationship has been established in an experimental setting[28] where experimentally induced maternal infection led to white matter damage in the fetus. In the human setting it is not yet clear whether the inflammatory response is neurotoxic, or whether primary ischaemia reperfusion injury induces the inflammatory response.

PVL may occur in association with IVH. IVH arises from bleeding in the sub ependymal germinal matrix in the floor of the anterior aspect of the lateral cerebral ventricles. PVL occurs more commonly in infants with IVH compared to those who do not. This may merely reflect the greater blood pressure variability in the IVH infants, but it also raises the possibility that there is a direct effect of

---

[25] Yoon, BH *et al*, Fetal exposure to an intra amniotic inflammation and the development of cerebral palsy at the age of 3 years, *Am J Obstet and Gynecol*, 2000, 182: 675-681; Counsel, S *et al*, Evidence for diffuse white matter injury in preterm infants following postnatal systemic infection remote from the brain. Neonatal Society of UK, Abstracts, March 2003; Willoughby, R and Nelson, KB, Chorioamnionitis and brain injury, *Clinics in Perinatology*, 2002, 29, 603-621.

[26] Nelson, KB *et al*, Neonatal cytokines and coagulation factors in children with cerebral palsy, *Ann Neurol*, 1998, 44, 665-675

[27] Zupan, V *et al*, Periventricular leukomalacia: risk factors revisited, *Developmental Medicine and Child Neurology*, 1996, 38, 1061-1067

[28] Yoon, BH *et al*, Fetal exposure to an intra amniotic inflammation and the development of cerebral palsy at the age of 3 years, *Am J Obstet and Gynecol*, 2000, 182: 675-681

haemorrhage on the adjacent periventricular white matter. In particular the presence of significant quantities of elemental iron arising from breaking down red cells in the ventricles could have a direct toxic effect on the white matter[29].

Spastic Tetraparesis

Spastic tetraparesis is responsible for 8% or so of the cerebral palsy population. Infants with spastic tetraparesis commonly have profound and multiple disabilities. There are usually severe to profound learning difficulties, cranial nerve deficits are common, there are severe feeding difficulties in the majority of these children, and reflux oesophagitis may complicate this problem. Many infants go on to require gastrostomy feeding because of oral co-ordination difficulties. Epilepsy and recurrent respiratory infections are common, and these infants often have a severely reduced life expectancy.

In this group primary cerebral malformation is commonly revealed by magnetic resonance imaging. Many of these conditions are genetically determined (eg see fig 10). A small proportion of children with spastic tetraparesis have disorders which arise in late pregnancy or in the early neonatal period due to the conditions listed in Table 3.

TABLE 3 – CAUSES OF SPASTIC TETRAPARESIS

Congenital cerebral malformations
Congenital infection, rubella, cytomegalovirus, toxoplasma, herpes simplex, HIV
Perinatal hypoxic ischaemic cerebral injury
Perinatal infection/meningitis
Intracerebral/extracerebral haemorrhage (various causes incl. trauma)

Of particular interest to the obstetrician are the hypoxic ischaemic causes. Broadly speaking two syndromes are relevant here:

- Prolonged partial hypoxic ischaemia.
- Abrupt onset near total asphyxia.

(a) Prolonged partial hypoxic ischaemia

Brain damage may arise in the perinatal period due to chronic deprivation of supply. The causes are listed in Table 4:

TABLE 4: CAUSES OF PROLONGED PARTIAL HYPOXIC ISCHAEMIA AT TERM

Recurrent umbilical cord obstruction
Chronic utero-placental insufficiency
Hypoxic ischaemia developing during periods of uterine hyper-stimulation

[29] Volpe, JJ, Neurobiology of periventricular leukomalacia in the premature infant, *Ped Res*, 2001, 50(5), 553-562

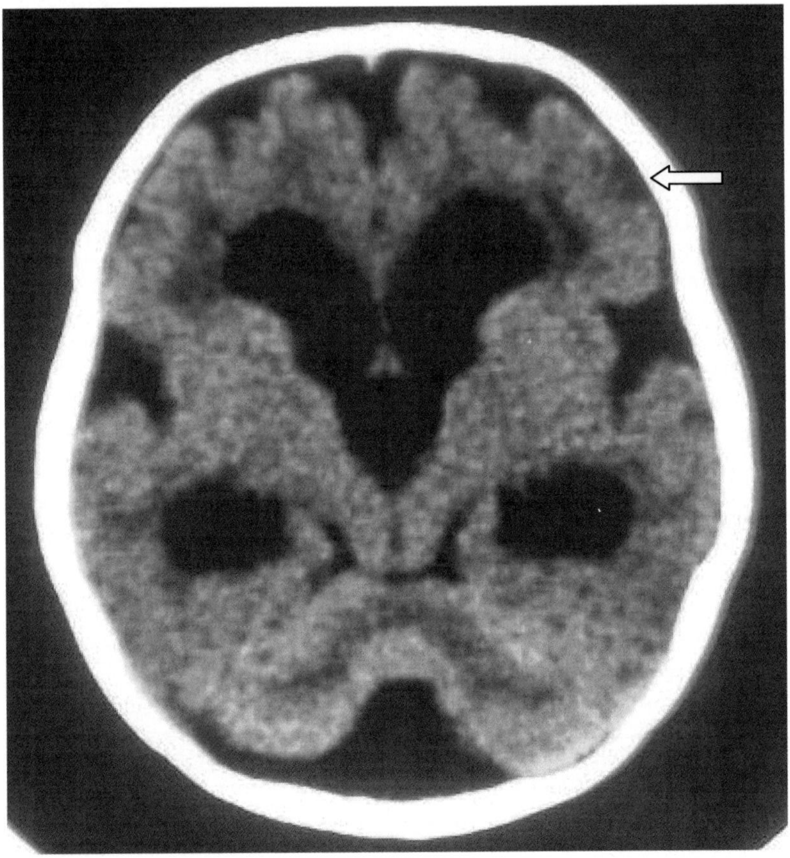

FIGURE 10 – TERM INFANT CT SCAN. FLOPPY AND UNRESPONSIVE FROM BIRTH. SEVERE LEARNING DIFFICULTIES. HYPOTONIA AND WEAKNESS, MUSCLE BIOPSY SHOWED CONGENITAL MUSCULAR DYSTROPHY. BRAIN SCAN SHOWS DIFFUSE PACHYGYRIA AND VENTRICULAR DILATATION

Hypoxic ischaemic brain injury in the newborn remains one of the major causes of long term disability. Hypoxic ischaemia refers to the reduction from normal in the cerebral oxygen delivery rate (hypoxia) as well as the reduction in cerebral perfusion with blood (ischaemia). Asphyxia refers to the combination of reduced oxygen level, increased carbon dioxide, reduced perfusion, and the biochemical abnormalities (acidosis) which follow from these changes. When hypoxic ischaemia passes a critical threshold, brain injury will be induced because the brain has limited intrinsic energy sources. Cerebral hypoxic ischaemia may produce a transient disturbance in brain function without necessarily inducing long term neurological damage (i.e. the death of brain cells). The extent of cerebral disturbance and injury is determined by the extent of reduction of critical supply, and the duration of that reduction.

A further important aspect of hypoxic ischaemic injury relates to the level of maturation of the brain at the time of the insult (that is, the stage of development reached by the brain which will be greater with greater post-conceptional age). Another important factor is whether the hypoxic ischaemic insult is global, (such as may occur due to general poor cerebral blood flow- for example due to low blood pressure), or focal, (such as may occur when there is an arterial occlusion due to, for example, an embolus from the placental circulation). A focal cause will result in the brain tissue in the distribution of supply of the artery becoming infarcted and necrotic. Tissue in the periphery of supply of the artery may be sustained by collateral circulation from adjacent arteries.

Profound oxygen deprivation will of course, if unrelieved, lead to the death of the individual. During profound oxygen deprivation, cardiac output will decline rapidly and effective cerebral circulation will cease. The failure of supply of oxygen to the brain will rapidly result in decline in the oxygen-dependent metabolic processes necessary for maintaining ionic gradients across neuronal cells. The consequence of this failure to maintain energy-dependent ion pumping systems results in depolarisation of brain neurons. The consequence of this depolarisation is a release of excitatory neuro-transmitters – in particular glutamate. This substance may achieve toxic levels, resulting in excessive opening of ion pores in neurones downstream of the depolarised neuron. The consequence of this excessive calcium influx is activation of a variety of intrinsic enzyme systems, resulting in cellular injury.

The hypoxic ischaemic insult in the above example may be reversed by resuscitation, but the trigger for the secondary processes of cellular destruction may already have been initiated. As a consequence, cellular injury may progress over the succeeding hours or days, resulting in a secondary destructive process (secondary energy failure).

In partial hypoxic ischaemia, where the hypoxic ischaemia is less severe than in the above example and is of a more chronic nature, energy failure may be progressive. Again, cellular injury may occur in the most deprived areas of the brain. These will tend to be those areas at the periphery of supply of the major cerebral vessels - the so-called watershed zones. These are the junctional areas between the anterior and the middle cerebral artery circulation territories and the middle cerebral and posterior circulation territories. Injury will tend to occur in these zones before the more central areas, since the blood supply to the central areas will be better preserved. (Fig 11). The cellular processes in partial hypoxic ischaemia, once the critical level of supply occurs, will be similar at a metabolic/pathological level to that in profound hypoxic ischaemia.

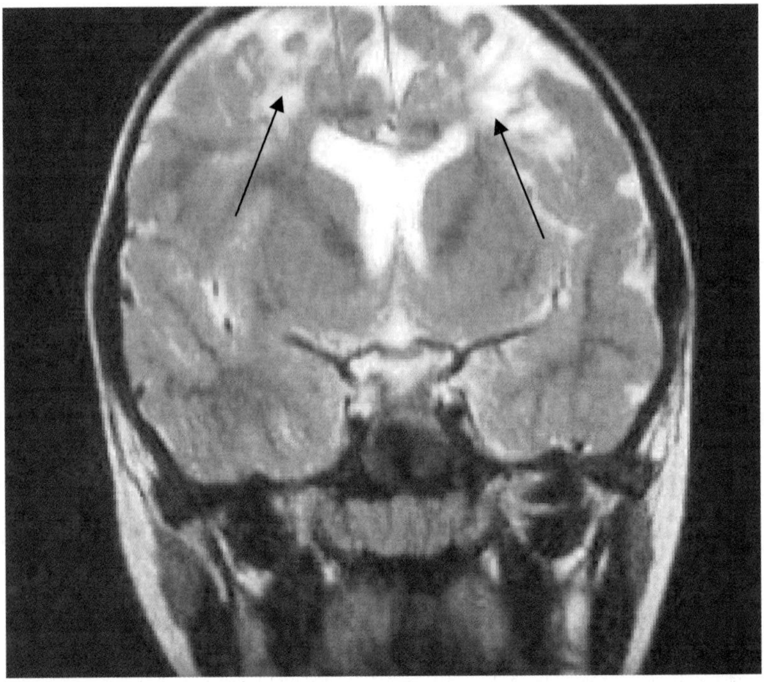

FIGURE 11 – TERM INFANT – PROLONGED PARTIAL HYPOXIC ISCHAEMIA SECONDARY TO UTERINE HYPERSTIMULATION. MRI T2 WEIGHTED IMAGE, CORONAL PLANE, SHOWING BILATERAL PARASAGGITAL 'WATERSHED' INFARCTION. THE WATERSHED IS BETWEEN THE AREA OF SUPPLY OF THE MIDDLE AND ANTERIOR CEREBRAL ARTERIES

Following resuscitation and restoration of brain perfusion (re-perfusion), there will be an initial increase in cerebral blood flow as the animal or infant recovers. However this is then followed by a reduction in cerebral perfusion (hypo-perfusion): this secondary cerebral flow reduction may become critical and cause further cellular injury

(b) Acute profound hypoxic ischaemia

This clinical situation is significantly different from partial hypoxic ischaemia. In profound hypoxic ischaemia there is a total or near total reduction in cerebral perfusion. This may come about as the terminal event in partial hypoxic ischaemia, where myocardial reserves are so depleted that effective cardiac output ceases. It may also come about where there is a sudden reduction in gas exchange for the fetus – commonly where there is uterine rupture, massive ante partum haemorrhage, umbilical cord prolapse with cord obstruction, or acute haemorrhage from vasa praevia. In this setting the fetus suffers an acute reduction in cerebral perfusion. Redistribution of flow to protect the high metabolic demand areas in the brain stem, basal ganglia, corticospinal tracts and hippocampi cannot occur, and as a consequence these high demand areas are primarily affected. If prolonged profound flow reduction occurs increasing degrees of brain injury will occur. It may be impossible to resuscitate the infant. If it is resuscitated, early death may follow. If it survives, it may have severe multicystic encephalomalacia (Fig 12). Fig 13 shows basal ganglia and thalamic injury after profound asphyxia.

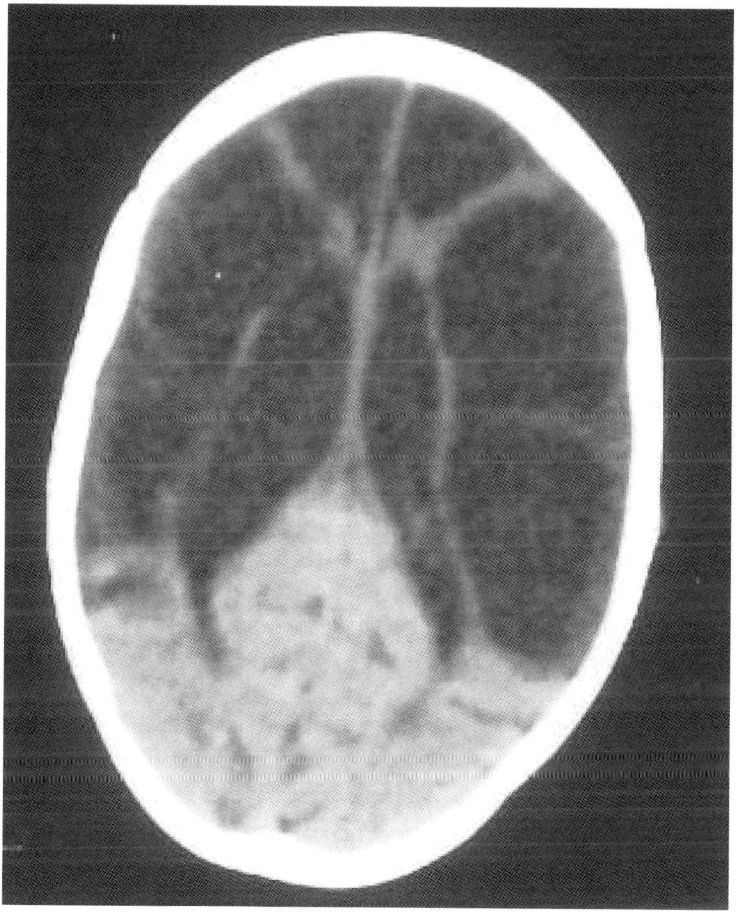

FIGURE 12 – CT SCAN, TERM INFANT; PROLONGED (>30MIN) PROFOUND HYPOXIC ISCHAEMIA FOLLOWED BY SEVERE NEONATAL ENCEPHALOPATHY WITH SEVERE CEREBRAL OEDEMA. MULTICYSTIC LEUCOMALACIA.

(c) Hypoxic ischaemic encephalopathy

Presentation

The mechanisms that may provoke cerebral hypoxic ischaemia during gestation, are listed above (Table 4). Where cerebral hypoxic ischaemia has been sufficient to cause neurological injury, there will be a period of post-insult neurological disturbance if the infant is born at or close to term. However, in pre-term infants,

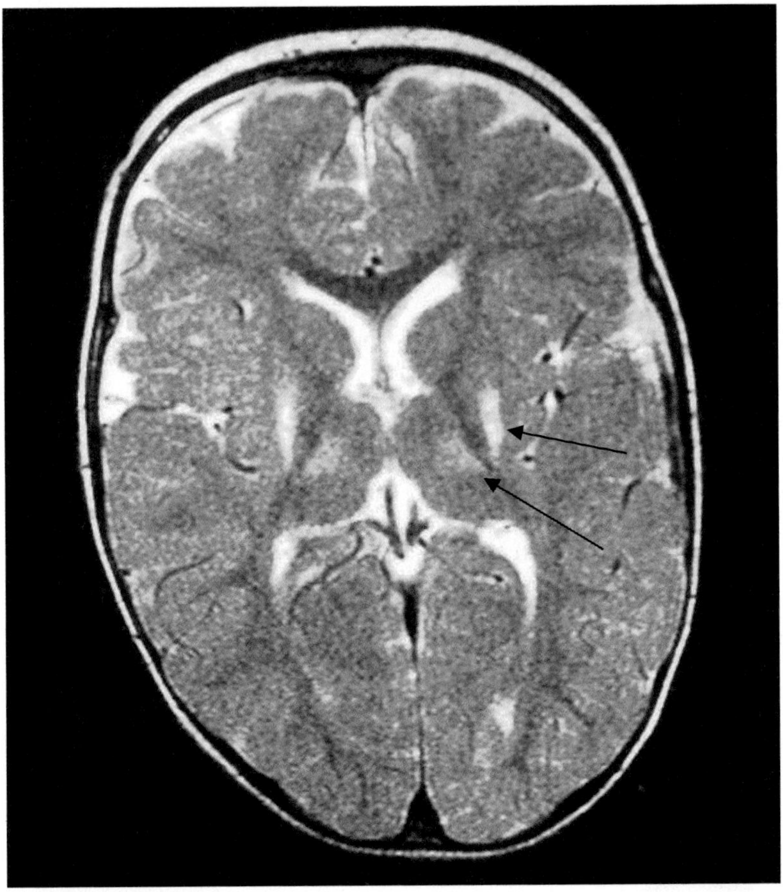

FIGURE 13 – T2 MRI, TERM INFANT, SHOWING BILATERAL DAMAGE TO THE POSTERIOR PUTAMEN (ABOVE) AND THE VENTROLATERAL THALAMI (BELOW, IN PICTURE). 21 MINUTES PROFOUND ASPHYXIA SECONDARY TO UTERINE RUPTURE. CHILD WITH CHOREO ATHETOID CEREBRAL PALSY

quite extensive cerebral injury may be apparently asymptomatic in the neonatal period.

Sarnat and Sarnat described the clinical features of hypoxic ischaemic encephalopathy[30]. In their initial study, three stages of HIE were observed -stages 1, 2, and 3 - of increasing severity. EEG data was also reported. Infants in Stage 1 HIE were hyper-alert, tachycardic and irritable. The duration of symptoms and signs was up to 24 hours. Stage 2 infants were more severely affected, tending to be lethargic to stuporose. Seizures were common in this group and duration was

[30] Sarnat, H and Sarnat, M, Neonatal encephalopathy following fetal distress, *Arch Neurol*, 1976, 33, 696-705

of 2-7 days. In Stage 3 encephalopathy children were comatose with depressed or absent deep tendon reflexes and commonly difficulties in maintaining satisfactory respiration. Since Sarnat and Sarnats' original description, their classification of HIE has undergone only minor modification. A number of authors[31] have observed that Stage 1 encephalopathy may be of up to 48 hours duration. It is often difficult to distinguish between Stage 2 and 3 HIE, particularly if anticonvulsant medication is used, and this may have a direct effect on respiratory function.

During the development of HIE there is commonly an initial period of relative normality following the birth and resuscitation. Seizures generally evolve during the first 8 hours after birth, but may be delayed beyond this time (up to 72 hours in some reports). The HIE when of Stage 2 or Stage 3 is generally at its most intense 24-96 hours after birth, following which there is commonly a gradual resolution of symptoms. Initial cranial ultrasound appearances may suggest normal brain structure (first 6-12 hours) followed by evidence of cerebral swelling (loss of definition of cortical sulci and effacement of cerebral ventricles). As the clinical encephalopathy subsides, resolution of cerebral oedema will be observed on ultrasound scan, usually by 5-7 days of age. A hyper-echoic cerebral texture may be observed in the acute phase. Some infants with HIE will show intra-ventricular haemorrhage and thalamic echodensity which may be diffuse, focal or intense, (the latter suggesting thalamic haemorrhage). Parenchymal haemorrhage may occur, and there may be extra-cerebral haemorrhage (subdural, subarachnoid).

In the pre-term infant the development of cerebral oedema may be less obvious, and on ultrasound haemorrhage and haemorrhagic infarction patterns are more commonly seen – in particular intraventricular haemorrhage (GLH/IVH) and periventricular haemorrhagic infarction.

In the term infant, diffuse echodensity may persist into the second week, to be followed by the development of multi-cystic encephalomalacia in the most severely affected cases (Fig 12).

HIE is commonly complicated by multi-organ injury. The most common associated organ damage is seen in the kidney, with oliguria and frequently haematuria in the initial phase of the HIE, accompanied by elevations in plasma urea and creatinine concentrations. After a variable period of time urine flow improves, and there is commonly a period of polyuria (excessive urine output) before renal function returns to normal. There are occasional cases where chronic renal impairment may follow HIE with persistently elevated and rising creatinine levels.

Multi-organ injury may also include hepatic damage (manifest as elevation of hepatic-derived transaminases), myocardial injury (manifest as hypotension,

[31] *e.g.* Levene, M *et al*, Comparison of two methods of predicting outcome in perinatal asphyxia, *Lancet*, 1986, 1: 67-69

cardiomegaly, poor myocardial contractility), and intestinal injury (manifest as haemorrhagic enterocolitis). Approximately 70% of children with moderate to severe hypoxic ischaemic encephalopathy will present with multi-organ injury: the commonest organ involvement is renal[32].

Further imaging studies in HIE. The advent of magnetic resonance imaging in the neonatal period has allowed description of characteristic patterns of brain injury both in the acute and long term settings. In the acute phase MRI may reveal[33] changes in the signal return in the internal capsule. The internal capsule comprises white matter tracts passing through the lower cerebral hemispheres close to the basal ganglia. These white matter tracts are myelinating in the term gestation infant and in the normal situation show as prolonged signal return compared to adjacent non myelinated white matter tracts. Disturbance of this differential myelination pattern is seen in hypoxic ischaemic injury (loss of prolonged signal in posterior limb of the internal capsule), and is commonly an indicator of later significant developmental disability.

Recent research in diffusion-weighted imaging, in which the molecular movement of water is assessed by MRI, show that precise estimation of compromised white and grey matter may be obtained with this technique which allows accurate timing of onset of the insult. This method is not available in clinical practice at the moment, but has yielded important information in research studies. For example, Cowan et al[34] have shown that a high proportion of infants presenting with neonatal encephalopathy show evidence on imaging of an acute (i.e. recent) brain insult. This observation is important because there has been uncertainty about whether infants with established (long standing) brain pathology will present with neonatal encephalopathy. This study suggests that most infants with an acute neonatal encephalopathy have acquired their cerebral disorder close to the time of birth. Brain imaging showed evidence of an acute insult without established injury or atrophy in 197 of 245 of infants who were born after 36 weeks gestation and presented within 72 hours of age with neonatal encephalopathy. The lesions were mainly bilateral abnormalities in basal ganglia, thalami, cortex or white matter, and there were 8 infants with focal infarction. 40 infants had normal scans, and 9 (4%) showed damage that additional to a recent hypoxic ischaemic insult. Only 8 (3%) had evidence of another disorder. These data suggest that in the majority of children presenting with neonatal encephalopathy, recent hypoxic ischaemia has occurred which is sufficient to cause the cerebral disturbance.

Dyskinetic Cerebral Palsy

This term refers to children who have a static movement disorder in which choreo athetoid movement patterns predominate, or where dystonia predominates. The

---

[32] Perlman, JM and Tack, ED, Renal injury in the asphyxiated newborn infant: Relationship to neurologic outcome, *J Pediatr*, 1988, 113: 875-879

[33] Rutherford, M, in *MRI of the neonatal brain*, 2002, London, WB Saunders, pp 102-105

[34] Cowan, F *et al*, Origin and timing of brain lesions in term infants with neonatal encephalopathy, *Lancet*, 2003, 361: 736-742

fundamental motor problem is that of co-contraction – a phenomenon where both agonist and antagonist muscles rotating a joint are contracted. This co contraction results in abnormal posture (dystonia) or abnormal motion of the limb or other musculature (face, oro pharynx etc) (choreo athetosis). The neuropatholigical origin of these movement and postural abnormalities is disease in the basal ganglia, the deep grey nuclei (putamen, caudate, globus pallidus, sub thalamic nucleus). The thalamus may also be involved. Approximately 10% of cases of dyskinetic cerebral palsy are secondary to profound asphyxia (see above, also Fig 13)[35]. A small number of cases are seen following severe neonatal hyperbilirubinaemia. In this latter group sensorineural hearing impairment may also complicate the picture. The specific area of damage in hyperbilirubinaemia is in the globus pallidus (see Fig 14). In theory hyperbilirubinaemia is avoidable through phototherapy and exchange transfusion. However in small pre term babies and sick more mature babies vulnerability to hyperbilirubinaemic brain injury shows wide individual variation. Evidence based guidelines for management of neonatal hyperbilirubinaemia are not available and therapeutic decisions are taken by consensus and opinion.

Children with dyskinetic cerebral palsy commonly have preserved intellectual function. In this authors experience up to 30% of children with post asphyxial dyskinesia have average or above average cognitive abilities. Simple and complex partial seizures may complicate the issue although response to anti convulsant medication is commonly good. In post asphyxial dyskinesia there may be a worsening of the movement disorder in mid to late childhood.

Ataxic Cerebral Palsy

These children present with ataxia intention tremor and dysmetria (past pointing). Commonly the children achieve independent walking by 4-6 years of age but have considerable difficulties in precision in gross motor movements and frequently have handwriting difficulties. In more severe cases learning difficulties may complicate the picture and seizures may also be present.

This group constitutes 7-15% of cases of cerebral palsy. Most of these cases are of pre-natal origin. In many cases there are strong familial patterns which may be autosomal recessive, dominant or X-linked in their inheritance pattern. Sporadic cases are also common. A number of series of cases of ataxic cerebral palsy have been published in relation to neuro-imaging findings. Between 38 and 50% of cases may show abnormalities in the posterior fossa, such as atrophy of the cerebellum, vermian hypoplasia, or atrophy, and some cases present with generalised cortical atrophy with prominent sulci. Pre-natal cytomegalovirus infection needs to be excluded in these children. Associations with perinatal hypoxia ischaemia are extremely rare. In the study reported by Esscher et al[36], a

[35] Rosenbloom, L, Dyskinetic cerebral palsy and birth asphyxia, *Developmental Medicine and Child Neurology*, 1994, 36, 285-289

[36] Esscher, E *et al*, Non progressive ataxia: Origins, brain pathology and impairments in 78 Swedish children, *Developmental Medicine and Child Neurology*, 1996, 38, 285-296

regional study of 76 children with congenital ataxia, there were three children whose disability may have arisen in the perinatal period. One child of 41 weeks gestation at birth had severe hypoxic ischaemic encephalopathy and later had ataxia and choreo-athetosis. A further child of 36 weeks gestation was ataxic following a cardiac arrest on the second day, and a third premature infant who was severely ill with hyperbilirubinaemia and sepsis was ataxic at follow up (a total of 78 patients). These findings suggest that the causal link between perinatal hypoxic ischaemia and congenital ataxia is very weak, if it exists at all.

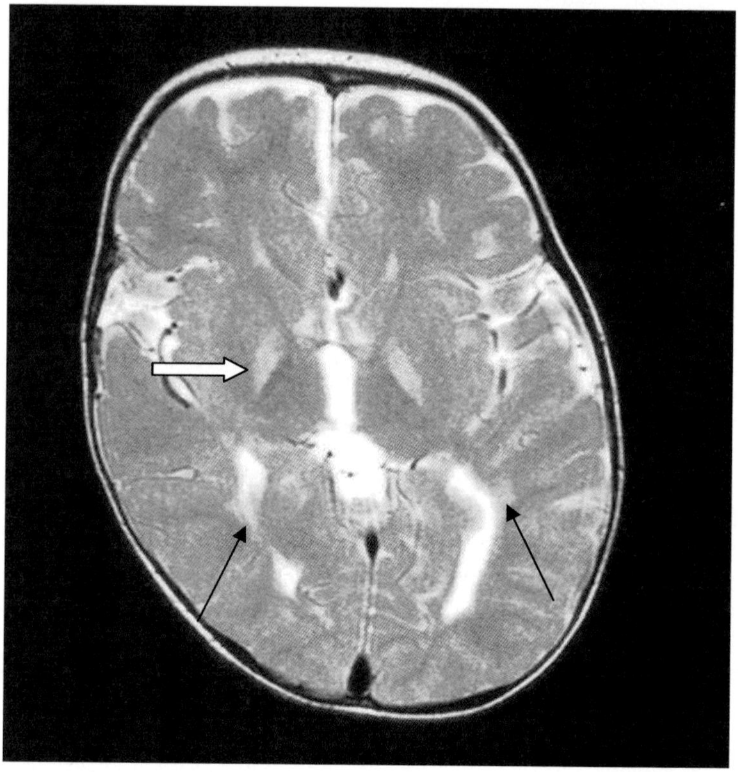

FIGURE 14 - T2 MRI SCAN, CHILD WITH DYSKINESIA AND SENSORINEURAL DEAFNESS. SEVERE NEONATAL HYPERBILIRUBINAEMIA. PROLONGED SIGNAL RETURN FROM GLOBI PALLIDI BILATERALLY (LARGE ARROW). NOTE ALSO PRESENCE OF HIGH SIGNAL RETURN FROM POSTERIOR WHITE MATTER, INDICATING PERIVENTRICULAR LEUKOMALACIA IN ADDITION (SMALL ARROWS)

Unclassifiable cerebral palsy

A number of cases of cerebral palsy will be of a mixed type and not readily classifiable into one of the above clinical syndromes. These children generally represent about 10% of the cases of cerebral palsy.

In summary

(i) A relatively small number of cases of cerebral palsy arise from perinatal adversity;
(ii) Preterm delivery continues to be associated with high mortality and significant long term morbidity;
(iii) Prenatal, perinatal and postnatal factors may all be relevant in the genesis of brain injury;
(iv) With the exception of basal ganglia injury, identification and timing of onset of single causative factors may be impossible in individual cases.

NEONATOLOGY AND PAEDIATRICS

Stephen Rose

INTRODUCTION

Damage a child, and you have damaged a person for life. That means that paediatric claims can involve many years of future loss, and therefore be very financially significant. Brain damage is the obvious example. Cerebral palsy has its own chapter in this book. Most cerebral palsy is a consequence of damage occurring during gestation or at the time of birth, but it should be remembered that babies suffering a traumatic birth should be handed over to a paediatrician as soon as they emerge. Failure by the paediatricians to salvage a child's brain, when that brain is teetering between normality and permanent injury, can be very expensive.

Another example of the potential for big paediatric claims is screening failures. Failures, early in the child's life, to screen properly for congenital hip abnormalities have attracted much recent legal attention.

This chapter is a survey of the most medico-legally significant parts of the neonatologist's and paediatrician's life.

NEONATOLOGY

Resuscitation

There are many types of maternity units across the country: some with full obstetric and paediatric service, some with obstetric medical staff but no paediatric medical staff, those run by general practitioners and those effectively run by midwife maternity units. In each of these establishments there must be a robust system for resuscitation of the unexpectedly compromised infant.

The type of personnel involved in resuscitation is not relevant; what is relevant is the level of training and expertise. There must be the expertise to recognise a compromised infant and then to respond appropriately and effectively to that problem. The standard approach to assessing the infant at birth is the Apgar Score. (See table 1). This gives an assessment of the state of the infant at 1, 5 and 10 minutes and should be used to determine the type of resuscitation required.

TABLE 1

Score	0	1	2
Heart rate	Absent	< 100bpm	> 100bpm
Respiratory effort	Absent	Weak cry	Strong cry
Muscle tone	Limp	Some flexion	Active movement
Reflex irritability	No response	Grimace	Cry
Colour	White	Blue	Pink

Infant resuscitation is no different from any other form of resuscitation and the basic life support principles of airway, breathing, circulation in that order should be observed.

For example, should there be meconium (infant stool) in the mouth, then the airways are compromised and should be cleared first. If there is little effort at breathing, then ventilation should be undertaken. Most infants will respond to bag and mask ("Ambubag") or T-piece ventilation; this is where a mask is applied by pressure exerted using a pressure controlled system with breaths produced by closing the open end of the T-piece with the finger. However, if this form of ventilation is unsuccessful then there must be skills available immediately for intubation of the neonate.

Neonatal intubation is not an easy task and requires considerable skill, practice and retraining. It is not negligent to attempt to intubate an infant and fail, or intubate the oesophagus as opposed to the trachea. However, it is negligent not to be able to ascertain that that is what has happened and to react appropriately.

Many infants, once successfully intubated and ventilated, will respond with increasing heart rate. However, those who have a very compromised heart rate, (that rate is not specifically defined), should have cardiac massage in an attempt to maintain circulation, improve tissue oxygenation, including that of the heart muscle so that the heart itself then responds appropriately with an increased heart rate.

In those units that do not have immediate access to paediatric staff, the personnel with neonatal resuscitation responsibility must be trained not only in the skills of immediate resuscitation but also in maintaining the stability of the infant until the paediatric team arrive. This will include, if necessary, maintenance of oxygen saturations with continued ventilation or supplemental oxygen and maintenance of the infant's temperature.

One of the complications of resuscitation (more so with bag and mask ventilation when very high pressures can be generated with the Ambubag) is a pneumothorax (rupture of the lung). The production of a pneumothorax is not necessarily negligent - it is a recognised complication of resuscitation - but there must be skills immediately available to recognise that a pneumothorax has occurred and appropriate treatment must be readily available.

Ventilation

Some neonates, once resuscitated, will require ongoing mechanical ventilation. This must be undertaken in a unit used to dealing with mechanical ventilation of neonates. This might require the movement of compromised infants on mechanical ventilation around a region or even around the country.

Movement of infants from place to place carries the risk of the endotracheal tube being dislodged. This can happen when moving the infant from the resuscitaire in the labour ward to the neonatal unit in order to be attached to the ventilator, or during transportation.

It is vital that the position of the endotracheal tube is correct. This means not only that the tube must be in the trachea but also that it must not be too high (allowing leakage of gases and inadequate ventilation) or too low (when one lung only is ventilated, causing difficulties with ventilation but also potential damage to that lung).

There must be a clinical assessment to ensure that the endotracheal tube is in the lungs, and the position should be checked with a chest x-ray.

Once an endotracheal tube is in position, the infant cannot cough, since the vocal cords are unable to close. Secretions, therefore, have to be removed mechanically with suction and these secretions may build up within the endotracheal tube. This is a recognised problem of mechanical ventilation and the signs of a blocked tube, (for example an increasing requirement for oxygen, and increasing levels of carbon dioxide in the blood), must be recognised and appropriate replacement undertaken.

Once on a mechanical ventilator the infant is normally totally dependent on mechanical ventilation: this is obviously the case in infants who have been paralysed in order to improve their ventilation. Individual ventilators have alarms which signify when things are going wrong. However, there must also be a clinical appreciation that the ventilator itself may be a problem and indeed the alarms may not be appropriate or may not sound off appropriately. This is even more of a problem in transport ventilation when the transport ventilator is considerably less sophisticated than the transport ventilator within the neonatal unit.

Only personnel with sufficient expertise and training should be involved in the care of ventilated infants. Further, personnel who are skilled in the transport of ventilated sick infants should only used for such transportation. These personnel must have sufficient skill to distinguish between a clinical deterioration in the infant's basic condition due to the underlying problem, and a deterioration related to the mechanical ventilation. There should be sufficient skill for the precise cause to be identified rapidly and appropriate treatment undertaken.

Neonatal Examination

Basics

Once resuscitation has been successful and the infant is stable and self-ventilating, thorough and careful examination is mandatory. The purpose of the examination is to look for obvious and not so obvious abnormal signs. Easily visualised aspects of the examination include the appropriate number of digits on hands and feet, normal facies (facial appearance) and normal genitalia. It is also important to establish that an anus is present and in the appropriate position, that the palate is complete and not cleft and that the red reflexes (reflection from the retina, back of the eye) are present and normal.

The fetal circulation changes considerably from being in utero to ex utero and there are changes in pressures on both sides of the heart. This means that heart murmurs may be present at birth, and then disappear, or may not be present at birth, and appear later. There is increasing pressure on obstetric beds, so many infants are discharged within 48 hours. Sometimes discharge occurs at 24 hours, but it may occur as early at 6 hours of life, with only one initial neonatal examination having been done. There must, therefore, be a process to ensure that these infants are rechecked at 6 weeks of life - normally when the mother returns for her postnatal check. At the 6 week check screening for heart murmurs and hips is particularly important.

Heart Murmurs

The commonest heart murmur to present after birth is a ventricular septal defect (VSD). This may not be audible at birth because of similar pressures in both of the pumping chambers of the heart, but as the right side of the heart pressure drops, the murmur becomes audible. Some of these infants will develop heart failure because of the size of the flow of blood between the chambers, and this usually occurs within the first 3 months of life. A VSD murmur will be present at 6 weeks of life and, therefore, cardiac examination is mandatory.

Developmental Dysplasia of the Hips

Developmental dysplasia of the hips, previously known as congenital dislocation of the hips ("CDH"), can be a devastating problem if diagnosed late, requiring operation towards the end of the first year. All infants must have an examination of their hips. There is still debate as to what is the most appropriate method for examination. The only agreement is that all infants must have some form of hip examination and those at high risk must have a more detailed examination. The Ortolani and Barlow tests are the standard tests used in physical examination of the hips in low risk infants. However, those infants at high risk, (those born breech, - either at term or pre-term - or by lower segment Caesarean section, those with a family history and those found to have an abnormality on physical examination), should have ultrasonography of the hips and appropriate treatment as necessary thereafter. The hips must also be checked at the 6 weeks check in case abnormalities not detected at birth are detectable later.

Hydration

The ratio of fluid requirement to body weight decreases massively as humans grow up. A pre-term infant may need 180 to 200/mls/ kg/day, a term infant 150 mls/kg/day and yet an adult only 30 ml/kg/day. Yet the requirement for other nutrients such as sodium, potassium and sugar does not vary so greatly with regard to body size. Therefore, the prescription and administration of fluids to infants especially, but also throughout the paediatric age range, requires knowledge of this considerable variation in fluid requirements. It is vital that those requiring high fluids are not deprived of fluid (leading to dehydration and possible organ failure), and that those with lower fluid requirements are not be over hydrated, (potentially leading to heart failure).

Fluid administration is trickiest during infancy.

The preferred route for fluid administration is by the enteral route, i.e. into the intestines. This can either be achieved by giving fluids by mouth or giving fluids via a nasogastric tube. If fluids are given this way then the body itself has some control over the amount of fluid absorbed from the intestines. However, if fluids are administered intravenously, there is no such intrinsic control; all the control is dependent on the medical and nursing staff.

The problems revolving around intravenous administration can be broadly divided into problems associated with volume, problems associated with the type of fluids administered, and problems associated with the mechanics of administration.

Infants require high fluid volumes/kg/day. They also require sugar as they may either have insufficient stores of sugar or glycogen or be unable to utilise them effectively. They also need electrolytes such as sodium, potassium, calcium etc. The volume of fluid must be worked out precisely given the weight of the child and then the appropriate amount of sugar, sodium and potassium must be given. Potassium is potentially a fatal drug if given as an overdose and recently Trusts have been issued with ready made bags containing different amounts of potassium to try to reduce the danger from excess potassium being added to intravenous fluids. Outside specialist units there can therefore be no excuse for potassium administration errors. In the highly specialised areas of neonatal and paediatric intensive care, the condition of infants and children may be such to demand unusual amounts of potassium, so necessitating the manual addition of potassium to the bags of intravenous fluid. Mistakes can occur there.

We all have a glucose demand, but most adults are able to maintain an acceptable glucose level despite starvation or just being given fluids without sugar. Infants find this much more difficult and it must be recognised that infants and children need glucose added to their intravenous fluids to prevent low blood sugar (hypoglycaemia).

Hypoglycaemia appears not to be too significant a problem in older children. However, in pre-term and term infants hypoglycaemia leading to seizures can cause neurological damage and must be avoided at all costs.

Administration of fluids is usually via a peripheral cannula, - a thin tube made out of soft silicone rubber inserted into a peripheral vein in the back of the hand or in the foot. Infants and children will not keep the limb in which the cannula has been inserted still and, therefore, it is almost inevitable that there will be rupture of the vein by the cannula at some point. As this is virtually inevitable, a process must be in place to determine as soon as possible that this has happened. When it does, fluid goes into the surrounding tissues instead of going into the veins. This can cause significant damage where the fluids contain substances which are corrosive to the surrounding tissues - for example calcium or sodium bicarbonate.

Those cannulae which are maintaining constant fluid infusion should be checked hourly and this should be documented on the nursing notes. Extravasation of fluids can occur at any time – for instance just after an inspection which appears to be (and is) normal. Thus, the child may suffer an hour of extravasation of fluids into the tissues. However, that is the most that should be considered acceptable.

Other cannulae may be used intermittently, for example for the administration of antibiotics or other drugs given as a bolus. These sites need not be inspected on a regular basis as no fluid is going through them. However, it is unacceptable to assume that a cannula through which fluid has not been going must still be in the vein. The siting of the cannula must be checked. Intravenous cannulae that are stabilised by being bandaged should have the bandage taken down so that the actual site of infusion can be inspected during the infusion of the bolus. Any extravasation of fluids, therefore, should be rapidly obvious; the infusion must be stopped. It is unacceptable to infuse a bolus of fluid into a cannula without first inspecting the site itself.

Unfortunately, there are still times when a large volume of fluid may have been infused into the surrounding tissues. This is potentially more of a problem with long lines. These are lines which are inserted into a peripheral vein and then pushed into some of the large veins around the groin or around the heart. These lines are made of very soft material and do not usually erode through the vessel wall, but this can happen. There is very little initially to be seen at the infusion site and although the intravenous pumps may register a pressure rise within the line, the pressure may not rise until quite a substantial volume of fluid is infused into the limb.

This again is a recognised complication of administration of fluids and, therefore, there should be protocols in place to try to minimise the damage done either by the corrosive nature of the fluid infused or because of the pressure effect of the volume itself.

There are no universally accepted techniques for dealing with the extravasated fluid, but there are techniques which are known to reduce damage. Examples include the application of GTN (glycerine trinitrate) paste to increase the local blood flow, multiple small incisions to allow local fluid egress and the administration of drugs to break down barriers within the tissues to allow diffusion of the extravasated fluids further - for example hyaluronidase. Each unit should have a policy appropriate to the expertise within that unit.

The administration of intravenous fluid is entirely dependent on the intravenous pumps or syringe drivers which pump fluid into the vein and measure the volume that has been administered. There are situations within paediatric intensive care and neonatal intensive care, when the volume per hour is very low - for example as low as 0.1 ml/hour. The accuracy of mechanical pumps cannot be assumed and, therefore, there must be an hourly visual check on the amount of fluid that has been infused in case a mechanical failure has caused administration of a far higher volume of potentially toxic medication than was prescribed. Such a mechanical failure can occur at any time between the hourly inspections. Therefore, one hour's abnormal fluid administration is acceptable but no more.

Neonatal Seizures

Seizures in the pre-term or term infant are relatively common and may or may not have the potential to cause neurodevelopmental abnormalities. It is vital, therefore, to try to determine the cause of the neonatal seizure. The causes are legion and will not be exhaustively listed. However, because there are so many causes it is important to have a rational approach. One approach is to consider categories causing seizures.

(i) *Metabolic Causes*: The common causes of metabolic seizures in neonates are either high or low sodium (hyper- or hyponatraemia), low calcium (hypocalcaemia) and low glucose (hypoglycaemia). The newborn infant is totally dependent on adults for nutrition and thus any of the above categories can be considered to be iatrogenic if occurring in hospital. However, normally only those caused by hypernatraemia and hypoglycaemia are associated with subsequent neurodevelopmental delay. There must, therefore, be considerable efforts to prevent the development of hypernatraemia or hypoglycaemia. The reduction in risk revolves around meticulous attention to fluid volume and content of sodium and glucose. Hypocalcaemia and hyponatraemia also cause seizures, but normally with no later sequelae.

(ii) *Infective Causes*: Neonates may undergo seizures for almost any form of infection, ranging from a severe infection in the head such as meningitis through to a urinary tract infection. Thus, any unexpected seizure should be subjected to the full rigours of investigation for possible infection.

(iii) *Trauma*: The commonest form of intracerebral trauma causing seizures in the neonate is in the pre-term infant suffering from intraventricular haemorrhage. There are many risk factors for intraventricular haemorrhage but it is not known what eventually causes one infant to have intraventricular haemorrhage and not another with apparently exactly the same predisposing risk factors. The occurrence of an intraventricular haemorrhage, therefore, does not necessarily connote negligence.

Despite such an approach the cause of the seizures may not be obvious. If there are concerns, therefore, that either an infective or a metabolic cause may be operating, it is appropriate to treat an infant for both unless and until further investigations make the cause clearer.

Jaundice

Jaundice is divided into two categories: so called conjugated or unconjugated hyperbilirubinaemia. Hyperbilirubinaemia simply means a raised level of bilirubin in the circulation. Unconjugated bilirubin has not yet been metabolised by the liver: conjugated bilirubin has been metabolised.

In the newborn, the dangerous form is unconjugated hyperbilirubinaemia, since unconjugated bilirubin is fat soluble and, therefore, can enter and damage the brain. If there are sufficiently high levels it may lead to a form of cerebral palsy.

There are groups of infants known to be at high risk of unconjugated hyperbilirubinaemia. These include pre-term infants, infants who have not fed, infected infants, and those with an incompatibility with their mother's blood group, (either the rhesus blood group or the AB and O blood type). However, there are many infants who become jaundiced for no obvious reason apart from normal so called physiological jaundice which relates to the immaturity of the liver. Thus, those infants at high risk must be observed carefully and frequently. Those at low risk must also be screened to determine whether they are becoming jaundiced. This screening must be performed initially in hospital, but with early discharge more screening occurs in the community health service than in hospitals. There must be processes, therefore, to allow rapid estimation of bilirubin levels both in hospital and in the community.

The causes of jaundice in the newborn are many and should be investigated and, if necessary, appropriately treated. However, the most urgent priority in high levels of jaundice is to treat the jaundice appropriately to minimise the risk of brain damage. The level of bilirubin at which brain damage occurs varies from infant to infant but also depends on gestation and age. The very premature infant has a low tolerance for bilirubin and, therefore, the level of bilirubin at which treatment should occur is very much lower than in a term infant. At any gestation the levels of bilirubin on day 1 requiring treatment are much lower than on day 5 and subsequently. Those caring for infants at risk of developing jaundice, should have access to or knowledge of the graphs that are available to allow determination of treatment levels. There are two basic treatment regimens: phototherapy using artificial sunlight; and exchange transfusion. The type of treatment is determined by the level of bilirubin.

Retinopathy of Prematurity

The advent and improvement of neonatal intensive care have meant that more preterm infants are now living. However, these infants if born pre-term have not completed their development. A clinically important example relates to the eye. The vascularisation of the retina is not complete until around 32 to 34 weeks gestation. Before that time the blood vessels growing into the retina are exquisitely sensitive to various stimuli, which may cause them to grow faster, then turn into scar tissue and pull the retina off the back of the eye causing blindness. This is so called retinopathy of prematurity. It has now become clear that there are various trigger factors for retinopathy of prematurity - not just high oxygen levels in the blood stream, which used to be thought to be the main cause. There are infants who seem to develop retinopathy of prematurity and who do not appear to have had high levels of blood oxygen. Thus, however well a pre-term infant may be, it should be considered to be at risk of developing retinopathy of prematurity if born at 32 weeks or less and should be subjected to regular screening by ophthalmologists with a special knowledge of retinopathy of prematurity. Such screening, and if necessary early treatment of retinopathy of prematurity, should minimise the chances of visual impairment or blindness. There can be no excuse for a lack of screening of these children when it is known that this group of infants is at high risk of this problem.

PAEDIATRICS

Paediatric Care in the NHS

Broadly, the care of patients within the National Health Service is divided into three levels: primary, secondary and tertiary care. Primary care is effected by general practitioners and is carried out within the community. Secondary care indicates a referral from the general practitioner to a hospital. The hospital could either be a district general hospital or a teaching hospital. Tertiary care is when a patient is referred from a hospital consultant to another hospital consultant. The referring hospital may either be a district general hospital or a teaching hospital and the hospital to which the patient is referred can again be either a district general hospital or teaching hospital.

The implication of these levels of care is that there is greater specialist care at each level. For example, a general paediatrician has more knowledge of paediatrics than a general practitioner who refers on to the hospital general paediatrician, and the specialist paediatrician has more expertise and knowledge in a narrower area of paediatrics than the general paediatrician who refers.

The appropriate place for care may be very obvious. For example all children with cancers should be and generally are looked after by a specialist paediatric cancer service, although there may be shared care with the local paediatrician. Similarly, children with severe liver disease will be looked after in the units with that expertise. However, it is not usually as obvious as this, and there are few generally applicable guidelines or protocols to help determine what the most appropriate level of care is for a particular child. For example, many children with asthma are looked after by their general practitioners, those with more severe asthma by a general paediatrician, and the most severe possibly in tertiary centres. However, there are no guidelines to determine where any particular child with asthma should be cared for. That decision may well depend on many factors, including the age of the child, the geography (ie how far away the family is from their local hospital), the severity of the asthma and the expertise of the particular doctor.

Any medical practitioner undertaking care must have sufficient confidence in his or her own abilities to care for a particular patient and, if challenged, should be able to mount an argument as to why it is appropriate for him or her to carry on caring for that child. Such a challenge generally only occurs if things go wrong. At that point the practitioner can only rely on surrogate markers, such as the number of patients who are cared for suffering from the same condition, attendance at recent training or update days and maintenance of continuing professional development. Awareness of the need for truly specialist care has led to increasing centralisation of paediatric care in larger paediatric units for some more specialist areas. The corollary of this is that district general hospitals may become de-skilled in certain areas of paediatrics, although children with those problems may well still arrive at that hospital.

This removal of expertise from local paediatric facilities means that there has to be even greater willingness for transfer of children to more specialist centres. It is not negligent to fail to recognise a rare problem or to fail to diagnose difficult illnesses. However, it is incumbent on the local paediatric facility to recognise the limits of their expertise and then either to gain access to that expertise via discussion with specialist centres, or, if necessary, to stabilise the child and move the child on to specialist services. Unless the child is in extremis, it is not acceptable to "have a go" in the face of ignorance rather than gain specialist expertise or refer.

National Guidelines for Paediatric Care

Traditional western medicine is based on clinical evidence, personal and collective experience, and that ethereal component, clinical acumen. The knowledge base of the medical profession has been built up over many generations and in many cases it is clear that there is more than one treatment option for any given diagnosis. This has meant that in very few instances are there agreed national guidelines for the investigation and treatment of specific paediatric conditions. Even when there are national guidelines it is acceptable to deviate from those guidelines as long as a robust argument for the alternative can be made.

There are agreed national guidelines for the treatment of asthma, both in children and adults, from the British Thoracic Society which have also been endorsed by the paediatricians. However, new drugs are introduced into clinical practice more rapidly than the guidelines can be changed. It is then up to the individual practitioners to decide how they wish to use the new medication.

There are, however, recognised approaches, albeit not blessed with the epithet of national guidelines. Some of those approaches are described in the sections on individual problems.

History Taking and Clinical Examination

The mainstay of paediatric care is a robust history taking. For younger children the history is obtained from the parents, and for older children from the children themselves and the parents. With teenagers the history may be taken exclusively from the teenager, especially if the teenager does not wish the parents to be present. A thorough history will frequently allow a diagnosis to be made before examination is undertaken, or at least open up a likely direction of further questioning or investigation in order to elucidate the diagnosis.

Paediatric history taking may also include details of pregnancy, birth and development – details which are rarely relevant in adult practice. An inadequately taken history may fail to open up the direction for diagnosis and compromise the care of that child.

The art of history taking is taught at medical school and refined in the years of medical training.

Medical students have much more experience of the clinical examination of adults than of children. The basic technique of examination in adults can be transferred to paediatrics. However, there are major differences. In infants, care must be taken to observe reaction during examination as questions cannot be asked. In toddlers and young children there may be enormous reluctance to be examined. Indeed there may be great distress whilst being examined: the child may cling desperately on to its parent. The paediatric practitioner must develop techniques and skills to examine and gain clinical knowledge from a child in all circumstances. This may mean deferring the examination until the child has calmed down and is more secure, or examining the child in an unconventional way. One has to be careful in interpreting non-compliance with examination. For example, the refusal of the child to walk may be because it is distressed and requires the comfort of its parent. It may also be because it has significant pathology which prevents it from walking, or discomfort which would only be apparent if techniques are employed to examine the child walking. Missing a brain tumour because a child refuses to walk because it is unsteady on its feet secondary to that brain tumour can never be acceptable.

It is not necessarily negligent to fail to reach a diagnosis. What is unacceptable is to come to a diagnosis or interpretation which cannot possibly explain the history and examination which has gone before. There may be several differential diagnoses. Further investigation will be required to shorten the list of possibilities.

Treatment: General Points

Many of the drugs used in paediatrics are not licensed for children and have not been subjected to the rigours of research to determine their safety and efficacy in children. However, by long term practice and experience the use of these drugs is generally safe. If paediatricians were not able to use drugs that had not been licensed for children it would severely curtail their ability to treat the many diseases of childhood. The dose of drug must, however, be scaled down from adult amounts. It is obvious that the amount of antibiotic needed to treat an infection in a baby would be considerably less than that to treat a large adult. Appropriate calculation must therefore be made to give the infant or child the appropriate amount of treatment, neither to over-treat, which may have severe side effects, nor to under-treat, which may lead to inadequate therapy. The prescribing doctor must be confident calculating the correct dose of any therapy for any child. In hospital, the treatment is normally administered by nurses, and the nurse should not only re-calculate the dose prescribed to check against the medical practitioner's calculation, but may also have to calculate the volume of fluid in which that dose of drug is contained.

There is debate as to the safest way for nurses to calculate drug dosages and volume. Many Trusts insist that two qualified paediatric nurses check drug dosages and volume. However, there is some evidence to suggest that more errors are made that way than if one nurse only is given the responsibility for checking drug dosage and volume. The reason for this is that if it is the responsibility of one nurse only, she takes greater care over her calculations than if two nurses are present – one of whom may rely inappropriately on the other.

Another check on the drug dosage is the ward pharmacist and many, if not all, Trusts will have pharmacists who check the prescription scripts on the ward and will query the drugs being used and the dosages, if necessary.

There are, therefore, several checks between the initial decision to treat a child with a drug and the administration of that drug. However, drug errors do occur and can never be considered acceptable.

A similar regimen of checks needs to be in place to minimise fluid administration errors, as described previously.

Acute Life Threatening Events (ALTE)

The term ALTE has been termed to cover all unexpected, worrying events in infants, the extreme end of which is sudden unexpected death syndrome (SUDS), formerly known as sudden infant death syndrome (SIDS). During an ALTE the parents may perceive the child as having died. The child may go very pale and limp, cease breathing or begin to choke in a way prejudicial to life. However, by the time the infant reaches a paediatric facility the event is over, and the child is often back to its normal perky self. The trigger factors for ALTEs are legion and may be related to abnormal rhythms of the heart, foreign bodies in or around the airways, secretions in the airways, seizures etc. A detailed history is, therefore, of great importance. Many of these events are, in fact, not ALTE but are caused by inhalation of fluid or secretions causing a child to choke or to cease breathing for a short period of time. A reasonable approach may be to observe the child in hospital for a period of time, especially during feeding when there may be some lack of co-ordination between sucking and swallowing of milk causing inhalation and choking. This may be sufficient to reassure the family and the clinicians that the child is essentially healthy.

Sadly, some of these ALTEs are related to bleeds within the head (subdural haematoma caused by non-accidental injury - shaken baby syndrome). There may be no external markers of any damage and the child may show no neurological abnormalities. This is especially a worry in those children under the age of 2 years. There should thus be a degree of suspicion of possible intracranial pathology, especially if there are potential risk factors - for instance multiple attendances at the hospital or previous episodes of ALTE. If there are concerns, appropriate investigations should be undertaken. It is better to investigate some infants unnecessarily than miss those infants who have been subjected to potentially fatal non-accidental injury.

Other methods of non-accidental injury, which may lead to ALTE, include partial smothering of the child. Again, there may be no external manifestations of this behaviour by the child's carer. There have been occasions when parents have been covertly filmed in hospital causing seizures by partial smothering of their infant. This is a highly controversial area of paediatric hospital care with debate raging as to the relative importance of care for the infant and the adult's right to be free from being spied upon. What is clear is that covert surveillance cannot be used without the clinicians being seriously and rationally concerned. It certainly cannot be used as a routine investigation for a child suffering from ALTE.

Foreign Bodies

A normal developmental stage in infancy and childhood is an oral phase when children gain information about their surroundings by picking up objects, feeling them and also putting them in their mouth. This is indiscriminate and there is no discrimination between food or non-food objects. The potential problem is that the object may be swallowed or may be inhaled causing a possible ALTE.

The majority of objects that are swallowed usually pass through the gut without any difficulty. Some extraordinary objects have been swallowed. They have included open safety pins, which have appeared later in a nappy or a potty with apparently no ill effects to the child. However, certain objects, for example mercury batteries, are potentially harmful. In these instances it is vital that the object is identified and removed .

The oesophagus, or gullet, is the narrowest part of the infant gut, and on occasions objects may be stuck in the oesophagus. This may result in refusal of solid food although drinking may continue. If a child does takes solid food, it tends to vomit. This leads to a refusal to take further food as the infant comes to recognise that it will vomit. A sudden change in eating habit such as this should alert the practitioner to the possibility of a foreign body even if there is no history of the child having taken an object into its mouth. The mobile infant can find objects scattered around its environment and put them in its mouth without any adult noticing.

Small objects are potentially much more dangerous as they can be inhaled into the lungs. This may cause death by suffocation if the object gets stuck at the vocal cords - the narrowest part of the trachea or windpipe. If, however, the object passes through the cords, it tends to fall into one of the lungs - normally the right lung. This leads to pneumonia and eventually a chronic cough.

Most objects taken into the lungs are not radio-opaque and therefore cannot be seen on x-ray. They may either be foodstuffs or plastic. What happens, though, is that the lung becomes expanded beyond the foreign body as air can be taken into the lungs but gets trapped. The appropriate investigation, therefore, is to take a chest x-ray when the child has breathed in fully (an inspiration film) and then another when the child has exhaled fully (an expiration film). This may take some skill, especially with an unco-operative toddler. The expiration film will show differences in the expansion of one lung against the other, which will give a clue that there is a foreign body in the over-expanded lung. If only one film is to be taken it should be an expiratory film.

Foreign bodies may end up not only in the gut or the airways, but also in any orifice such as the ear, the nose or the vagina. Any units looking after such young children must have a high level of suspicion in order to protect the child against the potential consequences of a retained foreign body.

Common Childhood Problems and Potential Pitfalls

Common symptoms can sometimes mask sinister underlying pathology.

Headaches

(a) General points

Young children tend to complain of "tummy aches" as a somatization of difficulties which they cannot enunciate. Around the age of 7 to 8 years the tummy ache is replaced by headache, a very frequent symptom. Rarely, however, a headache may mask a sinister diagnosis such as a brain tumour and it is the role of the secondary paediatrician to sift out those children with worrying symptoms or signs who should be investigated further from the majority of children who simply have tension headaches or migraine.

(b) Tension headaches

These can occur at any time during the day. They are not necessarily associated with any obvious cause of stress. They usually do not produce any facial colour change. They resolve spontaneously or with simple treatment such as paracetamol or Ibuprofen. There may be a very long history, (running into months, or even years), of tension headaches before the child is referred on by the general practitioner.

(c) Migraine

Younger children may have "abdominal migraine" which is associated with pallor and abdominal pain. Around the age of 7 to 8 years it can develop into cranial migraine. There is normally a family history. Around 70% of children with migraine have a close relative who also has migraine. Migraine occurs intermittently and never occurs on a daily basis, although rarely children may have cluster migraines, (a series of migraines close together, possibly on a daily basis but only for a few days - and then a gap before migraine occurs again). Migraine can be associated with vomiting and there are rarer types of migraine that may mimic epilepsy.

(d) Other causes of headache

Whilst most children with headaches may fit easily into one of these two common categories, a detailed history is important to elucidate those features which might potentially point to a more sinister pathology: this is typically the role of the secondary paediatrician.

Worrying features are a short history of headaches. Headaches which have a history of 8 months or longer are unlikely to be caused by intracranial pathology as it is likely that the intracranial pathology would have become manifest in other ways before that time. Both tension headaches and migraines are relieved by sleep, so any child who is awakened by the pain of headache should be viewed with suspicion. Headaches or "migraine" of a severe intensity which occur daily cannot be true migraine and should also be viewed with concern. Vomiting may be associated with migraine, but repeated daily vomiting with headaches, and especially the combination of early morning headaches (waking with headaches), and effortless vomiting should be recognised as a sign of raised intracranial pressure. However, by this time the intracranial pressure would be far advanced.

Headache may be caused by very high blood pressure. If this is found, the problem may be related to the kidneys rather than anything going on in the head.

A child presenting with headaches, however apparently benign, should have a full and detailed history taken and must be examined. As a minimum the examination should include taking the blood pressure, a full neurological examination concentrating on the cranial nerves and including an examination of the back of the eye (fundoscopy). Abnormalities of the optic disc at the back of the eye (papilloedema) are a late sign of increased pressure within the skull, but nevertheless fundoscopy is a vital part of the investigation of headaches or "migraine".

Fits, Faints and "Funny Turns"

Children may suffer from fits or sudden loss of consciousness which may be simple faints. Fainting is very common in adolescent boys and girls and children of late primary school age may develop primary epilepsy. The paediatrician is usually entirely dependent on the history given by a witness to a child having a fit. A child will have little or no memory of the event. Frequently the event happened with friends and was not witnessed by an adult, and even if it was, there is very rarely any corroborative evidence such as a video of the event. Rarely, intracranial tumours can present as epilepsy. As it is an uncommon presentation of intracranial tumours, it is now accepted that children suffering from generalised epilepsy are unlikely to have an intracranial tumour, whereas those who have focal epilepsy are more at risk of having sinister pathology.

Generalised epilepsy ranges from the well recognised shaking fit, so called tonic clonic epilepsy, to absences and behavioural changes but in each case the whole body is affected. Focal epilepsy is where only part of the body is affected - typically one limb or one side of the body or part of the face. It may then develop into a generalised seizure, but a seizure which starts in one part of the body. It is now accepted that such children must have imaging of the brain - either a CT scan or an MRI scan.

Faints and funny turns can also be the result of abnormal heart rhythms leading to loss of blood supply to the brain, causing loss of consciousness.

Classically, a faint is preceded by the child feeling dizzy, and possibly hot and sweaty. There is then a description of a curtain coming down in front of the eyes as the child loses consciousness and slides to the floor. There is no generalised fitting but there may be the occasional twitch of a limb. Once recumbent, blood supply is returned to the head and the child regains consciousness. The lack of blood to the head is normally associated with a drop in blood pressure - causing a simple faint. Reduced blood supply to the brain caused by abnormal heart rhythm manifests itself in the same way.

There are recognised patterns on heart tracing (echocardiogram, ECG) which are associated with abnormal rhythms so it is reasonable to undertake an ECG in children with apparently simple faints.

Children who give a history of loss of consciousness during exercise should be taken most seriously. Reduction of blood supply to the brain can be caused by a reduction in blood supply to the heart, and consequent reduced heart function. Children so affected may be at risk of sudden death during exercise and need expert investigation.

Most children presenting with fits, faints or funny turns have indeed just one of those. Most are normal on investigation or have primary generalised epilepsy. It cannot be stressed enough that a careful history is vital for identifying those children who have worrying symptoms and need to be investigated further. It is impractical to perform all possible investigations on all children presenting with common complaints.

Bedwetting (Enuresis)

Bedwetting is a very common problem which reduces with age. Around 2 to 3 years of age many children become dry during the day and between 3 and 4 years at night also. We do not actually know how we become continent as obviously babies cannot tell us.

If a child never becomes dry this is known as primary enuresis. If a child does become dry and then starts re-wetting, this is secondary enuresis.

Around 10% of 5 year olds and 2-3% of 10 year olds still wet the bed. The occasional adult still suffers. The great majority of these children have simple enuresis and can be treated for such. However bedwetting can be the result of other problems such as a urinary tract infection, (see below), kidney failure, the onset of diabetes mellitus or diabetes insipidus. Occasionally it can be the result of sexual abuse. It is medico-legally important to eliminate these causes.

The medical history may give some clue as to underlying pathology. Regular awakening at night to drink is abnormal in childhood. Excessive thirst, (which is difficult to define) should also raise concerns. Minimum investigation would be urinalysis for sugar or infection, and measurement of blood pressure. There is no consensus as to the need for genital examination although it could be argued to be good practice.

Constipation

This is another frequent problem, which is usually uncomplicated. Toddlers may present with true constipation or with stool withholding which eventually leads on to constipation. Stool withholding is when the toddler is straining to keep the stool in, as its passage is painful, as opposed to straining to evacuate. Unusual causes of constipation include underactive thyroid, hypothyroidism, Hirschprung's syndrome and sexual abuse.

Every infant born in the UK is screened for hypothyroidism, so the diagnosis should be known within the first 2 weeks of a normal life. However no screening program is 100% accurate and the method of screening will not pick up the admittedly very rare cases of hypothalamic hypothyroidism. Accordingly that possibility should be kept in mind.

Hypothyroidism presenting in later childhood usually has other features that suggest the diagnosis.

Hirschprung's syndrome is a condition where the nervous system of the gut is partly missing. The gut therefore can not propagate the waves of muscle activity necessary to propel its contents, leading to constipation.

96% of babies born at term open their bowels within 24 hours of life. Virtually all do so within 48 hours. Thus if there is a definite history of early opening of bowels, Hirschprung's is unlikely. If there is delay in bowel opening, the commonest causes are cystic fibrosis, a meconium plug and Hirschprung's. The situation is complicated, however, if the baby is initially unwell.

Sexual abuse may present with constipation. This association is probably more common than the association between enuresis and sexual abuse. If the history is of early passage of meconium in a well term infant with constipation evolving, uncomplicated constipation is the most likely diagnosis. However the examination of the child should involve visual examination of the anus to be sure that there are no concerning markers of physical damage.

Urinary Tract Infections

The main concern about urinary tract infections in infants is that there may be consequent kidney damage with permanent renal scarring. This kidney damage occurs because infected urine flows back up the ureters (tube connecting kidney and bladder) to the kidney, causing a kidney infection. If this is repeated, the consequent scarring makes the kidneys small and shrunken. This can result in high blood pressure and, potentially, kidney failure.

The diagnosis of a urinary tract infection in children under one is difficult. The child may have a temperature, it may be irritable, off its feeds and crying. These are also, note, the symptoms of many other common childhood illnesses. The body is often able to eradicate the urinary tract infection itself without antibiotics so that the infection may go undetected. Many, but not all, hospital paediatric departments will undertake a culture of a urine sample from all children under the age of one admitted to hospital for any reason. This approach has a low pick up rate for previously undiagnosed urinary tract infections.

Children may also be referred to outpatients by the general practitioner with a diagnosis of having had a urinary tract infection that has been treated and now requires investigation.

It is now universally accepted that any child of either sex who has had a urinary tract infection needs investigation. However, there is not a nationally accepted investigation algorithm and different units may have different ways of investigating children based on the same evidence. There is little debate, however, that all children under one year of age with a urinary tract infection need an ultrasound of kidneys and bladder, a DMSA scan of the kidneys, and a micturating cystourethrogram. The cystourethrogram may be urgent in male infants who might have had a urinary tract infection secondary to urethral valves. These are flaps of tissue within the male urethra which inhibit the flow of urine causing high pressure in the bladder and kidneys and may lead to damage to the kidneys secondary to the high pressure.

Infants under one year of age need appropriate antibiotic treatment and then need to go on to low dose antibiotics to reduce the likelihood of a further infection until the three basic investigations are undertaken and the results known.

Some units will undertake those three investigations in children until the age of 2.

Another common approach is to say that between the ages of one and 4 years, all children need an ultrasound and a DMSA scan and if both those are normal no further investigation is needed. However, if there are other abnormalities, it may be appropriate to undertake a micturating cystourethrogram.

Children older than 4 years will need an ultrasound scan only. If this is normal, no further investigation is needed. However, if there are abnormalities on the ultrasound, further investigations should be undertaken.

It is no longer acceptable to allow a girl to have a single urinary tract infection without investigation, as was previously thought. All proven urinary tract infections must be investigated, the purpose being to determine whether there are any predisposing features such as reflux (urine going back up towards the kidneys) which predisposes to urinary tract infection, with the potential for kidney damage, in order to try to prevent such kidney damage. It is also important to determine whether there is any kidney scarring. If so, further follow up will be needed as there is a potential for increased blood pressure in adult life.

ANAESTHESIA AND INTENSIVE CARE

Alan R Aitkenhead and Bernard Riley

INTRODUCTION

Anaesthesia may be considered as an unnatural state which carries inherent risks.

- Unconsciousness may result in airway obstruction, pulmonary aspiration and trauma of various kinds.
- Most anaesthetic drugs have undesirable side-effects on the cardiovascular and/or respiratory system, and many are lethal if given in excess dosage.
- The paralysed patient is dependent totally on the anaesthetist and his equipment for maintenance of oxygenation and ventilation, and any human or mechanical failure in this regard may result rapidly in cerebral damage or death.
- Paralysis also makes it more difficult to monitor depth of anaesthesia, and a paralysed patient may appear externally to be unconscious yet be completely aware of the operation if there has been a failure to deliver appropriate doses of anaesthetic agents.
- In some circumstances, deliberate trespass is made on the respiratory or cardiovascular system in order to enable surgery to be performed under optimal conditions (e.g. one-lung anaesthesia or induced hypotension).

Mistakes in clinical management of anaesthesia can result in many forms of injury, but a substantial proportion involve death or serious injury, rendering anaesthetists susceptible to large civil claims, to criticism at Coroners' inquests and to allegations of gross negligence in the criminal courts.

The health of the patient is also an important factor in the genesis of complaints about anaesthetic management. Most patients who undergo elective surgery are in good general health. While they are prepared to accept that surgery may not be entirely successful, or may be associated with a risk of complications, they anticipate perfection from the anaesthetist. Anaesthesia is now extremely safe; mortality associated with anaesthesia alone in developed countries such as Australia and the United Kingdom occurs in 1 in 120,000-180,000 administrations[1,2]. However, because of its apparent safety, surgeons offer increasingly heroic procedures to patients who may suffer from serious concurrent disease. In such patients, the risks of anaesthesia are increased significantly, but patients and their relatives are often unwilling to acknowledge that any risk from anaesthesia is acceptable.

THE PATTERN OF LITIGATION AGAINST ANAESTHETISTS

At least half of all claims against anaesthetists for minor injury relate to damage to teeth. The vast majority of these are dealt with by ensuring that the damage is repaired, either by hospital staff at no cost to the patient and at nominal cost to the hospital, or elsewhere, at no cost to the patient and at very modest cost to the hospital. Claims for dental damage are usually referred to expert witnesses only if the accused anaesthetist feels that his or her reputation is under threat as a result of the claim (very unusual) or if it is felt that the patient is trying unjustifiably to have a full 'makeover' of his or her dentition in the private sector at somebody else's expense. One report [Medical Defence Union, personal communication] found that dental damage was the basis of 63% of claims against anaesthetists, but accounted for only 1.4% of the costs incurred on behalf of anaesthetists.

Although dental damage is a frequent cause of complaint, the severity of the injury is usually very minor, the cost of correction is low and no detailed assessment of liability is usually conducted. Consequently, most in-depth reports of complaints against anaesthetists exclude complaints relating to damage to teeth. This distorts the perceived pattern of litigation against anaesthetists, who are often seen as a 'high risk' group. However, experience in the USA and in the UK over the last 15 years or so has indicated that the number of civil claims against anaesthetists which are pursued successfully is declining, in contrast to the situation pertaining to many other medical specialities. The reason for the decline in success by patients is probably a combination of improved clinical care and improved instrumental monitoring (resulting in improved patient safety), and improved record-keeping (which has no effect on patient safety but which may provide objective information which allows the allegations to be refuted with greater confidence).

Before the introduction of Crown Indemnity in 1990, claims against anaesthetists in the United Kingdom were, in common with claims against other hospital specialists, dealt with by the medical defence organisations, which analysed the claims and, from time to time, published large series which provided information about the pattern of injuries which led to litigation and the proportion which were deemed to have been due to error rather than misadventure. The last large

---

[1] Australian and New Zealand College of Anaesthetists, *Safety of Anaesthesia-Related Mortality*, 1997-99, http://www.anzca.edu.au/publications/reports/mortality/mort_97_1.htm.
[2] Buck N, Devlin HB, Lunn JN, *The report of a confidential enquiry into perioperative deaths*, Nuffield Provincial Hospitals Trust, London, 1987.

series[3] was published in 1987, and related to claims made between 1970 and 1982. Despite the fact that most clinical negligence claims in the United Kingdom since 1990 have been brought against NHS hospitals, and although all but the most trivial are dealt with centrally, there is only anecdotal information regarding the pattern of litigation. In our view, this is deeply regrettable. The lack of good information makes it impossible to know if trends in the pattern are changing. The only readily available sources of information, which are predominantly the lay and medical press, present a distorted view because they concentrate on claims involving serious or dramatic injury, and this may lead anaesthetists to fail to appreciate the importance of other, more frequent, avoidable complications which also result in litigation. As a result, there is a risk that defensive medicine is practised, which may be wasteful of resources, and important safety issues may be overlooked.

In the United States of America, the American Society of Anesthesiologists (ASA) has conducted a closed claims analysis continuously since 1984[4]. A closed claim is a claim that has been abandoned, settled or adjudicated by the courts. The ASA has been given access to the files of insurance companies which indemnify more than 60% of anaesthetists, and the files of closed claims are analysed by experienced anaesthetists who express an opinion on the standard of care provided. The number of anaesthetics given by the accused anaesthetists is not known. In addition, some injured patients do not sue, whereas others with no apparent injury do. Consequently, although the closed claims analysis provides a snapshot of anaesthetic liability, it does not give a comprehensive picture of all anaesthetic injury. There are other disadvantages of the ASA closed claims analysis, including its retrospective nature (claims may not be closed until more than 10 years after the event which caused injury) and the fact that the quality of the records may make it impossible to determine with confidence the cause of an injury. Nevertheless, the ASA closed claims analysis has generated large amounts of very useful information about the causes of litigation, and changes in the pattern of litigation, over three decades which have seen great changes in the way in which anaesthesia is delivered. While there are differences in practice between the United States of America and the United Kingdom, changes in practice in the two countries have, broadly, occurred in parallel, and our experience suggests that, in most respects, the findings of the ASA closed claims study probably reflect with reasonable accuracy the changing trends of litigation against anaesthetists in the United Kingdom.

In all fields of medicine, the quality of record-keeping has a great influence on the outcome of litigation. The quality of anaesthetic records has improved greatly in the last 15-20 years, and there has been a steady increase in availability of

---

[3] Utting, JE, Pitfalls in anaesthetic practice, *British Journal of Anaesthesia*, 1987; 59: 877-890.

[4] Weiskopf, RB, The American Society of Anesthesiologists Closed Claims Project: what have we learned, how has it affected practice, and how will it affect practice in the future? *Anesthesiology*, 1999; 91: 552-6.

automated records, which derive information directly from the monitoring systems and produce an objective record; it is known that records kept manually by anaesthetists are likely to have the data 'normalised', and that the records during the early stages of anaesthesia are (entirely reasonably, because the anaesthetist is very busy during induction of anaesthesia) completed retrospectively, which may lead to inaccuracy. In our experience, an automated record usually provides definitive evidence to support or refute a claim that injury occurred as a result of an inadequate standard of care during anaesthesia in cases involving death, cerebral damage or awareness.

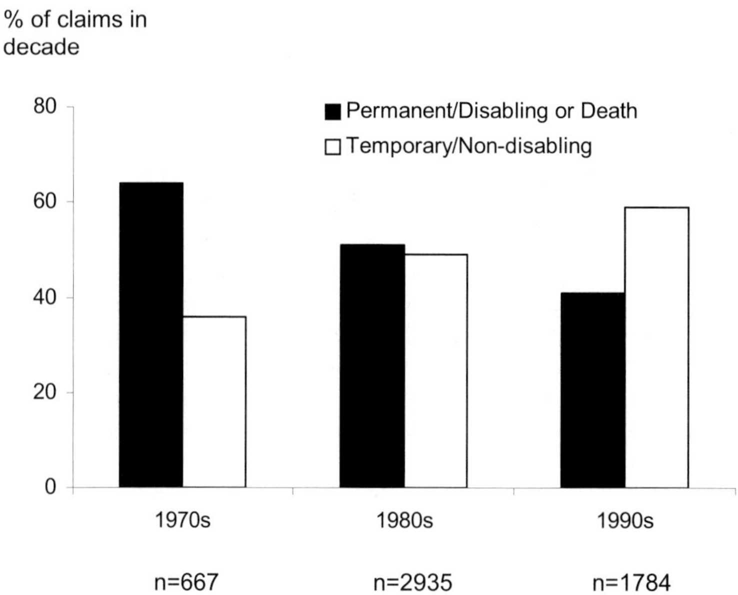

FIGURE 1 – TRENDS IN SEVERITY OF INJURY FROM ASA CLOSED CLAIMS STUDY (POSNER, 2001). THE PROPORTION OF CLAIMS RELATED TO PERMANENT AND DISABLING INJURIES (INCLUDING DEATH) HAS DECLINED PROGRESSIVELY. 'DECADE' IS WHEN THE ANAESTHETIC WAS ADMINISTERED. FROM POSNER, 2001 *(SEE FOOTNOTE 5)*, WITH PERMISSION.

The ASA closed claims study[5] has shown that there has been a dramatic shift in the severity of injury related to anaesthesia, and in the causes of injury, in the last three decades in the USA, and our experience suggests that changes in the UK have been similar. Figure 1 shows that the proportion of claims associated with permanent and disabling injuries (including death) has declined progressively, and Figure 2 shows that the frequency with which death was the cause of a claim

[5] Posner, KL, Closed Claims Project Shows Safety Evolution, *APSF Newsletter*, 2001, 16(2): 1-3

halved between the 1970s and the 1990s. Claims relating to brain damage also decreased, although claims relating to other nerve injuries, including injury to the spinal cord, increased, representing 21% of claims in the 1990s.

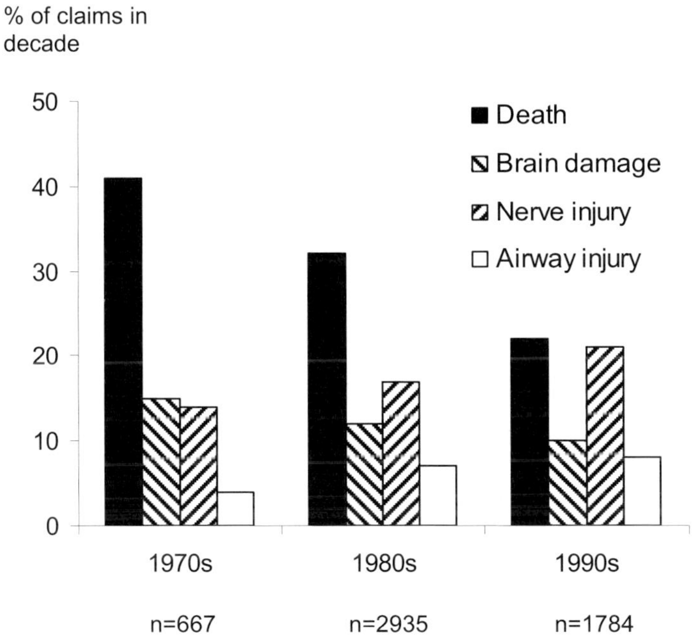

FIGURE 2 – MOST COMMON COMPLICATIONS IN ASA CLOSED CLAIMS STUDY. FROM POSNER, 2001 *(SEE FOOTNOTE 5)*, WITH PERMISSION.

Figure 3 shows the dramatic decline in respiratory causes of injury from 36% in the 1970s to 14% in the 1990s. There have been no significant changes in the proportion of claims related to injury caused by cardiovascular inadequacy, equipment malfunction or medication errors. The reduction in respiratory causes of injury has been offset by increases in complaints about less serious injuries with a variety of causes, such as burns, skin inflammation, awareness, eye injury, backache, headache, aspiration pneumonitis and injury to newborn babies.

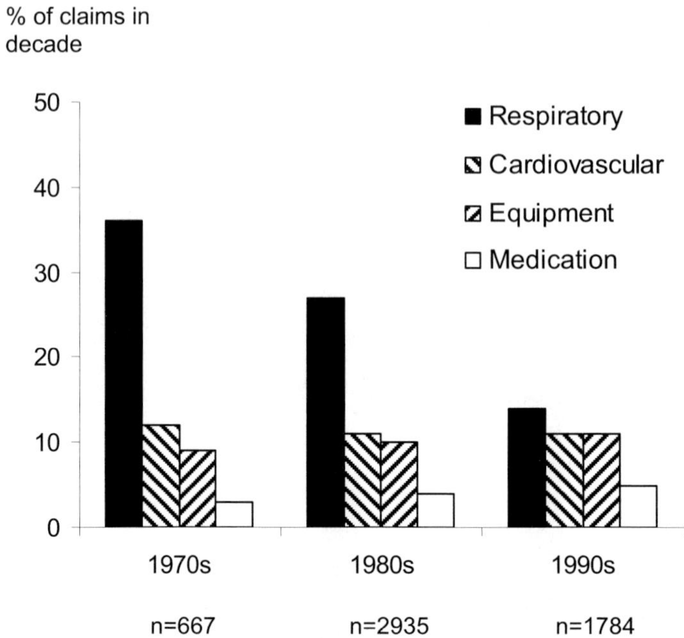

FIGURE 3 – MOST COMMON DAMAGING EVENTS IN ASA CLOSED CLAIMS ANALYSIS. FROM POSNER, 2001 *(SEE FOOTNOTE 5)*, WITH PERMISSION.

DEATH AND CEREBRAL DAMAGE

General considerations

In general terms, the causes of death and cerebral damage are the same. Any event which results in a severe reduction in the delivery of oxygen to the heart and brain has the potential to cause cerebral damage if the brain remains profoundly hypoxic for more than 3 minutes or so, and to cause death if severe cerebral hypoxia persists for longer or if cardiac arrest occurs and a spontaneous circulation cannot be restored rapidly or at all.

Death related to anaesthesia is a common source of complaint. In the report of the Confidential Enquiry into Perioperative Deaths (CEPOD) in 1987[6], there was a low incidence of death related solely to anaesthesia, but anaesthesia was deemed to have contributed to 14% of all deaths; in almost one fifth of these deaths, avoidable errors were deemed to have occurred.

[6] See above, footnote 2.

The incidence of serious morbidity related to anaesthesia is more difficult to assess. Numerous studies of specialised areas of practice have been published, but there is little information regarding the relative incidences of death and serious injury in relation to litigation. Data from the ASA closed claims study indicate (Figure 2) that the incidence of brain injury resulting in litigation is about 40% of the incidence of death[7], and that both have declined over the last three decades. Table 1 lists the causes of death or cerebral damage in cases reported to the Medical Defence Union in the United Kingdom between 1970 and 1982[8]; the majority were associated with errors.

TABLE 1 – CAUSES OF ANAESTHETIC-RELATED DEATH OR CEREBRAL DAMAGE IN 750 CASES REPORTED TO THE MEDICAL DEFENCE UNION BETWEEN 1970 AND 1982 [38].

Mainly misadventure		*Mainly error*	
Coexisting disease	14%	Faulty technique	43%
Unknown	6%	Failure of postoperative care	9%
Drug sensitivity	5%	Drug overdosage	5%
Hypotension/blood loss	4%	Inadequate preoperative assessment	3%
Halothane-associated hepatic failure	3%	Drug error	1%
Hyperpyrexia	2%	Anaesthetist's failure	1%
Embolism	2%		

Table 2 shows the detailed causes of the incidents which resulted from errors. In this series, 80% of the 750 cases of death or cerebral damage involved death, and death or brain damage accounted for 50% of all reports of untoward events. These proportions are not dissimilar to those found in the ASA closed clams study for the 1970s, and if the trends found in the United States have (as is probable) been reflected here, death and brain damage probably account for around one-third of litigation against anaesthetists (including damage to teeth) at the present time.

[7] See above, footnote 5.
[8] See above, footnote 3.

TABLE 2 – CAUSES OF ANAESTHETIC-RELATED DEATH OR CEREBRAL DAMAGE REPORTED TO THE MEDICAL DEFENCE UNION BETWEEN 1970 AND 1982 IN 326 CASES THOUGHT TO BE THE RESULT OF ERRORS IN TECHNIQUE.

Cause	*% of total*
Errors associated with tracheal intubation	31
Misuse of apparatus	23
Inhalation of gastric contents	14
Errors associated with induced hypotension	8
Hypoxia	4
Obstructed airway	4
Accidental pneumothorax/haemopericardium	4
Errors associated with extradural analgesia	3
Use of nitrous oxide instead of oxygen	2
Use of carbon dioxide instead of oxygen	2
Errors associated with Bier's block	2
Underventilation	1
Use of halothane with adrenaline	1
Mismatched blood transfusion	<1
Vasovagal attack	<1

Recently, death alleged to have been the result of a 'gross' degree of negligence by anaesthetists has resulted in allegations of manslaughter. Some of these allegations have been tested in Court, and several convictions for manslaughter have resulted. Serious incidents may result in serious physical injury, and may be followed by claims in the civil courts for financial compensation for alleged injury. Although, to our knowledge, no anaesthetist in the United Kingdom has faced the criminal courts charged with serious injury as a result of clinical care (excluding those charged with offences of a sexual nature), nursing staff have been convicted in the criminal courts of causing grievous bodily harm, and it may be only a matter of time before doctors face investigation by the police for such offenses with the potential for criminal prosecution for serious injury as well as death.

Damage to the central nervous system during anaesthesia and in the postoperative period may result in death, a variable degree of disability, or complete functional recovery. Causes related to anaesthesia itself, or to administration of drugs in the postoperative period, are associated almost exclusively with arterial hypoxaemia[9] or cerebral ischaemia[10]. Cerebral damage may also occur as a result of treatment in the Intensive Care Unit (ICU). All of these possibilities are considered below.

Hypoxaemia is the commonest reason for cerebral damage during anaesthesia and the postoperative period. It may arise from failure to deliver an adequate inspired oxygen concentration, a failure of ventilation, or an abnormality of the lungs which impairs oxygenation of pulmonary capillary blood. Most of the important causes are considered below.

Oxygen supply failures

Occasionally errors have occurred in the connections of pipelines at source, and nitrous oxide has been delivered through the oxygen pipeline; this is particularly hazardous, as the first instinct of the anaesthetist presented with a hypoxaemic patient is to ventilate the lungs with what he believes to be 100% oxygen. Although the pipeline system in the operating theatre is provided with fittings designed to prevent misconnection, there have been instances in which the nitrous oxide pipeline has been connected to the oxygen inlet of the machine and vice versa; these have occurred when hospital staff attempt to use non-standard or damaged equipment, or when old anaesthetic machines without pin-index systems or colour coding were serviced in haste. Occasionally, the pins on the yoke to which cylinders are attached have been sawn off, making it possible to attach a nitrous oxide cylinder to the oxygen supply to the patient. Deliberate interference with anaesthetic equipment to overcome safety features, and failure to check anaesthetic equipment before use to ensure that it is operating correctly, are regarded as very serious breaches of duty by an anaesthetist.

Flowmeter failures

Rotameter bobbins may give erroneous readings if the rotameter tube becomes contaminated with dirt, or if static electricity collects on the glass walls. The glass

[9] Hypoxaemia is a reduced arterial oxygen saturation.
[10] Ischaemia is deprivation of the blood supply to a tissue or organ such that inadequate oxygen is delivered to meet its metabolic needs, even though arterial oxygen saturation may be normal.

tubes are fragile, and occasionally break; if a leak develops above the bobbin either because of a fractured tube or a faulty O-ring seal, the flow rate of oxygen delivered is less than that indicated by the bobbin, especially if the nitrous oxide rotameter is positioned closer to the patient than the oxygen rotameter, and a hypoxic gas mixture may be delivered to the patient. Flowmeters in all contemporary anaesthetic machines contain an interlock which prevents a hypoxic mixture of gases being delivered to the patient as a result of inappropriate settings of the needle valves. On older machines it is possible to deliver a gas mixture containing little or no oxygen, although all anaesthetic machines should be fitted with a monitor which measures the concentration of oxygen in either the machine outlet or in the inspired gas mixture.

Failures in the breathing system

A hypoxic gas mixture may be delivered when a circle system is supplied with low flow rates of oxygen and nitrous oxide because, after the first few minutes of anaesthesia, oxygen is absorbed from the lungs at a greater rate than nitrous oxide. An inappropriately low flow rate of anaesthetic gases to other breathing systems, a leak within the breathing system at its connection with the anaesthetic machine, or a leak within the back bar of the anaesthetic machine may cause rebreathing of gases and inhalation of a progressively hypoxic gas mixture. It is now regarded as mandatory to measure the inspired oxygen concentration; consequently, an injury caused by a low inspired oxygen concentration usually means that the anaesthetist has failed to use this equipment, or failed to heed the values displayed.

Inadequate ventilation: general points

Inadequate ventilation, or total failure of ventilation, results in decreases in alveolar and arterial oxygen tension and an increase in carbon dioxide tension. The absolute value of arterial oxygen tension depends principally on the alveolar minute ventilation and the inspired oxygen concentration, although the presence of pyrexia may influence the values because of increased oxygen consumption and carbon dioxide production. In addition, hypoxaemia occurs more rapidly if the functional residual capacity (FRC) is low (e.g. pregnant or obese patients). Total failure of ventilation in a normal patient who has been breathing 33% oxygen (the usual inspired concentration during general anaesthesia) results in significant arterial hypoxaemia (PaO_2 < 6.5 kPa) in about 5 minutes, but this occurs in less than 2 minutes in a patient who has been breathing air (e.g. immediately after induction of anaesthesia) and in 1-1.5 minutes, and sometimes less, in a patient with reduced FRC or pulmonary disease.

Pharmacological depression

Hypoventilation, or apnoea, may be caused by a relative overdose of anaesthetic agent or opioid in the spontaneously breathing patient, and a degree of hypoxaemia may result during anaesthesia. In the immediate postoperative period, the residual effects of these drugs may cause hypoventilation or apnoea because of the absence of surgical stimulation. In the later postoperative period, excessive doses of opioid analgesics given to treat wound pain may cause ventilatory depression and hypoxaemia, especially in elderly patients. This is likely to occur particularly if a continuous infusion of an opioid is employed, as cumulation may take place. Respiratory arrest may be of relatively rapid onset.

It is now common to administer a local anaesthetic with an opioid analgesic intrathecally (into the subarachnoid space) or epidurally to provide postoperative pain relief after major surgery. Although these techniques often provide more effective analgesia than conventional systemic administration, there is a documented risk of sudden depression of ventilation many hours after the last administration of analgesic. This is true particularly when lipid-insoluble drugs such as morphine are used, but can occur after administration of any opioid in the vicinity of the spinal cord.

It is difficult to defend allegations of negligence related to respiratory depression caused by opioid analgesics if the patient has been nursed in an inappropriate area of the hospital. Nursing staff require training in the care of patients who are receiving intravenous morphine whether as a continuous infusion or intermittently, and additional training in the care of patients who have epidural analgesia, particularly when the drug mixture contains an opioid analgesic. In addition, because identification of trends is important in assessing risk of respiratory depression caused by opioids, accurate records should be maintained. Recent figures[11] indicate that, among hospitals which reported postoperative deaths which were investigated by the Enquiry, only 11% trained all nursing staff in the care of patients with an epidural infusion in surgical wards, and some trained no nursing staff; 37% of patients receiving epidural analgesia had no pain chart (a smaller percentage than when patient-controlled intravenous analgesia was employed) and 20% of the expected data was missing when a pain chart was used.

In the early postoperative period, residual neuromuscular blockade may cause hypoventilation, or occasionally complete paralysis and apnoea, even if an anticholinesterase drug has been given at the end of the operation to reverse the residual effects of a non-depolarising muscle relaxant. This is most likely when a long-acting relaxant has been given, or if renal function is impaired. The failure to record administration of an anticholinesterase has resulted in a number of claims relating to the subsequent development of alleged cerebral injury; the most common reason that administration has not been recorded is oversight in recording at a time when the anaesthetist is usually very busy.

Hypoventilation or apnoea may occur in association with the injection of local anaesthetic drugs for subarachnoid or extradural anaesthesia. For this reason, an

[11] National Confidential Enquiry into Perioperative Deaths, London, 1999.

anaesthetist should be present or in very close proximity after subarachnoid injection or after the first dose of local anaesthetic has been injected through an epidural catheter.

Airway obstruction

Anaesthetic breathing systems and connecting tubes may become kinked or obstructed by a foreign body or manufacturing fault. An amazing variety of objects have obstructed anaesthetic apparatus, including insects, items of equipment used for intravenous access, and spinal needles; in some cases, only sabotage could explain the presence of the obstruction. In a recent well publicised case, the plastic cap used originally to cover the end of an intravenous infusion set became impacted in a plastic angle-piece inserted between the anaesthetic breathing system and a laryngeal mask airway used when a child was anaesthetised. An equipment fault was suspected as a possible cause of an inability to ventilate the lungs normally, and all parts of the breathing system were changed – except for the angle-piece. The child died. The angle-piece was intended to be disposable, but in that hospital (in common with most hospitals at the time), the angle-pieces were re-used. This incident, and other similar reports from other hospitals (with much less serious consequences), led to a major police investigation into the possibility of sabotage (for which there was no reliable evidence), and has resulted in the Department of Health commissioning research to identify the reasons that 'disposable' equipment is re-used in operating theatres.

Most anaesthetic tubing is kink-resistant, but standard tracheal tubes may kink in the pharynx, particularly if the neck is flexed or rotated during surgery; reinforced tubes should be used for operations in which such movements are predictable. Overinflation of a tracheal tube cuff, or a weakness in the wall of the cuff, may result in its herniation beyond the end of the tracheal tube, where it may obstruct the tube lumen. The lumen may also become obstructed if the bevel abuts against the wall of the trachea; this may cause a ball-valve effect which will eventually prevent inflation of the lungs.

In the patient whose trachea is not intubated, airway obstruction may occur in the pharynx because of posterior displacement of the tongue or indrawing of the pharyngeal wall during inspiration. The pattern of ventilation is monitored closely during anaesthesia by observing the movement of the reservoir bag. However, monitoring is more difficult in the recovery room, where partial obstruction of the airway is a frequent occurrence, and total obstruction not uncommon. Continuous observation is never possible after discharge to a surgical ward, and a small number of patients each year die from acute upper airway obstruction as a result of loss of tone in the pharyngeal muscles and tongue due to the sedative effect of opioid analgesics and possibly residual effects of anaesthetic drugs. Usually, these patients are found to have been suffering chronically from obstructive sleep apnoea, whether officially diagnosed or not;

there is a history of loud snoring at home, and a short history of loud snoring before death.

Laryngospasm may cause total upper airway obstruction during anaesthesia, especially shortly after induction and during recovery. Severe laryngospasm results in the rapid development of hypoxaemia if appropriate measures are not taken; occasionally, hypoxaemia may occur later as a result of fulminant pulmonary oedema (see below).

Upper airway obstruction may be one of the presenting complaints of a patient undergoing anaesthesia, e.g. inhaled foreign body, acute epiglottitis. A skilled anaesthetist is required in the management of these patients because not only may tracheal intubation be extremely difficult, but total airway obstruction may occur as soon as consciousness is lost. Use of an inappropriate anaesthetic technique may increase the risk of hypoxaemia. Rarely, upper airway obstruction may result from inhalation of solid material (food or clotted blood) regurgitated from the stomach of the anaesthetised patient before a tracheal tube has been introduced.

Lower airway obstruction is usually the result of bronchospasm. This is commoner in the asthmatic patient, in whom it may be precipitated by administration of drugs which release histamine, or by the introduction of a tracheal tube. However, it may occur with no apparent precipitating factor, and can be so severe that ventilation of the lungs is impossible. Bronchospasm may occur in non-asthmatic patients as a result of aspiration of gastric contents, or as part of an anaphylactic or anaphylactoid reaction. Allegations relating to hypoxaemia caused by bronchospasm in patients with pre-existing asthma are often accompanied by suggestions that pre-operative treatment and preparation have been inadequate, particularly in patients who have, at some time, received corticosteroids. Allegations relating to hypoxic damage caused by aspiration of gastric contents are difficult to defend if appropriate steps have not been taken to elicit a history of predisposing factors (such as intestinal obstruction, hiatus hernia, recent food intake), and appropriate steps taken to minimise the risk. However, regurgitation and aspiration of gastric fluid can occur in patients with no predictable risk factors.

Difficulty in tracheal intubation: General

Tracheal intubation is usually straightforward. It is usually possible to see part or all of the larynx at direct laryngoscopy, and if it is, it is nearly always possible to insert a tracheal tube. However, in some patients, tracheal intubation is very difficult, and requires special equipment and techniques. Usually, difficult tracheal intubation is predictable from pre operative clinical tests, but on some occasions, difficulty arises unexpectedly. A number of injuries can arise during difficult tracheal intubation, including hypoxaemia due to inadequate ventilation of the lungs during prolonged attempts at intubation, awareness, and trauma to the mouth, teeth, pharynx and larynx.

Misplacement of the tracheal tube

This was for many years the commonest single cause of serious hypoxaemia resulting in death or cerebral damage (Table 2). Oesophageal intubation occurs most frequently in the hands of the inexperienced, and particularly where non-anaesthetists attempt to intubate the trachea at a cardiac arrest or in the emergency department. Every anaesthetist has intubated the oesophagus inadvertently at some time. This is not usually negligent. In some patients, it is impossible to visualise the larynx at direct laryngoscopy, and 'blind' intubation is necessary. Oesophageal intubation is not always easy to detect. Observation of the chest or auscultation of the lungs may be misleading, especially in the obese patient. The stomach may inflate and deflate in some patients when artificial ventilation is applied, although the pattern of refilling of the anaesthetic reservoir bag is seldom normal; however, when a self-inflating bag (e.g. Ambu bag) is employed, as often happens at a cardiac arrest or in the emergency department, the abnormal expiratory pattern is difficult to detect. Similarly, if the tracheal tube is connected immediately to a mechanical ventilator, ventilation may appear to be taking place normally. Small movements of the reservoir bag may occur during attempts at spontaneous ventilation when the oesophagus is intubated. Oesophageal intubation in the paralysed patient causes a progressive reduction in alveolar oxygen tension as the oxygen in the lungs is taken up by blood in the pulmonary capillaries. However, if the lungs have been pre-oxygenated (a manoeuvre used frequently when tracheal intubation is difficult, and before most emergency operations), it may be up to 10 minutes before alveolar oxygen tension decreases below normal and arterial oxygen saturation starts to fall; saturation then decreases very rapidly. If the effect of preoxygenation is not appreciated, the anaesthetist may waste valuable time in looking for other causes when hypoxaemia eventually becomes apparent.

The 'gold standard' test for correct placement of a tracheal tube is the use of a capnograph, which demonstrates the excretion of carbon dioxide from the lungs; oesophageal intubation is never associated with a normal capnograph trace. The use of a capnograph is now mandatory during general anaesthesia[12], and this has reduced the incidence of damage resulting from unrecognised oesophageal intubation. However, unrecognised oesophageal intubation continues to occur, albeit rarely, usually because the anaesthetist believes for other reasons that the tracheal tube has been inserted correctly, and chooses to ignore the absent capnograph trace. Failure to use a capnograph, or failure to heed the absence of a normal trace, are regarded as very serious breaches of an anaesthetist's duty of care.

Difficulty in maintaining the airway can occur during emergence from anaesthesia, and in the early postoperative period. Recent information from the ASA close claims study indicates that about 80% of claims relating to airway

---

[12] *Recommendations for Standards of Monitoring during Anaesthesia and Recovery*, Association of Anaesthetists of Great Britain and Ireland, London, 2000.

management arose during induction of anaesthesia or during surgery, 11% in association with removal of the tracheal tube and 5% in the recovery room[13].

Disconnection or ventilator failure

Most mechanical ventilators are robust and reliable, but occasionally they malfunction and fail to deliver gas to the patient. More commonly, a disconnection occurs at some point between the ventilator and the tracheal tube: it is common, particularly with the incorporation of monitoring devices, to have 10 or more sites at which disconnection could occur. A loose connection may cause gas to leak from the system, resulting in hypoventilation. However, the positive pressure in the system is likely to cause a loose joint to become completely disconnected, resulting in total failure of ventilation. Disconnections may occur because the tubing has been assembled carelessly, or if one of the operating theatre personnel dislodges a tube inadvertently while moving in the vicinity of the ventilator. Disconnection can be detected by all modern ventilators by capnographs and, in many anaesthetic monitoring systems, by absence of flow of gas either into or out of the patient's lungs. However, in many systems the alarms which should be activated when any of these abnormalities is detected can be disabled. Injury caused by disconnection of the breathing system can still occur, but is unlikely to be defensible.

Other causes of impaired ventilation

Ventilation may be impaired by increased diaphragmatic pressure during spontaneous ventilation, particularly if the abdomen is distended (e.g. during laparoscopy) or if the patient is placed in a steep head-down position. Occasionally, ventilation may be inadequate because of the presence of air or fluid in the pleural cavity (pneumothorax, hydrothorax). The commonest causes of pneumothorax during and shortly after anaesthesia are related to penetration of the pleura and, usually, the lung by needles used either to perform a local anaesthetic block (particularly supraclavicular brachial plexus block, intercostal block or interpleural block) or to insert a central venous catheter through the internal jugular or subclavian vein[14]. Attention has been drawn recently to the benefits of using an ultrasound scanner to assess the anatomy and guide insertion of needles in areas where adjacent structures may be damaged[15]. Allegations related to the development of pneumothorax are difficult to defend if multiple attempts have been made, if an inexperienced anaesthetist has made the attempts with inadequate supervision, or if the development of pneumothorax has not been diagnosed by reasonable clinical observation and radiological investigations.

---

[13] Peterson, GN, Posner, KL, Domino, KB, Lee, LA and Cheney, FW, Management of the Difficult Airway in Closed Malpractice Claims, *Anesthesiology*, 2003, 99. A1252.
[14] Cheney, FW, Posner, KL and Caplan, RA, Adverse respiratory events infrequently leading to malpractice suits, *Anesthesiology*, 1991; 75: 932-939.
[15] *Ultrasound locating devices for placing central venous catheters (NO 49)*, National Institute for Clinical Excellence, London, 2002.

Penetration of the right atrium by a central venous catheter usually causes cardiac tamponade and death, and may give rise to allegations of negligence, which are difficult to refute if the tip of the catheter has been positioned inappropriately[16].

Pulmonary disease

Patients with pulmonary disease may become hypoxaemic during anaesthesia unless a high inspired oxygen concentration is provided. During one-lung anaesthesia (used for thoracic operations, when one lung needs to be collapsed to allow surgical access), arterial oxygen saturation is often subnormal even when 100% oxygen is administered. This problem is accentuated if the bronchial portion of the double-lumen tube used to isolate the lungs occludes one or more lobes of the ventilated lung, which can result in severe hypoxaemia.

Pulmonary oedema may develop during or after anaesthesia. The commonest cause is cardiac disease, but excessive fluid administration may result in accumulation of fluid in the alveoli, and occasionally, and usually in fit, young adults, acute upper airway obstruction (e.g. laryngospasm) may result in pulmonary oedema because of the hydrostatic gradient generated across the pulmonary capillary membrane by the highly negative intra-alveolar pressures which occur when the patient attempts to breathe.

Analysis of claims in the ASA closed claims study[17] indicated that independent reviewers deemed the standard of care provided by anaesthetists to have been inadequate in the overwhelming majority of cases in which injury resulted from inadequate ventilation or oesophageal intubation (Figure 4), and in the majority of cases of difficult intubation. The standard of care was assessed as being inadequate in a much higher proportion of injuries associated with respiratory rather than non-respiratory causes.

[16] Fletcher SJ, Bodenham AR, Safe placement of central venous catheters: where should the tip of the catheter lie?, *British Journal of Anaesthesia*, 2000; 85: 188–91.
[17] Caplan RA, Posner KL, Ward RJ, Cheney FW. Adverse respiratory events in anesthesia: a closed claims analysis, *Anesthesiology*, 1990; 72: 828-833.

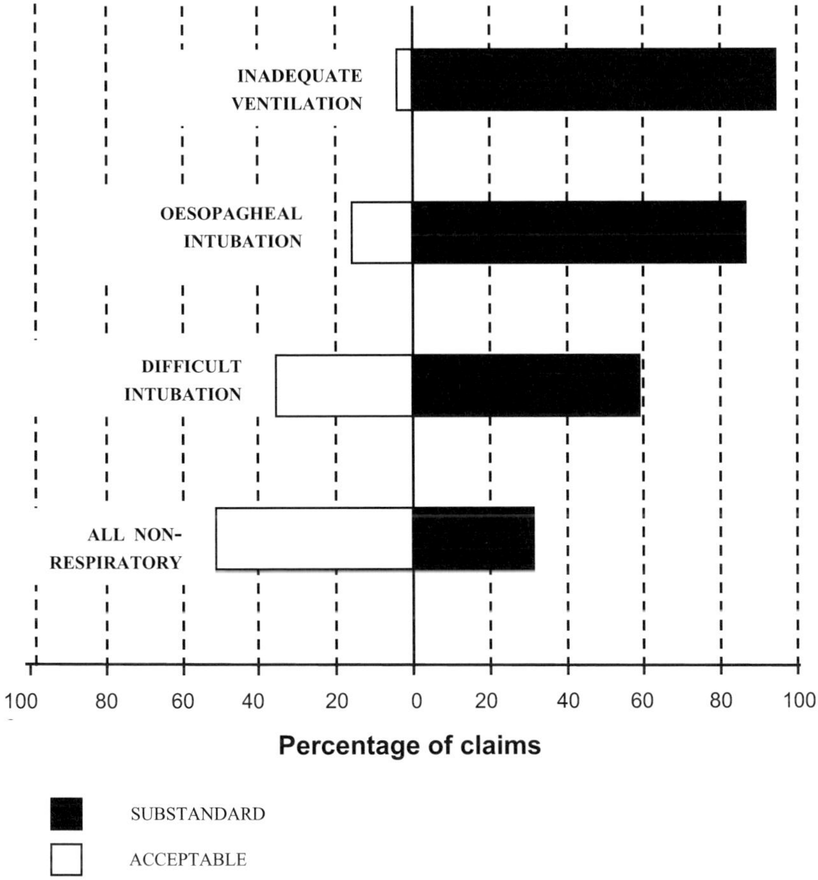

FIGURE 4 STANDARD OF CARE OF ANAESTHETISTS ASSESSED BY INDEPENDENT INVESTIGATORS CONSIDERING CLAIMS FOR INJURY ASSOCIATED WITH INADEQUATE VENTILATION, OESOPHAGEAL INTUBATION AND DIFFICULT INTUBATION, IN COMPARISON TO ALL CLAIMS WHICH DID NOT INVOLVE THE RESPIRATORY SYSTEM. REDRAWN FROM CAPLAN RA ET AL. *(SEE FOOTNOTE 14)*, WITH PERMISSION.

Failure of oxygen delivery and reduced tissue blood flow

This may result from impairment of cardiac output or extreme hypotension for some other reason. Severe anaphylactic reactions to drugs administered during anaesthesia may cause cardiovascular complications. Allegations are made from time to time that anaphylactic reactions should have been predicted by pre-operative screening; however, in most cases of anaphylaxis in which death or cerebral damage results, the allegations are centred on the management of the reaction, and particularly whether, and how promptly, adrenaline was administered.

Cardiac contractility

Many anaesthetic agents decrease cardiac contractility in a dose-related manner. This may result in a critical reduction of cardiac output if excessive concentrations particularly of inhaled anaesthetics are given, or if the patient has received other drugs (e.g. ß-blockers) with a negative inotropic effect. Inadvertent intravascular injection of local anaesthetics may reduce contractility, as does high (mid-thoracic or above) spinal or epidural anaesthesia. Patients with pre-existing cardiac disease may be more sensitive to the negative inotropic effects of anaesthetic drugs. Patients with ischaemic heart disease may suffer a reduction of cardiac contractility in the presence of otherwise innocuous degrees of hypoxaemia, tachycardia, hypertension or hypotension. Failure to elicit a history of cardiac disease and a history of use of drugs active on the cardiovascular system are important factors in rendering claims related to death or cerebral damage in such patients indefensible.

Cardiac arrhythmias

Probably the commonest arrhythmia during anaesthesia is sinus bradycardia, which results usually from vagal stimulation induced by surgical procedures. It may be exacerbated by the vagal effects of some anaesthetic agents and is more likely in the presence of ß-blockers. Cardiac output may be reduced by atrial or ventricular arrhythmias. However, these rarely result in serious hypotension unless a severe tachycardia is present. Hypoxaemia also predisposes to abnormal cardiac rhythm or conduction, as do electrolyte abnormalities. Death or cerebral damage may occur if it is not appreciated that, in the presence of an arrhythmia which severely impairs cardiac output (including severe bradycardia), external cardiac massage may be required to support the circulation; frequently cardiac massage is not started until after cardiac arrest has developed.

Cardiac arrest

Cardiac arrest during anaesthesia is unusual in the absence of a non-anaesthetic cause (e.g. profound hypovolaemia). Asystole may occur as a result of vagal stimulation, preceded usually by sinus bradycardia. It is also the usual terminal event in severe hypoxaemia. Ventricular fibrillation is less common, but may occur as a result of gas embolism, after the administration of adrenaline, in association with hypoxaemia or because of acute myocardial ischaemia or infarction. Cardiac arrest may also result from intravascular injection of local anaesthetics, particularly bupivacaine, either inadvertently while performing a regional block or in association with Bier's block if the tourniquet is applied inadequately or released prematurely, or if the drug is injected rapidly into a large vein. There have been at least two incidents in which an anaesthetist, intending to infuse intravenous fluid rapidly to increase blood volume during elective aortic aneurysm repair, inadvertently infused intravenously solutions of bupivacaine which were intended for slow infusion into the epidural space to provide postoperative pain relief; both patients developed intractable ventricular fibrillation and died. In most hospitals, epidural infusions are now prepared elsewhere, so that the bags containing bupivacaine are never present in the operating theatre unless already attached to the epidural infusion pump.

Electrolyte abnormalities, especially related to potassium, may precipitate cardiac arrest; abnormalities of serum potassium concentration may be exaggerated by acid-base changes induced by hypercapnia or hypocapnia. Pulmonary embolism may cause total failure of the circulation without causing cardiac arrest.

The outcome after sudden cardiac arrest (not associated with profound hypovolaemia) during anaesthesia is substantially better than that associated with arrest in other locations, probably because resuscitation is implemented rapidly and by skilled personnel, and because all emergency drugs and equipment are immediately available. However, claims for 'minor' cerebral damage (loss of memory, concentration or higher intellectual function), or post-traumatic stress disorder, often occur.

Electromechanical dissociation (or pulseless electrical activity; a condition in which there is electrical activity in the heart but no effective cardiac output) may precede asystole in patients with severe hypovolaemia, pneumothorax or prolonged hypoxaemia (and some other, less frequent, causes). It should be treated by external cardiac massage and, if possible, immediate diagnosis and correction of the cause.

In all forms of cardiac arrest, adrenaline should be given regularly because there is evidence that its administration increases the perfusion pressure resulting from cardiac massage, and because it may facilitate restoration of sinus rhythm. When cardiac arrest does occur during anaesthesia, injury is often attributed to delay in implementing cardiac massage and failure to administer adrenaline at appropriate intervals. Although anaesthetists are more knowledgeable than most hospital specialists regarding the management of cardiac arrest, there is evidence that not all consultants are familiar with contemporary guidelines for resuscitation, and some may treat cardiac arrest in a suboptimal manner unless they attend regular Advanced Life Support courses.

Hypotension

Almost all anaesthetic drugs produce some hypotension, by reducing cardiac output, promoting vasodilatation, or both. Hypotension is more marked in the absence of surgical stimulation (e.g. between induction of anaesthesia and the start of surgery) and in the presence of relative hypovolaemia (e.g. after haemorrhage or in the dehydrated patient). However, the presence of low blood pressure is not linked automatically to reduced tissue perfusion or oxygenation, provided that cardiac output is maintained. In the presence of a normal macrocirculation, autoregulation maintains flow despite moderate decreases in arterial pressure. Normally, cerebral autoregulation occurs down to a mean arterial pressure of 60 mmHg; below that value, cerebral blood flow decreases progressively. However, the threshold is increased in chronically hypertensive patients, and flow may be pressure-dependent in patients with atherosclerosis of cerebral arteries.

Tissue flow is reduced to a greater degree when hypotension is associated with reduced cardiac output and accompanied by vasoconstriction. Excessive hyperventilation causes profound hypocapnia, which also results in vasoconstriction, and may impair tissue perfusion further in the hypotensive patient.

Inadvertent hypotension during anaesthesia may be the result of a relative overdose of general anaesthetic agents, high spinal or epidural anaesthesia or inadequate replacement of blood and plasma losses. Deliberate induced hypotension to reduce surgical blood loss has become less popular, but the technique is still used by a proportion of anaesthetists, particularly for middle ear, nasal, pelvic and plastic operations. Anaesthetists vary in their enthusiasm for deliberate hypotension, and there have been cases of cerebral damage, myocardial infarction and death attributable to its use. There is no sudden 'cut-off' value of blood pressure below which serious complications occur predictably. However, there does appear to be an increased risk of complications if deliberate hypotension is used; the incidence of non-fatal complications has been estimated as 2.5%[18]. A large proportion of these complications can be prevented if deliberate hypotension is avoided in patients with pre-existing hypertension, cerebrovascular or ischaemic heart disease, hypovolaemia or anaemia. Hypotensive techniques associated with myocardial depression (by administration of high concentrations of volatile anaesthetic agents or ß-blockers) are associated with more complications than those that employ vasodilatation. The complication rate is also increased if mean arterial blood pressure is reduced to less than 70 mmHg, or if the anaesthetist is inexperienced. However, there may be some surgical procedures in which the risk of excessive blood loss warrants the use of lower values of blood pressure in otherwise healthy young patients and there is evidence that an adequate cerebral blood flow can be maintained in such patients at systolic blood pressures of 60 mmHg or slightly less[19].

Anaemia

Tissue oxygenation may be impaired despite a normal arterial oxygen saturation if the total amount of oxygen carried by blood is decreased by severe anaemia. The most common cause is massive haemorrhage, with replacement of blood volume by artificial solutions. It is a potential problem in any Jehovah's Witness

---

[18] Caplan, RA, Posner, KL, Ward, RJ and Cheney, FW, Adverse respiratory events in anesthesia: a closed claims analysis, *Anesthesiology*, 1990; 72: 828-833.
[19] Lindop, MJ, Complications and morbidity of controlled hypotension, *British Journal of Anaesthesia*, 1975; 47: 799-803.

who undergoes major surgery and refuses permission for blood transfusion. Most Jehovah's witnesses are prepared to accept cell salvage techniques, in which red cells are recovered from the operation site, processed, and infused intravenously; this has extended the range of major procedures which can be performed safely, although there is always a risk that recovery of red cells will not take place sufficiently rapidly to prevent a period of severe anaemia.

Embolism

Embolism of air or thrombus may result in cerebral ischaemia. Massive venous embolism causes a great reduction in, or cessation of, cardiac output. Arterial emboli may cause focal or generalised cerebral lesions. Massive pulmonary embolism is unusual during anaesthesia, but may occur in patients who have been immobile, or occasionally after release of a pneumatic tourniquet on the leg; postoperative embolism is much more common. Arterial thrombi may originate in the heart or great vessels, and are usually neither predictable nor preventable by the anaesthetist. Air embolism may occur during neurosurgery or operations in the pelvis if the patient is positioned in such a way that the operation site is above the heart. Oxygen emboli have caused cardiac arrest after instillation of hydrogen peroxide into surgical wounds[20]. Fatal carbon dioxide emboli have occurred during laparoscopy[21]. Emboli of air or clot, or reduced cerebral perfusion pressure, may cause focal or global ischaemia after cardiopulmonary bypass; microemboli of platelets, air bubbles or other substances result in a high incidence of minor neurological and psychological sequelae, the majority of which are of little clinical significance and most of which are temporary.

The consequences of cerebral hypoxia or ischaemia

The effects of these two insults are not identical. In the presence of an intact cardiovascular system, the brain is able to adjust for temporary episodes of even severe hypoxia by a compensatory increase in cerebral blood flow, thereby minimising the reduction in oxygen delivery.

If arterial Po_2 decreases to less than 6.5 kPa without circulatory arrest, there are increases in intracellular and extracellular brain lactate concentrations. More profound hypoxaemia results in a decrease in intracerebral phosphocreatine concentrations. However, even very severe hypoxaemia is not associated with a significant decrease in ATP concentrations because of a rapid compensatory vasodilatation, a resultant increase in blood flow (in excess of four times normal) and a sixfold increase in glucose metabolism. As long as increased cerebral blood flow is maintained, hypoxaemia must be very severe to threaten neuronal survival, although cerebral function may be impaired during the episode of

[20] Timperley, AJ and Bracey, DJ, Cardiac arrest following the use of hydrogen peroxide during arthroplasty, *Journal of Arthroplasty*, 1989; 4: 369-370.
[21] Beck, DH and McQuillan, PJ, Fatal carbon dioxide embolism and severe haemorrhage during laparoscopic salpingectomy, *British Journal of Anaesthesia*, 1994; 72: 243-245.

hypoxia[22]. However, prolonged moderate or severe hypoxaemia also affects the heart. There is an initial increase in heart rate and stroke volume as a result of sympathetic nervous system stimulation, but bradycardia or other arrhythmias, followed by cardiac arrest, supervene and permanent cerebral changes ensue. In severe hypoxaemia with circulatory inadequacy, the sequelae are similar to those caused by primary cerebral ischaemia.

Global ischaemia, as occurs in severe hypotension or cardiac arrest, results much more rapidly in neuronal damage. Brief episodes of ischaemia are often followed by complete recovery. However, as the duration of ischaemia increases, progressively more permanent damage occurs. Resulting lesions are more likely to affect grey matter than white matter, and are frequently bilateral and symmetrical; they may be confined to the parietal and occipital areas of the cerebral hemispheres, but in most cases involve both the supratentorial and infratentorial compartments. Fits may develop during or shortly after the ischaemic episode. A wide range of residual deficits may result, ranging from mild psychological symptoms or personality changes to a vegetative state or brain death. Cortical blindness is not uncommon. Outcome is influenced by the duration and extent of ischaemia and by age. Paradoxically, incomplete ischaemia (e.g. severe hypotension) may result in a worse outcome than a similar period of complete ischaemia; this is thought to be the result of continued delivery of glucose with an inadequate supply of oxygen in incomplete ischaemia, which causes increased lactate production and a lower intracellular pH.

Patients with cerebrovascular disease may develop localised neurological lesions attributable to ischaemic damage in the area of impaired perfusion.

Attempts at reducing the neurological sequelae of hypoxia or ischaemia have been disappointing. No specific treatment has been shown to ameliorate the condition in man. However, it is likely that prompt restoration of the circulation reduces secondary ischaemic damage, and moderate hyperventilation may be of theoretical benefit if there are signs of cerebral oedema. There is no clinical evidence that the use of routine artificial ventilation after cardiac arrest influences neurological outcome in man. Steroids are of no benefit.

If it is clear that an episode of severe hypoxaemia or profound hypotension has occurred during the peri-operative period, and if there is objective evidence of neuronal damage, it is usually difficult to deny a link between damage and peri-operative events; defence of a claim will then depend upon consideration of the cause of the peri-operative event, and whether it could have been avoided by reasonable practice. In some cases, allegations of cerebral damage are brought when there is no indication, despite adequate records, of any adverse event in the peri-operative period, where the alleged cerebral damage is psychological, intellectual or behavioural rather than physical, and when there is no indication in the records that there has been any abnormality of consciousness following

[22] Hypoxia is an inadequate oxygen supply to a tissue or organ.

anaesthesia. In these cases, it is often difficult to establish the patient's intellect and behaviour before anaesthesia. Successful defence is possible, but only if good records are available.

SPINAL CORD/NERVE ROOT DAMAGE

The commonest reason for complaint in patients who have suffered damage to the spinal cord or nerve roots relates to the use of subarachnoid or epidural anaesthesia. Insertion of a spinal needle at an inappropriate level of the vertebral column is usually a justified cause of complaint, as spinal anaesthesia should always be performed well below the level at which the spinal cord usually ends. Although described classically as a very rare complication of subarachnoid anaesthesia, one of the authors (ARA) has encountered 15 cases in which neuroradiological evidence has suggested that spinal cord damage has occurred as a result of insertion of a spinal needle, and another seven cases have been reported in the medical literature[23]. There is evidence[24] that anaesthetists frequently identify intervertebral levels incorrectly, usually concluding that the level is lower than the true level. Moderate spinal cord lesions produce symptoms and signs which are, in many but not all respects, similar to nerve root lesions, and it is probable that a proportion of injuries identified in the past as being peripheral in origin were caused by damage to the spinal cord; it is only because of advances in neuro-imaging that positive diagnoses have been made. Spinal cord damage may result also if an epidural needle, which is often inserted in the thoracic spine, and sometimes in the cervical spine, is advanced excessively, and there have been reports of cervical spinal cord injury associated with interscalene brachial plexus block if the needle is advanced in an inappropriate direction[25].

A substantial proportion of injuries to spinal nerve roots have no obvious cause. In many cases, allegations are made relating to injection of an inappropriate substance into the vertebral column. It is seldom possible to prove that this has occurred; however, it is also seldom possible to prove that it has not. A number of substances are known to cause neurotoxicity, including potassium chloride and calcium chloride. Local anaesthetic drugs used in the United Kingdom are rarely associated with neurotoxicity, although there are concerns about their use with adrenaline, and their administration through a subarachnoid catheter. There is suspicion that inadvertent subdural injection of local anaesthetic may be responsible for a proportion of unexplained neurological lesions in patients who have undergone epidural anaesthesia[26]; injection of radio-opaque dye through a

---

[23] Reynolds, F, Damage to the conus medullaris following spinal anaesthesia, *Anaesthesia,* 2001; 56: 238-47

[24] Broadbent, CR, Maxwell, WB, Ferrie, R, Wilson, DJ, Gawne-Cain, M and Russell R, Ability of anaesthetists to identify a marked lumbar interspace, *Anaesthesia*, 2000; 55: 1122-6.

[25] Benumof, JL, Permanent loss of cervical spinal cord function associated with interscalene block performed under general anesthesia, *Anesthesiology,* 2000; 93: 1541-4.

[26] Reynolds, F and Speedy, HM, The subdural space: the third place to go astray, *Anaesthesia*, 1990; 45: 120-123.

catheter placed inadvertently in the subdural space has demonstrated that fluid may produce compression of nerve roots and the spinal cord[27]. In the ASA Closed Claims study[28], 2.5% of claims against anaesthetists related to alleged damage to the lumbosacral nerve roots.

Damage to the spinal cord may occur also as a result of ischaemic lesions, either because of systemic hypotension, or local occlusion of the blood supply (usually in association with coeliac plexus block). Injection of steroids into the epidural space (usually without a product licence) has also resulted in a number of claims for damage to the cord or nerve roots.

AWARENESS DURING ANAESTHESIA

Allegations of awareness during anaesthesia account for a substantial proportion of claims against anaesthetists. Awareness is almost invariably the result of provision of inadequate concentrations of anaesthetic drugs in the paralysed patient. It has existed as a complication of anaesthesia since the introduction of muscle relaxants. The number of patients seeking redress through the courts increased dramatically in the late 1980s as a consequence of widespread publicity in the lay press about a patient who was aware during Caesarean section in 1981[29] and who received compensation in 1985.

One of the authors (ARA) has reviewed over 120 cases in which awareness during anaesthesia has been alleged. The most likely causes are shown in Figure 5. Broadly, the commonest causes of awareness are use of an inappropriate anaesthetic technique, and failure to check or monitor equipment with the result that less anaesthetic is delivered than the anaesthetist intended to deliver; these claims are, in our experience, indefensible. There are very occasional genuine equipment failures which can result in awareness despite a reasonable standard of care on the part of the anaesthetist, and there are, occasionally, situations in which a brief episode of awareness can be justified because a life-threatening event has occurred which requires, as part of its management, discontinuation of administration of anaesthetic drugs.

---

[27] McMenemin, IM, Sissons, GRJ and Brownridge, P, Accidental subdural catheterization: radiological evidence of a possible mechanism for spinal cord damage, *British Journal of Anaesthesia*, 1992; 69: 417-419.
[28] Kroll, DA, Caplan, RA, Posner, K, Ward, RJ and Cheney, FW, Nerve injury associated with anesthesia, *Anesthesiology*, 1990; 73: 202-207.
[29] Ackers v Wigan Health Authority, *Medical Law Reports*, 1991; 2 232-234.

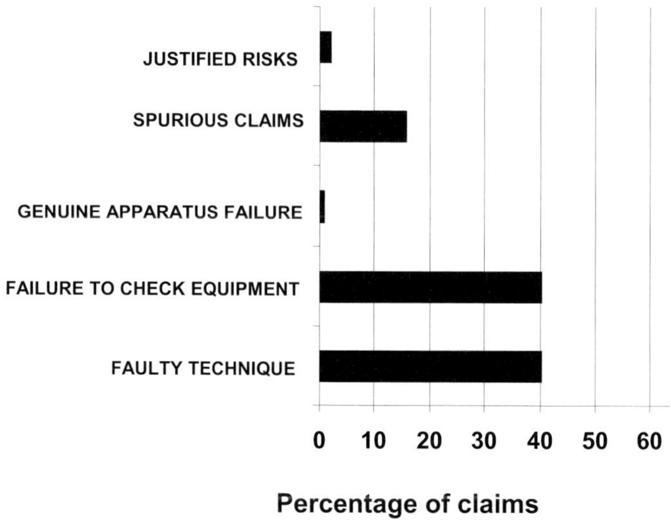

FIGURE 5 – ANALYSIS OF THE EXPLANATION FOR AWARENESS IN OVER 120 CASES REVIEWED BY ONE OF THE AUTHORS. SEE TEXT FOR DETAILS.

In obstetric anaesthesia, concerns regarding the effects of anaesthetic agents on the newborn baby and on the risk of haemorrhage from the uterus resulted in the use of anaesthetic techniques which would not be regarded as adequate in other areas of surgery. The perceived risks to the baby and the uterus have almost certainly been overemphasised, and a substantial reduction in the incidence of awareness has been achieved since the introduction of improved techniques. Most episodes of awareness now occur between skin incision and the delivery of the baby, and result from the short period between induction of anaesthesia and the start of surgery, and reluctance to use 'overpressure' to achieve a rapid increase in the concentration of volatile agent in the blood and brain. The vast majority of Caesarean sections are now performed under spinal or epidural anaesthesia because these techniques are associated with a much lower risk of death. Consequently, trainees now obtain little experience of undertaking general anaesthesia for Caesarean section, and this may also increase the risk of awareness.

A small proportion of patients who complain of intra-operative awareness have experienced events in the immediate postoperative period, but interpreted the events as having occurred during operation ('spurious claims' in Figure 5). Successful defence of such claims depends almost entirely on the use of an anaesthetic technique regarded as acceptable at the time of the incident, and the presence of adequate records showing the dosages and timings of drug administration, the pattern of administration of volatile anaesthetic agents and the absence of undue hypertension and tachycardia.

In the United Kingdom, there has never been, to the knowledge of the authors, an attempt to defend at trial an allegation of awareness when the Defendant accepted that the awareness occurred at a time when the patient should have been unconscious. In all but one case, the Defendant argued that the patient's memories related to events in the immediate postoperative period or were fictitious; in the remaining case, it was argued that awareness was justified because an emergency had arisen which resulted in discontinuation of administration of anaesthetic agents to preserve the life of the patient. In the large majority of claims for awareness during anaesthesia, it is accepted by both parties that awareness had occurred at a time when it should not, and the matter is settled out of court.

A number of devices are now available which provide information about depth of anaesthesia based on various analyses of the electroencephalogram (EEG) trace. One of these has recently been shown to reduce the incidence of awareness during surgery. However, these devices are not sufficiently sensitive to distinguish clearly between consciousness and unconsciousness, and cannot predict awareness in patients who are anesthetised and in whom surgery is about to start. When inhaled anaesthetic agents are employed, continuous monitoring of the inspired and end-tidal concentrations, with appropriate alarm values set, should minimise the risk of awareness caused by equipment errors.

Patients who have been aware during anaesthesia, and who have experienced pain and distress, may develop post-traumatic stress disorder. A number of recent claims have included allegations that, after learning of the episode of awareness, the anaesthetist did not refer the patient for psychological counselling. Advice to anaesthetists confronted with a patient who claims to have been aware during anaesthesia has been published[30].

REGIONAL ANAESTHESIA

In parallel with the increase in complaints of awareness during general anaesthesia in the late 1980s, there was a large increase in the numbers of patients who complained of pain during regional anaesthesia; these complaints are almost invariably associated with Caesarean section, and continue to occur, although less frequently. In many cases where complaint is made, the upper level of block has been predictably insufficient to produce adequate anaesthesia during the procedure. In others, there has been no record of the extent of the block, or whether the block has been tested, making defence of the claim impossible. In some cases, the anaesthetist has not been present during the operation! In general terms, spinal anaesthesia produces a denser block than epidural anaesthesia, and is the preferred technique for Caesarean section.

---

[30] Aitkenhead, AR, Awareness during anaesthesia: what should the patient be told?, *Anaesthesia*, 1990; 45: 351-352.

There have been several recent cases in which the patient has claimed to have been assaulted because regional or local techniques were employed without specific consent, and performed under general anaesthesia.

Severe headache can follow inadvertent dural tap during epidural anaesthesia. The incidence of dural tap is 0.5-1% in most units, and patients should be warned of the possibility of this complication. Dural tap usually occurs despite a satisfactory standard of care, and thus most allegations of negligence related to dural puncture can be denied. However, in some cases, treatment of the headache has been inadequate.

There have been many claims relating to persistent backache following epidural block, mostly in obstetrics. Current evidence suggests that there is no increased risk of prolonged backache associated with epidural block in the obstetric unit, beyond that associated with pregnancy itself, and no increased risk in other surgical patients beyond that associated with surgery undertaken under general anaesthesia.

Epidural analgesia is being used increasingly to provide pain relief after surgery. In addition to a small risk of direct neurological damage caused by insertion of the needle or by subdural injection (see above), there are risks of spinal cord compression if a large haematoma or abscess develops. Abscesses appear to be commoner in patients who have undergone bowel surgery and in whom the catheter has remained in place for several days; they are very rare in obstetric patients. Haematoma is more likely to occur if there is impaired coagulation, including that resulting from the administration of low doses of heparin administered to many surgical patients to minimise the risk of deep venous thrombosis and pulmonary embolism; the insertion and removal of an epidural catheter should be timed accordingly.

Estimates of the overall risk of persisting neurological lesions associated with epidural block range from more than 1:1,000[31] to less than 1:40,000[32]; in the latter study, the total frequency of serious complications was slightly more than 1:20,000. These risks are rare but, because the potential injuries are serious, they should not be dismissed lightly. Most anaesthetists in the United Kingdom do not volunteer the information that permanent neurological damage may result from the use of spinal or epidural techniques, but the Association of Anaesthetists of Great Britain and Ireland recommends that patients should be provided with an

31 Dahlgren, N and Tornebrandt, K, Neurological complications after anaesthesia. A follow-up of 18,000 spinal and epidural anaesthetics performed over three years, *Acta Anaesthesiologica Scandinavica*, 1995; 39: 872-80.
32 Aromaa, U, Lahdensuu, M and Cozanitis, DA, Severe complications associated with epidural and spinal anaesthesias in Finland 1987-1993. A study based on patient insurance claims, *Acta Anaesthesiologica Scandinavica*, 1997; 41: 445-52.

information booklet which includes uncommon risks, and any questions which a patient asks about risks or complications should be answered honestly[33].

PERIPHERAL NERVE DAMAGE

Peripheral nerve damage is usually the result of compression or stretching of the nerve. In a few cases, nerves are damaged by direct trauma from needles or extravasated drugs. Most lesions involve demyelination at a point of localised compression. In most cases, demyelination results in recovery in 6-8 weeks, but in some patients recovery is more prolonged, and in a few, the injury is permanent. In an early publication of the ASA Closed Claims study[34], 15% of claims against anaesthetists related to peripheral nerve injury, but more recently, this has increased to 21%[35]. Injury to the ulnar nerve represented about one-third of these claims, and brachial plexus injury just under one-quarter.

The ulnar and common peroneal nerves are particularly susceptible to damage because they lie, at some point, in a very superficial position close to bony promontories. However, there is evidence that many patients have pre-existing subclinical lesions of these nerves related to normal posture, often occupational, such as sitting with the legs crossed or leaning habitually on an elbow. In these patients, a brief period of normally innocuous stretching or compression may result in a clinical lesion. Often, electrophysiological studies in patients who develop a lesion in the postoperative period reveal that the nerve on the contralateral side is also abnormal. In these patients, it may be possible to defend allegations that the injury could have occurred only as a result of negligent treatment. Patients with a pre-existing general neuropathy are also at increased risk, but the presence of such a condition should be established at the pre-operative visit.

The brachial plexus may suffer injury if the arm is placed in any extreme position during anaesthesia, but particularly if it is abducted and externally rotated. In the supine position, the risk is highest if both arms are abducted, if an arm is abducted beyond 90º, if the arm is abducted and the head is extended and rotated to the opposite side, or if the arm lies below the horizontal plane of the body. In the prone position, there is a risk of damage to the brachial plexus if the arms are abducted excessively; this is most easily prevented by keeping the arms at the side of the body. There is also a risk of damage to the brachial plexus if shoulder braces are used to prevent a patient slipping from a steep head-down position on the operating table. Brachial plexus injury is most common after cardiac surgery, as a result of stretching during median sternotomy.

---

[33] *Consent for Anaesthesia*, Association of Anaesthetists of Great Britain and Ireland, London, 2006.

[34] Kroll, DA, Caplan, RA, Posner, K, Ward, RJ and Cheney FW, Nerve injury associated with anesthesia, *Anesthesiology*, 1990; 73: 202-207.

[35] See above, footnote 5.

Damage to the radial nerve in the upper arm occurs usually as a result of compression, for example under a pneumatic tourniquet. The sciatic nerve is at risk in thin patients placed on a hard operating table for a long operation, but may also be damaged by stretching in the lithotomy position, or by compression by a hard pad placed under the pelvis when patients are placed in the Lloyd-Davies position. The sciatic nerve may also be damaged by a needle during intramuscular injection of drugs into the buttock. Nerves injured less commonly include the tibial, femoral, obturator, saphenous, pudendal, supra-orbital and facial.

Uncommonly, peripheral nerves are damaged during performance of nerve block, probably either by penetration by the needle or as a result of direct injection of local anaesthetic into the nerve. Most nerve lesions which occur when the block has been performed in a conscious patient cause pain during insertion of the needle or during injection. Many anaesthetists perform peripheral nerve blocks after induction of general anaesthesia; the purposes of the block are to enhance intra-operative conditions and to contribute to postoperative analgesia. It can be argued that the risk of nerve damage is increased if the block is performed during general anaesthesia because a complaint of pain which might prevent injection of local anaesthetic into a nerve is, inevitably, absent. Many blocks of major, anatomically deep nerves are now undertaken with the aid of an electrical nerve stimulator which elicits a sensory response in conscious patients and a motor response in anaesthetised patients. However, it is possible for the tip of the needle to be lying in a sensory nerve when an appropriate motor response is obtained in an unconscious patient; this would result in injection of local anaesthetic into the nerve, causing nerve injury. Consequently, there are those who argue that, in adults, peripheral nerve blocks should be performed on conscious patients because feedback from the patient is likely to prevent the needle penetrating a nerve or injection of solution into a nerve. In the absence of firm evidence to support this contention, this remains an area of heated debate.

OBSTETRIC ANAESTHESIA

In addition to complaints against anaesthetists for alleged awareness and pain during regional anaesthesia for Caesarean section (see above), blame may be attributed by patients and, in some instances by obstetricians, for delay in obtaining satisfactory conditions for Caesarean section, resulting in death of, or cerebral damage to, the neonate. In a number of these cases, it has been alleged that general anaesthesia should have been administered in preference to extending an epidural block which was already almost satisfactory for Caesarean section or performing spinal anaesthesia, because the former course of action would be faster. Fetal death has also been attributed to failure to manage hypotension adequately during Caesarean section. Occasionally, operative delivery can result in massive haemorrhage, and complications such as amniotic fluid embolism and hypertensive disorders of pregnancy can cause rapid onset of serious illness: anaesthetists may be blamed for failing to provide rapid and effective resuscitation and intensive care when these events arise.

OTHER INJURIES

A few patients have sued because they suffered muscle pains after receiving the depolarising muscle relaxant suxamethonium, which is used routinely when rapid intubation of the trachea is required. Although these claims have been unsuccessful, muscle pain related to administration of suxamethonium is a very common complaint, and patients should be warned of the possibility at the pre-operative visit. Fractured ribs and other injuries have resulted from patients being dropped from the operating table on to the floor. Tissued infusions may result in damage to skin or nerves, and, in rare circumstances, ischaemic damage to an entire limb because of compartment syndrome; claims are difficult to defend if the anaesthetist has not checked an established infusion (often hidden under bandages) before injecting potentially toxic drugs such as thiopentone, or has not taken reasonable care to ensure that the infusion is functioning properly during anaesthesia (particularly when large volumes of fluid are infused under high pressure). Skin necrosis may occur if irritant drugs intended for deep intramuscular injection are delivered instead into the subcutaneous tissues. Skin damage may occur also as a result of burns, pooling of disinfectant, and pressure.

Laryngeal damage may be minor (e.g. granulomata) or major (e.g. dislocation of cartilages, or damage to nerves); in general, it is difficult to defend allegations that undue force was used if there has been substantial anatomical damage to the structures of the larynx. Trauma associated with tracheal intubation has also been alleged in relation to development of retropharyngeal abscess.

Allegations have been made that tracheostomy should not have been performed in patients whose trachea proved impossible to intubate by conventional methods, in hospitals without the facility to perform fibreoptic laryngoscopy; the expectations of patients (or their advisers) increase as technology advances.

Patient satisfaction with anaesthesia is high. In a recent study[36], 96.8% of patients were satisfied with their anaesthetic care; 2.3% were 'somewhat dissatisfied', and 0.9% were 'dissatisfied'. There were many factors which influenced the likelihood of satisfaction or otherwise. The authors calculated odds ratios for a number of these factors; for example, if the odds ratio for dissatisfaction was 2 for a patient who developed a specific complication, this means that a patient who fell into that category was twice as likely to be dissatisfied as a patient who had not suffered that complication. Patients who had suffered moderate or severe postoperative pain or severe postoperative nausea and vomiting had odds ratios

---

[36] Myles, PS, Williams, DL, Hendrata, M, Anderson, H and Weeks, AM, Patient satisfaction after anaesthesia and surgery: results of a prospective survey of 10,811 patients, *British Journal of Anaesthesia*, 2000; 84: 6-10.

of around 4. These were high in comparison to most other conditions tending to lead to dissatisfaction, but postoperative pain or severe nausea and vomiting are exceptionally rare sources of litigation. This may be related to expectation (pain, nausea and vomiting are anticipated by most surgical patients), or because they are transient. By comparison, the odds ratio for dissatisfaction in patients who had been aware during anaesthesia was 54.9. No other serious and lasting complications occurred in that series. High levels of dissatisfaction, and litigation, are probably related to whether the consequences of a complication are severe and protracted, and whether the complication is an anticipated risk. Risks which are not widely known by the public, and which are not explained by the anaesthetist, are unanticipated.

THE INTENSIVE CARE UNIT

General considerations

The Intensive Care Unit (ICU) is the hospital facility within which the highest level of continuous patient care and treatment is provided. In general terms, the patients in ICU are the most severely ill patients in the hospital. The Department of Health NHS Executive defines Intensive Care as 'a service for patients with potentially recoverable conditions who can benefit from more detailed observation and treatment than can safely be provided in general ward or high dependency areas'. The ICU and High Dependency Unit (HDU) are designated areas within the hospital staffed by specially trained medical and nursing staff. Recently, the concept of Intensive Care has been replaced by that of Comprehensive Critical Care which aims to provide ICU, HDU and provision of specialist advice, training and support to all critically ill patients wherever they are located in the hospital. This delivery of advanced care and support to patients on ordinary wards is termed Critical Care Outreach.

The nature of a Critical Care Outreach Team (CCOT) service differs among hospitals. Some provide designated nurses with medical support from the ICU, while in others, all the team members are based on ICU and attend ordinary wards when requested. The team attempts to detect deterioration early and intervene to pre-empt the patient requiring admission to ICU.

Ideally, the ICU provides a nurse to patient ratio of 1:1, together with a nurse in charge at all times of day and night, 24-hour cover by resident medical staff and the facilities to provide life support for organ dysfunction such as respiratory, cardiac or renal failure. HDUs are characterised as designated areas with a nurse to patient ratio of 1:2, a nurse in charge at all times, continuous availability of medical staff either from the admitting speciality or from ICU and an appropriate level of monitoring and other equipment. ICUs and HDUs may be either separate geographical entities or may be combined, with the beds occupied and staffed according to the prevailing need for ICU or HDU levels of care. Minimum standards for provision of space, storage, equipment and facilities have been recommended by the Intensive Care Society[37].

Why do medico-legal problems arise in the ICU?

The cost of provision of ICU services is usually the highest per patient in the hospital, and the resource is finite and subject to pressure of high demand. Delayed admission, premature discharge and transfer of patients to other hospitals may occur as a result. ICU care must be directed towards patients who are most likely to benefit. It is equally important to identify patients who do not require advanced care and who are likely to die despite ICU treatment.

Patients may be admitted from all areas within the hospital, including emergency admissions from the Accident and Emergency department, patients who have deteriorated on the wards, emergency admissions from the operating theatres where peri-operative complications may have occurred or transfers from other hospitals for specialist treatment. The provision of medical care can never be without risk, and this is particularly the case in ICU. The procedures required to provide life-sustaining treatment for prolonged periods are often invasive, and each has its own range of potentially life-threatening complications. The Risk Management review for the ICU in our hospital identified over 150 ICU-specific procedures which are potentially capable of causing major morbidity or mortality. A list of common iatrogenic events on ICU that have led to litigation is shown in Table 3.

The risk of complications arising from necessary treatment must be added to the risk associated with the illness that precipitated ICU admission. Prediction of mortality prior to admission to ICU is invariably subjective and often made on an opinion of the balance of probability. When the patient has been admitted to ICU, illness severity scoring enables mortality prediction to be calculated on a statistical basis by referral of an individual patient's score to large case-mix corrected databases.

For ICU survivors, discharge from such a highly monitored environment to the ordinary ward is a time of very high risk. Unrecognised deterioration following discharge is a well recognised cause of re-admission, morbidity or death. Death on the ICU poses further potential ethical and legal problems because, in the majority of ICU patients who do not survive, death results from decisions to withdraw life-sustaining therapy.

---

[37] *Standards for Intensive Care Units*, Intensive Care Society, London, 1997. (updated version available at http://www.ics.ac.uk/downloads/ICSstandards4302.pdf).

TABLE 3 – EXAMPLES OF CLINICAL RISKS IN ICU THAT HAVE LED TO LITIGATION

Risk	Consequence
Delayed recognition of illness severity	Increased morbidity and mortality
Delayed admission to Level 3/2	Cardio-respiratory arrest and death
Failed intubation	Hypoxaemia, hypotension, brain injury
Drug overdose during induction	Cardio-respiratory arrest and death
Lung injury due to mechanical ventilation	Hypoxaemia and death
Cuff over-pressure	Tracheal stenosis
Arterial line injuries	Aneurysm, haemorrhage, amputation, systemic sepsis and multiple organ failure
Central venous catheter injury	Tension pneumothorax and hypoxaemia, arterial injury and amputation, bleeding and haematoma formation leading to airway obstruction and death
Tracheostomy	Failure to cannulate trachea – death Bleeding into trachea – death Dislodgement – death Tracheal stenosis
Inappropriate use of inotropes	Peripheral gangrene Amputation of arm
Drug dosage/prescription errors	Death
Catheter embolism and atrial erosion	Death
Missed injury	Delayed surgery to brachial plexus leading to paralysis Gangrenous stomach due to diaphragmatic rupture
Missed cervical abscess	Paralysis
Missed spinal fractures	Delayed surgery
Withdrawal of life sustaining treatment	High Court injunction
Delayed diagnosis	Sepsis from infected breast reduction surgery Renal failure from TTP Pancreatitis – unnecessary surgery

Admission to and discharge from the ICU

The person who acts as the 'gate-keeper' to ICU is essentially performing a triage process to ensure that only those likely to benefit from ICU treatment will be admitted. If that person decides that, on the balance of probability, ICU admission would not save the patient's life, then the patient will not be admitted. The 'gate-keeper' role is generally performed by a consultant with a special interest and training in ICU[38]. Refusal to admit a patient on the grounds of futility should ideally be a consultant-only decision. Patients may also be refused admission to ICU on the basis that they do not require care in an ICU, and would be managed more appropriately elsewhere. Increasingly, it is the ICU consultant, sometimes termed an 'Intensivist' who acts as the arbiter in these matters. We are aware of several legal claims in which there has been a question as to whether delay in admission influenced outcome, but not of any case arising from a refusal to admit on the grounds of futility. This is surprising given that such decisions are not always clear-cut.

In the UK, a multi-disciplinary working party established criteria for admission to ICU based on the concept of organ systems failure. These were published by the Department of Health in 1996[39]. In general terms, patients should be admitted to ICU if they have a realistic prospect of recovery from an acute illness that results in:

- A requirement, or a likely requirement, for advanced respiratory support alone.
- A requirement for support of two or more organ systems.
- A requirement for support for an acute reversible failure of another organ system in the presence of co-morbidity.

There are specific categories of organ/systems failure and these are shown in Table 4. Some forms of organ system support (e.g. neurosurgery for insertion of invasive monitoring, or treatment of liver failure) are available only in specialist centres and, where appropriate, the patient must be transferred safely to the specialist unit. The decision to admit or transfer is not one that should be delegated to junior medical staff. The referral should ideally be on a consultant to consultant basis and no patient should be admitted or refused admission without discussion with the ICU consultant, one of whom must be available 24 hours a day.

---

[38] The parent speciality of consultants in charge of the ICU in the UK is most commonly anaesthesia, although some have trained as physicians and a very few as surgeons.
[39] *Guidelines on Admission to and Discharge from Intensive Care and High Dependency Units*, Department of Health, London, 1996.

TABLE 4 – CATEGORIES OF ORGAN SYSTEM SUPPORT.

1. Advanced respiratory support

Mechanical ventilatory support (excluding mask continuous positive pressure (CPAP) or non-invasive ventilation).

The possibility of sudden deterioration in respiratory function which requires immediate intubation and mechanical ventilation.

2. Basic respiratory monitoring and support

The need for more than 40% oxygen

The possibility of progressive deterioration to the point of needing advanced respiratory support.

The need for physiotherapy to clear secretions at least 2-hourly.

Patients recently extubated after a prolonged period of tracheal intubation and mechanical ventilation.

The need for mask CPAP or non-invasive ventilation.

Patients whose trachea is intubated to protect the airway but who do not need mechanical ventilation.

3. Circulatory support

The need for vaso-active drugs

Support for circulatory instability due to hypovolaemia from any cause unresponsive to modest volume replacement.

Patients resuscitated after cardiac arrest where ICU or HDU care is considered clinically appropriate.

4. Neurological monitoring or support

Central nervous system depression sufficient to compromise the airway and protective reflexes.

Invasive neurological monitoring.

5. Renal support

The need for acute renal replacement therapy

Delayed admission to the ICU

Delay in admission, and, linked to that, premature discharge or transfer of an existing ICU patient, are frequent sources of complaint. Each hospital has a finite number of ICU/HDU beds and admission may be delayed if all of these beds are occupied. In such circumstances, the prospective patient must be treated in situ until a bed is made available. The standard of care provided must be judged accordingly and not against the standard of care that would be received if immediate admission to ICU were possible. Either the new patient should be stabilised and transferred to another hospital where an ICU bed is available, or an existing ICU patient must be discharged prematurely to a non-ICU bed or transferred to another hospital. The transfer or discharge of an existing ICU patient exposes that patient to risk in order to provide benefit to the new patient. The decision to discharge or transfer a patient should be documented and the reasons for choosing that patient should be explained. If such procedures are followed, then the risk of a successful complaint is minimised.

Delayed admission may occur also as a result of failure to recognise the severity of illness of a patient who requires a higher level of care. If the patient's condition has deteriorated to the point where increased morbidity or death results, the chances of a successful action are high. The significance of delayed admission in causing increased mortality and morbidity is well documented in the medical literature. A clinical example would be a patient who has developed pneumonia at home, is treated initially by the general practitioner with oral antibiotics but who develops increasing respiratory difficulty and is admitted to hospital. The patient is seen in the Accident & Emergency department and admitted to a medical ward, after oxygen therapy and intravenous antibiotics have been prescribed. Not all such patients respond to this therapy and some continue to deteriorate. In such cases, the level of oxygen in their blood may fall (or carbon dioxide levels rise) to such an extent that the patient loses consciousness. The ability to maintain the airway may be lost, additional hypoxaemia may occur and the patient may inhale vomited gastric contents, further damaging the lungs. If hypoxaemia continues unchecked then cardiac arrest may occur. The resulting hypoxaemia and hypotension are potent causes of brain damage and, potentially, death. The failure to detect deterioration and the failure to intervene prior to cardiac arrest may be negligent if the appropriate level of observation was not carried out or the signs of progressive deterioration were ignored.

Refusing admission to the ICU

The reversibility of the patient's illness must be considered. If it is irreversible and incompatible with life then the patient should not be admitted. Such decisions are not made easily, and occasionally it is necessary to admit the patient and to provide appropriate treatment for a period of time to assess any response. The treatment must be of direct benefit to the patient; subjecting a patient who is dying to ventilation and resuscitation merely to preserve organs for donation to another patient is unethical.

Intensive care cannot reverse chronic ill health and admission may be inappropriate if a patient has significant co-morbidity which severely limits the quality and length of life. Such decisions are subjective and are generally based on the experience of the admitting consultant. Some patients adapt to co-morbidity to the extent that they accept a quality of life that others would regard as unendurable. Denying such patients admission based on the presence of co-morbidity alone is difficult to justify and the competent patient's views must be respected. Nonetheless, it is often possible to defend a consultant's refusal to admit a patient on the grounds that, on the balance of probability, no benefit would result. If the patient is competent, the consultant must discuss the range of treatment options and possible outcomes with the patient and the relatives.

Continuing with our example of the patient with pneumonia: should this patient be admitted to ICU for mechanical ventilation if he had longstanding chronic obstructive pulmonary disease, was normally on home oxygen and nebuliser therapy, was housebound and was unable to climb the stairs to go to bed due to breathlessness? The prospect of successful ICU treatment is so small that treatment might reasonably be limited to simple oxygen therapy, intravenous antibiotics and physiotherapy with non-invasive ventilatory support. If such a decision was reached then admission to ICU would be futile.

Some patients with such a degree of chronic ill health have experienced ICU admission and ventilation before and may have expressed a desire not to be treated aggressively in future. This is most commonly seen in illnesses which result in progressive neuro-disability, such as motor neurone disease. If a patient has made an Advanced Directive ('Living Will'), then its contents must be respected. The competent patient has every right to refuse life-sustaining treatment, the key issues being competence, understanding and belief that refusal will lead to their death. A difficulty arises if the patient (or more commonly, an unconscious patient's relatives) wants admission to ICU even though the Intensivist knows that death is inevitable. Treatment in such circumstances could be regarded as cruel and unusual, or torture, as it would be of no benefit to the patient.

Treatment modalities in the ICU

The aim of ICU care is to prevent the patient from dying from the effects of organ failure. The specific treatment(s) used is/are determined by the organ(s) that has/have failed to function. The ICU practitioner must recognise the presence of life-threatening organ failure, perform immediate life-saving interventions safely and in a timely manner, continually monitor the effects of interventions on the progress of the patient's illness, and modify treatment accordingly. The practitioner must be aware that more than one disease process may be present or that co-morbidity may be causative. A patient admitted with a head injury sustained in a motor vehicle accident patient may have crashed the car because of a heart attack. Trauma patients may have additional injuries which are unrecognised at the time of admission and which may cause significant disability in the future if recovery from the life-threatening injury occurs. The scope for error is enormous.

Continuing with the example of the patient with respiratory failure caused by pneumonia, if the patient's increasing hypoxaemia or hypercapnia is recognised to be a consequence of failure to respond to simple measures, then the use of mechanical ventilation may be appropriate and he may be admitted to the ICU. There, a number of potential complications may occur.

- This critically ill patient must be anaesthetised to allow the insertion of a cuffed tracheal tube. An overdose, or choice of the wrong drug, may result in cardio-respiratory arrest from which successful resuscitation may not be possible.
- The tracheal tube cuff pressure must be monitored to ensure it is not so high as to cause tracheal mucosal ischaemia and subsequent tracheal stenosis.
- A mechanical ventilator must be connected, a safe and effective mode of ventilation chosen, and appropriate end-points for oxygen levels set. Failure to react to low levels of oxygenation, particularly if accompanied by low blood pressure, may result in cerebral damage.
- The efficacy of ventilation is monitored frequently by serial arterial blood gas analyses. An intravascular catheter must be inserted into an artery to facilitate arterial blood sampling and to monitor blood pressure continuously. The catheter may become disconnected, resulting in haemorrhage, or may become infected, causing septicaemia. Inadvertent injection of drugs into a radial artery catheter may cause critical ischaemia to the hand, necessitating amputation.
- Continuous sedation is required to allow effective mechanical ventilation and this often requires the insertion of a multi-lumen central venous catheter. This may result in unrecognised or poorly treated pneumothorax, haemothorax, intra-pleural fluid administration, arterial damage, nerve damage, haemorrhage, cardiac tamponade, or sepsis leading to septicaemia and multiple organ failure.
- If mechanical ventilation is to be prolonged, the patient may need a tracheostomy which may cause death from bleeding, blockage or dislodgement. Any tube or device which passes into the body from the outside breaches the body's primary defence against infection. The presence of these devices, particularly when combined with broad spectrum antibiotic therapy, provides an ideal avenue of infection with multi-resistant strains of bacteria such as methicillin resistant staphylococcus aureus (MRSA).
- If such organisms are present in another ICU patient and appear in a new patient on the unit, the question may be raised as to whether the new infection is the result of the medical/nursing staff having failed to take adequate precautions to prevent cross-infection.

Other treatments involving specialised life support for head injury, spinal injury, multiple trauma, abdominal sepsis, renal failure, liver failure and neurological disease require additional techniques to those described above and are may precipitate further complications. The critically ill patient requires multiple therapies such as oxygen, mechanical ventilation, pharmacological control of heart rate, blood pressure, cardiac output, intra-cranial pressure and urine output, and biochemical and haematological support to be provided simultaneously for a considerable period of time. The effect of each intervention is monitored on a continuous basis and may change hour by hour. The records of changes in therapy and the patient's response to such changes are recorded on the ICU Daily Observation Charts. These must be analysed carefully before any conclusions about the conduct or standard of ICU care can be drawn. These A1 size charts are often filed separately from the medical records, often on the ICU itself.. A routine request for access to the medical records may not result in the ICU charts being disclosed.

Discharging the patient from ICU

The decision to decrease the level of care is not always obvious. The patient should be discharged when the condition(s) that necessitated admission have been treated successfully. Single organ system failure, provided that it does not require mechanical ventilation, can be supported in HDU or some specialised ward areas. Patients should be discharged to an appropriate level of care. It is unusual for an ICU patient to be discharged directly to the ward without receiving a period of 'step-down' high dependency care within the ICU to determine that the clinical course is evolving satisfactory. Thereafter, the patient may be discharged to either the HDU or the ward, as determined by clinical condition. Many ICUs now offer a Critical Care Outreach Team. One of its functions is to follow up recently discharged ICU patients. The standard against which the decision is taken is that described in Table 4. Premature discharge should ideally be accompanied by an enhanced level of supervision of the ex-ICU patient on the ward.

The care provided on ICU is termed Level 3 Care, with Level 2 referring to HDU and Level 1 to routine ward based care (Table 5)[40]. Staffing levels on ordinary wards have decreased progressively over the years and many complaints relate to the sudden reduction in supervision levels. Unrecognised dislodgement of tracheostomy tubes is a recurring problem, particularly in patients who are confused or have an altered level of consciousness.

Death on the ICU

Approximately 20% of all ICU patients die there. The majority die as a result of treatment limitation or withdrawal, the precise proportion varying from country to country. Such decisions account for around 70 80% of deaths in the USA and UK, less than 10% in Japan and Israel, around 30% in Spain and 60% in France. There is no distinction between treatment limitation (i.e. deciding not to offer an

[40] *Levels of Critical Care for Adult Patients*, Intensive Care Society, London, 2002.

increased level of life-sustaining treatment) and treatment withdrawal (i.e. removing/discontinuing a form of life-sustaining treatment already in place).

TABLE 5 – CLASSIFICATION OF CRITICAL CARE PATIENTS ACCORDING TO CLINICAL NEED

Level	
Level 0	Patients whose needs can be met through normal ward care in an acute hospital.
Level 1	Patients at risk of their condition deteriorating, or those recently relocated from higher levels of care whose needs can be met on an acute ward with additional advice and support from the critical care team (or CCOT*).
Level 2	Patients requiring more detailed observation or intervention including support for a single failing organ system or postoperative care, and those stepping down from higher levels of care.
Level 3	Patients requiring advanced respiratory support alone or basic respiratory support together with support of at least two organ systems. This level includes all complex patients requiring support for multi-organ failure.

*CCOT; Critical Care Outreach Team

Guidance to medical staff regarding these matters has been published by both the General Medical Council[41] and the British Medical Association (BMA)[42]. The BMA document states:

> *'Developments in technology have led to a misconception in society that death can almost always be postponed. There needs to be a recognition that there comes a point in all lives where no more can reasonably or helpfully be done to benefit patients other than keeping them comfortable and free from pain.'*

Neither organisation has published specific guidance for ICU patients but the principles are transferable. International guidance for ICU patients was published by the World Federation of Societies of Intensive and Critical Care Medicine in 1997:

> *'Respect for life should not be pushed to absurd limits. It is no part of the doctor's task to prolong suffering. A doctor has no obligation to sustain life*

[41] *Withholding and Withdrawing Life-prolonging Treatments: Good Practice in Decision-making*, General Medical Council, London, 2002. See http://www.gmc-uk.org/index.htm.
[42] *Withholding and Withdrawing Life-prolonging Medical Treatment: Guidance for Decision-making,* 2001, BMJ Books, London.

without meaning. Recourse to and continuation of life sustaining treatment are only permissible when there is a reasonable chance of success with an acceptable outcome for the patient.'

If a patient is competent, there is no problem in terms of the ability to request withdrawal of life-sustaining treatment. The problem occurs with non-competent (generally unconscious) patients when relatives wish to continue treatment and the ICU staff do not. This may occur after a diagnosis of Brain Stem Death has been made and the relatives look at a patient who has a normal colour, feels warm to the touch, has a beating heart and whose chest is rising and falling albeit due to mechanical ventilation. Brain Stem Death occurs rarely (around 4% of all deaths) in the ICU, even in ICUs with a large trauma workload.

The majority of treatment withdrawal decisions are taken as a consequence of continued deterioration in the face of maximal appropriate supportive therapy. This has been termed 'Imminent Demise Futility'. The concept of medical futility may be subdivided further into:

- 'Physiological Futility', in which the degree of injury is such that treatment will not succeed, e.g. performing a thoracotomy on a patient who has sustained an asystolic cardiac arrest following blunt chest trauma.
- 'Interactive Futility', in which the medical intervention will preserve physiological function but will not restore the individual's ability to interact e.g. Persisting Vegetative State.
- 'Qualitative Futility' in which the treatment proposed will sustain life but at a cost that the ICU staff consider to be unacceptable.

Decisions regarding withdrawal of treatment are subjective and based on opinion formed by experience on the balance of probability. The acceptance of Brain Stem Death and the concept of Futility are very variable between cultures and there is an increasing tendency in some sections of the community to seek an injunction regarding withdrawal of treatment.

When decisions about withdrawal of treatment are made, the reasoning behind the decision should be discussed with medical and nursing colleagues, a full explanation given to relatives, and their assent obtained. ICU staff aim to obtain the assent of relatives in all such cases and the discussions should be fully documented. The first step in the process of withdrawal of life-sustaining treatment is the implementation of a 'Do Not Resuscitate' order. Thereafter, all drug therapy other than sedation and analgesia is discontinued and the patient's lungs are ventilated with air rather than the much higher concentration of oxygen usually required in critically ill patients. In some units, if the patient is capable of breathing spontaneously, the tracheal tube is removed. If the patient shows any signs of distress, or if distress, pain and discomfort are known to be an inevitable component of their death, then the doses of sedatives and analgesics are increased to prevent this; the doses of these drugs should be designed to minimise the distress, pain and discomfort, but should not be so large that they are clearly intended to hasten death. Palliative, compassionate care should be continued on the ICU if death is imminent, but if death is inevitable but likely to be delayed, the patient should be transferred to a non-ICU/HDU area for terminal care.

CONCLUSION

The types of patient admitted, the severity of illnesses, the complexity of the treatment modalities necessary, the range of complications and the ability to cause lasting harm or death through action or inaction, result in critical care practice being potentially a major area of litigation. To date, most claims in this area relate to delay in admission or premature discharge from ICU, and the number of claims relating specifically to management in the ICU remains relatively small compared to other fields. However, changing attitudes and public expectations have resulted in a slow but steady rise in claims.

EMERGENCY MEDICINE

Roger Evans

INTRODUCTION

Accident and Emergency clinicians are no strangers to litigation. They are faced, often in understaffed and cramped departments, with patients suffering from all human ills from the cradle to the grave. Rather like GPs, they are expected to act as a filter between the public and the more specialised services, and, like GPs, they sometimes fail to admit patients who should be admitted and investigated further. They are also expected to perform a lot of treatment themselves. The law has to be careful not to require of them, in treating condition X, the standard of care expected of clinicians who spend the whole of their lives treating condition X. Some of the mistakes Accident and Emergency clinicians make can be catastrophic and very expensive – notably in the treatment of head injury and of chest pain.

It is impossible to discuss every medico-legally significant error which might occur in an Emergency Department (ED). This chapter outlines only those mistakes which occur most commonly and/or which result in the most serious sequelae.

FRACTURES: GENERAL

Basics

A fracture is defined as a broken bone, but there are many different types of fracture. Some are amenable to treatment, with the patient making a good recovery. Others will inevitably cause persistent pain and/or disability, even if diagnosis is prompt and treatment expeditious.

Some fractures require no treatment whatsoever other than pain relief, (e.g. a single, uncomplicated rib fracture), whilst others need complex open reduction and internal fixation (ORIF), with plates, screws, nails, etc; (eg a displaced and comminuted fracture of the shaft of the femur).

Techniques for imaging an injury and then correcting the damage are constantly and rapidly evolving. A fracture which today is diagnosable and treatable with relatively good results, may well not have been a few years ago.

Normally, when a fracture is diagnosed in an ED, the treatment, if simple (i.e. just immobilising the damaged bone in a plaster cast for a few weeks), is initiated in the ED. The patient is then followed up by the orthopaedic surgeons in a fracture clinic. It is then the surgeons' responsibility to see the healing process through.

Where a fracture needs ORIF, the patient is handed over immediately to the duty orthopaedic team, who admit and operate on them over the course of the next three or four days, stabilising the fracture with metal work before releasing them, to be followed up under outpatient supervision.

It is inappropriate for doctors trained in emergency medicine to look after significant fractures in the long term.

The diagnosis of fractures

When attempting to diagnose a fracture, the history is crucial.

Where an otherwise healthy patient has sustained a minor injury, such as inadvertently banging their thigh against the edge of a table, it is extremely unlikely that they have fractured their femur.

If however someone has come off a motorcycle, travelling at about 50 mph and has been stopped abruptly by a stone wall, the chances of bony damage are high.

When taking a history, the doctor must ensure that it is accurate and that it identifies the mechanism of injury and the extent of the forces involved. The damaged part of the body must be precisely identified, e.g. that the foot rather than the ankle is injured.

If the patient's history suggests the possibility of bony damage, careful examination must be undertaken, seeking the cardinal sign of a fracture - bony tenderness. Another feature which is diagnostic of a fracture is deformity. Where, for instance, the forearm is bowed at the midpoint between the wrist and elbow, a fracture is almost certainly present.

Fractures must be distinguished from sprains/strains, i.e. damage to the soft tissues supporting joints, such as the ligaments around the wrist or ankle.

Both fractures and sprains can cause swelling and bruising at the site of the injury, and hence these signs cannot be used to differentiate between a fracture and soft tissue damage. Inability to move an arm or bear weight on an injured limb, may again indicate either a fracture or a soft tissue injury.

Relevant positive and negative findings must be recorded, in order to justify the decision whether or not to X-ray.

Guidelines have been developed to help the ED doctor make a measured judgement as to whether or not X-rays are necessary for certain types of injuries, e.g. the Ottawa ankle rules.

The use of guidelines of this type helps to reduce the number of unnecessary X-rays taken, whilst ensuring that, where a fracture is present, radiographs are obtained.

Where X-rays are requested, it is important that at least two views of the injured part are obtained, as it is common for a fracture not to be apparent on a single view. Normally the two views taken are an antero-posterior (AP, i.e. a view from the front) and a lateral (a view from the side).

Why are fractures missed?

Fractures are missed for many reasons, but the three main ones are:

(i) Having obtained a proper history and examined the patient correctly, a decision is taken that it is very unlikely that the patient has a fracture and no X-rays are requested.

(ii) X-rays are misinterpreted. Physical signs suggestive of a fracture are identified and X-rays are obtained but when these films are reviewed, no bony injury is found. The patient is mistakenly reassured that they have only sustained ligament damage. Sometimes, for various reasons, fractures are not demonstrated on the initial X-rays. Occasionally the fracture is apparent but only to the highly trained eye and therefore the failure to identify the abnormality is forgivable where a junior doctor is involved. Unfortunately, on some occasions a fracture is quite obviously present and as the films have not been carefully inspected the injury is missed, the ED doctor being blameworthy.

(iii) The X-ray films are inadequate. X-ray films are like photographs: to get the best results the exposure must be perfect and all of the area under suspicion must be on the X-ray plate. If the film is under or over exposed or if part of the structure under suspicion is not visualised or is rotated, relying on such radiographs to exclude a fracture is unacceptable. In this situation the patient should be sent back to the radiology department for further views.

Reducing the risk of mis-reading x-rays

In order to minimise the risk of ED doctors misreading X-rays, two procedures have been initiated.

The so-called red dot system

The radiographer, (the technician who takes the X-ray and who is usually experienced in picking up abnormalities), scans the films as a quality control measure and, if the film does not appear entirely normal, marks the film in some way, e.g. with a red dot. This alerts the ED doctor to the fact that something unusual has been identified.

Subsequent review by the radiologists

After the x-rays are taken, the patient returns to the ED with his films and these are inspected by a member of the medical staff.

Having made his interpretation, the ED doctor will initiate treatment prior to releasing the patient. The X-rays are then returned to the radiology department, where at some time within the next twenty-four hours they will be reviewed by a radiologist, who will produce a definitive report. If this report is positive, (i.e. it identifies a significant abnormality), it is then returned to the ED, where a member of the clerical staff will link the report with the patient's ED record card

These two documents are then inspected by a senior member of the medical staff who will identify any discrepancy. If a subsequent review indicates that an x-ray abnormality has been missed, the patient would normally be contacted by telephone or first class post in order to arrange to review them and give any necessary treatment.

COMMONLY MISSED FRACTURES

Scaphoid

The scaphoid is one of eight small bones which make up the wrist. They are arranged in two rows. The scaphoid is the largest in the proximal row. Due to the frequency with which scaphoid fractures are missed, and the size of the subsequent settlements, it has been called the most expensive bone in the human body.

Classically the scaphoid is fractured in young men between the ages of 15 and 25, the cause being a hyperextension injury, e.g. a fall onto an outstretched hand. The patient complains of pain in the wrist, characteristically on the thumb side of the joint.

Where the scaphoid is fractured, the following physical signs are usually detectable.

(i) Some infilling of the "anatomical snuffbox" or scaphoid fossa on the injured side, when compared with the uninjured wrist.
(ii) Tenderness on deep palpation within the anatomical snuffbox.
(iii) Discomfort on telescoping the first metacarpal.
(iv) Tenderness over the scaphoid tubercle.
(v) Pain on wrist movement, particularly extension and ulnar deviation.

Where a scaphoid fracture is suspected, special X-ray views are requested, in order to give the best possible chance of detecting an injury. Scaphoid fractures have a baleful reputation for being missed on the initial films taken shortly after the injury, so good X-ray views are essential.

Where the radiographs are apparently normal, but physical signs are found which suggest that an occult fracture is present, the usual treatment would be to support the wrist and ask the patient to return in ten to fourteen days for further examination and re -X-ray.

If on the follow up visit physical signs suggestive of a scaphoid fracture are still present, then more scaphoid views are taken because by then the repair process will have started and any fracture which was present but which was not visible on the first films, will usually be identifiable.

If at this stage the patient still has clinical evidence of a scaphoid fracture, but again no bony damage is seen on the X-rays, an occult bony injury to the scaphoid is excluded, either by isotope or MRI scanning.

If a scaphoid fracture is missed, it is common for the fracture to fail to unite. This means that it goes on to non-union. Subsequently, due to damage to the blood supply to part of the bone, the portion of the scaphoid which has been deprived of blood undergoes what is known as avascular necrosis, i.e. the bone dies and crumples up - a problem which precipitates severe arthritis in the joint. The patient may well end up with an almost useless wrist. It should be noted that non-union and avascular necrosis can occur in a scaphoid fracture which has been promptly diagnosed and immobilised.

Cervical spine

Injuries to the cervical spine commonly occur at its lower portion, i.e. between the sixth and seventh cervical vertebrae or, sometimes, between the seventh cervical vertebra and the first thoracic or dorsal vertebra.

Injuries in the cervical region are commonly missed, because although X-rays are requested, the films do not include the whole of the cervical spine, i.e. from the first cervical vertebra at the base of the skull, to the junction between the cervical and dorsal vertebrae.

The potential problems that occur if an unstable cervical spine injury is missed are discussed below.

Dorso-lumbar spine

Elderly people, particularly females, sometimes suffer from a condition known as osteoporosis, in which there is a thinning/weakening of bone.

Such bones fracture more easily than the normally mineralised bones of younger people and the solid, square bodies of vertebrae in the lower dorsal and lumbar regions can sometimes compress, producing wedge or crush fractures after minimal trauma, e.g. slipping off a sofa and landing on one's bottom on a carpeted floor.

Usually these fractures do not cause any significant problems other than back pain. Spinal cord damage is not a feature of this type of injury and treatment is just with a period of bed rest, followed by mobilisation under analgesia.

Pelvis and hips

Hip fractures or, more correctly, fractures of the neck of the femur, are common in the elderly and are usually easily diagnosable. The patient complains of pain in the injured hip, they are unable to bear weight on that limb, and the leg is sometimes shortened and turned outwards (externally rotated).

X-rays demonstrate the fracture without difficulty in the vast majority of cases.

Occasionally however, the two fractured ends of the bone, particularly in the area just beneath the head of the femur, are driven firmly together by the force of the fall. The fracture is then said to be impacted.

Such patients, whilst they complain of pain in the hip, can often weight bear, though with a limp. Even when X-rays are obtained, the fracture is easily missed.

Some of these fractures go on to heal normally and the patients may never be aware that they have sustained a significant injury.

Unfortunately, in others, the fracture disimpacts suddenly whilst the patient is weight bearing, the fracture immediately becoming apparent. Surgery is necessary.

Tibial plateau

The tibia or shin bone has a flat top or plateau, which articulates with the lower end of the femur.

Following a heavy blow to the lateral (outer) side of the knee, the lateral portion of the plateau may be fractured and forced downwards (depressed).

As a result of this injury the knee swells due to bleeding into the joint, (a haemarthrosis) and the patient has great difficulty weight bearing. Even if X-rays are taken, the depression of the lateral part of the plateau is often missed and no immediate treatment is offered.

Treatment consists of the elevation of the depressed fragments and their fixation. The object is to restore the integrity of the joint surface and minimise the arthritic change which is likely to develop due to the disruption of the articular surface.

Elevation of the depressed fragment has to take place within ten days or so of the injury occurring if there is to be any hope of a significant improvement.

Facial bones

Fractures to the facial bones are common in contact sports and following assaults. The cheek bones are thin and light and built to withstand vertical stresses (i.e. those inflicted by chewing), but not direct blows.

The bones of the cheek and orbital region are the ones most often damaged. Normal assessment of these injuries would include careful inspection of the facial features, in order to detect such things as depression of one of the cheek bones, the face being asymmetrical when inspected from the front, the side or from above. Gentle palpation of the bony prominences might reveal depressions in the form of so-called "step deformities", or bony tenderness suggesting an underlying fracture. Sensation over the cheek should also be checked, as damage to the floor of the orbit can result in injury to the nerve supply to the face.

The eyes should be carefully examined to ensure no damage has been sustained to the globes and to check that the patient retains a full range of extra-ocular movement.

Because facial tissues swell rapidly following injury, it can be difficult to identify bony damage on clinical examination alone and therefore, when such damage is suspected, it is important to request X-rays. Because there are many intersecting lines on radiographs of facial bones, minor facial fractures can be difficult to identify.

Normal management of a depressed facial fracture involves early operation and elevation of the fracture. Where the orbital floor/walls have been damaged, they must be repaired.

The longer the fractured fragments are left in their abnormal position, the more difficult is the repair, as the healing process advances and the bones become fixed out of position.

If the soft tissues of the cheek are very swollen, the surgeon may delay the operative repair for a few days until the swelling has diminished.

DISLOCATIONS

Basics

A joint is where two different bones meet and move, one upon another, i.e. they articulate.

There are dozens of joints in the human body, some of which allow very little movement, whilst others permit a wide range, e.g. the gleno-humeral or shoulder joint.

A dislocation is said to occur when the articular surfaces of the two bones become completely separated.

The most commonly dislocated joints are those in the fingers. If this injury is recognised early following its occurrence, the dislocation can be easily reduced.

Where a dislocation at any joint is unrecognised, reduction of the dislocation gets progressively more difficult. After a week or two, if reduction is necessary, it has to be an open procedure, i.e. an incision has to be made into the structures around the joint and the dislocation reduced under direct vision.

Dislocation of the shoulder

The shoulder joint is the most commonly dislocated large joint. Diagnosis should be straightforward.

There are two joints in the region of the shoulder; the uppermost is the acromio-clavicular (AC) joint, which is formed by the outer end of the clavicle articulating with the acromion process of the scapula.

This joint is bound firmly in place by strong ligaments and does not normally permit much in the way of movement, though a heavy fall onto the point of the shoulder may result in a subluxation, i.e. a partial dislocation.

Immediately beneath the AC joint lies the gleno-humeral (GH) joint, which is formed where the rounded head of the humerus articulates with the shallow, glenoid fossa of the scapula.

The GH joint is free moving and has a large range of polyaxial movement, as a consequence of which it is relatively unstable.

The head of the humerus articulates with the shallow glenoid, which is deepened by having a rim of cartilage (the labrum) running around its edge. This is attached to the joint capsule, which together with the muscles in the area stabilises the joint.

The head of the humerus may be displaced or dislocated from the glenoid fossa, most commonly anteriorly, coming to lie in front of and beneath the glenoid.

When the head of the humerus dislocates, the supporting joint capsule is inevitably torn, part of the glenoid labrum may become detached, and there may even be a fracture to the rim of the glenoid, the tuberosity of the humerus, or the humeral neck.

Diagnosis of a shoulder dislocation is made by obtaining a history of significant trauma to the joint and subsequently examining the patient. The patient should be stripped to the waist for the initial inspection.

The patient is usually found to be supporting the damaged upper limb with the uninjured arm and when viewed from the front, the normal rounded contour of the shoulder on the affected side, is seen to be rather "squared off".

The patient is unwilling or unable to move the arm at the shoulder. There may be a patch of numbness over the "regimental badge" area on the lateral aspect of the shoulder over the deltoid muscle. This is due to damage to the axillary or circumflex nerve. This damage may also result in weakness/paralysis of the deltoid.

Normally the diagnosis would be confirmed by obtaining an X-ray of the shoulder from two different angles - an AP or antero-posterior and an axillary view, taken upwards through the arm pit.

Where the diagnosis is confirmed, then the dislocation may be reduced by one of several methods, under analgesic/anaesthetic cover.

Following a clinically successful reduction, it is appropriate to assess again the integrity of the axillary/circumflex nerve and confirm that the head of the humerus is back in the glenoid fossa, by taking a post-reduction film.

If damage to the capsule/glenoid labrum has been severe, then the patient may well go on to dislocate recurrently. This means that the shoulder dislocates with only minor trauma. This problem has to be dealt with surgically.

Whilst the vast majority of dislocations occur anteriorly, it is also possible for the head of the humerus to be pushed backwards out of the glenoid fossa and to lie almost directly behind that structure.

Posterior dislocations are traditionally seen in epileptics or patients who have had an electric shock which has caused muscle spasm. They account for no more than 5% of all shoulder dislocations.

A posterior dislocation is more difficult to diagnose clinically, and on an AP film the humeral head may appear to still be in place. It is therefore important that two views are obtained, as the posterior dislocation will be obvious on the axillary view.

Where a closed reduction is attempted within a day or two of the dislocation having occurred, it is usually a straightforward procedure. If however the dislocation is missed, then within two weeks or so at the most a closed reduction is no longer possible.

Dislocation at Lisfranc's joint

In the foot there is a series of joints between the tarsus, i.e. the seven bones that make up the lower part of the ankle and the metatarsals, the five bones that provide the skeleton for the sole of the foot.

This dislocation is an unusual injury but it is one that is often missed and is therefore of interest from a medico-legal point of view.

This type of injury occurs when someone stumbles, for instance putting only part of the foot on a kerbstone and applying differential pressures along the foot.

The whole of the midfoot then moves on the hindfoot and the joint subluxates, i.e. it partially dislocates.

The patient presents with a very painful, swollen foot. X-rays taken at the time are frequently passed as being normal because the subtle abnormalities produced by the movement of the metatarsals on the tarsus and the associated small, flake fractures in the region are missed, even by experienced observers.

Where there has been a good deal of movement of the midfoot on the hindfoot, the subluxation needs to be reduced. Reduction becomes more difficult or even impossible if there is a delay in diagnosis.

Unfortunately, even after early reduction of such a subluxation/dislocation, the patient is often left with significant ongoing symptomatology.

Dislocation at the scapho-lunate joint

A fractured scaphoid bone sometimes becomes dislocated and slips out of the joint that it makes with the lunate, another of the carpal bones.

This injury again is not a common one but as with scaphoid fractures, it seems to be missed regularly.

The AP view of the wrist often appears deceptively normal, but on the lateral view, the scaphoid can be seen no longer sitting in the concavity of the crescent-moon shaped lunate.

Again, prompt reduction is the treatment of choice. Even after expeditious treatment the patient is rarely asymptomatic.

SPINAL INJURIES

Basics

The spine is a structure made up of individual vertebrae, held together by stout ligaments that allow the structure to be flexible and yet stable, so that when the person bends there is no slippage of one vertebral body upon another, which might compromise the spinal cord, which runs within the spinal canal.

If damage occurs to the bony vertebrae and/or to the ligaments, this stability may be compromised: minor movements, such as flexing the neck to allow the chin to touch the chest, can result in abnormal movement of one vertebra upon another, with the sudden impingement of a hard, bony surface against the soft spinal cord, with resultant damage to the cord.

Injuries to the spine may be divided into two types:

- Stable
- Unstable

Stable injuries mean that, whilst there may be damage to part of a vertebra, the stability of the spine as a whole is not imperilled and therefore inadvertent movements of the neck/back will not damage the spinal cord.

Where the injury to the spine is severe enough to render it unstable, if the casualty is not protected by having the spine immobilised in a stiff collar or on a spinal board, any movement of the spine can result in the slippage forward of one vertebra upon another, with the bone of the vertebra crushing the cord.

Damage to the spinal cord is irreversible. Where one has a patient who has an unstable spinal injury but no abnormal neurology, failure to immobilize the spine in a hard collar, on a spinal board, or careless handling by doctors, nurses or ambulancemen, may transform the patient into a quadriplegic. Where a spinal injury has been sustained, one should assume that it is unstable until the contrary is proved. Extremely careful handling is mandatory. Unnecessary movements must be avoided. The spine having been immobilised, the patient is transferred into the emergency vehicle, and transported to the nearest ED. There the patient is moved gently into a resuscitation area.

Immobilisation is maintained until satisfactory cervical spine X-rays have been obtained, which either confirm or exclude a fracture/dislocation to the cervical spine. If the spine is found to be stable, the patient can be log-rolled, fully examined and a decision made as to whether further X-rays are necessary.

Cauda Equina Syndrome

The spinal cord, as it runs down the canal in the vertebrae, gives off pairs of nerves at regular intervals. These run down the limbs and around the torso.

In the lower back, these nerves form a leash, the so-called "horse's tail" or cauda equina.

If an intervertebral disc prolapses centrally in the lower part of the lumbar region, it presses upon these nerves, thus compressing them and interfering with their function.

The patient initially complains of back pain, which often radiates into both legs, because when the disc prolapses centrally, it not only compresses the cauda equina but also presses on nerve roots exiting on both the right and left sides, thus producing bilateral radicular leg pain (sciatica).

As a consequence of cauda equina compression, the patient also suffers with sphincter problems. These manifest initially with alteration of bladder function and painless retention of urine. When the anal sphincter is tested by examination of the rectum, tone is reduced and the patient is unable to tighten the sphincter musculature around the intruding finger. There is also a reduced ability to appreciate sensation in the perineal or saddle area.

Such patients need urgent investigation and treatment, as nervous tissue withstands compression badly and if the pressure on the nerves is not relieved swiftly, permanent problems will result.

SLIPPED UPPER FEMORAL EPIPHYSIS

Children's limbs lengthen at the growing points or epiphyses which are situated close to the ends of the long bones.

The epiphysis is a cartilaginous plate which lies between two sections of bone and is potentially a weak point. It may move or slip if subjected to excessive stress.

The bone in which this slippage characteristically occurs is the femur or thigh bone. The epiphysis involved is the one at the upper end of the bone - the so-called capital epiphysis.

Typically boys are more affected than girls. The left hip is affected more commonly than the right, and the slippage seems to occur most frequently between the ages of twelve and sixteen.

The classical presentation is of a rather fat boy in early adolescence, who begins to limp without having injured himself in any way. The complaint is of pain in the hip, radiating into the groin and down into the knee. It is well recognised that a patient may have a slipped epiphysis at the hip but present initially with pain only at the knee.

Where one is presented with a limping child in the 12-16 age group, proper examination on a trolley is essential, even if the patient only complains of pain at the knee. Such an examination involves the patient being undressed. The examiner must, before excluding a slipped epiphysis, be certain that the patient has a full range of pain free movement both at the hip and the knee.

If a slipped epiphysis is suspected, the patient needs the hips X-rayed. The abnormality will show up more easily on the so-called "frogs' leg view". Management consists of immediate referral to a paediatric orthopaedic surgeon, where one is available, so that the slippage may be stabilised.

HEAD INJURIES

Basics

The majority of patients who attend at EDs throughout the country with head injuries have only suffered minor damage. They can usually be discharged quite quickly, having been examined and perhaps X-rayed.

The two questions that have to be answered in relation to a head injured patient in the ED are:

Does the patient need to be x-rayed?

This would be done in order to identify a skull fracture. The skull fracture in itself is not necessarily that important but it is an indicator that complications are more likely to develop.

Does the patient need to be admitted?

Head injured patients are admitted because occasionally they develop a blood clot between the skull and the brain, which compresses and damages the brain.

When a patient sustains a head injury, the brain is often contused (bruised). This is *primary* brain damage. Generally speaking there is no surgical treatment available, to correct this.

A head injured patient is admitted to enable monitoring – the main purpose of which is to ensure that, if a clot is developing, it is detected early, thus preventing the occurrence of *secondary* brain damage.

Hospitals have various systems, but patients who have sustained ostensibly minor head injuries and are being admitted for observation commonly come under the care of the orthopaedic or general surgeons, though occasionally they are looked after by ED Consultants.

If a clot develops, it may be an extradural or subdural haematoma, depending upon its exact relationship to the dura, (one of the membranes surrounding and protecting the brain). Patients who are felt to be at even a slight risk of developing this complication are admitted and observed, for periods of between twelve and twenty-four hours.

The observations are usually performed hourly or half-hourly and record, on a neurological observation chart, such things as the patient's level of consciousness, his heart rate, blood pressure and the size and reaction of the pupils to light.

If there is deterioration in these parameters, it may be an indication that a haematoma is developing and the patient therefore needs urgent investigation and treatment. The deterioration occurs because brain function is adversely affected by a rise in intra-cranial pressure.

The investigation of choice would be CT scanning, which delineates the site and extent of the haematoma. The treatment is a craniotomy, i.e. opening the skull, draining the haematoma and stopping the bleeding. This procedure needs to be undertaken as quickly as possible, since the brain is an exceedingly delicate structure which tolerates compression and hypoxia very badly. Unfortunately neurosurgical units tend to be situated at larger centres and the vast majority of hospitals throughout the country will not have a neurosurgeon on site. This means that the patient often has to be transferred urgently, rather than being dealt with at the hospital which initially received him.

Transferring head injured patients is not merely a matter of putting them into the back of an ambulance and rushing them over as quickly as possible. The patients have to be intubated and ventilated, intravenous lines secured, monitoring equipment set up and appropriate staff released from other duties to accompany them, e.g. an anaesthetist. This whole procedure takes some time to arrange and it is unusual to be able to get it done in under an hour at best.

Conversely if the patient's condition remains stable after a reasonable period of observation and no abnormal neurological signs have developed, the patient is usually discharged to the care of their general practitioner.

Skull factures

Base of skull fractures

The skull is made up of several bones, (e.g. frontal, parietal, occipital, *etc.*), and may be divided into two parts:

- The base, which is the floor of the skull on which the brain sits. It has a large hole posteriorly - the foramen magnum - through which the spinal cord leaves the intra-cranial cavity.
- The vault, which is the concave oval portion of the skull. It covers the brain, forming the forehead, top of the head, etc.

The base of the skull is formed by bones which make up the roof of the orbit and nasal passages. Further back it contains the mechanism of the inner ear. The brain rests within the skull, surrounded and cushioned by cerebro-spinal fluid (CSF).

The following signs suggest a base of skull fracture.

(i) Rhinorrhoea, (leakage of CSF from the nose);
(ii) Otorrhoea (leakage of CSF from the ears);
(iii) Black eyes with no evidence of the patient having sustained a blow to the face;
(iv) Bruising behind the ear, (the so-called "Battle's sign") in the region of the mastoid process.

The CSF which is leaking out may be clear, blood-stained or may have a yellowish tinge, from coming into contact with wax from the ear.

Such fractures are usually impossible to pick up on skull X-rays, but where they are suspected the patient is treated with prophylactic antibiotics.

Depressed skull fractures

Depressed skull fractures are classically caused by blunt instruments. Instead of the usual linear fracture, bone is crushed, fragmented and pushed down into the intra-cranial cavity.

Depressed fractures are often more difficult to identify on skull X-rays than the usual fracture line that one expects to see following a head injury. They are often associated with a wound in the area and hence are by definition compound.

If a depressed fracture is not spotted, unless debridement has been meticulous, suturing of the wound can result in the development of an infection which has access to the intra-cranial cavity. A brain abscess or meningitis could follow. Such fractures also have a higher incidence of post-traumatic epilepsy than do linear bony injuries.

The normal management of a depressed skull fracture would be thorough debridement and elevation under general anaesthetic.

WOUNDS

Normal management of wounds in the EU

Any wound (even a surgical one) which breaches the integrity of the skin can get infected.

In traumatically inflicted wounds the reported infection rate varies between 1 and 31%, (depending on wound characteristics, wound site etc). This is despite proper treatment.

Where a foreign body (FB) is left within a wound, it is either:

- radio-opaque, i.e. it shows up on X-rays - for instance stone, metal or glass; or
- radio-lucent, i.e. it does not show up on X-rays - for instance wood or plastic.

Radio-opaque foreign bodies can usually be identified by X-raying the injured area.

Radio-lucent FBs can usually be demonstrated via ultrasound. Alternatively they may be found by careful exploration of the wound.

Initially, all wounds need to be cleaned and any dirt, grit or other foreign bodies removed. The extent of the cleaning depends upon the severity of the contamination. A relatively clean superficial wound would normally be treated with thorough cleaning using sterile normal saline or a mild antiseptic, whilst a deeper, heavily contaminated wound might require extensive debridement under general anaesthetic, with removal of not only any dirt/foreign bodies but also devitalised tissue.

If a foreign body is left in the tissues, (particularly an organic one such as a piece of wood), the usual result is a wound infection. The infection occurs because the FB acts as a focus for bacterial infection. Though a course of an antibiotic usually allows the infection to settle, it commonly recurs. This pattern of recurring wound infection despite otherwise adequate treatment, suggests strongly that there is an FB still within the tissues.

It cannot be said, however, that infection of a traumatically inflicted wound definitely indicates that the wound was inadequately cleaned. If, on subsequent exploration of the wound, dirt/grit/foreign bodies are identified and removed and the wound then heals, this does indicate that the injury was not properly cleaned.

If fine dust and grit are allowed to remain in a wound, the resulting scar is often blue or black in colour and much more obvious. This effect is known as tattooing.

Injuries caused by broken glass

Injuries caused by broken glass may be a problem if fragments of the glass remain stuck within the wound.

As glass is radio-opaque, (i.e. it shows up on X-rays), X-rays are normally requested.

Most X-rays requested from an ED are taken to confirm or refute a tentative diagnosis of a fracture. For such purposes the radiographer will take the standard two views: an AP and a lateral, and will use the exposure best suited to identifying bony damage.

If this standard procedure is followed when a doctor is searching for radio-opaque foreign bodies, it is quite possible that they will be missed, as a fragment of radio-opaque glass may overlie a radio-opaque bone and hence be obscured. Whilst AP and lateral views *may* show up the glass fragment, it is also quite possible that they will not.

Where the radiographer knows that glass is being sought in the soft tissues, the exposure will be changed. Also, extra views such as obliques will often be taken, in an attempt to catch the fragment "on the sky-line". The radiographer should also mark the site of the wound with a metallic arrow, so that the doctors who later review the films are aware of the point of entry of the foreign body.

Where glass foreign bodies are identified, it has to be decided whether or not to remove them. In certain circumstances it may be best to leave a tiny fragment in situ, as removing it might cause more problems than it is worth. Usually, however, most reasonably sized fragments are removed, particularly where they are in the hands or feet. A decision to leave the fragments should only be made after full discussion of the problem with the patient.

Severed nerves and tendons

Lacerations to the wrists/hands and feet/ankles caused by sharp objects are common. It is always possible that vital structures such as nerves or tendons, which lie very superficially beneath the skin in these areas, might have been damaged.

When such a patient presents, it should always be presumed that this complication has occurred, until meticulous examination has failed to reveal any abnormalities.

First, finger/toe movements should be checked, to ensure that the full range of movement is present. Next, sensation in the area beyond the wound should be checked to ensure that it is intact. The patient should be asked if his appreciation of sensation in the injured hand/foot is the same as in the uninjured one. Finally, having infiltrated the area with local anaesthetic, the wound edges should be drawn apart, bleeding stopped, and the depth of the wound assessed. Whilst this is being done, any exposed nerves/tendons may be directly inspected.

It is appropriate at this point to ask the patient to move his fingers/toes (i.e. flex and extend them) slowly. This will allow exposed tendons in the area to move beneath the examiner's gaze and any damage, such as a partial rupture, may be spotted.

If nerve or tendon damage is identified, the patient should be immediately referred to the local hand service so that the damage can be repaired primarily, i.e. within 12-24 hours or so. The results of primary repair tend to be better than those of a delayed or secondary repair.

It may be difficult to identify sensory loss over the twenty-four to forty-eight hours immediately following transection of a branch of a sensory nerve, in that if the cut ends are still closely opposed, some transmission seems to occur, so that the patient may tell the examining doctor that he is aware of a stimulus such as a pin prick, even though the nerve has been completely divided and sensation will disappear completely within a day or two.

If a flexor tendon or major nerve has been divided, even primary repair is unlikely to leave the patient with function as good as that prior to the accident.

CHEST PAIN

There are many causes of chest pain. Three of the most important are described below.

Ischaemic heart disease (IHD)

This means that the muscle of the heart - the myocardium - is not receiving as much blood, and hence oxygen and nutrients, as it needs to function normally. This occurs when the arteries which supply blood to the myocardium are narrowed by a fatty substance deposited in their walls (atheroma).

There are two types of ischaemic heart disease:

- The chronic form, stable angina pectoris, and
- The acute coronary syndrome.

These are considered in turn.

Stable angina pectoris

If a coronary artery is narrowed, the supply of blood (and hence oxygen and nutrients) to the area of myocardium served by this vessel is reduced.

Patients with ischaemic heart disease are unable to undertake tasks that require them to exert themselves without suffering chest pain (angina).When the patient is at rest, the work rate of the heart is low and the heart muscle can receive enough blood to function adequately, even though its supplying artery is narrowed. When the patient starts to exert himself, the heart has to work harder to pump blood around the muscles of the body, and hence the myocardium itself demands a greater blood/oxygen flow. Because the artery is narrowed, this necessary increase cannot be achieved. The heart muscle is now short of oxygen (hypoxic) but has to continue working, though under protest. This protest becomes manifest to the patient as chest pain.

Characteristically the pain is described as being a heavy/tight/crushing pain, which originates behind the sternum (retrosternal) and which may radiate into one or both shoulders, down the arms, (most commonly the left), or through to the back. Alternatively, the pain may radiate up into the neck, jaw and teeth.

Where angina is brought on by exertion, the pain can be relieved by stopping the activity and resting. Normally angina of effort settles within four to five minutes of the patient ceasing the activity which precipitated the pain.

The most common treatment used to relieve the pain of angina is Glyceryl Trinitrate (GTN) in tablet form. These are administered sublingually, i.e. they are allowed to dissolve beneath the tongue.

The pain of angina normally passes off within two or three minutes of the patient stopping and taking a GTN tablet.

The hypoxia causing effort angina is not sufficiently severe or long lasting to result in the death of myocardial cells.

The acute coronary syndrome

If angina occurs at rest it is viewed more seriously and the terms unstable or pre-infarction angina are used. Unstable angina is linked with myocardial infarction (MI) as one of the acute coronary syndromes. There are three sub-divisions to this syndrome: unstable angina, non-ST segment elevation MI (NSEMI), and MI.

Unstable angina is diagnosed when the normal pattern of a patient's stable angina changes and they develop pain at rest which is unrelieved by GTN.

In unstable angina myocardial necrosis does not occur, but patients have an increased risk of developing an MI over the course of the next three to four weeks.

When a diagnosis of unstable angina is made, the patient is admitted for intensive treatment and monitoring, as the condition may deteriorate and result in an MI or a serious arrhythmia (an abnormal rhythm of the heart). If the arrhythmia is a sinister one such as ventricular tachycardia or ventricular fibrillation, this will eventually lead to a cardiac arrest and death.

An MI occurs when the already narrowed coronary artery suddenly becomes blocked by the formation of a thrombus or blood clot. This completely fills the already stenosed lumen, stopping the flow of blood down the vessel. The portion of myocardium which is supplied by this blocked vessel becomes acutely short of oxygen and nutrients and the patient experiences a heavy retrosternal pain, similar in nature to that experienced during an attack of angina, though usually more severe. Radiation of the pain to the shoulders, neck, etc., is commonly described too. This pain presages the death of a portion of heart muscle, i.e. there is an infarct of some of the myocardium.

When an MI has occurred, the patient often collapses with severe chest pain and may become cold and sweaty, with a rapid pulse and reduced blood pressure. This is not an invariable picture: some patients who are having a heart attack walk into an ED.

Diagnosis is based primarily on a history of cardiac type pain, usually in a patient who has risk factors for ischaemic heart disease, such as hypertension, diabetes, heavy smoking, hypercholesterolaemia, etc.

The diagnosis may be confirmed by finding characteristic changes on a series of ECG traces or by identifying a rise in the level of certain chemical constituents (cardiac enzymes/markers) found in the blood, which indicate that there has been damage to the myocardium, e.g. creatine kinase, troponins, etc.

Unfortunately, in the early hours following an infarct, the ECG may be entirely normal, and it takes six to eight hours before the level of cardiac markers in the blood rises significantly. As the initial ECG may be normal, it is common practice to retain the patient for four or six hours and repeat the cardiogram on one or two occasions, as the changes observed where an infarct has occurred are usually diagnostic.

Up to 10% of people who turn out to have suffered an acute myocardial infarction, i.e. they have elevated cardiac enzymes, do not develop changes typical of infarction on their cardiograms.

Normal management of an acute myocardial infarct involves the administration of strong pain relieving drugs, e.g. morphine/heroin, together with oxygen. An attempt is made to dissolve the clot by the use of thrombolytic drugs such as streptokinase, and the patient is also given aspirin tablets to reduce clot formation. Ideally, thrombolytic drugs should be given as soon as possible in an attempt to preserve cardiac muscle. The usual target is a "door-to-needle" time of 30 minutes and/or a call to needle time of 60 minutes. This means that thrombolytic drugs should be administered within 60 minutes of the ambulance service receiving a 999 call, or within 30 minutes of the patient arriving in an ED.

Thrombolysis, however, is not entirely free of risk. It can result in the patient suffering a stroke which might well be fatal. Substances such as streptokinase and tissue plasminogen activator (TPA) are contra-indicated where the patient has a condition such as an active peptic ulcer.

A more recently developed method of treating MI's, is via a metal stent. This is a device which is inserted into the narrowed section of the coronary artery, dilates it and holds it open, thus restoring the blood supply to the endangered area of myocardium.

In NSEMI the patient does have myocardial necrosis, as identified by a rise in the level of sensitive cardiac markers in the blood, (e.g. troponins) but they do not develop the classical, progressive, ECG changes of ST segment elevation and pathological Q waves. Such a patient is sometimes said to have sustained minimal myocardial damage.

Deep vein thrombosis (DVT) and pulmonary embolus (PE)

Though these two conditions may exist separately, they are discussed together because usually a pulmonary embolus is secondary to the development of a deep vein thrombosis.

A deep vein thrombosis is a blood clot in veins deep within the patient's calf or calves. These clots form, when for certain reasons, including a congenital pre-disposition, the blood flowing through the deep veins spontaneously coagulates.

Conditions which favour clot formation include a period of immobilisation in bed or in a plaster cast, especially following surgery; a change in hormonal balance such as occurs in pregnancy or with the use of "the pill"; and obesity. Though the clot originates in the calf, it can propagate upwards, blocking off veins in the thigh and pelvis.

The patient typically complains of an aching pain in the limb associated with swelling. The calf may well be tender on palpation.

The main problem in making the diagnosis is that up to 50% of patients who have a DVT in the calf are symptom free.

The diagnosis may be made by venography, (i.e. injecting a radio-opaque dye into a vein in the foot) or, where the clot has extended above the knee, by Doppler ultrasound scanning.

Treatment of DVT is with anticoagulants such as warfarin. Failure to treat can result in two significant complications:

- The clot can damage the venous system of the lower limb, causing chronic problems with venous drainage, including varicosities, ulceration, eczema and persistent swelling.
- A large piece of clot in the veins of the thigh/pelvis may become detached and float up the inferior vena cava into the right side of the heart and on into the pulmonary artery, blocking part of that vessel.

This passage of the clot into the lungs results in what is known as a pulmonary thrombo-embolus (PE).

PE can present in a wide variety of ways depending upon the size of the embolus. Recurrent small emboli occurring over months/years can result in pulmonary hypertension and right sided heart failure, whilst at the other extreme, a large embolus which blocks off 40-50% of the pulmonary artery can result in sudden death.

The usual history with moderately sized pulmonary emboli is one of a series of collapses, with the patient complaining of chest pain associated with breathlessness.

The condition may be difficult to diagnose. A chest X-ray and ECG - the main non-invasive tests for chest pain undertaken in an A & E Department – are often normal. Approximately 85% of patients who suffer a PE complain of chest pain and shortness of breath, whilst 30% also cough up blood (haemoptysis) and in 15% of patients there is a history of syncope (fainting). On examination, the respiratory rate is almost invariably raised and there is often a tachycardia. If the embolus is large, the patient may be cyanosed and a check of the oxygen saturation will reveal that it is reduced.

The definitive investigations undertaken following admission are lung scanning using a radio-active gas, or a spiral CT scan of the chest.

Dissecting aneurysm of the thoracic aorta

The major vessel originating from the left side of the heart is the aorta. This large artery has three coats; the intima, media and adventitia.

The middle coat or media may, under certain conditions, become weakened. Due to the high pressures to which the aorta is permanently subjected, a split can occur in the intima. This defect allows blood to track between the intima and media thus "dissecting" the vessel and effectively producing two channels, down which blood flows from the left ventricle.

As the dissection progresses, blockage of certain vessels, such as those to the brain or the arm, often occurs. Eventually the aorta ruptures and death ensues.

Characteristically the patient is said to present with "tearing" central chest pain. This may be associated with features suggestive of a stroke if one of the arteries conveying blood to the brain is blocked. One of the upper limbs may become ischaemic if blood flow down that limb is impeded. A chest X-ray usually shows some widening of the mediastinum, (the area above the heart), but the ECG may well be normal.

The definitive diagnosis can be achieved by scanning the patient's chest. The appropriate treatment is usually surgical repair of the defect. This is a major surgical procedure and survival is far from guaranteed.

ABDOMINAL PAIN

In the writer's experience the commonly misdiagnosed causes of abdominal pain are as follows:

Acute appendicitis

The appendix is a vestigial portion of the gastro-intestinal tract (GIT). It lies low down in the abdomen, on the right side. It is a blind-ended tubular structure, which serves no useful function. If its entrance is blocked it can become infected and inflamed. If this problem is not adequately dealt with, the appendix may perforate, resulting in soiling of the abdominal cavity and the development of peritonitis.

Classically the patient with acute appendicitis is a young adult who becomes unwell with a complaint of discomfort/pain in the middle of the abdomen. This may be associated with a mild fever, anorexia, nausea and perhaps a couple of episodes of diarrhoea, followed by constipation. This sequence of events may extend over twelve to twenty-four hours or several days but eventually the pain moves to lie in the right iliac fossa, i.e. low down in the right side of the abdomen, over the appendix.

The severity of the pain increases and on examination the patient may be flushed, unwell and have a tachycardia, a mild fever and bad breath.

When the abdomen is palpated, the patient usually complains of significant tenderness in the right iliac fossa and tends to "guard the area" by reflexly tensing the anterior abdominal wall musculature in order to prevent pressure being applied over the inflamed appendix.

There are as yet no diagnostic tests which can definitely diagnose appendicitis. The patient usually has an elevated white blood cell count, but this is non-specific, (i.e. it can occur in appendicitis but could equally be related to an infection in another part of the body, e.g. the kidneys).

Whilst the presentation described above is a classical one, it probably occurs in no more than 50% of patients. Other signs and symptoms can be present and may confuse. For instance, the symptoms of appendicitis are often misdiagnosed as being caused by a urinary tract infection (UTI), as on routine urine testing there may be abnormal constituents in the sample, such as protein and white cells.

The normal management of an acutely inflamed appendix is its prompt removal. Generally speaking, the longer this is delayed, the greater the morbidity and mortality.

Peptic ulceration

Highly corrosive digestive juices are produced in the stomach, small intestine and pancreas, which help to break down food into small particles. The food particles are then absorbed through the wall of the gut and pass into the blood stream for distribution throughout the body.

The wall of the gut is protected against the corrosive action of these juices, but occasionally this protective mechanism breaks down and it becomes eroded or ulcerated. Normally such ulcers are found either in the stomach or the part of the duodenum immediately adjacent to it. These peptic ulcers give rise to abdominal pain, which can be persistent and may wake the patient at night.

If untreated, the corrosive fluid can erode either into a blood vessel running along the base of the ulcer, or occasionally right through the gut wall, perforating it. When an artery or vein is exposed by the ulceration and the arterial wall damaged, bleeding can occur. The blood pressure can fall, and the patient will classically feel ill, look sweaty, and vomit up blood, (haematemesis). Sometimes, if the blood has lain in the stomach for a period of time, it becomes partly digested and the vomitus looks like coffee grounds. If the blood is not all vomited up, it passes through the digestive tract in the normal way and is passed as black tarry motions known as melaena.

Where the ulcer erodes completely through the gut wall, leakage of gastric contents into the peritoneal cavity results in the patient collapsing with acute, severe abdominal pain. Such patients are frequently brought in by ambulance, with a low blood pressure and a rapid pulse, looking extremely ill.

When the abdomen is examined, characteristically the abdominal wall musculature is tensed - a phenomenon known as guarding. Patients who have perforated a peptic ulcer occasionally complain of shoulder tip pain. This is caused by acid gastric contents irritating the diaphragm. Pain is referred to the shoulder, because the two areas share a common nerve supply.

An important investigation in these circumstances is an erect chest X-ray. This often shows the presence of free air in the abdominal cavity, which when the patient is standing accumulates beneath the diaphragm.

Management is normally a laparotomy with repair of the perforation and lavage (washing out) of the peritoneal cavity. The patient is started on antibiotics and anti-ulcer drugs.

The longer the diagnosis is delayed, the poorer is the prognosis. Delay allows a more widespread dissemination of infection and the patient often develops a septicaemia.

Pelvic inflammatory disease

PID is a problem which is limited to females. It implies infection and inflammation of the internal genitalia (uterus, Fallopian tubes and ovaries).

The infection may be caused by a variety of organisms, including bacteria such as *Neisseria gonorrhoeae*, Mycoplasma, or intra-cellular organisms such as *Chlamydia trachomatis*.

The problem is usually sexually transmitted and is most common in adolescents. The patient is usually a sexually active young woman who complains of persistent, lower abdominal pain, associated with menstrual irregularity and an offensive vaginal discharge. There may occasionally be associated urinary tract symptoms such as dysuria (painful micturition).

If PID is left untreated, chronic problems develop which can result in infertility or, sometimes, the formation of a pelvic abscess or adhesions between the bowel and pelvic organs.

Abdominal aortic aneurysm

The aorta leaves the left ventricle and curves downwards to run along the back of the chest cavity. It passes through the diaphragm and then lies on the back of the abdominal cavity running close to the lumbar spine. As it proceeds downwards it gives off arteries to supply the kidneys, intestines, liver, etc. before dividing into the iliac arteries, one of which runs into each leg. In the area between the renal arteries and the bifurcation into the iliac vessels, the abdominal artery can dilate, forming a swelling or aneurysm.

Such aneurysms are usually asymptomatic unless a leak develops. If the leak is a torrential one, the patient rapidly exsanguinates into the abdominal cavity and dies. Where the leak is a minor one, the patient will complain of acute abdominal pain, which is often recorded as radiating through into the back.

On examination the patient may be guarding but if he/she is not, it is sometimes possible to feel the pulsatile swelling, i.e. the aneurysm, if the patient is slim.

A plain X-ray of the abdomen sometimes demonstrates the aneurysm due to calcification in its wall but the dilatation of the vessel can also be demonstrated neatly with an ultrasound scan.

Treatment is surgical: the weakened, dilated portion of the aneurysm is excised and replaced with a graft.

Torsion of the testicle

Though not an intra-abdominal organ, the testicle, when it torts, can sometimes present with abdominal pain and hence is included in this section.

As the testicles lie within the scrotum, they are supported by a structure known as the spermatic cord, down which runs the testicular artery.

Normally the spermatic cord does not allow any significant twisting movements of the testicle but in some men there appears to be weakness of the supporting structures. Occasionally this can allow the testicle to twist or tort, to the extent that the blood flow down the artery is closed off.

This condition, a torsion of the testicle, will, if unrelieved result in necrosis of the organ within six hours or so.

The usual presentation is in a young adult or adolescent, presenting with sudden onset of severe pain in the affected testicle. Occasionally the initial complaint may be of lower abdominal pain which radiates into the groin and outer part of the thigh.

When the patient is examined, the testis is characteristically swollen and riding high in the scrotum.

Urgent treatment is necessary to untort the affected testicle. Once the blood supply has been restored, the testicle is fixed in position. Where one testicle has torted, it is usually worthwhile also fixing the other one, as the congenital predisposition to torsion is usually bilateral.

Torsion occurs most commonly in very young babies, adolescents and young adults. It is rare over the age of twenty-five.

The condition which is most commonly mis-diagnosed in a patient with a torsion, is epididymitis. This is an infection of the epididymis, a structure which is situated close to the testicle.

Epididymitis is sometimes related to a venereal disease such as gonorrhoea. It most usually afflicts men between the ages of 15-30. They classically present with pain which has come on gradually over twenty-four hours and which may be associated with a urethral discharge or signs and symptoms of a urinary tract infection.

The only imaging procedure which is worth contemplating in order to confirm the diagnosis of a testicular torsion is colour Doppler sonography. It must be borne in mind, however, that waiting for this investigation to be undertaken may be counter-productive. There is a small window of opportunity for saving a twisted testicle.

Epididymitis should also be distinguishable from torsion or a testicular tumour by the fact that in epididymitis, acute-phase proteins such as C-reactive protein (CRP), should be significantly elevated. CRP levels should not be raised in torsion or tumour.

When a boy or young man presents with a history of sudden testicular pain, it should be expeditiously treated as a torsion until proven otherwise.

MISCELLANEOUS CONDITIONS

Peripheral vascular disease

Peripheral vascular disease (PVD) implies that arteries to the lower limbs are narrowed, thus preventing the flow of sufficient quantities of blood to the feet.

The major artery to the leg, the femoral artery, emerges from the abdomen in the groin and runs down the thigh, giving off smaller arteries en route. As it runs behind the knee, its name changes and it becomes the popliteal artery. This splits into two in the calf, emerging at the ankle as the posterior tibial and the dorsalis pedis arteries.

If the femoral artery gradually narrows, the patient often begins to complain of what is known as intermittent claudication. This is a cramp-like pain, usually in the calf, which comes on whilst the patient is walking. It gradually increases in severity, eventually forcing the patient to stop. After a period of rest, the pain disappears but will return if the patient starts walking again.

If however, the blood flow is occluded abruptly by a blood clot, the patient suddenly becomes aware of severe pain in the leg. The portion of the leg beyond where the clot has lodged becomes white, because no blood is flowing into. It often feels numb.

The chronic form of peripheral vascular disease is usually treated initially with drugs (of varying efficacy). If it becomes too severe, surgery to by-pass the narrowed portion of the artery may be necessary.

Where a significantly sized embolus has suddenly lodged in a lower limb artery, the artery has to be opened and the clot sucked out to restore blood flow down the leg. If this is not done quickly, the area of tissue which is robbed of its blood supply becomes gangrenous and an amputation may be necessary.

Sub-arachnoid haemorrhage (SAH)

The carotid arteries which run up the neck to supply blood to the brain subdivide once they have entered the skull and form a network of vessels to oxygenate and nourish the cerebrum. The walls of these vessels occasionally develop an aneurysm or berry-like bulge on the artery. This is a weak point.

If one of these aneurysms springs a leak, bleeding occurs beneath the arachnoid membrane which surrounds the brain and produces what is known as a sub-arachnoid haemorrhage. Where the leak is a catastrophic one, the patient may collapse and die within a matter of hours. More minor leaks are survivable.

The condition is more common amongst women (the female: male ratio is 3:2) and as with other cerebro-vascular accidents (CVAs) is predisposed to by hypertension (high blood pressure).

The characteristic presentation is of a middle-aged woman who complains of a severe headache of sudden onset. The patient often feels as if they have been struck on the back of the head. The headache may be described as the worst ever experienced. The headache may radiate down into the back of the neck and become associated with neck stiffness/rigidity. The patient may also start to complain of photophobia (an aversion to bright lights).

There is sometimes a transient loss of consciousness, during which the patient may fit. When consciousness is recovered, the patient complains of a blinding headache which is persistent. The leak which causes these symptoms is usually a small one and is sometimes referred to as a sentinel or herald bleed.

Whilst this leakage of blood is survivable, it is recognised as a warning sign. A significant percentage of patients go on to suffer a more major bleed within the next ten to fourteen days, often with catastrophic results. Sentinel bleeds occur in between 15-39% of patients who subsequently have a more major SAH.

Where the diagnosis is suspected, it can be confirmed or refuted by CT scanning. In some cases it may also be necessary to undertake a lumbar puncture (LP). If an SAH has occurred there will be blood in the CSF. The precise site of the bleeding aneurysm can be identified by carotid angiography (injecting a radio-opaque dye into the carotid artery and then X-raying the patient's head).

Initial management is conservative, with the use of the calcium channel blocker nimodipine. When the patient is stabilised, further investigation can proceed. When the aneurysm has been located, treatment is by inserting an intra-luminal coil into the bulge, thus thrombosing it, or alternatively by clipping the neck of the aneurysm.

There is no doubt that rupture of a berry aneurysm carries a poor prognosis: 28% of patients in whom this occurs die within forty-eight hours. Those who survive this first bleed continue to be at risk of a further deterioration. 45% of all patients who rupture a berry aneurysm die within thirty days: a major cause of death is re-bleeding. Even if the SAH is treated, there is a 25% mortality and a 50% disability rate. 66% of post-surgical patients fail to regain their pre-operative quality of life. Complications include re-bleeding, hydrocephalus and epilepsy.

Whilst CT scanning within twenty-four hours of the event should detect some 95% of bleeds, if there is a delay of three days or so following the bleed, up to 25% of haemorrhages may be missed on CT.

The British Society of Neurological Surgeons emphasises the importance of considering a lumbar puncture if the CT scan is negative, where the history and physical signs are highly suggestive of a bleed.

Meningitis

Meningitis, or perhaps more accurately acute meningo-encephalitis, is an acute, generalised viral or bacterial infection of the nervous system.

Clinically and pathologically there is almost always some degree of encephalitis, (inflammation of the brain), in acute meningitis, and some degree of meningitis (inflammation of the meninges) in acute encephalitis.

The common bacteria causing meningitis include *Neisseria meningitidis*, *Streptococcus pneumoniae* and *Haemophilus influenzae*. These bacteria usually gain access to the intra-cranial cavity via the blood stream from the nasal passages but direct spread can occasionally occur - for instance from infected sinuses.

Bacterial meningitis is pre-eminently a disease of babies and infants. It also occurs in young adults, often as a small "epidemic" in colleges and schools.

The patient presents feeling generally unwell and complaining of a headache, nausea/vomiting and drowsiness. The progression of symptoms can be frighteningly rapid. In extreme cases death occurs within 12 hours of the patient first complaining of feeling unwell.

Associated physical signs include neck stiffness, photophobia, drowsiness and a reduced Glasgow Coma Score (GCS). Meningeal irritation may result in a positive Kernig's and/or Brudzinski's sign. Where the patient has an associated significant septicaemia, as sometimes occurs in meningococcal meningitis, there may also be a florid, purpuric rash.

The major problem in diagnosing and treating meningitis at an early stage is the non-specificity of the symptoms and signs. Thousands of infants/children/young adults present with lethargy, irritability, fever, a mild headache and other cold/'flu like symptoms each day: perhaps one or two will have meningitis. Apart from a fever, there is often little in the way of abnormal physical signs. Diagnosis can be particularly problematic in neonates and young children. The diagnosis is confirmed by lumbar puncture and where there is a septicaemia, by blood culture.

Where the disease is suspected, and particularly if one is dealing with meningococcal meningitis/septicaemia, it is better to start treatment on a suspicion that the patient has the disease, rather than waiting for confirmation.

Unfortunately it is impossible to admit and observe all these patients. It would certainly be inappropriate to submit them to lumbar punctures, blood cultures etc. and start them on prophylactic antibiotics.

Meningococcal septicaemia

Meningococcal septicaemia is a widely disseminated infection caused when the bacterium *Neisseria meningitidis* gets into the blood stream. This organism is commonly found in the throat and nasal passages of otherwise well people. Problems only arise when it enters the cardio-vascular system.

The condition is a fulminating one which can kill a previously healthy patient within twelve hours of onset. It is not common. For instance, in 1998 there were only 2580 notifications of *Neisseria meningitidis* infections in the whole of the U.K.

Meningococcal infections usually involve the central nervous system, giving rise to meningococcal meningitis, but in some 20% of patients there is no central nervous system involvement.

Early diagnosis is difficult but important, as the disease progresses rapidly. It is a diagnosis which must be excluded when faced with a febrile/unwell patient.

Most cases occur in young children, who feel non-specifically ill. They complain of lethargy, irritability and fever. The classical sign of this condition is a purpuric, (i.e. non-blanching rash), in a child who is feverish and unwell.

Present opinion is that the catastrophic deterioration in the patient's condition with hypotension, multiple organ failure, vascular/coagulation problems, etc. is due to an abnormal reaction by the patient's own immune system. This causes huge quantities of proteins, known as cytokines, to be released into the bloodstream and the patient is overwhelmed.

The diagnostic investigation for this disease is a blood culture. Treatment, however, must be started urgently, before the results of the blood culture are available. Where there is a reasonable suspicion of meningococcal disease, the immediate treatment to be administered by the GP or ED doctor, would be the injection of 1,200 mg of Benzylpenicillin for an adult, and 600 mg for a child below the age of 10.

Even with prompt diagnosis and treatment, a significant percentage of patients will still die or be left with residual problems.

ORTHOPAEDICS

Stephen Norris

INTRODUCTION

The term "orthopaedic" comes from a Greek root and refers to the curing or correction of deformities in children. It has come to be associated with all treatment for afflictions of the musculo-skeletal system. Orthopaedic surgeons are responsible for the management of patients from birth to the grave. There is a huge diversity of work performed by orthopaedic surgeons in the United Kingdom.

In general terms orthopaedic surgeons are responsible for the management of bone and soft tissue injury and for the management of orthopaedic disease both acute and chronic.

Many clinical negligence claims are directed against orthopaedic surgeons. This is because in general patients submit themselves for orthopaedic surgery for painful and disabling conditions but not with life threatening conditions. Patients may succumb to the effects of multiple trauma but cases of multiple trauma occur only very infrequently. Similarly the number of patients who present with potentially life threatening malignant disease is also very low. Many people however, suffer from relatively minor non-life threatening injuries and the expectation of a return to normal function is very high. Similarly patients presenting with non fatal painful conditions of their joints expect to be able to return to all the activities they pursued before the condition developed. Unfortunately return to normal function cannot always be guaranteed and this often provokes a feeling of dissatisfaction.

Amongst all UK Independent sector surgical claims settled over the last 13 years, approximately 21% have related to orthopaedic procedures, and a similar proportion to obstetrics/gynaecology and plastic/reconstructive surgery respectively.

Approximately 16% of the orthopaedic claims result from spinal surgery. An almost equal number result from lower limb surgery. A further 13% (not counted in the lower limb figure) relate to total hip replacement.

In general terms there are three main areas in orthopaedic surgery which provoke claims for clinical negligence. These relate to errors of diagnosis, errors of treatment, and errors relating to consent. In general, trauma surgery and elective (non-trauma) surgery should be regarded as separate specialties.

TRAUMA

General

Patients suffering from trauma generally present initially to accident and emergency departments. For their initial assessment they are seen not by orthopaedic surgeons but by specialists in accident and emergency medicine. They are referred secondarily for orthopaedic care. The initial examination, assessment and diagnosis at the outset are therefore out of the control of the orthopaedic team.

Fractures

Errors of diagnosis

In most cases the diagnosis of a fracture is simple and straightforward. Patients typically present with a history of trauma and they complain of pain. Clinical examination reveals swelling of the part. There may or may not be a deformity, and clinical examination demonstrates local bony tenderness. There may be crepitus (a grating sensation) on movement of the limb. It is often relatively straight forward for the accident and emergency doctor to isolate the area of potential fracture and to arrange for the appropriate x-ray. In many cases, however, the diagnosis is less clear. The clinical signs of fracture may be equivocal and the x-rays may be difficult to read.

Unfortunately doctors in accident and emergency departments tend to be inexperienced. They have often not been qualified very long and they have very little clinical experience upon which to rely. Accident and emergency doctors need to understand the limitations of their own experience. The corner stones of good treatment and diagnosis are the taking and recording of an adequate history, and an appropriate and well recorded clinical examination.

The history should include a description of the events causing the injury and an analysis of whether the injury was high or low velocity. The examination should record the appearance of the limb, the presence or absence of swelling and deformity, and the presence or absence of local point bony tenderness. The doctor should also adequately examine and record whether the neurological function of the limb is intact and if the limb has adequate blood supply. The doctor should also record the x-ray appearances. If there is any doubt in the mind of the accident and emergency officer about the diagnosis, a further opinion should be sought, either from his supervisor, from a radiologist or from an appropriately qualified orthopaedic surgeon.

A typical example of an injury which may be difficult to diagnose is a fracture of the scaphoid bone.

Scaphoid fractures

The scaphoid is a small bone in the wrist. It lies at the base of the thumb and articulates proximally with the radius and distally with two other carpal bones, the trapezium and the trapezoid. It is frequently injured and has a relatively poor blood supply, particularly to the part adjacent to the radius.

Fractures of the scaphoid usually occur as a result of a fall on the outstretched hand. The fall may often be thought of by the patient as a very minor injury and the pain caused by the fall may be ignored. Many patients with fractured scaphoids do not present for several months.

When examined, patients with scaphoid fractures typically have tenderness in the area known as the anatomical snuff box which lies on the radial side of the wrist. The anatomical snuff box is bounded by the tendons which radiate towards the thumb. Tenderness in the anatomical snuff box is highly suggestive of a fractured scaphoid. Tenderness over the tubercle of the scaphoid situated on the front of the wrist may also be found in cases of scaphoid fracture.

Unfortunately, not all patients with injuries to the scaphoid present with the typical signs. Tenderness may be diffuse and by no means localised. The degree of tenderness may be extremely mild.

This can result in the patient being reassured that they have merely suffered a sprain, and therefore being offered no diagnostic test.

There is a standard series of x-rays to visualise the scaphoid bone. Signs of scaphoid fracture however can be extremely subtle, and fractures may either be missed or thought to exist when in fact the x-ray is normal.

Patients may therefore be under-treated if the fracture is not recognised, or they may be over-treated for a non-existent fracture. Both scenarios have the potential to cause frustration for the patient.

Problems are compounded by the variable natural history of scaphoid fractures. Undisplaced scaphoid fractures will in the majority of cases heal by immobilisation in plaster although immobilisation may in some cases be necessary for up to 12 weeks and occasionally longer. Displaced scaphoid fractures heal with less certainty. Inevitably therefore, some fractures of the scaphoid fail to heal as expected, thus prompting the need for surgical intervention. Surgical intervention usually involves some form of internal fixation together with a bone graft. Even then predicting the eventual outcome can be very difficult. The literature indicates that the outcome for an undisplaced scaphoid fracture is usually satisfactory provided the diagnosis is made within four weeks of the injury. It is not therefore necessary to immobilise every suspected scaphoid fracture in a plaster cast. It is however, important that accident and emergency officers recognise the possibility of a scaphoid fracture even if the x-ray findings are equivocal. There should therefore be an appropriate safety net, and all patients with suspected scaphoid fractures should be asked to return either to an accident and emergency review clinic or to a fracture clinic for clinical assessment and if necessary repeat x-ray. If repeat x-rays remain equivocal, further diagnostic tests should be undertaken in the form of either a radio isotope bone scan, CT, or an MRI scan.

Other fractures

Other fractures which can be difficult to diagnose include those of other wrist bones and the equivalent bones in the ankle. Fractures of the vertebrae are often extremely difficult to diagnose radiologically, particularly by inexperienced practitioners. Odontoid peg fractures of the second cervical vertebra and potentially unstable fractures of the spine not associated with spinal cord injury are frequently under-diagnosed at the outset. If there is any doubt at all about these injuries the involvement of more experienced practitioners is essential. Fractures at the ends of long bones in the epiphyseal and metaphyseal areas can also be difficult to diagnose both clinically and radiologically.

Soft Tissue Injury

Soft tissue injuries include any injuries to parts of the musculo-skeletal system not including bones. They comprise ligament injuries to joints, including dislocations, tendon injuries to the hand and feet, and soft tissue contusions.

Tendon injury

Missed tendon injuries –particularly in the hand - are a fertile source of clinical negligence claims. Flexor tendons can be injured as a result of open wounds, but closed injuries to flexor tendons can also occur in some cases. A typical example occurs amongst rugby players. A player grabs the jersey of an opponent in his clenched fist. His hand is prised away and he suffers a forced extension injury to a flexed digit. This can cause rupture of one of the long flexor tendons where it attaches to the bone. Early treatment for this type of injury will result in near normal function in most cases. If the injury is missed, however, the outcome of treatment is far less certain and residual disability is quite common. Once again the taking and recording of an adequate history, the recording of an adequate examination and a second opinion if necessary are essential if the injury is not to be overlooked.

Open injuries to the flexor tendons are more common. Injuries from knives or glass are the most frequent causes of flexor tendon damage. Unfortunately, flexor tendon injuries often occur late at night and alcohol may be a barrier to clinical assessment. Once again the accident and emergency officer should have the possibility of flexor tendon injury high on his list of diagnostic possibilities.

In some cases, however, injuries to flexor tendons can be incomplete: in other words the tendon is not completely severed. Function at the outset may appear to be relatively normal. This should not lull the doctor into a false sense of security.

A tendon which is lacerated through 80 or 90% of its thickness may eventually give way altogether, making surgical treatment far more complicated. Early referral to the hand specialist is therefore essential if normal function is to be preserved.

Referral to the surgeon does not occur until the patient has been clinically assessed by the accident and emergency doctor. If the injury is missed by the accident and emergency doctor there is not very much that the specialist surgeon can do about it other than advise and treat the patient accordingly. There is, however, a safety net for accident and emergency doctors in that all hospitals with accident and emergency departments have fracture clinics where patients can be seen within a few hours of the injury. In the overwhelming majority of cases if the injury is diagnosed within a relatively short period of time, no harm will follow. If the patient is discharged, then of course the safety net is missed and permanent damage may ensue. The concept of the safety net is therefore very important in minimising the risk of missed diagnosis and neglected care.

Penetrating injuries

Penetrating injuries from glass or other sharp objects are extremely common. There is an ever present risk of damage to deeper structures, (for example tendons and nerves) particularly if the penetrating injury has been to the hand. Patients with such injuries are often seen late at night and patients are often under the influence of alcohol. In the majority of instances glass will be seen on an x-ray as the density of glass is greater than the density of soft tissue. An x-ray should therefore always be taken in cases of glass injury. If there is any doubt at all about the severity of the injury or the diagnosis the patient should be asked to return within 24 hours for further assessment.

Cat and dog bites carry a high risk of infection. The same is true of human bites. These usually occur during fights when the clenched fist is in contact with a tooth resulting in an injury to the knuckle. These injuries require careful surgical treatment with cleaning and appropriate antibiotics.

Errors of management: fractures

Fractures may be either open or closed. An open fracture is a fracture with an associated wound such that the fracture at some time has been exposed to the external environment. The main complication of open fractures is infection. Infection in the early stages may be from gas gangrene or tetanus organisms and in the later stages from other bacteria such as staphylococci.

Patients with open fractures should have their tetanus immunisation checked, and they should immediately receive prophylactic antibiotics. Surgical treatment of open fractures involves the excision of the margins of the wound and wound debridement. All potentially infected and contaminated tissue is removed. The fracture is then reduced and stabilised.

It was once taught that to place internal fixation devices into an open wound was to invite infection. It is now believed that achieving stable fixation of a fracture reduces the risk of infection. The immediate priority however is the management of the wound.

Open fractures are classified by Gustilo into three grades.

(i) Gustilo I: There is a small clean puncture wound through which the bone has penetrated.
(ii) Gustilo II: The wound is more than 1 cm in length but there is no skin flap and not very much soft tissue damage. The fracture is not severely comminuted.
(iii) Gustilo III
  (a) There is extensive soft tissue damage but the bone can be adequately covered with soft tissue.
  (b) The fracture cannot be covered with soft tissue and there is also periosteal stripping and severe comminution of the fracture.
  (c) The above with vascular or neurological damage superimposed.

The higher the Gustilo grade, the greater the amount of energy which has been expended on the limb, and the graver the prognosis. The incidence of complications is far higher in high energy injuries than in low energy injuries. Infection, nerve injury, vascular injury, delayed union, non-union, joint stiffness, leg length inequality, and residual deformity are therefore more likely following Grade III open injuries than following Grade I injuries.

Management of these fractures must be very precise, and it is recommended that they should be managed jointly by orthopaedic and plastic surgeons. Plastic surgical care of the soft tissue by wound dedridement skin grafting and flap coverage converts the fracture into a closed injury and will reduce the risk of infection. Coverage of the wound should be carried out expeditiously and should have been completed ideally within 5 days. The orthopaedic surgeon can therefore deal with the fracture by using the most appropriate method of fixation - be that with a frame, nail or plate.

In general, fractures can be managed operatively or non-operatively. Non-operative management of fractures usually involves the application of an external splint of some kind - a plaster, a fibre-glass "plaster" or a splint. Non-operative management is usually reserved either (a) for fractures which are not displaced; or (b) for fractures which are displaced but which can be reduced into an anatomical position or are relatively stable (i.e. they are likely to remain in place once the plaster has been applied). Operative surgery, on the other hand, is used to maintain the reduction of a displaced fracture or to permit an early return to function.

Non-operative management is not free of risk. On the contrary some of the most serious complications of fracture management can arise when surgery is not the treatment of choice.

Compartment syndrome

This is a condition characterised by the presence of pain usually greater than can be explained on the basis of the original injury. The involved part, which might be the arm or leg, becomes swollen and there is often an associated colour change. Initially the affected part becomes either red or blue. There is associated paraesthesiae (altered sensation), and movements become limited. Pain elicited by passively stretching the affected muscles is a very suggestive physical sign.

Compartment syndrome is caused by swelling in the soft tissue envelope in which the muscles are contained. At the outset the swelling is caused by oedema and haematoma caused by the trauma. As the pressure in the muscle envelope rises, venous return is impeded. and this affects the normal oxygenation process of the muscles. The muscles thus become ischaemic, and this further compounds the swelling. Compartment syndrome is an emergency condition. If untreated the ischaemic muscles will die and this may result in virtually irreversible contractures of the digits - so called Volkmann's ischaemic contracture.

Initially the condition is diagnosed clinically. The diagnosis may be confirmed by measurement of the pressures within the compartment. Treatment is by fasciotomy –surgical division of the envelope surrounding the muscles. This alleviates the swelling, restores normal venous return and reverses the ischaemic process. Unfortunately, because of the swelling the fasciotomy wound tends to gape. This can make eventual wound closure difficult to achieve other than by the use of skin grafts. The ultimate cosmetic appearance can be quite poor.

Compartment syndrome can be a complication either of operative or non-operative management of fractures. It may also be a complication of elective surgical procedures. The fact that compartment syndrome occurs is not an indication that the treatment has been less than optimal. The condition should however be diagnosed as early as possible to avoid ischaemic contracture and long term disability.

Reflex sympathetic dystrophy or chronic regional pain syndrome

Reflex sympathetic dystrophy (or Sudek's atrophy as it is sometimes known) may be a complication of operative treatment, but may also be a complication of the injury itself. It may follow fracture or soft tissue injury. It can be a complication of elective orthopaedic surgery. The patient complains of pain. There is often associated swelling and colour disturbance of the limb. Neurological function may also be altered: there may be paraesthesiae. The affected joints become stiff. It is not an immediate complication of trauma but tends to occur during the healing phases. It is a difficult condition to treat. The mainstay of treatment is an early recognition of the condition and physiotherapy. Referral to pain management specialists may be useful.

The condition is often construed by the patient as an indication that the treatment has fallen below a satisfactory standard. Claimants need to be reassured that this is not the case and it is a natural complication of the fracture. Indeed the condition may occur not as a consequence of fracture but as a result of a soft tissue injury. The stimulus to the onset of reflex sympathetic dystrophy is a painful episode - not necessarily a fracture.

Problems of fracture union

The objective of an operation to reduce and internally fix a fracture is to effect adequate fracture reduction (i.e. the bone should be put back into as normal anatomical alignment as can reasonably be achieved), and fixation (so that the fixation will not fail - i.e. the plate and screws will not break and the fracture will unite).

This is often difficult to achieve. For example, displaced fractures of the radius and ulna must be perfectly reduced to permit normal rotational movement of the forearm. Even if anatomical reduction is achieved rotation can sometimes be affected. Cross union can occur between the two bones such that they become effectively welded together preventing normal rotation. Very minor degrees of mal-reduction are normally tolerated but significant degrees of mal-reduction can be a cause of great concern and initiate a clinical negligence claim. The humerus, for example is very tolerant of both shortening and of angular and rotational misalignment due to the wide range of movement of the shoulder which can compensate for these things. The tibia is less tolerant of rotational or angular misalignment or shortening.

The outcome of fracture management can be difficult to predict. Bone is a biological tissue and is subject to its own laws. Fracture healing can be delayed for a number of reasons. Smoking, for instance, influences fracture healing adversely. There may have been significant periosteal stripping of the bone or damage to the vascular supply to the bone. Notwithstanding appropriate fracture management, delayed healing or even non-union can sometimes occur. These must be recognised by the orthopaedic surgeon and dealt with correctly.

Neuro-vascular injury

Per-operative damage to a peripheral nerve during fracture surgery is fortunately an infrequent occurrence. When it occurs, it can be very serious. Damage to the radial nerve during an operation to plate the shaft of the humerus will result in very profound disability for the patient. There will be a lack of wrist extension, thumb extension and abduction and finger extension. Damage may occur to the posterior interosseous nerve during operations to fix fractures of the proximal radius, the median and ulnar nerves can be damaged during surgery on the radius and ulna; and damage can occur to the common peroneal nerve during operations on the knee and proximal fibula. These are just examples.

Nerves can be injured in a variety of ways. They can be stretched or cut. Simple stretching injuries to peripheral nerves are known as neurapraxia. There is temporary cessation of nerve function but eventual recovery is complete. If a nerve is stretched irreversibly or cut there is no chance of spontaneous recovery. Referral to a peripheral nerve specialist is then required. Specialist investigation by means of electro-myography is necessary to help determine the prognosis. Further surgery is almost always necessary with either a direct surgical procedure on the nerve itself, or reconstruction by means of tendon transfers.

ELECTIVE ORTHOPAEDICS

Errors of Diagnosis

The range of elective orthopaedic procedures is enormous. There are now orthopaedic practitioners practising in the sub-specialist areas of paediatric orthopaedic surgery, spinal surgery, rheumatoid arthritis surgery, joint replacement, sports medicine, upper limb surgery, hand surgery, foot and ankle surgery and bone tumours.

Diagnostic dilemmas in orthopaedic surgery are relatively infrequent. The clinical diagnosis is made on the basis of history, clinical examination and special investigations. Special investigations include plain x-rays, CT scans, MRI scans and radio-isotope bone scans. Haematological testing is also important if the patient is suspected of having an inflammatory condition, infection, tumour or metabolic condition.

Developmental Dysplasia of the Hip (Congenital Dislocation)

The incidence of developmental dysplasia of the hip is between 5 and 20 per 1000 live births. There may be a genetic pre-disposition to the condition. Girls are nine times more likely to be affected than boys. 60% of affected children are first born infants. There may be hormonal factors and intra-uterine mal-position: for example breach position with extended legs may favour hip dislocation. The socket of the hip joint may be poorly formed (acetabular dysplasia).

All infants should be tested at birth for hip instability. Unstable hips are further examined by means of an ultra sound test. If the hip is unstable and there is an abnormality on the ultra sound scan the hips are supported in splints with the hips flexed and abducted. Nevertheless, despite adequate screening programmes, some children do present late with congenital dislocation.

The diagnostic tests for instability include Barlow's test, in which the examiner attempts to push the head of the femur posteriorly out of the socket of the hip joint and Ortolani's test - a manoeuvre to reduce a recently dislocated hip. If positive, the examiner feels a clunk as the hip pops back into place. After age 2 this test is no longer useful, as the soft tissues around the hip have started to contract, thus preventing the hip from reducing. Late signs of dislocation include leg length inequality, asymmetrical thigh skin creases and abnormal gait.

The long term implications of a missed or untreated hip dislocation are very serious - leg length inequality and the potential for the early onset of hip arthritis.

Tumours

Benign tumours of the musculo-skeletal system are relatively more common than malignant tumours and seldom cause difficulty of identification or treatment.

Malignant tumours are far less common. An orthopaedic surgeon in general practice might see a malignant tumour perhaps once or twice each year. It is for this reason that the treatment of malignant bone tumours is centralised to specific orthopaedic centres.

Patients with suspected malignant bone tumours need careful diagnostic work up. Plain radiographs, MRI scans, bone scans and CT scans are indicated. Eventually, tissue diagnosis is necessary and this can be performed by means of fine needle aspiration or by an open incision and biopsy. Incisions need to be carefully planned to avoid seeding malignant tissues outside the treatment area. Ideally the complete diagnostic work up should be performed by the surgeon eventually responsible for providing treatment. Surgery should not be contemplated on either benign or malignant bone tumours unless there is a clearly identified radiological abnormality.

It must also be remembered that if bone is removed this may weaken the skeleton and necessitate prophylactic internal fixation to prevent subsequent fracture.

Back Conditions

Chronic neck and back pain is a frequent cause for orthopaedic referral. In the overwhelming majority of patients with neck and back pain the cause is relatively simple to identify and relatively simple to treat. Unexplained pain needs very careful investigation to avoid missing serious pathology.

Occasionally spinal pain can be a manifestation of more sinister pathology such as a tumour. Careful history-taking to identify, for example, night pain, loss of appetite or weight loss is essential. Pathology in the sacroiliac joints (for example tumour or infection) may present in many ways. Patient may present with back pain with or without sciatic radiation, abdominal pain or groin pain.

All patients presenting with back pain should undergo thorough neurological examination to assess whether there is compression of a nerve root. This may be caused by a prolapsed inter-vertebral disc, disc degeneration, infection or tumour.

Prompt recognition of neurological damage is necessary if irreversible damage is not to occur.

The spinal cord terminates at the level of the first lumbar vertebra. Below this level the lumbar and sacral nerve roots are contained within the spinal column as the cauda equina. Damage to the cauda equina can occur as a result of surgery on the lumbar spine, disc prolapse (frequently central), trauma, tumours of the lumbar spine and infection. It is a most serious event which can result in permanent neurological loss, manifested by paralysis, sensory loss and loss of bladder bowel, and sexual function. Patients present with bi-lateral (or, occasionally unilateral) leg pain, motor weakness, altered sensation in the buttocks and perineum, and paralysis of bowel and bladder. Pressure on the cauda equina must be alleviated quickly if permanent loss of neurological function is to be avoided. Careful monitoring of the patient's neurological status is essential so that if the condition does develop, appropriate treatment can be instigated.

Bone and Joint Infection

Primary bone infections (osteomyelitis) usually occur in children. Primary bone infection is very rarely encountered in adults although occasionally chronic infection (Brodie's abscess) is encountered. Infection can complicate the management of fractures.

Sepsis in joints is also usually only encountered in children. In adults, primary joint sepsis is usually caused by an underlying medical condition such as diabetes mellitus or rheumatoid arthritis. The diagnosis is in the majority of cases relatively straight forward as is the treatment. Both bone and joint infection can occur in patients with immunological compromise. Joint infection is common in intra-venous drug users.

Patients with soft tissue infections such as cellulitis frequently find their way into orthopaedic wards. Cellulitis is caused by strains of streptococci. Streptococci are normally sensitive to penicillin and respond quickly to treatment with intravenous antibiotics. There are, however, strains of streptococci which can cause very rapid and fulminating septicaemia resulting in shock and multi-organ failure. Necrotising fasciitis is one example of this. Prompt investigation with full blood count, erythrocyte sedimentation rate (ESR), C-reactive protein, urea and electrolyte estimation to determine the status of the kidneys, and blood cultures are essential. Treatment is by means of intravenous antibiotics. There must be careful monitoring of blood pressure, pulse, respiration rate, and urine output with appropriate fluid replacement and resuscitation if the patient requires it. Help and support may be needed from microbiologists to determine the correct antibiotic regime, anaesthetists if the patient requires intensive care, or physicians if the patient displays signs of organ failure.

Errors of treatment in elective orthopaedics

All surgical procedures can potentially be complicated by infection, respiratory difficulty such as atelectasis, deep vein thrombosis and pulmonary embolism. Patients need to be warned of these risks as part of the consent process.

There are, however, specific complications common to many patients undergoing orthopaedic surgery. These include the complications of diathermy and tourniquet application.

Diathermy

Diathermy is used in surgery to control bleeding. There are various types of diathermy, determined by the type of current used. The main complication is burning caused by poorly insulated diathermy leads. Diathermy can also cause the ignition and explosion of inflammable liquids used during the operation, such as the alcohol used to sterilise the operative field.

Tourniquets

Tourniquets are used widely in orthopaedic surgery to provide a bloodless field. A tourniquet can remain inflated at the correct pressure for as long as two hours, but it is normal not to leave it inflated for longer than this except in exceptional circumstances. If the tourniquet is inflated to the wrong pressure or if it is left in place for too long, ischaemic complications can result. These can include nerve injury and muscle ischaemia resulting in compartment syndrome. The tourniquet equipment requires regular maintenance to ensure that the pressures are correctly calibrated. The use of a tourniquet is contra-indicated in cases of vascular compromise sickle cell disease and other specific indications.

Complications of total joint replacement

Infection

Infection is the great enemy of successful joint replacement. Prophylactic antibiotics, ultra clean air operating theatres and special operating suits can help reduce the risk. Nevertheless some patients develop infection. This can be very serious and even life threatening. All patients undergoing joint replacement should receive antibiotics at the time of induction of anaesthesia and for between 24 and 36 hours post-operatively. Infecting organisms include gram negative staphylococci and, most seriously, antibiotic resistant staphylococci. The proportion of infected joints is less than 1%.

Treatment for infection is by antibiotics and surgery. Revision of the joint replacement is often needed and this can be done in either one or two stages.

Deep vein thrombosis and pulmonary embolism

The incidence of deep vein thrombosis in the veins of the leg below the knee after hip and knee joint replacement is between 40 and 60%. The sequelae of thrombosis in the lower leg are not especially serious, although venous ulceration can occur, rarely, as part of the so-called "post-phlebitic"syndrome. More serious are clots within the veins of the thigh and pelvis which can break off and result in pulmonary embolism.

Chemical prophylaxis to minimise the risk of deep vein thrombosis is widely employed by surgeons in the United Kingdom, but there is no wide-spread agreement about whether chemo-prophylaxis is indicated and which drugs should be used. The incidence of fatal pulmonary embolism is approximately 1%, and this is not affected by prophylactic treatment. Moreover complications can arise from anticoagulation. The most serious is bleeding. There are no national guidelines dealing with this issue. The British Orthopaedic Association, in a pamphlet distributed to members of the Association stated:

> *"There is no good evidence to suggest that the use of chemical prophylaxis reduces either overall mortality or pulmonary embolus. Furthermore in contemporary practice total hip replacement should be regarded as "moderate" risk for death from pulmonary embolism. Chemical prophylaxis may reduce the risk of non-fatal pulmonary embolism but rigorous scientific evidence is not available."*

Adjunctive means of reducing the risk of venous thrombosis include mechanical methods such as anti-thrombotic stockings, and foot pumps to maintain venous blood flow through the legs during surgery.

Leg length inequality

It is very difficult for the surgeon to ensure equal leg length following total hip replacement. The surgeon relies on specialised equipment for the implantation of the joint but there is no fool proof method of ensuring equal leg length at the end of the procedure. A leg length discrepancy of 1 cm is usually well tolerated and does not cause any particular functional problems. Discrepancies of more than 2 cms will, however, cause problems with gait, functional problems and sometimes back pain.

Nerve injury

Damage to the sciatic nerve can occasionally occur during hip surgery. Post-operatively the patient is aware of altered sensation in the leg and of weakness of the ankle and foot. There may be a foot drop. The nerve may be physically damaged. It may, for example, be cut or stretched by the use of retractors. Cement may leak from around the cup and burn the nerve. The nerve may also find itself physically distorted by prominent cement at the back of the hip joint. In many cases, despite careful investigation, it is impossible to identify the cause of the damage.

The prognosis for sciatic nerve injury is variable. Recovery may or may not occur. The patient may be left with permanent foot drop and permanent loss of sensation. This can be very disturbing and necessitate the use of appliances.

The common peroneal nerve winds round the neck of the fibula on the lateral aspect of the knee joint. It is very vulnerable to the effect of traction during knee replacement surgery, and the patient may wake up after the operation with weakness of ankle extension and eversion and sensory disturbance affecting the foot. The prognosis for the injury is similar for the prognosis for sciatic injury following hip replacement. Recovery may or may not occur.

Dislocation

Post operative dislocation occurs in a very small minority of patients following total hip arthroplasty. In the majority of these once the hip has been reduced there is no further problem. Recurrent dislocation can however occur, and this can cause a great deal of difficulty and anxiety both for the patient and for the surgeon. It may result from poor positioning of the components or by using a prosthesis of incorrect size. In many cases of dislocation, however, it is difficult radiologically to identify the cause. Treatment for recurrent dislocation is usually by means of a revision procedure.

Peri –operative fracture

Fracture of the shaft of the femur is a complication of total hip replacement in both primary and revision cases. The femur can fracture as the hip is dislocated to expose the diseased joint, as well as during reaming and at the time of relocation of the joint. It occurs more often in osteo-porotic bone than in normal bone. Fracture of the femoral shaft does not preclude satisfactory joint replacement, but additional steps may be necessary during the surgery to strengthen the bone. Internal fixation and sometimes bone grafting may be required A fracture will almost certainly delay recovery.

The tibial plateau can fracture during knee replacement. This generally happens during preparation of the bone for the stem of the tibial component, although the femoral condyles can also fracture if the bone is osteoporotic - particularly if the patient has rheumatoid arthritis. Fractures should be recognised at the time they occur. If necessary they should be supported with suitable internal fixation.

Arterial injury

The popliteal artery is a direct posterior relation to the knee joint and may be injured during knee replacement. It may be cut during resection of the tibial plateau or as the menisci are removed from the back of the knee joint. Damage to the popliteal artery may not be immediately manifest as the majority of knee replacements are undertaken in a bloodless field using a tourniquet. The pre-operative vascular status of the leg should be known and carefully checked post-operatively. Popliteal artery injury can cause pain and, sometimes, neurological injury. Examination may reveal colour changes in the limb, loss of sensation, weakness in the muscles distally, loss of peripheral pulsation and peripheral vascular failure (manifested by a drop in blood pressure and increase in pulse rate, with poor peripheral perfusion). If recognised peri-operatively, a vascular surgeon should assess the damage and carry out the necessary remedial surgery. If not recognised until after the operation has been finished, the vascular surgeon should give an opinion. Early recognition of the problem is essential if permanent damage is to be avoided.

Compartment syndrome

The physical signs of compartment syndrome are described above. The condition must be diagnosed early and treated by fasciotomy if permanent damage is to be avoided.

Complications of arthroscopy

Most soft tissue and ligament disorders of the knee are managed arthroscopically. Arthroscopy is increasingly common for disorders of the shoulder, elbow, wrist and ankle. The advantages of arthroscopic techniques are that surgery can be performed as a day procedure; the surgery can be performed through very small incisions; post operative recovery is quicker than if open surgery is performed.

Endoscopic procedures, however, are not without risk. Some of the risks are as follows:

Broken instruments

Instruments used in arthroscopic surgery have small cutting ends and are manufactured to fine tolerances. Breakage can occur, and may result in metal being retained within the joint. The surgeon should recognise what has happened and should take active steps to remove any retained fragments

Operations on the wrong joint

The joint should be marked pre-operatively to prevent this from happening.

Infection

The incidence of this is extremely low - probably less than 0.01%. There is no clear indication for the use of prophylactic antibiotics. It is incumbent on the surgeon to recognise the problem and treat it in the most expeditious manner with the appropriate medication and, if necessary by surgery with washing out of the joint.

Nerve injury

This can occur following arthroscopic procedures. The damage can be very severe. The nerves around the elbow seem particularly at risk - especially the ulnar nerve on the medial side. The brachial plexus can be injured during arthroscopic procedures on the shoulder.

Complications of shoulder surgery

The most frequently encountered complication of shoulder operations is damage to the brachial plexus.

The brachial plexus is the group of nerves running from the neck and into the arm. The nerve roots from C5 to T1 form a complicated network between the neck and upper arm. The nerves run into the arm in fairly close proximity to the shoulder joint. Any open operation on the shoulder exposes components of the brachial plexus to potential damage. Patients suffering brachial plexus damage may present with several types of neurological injury, including muscle weakness in the arm, forearm, wrist or hand, and sensory disturbance. The prognosis for such injuries can be poor. Permanent disability can result.

Complications of wrist and hand surgery

Specific risks inherent in wrist and hand surgery include nerve injury, tendon injury and stiffness. In particular, surgery on the fingers often results in stiffness. Nerves can be damaged during hand surgery, resulting in areas of numbness or muscle paralysis. Reflex sympathetic dystrophy is an ever present danger.

Complications of foot surgery

Pain and disability from disorders of the feet is very common. Deformities of the feet, bunions hammer toes and arthritic conditions are often an indication for surgery. Common problems causing anxiety for patients after foot surgery include persistent pain (particularly after operations to correct deformity of the great toe), persistent deformity, the wrong choice of operation to correct deformity, and post operative infection.

Hallux valgus can affect people throughout their lives. The condition often presents in adolescence. The choice of operation depends upon the degree of deformity, the patient's age and the presence of osteo-arthritis. The surgical choices include corrective osteotomy of the 1st metatarsal, fusion of the 1st metatarso-phalangeal joint, or Keller's procedure (which creates a false joint in the region of the 1st metatarso- phalangeal joint). Patient expectation may be greater than the operation can deliver. Management of those expectations is important. With increasing age there can be transfer of weight bearing from the 1st metatarsal onto the lesser metatarsals: this can be compounded by the wrong choice of operation. This must be made clear at the outset.

Osteo-arthritis of the great toe (hallux rigidus) can be treated surgically by fusion of the joint, by excision arthroplasty, or by the insertion of an artificial joint. Less severe pain can be treated by removal of the osteophytic rim from the margins of the joint. This can help to restore movement and delay the need for more radical surgery. Fusion of the joint involves the use of some form of internal fixation such as a screw. In time this may cause problems and need to be removed.

OBTAINING PATIENT CONSENT

Appropriately informed consent is a corner stone of good surgical practice. There are several important elements to the informed consent discussion.

First, the surgeon should explain the condition in easily comprehensible terms. Simple drawings and diagrams can help the patient to understand. Information booklets are helpful. The process should start in the out-patient clinic and should be continued throughout attendances at the pre-assessment unit. Information can be provided both by the surgeon and by trained nursing staff. The majority of information however, particularly relating to the operation should be given by the operating surgeon or by a surgeon trained in the procedure. It should not be left to a junior doctor untrained in the procedure. The patient needs to know why treatment is necessary and what might happen if the treatment is not provided.

Second, the available treatment options should be discussed, together with the risks and benefits of each.

Third, patients need to understand the post-operative regime. They need to know, for example, if they will require the removal of sutures or the application of plaster. They need to know if physiotherapy or occupational therapy might be necessary, and when, if ever, they can expect to return to normal function. They need to understand what functional restrictions might eventually be necessary. The long-term outlook and prognosis needs to be carefully discussed. So does the possibility and nature of future treatment. In relation to the contemplated surgery, patients need to know what might happen if the procedure is less straight forward than hoped.

Fourth, the specific complications of the procedure should be discussed fully, together with the implications of those complications for prognosis.

It is therefore important that the consent process involves careful planning of the procedure by the surgeon. The surgeon should understand what potential pitfalls might be encountered and communicate this understanding to the patient.

ACKNOWLEDGEMENTS

I am grateful to Helen Goodwin, Clinical risk manager at the Medical Defence Union, for her help in identifying areas of specific risk and furnishing me with MDU data.

REFERENCES

Guide to Clinical Negligence: The Legal Process Explained, Medical Defence Union

Managing Orthopaedic Malpractice Risk, American Academy of Orthopaedic Surgeons, 1996

Campbells Operative Orthopaedics, 2003, Mosby, 10th Edition

Rockwood, Green and Wilkins, *Fractures*, 2001, Lippincott Williams and Wilkins, 5th edition

Apley, A and Solomon, L, *Concise System of Orthopaedics and Fractures*, 1994, Butterworth and Heinemann, 2nd edition

The Management of Open Tibial Fractures, British Orthopaedic Association and the British Association of Plastic Surgery, 1997

Tonnis, D, *Congenital Dysplasia and Dislocation of the Hip in Children and Adults*, 1987, Springer Verlag

Total Hip Replacement a Guide to Best Practice, British Orthopaedic Association, 1999

RADIOLOGY

Sarah Burnett

INTRODUCTION

Radiology encompasses all forms of diagnostic imaging, i.e. plain films and fluoroscopy (screening), ultrasound (US), computed tomography (CT), magnetic resonance imaging (MRI), and isotope studies. Some of these tests require additional drugs to be given. In addition treatments may be carried out under imaging guidance (interventional imaging).

It would be impossible to describe all the potential causes of litigation. Radiology covers all anatomical systems. Some important general principles are outlined, together with a few specific conditions which commonly give rise to claims. The chapter does not cover obstetric scanning or the assessment of perinatal hypoxic damage.

Clinical radiological mistakes should be relatively easy to identify and, therefore, quantify, because (with the exception of ultrasound, where most of the images seen by the operator and used at the time for interpretation are not stored) the data are preserved for subsequent analysis. Audits have revealed an error rate of up to 5% in routine reporting of films. The error rate is related to the seniority of the reporting clinician, and studies have shown a vastly reduced error rate when 'double reporting' (i.e. the use of two clinicians) is used. However, few of these errors are clinically relevant: many reflect minor or coincidental findings.

Litigation against radiologists accounted for only 163 of the 8739 claims made through the NHS CNST claim system in 2002. This is less than 2% of the total. Radiology is, however, involved in a much larger number of claims, particularly in the field of trauma and orthopaedics. Unfortunately neither the NHLSA, the defence societies nor the Royal College of Radiologists keep precise records of the nature of the claims, but where the primary claim is against a radiologist claims related to interventional radiology predominate. Many different problems may arise from radiology. They can be classified as follows:

Errors of acquisition:

- Failure to obtain imaging at all
- Failure to image the correct body part or side
- Failure to image using the correct technique

- Failure to repeat the imaging as appropriate

Errors of interpretation:

- Failure to notice an abnormality
- Failure to interpret the abnormality correctly
- Failure to acquire a formal radiological report
- Failure to act on findings in an appropriate and timely fashion

Complications of the technique or procedure:

- Risks of ionizing radiation
- Risks of associated drug administration
- Failure to obtain appropriate consent
- Errors in interventional technique

Finally, radiological expert advice may be required to support or refute allegations of breach of duty. Imaging may, for instance, demonstrate inaccurate placement of an endotracheal tube, or spinal cord damage during surgery.

When instructing a radiologist it is important to have the best quality copy films available. Originals are preferable. One should also check that the radiologist is an expert in the subspecialty area of radiology in which advice is required. Radiologists vary in their desire to review clinical notes other than the request forms and reports, but in complex litigation, particularly if there is a question about who was requesting or who was responsible for acting on the results, the radiologist may need to see the whole bundle.

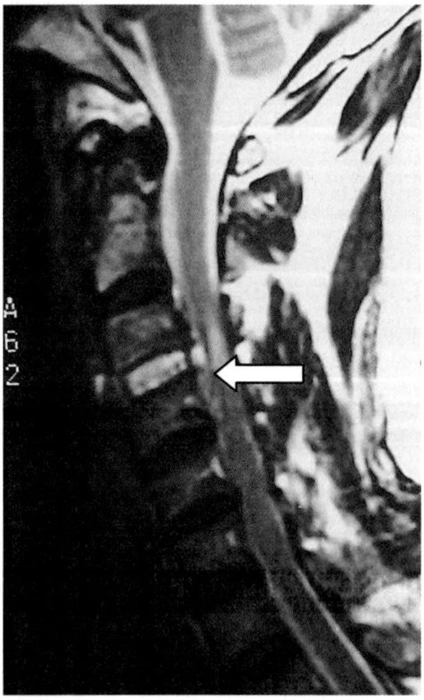

FIGURE 1. SAGITTAL T2 WEIGHTED MRI OF THE CERVICAL SPINE, TWO DAYS FOLLOWING SURGERY – This patient presented with arm pain and was diagnosed on MRI as having a cervical disc protrusion. He underwent surgery the next day. After the operation he developed weakness in both his upper and lower limbs. The image clearly shows an area of spinal cord damage that had not been present on the scan three days beforehand and therefore must have happened during the operation.

IMAGING TECHNIQUES

Plain radiographs (x-rays)

These are the mainstay of radiological imaging and provide a quick and rapid assessment. They are easy to generate and very reproducible, and are thus the starting point of investigation for many patients.

An x-ray beam is generated and passed through the patient. The beam is attenuated by dense structures within the patient, and the remaining beam is used to expose a piece of film to give a 'negative' image. The density of human tissue depends on the atomic number of the molecular components. Thus, for example, bone is dense due to the calcium content. Plain radiographs show the bony anatomy very accurately but do not demonstrate the soft tissues well - except in the lung where fine detail can be seen.

Most trauma and orthopaedic imaging is done using plain radiography. So is the routine assessment of the lungs and thorax. When continuous x-rays are used to assess moving structures or to guide intervention, this is described as fluoroscopy. The radiation dose from plain radiography is relatively low.

Contrast studies

This is where a radio-opaque agent (again with a high atomic number such as barium or iodine) is given enterally or parenterally to improve soft tissue visualisation. The enteral agents do not often produce adverse reactions, but severe adverse reactions can occur due to injectable iodine-containing agents. Severe allergic anaphylaxis may occur, sometimes with a fatal outcome. Although it can be impossible to predict which patients may suffer reactions, those with a history of asthma, or allergies to shellfish or iodine, should be given steroids prior to the procedure to reduce the risk of an allergic response. Severe previous reaction to contrast agents precludes their subsequent administration. All patients should therefore be asked specifically about previous reactions and allergies prior to any injections. In addition, diabetic patients who take metformin may go into renal failure following the administration of iodine-containing contrast agents. It is therefore suggested that metformin is stopped prior to contrast administration, and renal function checked after the procedure.

Ultrasound

No ionizing radiation is used in ultrasound. Instead, sound waves are produced by a piezo-electric probe. These waves pass through the patient and are reflected back at soft tissue interfaces. As the sound beam hits the piezo-electric crystal a small electrical impulse is generated which can then be measured and transformed into an image. Doppler shift analysis of beam frequency allows imaging of vascular structures. The beam is bounced back by air and bone, and therefore there are limitations on what can be seen. Images are selected by screen capture, and hence the value of the investigation is very dependent on which images the operator has chosen to capture. There are no known complications of the procedure itself. The technique can be used for therapy and biopsy.

Retrospective analysis of ultrasound data is extremely difficult. In many NHS institutions it is common practice not to acquire images unless any abnormality has been spotted. Hence there may be no documentary evidence to support a claimant's allegation of missed pathology, or indeed to support a defendant radiologist's denial.

Magnetic Resonance Imaging (MRI)

Again no ionizing radiation is used. Instead a strong magnetic field is combined with radio-frequency waves to produce changes in the oscillation patterns of hydrogen protons within the body. When the radio-frequency waves stop, the protons fall back to their original positions, releasing more radio-frequency waves as they move. These secondary waves are then detected, and highly complex mathematics is used to generate images of both the internal anatomy and the characteristics of the visualised tissue. The spatial resolution is not as good as CT or ultrasound. The images are digitally transferred to film.

The technique itself does not produce any complications, but there are risks associated with the magnetic field. Any ferromagnetic material may be accelerated into the centre of the scanner. Patients with electronic implants such as pacemakers and cochlear implants are unsuitable for scanning, and some heart valves, arterial clips or shrapnel may be pulled free by the magnetic field. At least two deaths have occurred in MRI suites from radiographic carelessness. One occurred when a technician walked into the scanner and scissors flew out of his top pocket, stabbing a patient. Another occurred when a patient was taken into the scanner in a metallic wheelchair. The wheelchair accelerated towards the scanner casing with sufficient force to cause a fatal head injury. Also the changing magnetic fields may produce heat in the target tissues. The real risk from this has not been quantified, but there is a theoretical risk to the unborn fetus and therefore MRI is not recommended in the first thirteen weeks of pregnancy.

Computed Tomography (CT)

This technique uses multiple beams of conventional x-rays in a circumferential pattern to acquire data about the relative densities within the patient. The radiation dose used is therefore much higher than with plain radiographs. A series of axial slices is acquired through the patient. These slices can then be reconstructed to produce imaging in different planes, or even a 3-dimensional reconstruction. The technique gives good soft tissue and spatial resolution. Again the images are transferred to film. CT can be used to guide therapy or biopsies.

Isotope studies

The patient is injected with, or inhales a material which is tagged with radioactive tracers. The tracer is then emitted by the patient and measured by a gamma camera. Although patients are often alarmed by the idea of being injected with radioactive tracers, the radiation dose is about the same as for a small series of plain radiographs. These tests tend to be quantitative and physiological, rather than giving anatomical data, and are very rarely implicated in litigation. However, particularly with bone isotope studies, the test is extremely sensitive. This means that it is likely to pick up irrelevant abnormalities. It is also highly non-specific. This means that it is often impossible to tell what the actual cause of the abnormality is.

WHO REQUESTS THE IMAGING?

In March 2000 the Ionising Radiation (Medical Exposure) Regulations (IRMER) came into force. They govern the requesting of any imaging technique using ionising radiation. The radiographers performing the techniques have to be satisfied that the request is 'justified' - in other words that there is a proper medical reason for taking the x-ray. Request forms must have the correct patient details, and be signed by someone who is allowed to request imaging. This will vary between units, as many hospitals now allow paramedical staff such as physiotherapy and nurse practitioners to request x-rays. However, many radiology departments will have a list of appropriate investigations, and patients may be refused an x-ray if the requesting clinician has provided an inadequate reason to image - such as 'routine' or 'at patient request'. It is imperative under these circumstances that the clinician is informed that the x-ray has not been taken.

WHO REPORTS THE IMAGING?

The IRMER stipulate that all imaging must have a written report. This is best done by a radiologist, who is a trained specialist in imaging, but initial interpretations are often made by Accident and Emergency doctors, orthopaedic surgeons, anaesthetists, and trained nurses and physiotherapists. All films should then be returned to the Imaging department for formal reporting by radiology doctors or by radiographers who have completed a qualification in reporting. Many legally significant errors in radiological interpretation occur when the images are assessed not by the radiologists, but by other clinicians.

A report should include recommendations for further imaging or follow up where necessary. The requesting clinician should follow those recommendations or take responsibility for pursuing a different course of action. Generally a radiologist should attempt to contact the clinician if urgent intervention is required. A classic example is where it has been radiographically demonstrated that there is an incorrectly placed endotracheal tube in an intensive care patient. Urgent replacement is required to avoid a lung collapse. Sometimes the radiologist fails to contact the requesting clinician in a timely fashion. Some general practitioners, for example, have an answering service where a message cannot be left, and do not provide a fax number. Here, the person who has asked for the imaging should make sure that they have seen the report and acted upon it.

A copy of the report should be safely stored within the department. Various things may happen to the films: some may be kept by the patient; some may be kept in the fracture clinic. Most, however, are stored in the x-ray department. Films are often lost, and this can cause problems during litigation. The loss of a film can lead to complete speculation about what may have been present on an original film. When data is acquired digitally, in CT, MRI or stored on a PACS system the original images can always be retrieved, and some post-processing may also be possible to resolve some questions.

ERRORS OF ACQUISITION

It is important that clinicians understand the limitations of any imaging technique and therefore what information they can expect to receive from it. For example, if the doctor wanted to know whether a patient had ruptured a major ligament in the knee, a plain x-ray would not be able to provide this information. The clinician would have to request an MRI scan. The failure of a clinician to know exactly what information can be expected from a test can lead to false reassurance and inadequate subsequent management.

Claims often arise from failure or delay of the primary clinician to request an x-ray. A GP may fail to send a patient with a persistent headache for an MRI scan of the head, so failing to diagnose a tumour which may have been treatable if detected early enough. Or a child with a limp may not be sent for x-rays soon enough to prevent a mild slipped upper femoral epiphysis progressing to an acute severe slip, with disastrous consequences.

From time to time litigation occurs because the area of pathology has not been imaged. The request form may specify the wrong side, or the radiographer can image the wrong side - possibly compounding the error by labelling the film as the correct side. On one occasion both shoulders were x-rayed, and the radiologist thought he had taken the film of each side out of the packet separately. He produced a report saying that both sides were normal. In fact he had taken the left shoulder film out twice, and completely failed to spot the huge tumour in the right clavicle that even the lawyers could spot! The wrong patient name can be put on the film. If the area that needs to be imaged is imprecisely described, the pathology may not be demonstrated on the film. A classic example of this is when the doctor asks for an x-ray of the radial head (elbow end of the main forearm bone), when he actually thinks that the fracture is at the wrist. He should ask instead for the distal radius. A correct report of 'no bony injury' would be given, but the patient may still have a fracture - with potentially long term disability.

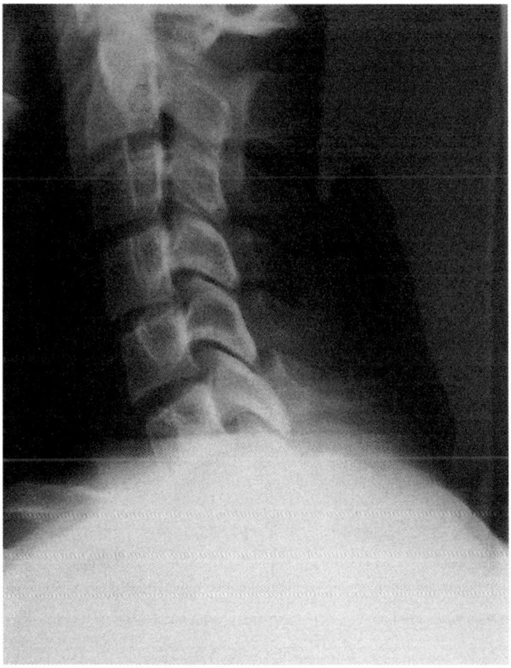

FIGURE 2. LATERAL PLAIN RADIOGRAPH OF THE CERVICAL SPINE – This x-ray of the cervical spine was taken of a patient in Accident and Emergency following a road traffic accident. Only six of the seven cervical vertebrae are demonstrated and no fracture can be seen. The patient was discharged from the department with no treatment.

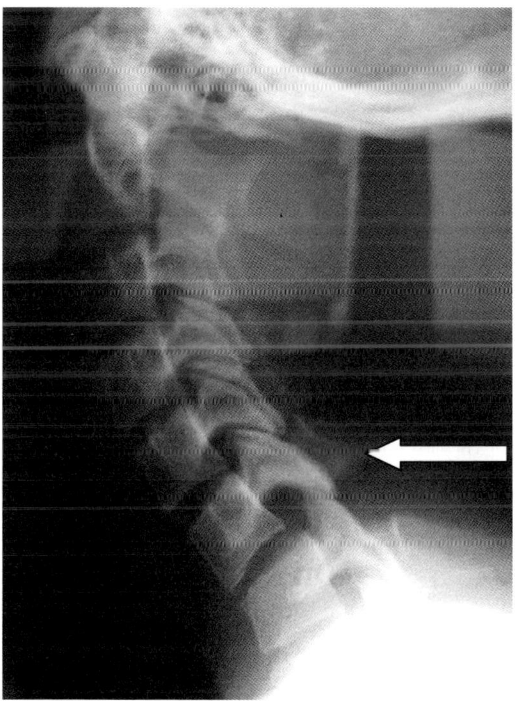

FIGURE 3. REPEAT LATERAL FILM OF THE CERVICAL SPINE WITH THE PATIENT'S SHOULDERS PULLED DOWN. – The subsequent day the patient returned to the department in severe pain and exhibiting generalized neurological symptoms. A further film, showing all of the cervical vertebrae, demonstrated bilateral dislocated and 'perched' facet joints (arrowed). The spinal cord was being compressed at the site of the dislocation.

The radiographer may not image the correct part of the patient, due to misinterpretation of the request form, inappropriate specification of views by the clinician, or inadequate technique. The classic example of this is where the lowest part of the cervical spine has been missed off an x-ray and there is a significant fracture at this level. It is then the responsibility of the person evaluating the films, whether she is an A&E officer or a Consultant Radiologist, to contact the radiographic staff to ensure that the correct views are subsequently taken.

The radiological features of some conditions develop slowly. This may be particularly relevant in brain damage. Both in diffuse axonal injury in the adult and premature neonatal brain disease, it is important for the clinicians to be aware of the need to repeat the imaging to make sure that no pathology is developing, as initial scans may be completely normal. Radiologists should bring this to the attention of the clinicians in their reports by suggesting repeat scans in 24 or 48 hours if there has been no improvement. A similar situation can arise in the irritable or infected childhood hip, where daily ultrasound scans may be required before an effusion develops.

ERRORS OF INTERPRETATION

The person reporting the scan may fail to notice that there is an abnormality on the film. Surprisingly, such missed abnormalities are not always subtle. Examples of this would be failure to notice a lung mass indicative of cancer on a plain x-ray, or failure to notice a fracture. A normal report would be generated, and the clinician then believes that no further management is necessary. In many cases only one reporter will ever see the films, and therefore the report is not questioned until it is too late.

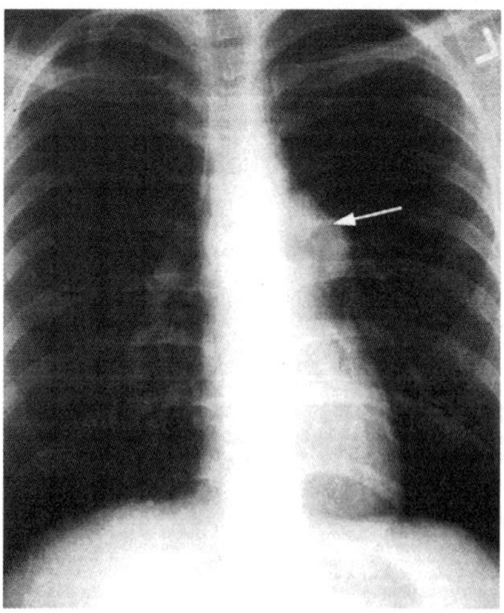

FIGURE 4. POSTEROANTERIOR (PA) CHEST X-RAY – This patient attended for a chest x-ray, having been referred from his GP with weight loss and haemoptysis. The radiologist completely failed to notice the large mass (arrowed) at the upper left hilum. The patient was sent away and reassured, only to return several months later with widespread metastatic disease. The primary bronchial cancer should have been diagnosed on the original film.

The chance of an abnormality being found depends not only on the training and experience of the reporter, but also on reporting conditions. Films should be viewed with high intensity transillumination on a proper viewing box in a room with low ambient light. They should never be held up to a window. An old radiological joke is: 'What do you call a doctor who looks at x-rays up against the window? Answer: The defendant.' Lighting conditions can be suboptimal, particularly in A&E departments, on the ward or in fracture clinics where it may be impossible to achieve low general lighting.

The Royal College of Radiologists recommends that no more than 70 sets of plain films should be assessed in one working session (3.5 hours) because it has been shown that the ability to detect abnormalities drops significantly with time. In some hospitals radiologists are expected to report up to 300 films in a session.

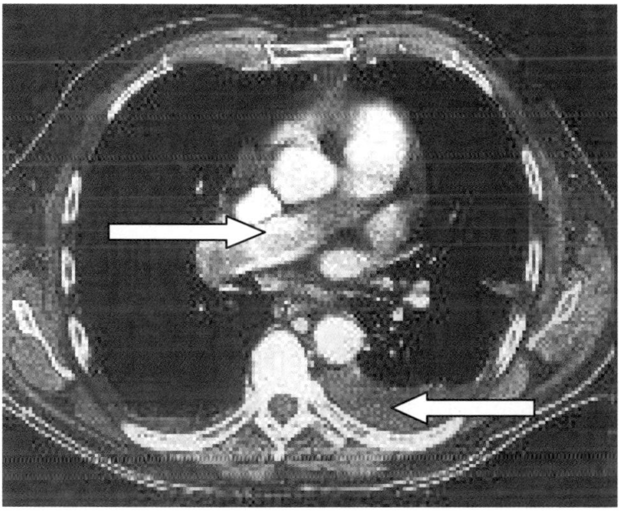

FIGURE 5. CONTRAST ENHANCED THORACIC CT – This patient attended the A&E department, complaining of chest pain and shortness of breath. The A&E officer suspected a pulmonary embolus (PE) and requested a CT scan. CT has now superseded isotope scanning as the most appropriate method of diagnosing PE. At it turned out, the A&E officer's suspicion was correct. The radiologist, however, noticed the left pleural effusion (arrow bottom right) and ascribed the patient's symptoms to this. She completely failed to notice the large clot sitting in the pulmonary trunk. Undiagnosed PE has a mortality rate of at least 50%. The patient died soon after the scan.

The abnormality may be identified, but the significance of the lesion may not be appreciated. For example a malignant tumour may be wrongly misinterpreted as benign and no follow up recommended, where a biopsy or further imaging may be needed. On occasion a normal variant or benign finding may be wrongly described as a significant fracture or malignancy. This then leads to traumatic and unnecessary treatment or surgery - for example a mastectomy being performed for a benign breast mass.

In a case that came to litigation recently a brain MRI revealed the presence of a small lesion in the pituitary gland. This was reported as being a pituitary tumour, and the patient was sent for minimally invasive surgery. It was only as the transphenoidal approach was made that the lesion was actually found to be an aneurysm. Profound bleeding occurred and an interventional radiologist had to be called to embolize the lesion. The patient survived.

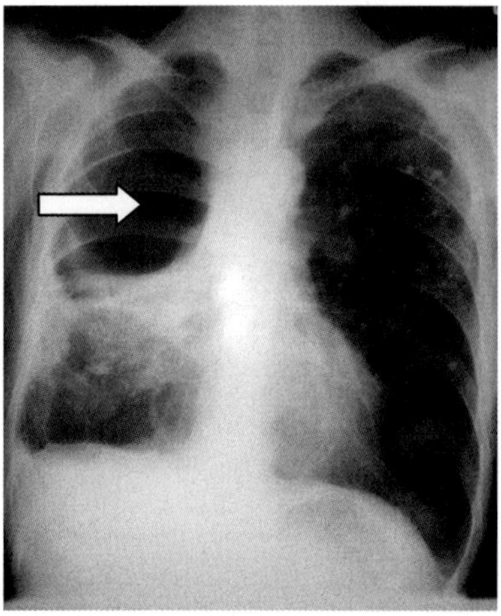

FIGURE 6. PA CHEST X-RAY – This elderly patient, with known chronic obstructive airways disease, was admitted with increasing shortness of breath. The admitting Senior House Officer interpreted the arrowed area as a pneumothorax and inserted a chest drain. The patient rapidly developed widespread surgical emphysema, respiratory failure and soon died. In fact the abnormality was a large bulla related to his existing lung disease.

COMPLICATIONS OF INTERVENTIONAL RADIOLOGY

Radiologists are often called upon to perform interventional techniques. These are either diagnostic, (such as biopsies and angiography), or therapeutic (such as steroid injections and angioplasties). These interventional techniques may give rise to complications such as haemorrhage and infection. In most cases these are unavoidable. It may sometimes be possible to impute negligence if it can be shown that the responsible radiologist has a very high personal complication rate. Evidence of this may be found by scrutinizing local audit results. It can be difficult to achieve adequate aseptic technique in a radiology department as the sorts of facilities found in operating theatres are not available.

Further complications such as false aneurysms, vessel rupture or pneumothorax may again be unavoidable. However some events, such as air embolism or injection of the wrong agent, should not occur if proper procedure is followed.

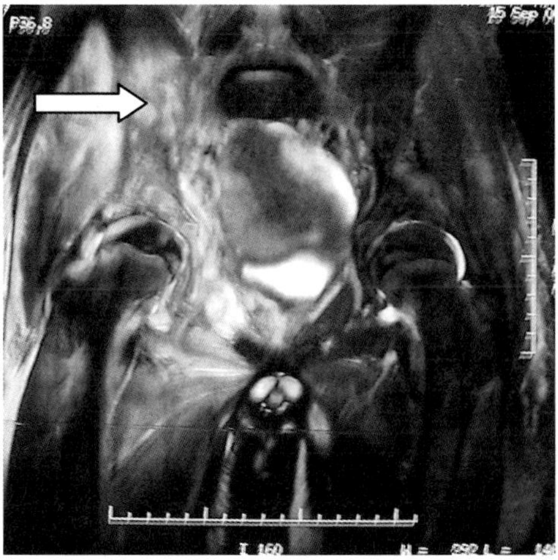

FIGURE 7. STIR WEIGHTED CORONAL MRI OF THE HIP – This child developed a severe septic arthritis of the hip with secondary osteomyelitis following hip aspiration of an originally sterile irritable hip effusion. The arrow shows the increased signal associated with bone infection and destruction of the hip joint which will leave the patient vulnerable to premature arthritis. Although joint aspiration or injection can on rare occasions result in infection even despite good technique, the claimant was able to demonstrate here that the Specialist Registrar performing the procedure had not used an adequate aseptic technique.

All patients undergoing interventions should be consented as for any other procedure, but there is potential for consent forms to be mislaid, as radiology departments often do not have a consistent policy on where to file them. If the patient notes are available, they may be put in the notes, but outpatient notes are often not available. A full description of the procedure should be made in a similar fashion to an operative note, and filed. Radiologists should confirm that consent has been obtained, describe the procedure and outcome, and indicate the presence or absence of short term complications within the body of their written radiological report. Instructions for post-procedural care and follow up should also be clearly documented.

Anaesthetists are increasingly convinced that patients should not be sedated in the x-ray department without an anaesthetist being present, as the radiologist cannot supervise patient sedation properly. This is partly due to lack of appropriate training, but also because of the need to concentrate on the procedure itself.

MISSED TUMOURS

Tumours missed at screening

The purpose of radiological screening is to identify potential serious conditions in the asymptomatic or minimally symptomatic patient. Examples of this are mammography, and 'routine' chest x-rays in smokers. The purpose of screening is to detect a lesion before it is too late for curative treatment. The significance of missing an abnormality really depends on the natural history of the disease process.

In screening mammography a radiologist may 'miss' the presence of a breast cancer either by failing to notice an abnormality, or by thinking that an abnormality is benign and not proceeding to biopsy or early follow up. At this stage the patient, or her physician, may be unable to feel a mass. Therefore the next investigation would only occur when a lump develops, or at the time of next screening. In this time it would be possible for the tumour to grow sufficiently to have metastasised, thus hugely reducing the likelihood of a cure. Claimants may sometimes think that a lesion has been missed on the original mammogram when in fact an 'interval' cancer has occurred, i.e. the cancer has actually developed since the original films. Careful comparison may be required to ensure that no abnormality was originally present.

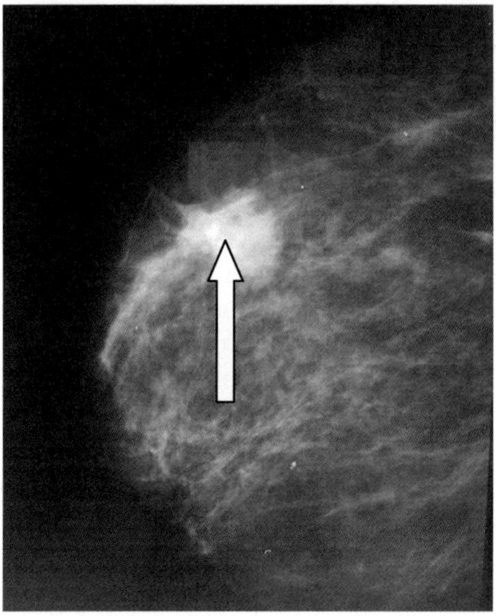

FIGURE 8. LATERAL OBLIQUE MAMMOGRAM – This breast cancer was wrongly thought by the radiologist to be a benign mass. The patient did not re-present until she had advanced disease requiring mastectomy and chemotherapy.

In the case of lung cancer, even a small delay in diagnosis can result in widespread metastatic involvement by the time of eventual diagnosis. The likelihood of a lung cancer being missed is proportional to the size of the mass on the chest x-ray, although one study assessed the average size of missed lesions at 1.6cm. By the time the cancers were detected, half of the patients had cancers which were staged as being more advanced, with a correspondingly reduced chance of cure. The likelihood of a cancer being missed does not seem to be related to its position in the thorax. Studies have suggested miss rates from 20% to 90%.

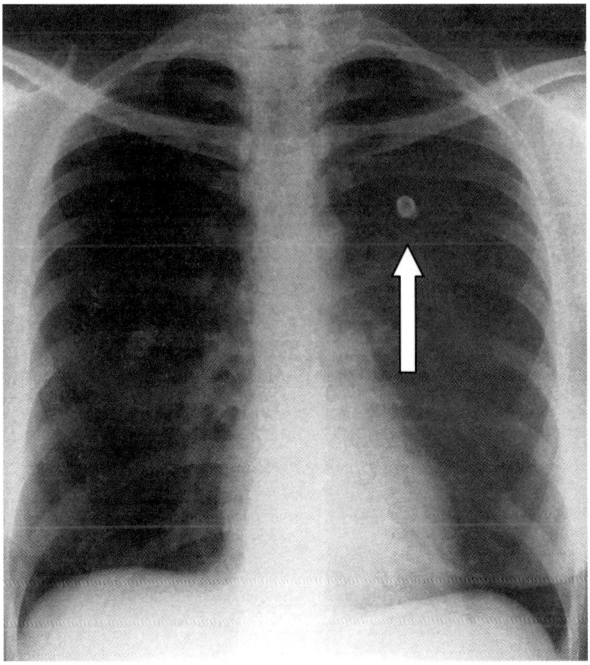

FIGURE 9. POSTEROANTERIOR CHEST X-RAY – This is an artificially produced example of a 1.6cm mass in the left upper lobe. This is a common site for lung cancer, but most lung cancer does not appear this dense on a plain film, and a lesion of this size could prove difficult to see.

Tumours missed in symptomatic patients

If a patient has symptoms, the radiological index of suspicion, (in other words how much one is expecting to see an abnormality), should be much higher. The error rate will be reduced by a clear understanding of what pathologies might produce the symptoms. If significant symptoms are described, such as haemoptysis, then even a normal investigation should still produce a recommendation for further investigation. For example, in a known long-standing smoker presenting with a hoarse voice, a normal chest x-ray is not particularly reassuring, as the loss of voice could be produced by a relatively small tumour in the mediastinum which would only be detected by CT. Therefore a follow up CT should be recommended.

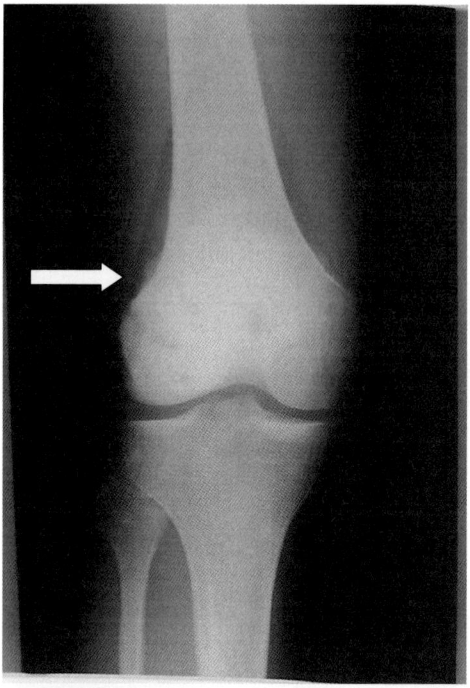

FIGURES 10A AND B: ANTEROPOSTERIOR AND LATERAL VIEWS OF THE KNEE – These were taken in a young man who complained to his football coach of persistent posterolateral knee pain - an unusual site for mechanical pain. The GP had refused to refer him for an x-ray for several months, stating that he had 'growing pains.' The x-rays clearly show areas of new bone growth representing on osteosarcoma. Unfortunately the reporting radiologist failed to spot the abnormality and the patient was sent away. A couple of months later, the football coach decided that the pain was sufficiently bad to arrange an orthopaedic referral. The films were retrieved and the correct diagnosis was made by the orthopaedic surgeon. Fortunately limb sparing surgery was still possible and there were no metastases.

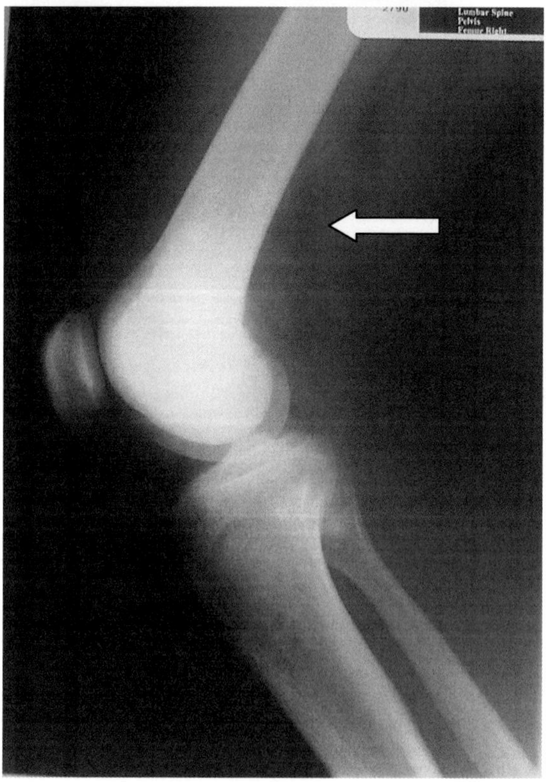

Missed Metastatic Disease

If a primary cancer is found, it is important that the patient undergoes proper staging. The type of staging which is appropriate depends on the cancer variant involved. For the majority of patients CT or MRI of the chest, abdomen and pelvis may be indicated. Practice in this area is changing rapidly. Staging should demonstrate the amount of local disease spread, and whether there is distant or metastatic spread. Certain tumours are likely to spread to liver, bones or lung, and imaging should be targeted appropriately. The limitations of each radiological technique should be assessed when deciding on the accuracy of staging.

Primary bone tumours are rare, and in a patient over the age of 50 even a solitary bone lesion is likely to be a metastasis. Many patients present with back pain and although the vast majority of cases are due to mechanical causes, there are certain 'red flags', (such as the presence of a known primary tumour, or night pain), that should alert the radiologist to the possibility of metastatic spinal disease. The elderly spine can be difficult to interpret as there is often widespread degenerative disease. Careful attention should be paid to checking that all of the pedicles can be seen, since the pedicles are a common site for bony deposits. 50% of bone has to be destroyed by tumour before it is visible on plain radiographs and therefore plain radiography is an insensitive test. The most accurate test is MRI, which will identify very small deposits.

A generalised reduction in bone density should alert the radiologist to the possibility of myeloma, as not all myeloma shows focal deposits and it is the most commonly found primary bone malignancy. Osteoporosis is common in post-menopausal women, but in other patients it should always raise the question of whether there is an underlying condition to account for it. Failure of radiologists or clinicians to be aware of this is another potential source of litigation.

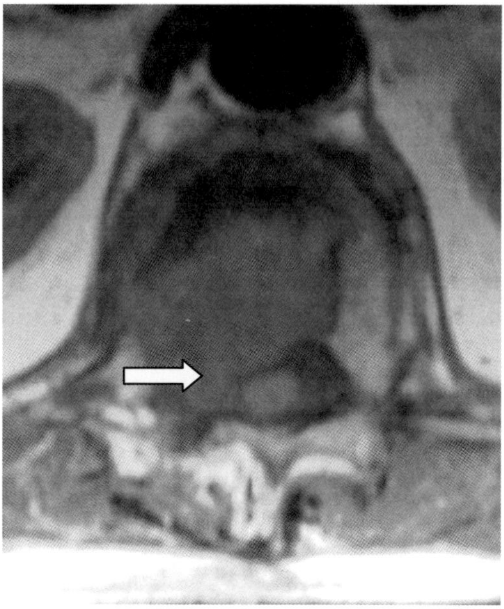

FIGURE 11. T1 WEIGHTED AXIAL MRI OF THE LUMBAR SPINE - The primary lesion in this 29 year old female patient was thought to be a plasmacytoma, which is a benign or solitary form of myeloma. Plain films were performed for staging. These were normal. The secondary deposits in the spine were not found until she presented with an acute spinal compression. The arrow marks the site of tumour extension posteriorly into the spinal canal. At the time of diagnosis it was common practice to perform an MRI at the time of staging and this had not been done. Despite bone marrow transplantation the patient relapsed and eventually died.

THE CHILDHOOD HIP AND KNEE

There are three childhood hip conditions which can give rise to very similar late radiological appearances and cause medicolegal confusion about the nature of the original pathology. These are developmental dysplasia of the hip (DDH), Perthes disease and Slipped Upper Femoral Epiphysis (SUFE). All these conditions are distinct clinical entities and the treatment of each condition is different. If untreated, all are later manifest by abnormal modelling around the hip and premature osteoarthritis. It should be possible for an experienced skeletal radiologist to distinguish between these conditions.

In SUFE the uppermost part of the femur may move medially and posteriorly before the growth plate has closed. This can be extremely difficult to see on the anteroposterior plain film, and in any child with hip pain a frog-leg lateral (with the hips abducted and externally rotated) is mandatory. Radiologists and clinicians should insist that this view is performed before giving a final diagnosis. The late appearances show a predominantly normal socket with a mushroom type deformity of the femoral head and increased amounts of bone in the femoral neck due to changed modelling. Late complications of avascular necrosis (AVN) can mimic Perthes disease, and therefore the sequence of pathological changes must be carefully noted. It is important to make a correct diagnosis of SUFE as the contralateral hip is also at risk and should be kept under review.

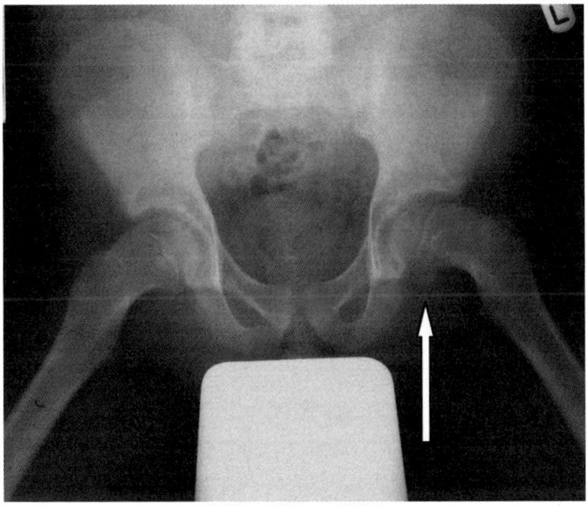

FIGURE 12. FROG-LEG LATERAL VIEW OF THE PELVIS – The right hip is normal and the left appeared normal on the frontal view. The child was sent away but suffered more symptoms. Fortunately the GP sent him back promptly for further views and the left sided SUFE was readily diagnosed on this film. The arrow shows the abnormal posterior and inferior tilt of the femoral epiphysis relative to the metaphysis.

In Perthes disease there is idiopathic interruption to the blood supply, which causes AVN. The characteristic changes of AVN at any site are a mixed picture of increase and loss of bone density, and subchondral collapse.

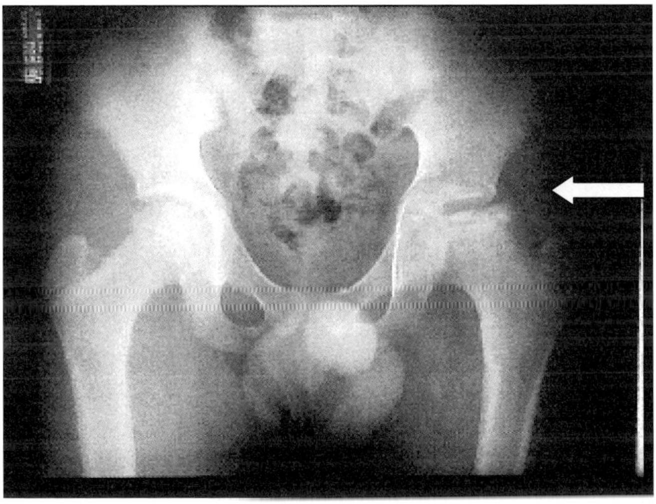

FIGURE 13. FRONTAL VIEW OF THE PELVIS – The arrow points to a characteristic area of flattening and increased density of the femoral epiphysis in this left sided Perthes disease.

In DDH the primary abnormality is in the formation of the hip acetabulum, which is defective and shallow. The femoral head is not adequately contained within the socket and therefore develops abnormally. It may be evident at birth or at the eight week clinical check through 'clicking' hips or abnormal thigh creases. At this stage it can be detected by ultrasound. Early treatment is both more effective and less likely to result in complications. In some children it is not evident at either of these times, and may genuinely develop later - hence the change in terminology from Congenital Dysplasia to Developmental Dysplasia.

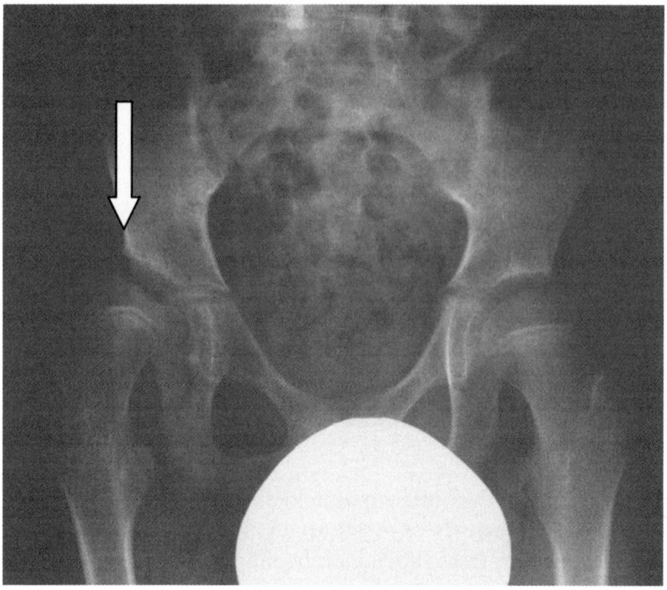

FIGURE 14. FRONTAL VIEW OF THE PELVIS – The arrow demonstrates the shallow socket and lateral slipping of the femoral head in the right sided DDH.

Radiologists and clinicians can either miss the diagnosis or make the wrong diagnosis both of which can lead to a poor clinical outcome and complications. When asking an expert to give an opinion on the nature of the original pathology, it is important both to have good quality copies and a sequence containing films that pre-date any clinical intervention.

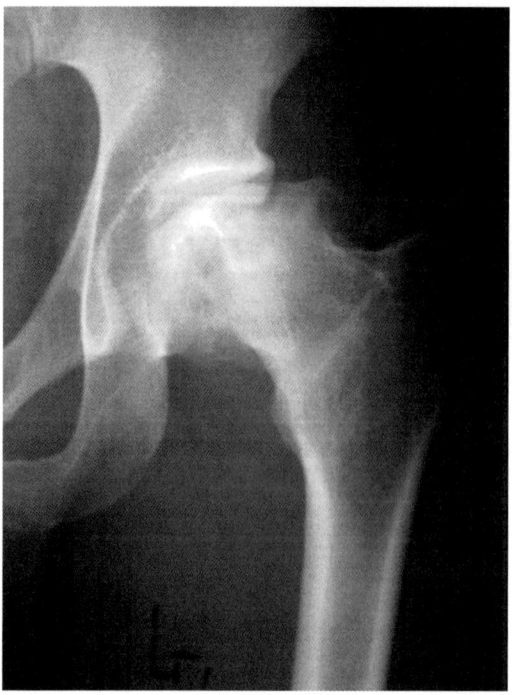

FIGURE 15. ANTEROPOSTERIOR VIEW OF THE LEFT HIP – There is abnormal modelling of the femoral head and premature osteoarthritis in this patient whose childhood hip disease went undiagnosed until late adolescence despite several trips to the GP. She was told that this was due to a missed SUFE which could have been treated effectively. In fact these appearances are due to previous Perthes disease, and her eventual outcome is unlikely to have been altered by early treatment.

In the knee there may be confusion between an acute fracture and osteochondritis dissecans. This in part arises because of the change in thinking about the pathophysiology of these conditions. It was originally thought that dissecans lesions were the result of repeated minor injuries in 'sporting' children. It is now thought that the lesion is the result of a single shearing injury cleaving off cartilage and a small layer of subchondral bone. This is not a fracture in the conventional sense. There may be some immediate pain but there is no short term biomechanical compromise. X-rays are often normal at the time of the initial event, apart from an effusion which can occur with low grade soft tissue injury. Claimants may be told that they have had a missed fracture which should have been dealt with at the time of injury.

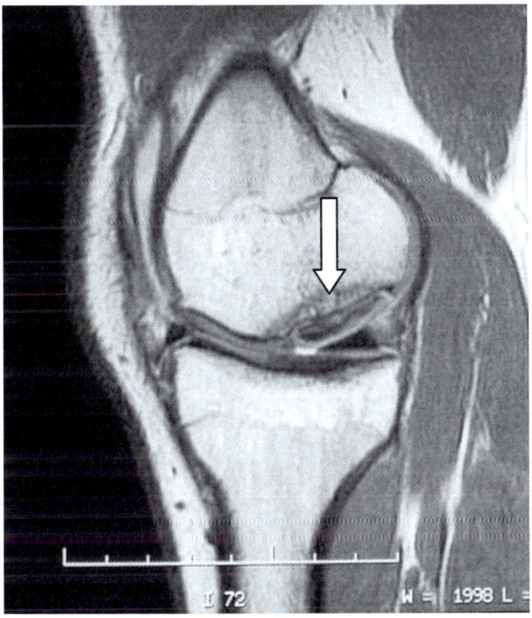

FIGURE 16. SAGITTAL STIR WEIGHTED MRI OF THE KNEE – This patient presented herself several times in her teens to the A&E department. Plain x-rays were apparently normal. Once she joined the forces her knee became increasingly symptomatic and she was discharged on medical grounds. The MRI shows a chronic osteochondral injury (arrowed), and a plain film at the time of the MRI showed the same abnormality. She was told that the A&E officer had missed a fracture and that she could make a claim. In fact her clinical outcome would have been similar had a diagnosis been made earlier, but she probably would not have attempted to join the Armed Forces.

Patients typically become symptomatic in later life when the fragment becomes loose or premature degenerative change develops. Both of these may then be evident on x-rays. Although in some cases early intervention can reduce the likelihood of long term sequelae, the condition can be extremely difficult to diagnose acutely.

MISSED FRACTURES

Fractures usually appear as radiolucent lines running through the bone and coming into contact with a cortical margin. At least two films should be taken in different orthogonal planes to maximise the chances of seeing the fracture line.

Fracture can however appear as white lines if the bone ends overlap, or as small linear flakes of bone or callus if the fracture is not fresh. Some fractures are impossible to see on plain films, and soft tissue signs such as an effusion, or a mixture of fat (which has escaped from trabecular bone marrow) and blood in a joint (lipohaemarthrosis) must be sought.

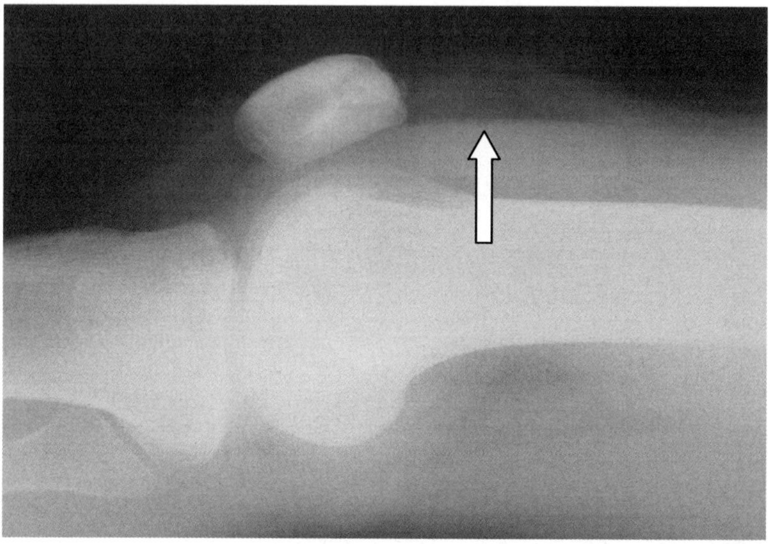

FIGURE 17. HORIZONTAL BEAM LATERAL OF THE KNEE – This film demonstrates the layer of fat floating on the layer of blood in this patient who was hit by a car on a zebra crossing. The fat floats because it is less dense than the blood. The primary fracture line was not visible. Both the A&E officer and the junior orthopaedic surgeon who saw her in clinic failed to appreciate the significance of this finding and she was discharged. She returned a year later with a very irregular joint surface due to impaction and displacement of the fracture.

The clinical signs of fracture include local bony tenderness and soft tissue swelling. On occasion it may be impossible to see a fracture on a plain film, and if the clinical index of suspicion of a fracture is high, further imaging should be considered. Clinicians should also be aware of the likely soft tissue damage that may be associated with any fracture and arrange further imaging as appropriate.

Many missed fractures are not mechanically compromising. Examples include rib fractures without soft tissue complications, and small avulsion fragments around the ankle. Although patients may become distressed to learn that these small fractures were initially misdiagnosed, there should be no long-term sequelae. Small fractures involving a joint surface (intra-articular) are significant because they may be associated with premature osteoarthritis. Isotope scanning was used for years to confirm a fracture, but because of the highly sensitive but non-specific nature of the test it should now be replaced with either MRI or CT.

A classic site for a missed fracture is the scaphoid bone, as discussed in the chapter on orthopaedics. In fact the initial films generally do show the correct pathology if properly assessed, although the fractures may be easier to see at ten days when some healing changes have occurred. It is important to diagnose a scaphoid fracture, as inadequate treatment can lead to non-union and avascular necrosis. If there is any doubt, the investigation of choice is an MRI scan which would clearly demonstrate any trabecular disruption.

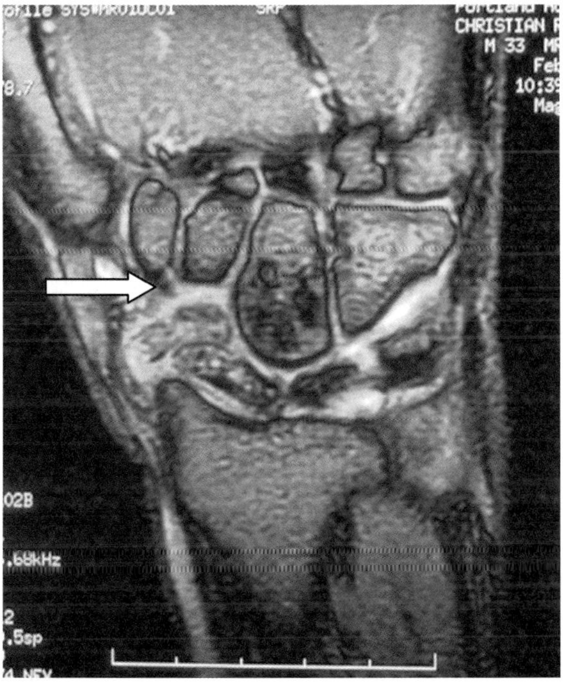

FIGURE 18. CORONAL STIR WEIGHTED MRI OF THE WRIST – The original plain films in this patient were wrongly reported as normal and the wrist was not immobilised. Six months later the patient returned with increasing pain. The MRI shows an established non-union through the waist of the scaphoid with avascular necrosis of the distal fragment.

In the elbow, radial head fractures are frequently missed because the plane in which the films were taken often does not demonstrate the fracture line. However, a joint effusion invariably accompanies this type of fracture in the acute phase. The same can be said for supracondylar fractures in children. The effusion is seen as a dark sail shape behind the distal humerus. This is because the effusion pushes out the normal fat pad at this site, which is dark on x-ray.

A similar situation can be seen in fractures of the tibial plateau. These are often caused in tripping or slipping accidents. The fracture line itself can be difficult to identify, but the presence of a lipohaemarthrosis in the joint is inevitable. It is important to make sure that the lateral view is performed with a horizontal beam so that the layering of the fat on top of the blood can be seen. If undiagnosed, a tibial plateau fracture can displace and collapse, leading to severe knee osteoarthritis. All tibial plateau fractures should be assessed for position using CT as soon as possible.

A frequent injury seen in the elderly or those with low bone density is the fractured neck of femur. The hardest of these, both to identify and treat, is the subcapital fracture - where the break occurs just at the junction of the head and neck of the femur. Delay in diagnosis or inadequate fixation (many patients will need a hip prosthesis) can lead to avascular necrosis of the femoral head. The fracture can be missed on plain films. A ring of osteophytes around the femoral neck can sometimes mimic a fracture leading to unwarranted intervention. If the diagnosis is in doubt, MRI should be performed.

The spine, and especially the cervical spine, is an area that causes a great deal of anxiety for clinical staff and radiologists. Fractures are relatively easy to miss, and the classically described associated soft tissues abnormalities, like swelling in front of the vertebrae, are often not present. The consequences of missed injuries can be disastrous due to neurological damage, and this is particularly the case in mechanically unstable fractures. There should thus be a low threshold for proceeding to further imaging (usually by urgent CT) if there is any question of injury. Damage to the spinal cord can occur in the absence of any bony injury. Where there is spinal cord damage MRI should be done as a matter of urgency.

Childhood fractures exhibit characteristic patterns. Unusual fractures should raise the possibility of non-accidental injury (NAI). Skull and rib fractures are extremely rare following conventional injury and should raise the suspicion of abuse. Transverse fractures of the long bones and fractures through the metaphysis are also indicators. In cases of NAI there are often multiple fractures of varying ages, the history does not correlate well with the clinical findings, and the child may be withdrawn and under-nourished. It is up to all of the staff involved with suspected NAI, including the radiologist, to document their suspicions and make others aware. Failure to do so often leads to grave consequences.

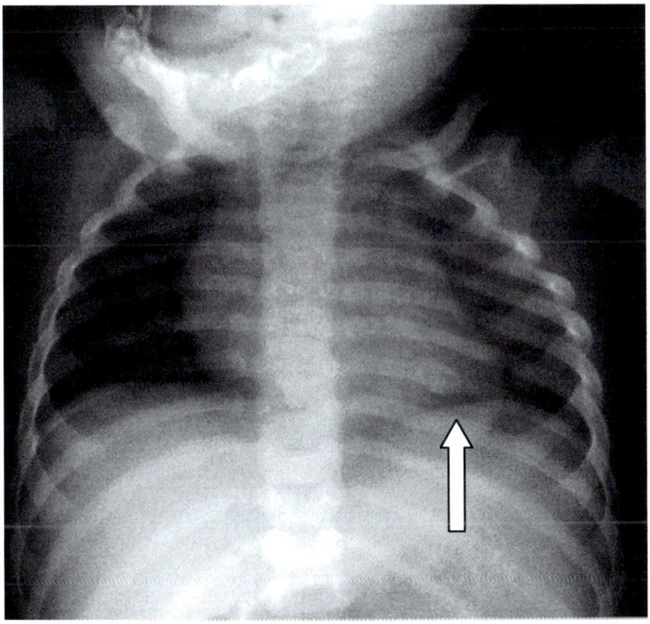

FIGURE 19. FRONTAL CHEST X-RAY IN A ONE YEAR OLD – The posterior rib fractures in this child were not seen by the paediatrician, and the films were never returned for reporting. The film was only reviewed when the child was brought in dead.

RADIATION EXPOSURE

In early 2004 a UK radiation report suggested that over 700 cancers a year were due to excessive medical radiation exposure. It is in order to reduce unnecessary medical radiation that the IRMER regulations were introduced. From a health perspective, radiation exposure is quantified in terms of dose, which is a measure of the amount of radioactive energy deposited in biological tissues. The commonly used units are mSv (milliSieverts). There is a certain amount of natural exposure to radiation, and together with artificial sources the average annual dose is 3.6 mSv, of which the majority is natural or 'background' radiation (80%). Very high radiation doses, of the order of 3,000 to 5,000 mSv are fatal, but at around 200 mSv the primary risk is of cancer or damage to the gonads. Almost all the available risk data is based on extremely high doses from atomic bombs or radiation accidents. All other risks are almost entirely based on statistical extrapolation and the real risks are not really known. However, pregnant women should not be exposed to radiation, especially in the first trimester. Particular efforts should be made to reduce the exposure of children with developing gonads.

The lifetime risk of cancer following a CT scan of the abdomen and pelvis in an adult is estimated at between 1 in 1,000 and 1 in 10,000. This should be weighed against the population risk of between 1 in 3 and 1 in 4 of developing a 'natural' cancer. There has as yet been no accusation of medical radiation producing cancer. It is important to keep medical radiation exposure to the minimum possible level, and to avoid unnecessary exposure in vulnerable groups such as women of childbearing age. In any decision to image using ionising radiation the benefits of the result must outweigh the risk of the procedure.

NEUROLOGY

W. J. K. Cumming

INTRODUCTION

While neurologists are sometimes sued (mainly for failing to diagnose), and when they are, awards against them can be very big, they are more commonly involved in litigation as commentators on causation.

Neurological practice has been revolutionised by magnetic resonance imaging (MRI). However, the increasing sophistication of investigation has led to an over reliance on investigation at the expense of the most important part of a neurological examination   the history. Frequently the history has been sacrificed to the "great God" of MRI, leading to elementary mistakes. The commonest of these is to assume that, because the MRI shows no abnormality, the patient's complaints are non organic.

Another common error is to assume that all neurological conditions are of acute onset. In fact most evolve slowly. A condition labelled as non organic in the early part of the illness may later display easily diagnosable neurological abnormalities.

Adherence to the basic rules of neurological history taking and examination will help to reduce the number of mistakes. Failure to diagnose a neurological rarity will rarely lead to litigation. Failure to diagnose, or wrong diagnostic labelling of common conditions, is a greater problem.

THE STRUCTURE OF THE NERVOUS SYSTEM

A detailed consideration of the structure, function and dysfunction of the nervous system can be found in Cumming (1998).

The nervous system can be thought of as a series of horizontal pathways and vertical pathways. The major descending vertical pathway is the pyramidal tract, which conveys movement to the limbs. The cell bodies arise in the motor strip of the cortex and the axons terminate at the level of the motor nuclei of the cranial and spinal nerves (Figure 1).

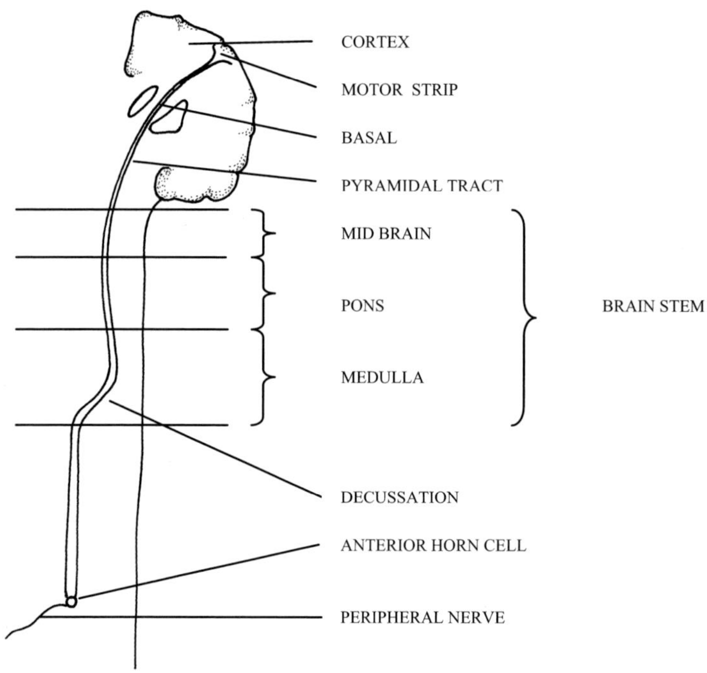

FIGURE 1

Sensation from the periphery is conveyed, via the spinal cord, to the brain in the major ascending sensory pathways. These are the spinothalamic pathway and the posterior columns. (Figures 2 & 3).

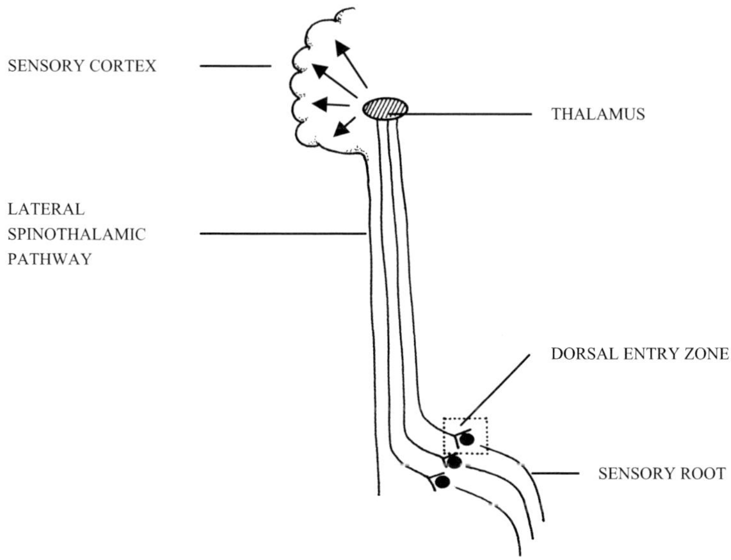

FIGURE 2

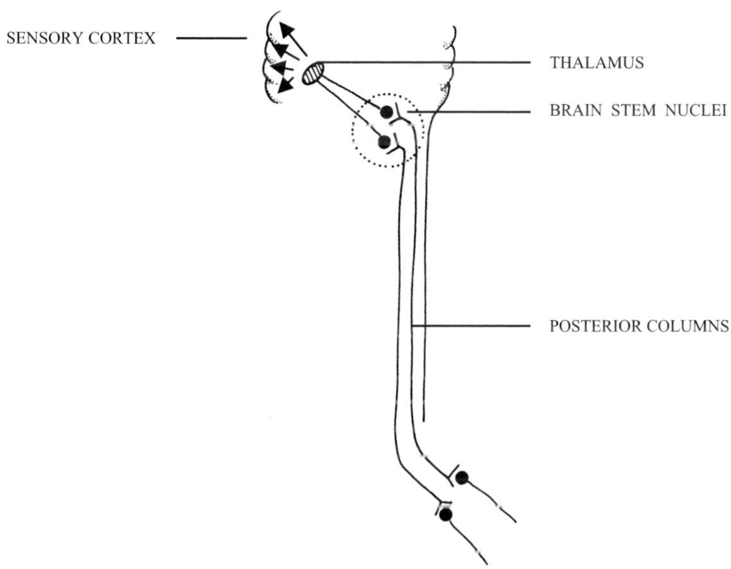

FIGURE 3

The central horizontal pathways comprise the cranial nerves (Figure 4).

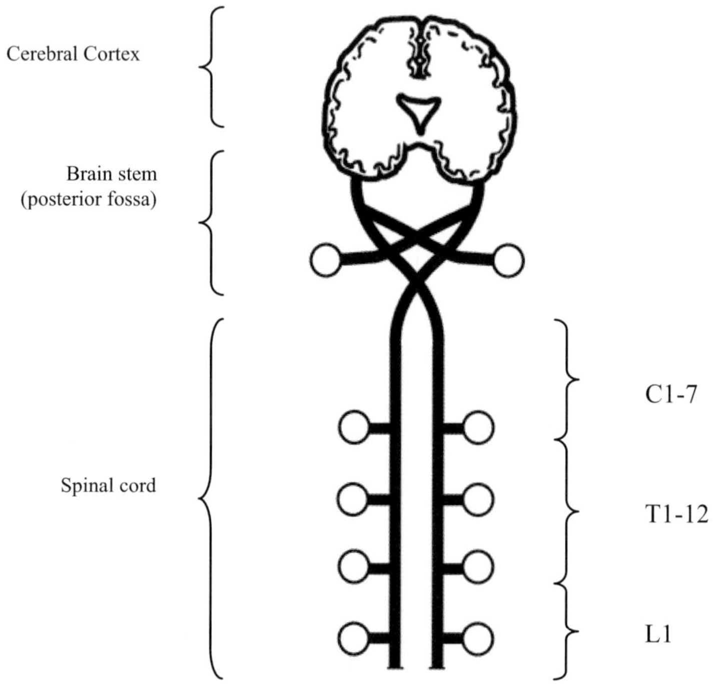

FIGURE 4 – CEREBRAL CORTEX, BRAIN STEM AND SPINAL CORD WITH ASSOCIATED HORIZONTAL PATHWAYS (CRANIAL NERVE/SPINAL NERVE ROOTS)

The horizontal pathways arising from the spinal cord are the individual nerve roots arising from each of the cervical segments supplying the muscles in the upper limbs. Having left the nerve roots between C2 and C7 these individual spinal nerves enter a plexus (brachial) (Figure 5) which can be thought of as a switching station, out of which emerge the main nerves to the arm (median, ulnar and radial).

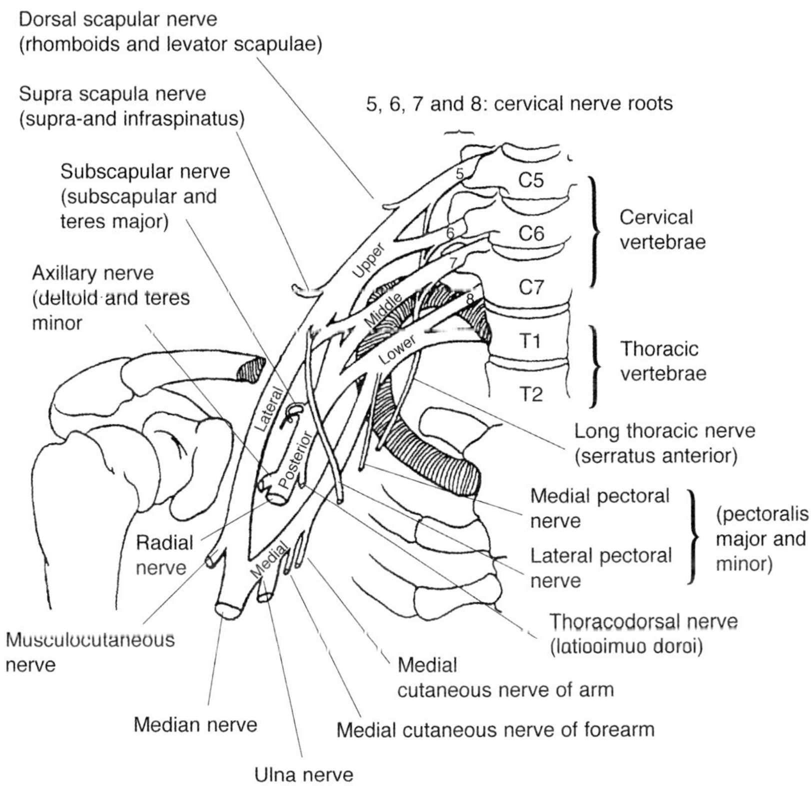

FIGURE 5

Similarly in the lumbosacral region, the nerve roots form the lumbosacral plexus (Figure 6) before emerging into the leg as the femoral and sciatic nerves, and into the pelvis as the pudendal nerves.

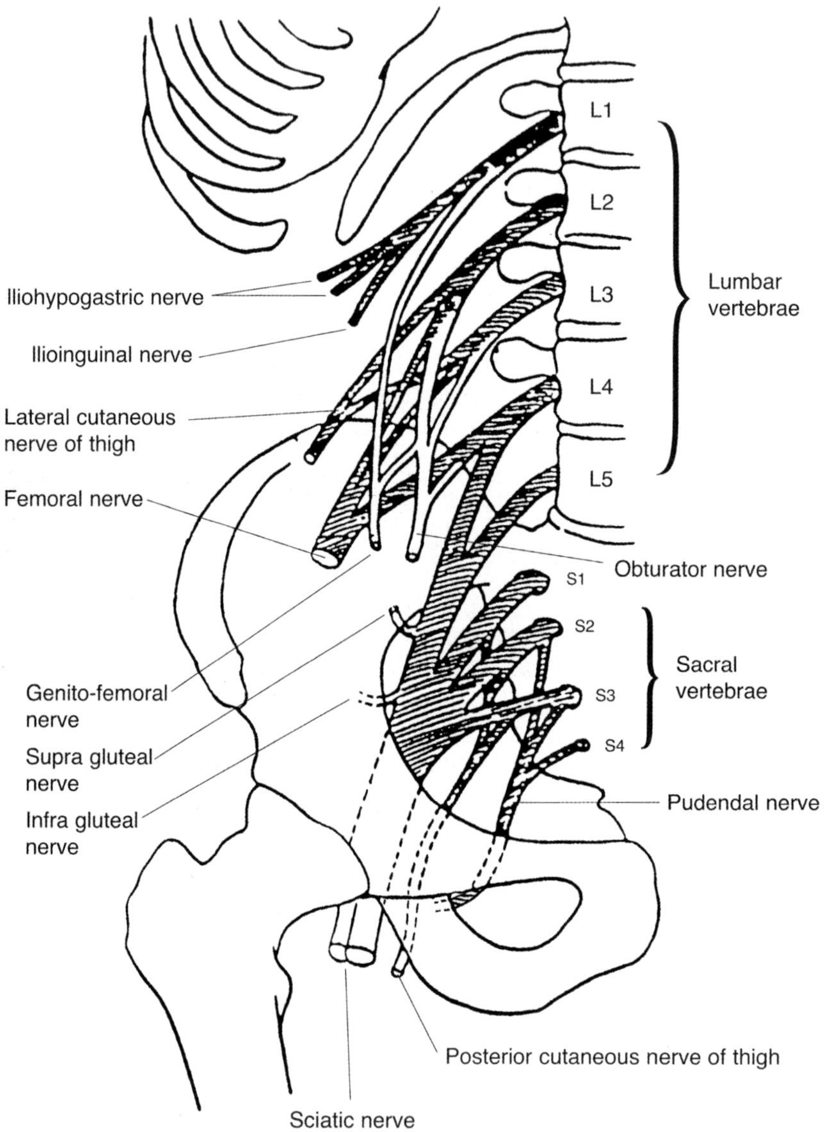

FIGURE 6

THE NEUROLOGICAL EXAMINATION

A neurological examination consists of history and examination, appropriate investigations and, if there is a suggestion of disturbance of cognitive function, a neuropsychological appraisal.

The aim of the history is to identify an intersect between the descending and ascending pathways and horizontal pathways to locate the lesion within the nervous system. At that stage, the tempo of the history gives a guide to the underlying diagnosis.

In the descending pathways, function is lost at the level of the lesion, and disturbed beneath the level of the lesion. Disturbance of function in the descending pyramidal pathway initially presents as an increase in tone (spasticity) which with time is followed by evolving weakness in a pyramidal distribution (arm extensors and leg flexors). Associated with an increase in tone is the finding of an increase in the reflexes. Eventually the plantar response will become extensor (positive Babinski's sign).

Lesions of the brain and spinal cord lead to more diffuse weakness, whereas lesions of the nerve roots leads to focal weakness, confined to the territory innervated by the relevant nerve.

Similarly, with the ascending sensory pathways, damage to a peripheral nerve will lead to focal sensory loss. The area of sensory loss is easily mapped by reference to standard diagrams. As sensation ascends the central pathways, integration takes place, and therefore involvement at the spinal cord, brain stem or cortical level leads to more diffuse sensory involvement - for example a whole limb or one side of the body.

IMAGING

Imaging of the nervous system is carried out by CT scanning and MR scanning. MR scanning gives much greater detail of brain structure – Figure 7 (a) and (b).

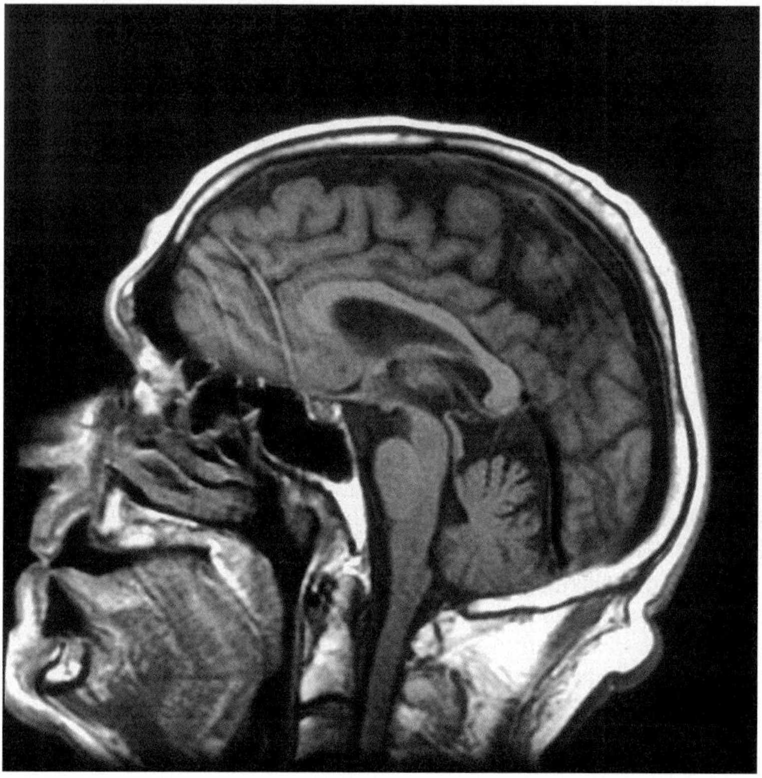

FIGURE 7 (A)

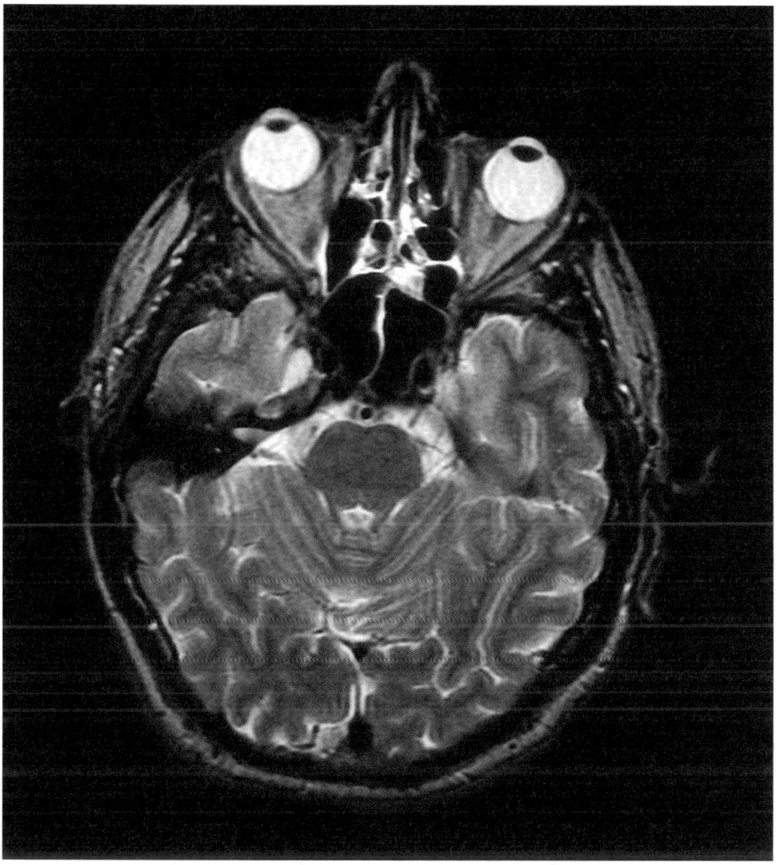

FIGURE 7 (B)

MR techniques can also be used for non invasive angiography of the carotid arteries, and hence the blood supply to the brain.

NEUROPHYSIOLOGY: GENERAL

The individual function of nerves and muscles is assessed using nerve conduction studies (NCS) and electromyography (EMG).

Disturbances of electrical function in the cortex of the brain are detected by an electroencephalogram (EEG).

EVOKED POTENTIALS

Evoked potentials give information about the integrity of electrical transmission, and therefore of the functional integrity generally, of the following pathways within the brain and spinal cord.

- Visual - eyes to the occipital lobes.
- Auditory – ears, through the brain stem to the temporal lobes.
- Somatosensory – periphery, through the spinal cord to the brain stem.

SIDE EFECTS OF THESE INVESTIGATIONS

Apart from CT scanning of the brain, which does expose the patient to ionising radiation, the investigations listed above do not have serious side effects. They may cause the patient some discomfort, but do not present any risk. This cannot be said for lumbar puncture, which is discussed below.

LUMBAR PUNCTURE (LP)

The fluid which surrounds the brain and the spinal cord, the cerebrospinal fluid (CSF), is accessed via a LP. LP is an important part of the diagnosis of infective diseases of the nervous system (meningitis, encephalitis), subarachnoid haemorrhage, some malignancies, multiple sclerosis, and neuropathies.

The likelihood of complications, and hence complaint, increases as the number of attempts at LP increases. Repeated attempts imply inexperienced staff.

The commonest complication of LP is postural headache. It occurs in about 40% of patients. Post LP headache usually begins within 48 hours of the procedure, and recovers within 72 hours in 90% of patients. The duration of the headache is less than 5 days in 80% of patients, though it occasionally persists for up to 14 days, and, rarely, for up to 12 months. The headache is described as bilateral. It can be at either the front or the back of the head, or may be generalised. It is described as a feeling of pressure which is maximal in the upright position and decreases or resolves when the patient lies flat. The headache is worse with movement, coughing, straining and sneezing. The longer the patient is upright, the longer it takes for the headache to subside when the patient becomes horizontal. It is probably caused by a slow leak through the dura (the lining of the spine and brain) where the rate of loss of CSF is greater than the rate of production.

Post lumbar puncture headache is twice as common in women as in men. The highest incidence is in the 18-30 year old age group. The risk is increased by a prior history of headache of any type, or a prior history of post lumbar puncture headache.

In most cases bed rest is all that is required. In severe cases an epidural blood patch may be needed to repair a tear in the dura.

The rarer complications of lumbar puncture include cranial nerve abnormalities. These are usually transient and thought to be due to decreased CSF pressure within the brain leading to a degree of traction. The III to the VIII cranial nerves are commonly involved. A very small percentage of patients (0.4%) report visual symptoms (double vision, blurred vision, spots before the eyes, intolerance of light and visual scintillation), and again a small percentage (0.4%) have auditory complaints including dizziness, tinnitus, popping ears and loss of hearing. Palsy of the IV cranial nerve follows 0.25% of lumbar punctures or spinal anaesthetics, and can be unilateral or bilateral. It produces a weakness of the muscles responsible for turning the eye downward and outward. The weakness occurs 4-14 days after the procedure and usually recovers over 4 –6 weeks.

When performing a lumbar puncture, the patient often complains of a transient "electric shock" or a sensation of pins and needles. This indicates a degree of contact within the spinal needle and the sensory root. This is recorded in some 13% of patients. Occasionally permanent sensory or motor loss can occur from the contact. Some 35% of patients complain of backache following a lumbar puncture. It typically lasts for several days, but can occasionally persist for months.

Bacterial meningitis is a rare complication of lumbar puncture. More common, but still rare, is discitis (infection of the disc), and local abscess formation.

A very rare complication of lumbar puncture is an intracranial subdural haematoma. It is classically seen in the context of typical post lumbar puncture headache. The haematoma can be unilateral or bilateral, and can be diagnosed any time from three days to several months after the lumbar puncture. The mechanism is again thought to be low CSF pressure causing traction of the blood vessels and tearing of the dural blood vessels. Subdural haematoma should be suspected when the post lumbar puncture headache lasts for more than a week, when the headache recurs after a headache free interval, or when the headache does not have a postural component.

In myelography the contrast medium is injected into the spinal cord following a lumbar puncture. It is used much less since the advent of MR techniques. Details of the complications of myelography can be found in Greenspan & Caldemayer (1998).

BIOPSIES

It is sometimes necessary to obtain a biopsy of nerve (Willison & Wiler 2003), muscle (Laconis 2004) or brain (Kros 1997). These techniques are the province of specialist neuroscience centres. They are only undertaken when other investigations have failed to provide a diagnosis.

There are few side effects to muscle biopsy other than discomfort.

A nerve biopsy is commonly taken from a sensory nerve. Because it involves removing part of the nerve, the patient is left with an area of loss of sensation. Occasionally this area can be painful (dysaesthetic).

Brain biopsies are usually undertaken for cerebral tumour. Their purpose is to ensure that the mass in the brain is not an abscess and, if it is a tumour, to identify the type. This is, of course, a dangerous procedure. The damage which results depends on the area of the brain which is biopsied.

NEUROPSYCHOLOGICAL EVALUATION

The field of neuropsychology has expanded dramatically over the past ten to fifteen years. Whereas previously neurologists would have provided an overview of neuropsychological dysfunction, this is now the province of the specifically trained neuropsychologist. It is possible, using their techniques, to quantify defects in cognitive function by comparing the results for the individual patient with normative values for patients of comparable age, sex and educational background. In addition, neuropsychologists have developed sophisticated tests to detect malingering.

HEADACHE

General considerations

Headache is amongst the commonest symptoms described by patients to their General Practitioners. Some 20% of males and 50% of females say that they have a headache on at least one day each week.

The problem is differentiating between headaches which indicate serious disease and those which are benign.

History taking is all important. No two patients mean the same thing by the word 'headache', and the meaning for the individual has to be established. Since some 300 causes of headache have been described, it is important that the history elucidates the cardinal features of the individual's headache.

The patient must be questioned to determine:

(a) For how long he or she has suffered from the headache.
(b) What words best describe the headache: for example, throbbing, pounding, stabbing, knife-like, bursting or aching.
(c) Whether the headache is increasing in severity, is static, or is improving.
(d) Whether the headache is constant, or comes and goes.
(e) If the headache is paroxysmal, at what time of day it comes on.
(f) Whether there are any factors which relieve or increase the headache.
(g) Whether the headache is associated with any disturbance of vision (e.g. visual obscuration or double vision).
(h) Whether there is any vomiting or nausea.
(i) Whether there is any local tenderness in the scalp.
(j) Whether there has been any recent head injury.
(k) Whether there are any symptoms suggestive of sinus disease.
(l) Whether the patient has a history suggestive of cervical spondylotic disease.
(m) Whether the patient is taking any drugs which are known to cause headache.
(n) Whether the patient has recently been depressed or anxious.

A purported history of headache which does not contain the above elements is insufficient to make a confident diagnosis.

Although most forms of headache can be identified by history taking alone, increasingly patients with headache are referred for neuro-imaging. This is entirely justified for the sake of patient reassurance. However, overall, the yield of neuro-imaging in evaluating patients with headache and a normal neurological examination is quite low. Even in large series (Evans 1996), brain tumours were found in 0.8% of scans, arteriovenous malformations in 0.2%, hydrocephalus in 0.3%, aneurysms in 0.1%, subdural haematoma in 0.2%, and strokes in 1.2%.
EEG is unhelpful in the evaluation of headache.

Some of the most important types of headache are considered below.

Tension headache

This is the commonest form of headache encountered in routine practice. Patients describe a generalised headache, occurring on more than 18 days per month. Any type of headache pain may be described. The headache tends to wax and wane, and is often present throughout the day. It is not associated with nausea, vomiting or visual disturbance. Response to analgesia is variable. There are no abnormal neurological signs on examination. Many patients have associated psychological disorders - predominantly depression.

Many patients are concerned that they have an intracranial problem - particularly a tumour - and reassurance by way of imaging with CT scanning is appropriate. Although there is a radiation risk from a CT head scan, in most cases the relief of the patient's anxiety far outweighs the potential risk of the scan.

Other forms of headache are frequently described wrongly as tension headaches simply because the patient is working in a stressful environment. To be safely diagnosed as a tension headache, the headache must conform to the features given above.

Analgesia induced headache

This type of headache is very similar in nature to tension headache but tends to occur daily, without remission. The headache is caused by overuse of "over the counter" analgesics. Typically, the history is that the patient starts off with a headache which initially responds to simple analgesia. However, with time the response to simple analgesia decreases, and there is a steady escalation through the range of analgesics. Eventually, addiction to the analgesia develops and, like addicts in other areas, patients will go to great lengths to hide their addiction. They will often use different pharmacies to buy "over the counter" medication so that no one pharmacist is aware of what they are taking. They hide their "over the counter" medication use from their medical attendants. Management is by psychological techniques.

This type of headache illustrates the importance of history taking and determining all the patient's medication - not just those prescribed.

Migraine

Ascribing headache to migraine is one of the commonest medical mistakes. Unquestioning acceptance of the patient's self report of "migraine" frequently leads to error. Patients often prefer to ascribe the headache to "migraine" than to tension, alcohol excess etc. Beware, too, of the assumption that because there is a family history of "migraine", the young adolescent with a headache must also suffer from migraine.

Migraine is a distinct disorder with a remarkably limited repertoire of symptoms. Patients often have a prodrome in the 24 hours before the onset of the attack. This consists of excessive yawning and tiredness. Some patients are hyper-excited, and in females there may be fluid retention. If the patient suffers from migraine with aura (formerly known as classical migraine), they can have visual disturbance and/or sensory disturbance affecting the side of the face and the arm (cherio-aura). In this presentation, the aura commonly lasts for about 15-20 minutes and then disappears before the onset of the headache phase. The headache can be unilateral (hemicrania), but can occur at any location of the head. It is described as throbbing and pounding. It is associated with nausea and vomiting. The headache is of sufficient severity to make it impossible to carry on with ordinary living. Most patients prefer a darkened room because of light intolerance, they prefer quiet because of noise intolerance, and many are intolerant of the smell of food - which leads to increased nausea and vomiting. The headache lasts anything from six hours to seventy two hours. It is inconstantly relieved by sleep. The 24 hours following a migraine is the obverse of the prodrome.

It follows that a patient who says they develop a migraine every other day does not suffer from the condition: nor does an individual who says that they have more than four migraine attacks per month.

Migraine with aura occurs in 15% of patients. Therefore migraine without aura (formerly known as common migraine) is the predominant headache type.

In the past great reliance has been placed on precipitating factors for the individual migraine attack, - particularly citrus fruits, chocolate, coffee etc. These factors are of much greater importance in childhood migraine. Common precipitants to the individual episode are disturbances of routine in terms of sleeping and eating.

Migraine is thought to be inherited in an autosomal-dominant manner with incomplete penetrance. It is generally considered that a "trigger" is required to convert the latent condition of migraine into the actual disease in those individuals predisposed to develop the disease. These triggers include emotional upset, physical disruption, or a combination of both.

Most migraine patients start developing attacks in the period between their late teens and their late twenties. Emotional factors such as the death of a grandparent, the death of a family pet, examination stress and puberty are well recognised triggers. In terms of trauma, the most common trauma is mild head trauma following, for example, an accidental blow to the head against an open cupboard door. Migraine may develop for the first time following a "whiplash". Such triggering events can be identified in 75% of all migraine patients.

In the female, migraine attacks may be more frequent at the time of menstruation, and there is a rare form of migraine (catamenial migraine) which occurs only at the time of menstruation.

Treatment is by explanation of the disease process, avoidance of precipitating events, treatment for the individual attack, and prophylactic treatment if required. If the history is as set out above, no further investigation is required unless, in patients who have migraine with aura, the aura extends into the headache phase, or develops during the headache phase. In such patients imaging of the brain is mandatory.

In patients with a diagnosis of migraine, neuro-imaging is, however, quite unproductive. Brain tumours are seen in 0.3%, arteriovenous malformations in 0.07% and saccular aneurysms in 0.07% of cases (Evans 1996). The commonest feature is that of so-called "white matter" abnormalities. The relevance of these is poorly understood.

Cluster headache

In this condition there is a marked male preponderance with a male: female ratio of about 6:1. Patients get clusters of attacks over a defined period, usually about three months, and then long periods of relief. During the attack the pain is in or around the eye. In most sufferers it is associated with reddening of the eye, increased lacrimation, increased nasal secretion and sometimes changes in the pupil size and shape. Some patients have a sensation of paraesthesiae immediately above the eyelid.

In contradistinction to the pain of migraine described above, the pain of cluster headache is so severe that often a patient will attempt to provide counter pressure by banging the head against the wall. The severe pain can last for anything from thirty minutes to three hours, and then subsides. Typically, the patient is woken from sleep at their first period of rapid eye movement sleep - usually between 2 and 4 in the morning. If the attacks recur, they tend to recur 12 hours later in the early part of the afternoon. Cluster headaches are triggered by smoking and by alcohol, and most patients have learned to avoid these precipitants before the diagnosis has been established.

Patients often present to the neurologists via the ENT Department where it is initially considered, erroneously, that the attacks are those of sinus headache. It is only when sinus wash outs have produced no relief that further referral is made.
Some studies have suggested that cluster headache can be precipitated by minor head trauma and by "whiplash".

Subarachnoid haemorrhage

The headache of subarachnoid haemorrhage (SAH) is absolutely characteristic. The patient will describe the abrupt onset of a headache, and will usually describe the activity which they are undertaking at the time. The headache may be unilateral or generalised, and the headache is usually described as being like "a kick in the head" or "the most severe headache I have ever had". Patients will often describe the headache coming on during a precipitating event, for example, lifting or bending (12%), defaecation (5%), sexual intercourse (4%), emotional upset (4%), head injury (3%), and coughing (2%).

50% of patients will experience vomiting at the onset, and 50% of patients will have an episode of loss of consciousness associated with the initial headache.

10% of patients arrive at hospital in a coma, and a further 10% are confused. Some 20% of patients will develop seizure activity at the onset of the bleed.

It is crucial to recognise SAH so that the patient is admitted to a Neurosurgical Unit for therapy prior to a second bleed.

Some 40-60% of patients with SAH will have had prior warning symptoms over the preceding few weeks. These usually consist of mild attacks of head, face or neck pain lasting for a few hours. It is thought that these headaches are brought on by either minor leakage from the aneurysm or stretching of the aneurysmal wall.

In a patient with a prior history of headache, these headaches will usually go unrecognised. In patients with no past history of headache they should be investigated thoroughly, particularly if the onset was sudden. In practice, however, few patients are identified prior to the definitive SAH.

Litigation is often associated with SAH. It often relates to a failure to heed the significance of warning headaches.

The CT scan in SAH will be positive in 95% of patients at day 0 (the day of the bleed), 74% of patients at day 3, 50% of patients at one week, 30% of patients at two weeks, and almost nil at three weeks (Evans 1996).

Intracranial tumours

The term 'space occupying lesion' (SOL) is used to identify any lesion which increases the volume of the intracranial contents, and thus leads to a rise in intracranial pressure. The terminology therefore embraces not only intracranial tumours (malignant or benign) but also vascular lesions (intracerebral haematoma) and inflammatory lesions (abscess).

The manifestations of intracranial tumour are those of increased intracranial pressure (ICP), and those due to the local effects of the tumour itself. For reasons that are not clearly understood, the signs and symptoms of raised ICP usually pre-date the signs of local disturbance.

The classical triad of raised intracranial pressure is headache, papilloedema and vomiting. Headache is present in 88% of patients, papilloedema in 75%, and vomiting in 65%, and all three occur together in some 60% of patients.

The headache caused by raised ICP is at first usually intermittent. It is described as a throbbing or bursting pain. It is typically worse first thing in the morning and wears off in minutes or hours, and it tends to recur towards the end of the day. As the tumour enlarges the headache becomes more persistent, eventually becoming continuous. The headache is increased by any activity which normally raises the ICP such as exertion, excitement, coughing, sneezing, vomiting, stooping, intercourse or straining at stool. Some patients find that posture plays a part - the headache being worse when lying down and relieved by sitting up. Headache is usually diffuse. It is rarely possible to locate the tumour by reference to the location of the headache.

Papilloedema is described as swelling of the optic nerve head and is observed by examination with an ophthalmoscope. This is an area where medical mistakes are common. It requires considerable experience to handle an ophthalmoscope appropriately so that maximum information is obtained. A cursory glance at the back of the eye is meaningless. An annotation saying “fundus not seen” does not mean that the fundus would not have been visible to an experienced examiner. When the history is suggestive of raised ICP but the examining doctor does not have sufficient experience to visualise the fundi adequately, a more senior member of staff should be involved until the fundi are adequately seen and the presence or absence of papilloedema can be confirmed.

When papilloedema is present, examination shows the blind spot to be enlarged, and the peripheral visual fields may show constriction. If the intracranial pressure is sufficiently elevated it may be higher than the arterial pressure of the blood vessels in the retina, and hence cause ischaemia. This leads to so-called visual obscuration - visual blurring or blindness. Frequently this occurs with mechanisms which elevate the intracranial pressure such as coughing, stooping or straining. Vomiting occurs at the time when headache is maximal. At first this is usually first thing in the morning and towards the end of the day.

Any patient presenting with a history suggestive of raised ICP requires urgent imaging of the brain by at least CT scan. This should be considered a medical emergency.

Coital headache

A small group of patients presents with severe headache of sudden onset which comes on at the point of orgasm. The headache is severe and commonly regresses over a period of about two hours. It has been shown that if the headache resolves within two hours, the likelihood of an intracranial vascular malformation is less than 1%. If the headache takes longer than two hours to regress, the likelihood of intracranial vascular malformation rises to around 25%. However, most patients who experience orgasmic headache seek the reassurance of negative investigation. Although most commonly referred to as coital headache, the term orgasmic headache is to be preferred, because the headache occurs irrespective of the mechanism by which orgasm is achieved.

EPILEPSY

There is perhaps no other area of neurology which causes greater diagnostic confusion than the epilepsies. The consequences both of failure to make a diagnosis and of wrong diagnosis can be far reaching.

The problems with epilepsy stem from its long history and its prior association in the minds of many individuals with "demon possession". The belief is still prevalent that patients who suffer from epilepsy are mentally incompetent.

A detailed history is the corner stone of diagnosis. Since the individual suffering from an epileptic seizure may be unaware or unconscious, a history from someone who has witnessed the seizure is important.

The epilepsies can be divided into two broad groups: the primary generalised epilepsies; and the partial epilepsies. These are considered below.

There are, too, many syndromic epilepsies which predominantly occur in children. Examples include Rolandic epilepsy, West's Syndrome and Lennox Gastaut syndrome.

Approximately one in 60 people will have a seizure at some time in their life, whereas established epilepsy, (defined as two or more seizures), has an incidence of approximately one in 200. The highest incidence of seizure activity occurs in the first few months of life, and by the age of 11, 50% of all people who will develop epilepsy will have done so. The incidence falls to approximately one in 200 throughout the teens to late fifties, and then rises again. This late rise is attributable to the increased incidence of vascular disease in the ageing brain.

The initial care and subsequent follow up of patients with epilepsy should be undertaken by medical practitioners with a particular interest in the condition. They should establish that the diagnosis is correct (some 20% of patients who have a label of epilepsy do not suffer from the condition), should arrange appropriate investigation, should discuss appropriate medication, should provide appropriate advice and, in the 20% of patients who have intractable epilepsy, should ensure prompt referral to more specialist units for consideration of specialised techniques such as epilepsy surgery.

The primary generalised epilepsies

The primary generalised epilepsies account for some 25% of all cases of adolescent/adult onset epilepsy.

The primary generalised epilepsies are thought to arise in the deeper parts of the brain, and the discharge spreads co-equally to all parts of the cortex (Figure 8). In the partial (or focal) epilepsies the seizure discharge arises from one area of the cortex (Figure 9).

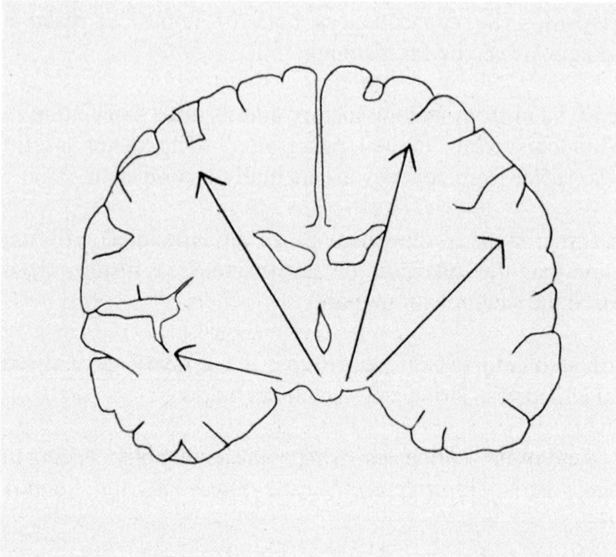

FIGURE 8

Generalised epilepsies comprise typical absence (formerly known as petit mal), atypical absence, tonic clonic seizures (formerly known as grand mal), and the myoclonic epilepsies (in particular juvenile myoclonic epilepsy).

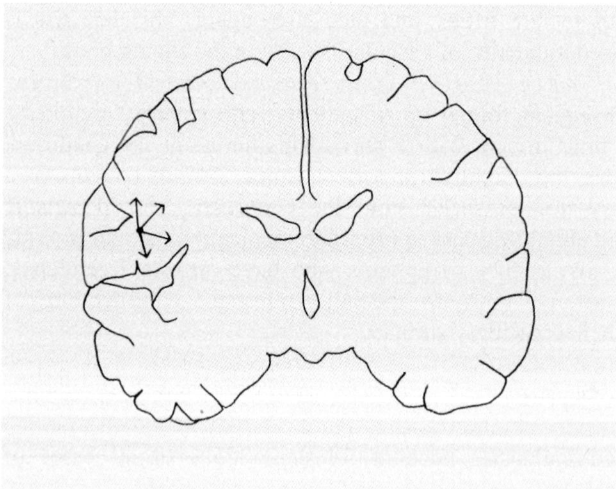

FIGURE 9

Absence seizures

These occur mainly in childhood, and rarely continue or develop beyond the age of 18. Children typically appear to "switch off" for a few seconds, and may be observed to have flickering of the eyelids. Commonly, the attacks start around the early part of the child's educational life, and they are often recognised first by teachers rather than parents. A proportion of children with absence seizures will go on to develop generalised tonic clonic seizures.

Tonic clonic seizures

Tonic clonic seizures are the most dramatic of all seizure types. Because the seizure discharge arises from the deeper structures within the brain and spreads out to all parts of the brain co-equally, there is an immediate loss of consciousness. The individual has no warning of the attack. The individual will usually become rigid first, and then go into the tonic clonic phase, where there is alternating relaxation and contraction of the musculature such that the patient appears to be shaking co-equally on both sides of the body (jactitation). There is a popular misconception that tongue biting must occur. However, this depends entirely on whether the tongue is between the teeth at the time of the onset of the seizure. It is not infrequent to read "this cannot be a fit because there was no incontinence of urine". Incontinence would only occur if the bladder contained urine at that time of the seizure. Tongue biting occurs in some 10% of patients, and 15% of patients will have incontinence.

In the tonic, (rigid) phase of a seizure, a patient is at risk of self harm, and may well fall to the ground. Most tonic clonic seizures are short-lived, lasting two to three minutes at a time. They can occur at any time of the day, although some sub-varieties have a predilection for the morning.
Following the seizure, a patient may be confused and restive, and then may sleep for several hours. If the patient has a second seizure, without regaining full consciousness, the condition is diagnosed as status epilepticus. It is important to realise that consciousness is impaired at the onset of a seizure. A patient who describes bilateral jactitation and claims to be aware of this is, by definition, not suffering from tonic clonic seizures.

The myoclonic epilepsies consist of short lived jerks which are symmetrical. They mainly affect the arms and the head, and may be associated with vocal utterances. They often occur in the setting of clear consciousness, and typically occur early in the morning. They may progress into generalised tonic clonic seizure activity.

Partial/focal epilepsies

The partial epilepsies account for some 75% of adolescent/adult onset epilepsy.

The partial epilepsies arise from differing areas of the cortex and are thus defined by the area from which they arise. Examples include frontal lobe seizures, temporal lobe seizures (previously known as psychomotor epilepsy or temporal lobe epilepsy), seizures of the parietal lobes, and seizures of the occipital lobes.

The manifestation of focal epilepsies depends entirely upon the area of the cortex from which they arise. They can exist in two states, known as simple partial and complex partial seizures.
In simple partial seizures, awareness is retained throughout the event. Patients are aware that something is happening to them, whilst still being aware of their surroundings. In complex partial seizures, awareness is lost and the patient is observed to be staring vacantly into space. They may have associated automatic movements (automatisms), which commonly consist of lip smacking or hand wringing. Volitional activity during an automatism is not possible, in that the automatisms themselves are primitive, stereotyped, repetitive movements, not driven by conscious demand.

Patients may progress from a simple partial seizure to a tonic clonic seizure, in which case the tonic clonic seizure is deemed to be a secondary generalisation (Figure 10), or they may progress to a simple partial seizure, a complex partial seizure, and then to a secondary generalisation. In the majority of cases, secondary generalisations occur nocturnally, whereas partial seizure activity occurs throughout the day, once again with a predilection for the early morning or early evening. Most partial seizures are of short duration (45 to 90 seconds). Not uncommonly, partial seizures are not recognised either by the patient or by their medical attendants, and it is the development of a secondary generalisation that brings the patient to clinical attention.

In frontal lobe seizures there is an aversive head turning away from the side of the electrical discharge. If the seizure arises in the motor strip there is a characteristic "march" of symptomatology known as the "Jacksonian march". Typically, the patient will develop focal jactitation which affects one or other hand, and then spreads up the forearm to the upper arm and to the face. The attacks are always unilateral. Focal sensory epilepsy arising from the sensory strip can occur but is much less common.

Following both of these focal seizures there will be a period of paralysis in the motor form (Todd's paresis), or a continued sensory abnormality in the sensory form. This rarely lasts beyond 24 hours.

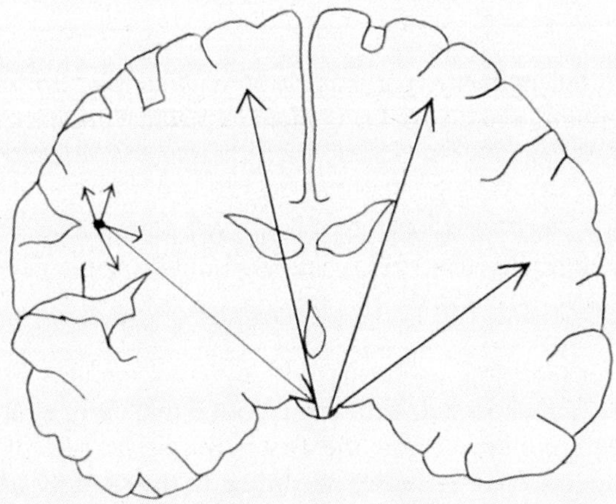

FIGURE 10

In parietal seizures there may be disturbances of body awareness, or perversions of language. By far the commonest manifestations of partial seizures are those arising from the temporal lobes and their associated structures. In this situation the patient often describes episodes of déjà vu (a feeling of intense familiarity with their surroundings as though they have been there before) which is always stereotyped. There may be a negative version of this: episodes of jamais vu, where the patient goes into a situation which they recognise well, but which feels strange to them. Perversions of smell and taste occur frequently, and are associated with the uncus. Visual hallucinations are common too. They typically involve a feeling of objects disappearing away from the individual as though they were looking down the wrong end of a telescope, or the converse of that, with things coming towards them, changing size and shape.

Perhaps the most common symptomatology is visceral symptomatology. The patient will typically feel as though their abdomen is churning and rising (giving a warm sensation) through the chest into the throat. This is often associated with a feeling of fear or panic. The patient may have episodes of depersonalisation, where they feel they are observing themselves from a distance or feel that the world is passing them by as if on a video. It is not uncommon for patients to have more than one symptom occurring at the time of their partial seizure. If a patient has partial seizure activity and then goes on to develop secondary generalisations, their partial seizure activity is often described as an aura.

During a complex partial seizure the patient is often seen to be staring vacantly into space and may show automatisms. It is at this stage that a witness to the event is of crucial importance since they can describe the patient's behaviour during the event whereas the patient can describe their subjective feeling during the event.

Patients who suffer from partial epilepsy, particularly if it is simple, are often embarrassed about their symptoms and do not bring them to medical attention.

Post Traumatic Epilepsy

It has been recognised since antiquity that, following head injury, some patients will develop seizures.

So called concussive seizures (seizures occurring within a few minutes of the original blow to the head) are not associated with any risk of either early epilepsy (within the first week) or late epilepsy (after the first week). The risk of the development of post traumatic epilepsy increases according to the severity of the head injury. Head injuries can be classed as mild, moderate or severe (Cumming 1998).

When set against population risk there is a very small increase in risk following a mild head injury. The risk is slightly higher for moderate injury, and highest for severe injury where the figure is some 15% of patients in a long term follow up of thirty years. (Annegers et al 1998; Annegers & Coan 2000).

Unfortunately these relative risks are not always appreciated and patients will frequently seek legal redress following even the most trivial head injury should they subsequently develop epilepsy.

The treatment of epilepsy

It must be realised that a simple partial seizure or a complex partial seizure is as significant as a tonic clonic seizure, whether primary or secondary. Unfortunately this understanding is not prevalent outside the field of neurology. Neurologists recognise that the earlier therapy is started the less likely the condition is to become refractory to therapy. The neurologist will pay attention to the frequency of partial seizures as well as tonic clonic seizures. Failure to bring partial seizures under control leads to chronicity.

80% of individuals with an otherwise normal brain who suffer from epilepsy, will have their seizures brought under control by a single anticonvulsant. It is therefore very important that the disease is not allowed to become chronic through lack of knowledge. Any patient who has a history suggestive of either a partial seizure or a tonic clonic seizure should be referred to the neurologist for further evaluation.

Careful consideration must be given to the institution of therapy because of the many side effects of the anticonvulsants. All of the anticonvulsants have side effects. The risk of treatment must be balanced against the risk of non-treatment. The patient must be fully informed of the potential side effects of the treatment and should be actively involved in the decision process.

In females of child bearing age special attention must be paid to the risk of fetal abnormality and to the possibility of the anticonvulsant crossing in breast milk. (Crawford et al 1999; Crawford & Hudson 2003).

Reassurance is an important part of the clinician's role.

The investigation of epilepsy

EEGs

An electroencephalogram (EEG), which records the electrical activity of the brain, is not very useful for diagnosing epilepsy. There are two exceptions to this generalisation. First: in typical absence seizures the EEG shows three cycle per second spike and wave activity which is diagnostic of the condition. Second: if the patient develops a seizure while their EEG is being recorded, useful information can be obtained. 70% of inter-ictal EEG's are normal.

Imaging

Neuroimaging gives little diagnostically useful information in the generalised epilepsies. It can, however, be very useful in partial epilepsies, particularly those thought to arise from the area of the temporal lobe. This is an area of the brain where developmental anomalies frequently occur and these can be the source of a seizure discharge. In the older patient (over fifty years of age) imaging will frequently show that the basis of the seizure activity is impaired blood supply or tumour.

Epilepsy and driving

The current regulations for non-vocational driving licences state that an individual who has had a single seizure or recurrent seizures is barred from driving for a period of twelve months from their last event. It is the patient's responsibility to notify the DVLA, and this must be explained to the patient. It is also prudent for the patient to advise their insurers. The rules for vocational licences are stricter. They change frequently. Current information can be found at www.dvla.gov.uk.

Epilepsy and employment

The diagnosis of epilepsy precludes an individual from becoming an airline pilot, prevents them holding a Public Service Vehicle Licence and precludes them from joining the Armed Forces.

Generally, the larger the employer the less likely the individual is to suffer discrimination. However, many patients believe their employment opportunities are severely affected by disclosure of the fact that they suffer from epilepsy.

Epilepsy's effects on recreational activities

Blanket restrictions on recreational activities (e.g. swimming cycling etc) are inappropriate. However, patients should be advised to take sensible precautions e.g. always being accompanied by someone else.

The concept of photosensitivity causes much misery because it is often misunderstood. Photosensitive epilepsy occurs in about 5% of all patients with epilepsy, although it is much commoner in childhood and juvenile absence epilepsy and in juvenile myoclonic epilepsy. It is a much rarer accompaniment of symptomatic generalised epilepsies, and is rarely seen in partial epilepsy. It is, therefore, inappropriate to say that an individual should not attend discos because of a presumed photosensitive response unless such a response has been demonstrated on an EEG.

HEAD INJURY

The acute management of head injury is discussed in the chapters on Accident and Emergency Medicine and Neurosurgery.

The obvious physical disabilities that can arise from brain injury (hemiparesis, aphasia etc) are easily identified in the early stages of recovery, and rehabilitation can begin then. However, this last decade has seen the recognition of a much more serious form of brain injury which can occur either independently or in association with hemiparesis etc. This is the frontal lobe dysexecutive syndrome.

The brain is a soft jelly like substance contained within the rigid confines of the skull. A blow to the head causes movement within the skull, with the brain being thrown forwards. The frontal lobes can come into contact with the frontal bones and the temporal bones can come into contact with the bones in the middle cranial fossa. This can lead to contusions at these sites. The continued movement of the brain can lead to shearing forces within the brain which disrupt the axons and lead to a pathological condition known as diffuse axonal injury. If this is severe it can disrupt the relay of information between the various parts of the brain. The frontal lobes, which are the most highly interconnected of all areas of the brain, are particularly affected.

It is important to recognise that this is a syndrome rather than one rigidly defined condition. This means that there are many ways in which it can present.

There are three major areas of the frontal cortex, being the dorsolateral, the medial/cingulet and the orbital. (Cummings & Mega 2003: see their figure 3). Each of these three areas tends to have a reasonably defined set of symptoms. Since more than one area may be damaged, symptoms attributable to damage of any of these areas may be present in one patient.

Patients with dorsolateral problems tend to have abnormalities of drive, attention and motivation.

They often display less alertness than normal people to events and persons in their environment, and lack the motivation to do things for themselves. Their ordinary life is sometimes driven by routine and a tendency to temporal concreteness. Their behaviour is therefore anchored in the here and now.

Their memory of recent events is faulty, and so is their capacity to plan for the future. In addition to the inability to formulate plans they are unable to execute them. This leads to lack of drive, an ability to make decisions, and faulty preparation for impending action.

The medial areas govern drive and motivation, and thus apathy is the dominant component of disorders of these areas. Patients classically lack of spontaneity in all aspects of action, including speech.

The orbital syndrome is characterised by failure to focus and concentrate. Patients are usually distractible and unable to block out interference from external stimuli. They may tend to show hyperactivity but be unable to inhibit spontaneous actions. The affect of patients with an orbital disorder is labile and unpredictable. They are usually unable to inhibit instinctual drives. Patients tend to fall into a spiral of increasing aggression, which leads to short term employment and eventually unemployment. Their apathy means that they are apparently content to do nothing. In addition to the cognitive deficits described above there are major non cognitive abnormalities – notably in terms of behaviour, which is often markedly antisocial.

Unfortunately it is usually only when litigation in relation to the head injury is well advanced that these abnormalities are recognised. Since these syndromes can be highly financially significant, it is important that they are recognised so that they are taken into account in the litigation. Early recognition is also therapeutically important. If the possibility of a frontal lobe dysexecutive syndrome, predicated either on the presence of contusions or diffuse axonal injury, is identified early, long term rehabilitation in the cognitive and behavioural domain can improve the outlook for these patients. This presupposes that the legal process will permit the costs of appropriate rehabilitative specialists during the process of litigation rather than at the end.

Occasionally the so called frontal lobe paradox is seen. This means that, in structured tests of frontal lobe function employed by neuropsychologists, the patients perform normally. This reflects the fact that many patients prefer a rigid structure to their lives. However, in real life they perform particularly badly.

WHIPLASH INJURY

From the neurological perspective, whiplash can be divided into two clear cut groups: those who have abnormal signs on neurological examination and those whose neurological examination is entirely normal. Ascribing patients to one or other of these groups depends on adequate history taking and adequate neurological examination.

Running through the cervical spine is the cervical spinal cord containing the descending motor and ascending sensory pathways. The horizontal pathways are the individual nerve roots arising from the cervical segments.

The commonest neurological abnormality following whiplash is the presence of radiculopathy - involvement of the nerve root. The symptoms of a radiculopathy are pain, parasthesiae (pins and needles) and weakness. Pain goes down the arm in the distribution of a given nerve root. It is often described as severe and may be precipitated and/or exacerbated by use of the limb.

With a more severe injury, as well as pain there is typically a complaint of paraesthesiae in the same distribution. With the passage of time this can progress to weakness of the muscles innervated by the relevant nerve root.

Examination of the upper limbs at the stage where the patient is complaining only of pain may well show no abnormality whatsoever. When paraesthesiae have supervened there may be altered sensation in the distribution of the nerve root, and weakness, when it develops, is demonstrable. A neurological examination conducted by non-neurologists, however, will often not distinguish between the varying degrees of sensory impairment and muscle weakness – noting only that sensation, weakness etc are present or absent.

If the spinal cord that runs through the cervical canal is damaged, the patient will complain of symptoms in the lower limbs indicative of cord compression. Initially this is a heavy feeling in the limbs exacerbated by walking and relieved by rest. Subsequently the patient is not able to walk as far as previously, and there may be diffuse sensory abnormalities in the lower limbs frequently associated with band like sensations around the limbs. These sensory abnormalities are exaggerated by heat, whether endogenous or exogenous. A cursory examination with a pin or piece of cotton wool does not suffice to exclude involvement of the ascending sensory pathways.

Late in the development of cord compression is the presence of weakness which is in a pyramidal distribution in the legs i.e. affecting the flexors. The tone will be increased. Increased reflexes will be seen. These may be symmetrical.

Later still a neurogenic bladder may result. This is manifested by frequency and urgency of micturition. It is unusual to find a record of the presence or absence of lower limb symptoms in an examination of a patient with whiplash other than an examination conducted by a neurologist.

Patients who have suggestive neurological symptoms and/or examination should be further investigated with MR scanning of the cervical spine.

Given that the evolution of neurological dysfunction is often slow, rapid resolution of personal injury litigation may well "miss" a genuine neurological whiplash.

SEVENTH CRANIAL NERVE (FACIAL NERVE) PALSY

This frequently features in clinical negligence litigation, usually because it has been wrongly attributed to benign Bell's Palsy.

This neuropathy results in weakness of the muscles of the face affecting both the muscles above and below the eye. If, after appropriate investigation, no definitive alternative cause can be found, the condition can be properly diagnosed as idiopathic facial palsy or Bell's palsy.

Unfortunately Bell's palsy is too often diagnosed when in fact there is a more sinister underlying condition. Both the history and the examination are important in distinguishing a Bell's palsy from a more sinister cause. Any history suggestive of impairment of the descending motor or ascending sensory pathways suggests a lesion in the brain stem. This may be associated with other cranial nerve palsies.

As the seventh nerve emerges from the brain stem in the cerebral pontine angle it can be distorted by the presence of tumours. This frequently leads to a complaint of unsteadiness when walking

A cholesteatoma can produce seventh nerve palsy, and the history therefore must include information regarding ear infections. The ear drum must be inspected. If it is covered in wax, the wax must be removed to ensure that a cholesteatoma is not present. Hearing tests have to be performed to ensure that the eighth nerve is not also involved. Eighth nerve involvement would make a tumour more likely.
A seventh nerve palsy can occur as one of the mononeuropathies associated with diabetes mellitus, and this must always be excluded.

There is no evidence to suggest that steroids improve the outlook for patients with idiopathic facial palsy. The early provision of euphatic facial stimulation is beneficial.

SPINAL ACCESSORY NERVE PALSY

As the spinal accessory nerve becomes extracranial, its spinal portion descends into the neck close to the internal jugular vein. It then passes deep into and innervates the sternomastoid muscle before coming through the posterior border of that muscle at the junction of the upper and middle third. It then passes obliquely into the posterior triangle of the neck to reach the upper trapezius muscle which it innervates.

In the posterior triangle the nerve is vulnerable and can be irreparably damaged by radiation, or resected during radical neck dissections. These are, however, recognised side effects. They may or may not be negligent. Whether they are negligent or not will be a matter for an expert from the relevant specialty – which will not be neurology. More commonly the nerve is injured at the transverse of the posterior triangle of the neck during minor surgical procedures such as a biopsy or excision of lymph nodes. Again, negligence cannot necessarily be inferred, but, again, a neurologist is not the right clinician to ask about breach of duty.

As a consequence of damage to the nerve the trapezius muscle loses its innervation and there is drooping of the shoulder and weakness of shoulder innervation.

REFERENCES

Annegers, JF, Hauser, WA, Coan, SP and Rocca, WA, A Population-Based Study of Seizures after Traumatic Brain Injuries, *The New England Journal of Medicine*, 1998; 338: 20-24.

Annegers, JF and Coan, SP, The Risk of Epilepsy after Traumatic Brain Injury, *Seizure*, 2000; 9: 453-457.

Crawford, P, Appleton, R, Betts, T, Duncan, JS, Guthrie, E and Morrow, J, Best Practice Guidelines for the Management of Women With Epilepsy. The Women With Epilepsy Guidelines Development Group, *Seizure*, 1999; 8: 201-217.

Crawford, P and Hudson, S, Understanding The Information Needs of Women With Epilepsy At Different Life Stages: Results Of The "Ideal World" Survey, *Seizure*, 2003; 12: 502-507.

Cumming, WJK, Head Injury, *Neurology*, 1998, London, Cavendish, 49-65.

Cumming, WJK, Symptoms and Signs, *Neurology*, 1998, London, Cavendish, 1-32.

Cummings, JL and Mega, MS, Frontal Lobe Dysfunction. In: Cummings, JL and Mega, MS (Editors), *Neuropsychiatry and Behavioural Neuroscience*, 2003, Oxford, Oxford University Press, 128-45.

Evans, RW, Diagnostic Testing for the Evaluation of Headaches, *Neurologic Clinics*, 1996: 14: 1-26.

Greenspan, SL and Caldemeyer, KS, Complications of Lumbar Puncture and Myelopathy, In: Biller, J (Editor), *Iatrogenic Neurology*, 1998, Boston, Butterworth-Heinemann, 1-24.

Kros, JM, Laboratory Diagnosis of Brain Tumours, In: Vecht, CJ (Editor) *Neuro-oncology*, Vol 67, 1997, Amsterdam, Elsevier, 217-33.

Lacomis, D, The Utility of Muscle Biopsy, *Current Neurology and Neuroscience Reports*, 2004; 4: 81-86.

Willison, HJ and Winer, JB, Clinical Evaluation and Investigations of Neuropathy, *Journal of Neurology, Neurosurgery and Psychiatry*, 2003; 74 (suppl II): 3-8.

NEUROSURGERY

Richard S.C. Kerr

INTRODUCTION

There are relatively few claims against neurosurgeons, but when they occur, they can be financially very large. There are often neurosurgical elements to claims against clinicians in other specialties – notably against Accident and Emergency clinicians and General Practitioners.

ANATOMICAL BASICS

The Brain

The central nervous system comprises the brain and spinal cord. These delicate structures are contained within the rigid skull or cranium, and the segmented, mobile, vertebral column or spine.

The skull is formed by the skull base, which lies behind the face through which all the nerves and arteries gain access to the central nervous system, and a series of interlocking plates of bone that form the top of the skull or skull vault (calvarium). This provides a rigid, protective box in which the brain itself is suspended in clear cerebro-spinal fluid (CSF). Lining the inside of the skull is a thick, fibrous membrane (dura) forming the outer layer of the meninges. The blood supply to the dura is predominantly via the middle meningeal artery, and damage to this structure, usually associated with a skull fracture, can lead to the development of a blood clot between the bone and the dura. This is termed an extra-dural haematoma.

Inside the dura lies the second layer of meninges, or arachnoid mata. A potential space exists between the dura and the arachnoid. Bleeding into this space results in the development of a sub-dural haematoma. Closely applied to the brain itself is the third layer of meninges or pia mata. This covers all the folds and convolutions (sulci and gyri) of the brain and forms a very fine vascular layer carrying minute blood vessels to the cerebral substance. Between the pia and the arachnoid is the fluid-filled subarachnoid space in which run all the major intracranial blood vessels and their various branches.

The cerebro-spinal fluid (CSF) is produced from within the hollow centre of the brain, circulating through a series of expansions, or ventricles, before emerging into the subarachnoid space. Its continual production and re-absorption over the surface of the brain allows the CSF to circulate via the subarachnoid space. Serving many functions, including protection, maintenance of homoeostasis, circulation of nutrients and hormones, the pressure in the CSF space is maintained around 5 to 15 cms of water. Bleeding from the large blood vessels within the subarachnoid space, most often from a cerebral aneurysm, results in the life-threatening condition of subarachnoid haemorrhage.

Having circulated through the brain, venous blood collects from both superficial and deep veins into a system of channels that lie within the dura. These large vessels eventually coalesce to leave the skull to form the internal jugular veins, which join with the external jugular veins to form the superior vena cava, this leading to the right hand side of the heart.

The brain itself is divided both anatomically and functionally into a series of lobes. These are connected to each other via a series of white matter tracts (the largest of which is the corpus callosum) and the spinal cord via the internal capsule and descending and ascending fibre pathways in the brain stem. They join the spinal cord at the level of the foramen magnum. The back part of the skull is occupied by the cerebellar hemispheres, which are mainly involved in modulation of movement and posture.

The cerebral hemispheres on each side are divided into four lobes. The frontal lobe is involved not only with the control of motor function, but also with higher mental functions, such as memory, concentration and personality. Behind this lies the parietal lobe, which comprises the sensory cortex and the sensory association areas. Lying at the back are the occipital lobes, vital for vision. On each side are the temporal lobes, areas involved with memory function, together with vision and also speech on the dominant side (usually the left).

From the brain stem arise the twelve pairs of cranial nerves conveying information to and from all the facial structures, including smell, sight and hearing, but also taste, swallowing, facial sensation and facial movement.

The Spine

Running from the tip of the brain stem to its termination at the top of the lumbar spine is the spinal cord. This is enclosed in identical layers of meninges with CSF in the subarachnoid space. The spinal cord lies in the centre of the spinal canal, partially suspended by CSF, but also by thickened suspensory ligaments (the dentate ligaments) from the side of the spinal cord to the dura. The spinal cord is swollen in the cervical region and at its termination or conus. From the spinal cord arise all the spinal nerves (motor and sensory) going out to the body, the arms and the legs. These emerge as mixed spinal nerves, leaving the spine via small foramina formed by notches in adjacent vertebrae.

The spinal canal itself is formed by a series of vertebrae, connected in front by the intervertebral discs, at the side by interlocking facet joints, and at the back by a series of strong ligaments. Surrounding this lie powerful blocks of muscle, which help provide stability to the spine and yet allow a large range of movement.

Running from the end of the spinal cord is a large sheath of nerves, descending through the lumbar and sacral areas, known as the cauda equina. The lumbar spine does not, therefore, contain spinal cord itself, but this large collection of nerves lying within the subarachnoid space. It should be noted that pathology directly affecting the spinal cord rarely produces pain, but a clinical picture of instability of gait and loss of co-ordination with, on examination, brisk reflexes and increased limb tone. A sensory deficit may also be evident according to the level of compression. Conditions affecting the nerve roots however, either within the cauda equina or as they emerge from the spine, result in severe pain which radiates into the area supplied by that nerve. Examination commonly shows reduced reflexes, reduced tone, sensory loss according to the area of distribution of that nerve, and power loss.

The blood supply to the spinal cord is derived from the descending anterior and posterior spinal arteries, enhanced by small segmental vessels at each spinal level.

Overall, the vertebral column is comprised of seven cervical vertebrae, the top two being highly specialised to articulate with the skull base (the atlas and the axis vertebrae), twelve thoracic vertebrae and five large, strong, lumbar vertebrae. The sacral vertebrae are fused to form the sacrum - an integral part of the bony pelvis.

THE PATHOPHYSIOLOGY OF RAISED INTRACRANIAL PRESSURE

Much of neurosurgery is concerned with the recognition and management of raised intracranial pressure. It is important, therefore, to appreciate how increases in intracranial pressure may occur and the impact that those changes will have.

As has already been indicated, the skull forms a protective but rigid structure that houses the brain, cerebro-spinal fluid and blood. Changes in any one of these components can lead to significant alterations in intracranial pressure. The speed of onset and the severity of change of intracranial pressure will dictate the pattern of symptoms and signs that develop as a consequence. For example, a spontaneous bleed from a blood vessel into the substance of the brain can render a patient unconscious from the effects of raised intracranial pressure. By contrast, a patient who has a very slowly growing tumour may gradually develop headaches. These are likely to occur particularly in the morning, or will wake the patient from sleep in the early hours due to a slow, steady increase in intracranial pressure during the night. In another, usually elderly group, intermittent rises in intracranial pressure can lead to a pattern of progressive loss of short-term memory, difficulty with balance and urinary incontinence. This triad of symptoms, which is due to very chronic intermittent raised intracranial pressure, is referred to as normal pressure hydrocephalus.

There is a relationship between intracranial pressure and volume, such that initially relatively large changes in intracranial volume produce very small changes in intracranial pressure. Compensatory mechanisms allow some reduction in cerebral blood volume, a significant reduction in the amount of cerebro-spinal fluid, both within the ventricular system and the subarachnoid spaces, and some shift of the cerebral substance itself. This enables us all to compensate for rises in intracranial volume. However, there comes a point where compensatory mechanisms are no longer able to cope with any further changes, the result being that any small change in volume at that stage leads to significant changes in intracranial pressure.

The importance of recognition of raised intracranial pressure is that without treatment, the sustained increase can result in neurological damage or death. This applies particularly to acute rises in intracranial pressure and to sub-acute rises, when compensatory mechanisms have been utilised and any further small changes in intracranial volume lead to large changes in intracranial pressure. The very chronic rises in intracranial pressure seen with normal pressure hydrocephalus rarely become life threatening.

The management of raised intracranial pressure depends initially upon recognition of its presence, arranging appropriate investigations to identify the cause and then treating the cause, whether it be by reducing the volume of the tumour, by draining excess cerebro-spinal fluid or using medication to reduce cerebral swelling and oedema. Failure to recognise increasing intracranial pressure will eventually lead to compression of the brain stem, with a risk of cerebral herniation and brain stem compression, either at the level of the mid-brain or at the level of the medulla. As that compression occurs, so cardiovascular changes will be observed, with an increase in the blood pressure and a fall of the pulse rate, producing the so-called "Cushing response".

THE PRESENTATION OF NEUROSURGICAL CONDITIONS

General

Patients with neurosurgical conditions may present with any one or any combination of the following groups of symptoms. When taking a history and examining a patient, it is often helpful to consider the symptoms and signs in this way, to try to enable an anatomical diagnosis to be made upon which a pathological diagnosis can then be superimposed. This will then be supported by appropriate investigations.

Raised Intracranial Pressure

Recognition of the symptoms and signs of raised intracranial pressure is vital. The most important sign is an alteration in the conscious level. Any patient whose conscious level is affected (particularly if their conscious level is deteriorating), should be diagnosed presumptively as suffering raised intracranial pressure and investigated and treated accordingly. To enable assessments to be made in a standardised fashion, the 15 point Glasgow Coma Score (GCS) is utilised almost universally. The GCS of patients with an altered conscious level should be assessed regularly so that changes can be identified.

For patients who do not have an altered conscious level, raised intracranial pressure should be suspected if there are symptoms of headache and vomiting with, on examination, papilloedema and neck stiffness. It should be noted, however, that patients could die from the effects of raised intracranial pressure without papilloedema ever developing.

The headache of raised intracranial pressure typically comes on in the early hours of the morning, when it will be present on waking or wake patients from sleep. The likely cause for this is a rise in the partial pressure of carbon dioxide due to relative hypoventilation at night, this causing dilation of the intracranial blood vessels and a relative increase in cerebral blood volume. As the patient gets up and walks around, so this will change and the pressure will come back to normal.

Vomiting associated with raised intracranial pressure will tend to occur at times when the pressure is increased and may be due to distortion of the brain stem.

Papilloedema may be visualised by examining the optic nerve as it leaves from the back of the eye using an ophthalmoscope. Increases in intracranial pressure results in venous engorgement and eventual swelling of the optic nerve head, with loss of the normal definition so producing a picture of papilloedema. If left untreated this in itself can result in atrophy of the optic nerve, but as previously mentioned, intracranial pressure can rise to a life threatening level without papilloedema ever developing. The absence of papilloedema, therefore, does not mean absence of raised intracranial pressure.

Neck stiffness can also be a feature of raised intracranial pressure. A patient who complains of pain in the neck and neck stiffness will either have local disease within the cervical spine, inflammation within the meninges or raised intracranial pressure. This applies particularly when the cause of the pressure is located in the back part of the brain

Meningeal Irritation

If the meninges (the coverings of the brain or spinal cord) become inflamed, this will result in the symptoms and signs of meningeal irritation. The causes of that inflammation can be many and varied. This equally applies to inflammation of the lining of the abdominal cavity or peritoneum, and the lining of the thoracic cavity or pleura.

Inflammation can be caused, therefore, by blood due to a subarachnoid haemorrhage, infection from bacteria causing bacterial meningitis, viruses causing viral meningitis, inflammation from air following trauma or open surgical procedures, and inflammation due to chemicals - either instilled as a form of therapy or following drainage of various tumours.

The resulting picture is one of severe headache and neck stiffness, temperature, vomiting and a feeling of malaise, with on examination a sensitivity to light (photophobia), neck stiffness and a limitation of straight leg raising due to stretching of inflamed meninges.

Recognition of meningeal irritation is vital, especially if the underlying cause is due to bacterial meningitis, as early treatment is necessary to prevent neurological damage.

Focal Signs

Abnormalities within the substance of the brain, or spinal cord, can present with signs consequent upon the functional activity of that area. As has been mentioned, the brain is divided into the cerebral hemispheres (each of these into four lobes), the deep structures, the brainstem divided into medulla, pons and mid brain, and the cerebellar hemispheres.

Abnormalities within the frontal lobe of the brain can be very difficult to recognise, particularly if anteriorly placed and unilateral. A large tumour that compromises the front or anterior part of both frontal lobes may result in patients presenting with symptoms suggestive of dementia, with abnormalities of behaviour and memory. Remember the olfactory groove meningioma, where the only clinical sign may be that of loss of the sense of smell. More posteriorly placed abnormalities within the frontal lobe will affect the motor strip and the motor association areas and result in a contra-lateral weakness with, on examination, brisk reflexes, an extensor plantar response and increased muscle tone. On the dominant side this may affect speech as well.

Lesions within the parietal lobe will produce contra-lateral abnormalities of sensation and an inability to recognise objects by touch alone. Eventually the patients will tend to ignore the contra-lateral side of the body as a result of this.

The occipital lobes are concerned with vision. The pathway from the back of the eye to the occipital cortex is long and complex. Vision is appreciated in terms of fields, and thus the right visual field is appreciated in the left occipital cortex, and vice versa. Abnormalities within the medial aspects of the occipital lobe will therefore result in a failure of vision in the contra-lateral visual field. There is significant overlap of the fields centrally, and unless specifically examined for, it is therefore easy to miss a contra-lateral field defect, particularly in its early stages. Involvement of the visual pathways from the retina back to the occipital cortex depends upon the anatomical site. Compromise of the optic nerve itself will lead to reduction of vision and eventual blindness in that eye. Involvement of the optic chiasm, where the two optic nerves join and crossover, will usually result in bi-temporal hemianopia (loss of the outer half of the visual field on either side). This will most often be due to a pituitary tumour. Loss of the optic tract behind the optic chiasm will result in field loss (homonymous hemianopia), similar to that seen with cortical anomalies.

The cerebellar hemispheres connected by the cerebellar vermis lie in the posterior fossa and are specifically concerned with co-ordination and modulation of movements. Their influence is ipsilateral. Therefore, an abnormality in the left cerebellar hemisphere will lead to a loss of co-ordination in the left arm and left leg. Equally, an abnormality in the right cerebellar hemisphere will tend to lead to inco-ordination in the right arm and right leg, whilst a centrally placed abnormality within the cerebellar vermis will affect the trunk itself and body posture, leading to abnormalities of gait and inco-ordination of walking. It should be noted that lesions within the posterior fossa may also compromise the circulation of cerebro-spinal fluid, (leading to a build-up of fluid), or obstructive hydrocephalus, (giving rise to a pattern of raised intracranial pressure in addition to focal signs).

Immediately adjacent to the cerebellar hemispheres is an area called the cerebellar pontine angle. Typically, benign, slow-growing tumours develop here from the 8th cranial nerve. As they enlarge, they can compromise other cranial nerves, in particular the 5th, 7th, 9th, 10th and 11th cranial nerves. They may also produce compression of the underlying cerebellar hemisphere and brain stem, leading to inco-ordination of gait and movement.

The last anatomical area is the brain stem. This comprises the descending motor pathways and ascending sensory pathways running from the spinal cord up to the cerebral hemispheres, together with the cranial nerve nuclei and connections to the cerebellar hemispheres. Abnormalities within the brain stem will tend to produce focal neurological change affecting the ascending and descending pathways, together with multiple cranial nerve palsies consequent upon involvement of the cranial nerve nuclei. The various different cranial nerve nuclei are found in mid-brain, pons and medulla, with the exception of the 5th nerve nucleus, which extends through all areas of the brain stem. Each of the cranial nerves has a specific function varying from control of eye movements and pupillary size, facial sensation, facial movement, control of swallowing, voice and tongue, and the 8th cranial nerve serving hearing and balance. Patients with neurosurgical conditions may present therefore, with any one or any combination of these groups of symptoms. When taking a history and examining a patient, it is often helpful to consider the symptoms and signs in this way, to try to enable an anatomical diagnosis to be made upon which a pathological diagnosis can then be superimposed. This will then be supported by appropriate investigations.

SUBARACHNOID HAEMORRHAGE:

Subarachnoid haemorrhage is a life-threatening condition affecting 10 per 100,000 of the population per year. The causes of subarachnoid haemorrhage include:

- Rupture of cerebral aneurysm – 80%.
- Rupture of arteriovenous malformation – 10% to 15%.
- Other causes, including bleeding from a tumour, anti-coagulants and connective tissue disorders.

In approximately 20% of patients, the source of the haemorrhage will not be identified.

The history is classical and very important.

The sudden onset of an unusual headache must be considered to be subarachnoid haemorrhage until proved otherwise. Like any other vascular event, it is sudden in onset and the severity of the headache is one that the patient will not have experienced before and will certainly never forget. The sudden eruption of blood into the subarachnoid space produces symptoms suggestive of meningeal irritation, including headache, nausea, vomiting and neck pain, and may cause a temporary loss of consciousness.

Diagnosis is based upon obtaining a good history from the patient or from other friends or relatives, being aware of the potential diagnosis and confirming this using a CT scan in the first instance. If that proves to be normal and there is no evidence of blood in the subarachnoid space, it is vital to go on and carry out a lumbar puncture. The cerebro-spinal fluid must be examined, not only for blood, but also for evidence of xanthochromic staining (which, if present, indicates that the blood has been present within the CSF for at least 6 hours). Lumbar puncture will also exclude sudden onset of bacterial meningitis. Failure to make the diagnosis will put the patient at risk from the effects of a further subarachnoid haemorrhage. Occurring mainly in the 6th decade of life, and in a ratio of female to male of 2 : 1, 30% to 40% of patients will die or be left seriously neurologically damaged as a consequence of their first haemorrhage. If patients go on to suffer a second subarachnoid haemorrhage, approximately 60% to 70% of patients will die or be left neurologically damaged. Furthermore, once a patient has bled from an intracranial aneurysm, it is known that every day there is a risk of a second haemorrhage occurring, the overall risk being approximately 30% in the first six months and 3% per year thereafter.

Having identified that a patient has suffered a subarachnoid haemorrhage, it is important that the patient is discussed with the regional neurosurgical unit so that an appropriate line of management can be arranged. This would normally include transfer to the regional neurosurgical unit for further investigation with CT angiograms and/or digital angiography with a view to treatment. This may be either surgical clipping of the aneurysm or endovascular coiling, depending upon the anatomy of the aneurysm and its location, together with the general well being of the patient.

Treatment of the aneurysm itself carries significant risk. Prior to surgery or endovascular therapy, there will need to be careful discussion with the patient and their family to ensure that they understand both the natural history following rupture of an intracranial aneurysm, and the potential risks of both morbidity and mortality associated with treatment.

Following rupture of an intracranial aneurysm, risks other than re-bleeding do occur. These include the development of arterial vasospasm and consequent cerebral ischaemia. This is a major cause of additional morbidity and mortality in patients following subarachnoid haemorrhage. It will usually occur within a few days of the onset of the haemorrhage, but may continue for several weeks afterwards. Hydrocephalus due to blood causing failure of proper circulation of the cerebro-spinal fluid through the subarachnoid space and failure of re-absorption of cerebro-spinal fluid at the level of the arachnoid villi, can also occur. This will lead to a fluctuating deterioration in the patient's conscious level. This can be confirmed with CT scan and treated by lumbar puncture or, if necessary, insertion of a shunt.

Whilst the overall management of aneurysmal subarachnoid haemorrhage remains controversial and complex, the initial diagnosis is paramount. I reiterate that in any patient with a sudden onset of an unusual headache, this must be considered to be subarachnoid haemorrhage until proved otherwise and investigated appropriately.

HEAD INJURY

In June 2003, the National Institute of Clinical Excellence published Clinical Guideline 4. This guideline details the management of head injury and includes information on triage, assessment, investigation and early management in infants, children and adults. In association with these guidelines were published several clinical practice algorithms. These relate to telephone advice for patients who have suffered a head injury, patients who require referral by community based medical services, selection of patients requiring CT imaging of the head following head injury, and selection of patients for imaging of the cervical spine following head injury.

The aim of these guidelines is to identify patients in whom there has been injury to the brain (and cervical spine) and to identify those patients who are at risk from the development of further complications which may lead to additional neurological injury.

The guidelines look at the best available evidence, the diagnosis and treatment of the head injury and make recommendations based on that evidence. The guidelines, therefore, include recommendations about:

- Management of a head injured patient before they get to hospital
- Who should go to hospital
- Initial assessment and the use of scans of the head and neck
- Who should be admitted to hospital
- Who requires surgery
- Discharge
- Information transferred to patients and their carers
- Problem solving following discharge
- Transferring patients between departments and hospitals.

Of the many hundreds of patients who are referred to hospital following a head injury, over 90% are considered to have minor problems, and they will be discharged home without requiring hospital admission. Of those admitted, the majority will be discharged home within 48 hours. Less than 1% of patients admitted suffer a severe brain injury consequent upon either the initial impact or the development of subsequent complications.

Management of head injury, therefore, requires not only recognition of those patients who have sustained a serious head injury, but also an appreciation of the risk factors that are likely to be associated with the development of subsequent complications.

This is well illustrated by the development and management of an acute extradural haematoma. This represents an injury to the coverings of the brain, rather than the brain itself, but if unrecognised and untreated this injury can lead to severe compression of the brain which may result ultimately in neurological damage or even death. If it is recognised and treated promptly the patient can recover completely. An acute extradural haematoma usually results from a skull fracture that causes damage to the blood vessel lying between the dura and the inner surface of the skull (middle meningeal artery). The initial injury may be sufficient to cause the patient to lose consciousness, but he would rapidly recover from that provided there has been no associated cerebral injury. Clinical examination at that time may reveal no abnormal neurological signs, the patient having apparently fully recovered from the head injury. However, the damage caused to the blood vessel allows a blood clot to accumulate between the dura and the inner side of the bone, and as it enlarges so it causes more bleeding, which causes further enlargement. Unchecked, eventually the presence of the blood clot could cause compression of the underlying brain and an associated increase in intracranial pressure. This results in an alteration in the conscious level. As the pressure increases further, so other neurological signs develop, including compression of the ipsilateral 3rd nerve leading to dilatation of the pupil, herniation of the medial side of the temporal lobe into the tentorial hiatus causing mid-brain compression, and ultimately brain stem compression which can result in brain death. It is known that the risk of a patient developing an intracranial blood clot is as high as 1 in 4 in patients who have a skull fracture and a persistent alteration in conscious level. The guidelines are aimed, therefore, at trying to identify those at risk of developing complications after head injury.

The guidelines say that any patient should be taken directly to an Accident and Emergency Department if:

- They have suffered loss of consciousness from which they may have recovered
- Any problems with memory
- A persistent headache
- Vomiting and sickness
- Previous brain surgery
- A history of bleeding and abnormalities or are taking anti-coagulant medication
- Over 65 years
- Altered behaviour including lack of interest in what is around them
- Being drunk or having taken drugs
- Suspicion of injury that was caused intentionally, either by the patient or someone else

Following admission to hospital, basic and immediate assessment of airway, breathing and circulation should be carried out, with specific attention being paid to the cervical spine in any patient who has suffered head injury.

A neck collar should be positioned if there is:

- Persistent alteration in Glasgow Coma Score
- Neck pain and tenderness
- Difficulty understanding, speaking, reading or writing
- Alteration in feeling in any part of the body
- Problems balancing or walking
- General weakness
- Changes in eyesight
- Suspicion of injury

If there is concern that the patient is at risk of developing an intracranial blood clot, then a CT scan should be performed immediately. There should be such concern where any of the following applies:

- Glasgow Coma Score of less than 13 since the time of the injury;
- Glasgow Coma Score of 13 or 14 two hours after the injury (patient has not fully recovered);

- Fracture of the base of the skull, with cerebro-spinal fluid leaking from ear or nose, deafness or the development of a black eye or bruising behind the ears;
- Damage to the skull, particularly if a penetrating injury is suspected;
- Vomiting;
- Over age 65, provided there has been loss of consciousness or amnesia
- Convulsions or seizures;
- History of bleeding problems, or taking medication;
- Problems of understanding, speaking, reading or writing;
- Loss of feeling in any part of the body;
- Problems with balance and walking;
- General weakness;
- Any changes in eyesight.

If there is concern about injury to the cervical spine, a neck X-ray should be done. Alternatively (and particularly if the lower part of the cervical spine cannot be visualised on plain X-ray) a CT scan should be done. It is vital the whole cervical spine is covered down to, and including, the C7/T1 junction.

The use of guidelines such as this will hopefully allow not only recognition of damage caused by the head injury, but also anticipation of further complications that could develop, and that if treated promptly will allow complete recovery of the patient.

For those patients who do suffer a severe head injury, it is likely that their recovery will be associated with long-term sequelae, not only for the injured person, but also for their family and carers. Recognition of this in the very early stages will often help long-term management. The patient, the family and the carers need to be advised that recovery can take 18 months to 2 years, and only at that stage will the final picture emerge. Clearly, in children there may be further changes that will occur in the years thereafter as well. As much information should be given to patients and their families as possible about the long-term effects of head injury. Attention should be paid to changes in higher mental function, in terms of memory, concentration and personality and, where required, patients should be referred early for neuropsychological assessment and advice. Self-help groups such as HEADWAY provide invaluable support and guidance.

Finally, patients should be advised after a major head injury that they should contact the DVLA in Swansea, as there may be restrictions on their ability to return to driving. If they have suffered an intracranial blood clot that required surgery, if they have suffered seizures or if they have major residual neurological deficits, it is likely that a driving restriction will be applied for a period of time.

Prior to discharge from hospital, any patient who has suffered a head injury should be given information about what to look out for, and particularly the following:

- Unconsciousness or lack of full consciousness
- Confusion
- Drowsiness
- Problems understanding or speaking
- Difficulty with balance or walking
- Weakness of arms or legs
- Difficulty with eyesight
- Severe headache that will not resolve
- Vomiting
- Seizures
- Evidence of CSF leak through the ear or the nose

Should any of these occur, the patient should go straight to the nearest hospital Accident and Emergency Department.

Some complications following head injury take weeks to develop. This is particularly with chronic collections of fluid in the subdural space or hydrocephalus. This should always be borne in mind by the patient's general practitioner and hospital practitioners if the patient returns to the Accident and Emergency Department.

Finally, it should be appreciated by the patients, their families and carers, their general practitioner, their employers and, in children, teachers at school, that recovery from a head injury can take many weeks or months, even in those patients who have no obvious neurological deficit. Patients will often feel very tired, have difficulty with short-term memory, and have problems concentrating, planning and taking executive decisions. Many of these symptoms will resolve when a suitable period of time has lapsed, which may run into many weeks, with appropriate understanding by the patient and those around him.

INTRACRANIAL TUMOURS

General

Tumours within the brain are usually described according to a classification from the World Health Organisation. It is easier to consider them as either benign or malignant, the malignant tumours either arising from within the substance of the brain or its coverings, or coming from outside the brain (metastases). The tissues within the brain include the glial supporting cells, nerve cells, blood vessels, the lining of the ventricles or ependyma, the nerves emanating from the brain and the coverings of the brain. All of these structures can have tumours associated with them.

Presentation of intracranial tumours will usually be a combination of focal signs due to the presence of the abnormality, and symptoms of raised intracranial pressure often due to the size of the tumour. For those tumours that are within the brain itself they may present with epilepsy, the pattern of the epilepsy often suggesting the anatomical location of the lesion itself.

The most common benign tumours seen are meningiomas and nerve sheath tumours or schwannomas.

Meningiomas

These can arise anywhere within the skull, either from the convexity or the skull base. Invariably slowly growing, they are seen more commonly in women than in men and will usually present with focal neurological signs, associated eventually with symptoms of raised intracranial pressure if the presentation is delayed. Specific sites of diagnosis can be difficult, and include the floor of the anterior cranial fossa, where the only sign may be that of the lack of sense of smell and unless specifically tested for that will be missed. Tumours within the region of the body of the sphenoid can present with subtle visual field defects that require careful visual assessment. Tumours of the foramen magnum, whilst usually presenting with progressive brain stem compression, can present simply with wasting of the small hand muscles on both sides. Management depends upon recognition of the signs and symptoms, arranging appropriate investigations and having a detailed discussion with the patient and their family about the options of treatment. For meningioma this includes conservative treatment with simple observation, surgery to remove the tumour and focussed radiation. All of these options need to be discussed and considered before the final decision is made.

Schwannomas

These can be found on most cranial nerves, but are frequently associated with the 8th or vestibulo-cochlea nerve, giving rise to the so-called acoustic neuroma. Invariably unilateral, except under very specific circumstances, these tumours grow on average 2 to 3 mm per year, presenting with unilateral sensory neural deafness, often with associated tinnitus and balance difficulties. Faced with a patient with unilateral deafness, an MRI scan must be arranged to exclude the presence of an acoustic neuroma. Having established a diagnosis the patients will usually be referred through to a specialist clinic where the options of treatment can be considered, which again include conservative treatment with observation, surgery to remove the acoustic neuroma or focussed radiation. The relative merits of observation, surgery and radiation therapy need to be carefully discussed so that patients can come to a judged decision about how best to proceed. Information from the British Acoustic Neuroma Association may also be invaluable and should be given to the patients.

Gliomas

These arise from the glial or supporting cells in the brain. They can be low-grade tumours with a long natural history, high-grade tumours that will grow rapidly and without treatment lead to a very short life expectancy, or anything in between. Presentation will usually be with focal neurological signs, although with high grade tumours raised intracranial pressure will often occur, but can be rapidly helped using steroid therapy. If suspected, a CT scan and/or an MRI scan should be carried out and the patient referred to the neurosurgical unit. The treatment possibilities include the use of image guided biopsy, the use of surgery to remove the tumour and the subsequent use of both radiotherapy and chemotherapy. Unfortunately, the natural history of high-grade glioma is to recur, often within a 1 to 2 year time period.

Secondary or metastatic intracranial tumours

These spread most commonly from the breast, gut and lung. Again, they will usually present with focal signs and raised intracranial pressure of rapid onset, in keeping with their aggressive nature. Biopsy or the presence of multiple lesions on scan can confirm diagnosis. Treatment depends upon the general condition of the patient, together with the distribution of the disease, but is often by surgery with adjunctive radiotherapy.

Colloid cysts

These are very unusual tumours, which are derived from the ependymal lining of the third ventricle and usually occur in the anterior part of that ventricle. As they enlarge they block the outflow from the lateral ventricle into the third ventricle and cause hydrocephalus. This can be acute and sufficient to cause rapid loss of consciousness of the patient. Often the patient will recover and regain consciousness, but if the diagnosis is not made and recognised, the patient remains at risk from further such hydrocephalic attacks from which they may not recover fully in the future. Management requires not only recognition of the presence of raised intracranial pressure and that these attacks are hydrocephalic in nature, but subsequent imaging with MRI, neuropsychological assessment to measure memory function, and then treatment. This is either by insertion of a shunt to treat the hydrocephalus, or by direct approach to the colloid cyst, (either using a ventriculoscope or by open operation) to drain and excise the cyst. The anatomy of the colloid cyst is such that the memory pathways carried in the fornices will often lie immediately over the colloid cyst and treatment therefore carries significant risk to the patient in terms of short-term memory. They should be advised of that prior to surgery, as should their family.

Tumours of the pituitary gland

The pituitary gland lies in a small bony depression in the middle of the floor of the skull. From the pituitary gland are released many hormonal precursors, including ACTH, TSH, prolactin growth hormone and gonadotrophins. Tumours within the pituitary gland can therefore be associated with either over- or under-production of any one or combination of these hormones. In addition, if a tumour enlarges it may cause compression of the overlying optic chiasm, producing a visual field defect where the field loss is in the outer aspect of the field on both sides. This forms a so-called a bi-temporal hemianopia. Again, unless specifically examined for, such a visual field defect will be missed and delay in treatment may result in progressive visual loss that cannot be recovered once the diagnosis has been made.

Investigation, therefore, requires appropriate endocrine tests to establish the hormonal changes, an ophthalmological examination with appropriate radiology, usually with MRI scan.

Treatment involves management by a multidisciplinary team used to attending patients with pituitary disease and may require a combination of medical therapy, surgery (usually transphenoidal) and/or radiotherapy. The results are very much dependant upon the experience of that team and there is no place for the occasional pituitary surgeon, except in specific circumstances.

SPINAL CORD AND CAUDA EQUINA COMPRESSION

The clinical pictures that emerge due to compression of the spinal cord or compression of the cauda equina are very different, but delays in their diagnosis and treatment can be equally devastating. The causes of compression of these neurological structures are many and varied and include degenerative disease and acute disc prolapse, compression due to tumour, epidural infection and epidural haematoma, either spontaneous or following trauma.

Spinal cord compression

The spinal cord extends from the foramen magnum down to the L1/L2 junction. Pathology between these sites can lead either to compression of the spinal cord, or to compression of the exiting nerve roots, giving rise to severe pain in the distribution of that nerve root.

Spinal cord compression may present with pain at the site of the pathology. As regards neurological change, this will usually be manifest initially as a gritty numbness in the fingers and toes, progressing to a glove and stocking sensory loss, and eventually an ascending sensory level if the compression is unchecked. In association with this, patients will complain of increasing unsteadiness of gait with difficulty going upstairs or rising out of a chair and increased spasms of cramps in their legs. Certainly the examination would usually reveal signs of an upper motor neurone lesion, with brisk reflexes, increased tone with a sensory level according to the area of compression. Early recognition of this is vital. The major aim of treatment of spinal cord compression is to try to prevent further deterioration of the symptoms and it is important, therefore, to recognise that the clinical picture present at the time of surgery may well be the clinical picture which remains once the decompression is achieved. Surgery aimed at relieving pain from degenerative disease within the spine is rarely successful and still carries the same risks as operations aimed at relieving spinal cord compression.

Prior to surgery it is important that these risks are carefully described to the patient and their family. Any surgery to the spine carries with it the risk of neurological injury to the point of paralysis, whether that is due to direct injury to the spinal cord at the time of surgery, or delayed effect due to post-operative haematoma or infection. The risk of such devastating neurological injury is very low (less than 1%) but it is still of such consequence that it needs to be carefully described.

Any patient who presents with spinal pain which is unremitting, and especially if it is pain that tends to wake them at night and make them try to sleep in a chair to get some relief, should be investigated with MRI to exclude the presence of a tumour. Benign tumours such as meningioma or neurofibroma often present with a very long history of gradual onset of symptoms of this nature that, at a later date become associated with symptoms suggestive of spinal cord compression. Under these circumstances, the sooner the tumour is identified and dealt with, the easier it is to deal with and the less the risk to the spinal cord. Delayed diagnosis will therefore enhance those risks. For the patients with malignant tumours, they will often present with a very short history of severe pain, which requires them to sleep in a chair at night before the symptoms of spinal cord compression start. Again, it is vital to try to establish the diagnosis before patients begin to lose leg motor function, and especially bladder and bowel function, as it is very rare for these to be restored following treatment. Early diagnosis, therefore, and an awareness of the history followed by careful examination will allow treatment before irreversible neurological damage ensues.

Traumatic spinal cord injury must always be considered in patients with head injury or other multiple injuries. Adherence to the guidelines described in the Head Injury section of this chapter will hopefully avoid the clinical mistake of missing a cervical spine injury associated with head trauma. The guidelines need to be considered and appropriate local arrangements put in place to enable such injuries to be identified.

Cauda Equina Compression

The cauda equina extends from the tip of the conus at the L1/L2 junction, through the lumbar sac and into the sacral canal. It is rare to see pathology within the sacral canal and the majority of disease occurs within the lumbar sac. Whilst tumours do occur here, as do infection and blood clot, by far the most common pathology relates to degenerative changes within the lumbar spine leading, either to acute soft disc prolapse (slipped disc) or to nerve root or cauda equina compression due to narrowing of the canal or lumbar canal stenosis.

Back pain with pain radiating into the leg in a sciatic distribution is a very common problem faced by general practitioners, and indeed by hospital practitioners. In the majority of patients this is due to an acute soft disc prolapse and will resolve spontaneously without residual neurological compromise. Often this will take 4 to 6 weeks before resolution of the symptoms will begin to be apparent, and during that time it is important that patients rest and allow the pain to settle down before returning to their previous activities. If the symptoms do not resolve patients should be referred for further investigation, with imaging in the form of MRI scan. Earlier referral is required for patients who have severe and increasing pain, early and progressive neurological deficit, for example a foot drop, and for patients who have symptoms and signs of cauda equina compression, with pain in both legs and any disturbance of bladder and bowel function.

The disc prolapse can become so large, especially in patients who have a naturally narrow spinal canal that direct pressure on all of the nerves travelling through the lumbar sac can result in loss of bladder, bowel and sexual function. Relief of that compression should be carried out as soon as possible. There is controversy within the literature as to how quickly such decompressive surgery should be effected. Whilst some papers would suggest that time is not of the essence, the majority of surgeons would treat this as a neurosurgical emergency and bring the patient into hospital as soon as possible, arrange for an MRI scan and if appropriate and after discussion with the patient, deal with this by a decompressive laminectomy and removal of the central disc prolapse. Recovery undoubtedly depends upon how advanced the cauda equina syndrome was prior to surgery. This applies not only to patients who have compression due to an acute soft disc prolapse, but also patients who, following spinal surgery, develop an acute blood clot leading to compression of the cauda equina. For the post-operative patients, careful neurological observations immediately following surgery are aimed specifically at identifying whether or not surgery has been associated with any additional neurological change and at identifying any deterioration which would suggest the development of a post-operative wound haematoma. If a patient has experienced progressive deterioration in function following surgery, the presence of a blood clot must be excluded, either by appropriate imaging, using MRI, or myelography if that is not available, or failing that to re-explore the wound. The identification of cauda equina compression in post-operative patients is one that may require careful neurological examination. Often the patient in the post-operative phase will feel that the changes they are experiencing are to be expected. Furthermore, local pain may make it more difficult to assess and the development of post-operative retention, especially in male patients following lumbar spine surgery, complicates the issues even further. Anybody undertaking spinal surgery, therefore, needs to be very vigilant of these factors and err on the side of caution if there is any concern about the patient's post-operative recovery.

As regards the development of an acute central disc prolapse with cauda equina compression, anyone harbouring a disc giving rise to sciatica needs to be advised that the development of a cauda equina syndrome is possible. The patient should be advised about what to look out for, and told that they need to bring this to the attention of either their general practitioner or the hospital doctor as soon as possible, so that appropriate investigations can be instigated.

REFERENCES

Youmans, J R, *Neurological Surgery (3rd Edition)*, 1990, WB Saunders Company

Hunt Batier, H, and Loftus, CM, *Textbook of Neurological Surgery – Principles and Practice*, 2003, Lippincott Williams and Wilkins

Apuzzo, MJ, *Brain Surgery – Complication Avoidance and Management*, 1993, Churchill Livingstone

Garrard, C, Foex, P and Westaby, S, *Principles and Practice of Critical Care*, 1997, Blackwell Science

Kaye, AH and Laws, ER Jr, *Brain Tumors*, 1995, Churchill Livingstone

Russell, RGC, Williams, NS and Bulstrode, CJK, *Bailey and Love's Short Practice of Surgery (23rd Edition)*, 2000, Arnold

ENT SURGERY

John R. Cherry

INTRODUCTION

ENT surgery is a large and complex specialty today, covering the medicine and surgery of disorders of the ears, including the acoustic nerves, the nose and sinuses, the throat and vocal apparatus and large parts of head and neck surgery. This chapter is divided into three sections: ear disease (including hearing loss and imbalance); nasal and sinus disease; and laryngology/head and neck surgery.

EAR DISEASE, HEARING LOSS AND IMBALANCE

Basic structure and function

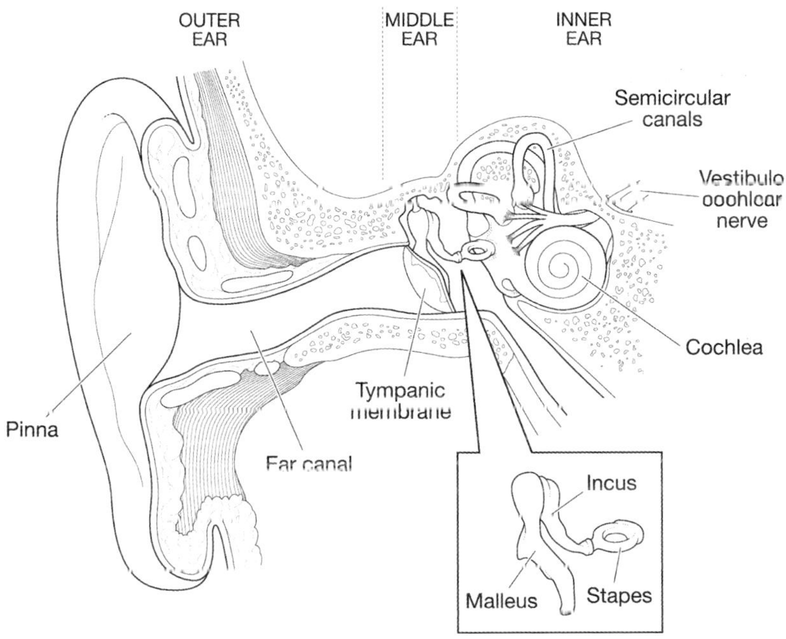

FIGURE 1

The ear has three parts: the outer ear, the middle ear and the inner ear. The outer ear consists of the pinna (the visible external ear, composed of cartilage and skin) and the ear canal, lined with skin and wax-producing glands, leading to the tympanic membrane (eardrum). The outer ear's only function is to allow sound waves access to the tympanic membrane.

The middle ear consists of the tympanic membrane, the middle ear cleft (a space in the temporal bone lined with mucous membrane) and its contents: three tiny bones (auditory ossicles, the malleus, incus and stapes) and two muscles (stapedius and tensor tympani). The footplate of the stapes fits into the oval window, a defect in the medial wall of the middle ear, and movement of the stapes' footplate agitates the inner ear fluid. The middle ear communicates behind with a honeycomb of air cells in the mastoid. The function of the middle ear is to amplify sound waves so that they can create motion in the inner ear fluid. It is maintained at atmospheric pressure by a ventilation tube (the Eustachian tube) which runs from the front of the middle ear to the nasopharynx (postnasal space), and opens on swallowing or yawning to allow air in or out.

The inner ear is a complex labyrinth of passages containing fluid (perilymph and endolymph). The cochlea is the organ of hearing. It converts movements of the perilymph into displacements of the basilar membrane, which stimulate hair cells. These in turn generate nerve impulses which travel up the vestibulocochlear nerve to the brain, where they are perceived as sound. The vestibular system (which includes the semicircular canals) uses hair cells to produce neural information about the position of the head in space, both at rest and in motion.

There are two main types of hearing loss: *conductive loss*, where sound passage through the outer ear is impeded (e.g. by a dense wax plug) or the function of the middle ear is abnormal (e.g. because of a perforated tympanic membrane, glue in the middle ear or fixation of the stapes), and *sensorineural loss*, where the cochlea or nerve of hearing fails (e.g. the deafness of ageing).

Common legal issues concerning the ear

In the *outer ear*, problems arising from ear syringing are commonest. Syringing is an accepted and common method of removing obstructing ear-wax, often performed by GPs or their nurses. Preparatory softening with olive oil or sodium bicarbonate drops is required for a week or two before the procedure. Ideally, the wax should be loosened manually to allow a channel for the water to penetrate beneath the wax, thus forcing it outward. The syringe should be angled at the back wall of the ear canal, not straight at the drum. Electric syringes produce a very strong jet of water, and should be used cautiously on the lowest power setting. The main risk is *perforation* of the tympanic membrane. This almost always causes marked pain and bleeding, with dizziness, and water typically enters the throat by way of the Eustachian tube. Any of these features require the operator to stop at once. The ear should then be examined by a doctor. An acute perforation will normally heal spontaneously, but ENT referral is wise.

Persistence with syringing *despite* pain or other features of injury may cause damage to the middle ear, including scarring with persisting hearing loss. This is not defensible.

In middle ear disease, the overwhelming majority of litigation cases arise from the diagnosis and treatment of *cholesteatoma*[1], which must be described in outline. A cholesteatoma is an infected bag of skin, arising in the upper or posterior part of the tympanic membrane, and progressively invading the middle ear and mastoid. It is a benign condition, but untreated it causes worsening conductive hearing loss and persisting discharge. It may be complicated, in the long term, by facial paralysis, damage to the inner ear with dizziness and permanent sensorineural deafness, and intracranial complications including brain abscess[2]. Treatment requires surgery to the middle ear and mastoid.

Litigation cases arise in two areas: delayed diagnosis, and complications of mastoid surgery.

Delayed diagnosis is usually claimed in children. The problem is that recurrent acute middle ear infection (otitis media) is common in children, because of the high incidence of viral respiratory infections and persisting glue ear in childhood. Although cholesteatoma typically presents with persistent smelly discharge from one ear, childhood cases often declare themselves with recurrent acute infection, and this may be seen as normal and unimportant in general practice. Experts generally agree that children who experience more than four or five middle ear infections should be seen by an ENT surgeon, unless these are spaced out over several years. All cases of persisting infection and discharge must be referred, although many will prove to relate to simple uncomplicated perforations of the eardrum without cholesteatoma.

An allegation of negligence related to delayed diagnosis is often based on a claim that infection was neglected for so long that mastoid surgery and removal of the ossicles became necessary. In fact, mastoid surgery is required in almost all cases of cholesteatoma, and the ossicles involved with the infection (typically the incus and the head of the malleus) are often damaged by disease and are routinely removed. Techniques of surgery vary, but perfect hearing rarely results, and the operation most popular in the UK, a modified radical mastoidectomy, leaves an ear which typically has some conductive loss and needs periodic cleaning in the clinic. It is virtually impossible to succeed in a litigation claim where the disease was not complicated, as it cannot be shown that earlier intervention would have required less extensive surgery, although there may be a claim for avoidable pain and suffering.

---

[1] Youngs, R, Chronic suppurative otitis media – cholesteatoma in Ludman, H and Wright, T (Eds), *Diseases of the Ear*, 6th edition, 1998, Edward Arnold, London, 386-397

[2] Youngs, R, (1998) Complications of suppurative otitis media in Ludman, H and Wright, T (Eds), *Diseases of the Ear*, 6th edition, 1998, Edward Arnold, London, 398-412

If, however, an unacceptable delay in diagnosis has been followed by a complication such as facial paralysis, total loss of hearing in the ear, or, worst of all, an intracranial abscess, causation will be easier to establish.

The complication of mastoid surgery typically leading to litigation is facial nerve injury. The facial nerve actually runs through the medial wall of the middle ear, and is at risk during all mastoid operations. The typical site of injury is the point where the nerve runs above the oval window and then turns downward to pass into the mastoid (known to surgeons as the second genu). All patients undergoing mastoid surgery (or their parents, if children) must be warned of the risk of facial paralysis. Liability will depend on the nature of the injury and the reason for it. This is most simply explained by giving two real examples.

First, consider an appropriately counselled patient with longstanding middle ear disease, where the facial nerve has been exposed by the infection, and trapped in scar. While gently elevating the cholesteatoma, the surgeon tears across the exposed and vulnerable nerve. The injury is immediately noted, and a cable graft using a donor nerve is performed promptly. There is partial recovery of facial nerve function, but the long term result is poor. The surgeon refers the patient on for facial reanimation. This case represents a nerve injury resulting from the pathology and the altered anatomy. The surgeon has not lost control of the operative field, and all appropriate steps have been taken to mitigate the effects of injury. This case is defensible.

Now consider a contrasting case. The surgeon performs mastoidectomy, without noting any operative complication. Postoperatively, the patient has a complete facial paralysis, temporary dizziness and a dead ear on the operated side. Re-exploration by a second surgeon reveals that several millimetres of the facial nerve have been removed during the earlier operation, and the inner ear has been entered with the drill and thus destroyed. The first surgeon was unaware of having made either error. In this case, the surgeon has failed to follow appropriate landmarks, lost control of the operative field, damaged important structures and failed to realise that he has. The case cannot be defended.

Litigation may also follow *reconstructive middle ear surgery* for perforations of the tympanic membrane or loss of part of the ossicular chain following simple infection. Even a simple procedure to graft a perforated tympanic membrane carries a very small risk of severe or total sensorineural hearing loss on the operated side, of which the patient should be warned. Where the operation was straightforward, failure of duty of care cannot be established. The situation may be different where a complex reconstruction of the ossicles has been undertaken. All such procedures inevitably involve some manipulation of the stapes. Since an excursion of a millimetre or two equates to exposure to a very loud sound (such as an explosion) the potential for damage to the inner ear is far greater. A realistic estimate of risk for significant sensorineural deafness after such surgery is around

3%[3]. In one litigation case, the claimant consented specifically for *revision* myringoplasty (re-grafting of the drum), but the surgeon also performed ossiculoplasty. The claimant understood the difference, and his purpose in having the operation was to obtain a dry ear, free of infection, not a hearing gain. In the event, he was very unfortunate to sustain both a dead ear and persisting disequilebrium and dizziness with serious consequences. Reference to notes from the original graft operation would have shown the surgeon that the ossicular chain had been noted to be out of continuity even then, and allowed a discussion of the risks and benefits of rebuilding it. The claimant won the case, not on the basis of unsatisfactory surgery (which was not alleged) but on the basis of inadequately informed consent.

Surgery to replace a fixed stapes, causing conductive deafness, in the condition *otosclerosis***,** carries a significant risk of a dead or severely deafened ear. The position is complicated because this risk is surgeon-dependant. Some large European series produce a severe sensorineural loss in the operated ear of 1-2%[4] or even less[5], but a typical general ENT surgeon in the UK may have a higher incidence with a relatively small series of procedures.. Provided the patient has been warned of the risk, and the surgeon is appropriately trained and performing at least ten stapedectomies a year, litigation can generally be defended.

In the field of otoneurology, one allegation surfaces repeatedly. This concerns the diagnosis of *acoustic neuroma*. This benign tumour, otherwise termed acoustic or vestibular Schwannoma, arises from the nerve sheath of the eighth cranial nerve where it passes from the inner ear into the brain. Although benign, the tumour is potentially lethal, as it may enlarge slowly but progressively within the cerebellopontine angle of the brain, ultimately causing raised intracranial pressure and death if neglected. The incidence of the tumour is around one per 100,000 per year in the UK, and the usual presentation is with unilateral sensorineural deafness of gradual onset, although in about 10% of cases the onset is sudden[6]. There may be associated dizziness, and progressive imbalance occurs with large tumours compressing the brainstem.

The diagnostic problem is that unilateral sensorineural deafness is relatively common as a result of injuries and diseases affecting the cochlea, not all of them well defined. In the past, diagnosis of acoustic neuromas was difficult, and involved complex investigative protocols culminating in invasive radiodiagnostics[7]. Now it is simple, with the use of magnetic resonance scanning, which will define the smallest tumours. The difficulty then becomes the definition

---

[3] Strauss, P, Hearing results following tympanoplasty, *HNO*, 1979, 27(7): 217-20

[4] Mann, WJ, Amedee, RG, Fuerst, G and Tabb, HG, Hearing loss as a complication of stapes surgery, *Otolaryngology-Head & Neck Surgery*, 1996, 115(4): 324-8

[5] Causse, JB, Causse, JR, Wiet, RJ and Yoo, TJ, Complications of stapedectomies, *American Journal of Otology*, 1983, 4(4): 275-80

[6] Moffat, DA, Baguley, DM, von Blumenthal, H, Irving, RM and Hardy, DG, Sudden deafness in vestibular Schwannoma, *Journal of Laryngology & Otology*, 1994, 109:381-4

[7] Cherry, JR, *Acoustic nerve tumours: diagnosis* in Medicolegal Practitioner Series, Volume 7, 1997, Cavendish, London, 187-89

of what constitutes a significant difference between the two ears. There is little literature to help, and it is perhaps surprising that even a large acoustic tumour may present with a mild hearing loss. Protocols have been developed. The writer uses a strict one which dictates a scan if there is a difference of 20dB or more, averaged over the worst two frequencies for the suspect ear.

Where an unacceptable delay in diagnosis results in a bad outcome (neurological disability or even death), the case will succeed easily. It must be recognised, however, that invasive surgery is generally regarded as the best treatment, and conservation of useful hearing in the operated ear is rare, so that a claim based on post-operative loss of hearing in the ear cannot usually succeed. Perhaps the most difficult cases are those where facial nerve paralysis follows surgery. This is the commonest complication, but its incidence increases with tumour size[8]. It is thus possible to claim for facial paralysis when diagnosis has been delayed, but this requires back-projections of the likely tumour size at the appropriate time for diagnosis, which are bedevilled by variable growth rates of these tumours, some of which remain static for long periods. Such calculations can be made on the basis of *average* growth rates[9], and an action for avoidable facial palsy may therefore succeed if the tumour can be shown, on the balance of probabilities, to have been of small size at the point when failure to diagnose occurred.

[8] Arriaga, MA, Luxford, WM, Atkins, JS Jr and Kwartler, JA, Predicting long-term facial nerve outcome after acoustic neuroma surgery, *Otolaryngology-Head & Neck Surgery*, 1993, 108: 220-4

[9] Shin, YJ, Fraysse, B, Cognard, C, Gafsi, I, Charlet, JP, Berges, C, Deguine, O and Tremoulet, M, Effectiveness of conservative management of acoustic neuroma, *American Journal of Otology*, 2000, 21(6): 857-62

NASAL AND SINUS DISEASE

Basic Anatomy

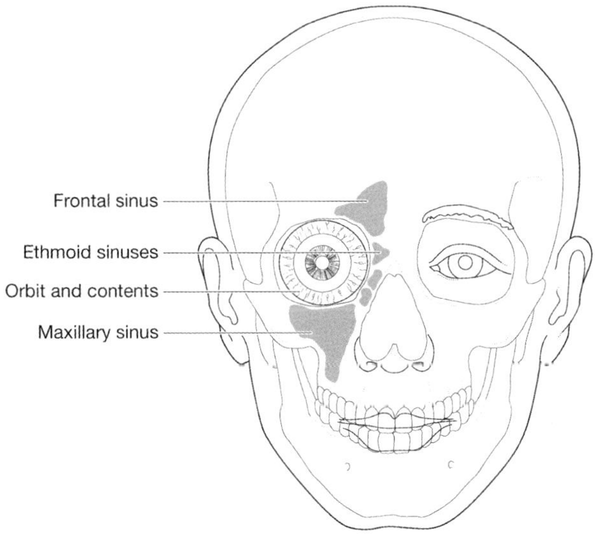

FIGURE 2

The external nose consists of bone and cartilage draped with skin. Internally, the nasal cavity is divided into two by the *septum*, a partition of cartilage and bone. Scroll-like bones covered in mucous membrane, the *conchae* or *turbinates*, project into the nasal fossae from their lateral walls, and moisten and warm the inspired air.

The *paranasal sinuses* are cavities in the skull bones, lined with mucosa and communicating with the nasal fossae. Paired *frontal, ethmoid, maxillary and sphenoidal sinuses* exist, although the frontals are rudimentary until adolescence. The function of the sinuses is unknown, but their potential for infection makes them of great importance.

Common legal issues concerning the nose and sinuses

At present, the commonest allegations of negligence in this area result from complications of endoscopic ethmoidectomy (otherwise termed FESS) for chronic rhinosinusitis and nasal polyposis. The structures at risk during these sophisticated procedures are the orbit, the optic nerve, the anterior cranial fossa and overlying brain of the frontal lobe and the internal carotid artery[10].

Anatomical factors predisposing to injury in a particular case should be revealed by preoperative CT scanning, which is mandatory.

Minor injury to the orbit, in the form of penetration of the orbital periosteum, the membrane lining the eye socket, is a frequent occurrence (of the order of 10% in the writer's practice), and causes no long term problem if recognised. The appearance of a prolapse of orbital fat into the operative field should be noted at once and work in the immediate area discontinued[10]. Bruising of the eyelids may follow. The patient must be cautioned against nose-blowing, which may lead to the eyelids being inflated with air. Even then, swelling of the lids and any temporary double vision will subside within a few days. Successful litigation is unlikely.

Deeper penetration into the orbit may have very serious consequences, however. If the surgeon fails to recognise this, injury to the ocular muscles (especially the inferior or medial rectus) may occur, with persisting double vision not amenable to surgical correction. Generally speaking, such injuries indicate loss of control of surgical anatomy, and cannot be defended. Use of a powered microdebrider with its aperture directed laterally may draw in the medial rectus through a periosteal injury, and caution is required with these very useful instruments[11]. In the writer's opinion, any injury causing permanent double vision is very hard to defend.

The situation is even worse where the optic nerve is damaged, for blindness occurs in the affected eye. There are two ways in which such damage can occur. First, a surgeon who has penetrated the orbit may so lose control of the operation that the medical rectus is transected and the deeper optic nerve then injured as well. This is clearly indefensible. Secondly, the optic nerve may be vulnerable in the posterior ethmoid, lying within a large ("Onodi") cell, and may be directly injured in dissection[12]. Good CT scans should warn of this risk, and again no realistic defence is possible. The nerve may also lie uncovered in the sphenoid sinus, but injury here is less likely as most surgeons do not actually work within the sphenoid except under unusual circumstances.

Injury to the anterior ethmoidal artery during dissection may produce a major bleed into the orbit. Immediate recognition and decompression are needed, as an untreated orbital haematoma may cause blindness.

The internal carotid artery may lie uncovered in the sphenoid sinus. Injury here produces a catastrophic bleed. Control by packing is sometimes possible, but the usual outcome is death from haemorrhage or from acute stroke. The exposed artery should be recognised both on scan and at surgery, and there is no realistic

---

[10] Lund, VJ, Wright, A. and Yiotakis, J, Complications and medico-legal aspects of endoscopic sinus surgery, *Journal of the Royal Society of Medicine*, 1997, 90: 422-28

[11] Graham, SM and Nerad, JA, Orbital complications in endoscopic sinus surgery using powered instrumentation, *The Laryngoscope*, 2003, 113: 874-78

[12] Bhatti, MT and Stankiewicz, JA, Ophthalmic complications of endoscopic sinus surgery, *Survey of Ophthalmology*, 2003, 48(4): 389-402

defence unless the operation was for biopsy of a malignant tumour of the skull base which had distorted the anatomy and exposed the vessel.

Finally, the roof of the ethmoid may be penetrated. The usual result is a leakage of cerebrospinal fluid. This may be recognised by the surgeon as a flow of clear fluid, washing away blood from the field. Repair may be performed by insertion of a free graft of turbinal bone and mucosa into the defect. Antibiotics should be given to prevent meningitis, and the likely result is simply an unexpected stay in hospital, on bed rest, until it is certain that the leakage has ceased. If primary repair fails, a secondary repair will be needed, and is best delegated to a surgeon with experience in closing CSF leaks. To cause a CSF leak may denote poor technique, but proper management will minimise the consequences. Successful litigation is much more likely to follow a failure to identify the injury, with subsequent meningitis. Death or permanent neurological disability can follow, and damages may be large.

Deeper penetration of the anterior fossa will cause bleeding from intracranial vessels, with a high risk of stroke or death. Defence is impossible.

Precautions to minimise risks include familiarity with the preoperative CT scans, which should be displayed in the theatre, and control of bleeding by preparation of the nose with vasoconstrictors. The procedure must be abandoned if intractable bleeding obscures the operative field. Exposure of the orbital periosteum, either by nature or by the surgeon, can be confirmed by gentle pressure on the closed eye, which will produce bowing of the orbital boundary into the field. Some surgeons prefer to have the eye watched by an assistant throughout every FESS procedure, so that any movement of the eyeball (indicating pressure or traction on the orbital periosteum or contents) can be reported at once. Others take this precaution when working laterally in the ethmoid labyrinth, or if in any doubt as to the closeness of the orbit. If material has been withdrawn from the ethmoid and its nature is in doubt, it may be placed in saline solution, where mucosa of the sinus will sink, but orbital fat (and indeed brain tissue) will float. Computer-guided systems are now available, which combine virtual views of the CT scans, showing the position of a hard-wired surgical instrument, with the endoscopic view of the operative field. At present, evidence that they improve safety is lacking[13].

What of informed consent? As recently as 2001, a survey indicated that only about one third of British surgeons responding to a questionnaire routinely warned of a risk of double vision after FESS[14], although the authors noted that the Medical Protection Society considered all the recognised orbital complications so severe as to warrant a warning, however low their incidence. The writer agrees with the MPS, and could not defend a failure to warn.

---

[13] Reardon, EJ, Navigational risks associated with sinus surgery and the clinical effects of implementing a navigational system for sinus surgery, *Laryngoscope*, 2002, 112 (7:2): 1-19

[14] Sharp, HR, Crutchfield, L, Rowe-Jones, JM and Mitchell, DB, Major complications and consent prior to endoscopic sinus surgery, *Clinical Otolaryngology*, 2001, 26: 33-38

As to technique, there are several acceptable options. Surgeons can choose whether to use power tools or conventional instruments, and whether to view directly through the endoscope or on a TV monitor. Intranasal ethmoid surgery performed under direct vision, without endoscopes, is still practised by some surgeons, and is acceptable given suitable experience. The risks and legal implications are for practical purposes identical.

Another frequent cause of litigation in rhinology is failure to diagnose a malignant tumour of the paranasal sinuses. Such tumours occur most frequently in the maxillary sinus, but may arise in the ethmoid labyrinth. Within the maxillary sinus, they may grow concealed for some time before presenting with invasion of adjacent structures.

The rule is that any masses within the nasal cavity must be biopsied. Endoscopic biopsy is usual today. This rule also applies to cases of nasal polyps confined to one side of the nose. Nasal polyp disease is generally bilateral, and where outpatient endoscopy confirms a polyp (or polyps) to be unilateral, removal and submission to histology is mandatory. It is also advised that, during all operations for nasal polyposis, representative specimens from both sides should be submitted for histology as a minimum requirement. Some surgeons prefer to send all material excised for examination.

Two examples of litigation cases will illustrate the topic. In one, a patient underwent serial operations for nasal polyps, and the pathologist reported these to be transitional papillomas (benign tumours with a strong tendency to recur). When a report diagnosed transitional papilloma on both sides of the nose (excessively rare), the surgeon was alerted to possible misdiagnosis. Review of the slides indicated a malignant olfactory neuroblastoma, arising in the olfactory neuroepithelium of the nasal roof. Radical craniofacial resection and radiotherapy were required, and the extent of the tumour, after several years' delay in diagnosis, was such as to invade the brain and compromise resection, with poor long term prognosis. Medicolegal review of CT and MR scans showed that the radiologist had failed to note erosion of the skull base on the first scan series, with appearances consistent with malignancy. The case was settled.

In a second case, a young woman had a diagnosis of olfactory neuroblastoma of the maxillary sinus (an excessively rare and questionable diagnosis) made by a surgeon in private practice who was not a subspecialist in head and neck cancer. He referred her for radiotherapy. The surgeon and radiotherapist chose to ignore scans and reports indicating recurrent disease during follow up. After a long delay, the tumour invaded the orbit, and the patient was finally referred to a specialist head and neck oncology clinic. The diagnosis was revised to one of chondrosarcoma of the maxillary sinus. Extensive craniofacial resection was performed, with sacrifice of the eye and much facial skin, and severe disfigurement of a woman still in her early thirties, all of which could be shown to result, on the balance of probabilities, from the delay in diagnosing recurrence initially confined to the sinus. A large sum was given in settlement.

These cases indicate the importance of excellent pathology and radiology, meticulous management, and, certainly in the case of the less usual tumours, treatment in a combined head and neck oncology clinic.

LARYNGOLOGY AND HEAD AND NECK SURGERY

Anatomy

The anatomy of the head and neck is very complex, and space does not permit a description here. Line drawings of the structures relevant to what follows must suffice, but the reader is referred elsewhere for further detail[15].

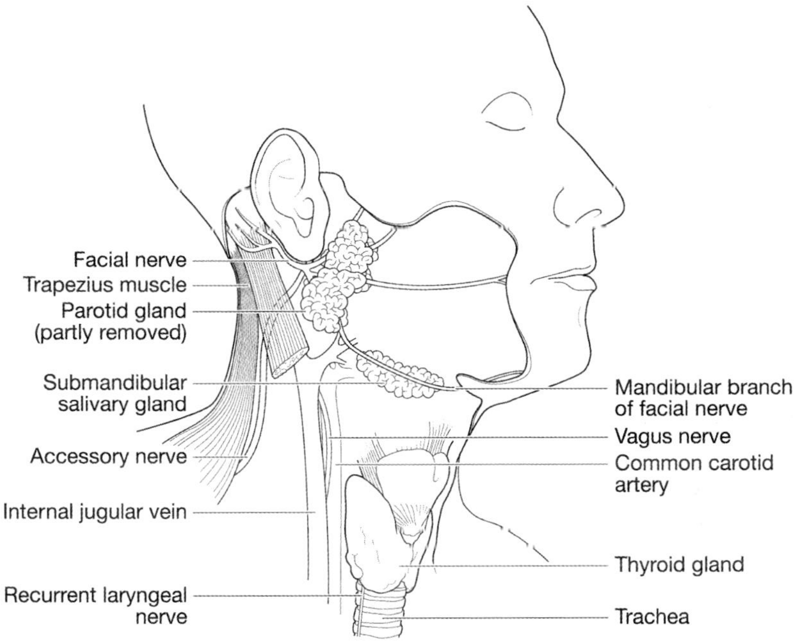

FIGURE 3

Common legal issues in laryngology and head and neck surgery

Three themes recur in these areas, namely, nerve injuries in head and neck surgery, delayed diagnosis of certain head and neck cancers, and perforation of the oesophagus.

[15] Cherry, JR, *Anatomy and physiology of the larynx, pharynx and head and neck*, in Medicolegal Practitioner Series, Volume 7, 1997, Cavendish, London, 331-349

Nerve injuries

Three motor nerves are usually concerned: the spinal accessory (XIth cranial nerve), the vagus (Xth cranial nerve), and its important recurrent laryngeal branches, and the facial (VIIth cranial nerve).

The spinal accessory is typically injured either at the skull base or, more frequently, in the posterior triangle of the neck. The nerve leaves the skull base at the jugular foramen, pierces and supplies the sternomastoid muscle, and then pursues a long course across the posterior triangle, where it lies very superficially, on its way to enter and supply the trapezius.

Injury at the skull base typically occurs during operations for branchial cysts, lymphangiomas, or other high benign neck lesions deep to sternomastoid. The nerve may be exposed during dissection of the structure to be removed, or may be adherent to it. Avoidance of injury is by awareness and careful demonstration of the course of the nerve at operation. Patients should be warned of the risk of injury. Such injuries may be defensible (as with a nerve trapped in scar tissue, identified and repaired after injury), but where surgery has presented no particular difficulty and the injury gone unnoticed, defence is difficult. Injury of the XIth nerve at the skull base is also a risk of selective neck dissection for malignant disease. When dealing with malignant glands the risks are higher, and defence of an injury therefore easier.

Injury within the posterior triangle typically occurs during biopsy of a lymph node or other structure in this region of the neck. Enlarged lymph nodes often overlie the course of the nerve, and the nerve may be to be in contact with or adherent to the capsule of the node. Nodes should not be biopsied without good reason, nor before full clinical examination of the upper air and food passage and fine needle aspiration for cytology[16 17]. The surgeon must be aware of the danger. Biopsy of the posterior triangle should not be carried out under or with local anaesthetic, as this will temporarily paralyse the nerve and make recognition harder. In the writer's experience, EMG monitoring of the nerve during surgery is of great value.

The important consequence of division of the XIth nerve is paralysis of the trapezius. Division above the sternomastoid will also paralyse the sternomastoid, but this is not of great functional importance. Paralysis of the trapezius causes weakness of abduction of the upper limb, shoulder drop, winging of the scapula, brachial plexus traction, a painful arc, and severe pain and dysfunction of the shoulder and arm. When such an injury results from biopsy of a benign lesion of the posterior triangle it is a catastrophe for the patient. This is a common cause of litigation. Furthermore, there is often a surprising delay in diagnosis - the surgeon failing to note the injury at surgery, or to recognise that the pain and stiffness

---

[16] Martin, H, Untimely lymph node biopsy, *American Journal of Surgery*, 1961, 102: 17-18

[17] Watkinson, JC, Gaze, MN and Wilson, JA, Assessment of cervical lymph nodes in *Stell & Maran's Head and Neck Surgery*, 4th edition, 2000, Butterworth Heinemann, Oxford, 204-6

result from such injury. Since early repair or grafting of the accessory nerve produces improvement or full recovery in most cases[18], this is a serious omission, and such cases cannot be defended.

In radical neck dissection for malignant cervical lymph nodes associated with head and neck cancer, the XIth nerve is sacrificed. Most modern surgeons, however, perform modified radical dissections where possible, exposing the entire nerve from trapezius to skull base. Some 50% of these nerves will function normally after such surgery, but the remainder do not, presumably because of interference with blood supply. Litigation (which is unlikely) is unlikely to succeed.

Injury to the vagus or to its important branch, the recurrent laryngeal nerve, produces the same result: paralysis of the vocal cord of the same side. The vagus has other functions, supplying autonomic nerves to the heart and the gut, but division of one vagus in the neck has no clinically noticeable effects apart from vocal weakness. Division of one vagus is rare, and most likely to occur during radical surgery for malignant neck glands which are invading the nerve. Under such circumstances, injury is unlikely to be seen as negligent. Injury during operations on benign lesions (such as branchial fistulae) is unusual, but would be hard to defend save in the rare case (*eg* where the lesion proved to be a neuroma of the vagus itself[19]).

The recurrent laryngeal nerve arises from the vagus in the thorax on the left and at the root of the neck on the right. The nerves run back up into the neck, from lateral to medial, finally lying between the cervical oesophagus and the trachea, behind the thyroid gland. They are at risk in operations on the thyroid and parathyroids, and in open procedures for removal of pharyngeal pouch. Identification is mandatory in thyroid surgery. If one lobe is to be resected, the nerve of the same side should be identified before division of the inferior thyroid artery, to which it is often intimately related. In subtotal thyroidectomy, both nerves must be identified, and the same applies to total thyroidectomy for cancer, and to exploration of the parathyroid gland[20]. In as many as 1% of individuals, the *right* nerve is non-recurrent, arising directly from the vagus and passing behind the common carotid artery to reach the larynx or the tracheo-oesophageal plane, and the surgeon must be aware of this anomaly and search for such a nerve if the right recurrent is not found in its expected place[21].

Division of one recurrent nerve causes paralysis of the homolateral vocal cord, with hoarseness and vocal weakness. This is problematic for any subject, but for

---

[18] Williams, WW, Donell, ST, Twyman, RS and Birch, R, The posterior triangle and the painful shoulder: spinal accessory nerve injury, *Annals of the Royal College of Surgeons of England*, 1996, 78: 521 5

[19] Gilmer-Hill, HS and Kline, DG, Neurogenic tumours of the cervical vagus nerve, *Neurosurgery*, 2000, 46(6): 1498-1503

[20] Shaheen, OH, *Thyroid Surgery*, 2003, Parthenon, Boca Raton, pp 87-95 and 166-171

[21] Henry, JF, Non-recurring recurrent laryngeal nerve, *Surgery*, 1988, 104: 977-84

professional voice users, and especially singers, it is a disaster. Some improvement in vocal quality may be achieved by speech therapy exercises, or by surgery to move the paralysed cord closer to its opposite number. Division of both recurrent laryngeal nerves leads to paralysis of both cords in a paramedian position[22], with noisy obstruction to the breathing (stridor). Tracheostomy is required to secure the airway, which may later be widened by laser arytenoidectomy, with sacrifice of vocal quality.

Temporary weakness of one cord after thyroidectomy results from bruising, and does not indicate breach of duty. Accidental division of one nerve is a recognised operative complication (of which all patients must be warned), but liability is usually accepted. Division of both nerves inevitably indicates failure of surgical technique, and liability is easily established.

The facial nerve has already been mentioned in the context of the middle ear. Having coursed downward through the mastoid, it leaves the skull base at the stylomastoid foramen and immediately enters the parotid salivary gland. Here it divides into branches, finally leaving the gland at its anterior border as five named nerves, which supply all the muscles of facial expression: those of the forehead, the eyelids and the mouth. The nerve is at risk in operations on the parotid gland for benign tumours, and in operations on high neck masses. Its mandibular branch, which supplies the depressors of the lower lip, is at hazard in operations on the submandibular triangle.

The classical operation for benign parotid tumours is superficial parotidectomy. The nerve is deliberately exposed at the skull base and followed through the parotid gland, with dissection of its divisions and branches. The tumour, usually lying superficially, is delivered from the nerve with (where possible) a surrounding cuff of normal parotid tissue. Since the nerve has no distinct plane within the gland, since tumours may lie directly in contact with or displace it, and since the commonest benign tumour (the pleomorphic adenoma) has a tendency to recur if not excised widely, the operation demands much technical skill. Some surgeons use continuous intraoperative nerve monitoring as an aid to location and preservation, and some use microscope magnification. Neither approach is seen as mandatory. All patients must be warned of the risk to the nerve, which should be under 3% or less in experienced hands[23].

What is the legal situation where injury occurs? In the writer's view, injury to the main trunk or a major division can be defended if the following conditions obtain: the patient was warned of the risk, the surgeon was appropriately experienced, the injury was noted at surgery, repair was performed promptly (either by the surgeon or a colleague with suitable experience) and good rehabilitation was offered,

---

[22] Shaheen, OH, *Thyroid Surgery*, 2003, Parthenon, Boca Raton, 192

[23] O'Brien, C, Morbidity following surgery for benign parotid disease, in McGurk, M and Renehan, A (Eds), *Controversies in the Management of Salivary Gland Disease*, 2001, Oxford University Press, Oxford, 133-39

including referral for facial reanimation if the results of repair proved poor. An unrecognised injury or one left untreated would not be defensible.

Bruising of the nerve at surgery frequently produces temporary facial weakness, resolving over two to three months[24]. Again, patients must be warned of this possibility, but there are no legal implications.

In the treatment of malignant parotid tumours, sacrifice of the nerve may be inevitable (although it is avoided where possible today), and litigation is unlikely.

High lateral neck lesions, such as branchial cysts, may come into contact with the facial nerve, particularly its lower division. The risk of injury must be recognised before surgery, the patient warned, and the operative incision extended to encompass dissection of the facial nerve within the parotid, so that the relevant branches can be identified and conserved. Unrecognised division of the lower part of the nerve during such surgery is indefensible.

Finally, the mandibular branch may be injured during operations to remove the submandibular salivary gland or adjacent lymph nodes or masses. The branch descends below the mandible and overlies the submandibular gland. It is small in size, and easily overlooked. Even in the experienced hands, there is a risk of injury, with weakness of the lower lip, of around 8%[25], and damage is therefore to be seen as an operative complication which is unavoidable in some cases. Methods of conserving the branch include nerve monitoring, a low approach with elevation of the deep cervical fascia from the level of the hyoid bone, and early ligation and upward rotation of the facial artery. None is perfect. Provided proper informed consent has been obtained, litigation generally fails.

Delayed diagnosis of head and neck cancer

Delay in diagnosis of malignancy affecting the upper air and food passage may occur in general or in specialist practice.

In general practice, the commonest cause of delay remains failure to refer with persisting hoarseness or throat pain. Any patient with hoarseness persisting for more than four weeks should be referred for specialist examination of the vocal cords by an ENT surgeon. The patients at particular risk of head and neck cancer are smokers in middle life and beyond. A typical litigation case would involve a patient whose hoarseness has been disregarded by the GP for many months, and who then presents with upper airway obstruction requiring urgent surgery to remove the larynx. Since the majority of early tumours of the vocal cords are curable by radiotherapy, and since tumour volume doubling times may be estimated (averaging about eight weeks), causation in respect of the major surgery and resulting disability is not usually difficult to establish. The same

---

24 *Ibid.*

25 Hald, J and Andreassen, UK, Submandibular gland excision: short- and long-term complications, *Journal of Oto-Rhino-Laryngology & its Related Specialties*, 1994, 56(2): 87-91

applies to avoidable death from advanced disease. Persistent throat pain referred to one ear may indicate a tumour of the tonsil or of the laryngopharynx. Again, specialist referral is dictated, but the legal issues regarding major surgery and failure of cure are more difficult, since many surgeons advocate radical surgery for relatively early tumours in both sites. Each case requires careful individual analysis.

In specialist practice, there are three specific tumours which may be overlooked despite careful assessment: carcinoma of the posterior third of the tongue, of the supraglottic larynx and of the nasopharynx.

The posterior third of the tongue consists of mucous membrane, muscle and lymphoid tissue. It always appears irregular and lumpy on examination with a mirror or flexible endoscope. Tumours here are uncommon (incidence around 3 per million in the UK)[26], and may be difficult to identify. Typically, they present with pain in the throat referred to the ear, or pain felt in the ear alone. Unfortunately, chronic pain around the ear is not uncommon in middle life, often being referred from the cervical spine or the jaw joints, and hemifacial neuralgias and cases of "atypical" facial pain are frequently seen in ENT and maxillofacial practice[27]. It is mandatory to examine the whole mouth, tongue, oropharynx and larynx when such symptoms are present, but a tumour buried within the irregular tongue base may be overlooked. It is this which accounts for occasional cases appearing under press headlines of the "seven doctors missed throat cancer" type. These cases give rise to more questions than answers. Should every smoker with ear pain apparently related to arthritis of the cervical spine be examined under anaesthetic, with "blind" biopsies of apparently normal areas of the posterior tongue? Such an approach would be excessive and not without risk. Again, each legal case must be carefully assessed, but a specialist who has thoroughly and repeatedly performed clinical examination of the mouth and throat will generally escape liability for missing what is undoubtedly the most difficult diagnosis in head and neck oncology.

The supraglottic larynx is that part of the voice box above the vocal cords. Whereas tumours of the true vocal cord produce hoarseness as an early symptom, tumours of the supraglottis have considerable room to expand before causing symptoms. They may then present with some swallowing difficulty, or with hoarseness if they grow into the vocal cord, or invade deeply and paralyse it. Some such tumours may infiltrate the false cords or epiglottis without producing obvious distortion or ulceration, and it is in these cases that specialist diagnosis may be delayed. Radiotherapy remains the usual treatment modality for early supraglottic cancer in the UK, so there will be little liability where radiotherapy produces cure despite delayed diagnosis. If laryngectomy has to be performed, or death ensues, the legal outcome will require careful consideration of the

---

[26] Watkinson, JC, Gaze, MN and Wilson, JA, Base of tongue tumours in *Stell & Maran's Head and Neck Surgery*, 4th edition, 2000, Butterworth Heinemann, Oxford, 320-21

[27] Cohen, Lord, Facial Pain in Stell, PM and Maran, AGD (Eds) *Clinical Otolaryngology*, 1979, Blackwell, London, 279-287

surgeon's approach. In general, smokers with suspicious symptoms which persist should have repeated clinical examination supplemented by examination under anaesthetic or high definition scanning.

The nasopharynx lies behind the nasal cavity and contains the adenoid in childhood. Carcinoma is uncommon in UK practice (although the tumour is common in Cantonese and certain other racial groups). Because the nasopharynx is invisible except to specialist mirror or endoscopic examination, and because tumours do not produce any early localising symptoms, delay in diagnosis is always a hazard. Tumours may present with glue ear, neck masses (lymphatic metastasis), double vision and facial pain (invasion of the middle cranial fossa).

Any adult with a new case of glue ear must be regarded as potentially having a nasopharyngeal tumour. The mechanism is invasion of the Eustachian tube (which ventilates the middle ear) by the tumour. Glue ear is very frequent in childhood, but rare in the adult. Every adult with glue ear must have a full clinical examination of the nasopharynx using a flexible or rigid endoscope. Even with normal findings, many surgeons prefer to insert a grommet under general anaesthetic and biopsy the nasopharynx at the same time. If the alternative – grommet insertion under local anaesthetic – is selected, then the nasopharynx should be re-examined clinically on one or more occasions over the succeeding months. Delay in diagnosis of nasopharyngeal cancer where the postnasal space has not been visualised is indefensible. Causation will depend on the extent of the delay and the stage at final diagnosis. Possibilities include a claim for a radical neck dissection which could have been avoided with earlier diagnosis, or one for worsening of prognosis (eg from 5 year survival of 90% in Stage I disease to 40% or less in Stage IV disease).

Perforation of the oesophagus

Oesophageal perforation is a frequent cause of litigation. The oesophagus is a thin-walled structure composed of mucous membrane and muscle. It commences at the cricopharyngeal sphincter, opposite the sixth cervical vertebra, courses downwards through the neck and chest, and finally reaches the stomach, typically some 40 cm below the incisor teeth.

Internal examination of the oesophagus is needed when there is suspicion of a foreign body (eg a meat bone or coin) lodged therein, where there is suspicion of tumour, and as part of the investigation of cancers of the larynx and pharynx. Diseases of the lower oesophagus are the province of the gastroenterologist, and are diagnosed by flexible oesophagoscopy, not to be discussed here. Removal of foreign bodies is generally carried out by ENT surgeons, as many of them lodge in the pharynx or upper oesophagus. For this, and for the examinations associated with tumours of the upper food passage, rigid oesophagoscopes are still employed.

The modern rigid oesophagoscope is a hollow metal tube, lighted at its distant end by a powerful light from a halogen source, and marked externally with distance in centimetres. Various lengths are available. It is ideal for removal of sharp or metallic bodies, and for examination of the upper gullet, but perforation is an ever present risk. A gentle technique must be employed, without application of heavy pressure, in inserting and manoeuvring the instrument. Even so, perforation will occur occasionally, especially where strictures or other abnormalities make examination difficult.

Perforation is a life-threatening emergency. Early diagnosis is vital, for infection in the connective tissues of the chest (mediastinitis) is rapidly fatal if untreated. Perforation, if not noted at operation, declares itself early after awakening from anaesthetic, with severe chest and back pain. There will be signs of pleural effusion at an early stage, there may be air (surgical emphysema) palpable in the neck, and chest x-ray may show basal effusion, mediastinal widening or mediastinal air. If confirmation is needed, a contrast swallow using non-irritant contrast will clarify the site and size. Intravenous antibiotics must be started as soon as diagnosis is suspected. If the perforation is in the neck, this (together with drainage if needed) will be sufficient treatment. If it is in the thorax, exploration of the chest and repair of the oesophagus by a suitably experienced surgeon is seen as mandatory.

Perforation of the oesophagus is an operative complication which occurs inevitably once or twice in any large series. Patients should be warned of the risk, but it is not necessarily negligent, and provided prompt diagnosis and appropriate treatment were performed, litigation will be difficult. Successful litigation is likely where there has been delay in diagnosis, where typical symptoms and signs have been ignored, where antibiotics have not been started promptly, and where the chest has not been explored in the case of a thoracic oesophageal perforation. Since thoracotomy is mandatory for intrathoracic oesophageal perforation, a claim for thoracotomy cannot succeed if the initial perforation was not negligent. Specific complications related to delay in diagnosis include protracted intensive care and broncho-oesophageal fistula.

OPHTHALMOLOGY

Jane Leitch

INTRODUCTION

Ophthalmologists often find themselves at court, but claims against them are relatively uncommon. Much more commonly, ophthalmologists will be giving evidence in cases involving mistakes by other specialities – notably general practitioners and neurosurgeons. But of course ophthalmologists make mistakes themselves, and when they do the results can be tragic and expensive. This chapter looks at the main things which trouble ophthalmologists' underwriters.

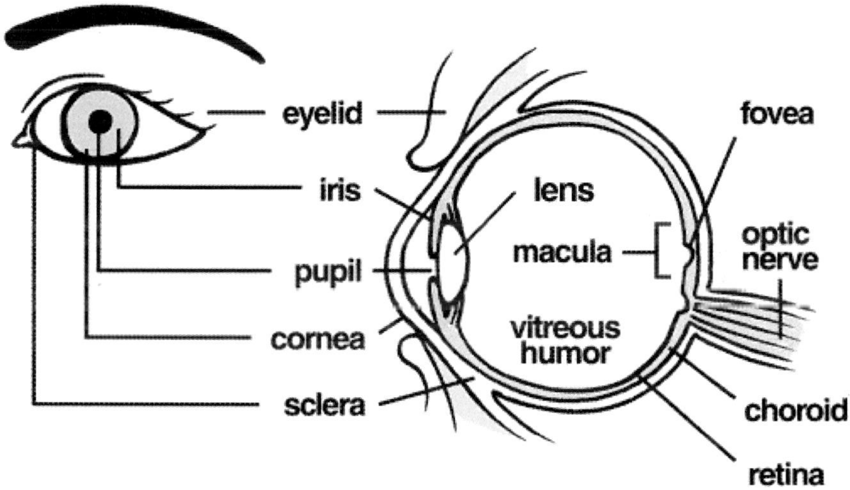

FIGURE 1: THE BASIC ANATOMY OF THE EYE (WWW.MVRF.ORG: BASED ON AN ILLUSTRATION FROM THE NATIONAL EYE INSTITUTE/NATIONAL INSTITUTE OF HEALTH)

REFRACTIVE SURGERY

The correction of refractive errors with surgery or laser has become increasingly frequent. The idea is to get rid of glasses or contact lenses.

The principle behind this type of surgery is that by changing the shape of the cornea one changes the focus of the eye – so eliminating the need for any artificial lens.

This type of procedure was initially performed with surgery in the form of radial keratotomy (cuts in the cornea to change its shape) and more recently has been replaced with laser treatments including LASIK (Laser-In-Situ Keratomileusis), and the placement of implants such as intrastromal corneal rings, intracorneal lenses and phakic intraocular lenses. A phakic intraocular lens is an artificial lens implanted without removing the patient's own lens. In LASIK a knife, called a microkeratome, is used to cut a flap in the cornea. A hinge is left at one end of this flap. The flap is folded back revealing the stroma, which is the central section of the cornea. A portion of the stroma is vaporised using pulses from a computer-controlled laser and the flap is replaced.

All these procedures, whether laser or implant based, are surgical interventions. Although the risks are small, complications can occur.

Typical complications of the procedures themselves include:

- Over- or under-correction, which may require glasses or contact lens itself
- Infection of the cornea or other parts of the eye
- Scarring of the cornea
- Perforation of the eye
- Flap formation which is too superficial or deep (in LASIK)
- Reaction to the local anaesthetic.

Regardless of complication it is important to be aware that these procedures are unlikely to get rid of glasses or contact lenses for good. They do not abolish the normal effects of ageing. With increasing age the depth of vision reduces (presbyopia) and reading glasses are likely to become necessary.

There are several contraindications to refractive treatment. Refractive treatments for high refractive error have problems with accuracy and accurate assessment of corneal thickness is vital.

People with glaucoma, dry eye, Rheumatoid arthritis and connective tissue disorders such as systemic lupus erythematosis should not be treated, and those taking immunosuppressant drugs and steroids are well advised to avoid laser treatment.

Many of the complaints in relation to refractive surgery are against High Street practitioners. Patients may have unrealistic expectations. Consent is often taken by a specially trained nurse or assistant rather than the operating surgeon; there may be financial pressure to treat. There are often problems with continuity of care, particularly in the event of post-operative complications. The treating doctor sometimes seems very elusive. The qualifications required for treating surgeons are laid out in the Royal College of Ophthalmologists' guidelines for refractive surgery (2004).

Information for patients, and the national guidelines are all available via the College of Ophthalmologists' website at www.rcophth.co.uk.

RETINAL DETACHMENTS

Basics

The retina is the photoreceptive membrane lining the eyeball. Its function is similar to the photographic film in a camera. The eye focuses light onto the retina and the retinal image is then transferred to the visual cortex along the optic nerve and visual pathways. The central area of the retina, called the macula, is used for detailed central vision. The rest of the retina is for peripheral vision. A retinal detachment is where the retina comes away from the underlying surface. This is usually caused by the development of a hole in the retina through which fluid may pass, forcing the retina away from the underlying tissue. This is called a rhegmatogenous detachment.

Retinal detachments occur under a number of different circumstances:

- As part of the ageing process within the eye. This is associated with a posterior vitreous detachment. This is where the vitreous jelly, which fills the back cavity of the eyeball, collapses and becomes fluid, pulling away from the retina and causing a hole to form. If the process is not identified and arrested, a retinal detachment is likely. In most circumstances, however, the vitreous may detach without causing a retinal hole.
- Secondary to blunt or penetrating trauma, either immediately, or more commonly, as a secondary event up to six weeks later.
- In eyes predisposed to detachment, *e.g.* with myopia or degenerative vitreoretinopathy such as Stickler's syndrome, or complicated cataract surgery.

Symptoms and signs

The cardinal features are flashing lights and floaters of sudden onset, with a curtain or obstruction to vision that advances as the detachment progresses.

Pigment cells in the anterior vitreous are suggestive of a retinal hole which has not yet caused a detachment. These are seen behind the lens by slit lamp examination. This sign is not reliable if there has been previous ocular surgery or ocular inflammation.

Examination

When a patient presents with symptoms of a retinal detachment, the examination should include recording of the visual acuity, slit lamp examination of the anterior and posterior segments of the eye and measurement of the intra ocular pressure. The intra ocular pressure may reduce in an eye with a retinal detachment. Both eyes should have the pupils dilated for peripheral retinal examination with indirect ophthalmoscopy and indentation as gold standard. Both eyes should always be examined even if symptoms are confined to one. The pathology which causes a retinal detachment may frequently occur in both eyes.

When a patient first presents with symptoms of flashes and floaters and an examination is performed but no retinal hole is detected, the patient needs to be advised of the symptoms of a retinal detachment and what to do if symptoms persist.

If a previously symptomatic patient is examined and no abnormality found, but a retinal detachment subsequently occurs, it cannot necessarily be concluded that the examining clinician was at fault. The examination could have taken place early in an evolving process.

Principles of treatment

If a retinal hole is detected prior to a detachment occurring, laser or cryo therapy to the retinal hole is the treatment of choice. Laser treatment is currently the preferred option in most cases. It can be delivered in a variety of different ways. The exact type of laser and approach will depend upon the surgeon's preference and what is available locally. Argon lasers are the most commonly used.

The best surgical results are obtained by specialist retinal surgeons.

At a first assessment a retinal hole, if present, should be detected and appropriate treatment advised and carried out immediately. Any detachment or retinal hole which has not involved the macula, (the area of central vision), should be treated as an emergency. This usually means that surgery is carried out on the next available operating list. If the macula has been involved, the visual prognosis is less good and a modest delay in treatment is acceptable. In longstanding retinal detachment complex surgery is required. A good anatomical outcome does not guarantee good vision.

Retinal detachment surgery does not carry absolute guarantees, but with increasing sub specialisation there has been an increase in the percentage of good anatomical results. A recent triple cycle audit cycle showed an increase in the rate of primary anatomical success from 64% in1987-1989 to 71% in 1990-1993 and to 87% in in1996-1997. The final success rate likewise showed an improvement in the corresponding years from 83% to 90% to 97%. A success rate of 100% has not been achieved. It is likely that the reason for this is the scarring reactions within the retina. If primary surgery is unsuccessful, the most likely reasons are new or missed retinal breaks or holes. It should be possible to overcome the problem of missed breaks, but new breaks cannot currently be predicted.

Poor prognostic factors

Prognosis worsens with increased the size of the retinal hole, increased numbers of retinal holes, the presence of vitreous haemorrhage and a scarring reaction within the retina called pre retinal fibrosis or proliferative vitreous retinopathy. These factors are important in determining the type of surgical approach.

Other forms of retinal detachment

These include exudative detachments, which are seen in inflammatory conditions, and tractional detachments, which are secondary to scar formation (which occurs in diabetes, retinopathy of prematurity or where there is an existing, longstanding detachment). These types of retinal detachment are by definition complex. Surgery in patients with diabetic retinopathy should be handled by specialist retinal surgeons.

Surgery in cases of retinopathy of prematurity has very disappointing results. Even if an anatomical correction is achieved, vision still fails to develop. Most specialist surgeons advise against this type of intervention as one is exposing a young baby to complex surgery and associated complications with no prospect of improved vision even if surgery is successful in flattening the retina.

GLAUCOMA

Acute glaucoma

This is where there is a rapid increase in intra ocular pressure (pressure within the eye). This is provoked by an obstruction to the usual flow of aqueous humour (the clear fluid circulating within the eye which is usually formed and drained at a rate of approximately 2 microlitres per min). The pressure builds up inside the eye causing pain, redness, nausea and vomiting. The vision becomes blurred, and haloes are seen around lights.
This is a condition of the elderly and may be misinterpreted as a gastric upset in an otherwise debilitated patient. Usually medical treatment with drops and intravenous Diamox (a diuretic) will deal with the immediate threat. The definitive treatment is with laser iridotomy. Sometimes surgical intervention will be required.

Acute Glaucoma is usually associated with a good clinical outcome unless it has gone unrecognised and high pressure within the eye has been experienced for a prolonged period of time. In these cases there may be permanent visual loss in the affected eye.

Chronic Open Angle Glaucoma

This is where there is a more subtle increase in intra ocular pressure over a long period, resulting in damage to the nerve fibre layer of the retina and secondary optic nerve changes. There are no early symptoms and detection is usually at a routine examination by an optician. The clinical signs are elevated intra ocular pressure (>21mmHg), loss of peripheral visual field and a cupped appearance of the optic disc. A variant of this condition is normal tension glaucoma where glaucoma occurs at a pressure that is within the normal range. This can be difficult to diagnose and MRI or CT imaging of the brain is usually required to exclude another cause of visual field loss.

Risk factors include a family history of glaucoma and cardiovascular disease. There are a number of other situations that can predispose to glaucoma, for example previous ocular trauma, pseudoexfoliation and pigment dispersion. These forms of glaucoma should be identified at examination. Treatment is primarily medical, with eye drops, but surgical intervention may be required. Chronic open angle glaucoma requires on-going monitoring of the intra ocular pressure and visual fields, (from 3 monthly to annually depending on the signs of progression). A target pressure for a patient is usually identified at presentation and usually represents a 1/3 reduction from the presenting pressure. This may need to be modified if there is seen to be progression of visual field loss. A combination of topical drops may be required and changes in medication may have to be made to find an appropriate combination for a patient. Side effects to medication occur commonly and vary from some ocular discomfort and mild redness to shortness of breath in patients prone to asthma. Beta blockers should usually be avoided in those with a history of chest disease. Patients at risk of this complication should be identified prior to treatment being commenced.

Any patient with advanced glaucoma, who has loss of visual field approaching the central area and who needs to undergo surgery for cataract is at risk of further loss of vision related to the surgery. This risk should be identified preoperatively and explained to the patient.

Rubeotic glaucoma

This is a type of end stage glaucoma that can complicate conditions such as central retinal vein occlusion, diabetes and certain inflammatory conditions. The visual prognosis in these patients is almost always poor. Treatment is aimed at preventing the development of a painful blind eye. The treatment of this condition involves eye drops, laser treatment to the retina and laser treatment to the ciliary body (the structure responsible for the production of the aqueous fluid). A variety of different lasers can be used. Before lasers were so well developed, cryotherapy (freezing) treatment was used. A patient should be appropriately counselled about the poor visual prognosis if faced with this situation.

DIABETIC RETINOPATHY

Basics

Type 1 diabetes presents in the younger population, and requires insulin for its control. After 10 years of diabetes the incidence of retinopathy and other microvascular complications increases in frequency. The presence of retinopathy is directly related to the efficacy of diabetic control and other clinical factors such as high blood pressure. Any patient presenting with advancing retinopathy should have all risk factors reviewed by a medical team specialising in diabetes.

Diabetic retinopathy is subdivided into different groups according to the risk to vision created by the disease. In type 1 diabetics the background diabetic retinopathy is not visually significant and does not require treatment although continued screening and review of risk factors is advisable. Pre-proliferative disease is important to identify by screening as both medical treatment of the diabetes and laser treatment for the eye may be required. At this stage, assessment of the ocular microvascular circulation with angiography is frequently needed. This is where photographs of the retinal circulation are taken after the intravenous injection of a dye - usually fluorescein.

The classification of Diabetic retinopathy

- No retinopathy
- Pre-proliferative: mild, moderate and severe
- Proliferative
- Maculopathy

Any patient who has progressed to the stage of proliferative diabetic retinopathy requires intervention with laser treatment. The most commonly used laser is the argon, and the aim is generally to complete pan-retinal photocoagulation within a few weeks. This should consist of approximately 2000 burns to the affected eye. This is ideally completed at one treatment session, but two sessions are commonly required. Some patients may require up to double this amount of treatment to achieve control. Control is defined as the disappearance of the abnormal new retinal blood vessels. The ability to treat with laser may be compromised by the presence of blood in the vitreous cavity of the eye. This is called vitreous haemorrhage and is caused by bleeding from the abnormal proliferative new vessels that grow secondary to ocular ischaemia (lack of oxygen). Where there has been vitreous haemorrhage that has not cleared within a few weeks, surgical intervention with vitrectomy (removal of the vitreous with any blood) and inter-operative laser treatment may be required. Patients with proliferative changes within the retina are at risk of the scarring reactions that can cause tractional retinal detachments.

Type 2 diabetes is late onset and may be controlled by diet, oral hypoglycaemics (tablets), or insulin. This affects an older population and is associated with obesity. In this type of diabetes the common form of retinopathy affects the macular area which is the part of the retina used for precise reading vision. This retinopathy can commonly occur within 2 years of diagnosis and is again influenced by good diabetic control and good control of blood pressure. This type of retinopathy includes, retinal haemorrhages, exudates and oedema. Treatment of this type of retinopathy is with laser treatment focussed on the macular area, however if there is pronounced macular ischaemia treatment is unlikely to be helpful.

Cataract has an increased incidence in both forms of diabetes and may interfere with laser treatment. Cataract extraction may be advised to allow both accurate assessment and treatment of retinopathy.

Retinal laser treatment for proliferative retinopathy can be extensive and cause a reduction of the field of vision. A patient holding a driving licence should be counselled in advance of possible problems in maintaining a driving licence if extensive bilateral treatment is required to control the disease. Retinal and vitreous haemorrhage can occur as complications of laser treatment, overzealous laser treatment can lead to damage to the macular. These complications can lead to temporary or permanent loss of vision. Such complications need to be explained clearly to patients.

The obligation to screen for diabetic retinopathy

The National Health Service framework for Diabetes was published in 2003. This makes recommendations for the screening of diabetic retinopathy. Schemes for screening are being developed throughout the country and depend upon the presence of a comprehensive diabetic register with efficient call and recall systems. Screening is based on retinal photography. The photographs are graded and referred on for specialist opinion. Inbuilt validation systems are important. Patients must also understand that they should have their eyes examined once a year and must take responsibility for attending appointments.

RETINOPATHY OF PREMATURITY (ROP)

Basics

ROP is a condition of the developing blood vessels in the retina. The retinal vessels continue to develop until term (40 weeks gestation). In premature infants, retinal vessel development takes place after birth and can be disrupted, leading to tractional retinal detachment and blindness. Premature infants at risk of ROP need to be identified, monitored and offered treatment. High standards of neonatal care with appropriate monitoring of oxygen reduce the incidence of ROP. Prematurity and multiple complications related to this are now the greatest risk factors for developing the disease. In the multicentre cryotherapy for ROP study, 85% of the infants developing ROP regressed spontaneously. Racial differences in the incidence of ROP, and hence the possibility of a genetic predisposition to it, have been discussed in the literature. Research continues. A gene responsible for a condition called Norrie's disease is attracting particular attention. Molecular analysis of 16 children with advanced ROP showed that 4 had miss-sense mutations of the Norrie's gene

Screening should be carried out on those born at 31 weeks of gestation or less and/or with a birth weight of less than 1500g. Those most at risk are the smallest sickest infants (<28 weeks <800g). Screening should start 6 weeks after birth. Examinations are performed 1-2 weekly if no ROP is detected. Examinations are performed weekly if active disease is detected. Screening should continue until the peripheral retina is fully vascularised or until all the changes of ROP are seen to have regressed.

The treatment threshold referred to below is that severity of disease which would result in blindness in 50% of cases if left untreated.

The classification of ROP

Stage 1: visible demarcation line
Stage 2: a visible ridge
Stage 3: retinal vessel proliferation into the vitreous
Stage 4: partial retinal detachment
Stage 5: total retinal detachment.

"+ disease" is characterised by pupillary rigidity, vascular tortuosity and engorgement, vitreous haze, preretinal and retinal haemorrhage and rubeosis (new vessel formation on the iris).

"Threshold disease" (in which treatment is indicated), is characterised by stage 3 changes in 5 contiguous clock hours or in 8 non-contiguous clock hours. Posterior, rather than peripheral changes are particularly significant, as is the presence of "+ disease".

Screening for ROP

There were national guidelines for screening and treatment published in 1995. Local screening programmes are expected to comply with these standards.

Each neonatal unit should have a system for identifying at-risk infants and for informing the local ophthalmologist responsible for screening so that timely examinations can be done. It is then the responsibility of the ophthalmologist to continue to screen the infant until the risk of ROP has passed. Accurate information on the presence of ROP or the date the next screening examination is required must be included in the transfer record of infants transferred between neonatal units. Infants showing signs of ROP must be monitored on a weekly basis to see if the threshold for treatment is reached or if, as occurs in most cases, the disease regresses spontaneously. If the treatment threshold is reached there is a window of opportunity for treatment of only a few days. If changes progress rapidly the frequency of examination may need to be increased. Rapid progression tends to mean a poor prognosis - especially if it occurs when retinal vascularisation has not progressed very far toward the retinal periphery (zone 1 or posterior zone 2).

Treatment

Treatment for ROP does not ensure a good visual prognosis. Premature infants in any event have a high risk of refractive error, and in particular myopia (short sight). The risk of refractive error increases if the infant has treatment for ROP. The risk is increased less with laser than with cryotherapy. There is also a higher risk of squint and amblyopia (lazy eye) in premature infants. The visual system can also be compromised by intracerebral haemorrhage and hydrocephalus, which can lead to damage of the optic nerves and pathways.

When a child becomes blind as a consequence of retinopathy of prematurity, expert opinion on liability is often sought. Screening was not strenuously advocated until the mid 1980s, when the early results of a cryotherapy study became available. This study showed that treatment could reduce the risk of blindness by 50% in babies reaching threshold disease. A number of ophthalmologists were, however screening for retinopathy of prematurity, and some specialist centres were also offering treatment for severe retinopathy, by the early 1980s. Screening was patchy until 1986.

Before the advent of treatment, most claims about ROP were related to neonatal care and, in particular, exposure to oxygen. High oxygen levels are known to be associated with an increased risk of ROP. Questions of whether oxygen was negligently administered, will, of course, need to be assessed against the standards relevant at the time. Oxygen should always be administered with some definite clinical indication. Once arterial monitoring of blood gases became available it should have been used where oxygen levels of over 40% were administered. Premature babies should have been transferred to units with the appropriate expertise to care for them.

AMBLYOPIA

Hippocrates said that amblyopia was where both the physician and the patient see nothing. Amblyopia is caused by a disruption to visual development. The most common reasons are squint (where the 2 eyes are not aligned), anisometropia (where the 2 eyes have different focus), and sensory deprivation. Sensory deprivation is typically the result of organic interference with visual development, such as congenital cataract in one eye or some other form of congenital anomaly. This type of amblyopia is rare, but is potentially the most difficult to treat.

When a baby is born the visual system is not mature. The system relies on visual input to develop. Visual development progresses very rapidly until 4 months of age, rapidly to 2 years and then at progressively slower rates from age 2 to age 8 –10 years. If an early stage of visual development is missed, irreversible changes occur within the visual system and vision cannot be influenced at a later date. The work of Hubert and Weisal demonstrated this well. They demonstrated that kittens deprived of vision in one eye did not develop the central visual connections to the visual part of the brain from the sensory deprived eye. Opening the eye at a later date could not reverse this process. Accordingly vision in the closed eye was irretrievably lost. If, however, both eyes were deprived of vision, the period in which vision could be developed could be extended. This landmark work confirmed that there were both structural and functional elements to amblyopia.

How does this relate to the clinical situation? If a child has either of the first two types of amblyopia (strabismic or refractive) the central visual connections have usually had the chance to develop for each eye, and visual development is affected at a later stage. For example, a baby with an early onset squint (onset before 6 months of age) usually uses both eyes. Visual development is less influenced under these conditions. A child who develops a squint at an older age may develop a preference for using one eye: this may cause visual development to slip back in the less preferred eye. As long as central connections for vision have developed earlier this can sometimes be corrected by occluding the better seeing eye with a patch. Before patching it is essential that the refractive error of both eyes is assessed and any appropriate glasses prescribed. The correction of refractive error can assist with both the correction of amblyopia and squint.

Refractive amblyopia, when not accompanied by a squint, will go undetected unless the vision is tested in each eye individually. In some parts of the country there is routine pre-school vision screening, and this is now recommended to take place at around the age of 4 years. There is no mandatory requirement for screening of this type. If screening is carried out there should be a robust system for follow up and parents should be fully informed of the results and their implications. Studies have shown that orthoptists are the most efficient screeners, but a range of professionals, including health visitors and medical officers may do this work.

Where amblyopia is detected after the age of 6 to 8, the treatment options are limited. Aggressive patching can lead to complications such as double vision. The most recent studies suggest that in cases of moderate and severe amblyopia treatment with glasses and patching is appropriate and helpful.

The sensory deprivation form of amblyopia is much more difficult to treat. Causes of this type of amblyopia include dense uniocular cataract from birth, occlusion of the visual axis by a haemangioma, or ptosis of other cause. Treatment of the underlying problem and treatment of the amblyopia needs to be started as soon as diagnosis is made. Even with early surgical intervention, there can be no guarantee of a good visual result with uniocular congenital cataract, since correction of the resultant refractive error is so difficult that dense amblyopia may still intervene. Correction of focus after congenital cataract surgery has traditionally been achieved with contact lenses. When there has been unilateral cataract surgery, glasses have to be so strong that they lead to a reduced quality of vision in the affected eye and the trigger for amblyopia is still present. An increasing practicable alternative is an implanted lens. An infant, however, requires a more optically powerful implant than an adult. It is possible for an implanted lens to be exchanged for another, but this can be technically difficult. When a lens is implanted, an over correction with glasses or a contact lens will be required. In addition to this, patching will be required for up to half the waking day for approximately the first 6 to 8 years of life.

It is important to remember that a person with poor vision in one eye or no vision in one eye is, for most practical purposes, visually normal. They will be able to hold a standard driving licence, but will not achieve the visual standards for a commercial or HGV licence.

Children with a squint or dense amblyopia who cannot perform stereovision tests are still able to judge depth and speed of movement, etc. They can be expected to participate in ball games and other sports with their peers without a problem. A person who has previously had binocular vision who loses vision in one eye will have to undergo a period of adaptation. Some people adjust to their changed visual status more quickly and fully than others. Any person with good vision only in one eye should use appropriate eye protection for sports such as cricket, squash and badminton and would be well advised to avoid boxing and other contact sports.

NON-ACCIDENTAL INJURY (NAI)

Ophthalmologists are frequently asked to comment on the eyes of children who are believed to have been victims of violent shaking injuries. The purpose of this is to look for the presence of retinal haemorrhages. The Ophthalmology Child Abuse Working Party is about to publish its interpretation of the current literature on this subject.

Recent articles have been interpreted in some forums as supporting a theory that less violent injury could be associated with the classic picture of subdural haemorrhage and retinal haemorrhage seen in NAI. Extra-dural haemorrhage seems to be associated frequently with accidental head injury in children.

High cervical injuries may be associated with transient apnoea (stopping breathing), but this does not lead to the cascade of events seen in the shaken baby syndrome. Hypoxic ischaemic encephalopathy will only occur where there is circulatory collapse and consequent hypoxia. The incidence of retinal haemorrhages in this group is unknown.

Where subdural haemorrhage is seen in conjunction with retinal haemorrhage and there is no clear history of a high velocity injury, the child should be fully examined for evidence of other causes of haemorrhage. If no other causes can be found, the most likely explanation remains non-accidental injury, and a full clinical examination for other signs of injury should be completed.

REFERENCES

Retinopathy of Prematurity: Guidelines for Screening and Treatment, The Royal College of Ophthalmologists and British Association of Perinatal Medicine, The Report of a Joint Working Party, 1995.

Guidelines for the Management of Strabismus and Amblyopia in Childhood, The Royal College of Ophthalmologists, February 2000.

Guidelines for Diabetic Retinopathy, The Royal College of Ophthalmologists, 1997.

Guidelines for the Management of Ocular Hypertension and Primary Open Angle Glaucoma, The Royal College of Ophthalmologists.

Child Abuse and the Eye, The Ophthalmology Child Abuse Working Party. Eye, 1999; 13: 3-10.

GENERAL SURGERY

James R.H. Scurr and John H. Scurr

INTRODUCTION

General surgery covers a huge number of organs, anatomical areas and conceptual areas. Generalism throughout medicine is under threat, but still a large amount of surgery, especially in District General Hospitals, is performed by true generalists. The law is sympathetic to them. It does not, or should not demand superspecialist standards of treatment where a case can properly be dealt with by a general surgeon. If you spend your life operating on the colon you get better at colons than someone who deals with colons amongst a lot of other things. But patients increasingly expect superspecialist treatment. Litigation increasingly centres around allegations that a case was not properly the province of the general surgeon in the first place. If a case has been wrongly allocated to a generalist, or wrongly accepted by him, and the evidence suggests that a specialist would have avoided the poor result which the claimant is complaining of, liability is likely to be established.

This chapter considers the areas of medico-legal significance which are traditionally regarded as the province of the general surgeon.

THE ACUTE ABDOMEN

General

In the acute abdomen appendicitis, perforated peptic ulcer, perforated diverticular disease, intestinal obstruction and strangulated hernias form the majority of surgical emergencies.

Presenting symptoms include pain, (colicky, persistent, generalised or localised), nausea, vomiting, abdominal distension and absolute constipation.

When any patient presents with an acute abdomen, a full history must be taken and a full clinical examination performed. Then, if appropriate, there must be further investigations to make, confirm or refute the preliminary diagnosis. Treatment should then follow. Delay, failure to diagnose, failure to refer, inappropriate investigations, incorrect surgical management and poor follow-up can all lead to legal claims.

Breach of duty is often clear. Causation is often not.

Pathophysiology

The abdomen is essentially a box containing organs. The pancreas and kidneys are really outside the abdominal cavity (retro-peritoneal). The abdominal cavity is surrounded by a peritoneal lining and this lining is reflected over the surface of abdominal organs like the liver, the spleen, the uterus, ovaries and the large and small bowel.

Most of the functions which go on inside the abdominal cavity are autonomic, and so the patient is unaware of what is happening there until something goes wrong. When structures become distended they become painful. Distension of the bowel gives rise to central abdominal pain. This is often colicky in nature, since the bowel contracts to try to overcome the obstruction. The covering over the structures - the peritoneum - can become inflamed and, when inflamed, this too becomes painful. Inflammation of the peritoneum gives rise to quite severe localised pain at the site of inflammation.

Appendicitis

The appendix is a small finger-like projection from the caecum (the first part of the large bowel). The appendix is situated in the lower right hand corner of the abdomen. It may point towards the pelvis, or it may point behind the caecum (retrocaecal) up towards the liver.

Inflammation of the appendix is quite common, and may settle. If the lumen – the channel running through the appendix – becomes blocked the appendix will swell and perforate. The first sign of any trouble is centralised colicky abdominal pain. As the appendix swells and becomes inflamed it irritates the lining of the peritoneal cavity, causing localised pain: thus the pain moves from the centre of the abdomen towards the lower right hand corner. In the early stages of appendicitis, patients may go off their food, lose their appetite and develop nausea. Vomiting, diarrhoea or absolute constipation are unusual features of appendicitis, but can occur. If the appendix is in the pelvis it can cause irritation to the sigmoid colon, resulting in diarrhoea.

There are no classic signs of acute appendicitis that can be relied on. The textbook presentation is centralised colicky abdominal pain localising to the lower right hand corner of the abdomen. But the appendix has not read the textbook. Most cases of appendicitis do not present like this.

There are no tests which confirm or refute the diagnosis of appendicitis and therefore it is important that a proper history is taken and a proper examination performed. This will usually be done by the general practitioner but if the patient goes to the accident and emergency department it will be done there.

Classically a patient with acute appendicitis will have tenderness in the lower right hand corner of the abdomen. There may be guarding (where the muscles become tensed on palpation) or there may be rebound tenderness, (tenderness when the abdomen, having been pressed, is then released). Rebound tenderness is a very good indicator of peritoneal irritation secondary to inflammation.

An ultrasound scan will sometimes show an enlarged appendix. More importantly, in females, it will exclude a gynaecological cause such as an ovarian cyst, inflammation of the Fallopian tubes, or a tubo-ovarian abscess. A pregnancy test in women of child bearing age is essential to exclude the possibility of an ectopic pregnancy.

The diagnosis of acute appendicitis is difficult in the very young and the very elderly. It is also the young and elderly who suffer most from any delay in making the diagnosis.

Once acute appendicitis is diagnosed the appendix should be removed. It is far safer to remove a normal appendix than to leave an inflamed appendix which subsequently goes on to rupture and cause generalised peritonitis. The writers are unaware of any successful clinical negligence cases against surgeons who have removed a normal appendix.

Removing the appendix involves making a small incision (about 4 cm in length) in the lower right hand corner of the abdomen. The muscles are split, the peritoneum incised and the appendix appears in the wound. If the appendix is retrocaecal it can be difficult to mobilise, but in most instances can be delivered through the wound. Very occasionally it is necessary to extend the wound by 1 or 2 cm. The appendix is removed and the stump invaginated and covered with a purse string suture. When carrying out an appendicectomy it is normal practice to check to make sure there is no other problem within the abdominal cavity. This includes looking at the right ovary, the right Fallopian tube and excluding a Meckel's diverticulum, (a small pouch which can occur in the small bowel about 2 feet from the ileo-caecal valve). Any pus or free fluid should be removed before closing the abdominal cavity. Care should be taken to avoid incorporating the bowel in the wound. Stitching the bowel into the wound is negligent. The wound is then closed.

Following a routine appendicectomy, most patients will start drinking the following morning, eating the day after that and will go home within two to three days. Most will be back to normal within two to six weeks.

Antibiotics, (particularly metronidazole as well as another broad-spectrum antibiotic to go with it), have significantly reduced the risk of wound infection. The incidence of wound infection prior to the use of antibiotics was in excess of 30%. The incidence of wound infection now is less than 5%. Although there may still be a small body of medical opinion which supports not giving prophylactic antibiotics, there is rapidly accumulating evidence to demonstrate the utility of prophylactic antibiotics in any case of appendicitis.

If a patient presents with very advanced appendicitis they may already have formed an intra-abdominal mass. This occurs when the omentum, (fatty tissue within the abdominal cavity), surrounds the appendix, creating a mass in the lower right hand corner. In some situations it is not possible to remove the appendix, and all that can be done is to insert a drain. The appendix can then be removed three months later.

Problems do occasionally occur with the appendicectomy wound. These problems include local infection, incisional hernia and persistent pain.

Laparoscopy is now commonly used to manage patients with acute appendicitis. It can be used to make the diagnosis and to remove the appendix. If the appendix is severely inflamed, removal through a small incision is usually quicker and safer than persisting with a laparoscopic procedure. Although there are benefits from laparoscopy, there are also risks. These risks are greater with the severely inflamed appendix.

If the diagnosis of appendicitis is missed and the patient presents late, the surgeon may be faced with a very different situation. There may be much more inflammation within the abdominal cavity, and it may be much more difficult to remove the appendix. It may be necessary to remove it through a laparotomy incision, (a vertical incision either in the midline or slightly to the right of the midline). If it is necessary to perform a vertical incision there are obvious cosmetic implications.

The recovery following a formal laparotomy is always longer than that following a simple appendicectomy. In the absence of gross peritonitis the normal recovery after laparotomy would be four to eight weeks. Gross peritonitis and generalised infection can occur. This can delay recovery for several months. In extreme cases the patient may need to spend some time in the intensive care unit.

Most medico-legal cases relating to the appendix relate to delayed diagnosis and delayed treatment. Since many cases of acute appendicitis are preceded by a prodromal illness such as acute tonsillitis, or gastro-enteritis, it is often quite difficult to define when the appendicitis actually started and when the patient should have been referred to the hospital.

The use of antibiotics in this period will often mask signs and symptoms, making the ultimate diagnosis more difficult. The easiest time to make the diagnosis of acute appendicitis is when the patient first presents with centralised abdominal pain. The most difficult time to make the diagnosis is one week to ten days into the illness, when a confusing variety of symptoms may have appeared.

Other medico-legal cases have involved failure to remove the appendix, failure to remove the whole appendix, difficulties in subsequent diagnosis with recurrent abdominal symptoms, incorporation of the small bowel in the wound, and other wound problems such as infection, herniation and nerve entrapment.

Peptic Ulcer

Peptic ulceration used to be a very common condition in the United Kingdom. Until 1980 most cases were treated surgically. The advent of H2 antagonists, proton pump inhibitors and *Helicobacter pylori* eradication therapy has reduced not only the instance of peptic ulcer disease but also the complications.

An ulcer may bleed or perforate. If it perforates, it does it spontaneously and the patient will time the onset of symptoms to the nearest minute. When an ulcer perforates, gastric juices enter the peritoneal cavity causing irritation. This chemical irritation is followed fairly quickly by infection. The patient typically presents with a history of sudden onset of severe abdominal pain, often with associated shoulder-tip pain. There may already be a history of a peptic ulcer, and the patient may be receiving treatment for that. Another relatively common history is that of taking non-steroidal anti-inflammatory drugs. These can cause gastric irritation and ultimately lead to a peptic ulcer. It is important to take the history, (particularly the drug history) and to examine the patient.

Typically, the patient will have marked abdominal signs with very pronounced tenderness, guarding and rebound tenderness. An erect chest x-ray may reveal air beneath the diaphragm. A CT scan may be requested to confirm the diagnosis before proceeding to a laparotomy through a midline incision or a paramidline incision. The free fluid and gastric contents can be removed from the abdominal cavity and an omental patch (fat) sewn over the perforation. The stomach can be emptied with a naso-gastric tube and the patient started on anti-ulcer medication. There are virtually no indications for carrying out an anti-acid operation (vagotomy and pyloroplasty) with current medication.

There is a significant incidence of wound infection and the late formation of incisional hernias.

Medico-legal issues arising from a perforated peptic ulcer include whether the patient received appropriate treatment for pre-existing symptoms, the appropriateness of administering non-steroidal anti-inflammatory agents, and any significant delay in making the diagnosis and effecting treatment.

Perforated Diverticular Disease

Diverticular disease is extremely common. Most people over the age of 50 have some diverticuli in the large bowel. There may be one or two in the sigmoid colon, extensive changes throughout the colon, or anything in between. If a diverticulum becomes obstructed and inflamed (diverticulitis), a local abscess may form and eventually perforate. A perforated colonic diverticulum gives rise very rapidly to faecal peritonitis. The patient may have a history of diverticular disease. Pain is often left-sided but can be generalised. It often comes on suddenly. Diverticulitis itself is a common medical condition treated by fluids, a low residue diet and antibiotics. When the condition settles the patient is encouraged to take a high residue diet and may, if appropriate, undergo investigations to determine the extent of the disease. If the inflammation does not settle and perforation occurs, it becomes a surgical emergency.

A rising white cell count may indicate the presence of generalised infection. A CT scan of the abdomen will confirm the presence of diverticuli, identify an abscess or perforation, as well as excluding other possible causes of the acute abdomen. A laparotomy through a midline or left paramedian incision will be required if the bowel has perforated or an abscess requires drainage. If the diverticular disease is not extensive and there is very little evidence of infection, a primary bowel resection can be carried out. There are hazards to carrying out large bowel resections on unprepared bowel - notably a very significant increase in the incidence of anastomotic leakage. In an ill patient the safest procedure is to resect the segment of bowel involved with diverticular disease and bring out the proximal end as an end colostomy. Three months later, when the inflammation has settled, the colostomy can be taken down and a bowel anastomosis carried out, safely joining the bowel end to end.

The writers have seen relatively few cases claiming negligence in the management of diverticular disease. Even in patients with an established history of diverticular disease there may be no indication for surgery until a perforation occurs. Any delay in recognising the perforation is unacceptable.

Perforation of the colon can occur in patients with diverticular disease during colonoscopy. This is a well-recognised complication and does not necessarily connote negligence. It must, however, be recognised and appropriate action taken. A patient who has undergone colonoscopy in the presence of severe diverticular disease who develops severe abdominal pain and is still discharged from the endoscopy unit only to be re-referred by his general practitioner 24 to 48 hours later has had unacceptable care.

Early treatment of a perforated diverticulum is likely to lead to a good outcome.

Intestinal Obstruction

Intestinal obstruction is a common surgical emergency. Fifty years ago the most common cause of intestinal obstruction was a strangulated hernia. Now most patients receive treatment for their hernia long before the hernia strangulates, and a strangulated hernia is a relatively rare surgical emergency. Most cases of intestinal obstruction seen today relate to intra-abdominal adhesions causing small bowel obstruction and tumours that cause large bowel obstruction.

Intra-abdominal adhesions can be congenital, (present from birth), or they can occur following intra-abdominal surgery. Generally, the more extensive the surgery and, in particular resecting large bowel will result in fairly extensive adhesion formation. Adhesions are usually asymptomatic and only cause symptoms when the bowel twists or kinks around them. If the bowel does kink it becomes obstructed and distends, giving rise initially to colicky abdominal pain, nausea and then vomiting. This will be accompanied by absolute constipation. Small bowel obstructions can initially be treated conservatively for 24 to 48 hours. A mechanical large bowel obstruction usually requires treatment within 24 hours if perforation of the colon is to be avoided.

When a patient presents with intestinal obstruction it is important to take a history, to examine the patient and to obtain abdominal x-rays. The distribution of fluid levels and gas on these x-rays will determine whether it is a small or large bowel obstruction, and give some indication as to the severity of the obstruction.

Once the diagnosis is established, intravenous fluids should be administered, a naso-gastric tube may be passed and the patient should be observed. Any patient showing signs of deterioration should undergo a laparotomy. Where there is clear evidence of a large bowel obstruction early surgical intervention is advisable.

Most of the clinical negligence cases concerned with intestinal obstruction that the writers have been involved with have related to the development of adhesions following a previous major surgical procedure, and the allegation that those adhesions should never have occurred. In most instances adhesions remain asymptomatic. Perhaps as few as 5% of patients with extensive intra-abdominal adhesions will develop symptoms and perhaps no more than 1% of those will require further surgery. Relatively few claims relate to the failure to make the diagnosis of intestinal obstruction or the failure to provide appropriate treatment. Most cases of intestinal obstruction have fairly clear-cut presentations and in general their management is fairly straightforward.

HERNIAS

Hernias are an important general surgical condition. Very few hernias now present as an acute surgical abdomen. The majority of hernias (inguinal and femoral hernias) present as swellings in the groin, with or without pain, and are treated electively.

When a hernia does present acutely, it may present with a painful lump in the groin, or it may be an incidental finding in a patient who presents with intestinal obstruction.

Failure to examine the groins and failure to make the diagnosis of a hernia in a case of intestinal obstruction may result in delayed treatment. In many cases it is the very small hernias and in particular the femoral hernias which present with obstructive symptoms.

Patients presenting with hernias should have them repaired to avoid the situation where the hernia may become irreducible and then strangulate. Once a hernia strangulates, the blood supply to the contents of the hernial sac (a loop of bowel or fat), becomes cut off and the bowel or fat dies. This may result in a perforation of the bowel and generalised intra-abdominal peritonitis. If a patient presents with a tender irreducible lump in the groin this should lead to immediate surgical exploration. If there is evidence of plum coloured fluid on exploration of the groin, an intra-abdominal inspection of the gut should be carried out.

Most hernias are repaired fairly uneventfully. There are four major complications. These are recurrence of the hernia, loss of a testicle, persistent pain and infection.

Recurrence is a recognised complication of hernia surgery. In experienced hands the recurrence rate should be no greater than 1%. The incidence of recurrence increases for recurrent hernias.

Testicular loss following hernia surgery provides a constant stream of complaints. The overall incidence of loss of testicle should be no greater than 1 in 1000. Occasionally, with the patient's consent, a testicle is removed to make a more complete repair in a patient who has had two or three previous repairs. The loss of one testicle, although a cosmetic and psychological disaster, has very little physiological effect. The loss of two testicles requires hormone replacement therapy and results in infertility.

The reason why testicles are lost include damage to the arterial supply to the testicle at the time of surgery (which is negligent), damage to the main veins at the time of surgery by division (which is negligent), and occlusion of the veins due to pressure. Occlusion of the veins is not necessarily negligent. A very large haematoma can cause this: it can be argued strongly that this should be drained. Where occlusion results from a small haematoma or a slow thrombosis of the veins due to local pressure, negligence is much more difficult to establish. Where a surgeon can be shown to have been rough in handling the veins, so causing the thrombosis, venous obstruction and the loss of the testicle, this may well prove negligent.

Persistent pain following a hernia operation can be due to nerve entrapment. The ilio-inguinal nerve runs through the region of the repair. If the ilio-inguinal nerve is caught in the repair i.e. lassoed by the nylon used to carry out the repair, this probably represents negligence. If the ilio-inguinal nerve becomes incorporated in the healing scar tissue over a period of three to six weeks following the surgical repair, this is an unfortunate but well recognised event. It does not represent negligence. It is therefore crucial to determine when the pain comes on - whether at the time of surgery or about three weeks later. Where the pain comes on several weeks after the repair it is probably due to nerve incorporation in scar tissue and not due to negligent incorporation of the nerve in the surgical repair.

Infection following a hernia repair can be superficial or deep. Superficial infections usually heal without any problems. A deep infection may prove a disaster. It may require the removal of any foreign material, including the mesh used to reinforce the posterior wall. The incidence of infection can be reduced by the use of prophylactic antibiotics. Although the evidential basis for the use of prophylactic antibiotics is still discussed, most surgeons inserting mesh will now use prophylaxis. It is extremely difficult to justify not using prophylaxis, and if the mesh becomes infected and requires removal then the patient may have a justifiable claim.

Haematoma formation can occur following any surgical procedure. The development of a haematoma is a well-recognised and unfortunate event. It is the failure to recognise the haematoma and the failure to drain large haematomas which gives rise to problems. A haematoma may lead to local infection, and local infection can then cause problems. A large haematoma may cause pressure on the vessels, giving rise to venous compression. In severe cases it can result in the loss of the testicle.

The modern technique of repairing a hernia involves reducing the hernia back into the abdominal cavity, closing the defect and inserting a polypropylene mesh across the defect to act as a scaffold. The body then heals, laying down fibroblasts which mature over a six-week period. If the repair is stretched during the healing process, the risk of recurrence increases. Patients should be encouraged not to do anything too strenuous for this period of time. Any patient undergoing the repair of a recurrent hernia should be advised to avoid strenuous exercise for twelve weeks. Hernias can also be repaired laparoscopically.

LAPAROSCOPIC SURGERY

The history of laparoscopy in the UK

Laparoscopic surgery (keyhole surgery) really started in the United Kingdom in 1990. For 20 years before this, laparoscopy was widely used by gynaecologists for investigative procedures and simple intra-operative procedures such as tubal ligation. By 1990 there had been developments in both the surgical instruments involved and in video imaging. Partly driven by public demand, a large number of conventional surgical procedures suddenly became targets for laparoscopy. The first and by far the most successful general surgical procedure carried out laparoscopically was cholecystectomy.

Laparoscopic cholecystectomy

In 1990 100% of cholecystectomies were carried out using an open surgical procedure. By 1995 85% of cholecystectomies were carried out laparoscopically, and that percentage continues to increase. The old adage that you can't teach old dogs new tricks should have been applied to laparoscopic procedures. In 1990 every surgeon who wished to carry out laparoscopic procedures could do so provided they could get the equipment. It was in the early '90s that proper training programmes were set up and surgeons gained experience using simulators and animal models before undertaking cholecystectomy.

The principle of laparoscopic cholecystectomy is exactly the same as open cholecystectomy. The main indication for removing the gallbladder is gallstones. A patient presenting with gallstones may present with abdominal pain with or without jaundice. Investigations include liver function tests, ultrasound scanning, ERCP (endoscopic retrograde cholangio pancreatography), MRI and isotope scans. In most cases the diagnosis can be made by simple ultrasound scanning.

Removal of the gallbladder involves identifying the anatomy, dividing the cystic duct, the cystic artery and peeling the gallbladder off the liver. Failure to identify the anatomy adequately can lead to inadvertent division of the common bile duct, the common hepatic duct or indeed other structures. This is not acceptable. No structure should be clipped or divided until it has been clearly identified.

Laparoscopy involves injecting gas into the abdominal cavity to create a pneumoperitoneum. This can be done using a small Verres needle. When the needle is inserted into the abdominal cavity care has to be taken to make sure that it does not perforate the bowel. The needle is very fine and small perforations may go unnoticed. Having created a pneumoperitoneum, the surgeon inserts a much larger trocar and port. The laparoscope with the television camera attached is inserted through this port and all other operating ports are inserted under direct vision. Damage to the bowel can occur, particularly if the bowel is adherent to the anterior abdominal wall. The alternative technique to establish the pneumoperitoneum, involves dissecting down to the peritoneum and inserting the trocar and port under direct vision. This technique is now commonly practiced and does help avoid the risk of inadvertent damage to the bowel during the insertion of the initial laparoscopic port.

Damage to the bowel remains a recognised complication. Provided it is recognised and dealt with at the time of injury, negligence will be difficult to prove. Damage to internal organs (including the liver and the spleen) and in particular damage to retro-peritoneal structures, (notably the aorta, the inferior vena cava and the kidneys) is unacceptable.

Following a laparoscopic cholecystectomy, bile may leak from the liver and collect in the abdominal cavity. Again, this is usually recognised and treated by the insertion of a percutaneous drain.

Most patients undergoing a laparoscopic cholecystectomy will leave hospital within 24 to 48 hours. Patients following a laparoscopic cholecystectomy should have made a full or almost full recovery within 48 hours. Any patient who is not making the expected recovery should be considered likely to have a complication and should undergo urgent investigations including liver function tests, an ultrasound scan and, if appropriate, an ERCP (endoscopic retrograde cholangio pancreatography).

There are a number of complications which can follow a laparoscopic cholecystectomy. These include biliary leakage from the cystic duct, bleeding and infection. Most of the complications do not connote negligence. Clinical negligence will most commonly be proved when the complications are not recognised, or are dealt with inappropriately.

The most common claims relate to inadvertent damage to the bile ducts. This is usually a result of failure to define the anatomy correctly or failure to convert to an open surgical procedure when the anatomy is obscure or there is significant bleeding. Damage to intra-abdominal structures during laparoscopic procedures again grounds a substantial number of claims - usually because the damage is not recognised at or shortly after the time of surgery.

Where damage to major structures occurs, a laparotomy, and in some instances major bile duct reconstruction, is required. Major bile duct reconstructions will involve dividing the bowel and creating loops and anastomoses. The loops can twist, adhesions can form and the anastomoses can narrow, giving rise to potential long-term complications. For the best long-term results patients should be referred to hepatobiliary centres for these reconstructions

Patients being consented for laparoscopic cholecystectomy should be told that under certain circumstances it may be necessary to convert to an open surgical procedure. This involves making an incision in the anterior abdominal wall and carrying out a procedure under direct vision. Indications for conversion to an open procedure include difficult or uncertain anatomy, obscured vision due to moderate bleeding, or any other circumstances where the surgeon feels that he cannot complete a laparoscopic procedure safely. Nobody can be criticised for converting to an open surgical procedure. A surgeon who converts too late or not at all, causing intra-abdominal damage, certainly can.

BOWEL CANCER

Cancer of the bowel remains a very common condition. The majority of bowel cancers are in the colon. Cancers of the small intestine are rare. Cancers of the stomach and oesophagus are also relatively uncommon, and are usually associated with a very poor outcome. Large bowel cancer can affect the colon, including the caecum and the rectum. Most clinical negligence cases arise from a failure to make the diagnosis or undue delay. Relatively few cases arise as a direct result of technical complications arising from surgery.

Large bowel cancer usually, but not always, presents in the over-forties. Incidence increases with age. Certain conditions may predispose to the development of cancer. These include a congenitally acquired condition (familial adenomatous polyposis) and longstanding total ulcerative colitis. Other factors thought to be important in the development of colon cancer include diet, environmental factors and a family history. Colon cancer can present with an alteration in bowel habit, bleeding, weight loss and/or abdominal pains.

Although some cases are picked up on routine screening (colonoscopy), by far the majority of patients present to their general practitioner with a history of rectal bleeding and/or alteration in bowel habit.

Since bleeding from the back passage is an extremely common symptom and often associated with haemorrhoids, it is not difficult to see why some genuine cases are dismissed at an early stage.

Any patient presenting with rectal symptoms warrants investigation. These investigations should include history, physical examination including a rectal examination, proctoscopy (examining the anal canal with a proctoscope), sigmoidoscopy (examining the lower part of the rectum with a sigmoidoscope) and if necessary a colonoscopy (examining the colon with a colonoscope). Many claims have been based on a failure to carry out these investigations and a subsequent diagnosis of bowel cancer.

The prognosis with bowel cancer is improved by early diagnosis, and therefore any delay may be an important factor in any potential damages claim.

The diagnosis of bowel cancer usually involves colonoscopy. Colonoscopy is a commonly performed procedure, usually performed under sedation but occasionally under a full general anaesthetic. The diagnosis is made by histological examination of tissue (biopsy) taken at the time of colonoscopy.

Perforation of the colon can occur during colonoscopy - particularly in patients with extensive diverticular disease. Provided this is recognised and treated appropriately, it does not constitute negligence. It is the failure to recognise the perforation which leads to claims. If a colon is perforated at the site of a cancer this can adversely affect the prognosis, but in most cases the cancer is so advanced that this does not have a significant effect.

Before undergoing surgery a patient can be staged using CT or MRI scanning to determine whether or not metastatic disease is present in the lymph nodes or the liver and, if it is, the number and size of those metastases.

When cases of colo-rectal cancer are caught early (confined to the bowel wall or at the very most spreading to local lymph nodes) the first line of treatment is surgical resection of bowel. The exact nature of the resection will depend on the position of the cancer, but it will involve resecting the whole segment of bowel supplied by the arteries running to the region of the cancer. For this reason one sees the right half of the colon resected (right hemicolectomy), the left half of the colon resected, the whole of the sigmoid colon resected or, in the case of an anterior resection, part of the rectum and the sigmoid colon. With cancers involving the rectum it may be necessary to remove the rectum in its entirety and give the patient a permanent end colostomy.

Prior to carrying out surgery some form of bowel preparation is required to empty the bowel, and prophylactic antibiotics are administered. A primary resection with an anastomosis may be carried out. In situations where the anastomosis is difficult or the bowel poorly prepared, it may be necessary to cover the anastomosis with an ostomy (a temporary opening in the bowel upstream of the anastomosis).

Following major bowel surgery, patients recover rapidly and progressively. Any patient whose initial recovery stalls should be monitored carefully for the presence of an intestinal anastomotic leak. Anastomotic leaks dealt with early are a recognised complication of colo-rectal surgery and do not constitute negligence. An anastomotic leak which is missed, and goes on to produce generalised intra-abdominal sepsis, septicaemia and in some instances death, usually represents unacceptable medical practice.

Radiotherapy and chemotherapy may be indicated. The decision to administer radiotherapy or chemotherapy is decided by a multidisciplinary team, including an oncologist. It is not possible to give generalised guidelines on who should or should not receive it. Many patients with colo-rectal cancer are entered into clinical trials and followed-up for long periods of time. All cases really need to be assessed on their own merit.

Following major colonic surgery there is a high instance of intra-abdominal adhesions, and sometimes these become symptomatic. The presence of adhesions themselves does not indicate sub-standard clinical practice.

VARICOSE VEINS

General

The surgical treatment of varicose veins is one of the commonest surgical procedures performed in the United Kingdom. The various treatments are considered to be amongst the easiest surgical procedures, and have been commonly delegated to junior staff. Unsurprisingly, there are many claims relating to varicose veins. Only in relatively few centres is the treatment for varicose veins carried out by surgeons with a specific interest, vascular surgeons. In many centres it is carried out by general surgeons with no specific interest.

After a brief examination, most varicose veins undergo surgical treatment or, in some instances, injection treatment (sclerotherapy). It is now generally recognised that all patients presenting with recurrent varicose veins should undergo a proper venous duplex ultrasound assessment. In many centres a venous duplex assessment is carried out on all patients who present with varicose veins prior to any form of treatment.

Treatment of Varicose Veins

Most varicose veins are treated either by surgery or by an injection technique (sclerotherapy). There are now a number of new minimally invasive percutaneous techniques that have been introduced as an alternative to surgery with stripping. These include endovenous laser therapy (EVLT) and radiofrequency ablation (RFA) techniques. Ultrasound guided foam sclerotherapy (UGFS) is being increasingly used, not only to treat residual varicosities but also for truncal incompetence. The complication rates for these new procedures are atarting to be seen and understood. Although randomised trials have not yet shown a clinical advantage to these new forms of treatment, they are popular with patients as they are less invasive than surgery with stripping.

With Duplex ultrasound imaging the veins can be outlined. This means that before offering treatment the surgeon will know where the veins are filling from and can then advise better on the alternatives. Surgical treatment remains the treatment of choice for patients with significant reflux in major superficial veins. Prior to undergoing surgery, patients should be aware of the purpose of the operation, what the operation involves and the likely outcome. No guarantee can be given that all the superficial veins will be obliterated. Patients must be aware that there will be significant bruising, and that there is a 10% incidence of small cutaneous nerve injuries giving rise to small areas of altered sensation up to the size of a fifty pence piece. Injury to major nerves should not occur. Removal of the long saphenous vein to the ankle has now been abandoned because of a high incidence of sensory nerve injury affecting large areas over the inside of the leg and the foot.

Sclerotherapy is widely practised. It has the advantage that the treatment can be repeated until a good outcome is achieved. Sclerotherapy in large veins with significant reflux may be associated with superficial thrombophlebitis and some skin staining. The superficial thrombophlebitis and the skin staining are reversible, but often only over quite a long period of time.

Most claims arising from the treatment of varicose veins relate to poor outcome and nerve injuries. Motor nerve injuries are indefensible. Sensory nerve injuries are very common and, provided the patient has been given appropriate advice pre-operatively, are often defensible. Haematoma formation is a recognised complication and not one which warrants action. Infection is extremely rare (occurring in probably fewer than 1% of cases) and does not necessarily indicate inadequate care.

Damage to important structures including the femoral vein and the femoral artery occur rarely. When these structures are damaged there can be no defence. A clear proper dissection of the groin avoids these complications. These complications are always associated with a relatively poor outcome even if immediate reconstruction takes place.

The writers have recently reviewed 200 medico-legal cases involving varicose veins. 46% of these cases related to nerve or major vascular injury. 15% arose following sclerotherapy. The remainder related to outcome, venous thromboembolism and recurrence. Less than half of the procedures carried out on the varicose veins were done by consultant surgeons (47%) with 53% being carried out by registrars, associate specialists or senior house officers.

Of the operations carried out by consultant surgeons, 82% were carried out by consultant general surgeons and 18% by consultant vascular surgeons. There were 24 cases of injury to the femoral vein: one case was carried out by a consultant vascular surgeon, 3 cases by a consultant general surgeon and 20 cases by registrars or senior house officers. There was one case of femoral artery injury caused by a consultant surgeon and 3 cases of femoral artery injury caused by junior surgeons. Awards for sural nerve injuries ranged from £4000 to £86,700. For common peroneal nerve injuries awards ranged from £26,500 to £90,000. Compensation for femoral vein and femoral arterial injuries ranged from £6,600 to £135,000. 89% of the claims arose from varicose veins operated on within the National Health Service and 11% of claims arose from patients being operated on in the private sector.

WOUND INFECTION

The rate of wound infections following appendicectomy used to run at over 30%. Using prophylactic antibiotics the rate is now under 5%. The incidence of infection following mesh repair of inguinal hernias should be under 1% when prophylactic antibiotics are given. If prophylactic antibiotics are not given a wound infection rate between of 5% and 10% occurs.

What then are the consequences of wound infections? First, there is delayed discharge. This increases costs and reduces the number of patients who can be treated. Second, there is delayed recovery and this may lead to a loss of income. If the delayed recovery amounts to many months there may be a substantial claim. Third, infection can result in systemic illness, with the possibility of septicaemic damage to many organs, and even death. Fourth, the cosmetic effects of wound infection can be significant.

DEEP VEIN THROMBOSIS

Many major surgical procedures are accompanied by the development of a deep vein thrombosis (DVT) and the risk of a pulmonary embolism. This risk, and the benefits of using DVT prophylaxis, has been known for many years. If a patient develops a deep vein thrombosis following a major surgical procedure and no prophylaxis is given, one can argue that a known risk was not addressed.

All patients entering hospital should have their risk of deep vein thrombosis assessed. If a patient is at significant risk, appropriate DVT prophylaxis should be provided. The level of provision will be determined by pre-established protocols. These protocols may accord to the SIGN guidelines (Scottish Intercollegiate Guidelines Network) or they may be locally derived protocols. The National Institute of Clinical Excellence (NICE) is due to issue guidelines on venous thromboprophylaxis in 2007.

REFERENCE

Connor, S and Garden, OJ, Bile duct injury in the era of laparoscopic cholecystectomy, *Br J Surg*, 2006; 93: 158–168.

Ellis, H, Medicolegal consequences of adhesions, *Hospital Medicine*, 2004 65(6):348-50.

Geerts, WH, Pineo, GF, Heit, JA, Bergqvist, D, Lassen, MR, Colwell, CW and Ray, JG, Prevention of Venous Thromboembolism: The Seventh ACCP Conference on Antithrombotic and Thrombolytic Therapy, *Chest*, 2004;126 (3 Suppl):338S-400S.

Goodwin, H, Litigation and surgical practice in the UK, *Br J Surg*, 2000; 87:977–9.

Kavanagh, S, The acute abdomen – assessment, diagnosis and pitfalls, *Casebook* 2004; 12(1): 11–7 (www.mps.org.uk)

Kavanagh, S, Mistakes in vein, *Casebook*, 2005; 13(4): 11-14. (www.mps.org.uk)

The National Institute for Clinical Excellence (2004) Laparoscopic surgery for inguinal hernia repair, *NICE Technology Appraisal Guidance* No. 83., London. (www.nice.org.uk).

Scottish Intercollegiate Guidelines Network (SIGN), Prophylaxis of venous thromboembolism. 2002; (SIGN Publication No. 62), (http://www.sign.ac.uk/guidelines/fulltext/62/index.html)

Scurr, J, *Vascular surgery* in Medico-legal practitioners series, London, Cavendish Publishing Limited, 1999.

Scurr, JR and Scurr, JH, Varicose veins: a review of 200 consecutive medicolegal claims, *Clinical Risk*, 2005; 11(6): 225–230.

Scurr, JR and Scurr, JH, 100 Consecutive Claims of Alleged Negligence in Elective Open Inguinal Hernia Repair in UK, *Clinical Risk*, 2006.

GYNAECOLOGY

Stephen Kennedy

INTRODUCTION

This introduction outlines the basic principles of pelvic anatomy and reproductive physiology relating to benign gynaecology. The subject includes a wide range of conditions such as menstrual problems, pelvic pain, vaginal prolapse, infertility treatment and fertility control. Problems associated with the management of gynaecological cancers are not covered. These are dealt with in the chapter on oncology.

The remainder of the chapter covers legally important mistakes in the specific areas of female sterilisation, intra-uterine contraceptive devices, early pregnancy problems (miscarriage and ectopic pregnancy), surgical termination of pregnancy, laparoscopic surgery and ureteric damage. The choice is deliberately limited, but it reflects the most common problems encountered and the emphasis on laparoscopic surgery reflects the increasing tendency for operations to be carried out laparoscopically rather than at laparotomy.

The majority of legally important mistakes in the field arise because of communication failure and/or surgical complications. In only a few surgical cases do the mistakes occur because the gynaecologist has been inadequately trained or is insufficiently experienced to perform the procedure. In most cases, the complication occurs despite reasonable attempts being made to avoid it happening: in other words, gynaecologists generally follow established practice and use standard techniques.

The introduction of a new Department of Health consent form in the UK in 2000[1] has emphasised the necessity of communicating risks to patients, although it remains unclear whether *all* possible complications, including very rare ones, should now be mentioned. It is not standard practice to do so for non-surgical treatments (e.g. prescribing drugs), but it can easily be argued that it is in the best interests of patients and clinicians that it is done. Hence, it should be documented clearly in the notes, and/or in a letter to the patient, what options were discussed; why the decision to treat was made; what the aims of treatment are, and what side-effects and risks were mentioned.

[1]http://www.dh.gov.uk/PolicyAndGuidance/HealthAndSocialCareTopics/Consent/fs/en

ANATOMY AND PHYSIOLOGY

Pelvic anatomy

The female external genitalia are described as the vulva, which is bordered by the mons veneris anteriorly and the labio-crural folds posterolaterally. The introitus (vaginal entrance) tends to be open in parous women (i.e. those who have had children) but otherwise appears closed by the apposing labia majora. The labia minora are folds of skin which fuse anteriorly to form the clitoris, containing erectile tissue similar to the penis. The fourchette is the posterior part of the introitus, which must stretch considerably to allow the delivery of a baby.

The vagina is an elastic, distensible tube, approximately 10 cm long, passing upwards and backwards from the introitus. The cervix (neck of the womb) protrudes into the vault (top) of the vagina, dividing it into anterior, posterior and lateral fornices. Pelvic structures can be felt by placing fingers in the posterior and lateral fornices, as the vaginal vault sits just below the pouch of Douglas (the area at the bottom of the pelvic cavity bordered by the uterus in front and the rectum behind). The urethra and bladder neck sit above the anterior wall of the vagina; the perineal body and rectum behind the posterior wall.

The uterus, consisting of a body and a cervix, is a pear-shaped structure that is flattened anteroposteriorly giving its cavity a flat, triangular shape. The uterus is supported partly by ligaments attached to the cervix (transverse cervical, pubocervical and uterosacral) consisting of condensed connective tissue. The cervix is a canal, approximately 2 cm long, connecting the external os (opening), which can be seen on speculum examination, to the internal os where the cervix enters the uterine cavity. The length of the uterine cavity, including the cervical canal, is approximately 6 cm in nulliparous women (i.e. those who have not had a child) and approximately 8 cm in parous women. The walls of the uterus are 1-2 cm thick and composed of muscular tissue (myometrium). The uterine cavity is lined with endometrium, a tissue that undergoes cyclical changes in response to ovarian hormones (see Reproductive physiology section below).

The top of the uterus is called the fundus; on either side (cornu) at the top, the uterus is connected to a fallopian tube. These are thin, muscular tubes, approximately 10 cm long, which connect the peritoneal and uterine cavities. They are divided into four parts: intramural (within the uterine wall), isthmus, ampulla, and fimbriated opening which picks up the oocyte (egg) following its release at the time of ovulation. The tubes are very narrow in the isthmic and intramural parts, but they widen in the ampullary region. Each tube is contained within the upper part of the broad ligament, a fold of peritoneum on either side of the uterus which also contains blood vessels and the round and ovarian ligaments. The fimbriated opening and part of the ampulla, however, are free and closely associated with the ovary on either side. The ovaries are flattened, ovoid structures that contain eggs. They are approximately 3-4 cm long and suspended from the back of the broad ligament on either side of the pelvis. The ovarian blood vessels are contained within the infundibulopelvic ligaments, which are continuations of the broad ligaments to the pelvic brim on either side.

The cervix is located in the centre of the bony cavity of the pelvis and the uterus can be pivoted around this point. It is usually angled forwards at approximately 90° relative to the vagina, in which case it is called anteverted. However, it is usually freely mobile, however, and filling of the bladder or changes in position may rotate it backwards. In some women, the uterus is tilted backwards (retroverted) either because of weak ligaments or because the uterus becomes stuck due to a disease process such as endometriosis (defined as the presence of endometrial-like tissue outside the uterine cavity). The uterus may also be angled forward (anteflexed) relative to the cervix when anteverted, or backwards (retroflexed) when retroverted in which case it can usually be felt in the pouch of Douglas on vaginal examination. The commonest cause of an enlarged uterus, aside from pregnancy, is the presence of fibroids (benign tumours of the myometrium) growing inside or outside the uterus. In such cases, the size of the uterus is described in terms of weeks of pregnancy as it expands forwards and upwards into the abdominal cavity with increasing gestational age.

Reproductive physiology

The menstrual cycle is under the control of hormones produced in the brain, which are carried around the body in the blood. Thus, gonadotrophin releasing hormone (GnRH) produced in the hypothalamus stimulates the pituitary to produce follicle stimulating (FSH) and luteinising (LH) hormones, which in turn control how the ovary produces an egg on a monthly basis, and also the hormones, oestrogen and progesterone. These hormones have an effect on many structures in the body, but principally on the endometrium (the tissue that lines the uterine cavity).

The endometrium prepares itself to receive a fertilised egg during the course of the menstrual cycle. In the first half (proliferative or follicular phase) of the cycle, following menstruation, the endometrium starts to regrow or proliferate in response to oestrogen, the hormone produced as an egg develops within a small, fluid-filled, cyst in the ovary called a follicle. The endometrium becomes thick and spongy during the follicular phase of the cycle and grows extra blood vessels.

At mid-cycle, on approximately day 14 (day 1 of the cycle is defined as the first day of menstruation), the egg is released from the ovary - the process known as ovulation. The follicle is then transformed into the corpus luteum. Following ovulation, in the second half (secretory or luteal phase) of the cycle, the endometrium thickens even more in response to the hormone progesterone, which is produced by the corpus luteum.

If fertilisation occurs, the fertilised egg is transported along a fallopian tube into the uterine cavity and then attaches itself to the endometrium - the process known as implantation. If fertilisation does not occur or if the fertilised egg fails to implant, the endometrium is shed and menstruation occurs. Bleeding (a 'period') tends to last 4 days but can range from 2-6 days. Typically, about 40 ml blood is lost during each period; if the bleeding is heavy (i.e. greater than 80 ml), blood clots may form. The whole process then starts again in the next menstrual cycle.

If fertilisation does occur, the duration of the pregnancy (gestational age) is traditionally calculated from the first day of the last menstrual period (LMP). However, ovulation may occur earlier or considerably later than day 14, or the woman's recollection of the date of the LMP may be incorrect, which means that calculating gestational age on the basis of the LMP alone may be inaccurate. This explains the alternative practice of calculating gestational age using ultrasound measurement of fetal size.

FEMALE STERILISATION

Basics

The aim of sterilisation is to occlude the fallopian tubes permanently so as to prevent subsequent conception. The procedure is performed at laparoscopy, Caesarean section or mini-laparotomy (i.e. via a small abdominal incision). In certain parts of the world but not the UK, access to the fallopian tubes is obtained by opening the vaginal vault.

At laparoscopy, the commonest device used in the UK to occlude the fallopian tubes is the Filshie clip – a clamp-like device that is applied to each fallopian tube at laparoscopy. However, the tubes can also be occluded with rings, or by using diathermy, a method that is difficult to reverse because it causes more permanent damage. In addition, if the tubes are occluded with diathermy and the method fails, the pregnancy is more likely to be ectopic. Sometimes, it may be necessary to remove the tubes completely (salpingectomy); this is not done routinely because it takes more time, is obviously irreversible and because the risks, mainly bleeding, are slightly greater. At Caesarean section or mini-laparotomy, several methods may be used. They usually involve removal of part of each tube.

Pre-operative counselling

It is standard practice to counsel the patient that:

- sterilisation should be considered a permanent and irreversible form of contraception, especially as reversal of sterilisation is no longer available as an NHS patient.
- there is a small risk that a laparotomy might be required, if sterilisation by laparoscopy proves difficult or if a complication arises (e.g. bowel damage).

- there is a well-recognised failure rate (quoted as 1 in 200 procedures in the RCOG patient information sheet[2]).
- vasectomy is an alternative form of permanent contraception.
- it is advisable to continue using contraception at least up until the time of the operation, and, in the case of the 'pill', up until the end of the packet.
- sterilisation is not associated with an increased risk of heavier or irregular periods when performed after the age of 30, although stopping the 'pill' may lead to periods becoming heavier again and there is an increased hysterectomy rate following sterilisation.

It is also standard practice to use a separate consent form for sterilisation, which clearly refers to the irreversibility of the procedure and the risk of failure. To exclude the possibility that the patient might be pregnant at the time of the sterilisation, it is standard practice to ask:

- the date of the LMP
- the method of contraception currently being used
- whether the current method of contraception might have failed

These questions aim to determine whether the woman had unprotected intercourse since her LMP, in which case conception might have occurred. In addition, it is prudent to ask the woman whether she believes there is any possibility that she might be pregnant.

In some hospitals, a urinary pregnancy test is performed routinely, in keeping with the RCOG Guidelines[3]. However, this is not universal practice because of the cost involved and because the conception will not be sufficiently advanced to produce a positive test if the procedure is being performed in the luteal phase (i.e. in the second half of the menstrual cycle).

Why does sterilisation fail?

A failure of the operation is defined as a pregnancy occurring any time after the menstrual period following the procedure. The pregnancy can be intra- or extra-uterine (i.e. an ectopic), and can occur immediately or several years after the failed operation.

The most common reasons for failure are:

(a) one or both clips are applied not onto the fallopian tubes, but onto some other structure within the pelvis, such as the round ligament
(b) one or both clips are not applied completely across the fallopian tubes

---

[2] http://www.rcog.org.uk/resources/Public/pdf/PI_sterilisation_women_men.pdf
[3] http://www.rcog.org.uk/resources/Public/pdf/Sterilisation_summary.pdf

(c) one or both clips do not completely occlude the fallopian tubes, despite being applied properly
(d) one or both clips become loose, despite being applied properly to the fallopian tubes

It is usually possible to determine the reason at a later laparoscopy if the woman undergoes a repeat sterilisation. Reasons a) and b) represent operator failure, whereas reasons c) and d) represent a technical failure of the method.

Sterilising a woman who is pregnant is strictly speaking not a failure of the method, but nevertheless something to be avoided if possible. It occurs most often when a sterilisation is performed in the luteal phase, following conception earlier in the same cycle. To avoid such an occurrence, it was common to perform a dilatation & curettage (D&C) of the uterine cavity at the same time to disrupt the endometrium. However, the practice ceased because of the high percentage of failures (i.e. continuing pregnancies) and because it could be interpreted as an attempt to procure a termination of pregnancy.

INTRA-UTERINE CONTRACEPTIVE DEVICES

Basics

An intra-uterine contraceptive device (IUCD) or 'coil' consists usually of a small, copper-wire bearing device, which is placed through the cervix into the uterine cavity. The IUCD is designed to be folded up within a fine tube to allow insertion; once inside the uterine cavity its original shape is then restored. The device has threads attached to its lower end, which descend through the cervix allowing easy removal. The threads also provide a means of checking that the IUCD remains *in situ*. The IUCD produces a foreign body reaction within the uterine cavity and prevents a fertilised egg implanting. In recent years, another type of device - the Mirena coil or intra-uterine system (IUS) - has been developed which slowly releases a small amount of a hormone like progesterone into the uterine cavity. Aside from providing contraception, the Mirena IUS also reduces menstrual bleeding or stops it altogether: it is therefore used as an effective treatment for heavy periods.

The commonest, legally important, problems associated with the IUCD are:

- uterine perforation at the time of insertion (primary) or subsequently because of muscular contractions expelling the IUCD through the uterine wall (secondary)
- ascending infection which can result in tubal damage and abscess formation: consequently the IUCD should be avoided in women at risk of sexually transmitted diseases, e.g. young, nulliparous women with multiple sexual partners
- pregnancy (intra- or extra-uterine)

All patients should be counselled and given written information about the effectiveness and failure rates of IUCDs and the known complications, including pelvic infection and menstrual disturbances.

Uterine perforation

The frequency of primary perforation, i.e. pushing the IUCD through the uterine wall into the peritoneal cavity, is approximately 1 in 1000. In theory, perforation is avoidable if:

- the size and position of the uterus have been adequately assessed on bimanual examination.
- the uterus has been sounded beforehand to measure the length of the uterine cavity.
- excessive force inserting the IUCD has been avoided.
- traction is placed on the cervix to straighten the cervical canal during insertion.

Perforation often occurs as a result of mistaken assessment of the position of the uterus: thus, the anterior wall can be perforated, if the operator believes that a uterus is anteverted when it is in fact retroverted, because the IUCD is introduced in the wrong direction.

Secondary perforation, however, with a frequency of 3-15 in 100 at 1 year, like expulsion, is usually unavoidable.

To check that the IUCD remains *in situ*, the woman should be examined 4-6 weeks after the insertion and approximately every 1-2 years thereafter to see that the threads are still visible, or if she herself cannot feel the threads on self-examination. If the threads are not visible, it is logical to assume that:

- the IUCD is still in the uterine cavity or embedded in the uterine wall and the threads have been drawn upwards, or
- it has been pushed out of the uterus into the abdominal cavity, or
- it has been expelled altogether from the body

The uterus should be sounded (the most commonly used device is an Emmett Thread Retriever) and if the IUCD is not found within the uterine cavity, an ultrasound scan of the uterus should be performed.

There are two reasons why it is important to localise the IUCD:

- to ensure that the woman still has adequate contraception - clearly if the IUCD is not within the cavity she needs an alternative form of contraception.

- to remove the IUCD, preferably at laparoscopy, if it is within the abdominal cavity as an IUCD can cause the pelvic organs to become adherent to the omentum or bowel.

There have also been cases where a second IUCD has been inserted on the assumption that the first has been expelled, leaving two in the uterine cavity. Removing the second when the woman wishes to conceive has then resulted unknowingly in infertility.

What happens if the woman becomes pregnant?

If pregnancy occurs, an ectopic should be excluded as soon as possible by performing an ultrasound scan. If the pregnancy is intra-uterine and the woman wishes it to continue, the IUCD should be removed if possible because of the increased risks of miscarriage, antepartum haemorrhage and premature labour.

PROBLEMS IN EARLY PREGNANCY

Miscarriage

A miscarriage is defined as the spontaneous loss of an intra-uterine pregnancy. It occurs much more commonly than an ectopic pregnancy. A miscarriage usually starts with painless vaginal bleeding, at which point it is defined as a *threatened miscarriage*. The bleeding then becomes heavier with associated uterine cramps, at which point it becomes an *inevitable miscarriage*. Blood clots and products of conception (i.e. fetal and placental tissue) are then passed through the cervical os until the uterus is emptied (defined as a *complete miscarriage*). Sometimes, not all the products of conception are passed spontaneously (defined as an *incomplete miscarriage*) and the woman requires an operation, called an evacuation of retained products of conception (ERPC), to remove what is left of the pregnancy. The operation involves passing a plastic suction curette through the cervix into the uterine cavity. The risks of the procedure are described in the termination of pregnancy section.

On vaginal examination, there is typically no cervical excitation (pain on moving the cervix) or tenderness in the lateral fornices (i.e. tenderness in the vicinity of the fallopian tubes), which are signs associated with an ectopic pregnancy. The uterus feels the right size or smaller for the gestational age. The internal cervical os, by definition, is closed if the miscarriage is threatened or complete, and open if the miscarriage is inevitable or incomplete. If the fetus has not developed (defined as a *missed abortion*), the uterus will feel small and there may have been no bleeding, in which case the os will be closed. In such circumstances, the os will need to be dilated before performing the ERPC.

An ultrasound scan is usually performed to determine whether there is a viable intra-uterine pregnancy present or not. However, it is still not uncommon, especially in early pregnancy, to make the diagnosis of a miscarriage on clinical grounds alone, such as:

- heavy vaginal bleeding with clots and associated uterine cramps
- no history of abdominal pain
- no cervical excitation or tenderness in the vaginal fornices
- no risk factors for an ectopic pregnancy e.g. a past history of pelvic inflammatory disease or previous tubal surgery

Ectopic pregnancy

An ectopic pregnancy is one that grows outside the uterine cavity, almost always in a fallopian tube. As the ectopic grows, the placenta infiltrates blood vessels within the fallopian tube which can cause bleeding within the tube and bleeding into the peritoneal cavity. Further growth of the ectopic can rupture the fallopian tube causing substantial blood loss into the peritoneal cavity and, rarely, death.

An ectopic pregnancy may be suspected on clinical grounds but making the diagnosis can be difficult because the presentation is so variable and can mimic that of a miscarriage. There may be a history of lower abdominal pain with a small amount of vaginal bleeding at 4-6 weeks' gestation. On vaginal examination, there may be cervical excitation and tenderness in the vaginal fornices; the cervical os is closed. Alternatively, the woman may not have any symptoms or physical findings. The urinary pregnancy test is usually positive.

An ultrasound scan will be performed if the diagnosis is suspected. The complete absence of an intra-uterine gestational sac with a positive pregnancy test increases the probability of an ectopic pregnancy unless the pregnancy is not sufficiently advanced for the sac to be seen on ultrasound. An ectopic is more likely if fluid (i.e. blood) is seen on ultrasound in the pelvis or an adnexal mass (i.e. a mass on either side of the uterus) is seen on ultrasound.

In equivocal cases, measuring blood levels of βhCG (a pregnancy hormone) can help to establish the diagnosis. βhCG levels usually double every 48 hours if the pregnancy is viable and intra-uterine. Levels tend to be static or the rise is less than double over a 48 hour period if the pregnancy is ectopic. A single level above approximately 1,500 iu/l in association with an empty uterus on ultrasound is highly suggestive of an ectopic pregnancy.

The best diagnostic test is laparoscopy, but it is not always accurate if the ectopic pregnancy has not advanced sufficiently to be seen in the tube. There is also a view that a laparoscopy should only be performed once a miscarriage has been excluded because of the surgical and anaesthetic risks associated with the procedure (see section on laparoscopy).

Once an ectopic pregnancy is diagnosed at laparoscopy, a salpingectomy is usually then performed, i.e. the tube and ectopic are removed. A salpingostomy (removal of the ectopic with conservation of the tube) may be performed instead as some gynaecologists maintain that subsequent intra-uterine pregnancy rates are higher and recurrent ectopic rates lower following conservative surgery, even though the literature would appear not to support this view. In the past, these operations were performed exclusively at laparotomy, but increasingly they are now done laparoscopically.

In practice, the type of operation chosen depends on factors such as:

- the amount of bleeding - an immediate laparotomy may be required if the woman has lost a great deal of blood.
- the state of the tube, i.e. the size of the ectopic and whether it has ruptured or not (in general, if the ectopic is too large the chances of conservative surgery being successful are small; if it has ruptured there is little point in trying to be conservative).
- the state of the other tube - as one usually tries to be as conservative as possible if the other tube has been affected by pelvic inflammatory disease (i.e. it is closed or densely adherent to other pelvic organs).
- previous ectopic pregnancy or tubal surgery - as one usually performs a salpingectomy if a woman has had a previous ectopic or tubal surgery in the same tube.
- the woman's fertility intentions - as one usually performs a salpingectomy if a woman does not want more children.

Sometimes, the ectopic is located at the very end of the tube, in which case it may be possible simply to 'milk' it out, thereby conserving the tube. The principal disadvantage of the method is that some residual trophoblastic tissue (placenta) can be left inside the fallopian tube. The tissue often survives and continues to grow. The presence of residual trophoblastic tissue inside the fallopian tube can cause problems such as internal bleeding. The best method for determining whether all the tissue has been removed is to take serial blood samples after the operation to measure βhCG levels: levels fall to zero over time if all the tissue has been removed at surgery. However, βhCG levels remain constant or rise if there is residual trophoblastic tissue, which may necessitate another laparoscopy to remove the tube.

In the USA, many women avoid surgery altogether by being treated with intramuscular injections of methotrexate, which is toxic to trophoblastic tissue. The drug has some side-effects and the treatment carries the risks associated with residual trophoblastic tissue, namely internal bleeding and the eventual need for a laparoscopy. In the UK, methotrexate seems to be used only in those patients who are a surgical risk (i.e. the morbidly obese or those with extensive pelvic adhesions).

After treatment, the patient who still has one or both tubes should be warned that she is at increased risk of another ectopic pregnancy. She should therefore be encouraged to present as early as possible in a subsequent pregnancy so as to rule out the diagnosis.

SURGICAL TERMINATION OF PREGNANCY

Surgical termination of pregnancy (STOP) by vacuum aspiration (otherwise known as suction termination) is performed under general or local anaesthesia typically from 7 to 12 weeks gestation, although some centres will offer the service up to 15 weeks. The cervical canal is dilated using graduated metal rods until a suction tube can be inserted into the uterine cavity to remove the pregnancy. The more advanced the pregnancy, the more the cervix has to be dilated; usually therefore a drug is inserted into the vagina pre-operatively to soften the cervix which makes the dilatation easier to perform.

The principal complications and their approximate rates are shown below. In general, the rates are lower when STOPs are performed early in pregnancy and by experienced clinicians. It should be remembered that STOP is safer for most women than carrying a pregnancy to term and having a baby.

- *Uterine perforation* (1 - 4 in 1000): may cause damage to pelvic organs and/or bleeding, and necessitate a laparotomy
- *Haemorrhage* (1 - 2 in 1000) may manifest as vaginal or intra-abdominal bleeding
- *Cervical trauma* (no greater than 1%) may later result in an incompetent cervix predisposing to mid-trimester miscarriage
- *On-going pregnancy* (1 in 1000 at ≥7 weeks gestation) may result from:
    i. a failure to access the uterine cavity
    ii. incomplete emptying of the cavity, e.g. removal of only one of a twin pregnancy
- *Infection* (up to 10%) manifesting as genital tract infection of varying severities, including pelvic inflammatory disease. The risk is reduced when prophylactic antibiotics are given or when lower genital tract infection has been excluded beforehand by bacteriological screening.

LAPAROSCOPY

Diagnostic laparoscopy

Diagnostic laparoscopy is usually performed to investigate infertility and/or the cause of pelvic pain. In both instances, the findings may be normal or there may be pathology present such as pelvic adhesions and/or endometriosis. Most diagnostic laparoscopies are performed under general anaesthesia, although a few patients have the procedure while awake to try to determine which parts of the pelvis are causing pain (conscious pain mapping).

Typically, the steps involved are:

(a) Empty the bladder, unless the patient has emptied her bladder just before the procedure.
(b) Attach a manipulator to the cervix, which enables the uterus to be moved from side to side, and backwards and forwards. One part of the manipulator is placed in the uterus. This may be used later to pass blue dye into the cavity to check whether the fallopian tubes are open by seeing if dye spills out of the tubes into the pelvis.
(c) Make a tiny incision in the abdominal wall for the insertion of the Veress needle (sometimes also known as Verres needle).
(d) Insert the Veress needle through the abdominal wall – the needle consists of an outer cannula, a few mm in diameter, with a bevel cutting edge, inside which is a spring-loaded, central tube. As the needle enters the abdominal cavity, the central tube protrudes beyond the cutting edge of the outer cannula, helping to protect underlying structures from damage during insertion.
(e) Create a pneumoperitoneum by filling the abdominal cavity with carbon dioxide via the Veress needle (producing a gas layer which keeps the abdominal wall away from the bowel).
(f) Via a 10 mm incision inside/just below the umbilicus, insert a metal trochar through the abdominal wall (typically a metal sleeve containing an inner, pointed, metal introducer).
(g) Remove the introducer and pass the laparoscope (a rigid telescope usually 10 mm in diameter) down the trochar sleeve. The pneumoperitoneum is then maintained by instilling gas into the abdominal cavity via the trochar.
(h) Connect the laparoscope to a video monitor allowing everyone in the operating theatre to see the pelvis.
(i) Insert an additional, instrument trochar (similar to, but thinner than, the laparoscope trochar) under direct vision, via a 5-10 mm incision in the midline or on one side of the lower abdominal wall.
(j) Remove the introducer and pass a grasper/manipulator down the trochar sleeve. The grasper/manipulator is used to move the pelvic organs around to obtain as good a view of the pelvis as possible.

The Veress needle can be inserted vertically into the pelvis from just above the pubic symphysis or at an angle into the pelvis from inside/just below the umbilicus. Provided that the patient is not pregnant, the bladder is empty and the needle does not stray from the midline, the former approach is probably safer because the uterine fundus is the only structure the surgeon is likely to hit by mistake, with little undue consequence other than some bleeding which usually stops spontaneously. However, the latter approach has the advantage that, at this site, the abdominal wall is thin, the peritoneum is close to the skin and there is minimal peritoneal fat.

If there is a laparotomy scar, especially in the midline, the bowel might be adherent to the undersurface of the abdominal wall, in which case another site is usually chosen for the insertion of the first trochar, such as the upper left abdominal quadrant just lateral to the rectus sheath (Palmer's point). The undersurface of the abdominal wall near the umbilicus can then be inspected with a small laparoscope inserted at Palmer's point to determine whether a laparoscope can be safely inserted at the umbilicus.

Insertion of both the Veress needle and the laparoscope trochar is performed blindly, i.e. the surgeon is unaware precisely what lies underneath the abdominal wall when these instruments are inserted. Therefore, damage to underlying structures can occur even in the most competent hands. An alternative approach is an open technique which involves extending the abdominal wall incision down to the peritoneum, i.e. entering the cavity under direct vision to minimize the risk of damaging underlying structures. A major problem with the technique, however, is that it can be difficult to maintain a pneumoperitoneum thereafter because the hole in the abdominal wall cannot be sealed well enough around the trochar, which may explain why few gynaecologists in the UK use the method.

Once the Veress needle has been inserted, several techniques are used before instilling gas to try to ensure the needle tip is in the abdominal cavity. This may involve filling a 10 ml syringe attached to the Veress needle with saline; injecting approximately 5 ml saline down the needle and then withdrawing the plunger of the syringe. If the needle tip lies in the abdominal cavity, no aspirate should be obtained on withdrawing the plunger as the fluid will have dispersed. If the aspirate is red or brown, it suggests that a blood-vessel or the bowel has been perforated. Such techniques, although recommended, are not universally used because they are not always accurate and because an experienced surgeon can usually feel whether the needle is in the correct location.

Bowel can be perforated by the Veress needle and/or the laparoscope trochar during their insertion. The surgeon may not recognise during surgery that the perforation has occurred. It usually becomes obvious in the immediate post-operative period, however, because the woman develops peritonitis. A blood vessel in the pelvis may similarly be perforated: the consequences then depend entirely upon the vessel's calibre. They range from the need, under rare circumstances, for an immediate laparotomy to stop massive internal bleeding to doing nothing if a minor vessel has been damaged as the bleeding usually ceases spontaneously.

Superficial and deep epigastric blood vessels in the lower abdominal wall can also be damaged as the instrument trochar is being inserted. There are standard techniques to try to avoid damaging blood vessels in the abdominal wall, which include:

being familiar with the normal anatomy of the vessels, so as to make the skin incision away from their normal position in the abdominal wall.

- trans-illuminating the abdominal wall with the light at the end of the laparoscope before making the skin incision so as to visualise the course of the superficial blood vessels.
- using the laparoscope to visualise the course of the deep blood vessels along the undersurface of the abdominal wall so as to avoid inserting the instrument trochar near them. These vessels are often, but not always, seen between the insertion of the round ligament at the inguinal canal and the obliterated umbilical artery.

If it is impossible to trans-illuminate the abdominal wall and/or visualise the course of the blood vessels along the undersurface of the abdominal wall, which can occur if the patient is overweight, the surgeon should rely upon his/her knowledge of normal anatomy and insert the instrument trochar lateral to their usual location.

Damage to the deep blood vessels can lead to abrupt and significant blood loss. This usually requires making a larger skin incision to isolate and ligate the bleeding blood vessels. The damage may be apparent during the operation because of bleeding from:

- the skin incision onto the abdominal wall.
- around the instrument trochar into the abdominal cavity.
- the trochar site into the abdominal cavity (after the instrument trochar has been removed at the end of the operation).

Sometimes, the damaged vessels do not bleed into the abdominal cavity. The bleeding may only occur in the abdominal wall, producing a haematoma (blood clot) over time.

The insertion of the instrument trochar through the abdominal wall should be visualised with the laparoscope (i.e. it is not a blind technique). Thus, bowel perforation should be avoided with careful surgical technique and adequate visualisation of the instrument trochar throughout its insertion through the abdominal wall, even if bowel is stuck to the undersurface of the abdominal wall at this site.

How common are the complications?

The list in Table 1 is taken from a large French study: it summarises the commonest complications during nearly 6,000 diagnostic laparoscopies[4]. To simplify matters, the frequencies are rounded up and expressed as a number per 10,000 operations rather than as a percentage or a number per 6,000 operations. The exception is the rare complication of death, which is expressed as a figure per 100,000 operations.

---

[4] Chapron, C *et al.*, Surgical complications of diagnostic and operative gynaecological laparoscopy: a series of 29,966 cases, *Human Reproduction*, 1998, 13, 867-72.

If it is recognised during the operation that damage has occurred, it may be possible to repair the damage laparoscopically. It is more likely, however, especially if bowel is damaged, that a laparotomy will be necessary to repair the damage. Depending upon the type of damage, this may involve making an incision approximately 10 cm long just above the bikini line, or a vertical incision 10-15 cm long from the umbilicus downwards.

TABLE 1: COMPLICATIONS RECORDED IN A FRENCH STUDY OF NEARLY 6,000 DIAGNOSTIC LAPAROSCOPIES

Type of complication	How often did it occur?
Bowel damage	5 in 10,000 operations
Bladder damage	2 in 10,000 operations
Major blood vessel damage *	2 in 10,000 operations
Minor blood vessel damage †	10 in 10,000 operations
Death	3 in 100,000 operations

Note: blood vessel damage is usually caused by accidentally hitting a large (major) blood vessel in the abdominal cavity (*) or a small (minor) blood vessel in the abdominal wall (†).

However, in about 25% of cases complicated by accidental damage, it is not recognised during the operation that a structure has been damaged. This particularly applies to bowel damage, in which case the patient is likely to become increasingly unwell, with nausea, marked abdominal pain and a fever due to the leakage of bowel contents into the abdominal cavity. A laparotomy via a midline incision is usually then required to repair the damage. The patient may need to have the damaged area of bowel removed and a temporary colostomy formed. This would normally be reversed some months later, which would necessitate another laparotomy.

Lastly, there are minor complications of surgery which include:

- urinary infection as a result of catheterizing the bladder
- infection at the site of, or bleeding from, the abdominal wounds
- bleeding from the cervix as a result of minor damage caused by the attachment of the manipulator
- shoulder-tip pain as a consequence of trapped gas irritating the diaphragm

Laparoscopic surgery

Diagnostic laparoscopy is simply a way of determining whether a woman has a normal pelvis or not, i.e. it is only a diagnostic test – no actual treatment is involved. On the other hand, laparoscopic surgery, which is sometimes called 'key-hole' or 'minimal-access' surgery, involves treating conditions like endometriosis or ovarian cysts at the same time as the diagnostic procedure.

Over the last 25 years, gynaecologists have increasingly been able to offer laparoscopic surgery as an alternative to laparotomy, which involves making larger incisions in the abdominal wall and operating with conventional instruments. Some of the advantages of having surgery performed laparoscopically include:

- faster recovery time after surgery and shorter stay in hospital
- lower infection rates
- less chance of post-operative adhesions
- better view as the laparoscope can be placed a few mm away from pathology

In most UK hospitals, the two operations are clearly distinguished from each other, mainly because there is not time on most operating lists to convert a diagnostic laparoscopy into a surgical procedure. However, increasingly more women are being offered minor surgical treatment, such as diathermy to small areas of endometriosis, at the time of a diagnostic laparoscopy. This should be made clear on the consent form if it is an option.

As with diagnostic laparoscopy, all laparoscopic surgery has its risks and it is important that the patient is made aware of these before giving consent. There are risks relating to simply having a laparoscopy, which are the same as those described for diagnostic laparoscopy, plus risks relating specifically to laparoscopic surgery such as:

- damaging a structure such as the bowel, bladder or ureter as the surgery is being performed.
- losing an ovary during an ovarian cystectomy (removal of an ovarian cyst).

How common are the complications?

Table 2 is taken from the same French study shown in Table 1. It summarises the most common complications during approximately 21,000 laparoscopic procedures. Rates are directly related to the complexity of the surgery. Therefore, the table is divided into minor and major surgery: examples include diathermy to minimal endometriosis (minor) and ovarian cystectomy and treatment of moderate-severe endometriosis (major).

TABLE 2: COMPLICATIONS RECORDED IN A FRENCH STUDY OF 21,000 LAPAROSCOPIC PROCEDURES

	How often did it occur?	
Type of complication	**MINOR SURGERY**	**MAJOR SURGERY**
Bowel damage	3 in 10,000	24 in 10,000
Ureter/bladder damage	None ‡	5 in 10,000
Major blood vessel damage *	None ‡	2 in 10,000
Minor blood vessel damage †	5 in 10,000	10 in 10,000
Death	3 in 100,000	

Note: blood vessel damage is usually caused by accidentally hitting a large (major) blood vessel in the abdominal cavity (*) or a small (minor) blood vessel in the abdominal wall (†). This list does not include complications for advanced surgery, e.g. hysterectomy and endometriosis involving bowel.

Statistics can be misleading: there were no injuries (‡) to the ureter/bladder or major blood vessels in those patients undergoing minor laparoscopic surgery. That does not mean these complications cannot occur. It probably makes sense to consider the risk of these complications occurring as being the same as during a diagnostic laparoscopy, i.e. 2 in 10,000 operations for each complication (see Table 1).

Lastly, there are some additional risks associated with laparoscopic surgery related to the removal of ovarian cysts. The aim in such operations, especially in women who are still in the reproductive years, is to shell the cysts out of the ovary, like peas out of a pod, thereby preserving as much normal ovary as possible. However, if the cysts have grown so large that no normal ovary can be found, the whole ovary may need to be removed. The other rare occasions when removing the whole ovary might be necessary are if a cyst looks cancerous or there is uncontrollable bleeding. The possible need for an oophorectomy (removal of an ovary) in the event of these circumstances should clearly be highlighted on the consent form.

URETERIC DAMAGE

The ureters are thin, muscular tubes passing urine from the kidneys to the bladder. They enter the pelvis beneath the infundibulopelvic ligament on either side, pass down the pelvic side wall to the ischial spine underneath the peritoneum and then turn forwards and medially below the uterine artery in the base of the broad ligament to reach the bladder. They pass close to the sides of the cervix, just above the lateral fornices of the vagina, where they are crossed by the uterine arteries.

Per-operative damage to the whole or part of the ureter can result from:

- cutting with or without ligation with a suture
- ligation with a suture alone
- a crushing injury from a haemostatic clamp
- a burn from diathermy applied to the ureter or a nearby structure
- interference with the blood supply to the ureter

The ureters can be damaged at any point along their course through the pelvis. However, damage occurs most commonly:

- when the uterine arteries are cut and ligated during a hysterectomy
- during surgery on a densely adherent mass at the base of the broad ligament
- when the ovarian vessels are cut and ligated in the infundibulopelvic ligament during an oophorectomy

Ureteric damage may become apparent in the post-operative period because of:

- external leakage of urine, i.e. through the vagina
- leakage of urine into the abdominal cavity presenting as a pelvic collection or peritonitis, with reduced urine output
- symptoms/signs of ureteric obstruction, i.e. loin pain and constitutional symptoms (such as fever) if the urine is infected

As a general rule, if the ureter has been cut and not ligated, it will become apparent in the immediate post-operative period. If the ureter has been cut and ligated, it may take a few days for the suture to slough and permit drainage of urine.

If the ureter has been ligated and/or clamped completely, the signs of obstruction usually present within a few days and loin pain is a predominant feature. The ureter and kidney appear enlarged on radiological examination because of back-flow caused by the obstruction. Occasionally, the patient does not experience any problems following complete ligation. It may remain undetected for many years until the woman is investigated for an unrelated problem and is found on ultrasound to have a malfunctioning kidney secondary to the obstructed ureter.

If the damage has resulted from partial clamping, a burn or interference with the blood supply to the ureter, it may take a few weeks for the ureteric wall to become devitalised and slough off, and then for a fistula to form. A fistula is a communication or track between two structures such as the ureter and the vagina (e.g. uretero-vaginal fistula). In such circumstances, there may be very few symptoms or signs of ureteric damage other than fever in the time between the operation and the appearance of urine leaking from a fistula weeks later. There may then be radiological signs of ureteric obstruction until the fistula forms and the obstruction is relieved.

Damaging a ureter during a hysterectomy ± bilateral salpingo-oophorectomy (removal of uterus ± both fallopian tubes and ovaries) is one of the commonest mistakes in gynaecology. Clearly, there is a view that it should never occur during a routine operation as the ureters should always be identified in the operating field and standard techniques should be used to avoid its occurrence such as:

- pushing the bladder down from its normal position so as to move the ureters away from the side of the cervix
- ensuring that any sutures inserted into the vaginal cuff (i.e. the upper portion of the vagina that is closed after removal of the uterus and cervix) are placed medial to the two outermost sutures in the vaginal cuff (i.e. within a well-defined area away from the ureters).

However, identifying the ureters can be difficult if the anatomy is distorted because of adhesions and/or endometriosis. In such circumstances, there is a view that ureteric damage is an acceptable risk provided that it has been explained to the patient beforehand.

SUMMARY

Health care is increasingly being provided in the UK in a more open and less paternalistic way, as expressed in the quotation from the Department of Health document entitled Expert Patient: A New Approach to Chronic Disease Management for the 21st Century[5]:

> *'The era of the patient as the passive recipient of care is changing and being replaced by a new emphasis on the relationship between the National Health Service and the people whom it serves – one in which health care professionals and patients are genuine partners seeking together the best solutions to each patient's problems, one in which patients are empowered with information and contribute ideas to help in their treatment and care'.*

This is leading to a fundamentally different way of practising medicine especially in the field of benign gynaecology, given that none of the clinical problems, by definition, are life-threatening. Symptoms such as heavy periods or pelvic pain affect quality of life but they rarely require immediate treatment. Therefore, women have time to make fully informed decisions about their care provided that they have access to high quality information about their options, and the benefits and risks associated with both treatment and the decision not to be treated. Only time will tell what effect allowing patients to participate so actively in the decision making process will have on the medico-legal issues discussed in this book.

---

[5] http://www.doh.gov.uk/healthinequalities

COSMETIC SURGERY

Chris M. Ward

INTRODUCTION

Cosmetic surgeons quite often find themselves in court, and when they do, their cases tend to attract disproportionate media attention. Very often the root of the claim is an actual or perceived discrepancy between the result promised or hoped for, and the result achieved. Good communication is crucial in all medicine and surgery: it is perhaps even more crucial in the management of patient expectations in cosmetic surgery.

The popular image of cosmetic surgery is synonymous with plastic surgery. Indeed, many plastic surgeons are cosmetic surgeons, but there are some plastic surgeons who do not practice cosmetic surgery and an increasing number of cosmetic surgeons who are not plastic surgeons. To understand the evolution of cosmetic surgery it is helpful to reflect on selected surgical episodes in surgical history relating to interventions intended to improve appearance.

The recorded story of cosmetic surgery starts around 600 BC with the Indian surgeon Susruta. He described sixteen different methods of repairing the earlobes of women which had split as a result of wearing heavy earrings. In the 4th Century BC Hippocrates suggested ways in which abnormal scarring could be improved. Later, in 150 AD, Galen also commented on the surgical correction of scarring, and also described the correction of eyelid deformities. During the Chinese T'Ang dynasty of 618 to 907 AD Fang Kan acquired a reputation for repairing cleft lip and other facial defects. Several centuries later, the legendary Italian surgeon Gasparo Tagliacozzi devised a method of reconstructing the nose by means of a flap of tissue raised from the patient's upper arm. He was well aware of the benefit of restoring facial appearance, and in his apologia of 1597, *De Curtorum Chirurgia per Insitionem*, he writes: "We restore, repair and make whole those parts of the face which nature has given, but fortune has taken away, not so much that they may delight the eye but that they may buoy up the spirit and help the mind of the afflicted". In his lifetime Tagliacozzi was accused of meddling with the destiny of man and the handiwork of God, and even after his death his published work continued to arouse such animosity among the clergy that his remains were ordered to be exhumed from their convent burial site and reburied in unconsecrated ground. Reconstructive surgery fell into disrepute in Europe, and in 1788 the Paris Faculty of Medicine banned the teaching and practice of facial surgery.

Many major advances in reconstructive surgery evolved through the ingenuity of military surgeons in wartime over the last two hundred years, and it is on the shoulders of some of these giants that modern plastic surgeons stand. In the course and the wake of the horrors of trench warfare in the First World War, surgeons focussed on the restoration of appearance and function. New surgical techniques evolved and established techniques were refined, leading to universal recognition of the art and craft of plastic and reconstructive surgery. This was the true plastic surgery, concerned with the restoration of form distorted by disease or trauma. Many of the early plastic surgeons realised that the new surgical methods at their disposal could also be put to good use in civilian life for less essential problems such as disproportionate physical features or the consequences of aging or pregnancy. So emerged the subspecialty of cosmetic surgery which has been defined as operations or other procedures that revise or change the appearance, colour, texture, structure or position of physical features in order to match the patient's own concept of what is normal or desirable. The goal of cosmetic surgery can be summarised in a bastardized version of Tagliacozzi's declaration: "To improve on what nature has given in order to delight the eye, buoy up the spirit and help the mind of the afflicted".

Professional colleagues and patients alike may be confused by a contemporary trend for some cosmetic surgeons to call themselves *aesthetic* surgeons – a somewhat misleading and pretentious title and one to which no surgical specialty has an exclusive right. Further potential confusion and conflict may also arise from the number of surgeons from various backgrounds who indulge in cosmetic surgery such as plastic, ophthalmic, ear, nose and throat, maxillo-facial, vascular and breast surgeons, urologists, dermatologists and GPs. There is no justification for some plastic surgeons to resent other surgical specialties encroaching on to what was traditionally regarded as their territorial monopoly of cosmetic surgery. After all, plastic surgery is a relatively recent discipline derived from the older schools of ear, nose and throat surgery, ophthalmic surgery and general surgery. It is far better to share the main concern of the public, which is not about a surgeon's pedigree but about his competence. It therefore makes sense to include all the families of surgeons interested in surgery for the sake of appearance under a common title of *cosmetic*.

THE COSMETIC SURGERY MARKET

There was a time when most of the traditional forms of cosmetic surgery were available within the NHS, mainly for the benefit of carefully selected patients, but also to teach and train future generations of surgeons; but contract exclusions, restricted access policies and priority setting (rationing by any other name) have excluded cosmetic surgery from the National Health Services menu. It is not offered, either, under most medical insurance policies except under very restricted circumstances. It follows that cosmetic surgery has to be bought privately.

The range of available cosmetic surgical services has burgeoned: society is increasingly persuaded that good looks matter, and promotes and even expects conformity of appearance. The surgical categories can be broadly described as follows:

Traditional

(a) Scalp and facial

(i) Hair transplants
(ii) Browlift
(iii) Eyelid reduction (blepharoplasty)
(iv) Face and neck left
(v) Rhinoplasty (change of nasal shape)
(vi) Otoplasty (prominent ear correction)

(b) Breasts

(i) Augmentation
(ii) Reduction
(iii) Mastopexy (breast skin tightening)
(iv) Developmental asymmetry (correction of unequal size and shape)
(v) Correction of inverted nipple

(c) Trunk and limbs

(i) Abdominoplasty
(ii) Arm and thigh reduction
(iii) Liposuction

(d) Skin

(i) Removal of unwanted lesions: e.g. moles, skin tags, etc.
(ii) Resurfacing and smoothing by chemical peel, dermabrasion or laser
(iii) Improving contour with injectable material such as collagen
(iv) Reduction of skin creasing through botulinum toxin (Botox) injections

Implant Surgery

Apart from breast augmentation, a variety of tailored implants can be used to augment the nose, cheeks and chin, buttocks and calves and the male chest wall.

Surgery at the limits

The list continues to lengthen through the inventiveness of surgeons and the resolve of patients, and includes such interventions as penile lengthening, female labia majores reduction and surgery on the aging hand (skin lift and venous stripping).

The place of treatment and the style of anaesthesia is determined by the nature of the procedure. Thus a patient undergoing breast reduction will remain in hospital overnight and have a general anaesthetic. Eyelid reduction can be performed as a day patient under general anaesthetic (so occupying a bed), or under local anaesthetic combined with sedation, or under local anaesthetic alone. Skin lesions are removed under local anaesthetic in a minor operating theatre on a walk-in-walk-out basis, while botox and collagen are injected without anaesthesia in a consulting room.

The cosmetic crock of gold attracts surgeons and doctors of various backgrounds and of various levels of training and experience. Furthermore the relative underservicing of the cosmetic surgery industry in the UK attracts doctors and surgeons from abroad to add to the ranks of professionals who have never completed training and accreditation in any specialty, let alone in cosmetic surgery, although they may have attended a course and have a certificate to prove it.

Patients with cosmetic surgery in mind might reasonably expect that if they see a cosmetic surgeon they are likely to be in safe hands; but private hospitals or clinics do not always operate the mechanisms intended to ensure patient safety which are commonplace in the NHS. There is always a risk of jeopardising standards of care by cutting overheads and taking shortcuts to cut other costs. The Care Standards Act 2000 should help to reduce the disparity between NHS and private hospitals. The picture is not all black. There are places of genuine clinical excellence. The problem is that not all GPs and self-referring patients know where they are. There is no comprehensive register of specialty interests and performance indicators in the private sector.

Table 1 compares the ideal independent hospital which matches the standards expected within the National Health Service with a clinic devoted exclusively to cosmetic surgery.

TABLE 1

Ideal independent Hospital	**Sub-optimal cosmetic surgery clinic**
GP referral	Self referral
Served by accredited surgeons	Served by unaccredited surgeons
Peer review	No peer review
Team care and interspecialty collaboration	Restricted team care
Effective accountability, audit and outcome measures	Weak accountability, no audit or outcome assessment
Appropriate patient selection and monitoring of standards with no financial incentive	Patient selection may be influenced by financial incentive
Specialists working within areas of expertise	Temptation to work outside limits of competence.
Facilities to manage serious complications e.g. intensive care unit	No high dependency unit or intensive care unit.
Clear route for redress in the event of complications	Poor opportunity for redress in event of complications.

WHAT DO COSMETIC SURGEONS GET SUED FOR?

Which operations lead to the greatest source of patient complaints and what is the nature of the complaint? In order to find some of the answers enquiries were made of the Medical Defence Union and the Medical Protection Society. Both provided lists of patients who, within a particular timescale, had initiated an action in medical negligence relating to cosmetic surgery which eventually led to settlement of the claim. The range and frequency of procedures and complaints were virtually identical from both sources.

Operations on the face and scalp provoked the greatest number of actions, of which those involving the soft tissues of the face, such as facelift, were most frequent, followed by rhinoplasty and then, (a very small category), operations involving the treatment of male pattern baldness. Next came cosmetic breast surgery, in which breast augmentation initiated more complaints than breast reduction or mastopexy. The second smallest group of claimants were those who underwent body or limb contouring such as abdominoplasty, liposuction and thigh reduction. The smallest group were those who had had the rarely performed surgical procedures at the limits (see category 3 above).

In terms of the nature of the complaint, the overwhelmingly important reason was failure to reach the aesthetic goal. This is no great surprise. After all, cosmetic surgery is very different from other forms of surgery in that the procedures are self-demanded and self-judged. Thus the indications are solely subjective. The patients are also the ultimate arbiters of the results[1]. The range of aesthetic shortcomings complained of include the siting and appearance of scars, contour irregularities, asymmetry and altered pigmentation.

Surgical complications constitute the next most frequent source and follow the usual pattern of infection, skin necrosis, haematoma, nerve damage, retained foreign bodies, etc. One patient sustained the ultimate complication: death.

Issues of inadequate consent featured in about 10% of the claims. Of significance was a handful of patients who were found to be suffering from psychological problems. Clinical depression was the most common of these problems, but a few patients were identified as suffering dysmorphophobia. This is body dysmorphic disorder: a preoccupation with an imagined defect in appearance. If a slight physical anomaly is present the person's concern about this is markedly excessive. Although it is a rarely encountered syndrome it is very important to recognise, as not only is any form of surgical intervention useless, but is likely to be disastrous for both patient and surgeon[2].

The papers and reports of 105 consecutive female claimant patients who had undergone breast surgery were examined and analysed. There were three groups - those for restoration of a breast mound following mastectomy; those for reduction of disproportionately large breasts contributing to neck and breast pain and skin infections; and cosmetic breast augmentation[3]. Once again, a dominant reason for complaint was inadequate information and preparation for surgery (23 patients). Of greater concern were the 11 patients, with the exception of the breast augmentation group, who not only believed that they had been ill-informed but subsequently, following a complication, experienced a sense of abandonment. They claimed that there was no apology and no explanation. An infected or disintegrating breast following a procedure originally intended to improve appearance was attended to by a variety of nurses and trainee surgeons. Confusing and conflicting advice was given as to the nature of the problem, the best line of management and the possible end result. It is possible that the patient perception was not the reality, but patient perception matters. Intelligent surgical management will involve management of patient expectation and, wherever possible, perception.

---

[1] Hyman, DA, Aesthetics and Ethics: the implications of cosmetic surgery. Perspectives, *Biol. and Med.*, 1990; 33:2: 190-202.

[2] Crisp AH, Dysmorphophbia and the search for cosmetic surgery, *Brit.Med.J.*, 1981; 282 : 1099-1100.

[3] Ward, CM, Why do patients sue? An analysis of 105 consecutive actions in alleged medical negligence relating to breast surgery, *Clinical Risk*, 2002; 8 : 173-176.

Eight patients had a history of persistent and recurrent complaining and litigation. Their complaints were about lots of trivial issues, such as the standard of food or minor delays in appointments, and they also made unsubstantiated and repeated complaints of poor clinical management. One gains the impression that the expectations of these patients could never be satisfactorily fulfilled. In six cases surgical arrogance emerged from the notes and patient interviews. Such an attitude provokes and enrages patients enough to lead to a complaint, although it cannot ground a claim. Among seven patients it was apparent that the surgeons were occasional operators and that they and the members of the team were out of their depth in all aspects of care.

In analysing the cases the author assessed the standard of care as either acceptable or unacceptable according to the standards expected of surgeons routinely carrying out that particular style of breast surgery. All but a few of the women undergoing reconstruction or breast reduction were treated in the NHS. 40% were judged to have received substandard treatment. All the women with breast augmentation were treated as private patients: only 27% were assessed as having had substandard care. Furthermore, 24% of this group were considered to have no obvious damage on objective assessment, while any obvious damage was trivial compared to that suffered by the women in the other two groups - all of whom had good reason to initiate a complaint.

TOWARDS MORE REALISTIC EXPECTATIONS

The contributions from the Medical Defence Union and Medical Protection Society and the study on women following breast surgery[4] provide evidence that patients seeking cosmetic surgery have a low threshold of complaint, and that a dangerous gap between the patient's and the surgeon's expectations of surgery opens up if the overall care falls below the expected standards. How can the gap be narrowed and why should the patient have such high expectations in the first place?

In spite of efforts by advertising standards authorities to ensure more realistic information about patient services, advertisements for cosmetic surgery in magazines, newspapers and handouts tend to dwell only on the positive aspects rather than offering a balanced view. The advertisements are not dishonest but, through before and after photographs of the best results, and by failing to put over the full picture, a potential patient can gain the impression that cosmetic surgery is a simple quick fix. The advertisements provide a contact number for making the first appointment but make no mention of the advisability of consulting their GP in the first instance in order to discover for themselves the facts about cosmetic surgery, and to allow the GP to pass on relevant information about the patient to the clinic and the surgeon. Self-referral to named clinics in advertisements is not discouraged.

[4] See above, footnote 3.

Cosmetic surgeons employed by the clinics, as well as surgeons working independently, are not necessarily aware of the level of ignorance or misplaced motivation of patients consulting them. Information sheets relating to the proposed surgery are provided and the consultation process gone through, but there is always a danger that such a general formulaic approach fails to address the specific vulnerabilities of the patient and the particular benefits and hazards of the treatment options. The consultation can be acted out in a way that is viewed by the patient as a tedious but unavoidable step to a predetermined end rather than an essential dialogue in the preparation for the best possible outcome. On some occasions the best outcome could be no treatment at all.

It is the intrinsic psyche of the patients themselves that dominates the shaping of their behaviour and fate. Consider the act of cosmetic surgery itself. Patients without any form of illness, but simply a desire to have their appearance surgically adjusted, are prepared to be rendered unconscious by an anaesthetist, whom they will meet for the first time on the day of surgery and whose competence is unknown to them. They will previously have given permission for a relative stranger to incise, dissect and surgically rearrange a part of their body, without having any convincing evidence about that surgeon's experience, technical skills or personality. These facts evidence either an extraordinary expression of trust or an unusually high degree of motivation to change their appearance. Motivation does indeed seem to be very high. A psychological analysis of patients undergoing cosmetic surgery identified a significantly higher measurable level of self-consciousness compared to patients without cosmetic surgery in mind[5]. This heightened and sensitive self-consciousness has been likened to the supersensitivity of those with a sensitive musical ear or high level of 'musicality': in the context of aesthetic surgery it is termed 'aestheticality'. Further support for this view comes from the revelation that a quarter of patients undergoing breast augmentation as private patients and who initiated an action in alleged medical negligence were judged objectively as having sustained no damage[6]. Indeed it was demonstrated 25 years ago that women seeking breast augmentation have higher personal aesthetic aspirations compared to other groups of women[7]. It has subsequently been argued that in all cosmetic surgery, let alone breast augmentation, the standard of care should be particularly high, and disclosure of information about any risks particularly thorough[8].

For the purposes of further discussion, let us assume that all patients seeking cosmetic surgery have unrealistic expectations. While acknowledging that ideal standards intended for the safety and best interests of patients cannot be consistently reached they can, at least, be aspired to. What steps must be taken? The answers should be obvious, but within a commercial surgical enterprise

---

[5] Harris, D, The benefits and hazards of cosmetic surgery, *Brit.J.Hosp.Med*, 1989; 41 : 540-545
[6] See above, footnote 3.
[7] Helter, G, Satisfactions and dissatisfactions of patients with augmentation mammoplasty, *Plast.Reconstr.Surg.*, 1979; 64 : 151-154
[8] Brahams, D, Cosmetic Surgery: a greater duty to warn of risks, *Lancet*, 1988; 331 : 1434

which remains unaccredited, unaudited and unregulated a practical solution is not so easy.

The least that any patient and relative should expect is that cosmetic surgery should be performed in a secure environment with all the failsafe mechanisms that are listed in table 1 in the column relating to the ideal independent hospital. The National Care Standards Commission, spawned by the Care Standards Act 2000, is delegated to take on regulation and inspection functions in the private sector[9]. Its impact remains to be seen.

It is an indictment of the 'system' that one should even have to mention the obvious expectation of being treated by a reliable surgeon using safe, well-tested techniques and working with a competent surgical team. However, despite the Care Standards Commission, clinical governance is often absent or rudimentary in private hospitals and clinics. Similarly there is no obligation to submit any inadequately evaluated technique, tool or gimmickry to the Safety and Efficacy Register of New Innovative Procedures. The revalidation process is irrelevant to activities that have never been validated in the first place. There is hope of change: A cosmetic surgery working group has been convened to ensure that a common set of standards is in place, that there is proper patient selection and that surgeons are adequately qualified and trained, meeting GMC requirements[10]. It has already drafted a document on Good Medical Practice in Cosmetic Surgery, but it is not clear how the recommendations are to be implemented and monitored and whether they apply to established or new surgeons or both.

Clinical audit and review are crucial, but they can only improve clinical standards if their findings are acted on. For example, if it becomes evident in a private hospital that members of a cosmetic surgical team repeatedly create unacceptable problems and complications because their attitudes or communication are flawed, or that they put patients at risk by substandard care, steps have to be taken either to improve the necessary skills or to compel the defaulting individual to work only in those areas in which they are proved to be skilful. Also, if there is evidence that standards are compromised by inadequate facilities and resources, action has to be taken. In the breast surgery survey[11] it was noted that of the seven surgeons who performed an operation outside their area of expertise, five operated in the unregulated private surgical healthcare market where financial incentive is a factor. The quality of surgical care must be determined by clinical need and the expertise and experience of the surgeon, rather than by the financial rewards to be gained from the patient; but it is not easy to regulate against greed.

Finally, the recurring theme of consent cannot be over-emphasised. Doctors are not short of instructions and literature on duties relating to consent.

---

[9] Taber, S, Private Healthcare: clinical risk in the independent sector, *Clinical Risk*, 2001; 7 : 68-70

[10] *Ibid.*

[11] See above, footnote 3.

The special issues within the framework of consent relating to cosmetic surgery have been described at length elsewhere[12], but a few threads can usefully be teased out. There can be no good reason for withholding any information that relates to an entirely elective, inessential form of treatment which is not prescribed but willed solely by the patient. It follows that the consultation should be comprehensive and expressed in such a way that the patient cannot fail to understand. The patient should never be given the impression that the end of the consultation marks the end of the opportunity to ask more. The door must always be open. It is sometimes worth arranging a second visit so that, in the interim, the patient has a chance to mull over what has already been discussed. If there is any doubt about the motivation for cosmetic surgery, the views of a colleague in clinical psychology with skills relating to matters of appearance can be invaluable. There is always time for proper consideration. Cosmetic surgery is not emergency surgery. It is also sometimes in the patient's best interests not to have surgical treatment at all. But it can take a lot longer to say 'No' than to agree to proceed. It should go without saying that record-keeping must be meticulous. It should include notes of the consultation, clinical photographs, sketches and every subsequent encounter by telephone or in person. These are not the actions of a practitioner watching his back, but just good surgical practice.

In conclusion: "For surgery to be successful there must be a relationship of trust and confidence between surgeon and patient. Surgeons must be sensitive to the vulnerability of patients. Morally, therefore, surgeons should always act towards patients in ways in which they would wish other surgeons to treat themselves, their families and friends"[13].

ACKNOWLEDGEMENTS

The author wishes to acknowledge with thanks the information and advice from the Medical Defence Union and the Medical Protection Society.

---

[12] Ward, CM, Consenting and consulting for cosmetic surgery, *Brit.J.Plast.Surg*, 1998; 51 : 547-550.

[13] The Senate of Surgery of Great Britain and Ireland, *The surgeon's duty of care: guidance for surgeons on ethical and legal issues*, Senate Paper 2, 1997: 4.

UROLOGY

P.H.L. Worth

INTRODUCTION

The boundaries of urology are difficult to sketch. It is pre-eminently a surgical specialty, broadly concerned with the urinary and the male reproductive tracts. Renal medicine, however, is definitely a separate specialty, (see the chapter on Nephrology), and Gynaecologists will do many procedures involving the female urinary tract.

Claims against urologists used to be much more financially significant than they now are. The change is a result of a change in the law, discussed in the Introduction, which has reduced hugely the damages payable in relation to children born as a result of failed sterilisation.

This chapter considers the main urological conditions and procedures that occupy the courts.

SCROTAL CONDITIONS

Hydrocele

Hydrocele develops in a peritoneal space which descends into the scrotum as the testicle descends. If it never closes the child has a congenital hernia. When the peritoneal end seals, a space is left around the testicle. There is always some fluid in it. This is a naturally occurring hydrocele space.

Often there is an increase in the amount of fluid around the testicle. This is often not due to any pathology. It is, however, important to be certain that there is no disease in the testis or epididymis, so it may be necessary (but is generally not mandatory) to do an ultrasound examination if it is difficult to feel these structures.

If the proximal end subsequently opens, an indirect inguinal hernia forms. If a space is left in the cord it is known as an encysted hydrocele of the canal of Nuck. It should be treated by excision if symptomatic.

There are some congenital structures sometimes found around the testis which can give problems. The appendix testis and the appendix epididymis may twist and cause severe pain. A swelling can usually be felt. It may be necessary to operate, but often the swelling resolves. If an appendix testis is found to be present when the tunica is opened for other operations it should be removed. The operation consists of opening the space around the testicle and everting the cover (Jaboulay procedure). If the appendix is very big it is usually better to remove some of the excess tissue. It is very important to be certain that all bleeding points are controlled, or a haematoma will develop.

Conditions affecting the epididymis

Cysts are very common in the epididymis, but should only be operated on if they cause trouble. It should not be assumed that if a patient has pain and is found to have a cyst that the cyst is the cause of the trouble. Also if a cyst is operated on, the patient should be warned that the pain may not be eliminated.

Operation on the epididymis carries a risk of damaging sperm conduction through the epididymis, so it is unwise to operate on a small asymptomatic cyst. It is well recognised that operating on bilateral cysts may cause infertility (obstructive asospermia)

Epididymitis is a painful condition. When severe, the testicle may also be involved. Occasionally an abscess forms. Drainage of that abscess is important. The end result may be a small, atrophic, non-functioning testicle. Delay in undertaking drainage can be criticised.

Malignancy very rarely occurs in the epididymis, but if an abscess develops tuberculosis should always be considered T.B. is usually secondary to disease elsewhere, and therefore the urinary tract should be investigated by ultrasound and an x-ray intravenous pyelogram.

A painful epididymis should initially be treated conservatively with antibiotics. Management in a pain clinic may help. Surgery on the epididymis may ultimately be inevitable. If this fails to cure the pain the patient may seek to have the testis removed: this is also unlikely to cure the pain.

Varicocele

This is a collection of veins in the scrotum. It is usually found on the left side because on this side the veins drain into the left renal vein (a relatively low bore vessel), whereas on the right they drain into the inferior vena cava (which, being a larger vessel, effects better drainage with a consequently lower back pressure). A patient may present with an asymptomatic swelling, a painful swelling, or may have a low sperm count.

Surgical treatment consists of dividing the testicular vein where it enters the abdomen through the internal ring, by an incision in the groin. It is also important to divide the cremasteric vessels which run from the cord into the external iliac vein. The practice of embolising the testicular vein (which is performed by injecting the vein via a catheter passed up the vena cava and through the left renal vein) does not give such good results because these small tributaries are not occluded.

It cannot be guaranteed that an operation on a varicocele will either cure pain or improve fertility.

Occasionally the testicular artery may be damaged when the testicular vein is mobilised and divided. This will leave the patient with an atrophic testicle. This should not happen and cannot be defended.

Testicular torsion

This occurs commonly in adolescent boys. It often starts at night when the patient is resting, but may follow minor trauma.

It should be assumed that a young boy presenting with testicular pain has a torsion until proved otherwise. To treat a boy with antibiotics on the assumption that the pain is due to epididymitis is wrong and indefensible. Ultrasound scanning to check on blood flow is theoretically a sensible thing to do. However, it is unreliable - especially since the examination is usually done out of hours by inexperienced staff. The writer does not believe that it is mandatory. Where there is a presumptive diagnosis of torsion, no clinician who explores the testicle should be criticised. Not to do so may lead to testicular death. The testis will not survive if the blood supply is occluded for six hours. Unfortunately it is often too late to operate when the boy presents with pain.

A clinical sign that should be looked for is whether the contralateral testicle is lying horizontally rather than vertically. A horizontal position predisposes to torsion. It is important when operating for torsion to fix the contralateral testicle. Not to do so at the time is not necessarily wrong, but the boy should be told that he will need to have the testis fixed as soon as possible.

Undescended testicle

The testicle may be in the wrong place (ectopic). It may be in the superficial inguinal pouch, or (very occasionally) in the perineum (where elephants keep their testicles) or mal descended (when it has stopped somewhere along the line of normal descent).

If a testicle is not in a satisfactory position in the scrotum when a child is a year old then surgery will be needed to position it properly.

Retractile testicles are pulled up into the groin by a hyperactive cremasteric reflex (as practised by Sumo wrestlers). If it is only possible to position the testicle in the lower scrotum in ideal circumstances (e.g. after the boy has had a hot bath), it may be better to operate. The risk of damaging the testicle from the surgery has to be weighed against the risk of decreased fertility which is created by its wrong position.

To give a child pituitary hormones to encourage the testicle to descend is probably not appropriate in the young child. It is appropriate in the pre-pubertal child if previously the undescended testicle has not been identified.

Surgery aims to position the testicle correctly without damaging the blood supply. Damage is more likely to occur when a hernia is operated on as well. To end up with an atrophic testicle is unacceptable.

There is a significantly increased risk of malignancy developing in an undescended testicle – even when the position of the testicle has been surgically corrected. If an older child or adolescent presents with an impalpable testicle, CT scanning should be performed to try and identify its position. An absent kidney is often associated with an absent testis.

Complex surgery may be needed to position the testicle in the scrotum. If the testis is found adjacent to the kidney, the testicular artery will have to be divided and the testis brought down on a peritoneal flap. If an appropriate surgeon is available it may be possible to do a vascular anastomosis between the testicular artery and the mobilised inferior epigastric artery. If the testicle is found to be atrophic or very abnormal it is better to remove it.

Hernia

Hernia operations are not discussed here. Their urological significance is that testicular pain may develop if the cord is obstructed, and occasionally the testicle atrophies if the blood supply is damaged either by sutures or by other cord obstruction. Any testicular damage is unacceptable.

Vasectomy

This operation involves dividing the vas deferens. It should be an easy procedure but it is fraught with a variety of complications.

The writer believes that the general practitioner should explain the procedure to a man in simple terms before referring to the surgeon. It is preferable for the surgeon to see the man before the operation and examine him very carefully to see, amongst other things, whether he is a suitable candidate for a procedure under local anaesthesia.

It is helpful but not essential to meet the couple together. It is important to be satisfied that the vasectomy is wanted for the right (contraceptive) reasons. The surgeon should also explain the technique used and discuss all the complications, including the possibility and mechanism of early and late failure.

There is no evidence that vasectomy predisposes to testicular tumours. It is uncertain whether there is an association with late prostate cancer.

The operation is usually done under local anaesthetic. It is necessary to anaesthetise the skin and the tissue around the vas because they have different nerve supplies. The writer does the operation through two separate incisions, fixing the vas between the fingers against the skin through which the incision is made.

The patient should be warned that local anaesthetic abolishes sharp pain but not pressure or pulling. It is important to give the local anaesthetic time to work. The writer strokes the skin with the scalpel to be certain that the local has worked. An anxious patient will perceive any sort of pressure and may complain of a pulling sensation in the groin if too much tension is put on the vas.

It is important to warn the patient about bleeding, infection and post-operative discomfort. Intercourse will be painful if performed too soon. It will be painful because the epididymes are swollen. Usually this pain lasts for about a week. It is unclear why some people get post vasectomy pain, but all patients should be warned of the possibility. It may occur years after the operation. It may occur due to rupture of the tubules in the epididymis, with sperm granuloma formation. A complicated vasectomy does not necessarily predispose to post vasectomy pain. Although in some cases the pain may be very severe, the surgeon cannot be criticised if the possibility of postoperative pain has been discussed. Treatment is very difficult. Sometimes a swelling (a sperm granuloma) can be felt at the site of vas transection, but excising this will not necessarily cure the pain. In addition the epididymis will be swollen because of the nature of the procedure, but removing the epididymis is unlikely to cure the pain. It is best to arrange for the patient to be seen in a pain clinic, and to avoid surgery.

A patient is not sterile the day the operation is performed because sperm are present in the proximal end of the vas and in the seminal vesicles. It is important for the patient to ejaculate at least ten times to clear the system.

A sperm test should be done at 8 and 12 weeks. Since a sperm lives for about 100 days, motile sperms found at this time suggest the operation has failed. The operation should be redone on both sides even if specimens of the vas were successfully excised at the surgery and proven histologically (as they should be). Very occasionally a third vas is present.

If immotile sperm are present, tests should be repeated until they disappear. The patient should be encouraged to ejaculate in order to help clearance. Some surgeons accept the presence of the occasionally non motile sperm and take no further action.

Early failure may be due to failure to remove an adequate segment of the vas. It is important to try to separate the ends of the vas by interposing tissue or turning each end back on itself. If there has been a complication of the surgery there may be an increased risk of early failure.

Using a non-absorbable suture such as silk should guarantee that the cut end remains closed, but silk increases the risk of infection, and so absorbable sutures are used. They need to last for at least two weeks and therefore should not be too small. Minimally invasive techniques usually use a clip.

Why late failure occurs is difficult to say, but it is recognised that it occurs between every 2-3,000 cases. Sperm counts are usually negative in cases of failure, but occasionally a sperm may be identified.

There is no point in doing sperm tests ad infinitum, but a couple should be warned that even if they have had two negative sperm tests pregnancy cannot be discounted. If the woman becomes pregnant but sperm tests are negative, there may be acrimonious discussion about paternity, which DNA testing can resolve.

Vasovasostomy

Changed family circumstances often result in requests for reversal of vasectomy. Occasionally it is offered to men who have persistent post-vasectomy pain, in whom there may be improvement following surgery.

Reversal is technically more difficult than vasectomy. An operating microscope should be used, and a two layer anastomosis performed. A return of fertility depends on three factors:

- The patency of the anastomosis. Patency can be achieved in approximately 90% of cases
- Whether or not the seminiferous tubules have been damaged by the obstruction
- The level of anti-sperm antibodies which develop as a result of vasectomy. These can be measured, and if high, a course of steroids can be prescribed

Complications of scrotal surgery

There are some complications which are common to all surgical procedures. Those are not discussed here. Some of the complications which are specific to particular urological procedures have been discussed above.

Since the skin of the scrotum can stretch and it is very difficult to apply adequate pressure postoperatively, significant swelling can occur. When a large cyst or hydrocele is treated, there is a potential space which can be very difficult to obliterate. In such a situation a patient should be warned about the possibility of swelling - which usually results from venous bleeding.

When a patient is lying down on the operation table the venous pressure will be low and careful inspection of the operation site may not reveal any bleeding. However, once the patient gets off the table or coughs when waking from the general anaesthetic, the venous pressure rises and small veins will open up. Oozing occurs which may produce significant swelling.

Arterial bleeding is more serious, but should be recognised during the operation and controlled.

With venous bleeding, bruising will be obvious in the inguinal region. This usually spreads onto the shaft of the penis as well. If the swelling is not excessive it is better to leave it alone, but a broad spectrum antibiotic should be given for five to ten days to reduce the risk of infection. The swelling may take at least six weeks to resolve.

If the swelling develops rapidly postoperatively, it is better to arrange for exploration under general anaesthetic. Very often, once the haematoma has been evacuated, the source of the bleeding is not easy to identify. It is best to leave a corrugated drain in situ for twenty four to thirty six hours, and to keep the patent rested. Sometimes the haematoma can discharge through the wound. A patient who has developed a significant haematoma post-operatively may expect it to be drained surgically, but the less interference the better since each intervention increases the risk of infection.

Provided the patient has been warned that there is a risk of bleeding, and the surgeon has taken proper care to control the bleeding, no criticism can legitimately be levelled at the surgical technique.

Because it is difficult to sterilise the scrotal skin, minor infections may occur. These are not usually serious. However, infections with unusual anaerobic organisms occasionally occur, and can result in gangrene of the scrotum (Meleney's synergistic gangrene).

SURGERY ON THE PENIS

Circumcision

Apart from religious circumcision, circumcision is now rarer than it was. It should not be done on demand, and an adult demanding circumcision for hygiene or cosmetic reasons should be discouraged from having the procedure. It may take at least two years for the foreskin to separate in a child, but if the opening is tight and produces ballooning of the foreskin (phimosis), it may be possible just to do a simple stretch. If it is not possible to retract the foreskin fully, and there is chronic infection, circumcision is justified.

Patients not needing the operation are much more critical of the result. There are many ways of doing the operation, but it is important to leave a symmetrical rim of skin at the base of the glans, and to realign the mid-line raphe to the frenum. It is also important to remove the right amount of tissue. It is better to err on the side of caution than to be too radical. Sometimes a revision of the operation is necessary, but a patient complaining bitterly about the cosmetic result is unlikely to be satisfied by further attempts to improve what he thinks is wrong.

Fine absorbable sutures should be used, small amounts of tissue should be incorporated and the edges of the skin everted and not rolled in. The sutures should not be tied too tight, or the suture line becomes irregular.

Following the surgery, the glans will be more sensitive for some time, and patients should be warned about this. However, it is usually the patient who is dissatisfied with the cosmetic appearance of his operation who will complain bitterly about the altered sensation, which does not usually seem to improve.

Diathermy should be used with caution in circumcision in younger boys. Monopolar diathermy should not be used, as necrosis of the corpora has been described. Arterial bleeding from the frenal artery may occur. It will require suturing rather than firm pressure. A firm circumferential dressing may reduce the risk of venous bleeding, but it is usually difficult, and is potentially dangerous, to apply very firm pressure.

Placing a suture through the skin and into the urethra, so causing a fistula, is unacceptable.

Circumcision techniques which involve removing the foreskin without exposing the glans may result in removal of part of the glans: this is unacceptable.

If a man has troublesome venereal warts not responding to local applications of chemicals, circumcision may cure the problem.

There is a condition called balanitis xerotica obliterans (BXO), which causes whiteness of the skin and scarring causing phimosis. The meatus may be involved and requires dilatation or occasional meatoplasty. The urethra may need to be inspected because sometimes it is involved. If strictured, a urethroplasty may be necessary.

If the glans is badly affected, skin grafting may be necessary. The association of BXO with subsequent squamous carcinoma is unclear, but warrants careful follow up of the condition.

Peyronie's Disease is a condition which results in scarring of one or both the corpora, resulting in variable deformity of the erect penis. Erection may be painful and intercourse may be impossible. It is a self limiting disease. If treated early with ultrasound, shock waves, hydrocortisone injections, or medication, the amount of scarring can be controlled. Surgical correction should be considered only if the disease has stabilised, (usually after about 2 years), and intercourse is impossible.

Various procedures are used. They all correct the deformity rather than removing the plaque. An uncircumcised patient should be advised that circumcision is a necessary part of the operation. He should be warned that the operation will shorten the penis. Also, if there is an extensive scar, the quality of the erection in the distal part of the penis will not improve. It may be considered necessary to implant a penile prosthesis rather than trying to correct the deformity.

Some of the suturing techniques are difficult, leading to failure of the operation. It is important to bury the knots, otherwise the patient will complain of lumps under the scars. The sensory nerves need to be avoided, otherwise the patient will complain of decreased sensation in the distal penis.

Penile augmentation

This is an operation that probably should not be done. It may only produce some lengthening of the flaccid penis, by division of the suspensory ligament. Certainly the quality of the erection cannot be improved. Injecting autologous fat may give some improvement in the girth.

No surgeon should consider penile augmentation without obtaining a full psychological assessment of the patient. More often than not, no surgery is needed.

Private clinics often offer advice about penile augmentation to self referred patients, without getting proper assessment, and an itinerant surgeon arrives to do the operation. This often produces a perceived or actually unsatisfactory result.

Impotence

A man may be impotent for many reasons. If he does not have spontaneous nocturnal erections, he is likely to have an organic problem. There are techniques available to assess this.

Impotence due to neurological damage from pelvic trauma, pelvic surgery, radical prostatectomy or diabetes, does not usually respond to medical treatment.

Various mechanical devices can be used, but if these techniques are unhelpful, penile implants can be considered.

There are several types of implants available: rigid, semi-rigid, and inflatable. The patient should be carefully advised on the pros and cons of each.

Meticulous surgical technique and anti-sepsis are important, because there is about a 10% risk of infection when implanting a foreign body. Failure to treat the infection adequately will lead to removal of the prostheses, and subsequent implantation can be extremely difficult due to the scarring produced.

Priapism (a prolonged painful erection), may be the presentation of a disease like acute leukaemia, often occurs in people with sickle cell disease, and may occur after an injection of prostaglandins for impotence. It is a rare consequence of medical management. It should be treated urgently by aspirating the static blood or shunting procedures between the corpora. An unnecessary delay will result in fibrosis, and the only treatment, will be the use of implants.

TESTICULAR TUMOURS

More often than not, testicular tumours present as a painless swelling. The swelling may have been found by chance by the individual or his partner: very often the man will have been aware of an abnormality for some time. Occasionally an injury to the testis draws attention to an already present abnormality. Since the lymphatics from the testis drain into the para-aortic region, by-passing the groin, the individual may present with abdominal pain or an abdominal swelling, or back pain.

Any patient found to have a solid swelling of the testis should have an ultrasound performed. This is particularly important if a secondary hydrocele is present, because this makes assessment of the testis difficult. The tumour may be circumscribed or diffuse, and not infrequently some calcification may be present.

If a tumour is suspected, markers (alpha-fetoprotein and beta human chorionic gonadotrophins) should be measured. They will be negative in the presence of a pure seminoma, but are usually positive if a yolk sac element is present, as in a teratoma. Negative markers therefore do not exclude a tumour, but if the markers have been positive, they are helpful in monitoring progress because they will become negative when the disease is eradicated, and become positive in the event of a recurrence.

Pre-operation trans-scrotal biopsy is not recommended because:

(i) the biopsy may miss the tumour if it is small
(ii) the pathologist may have difficulty interpreting the biopsy
(iii) the needle track transgresses anatomical planes

Not all testicular lumps are malignant. Sperm granuloma is one example of a non-malignant lump. If there is any doubt about the diagnosis, it is correct to advise exploration.

Testicular tumours are treated by radical orchidectomy. This means removal of the testis and the cord through a high inguinal incision. The cord is clamped with a non crushing clamp and the testis delivered out of the scrotum. The hydrocele sac can be opened, and the testicle inspected and palpated. Very often there will be abnormal veins on the surface of the testis. When there is clinical doubt about the condition, the testis can be opened and the tumour inspected (the Chevasseu manoeuvre).

Pathologists do not like reporting on frozen sections, so if there is any doubt, a formal biopsy should be obtained and the testis closed and replaced in the scrotum. If a tumour is subsequently demonstrated by the histology, the orchidectomy should be undertaken as soon as possible.

Sometimes the surgeon makes a decision to do an orchidectomy even when there is uncertainty about the diagnosis. Subsequent histology may prove the lesion to be benign. Provided he proceeded along the lines outlined above, his action can be defended.

Primary removal of intra-abdominal lymph nodes is not undertaken in this country. Further management after the diagnosis has been made is undertaken by a medical oncologist, and may include radiotherapy or chemotherapy.

If there is evidence of spread to the abdomen or the lungs, and chemotherapy fails to control the disease, removal of the intra-abdominal nodes should be undertaken at a later date. This is a difficult operation, and should only be done in specialist centres. If chest secondaries remain, a thoracic surgeon should be asked to do a thoracotomy.

Prior to chemotherapy, patients should be advised to store sperm, although very often a patient presenting with a testicular tumour is infertile. If retroperitoneal lymph node dissection is required, there is a risk of damaging the sympathetic nerves, and retrograde ejaculation may occur. Potency however will not be affected.

At the time of orchidectomy, it can be argued that a biopsy should be taken from the contra-lateral testicle because of the possibility of carcinoma in situ - a pre-malignant condition. If present, it means that very careful follow up is necessary.

Asynchronous bilateral testicular tumours do occur. They may be of different histological types.

The presence of micro calcification on ultrasound can present problems of interpretation. Calcification is common. It does occur in the presence of a testicular tumour, but cannot be considered to be pre-malignant.

THE URETHRA

Urethral catheterisation

This is a very common procedure. It is not entirely risk-free. The urethra may not be sterile and urine may be infected. In an ideal world, the result of a recent urine cultures should be available before catheterisation is undertaken.

It is therefore good practice to cover a urethral instrumentation with a single intravenous shot of an antibiotic. The reason for doing this is to prevent septicaemia developing. Septicaemia can kill. The incidence of septicaemia will be reduced, but not abolished.

Any patient who has had an indwelling catheter, has recently had a urinary tract infection, or has a prosthetic heart valve or an orthopaedic joint, should certainly have antibiotic cover.

Logically, if an antibiotic is given when the catheter is introduced, an antibiotic should be given when a catheter is removed.

In the female, urethral catheterisation is not usually difficult provided that the urethral meatus is visualised. Putting local anaesthetic into the urethra is not usually necessary. In the male the exposed meatus should be carefully cleaned and local anaesthetic instilled.

A size 14-18 catheter should be used, and passed using a forcep or a gloved hand. If the catheter will not go beyond a few centimetres, it is likely that a urethral stricture is present. A smaller catheter should be tried, but if this still will not pass, advice should be sought from a senior doctor.

The catheter should be passed in as far as it will go, and the balloon inflated with 5-10 mls of water. The catheter should then be withdrawn until the balloon can be felt to reach the bladder neck. It is then important to be satisfied that it is correctly placed, and that urine flows. If it does not, light suprapubic pressure should be applied.

If no urine comes out, the bladder may be empty (unlikely), or the catheter may not be correctly placed. In a male with a big prostate, it may be difficult to manoeuvre the catheter past the prostate into the bladder: using a smaller catheter does not make it any easier. If the catheter is not in the bladder, it will be difficult to inflate the balloon, it may cause pain, and the catheter will not move when gentle traction is applied. If this is the case, the balloon should be deflated and a further attempt made to pass a catheter. If blood appears at the external meatus, the urethra has probably been traumatised.

It is reasonable for a junior doctor or a trained urological nurse to try to introduce a catheter, but if the catheter cannot be passed easily on the second attempt, he/she should seek more expert help – typically from a Specialist Registrar in Urology. The Specialist Registrar, faced with a catheter which will not pass, has three options:

(a) To attempt urethral catheterisation in the usual way himself. He will be able to establish whether or not there is an obstruction or perhaps a false passage has been created.

(b) He can try to pass a catheter with a metal introducer. This has a curved end, and it will be possible to direct the end of the catheter and help it through the prostate and over the bladder neck. Because he can "feel" the end of the catheter, he should be able to tell if and where there is a problem.

A false passage can be made, either in the prostate or below the bladder neck area where the catheter will pass behind the trigone. Even if a false passage has been made, if a catheter can be passed into the bladder, catheter drainage will allow healing to occur without any long term problems. If damage has been done to the urethra, and extravasation into the perineum and scrotal tissues occurs, a suprapubic catheter must be placed.

(c) If the bladder is palpable, local anaesthetic should be put into the skin of the abdominal wall and into the wall of the bladder, about 5-10 cm above the symphysis pubis, and a suprapubic catheter inserted. Since the bladder is extra-peritoneal and is palpable, no damage will be done. If the bladder is not full, and the patient has had lower abdominal surgery, it is possible to damage the small bowel. If it is essential to place a suprapubic catheter, and there are difficulties, it can be done with the help of ultrasound imaging.

Using a suprapubic catheter is not an admission of defeat. It is very safe, causes less infection than a urethral catheter, and is often used as primary treatment for a patient in urinary retention.

If a suprapubic catheter is placed when a bladder operation is done, it can be clamped at an appropriate time, the patient's voiding assessed, and the residue measured. When this is acceptable, and usually less than 100 mls, it can be easily removed. The track will close without any suturing provided there is no urethral obstruction.

If urethral damage occurs as a result of catheterisation, the circumstances of the need to catheterise and the experience of the doctor doing it have to be considered.

Urinary obstruction in men

The commonest cause of urinary obstruction in a male is benign enlargement of the prostate. Because it lies below the bladder neck and urine passes through it, any alteration in the size of the prostate may cause obstruction. The prostatic urethra is not a tube with the prostate outside it: the prostate is the tube. However, the amount of obstruction does not relate to the size of the prostate. Some prostates may be small, may contain more muscle than glandular tissue, and may cause more obstruction than a very large gland.

In order to pass urine, the bladder neck must relax and the bladder contract. This is a neurologically controlled event, and it is not really possible to increase the flow rate by straining.

Bladder neck dysfunction occurs in younger people, and may cause significant obstruction. If not treated correctly, the bladder will become sacculated and poorly emptying, and may contain stones.

No patient should be advised to have an operation for obstruction without appropriate investigations. Measuring the flow rate on an adequate voided volume (at least 150 mls) is necessary. An ultrasound scan of the bladder when full and when empty will show how thick the bladder wall is, and whether or not stones are present. A residue of under 100 mls is acceptable. It is usually unnecessary to image the kidneys, but in fact this is usually done because kidney abnormalities unrelated to any obstruction from the prostate may be present in 10% of patients.

Urethral strictures

If a urethral stricture is suspected, an ascending urethrogram should be performed. This will identify the anterior extent of the stricture, but may not show how severe it is. If contrast can be introduced into the bladder, a voiding study will show the proximal extent of the stricture and how tight it is.

Urethral strictures may be traumatic in origin, infective, or may follow a prostatic operation or the use of an indwelling catheter.

Uncomplicated strictures can be treated by urethral dilatation with sounds, or by internal urethrotomy under direct vision. The stricture will usually not be cured by these manoeuvres. Too many urethrotomies cause increasing damage and may make subsequent surgery more difficult.

More serious strictures should be treated by surgery. It may be possible (it depends on the position) to excise the stricture and re-anastomose the urethra. If the defect is extensive a graft will need to be used. A buccal mucosal graft is currently the most popular.

In pelvic trauma, potency may already have been affected by the injury. The patient may not be aware of the problems because sexual activity is not a high priority after a major accident.

If carried out around the apex of the prostate, surgery may compromise potency further, although ejaculation will probably continue to be possible. Any impotence is likely to be the inevitable consequence of the necessary surgery, not of sub-standard surgery.

THE PROSTATE

Prostatic surgery: General

Any patient having an operation for a benign prostate should be warned about retrograde ejaculation. The reason for this is that the bladder neck, which needs to be competent for ejaculation to occur, is compromised by the surgery.

There are now many ways of treating benign disease. Patients with minor symptoms can have alpha blockers which relax the muscles of the bladder neck and prostate. If the prostate is big, a 5 alpha reductase inhibitor, which blocks testosterone breakdown, will help to shrink the prostate, but this takes weeks to work. If a patient is obstructed, prostatic tissue must be removed for a good result, but smaller prostates can be treated by various types of laser. Microwave has been popular. Balloon dilatation of the bladder neck is a waste of time. Various stents have been used, but they need to be very accurately placed. If they extend into the bladder, stones may form: if they are placed too low they may cause incontinence. These lesser procedures are unlikely to cause retrograde ejaculation, but they are also less likely to cure the obstruction.

If ejaculation remains after prostatectomy, the prostatectomy has probably been done inadequately, but if the flow rate is better, the patient may not complain.

If the bladder neck is the primary cause of the obstruction, then it can be incised unilaterally in an endoscopic procedure. Ejaculation is preserved in up to 80% of cases.

Other complications of operating on the Prostate

When the prostate is resected endoscopically, complications are avoidable, but need to be recognised.

Capsular perforation occurs because it is not possible to gauge the thickness of the capsule, although it can be recognised as being distinct from the prostate. Fluid may extravasate extra-peritoneally (which does not really matter). Big veins may be opened, causing significant bleeding which is difficult to stop. It is necessary to control the bleeding with diathermy as well as possible. A three way catheter should then be inserted with at least 30 mls in the catheter balloon. Traction should be applied to the catheter so that it is positioned at the bladder neck. This usually stops the bleeding.

Very occasionally a patient has to be taken back to theatre for a further inspection. Even after having washed out the clots, the cause of the bleeding may not be visible. If the bleeding continues, the patient may need to be opened up and the prostatic cavity packed through the opened bladder.

Major bleeding may also occur for no obvious reason. Provided that aspirin and anti-coagulants were stopped pre-operatively and the patient's clotting parameters were normal, it is difficult to criticise the surgeon.

When resecting the prostate it is sometimes possible to undermine the trigone. Provided this is recognised and great care taken in positioning the catheter in the bladder, no long term problems will result. However, if it is not recognised, or the catheter is placed behind the trigone and the balloon inflated, urine will not drain. This should be obvious and should be recognised. It can be very difficult to place the catheter correctly once the patient has left the operating theatre. An introducer may help to get the catheter into the bladder.

The TUR syndrome occurs because irrigating fluid used for the operation enters the circulation via the prostatic veins. Since the fluid is approximately isotonic, haemolysis will not occur, but haemo-dilution occurs, with lowering of the serum sodium and an increase in circulating volume. A syndrome similar to water intoxication may occur. The patient may remain unconscious at the end of the operation with a high blood pressure. It is very difficult to measure how much fluid enters the circulation during an operation. One ingenious way is to add alcohol to the irrigating fluid, and to breathalyse the patient. Provided the situation is recognised, and saline given intravenously, plus a diuretic, the situation can be quickly reversed. In older men with poor circulation, the secondary circulatory effects can be very serious.

Incontinence is a very rare event after resection, but a patient should be warned of this possibility.

Since the prostate has nothing to do with potency, impotence should generally not occur, but it occasionally does. The patient should probably be warned there is a very small risk of this occurring. If carried out around the apex of the prostate, surgery is more likely to compromise potency, although ejaculation will probably be intact. Impotence should not be considered to be due to sub-standard surgery.

It is important to understand that the patient's potency may not be particularly good prior to the surgery on account of his age.

A urethral stricture may develop as a result of a resection, but not present for some time. It may result from poor technique - using too large an instrument or too large a catheter post-operatively - but its cause may not be obvious.

Resecting the prostate does not remove the entire prostate. It is wise to warn a patient that he is still at risk of developing cancer although the histological examination of the resected prostate shows it all to be benign.

Cancer of the Prostate

This disease has an increasing incidence and detection rate. It may cause outflow obstruction and the symptoms are no different from benign enlargement. There has been great interest in trying to diagnose the disease when it is still curable, by measuring Prostatic Specific Antigen (PSA). The result can be difficult to interpret because the level may be raised in the presence of urinary tract infection, and with a very large prostate. Even with a PSA level below the upper limit of normal of 4ng/l, cancer may be found, but probably 50% of patients in whom a level of 4-10 is found have a negative biopsy. A level below 20 is unlikely to be associated with metastatic disease.

To diagnose cancer a biopsy has to be performed. This is done under ultrasound control, but because only a small amount of tissue can be sampled, a negative biopsy does not necessarily exclude disease.

There is a common misunderstanding that if a diagnosis of cancer is missed, the disease becomes more malignant. This is generally not the case. A low grade disease tends to remain low grade, and does not progress.

In cancer of the prostate, the grades are described as Gleason grades 1-5. Two scores are given, representing different parameters. The two scores are then added together, giving an overall index of seriousness.

Once the diagnosis has been made, the treatment options are watchful waiting, (with very low grade small volume disease), hormone manipulation, radiotherapy or localised brachytherapy, or radical prostatectomy.

The clinician treating the patient will have to decide on what he thinks best for that particular individual, but the patient himself may have strong views about what he wishes to have done. In fact the place of radical prostatectomy is much debated, but it is a popular form of treatment. Patients should be warned of a significant risk of incontinence, (about 5%), and a very high risk of impotence, (at least 60%). Complications of the procedure include damage to the rectum (which is avoidable), and bladder neck stenosis - which is relatively easy to treat.

If the disease is not eradicated by the prostatectomy, (as evidenced by a PSA that does not fall to well below 1 nanogram), radiotherapy to the prostatic bed or treatment with hormones may be indicated. It may not be possible to say that a patient has been cured of his prostate cancer for at least 10 years after the surgery.

THE BLADDER

Cystitis and miscellaneous bladder conditions

Bladder infection with bacteria is very common. The presence of blood in the urine, associated with infection, does not mean that the cystitis is more serious. Cystitis is inflammation of the bladder, manifested by urinary frequency, and painful passage of urine.

Cystitis in the female is very common, and investigation is only needed if it is recurrent and associated with kidney pain and fever.

If a man has cystitis, even once, he does need to be investigated in case there is an obstructive element present. He needs to be shown to have a normal flow rate and to have no urine remaining in the bladder after micturition.

The male with cystitis probably should be cystoscoped, but a female does not need a cystoscopy if no anatomical abnormality is identified. However, very often, cystoscopy and urethral dilatation are performed empirically with some improvement in symptoms.

Where there is a painful bladder and urinary frequency but no infection, the clinician should consider an inflammatory condition of the bladder wall. Many patients with these symptoms ascribe their condition to interstitial cystitis, sometimes wrongly. Where there is true interstitial cystitis, self help groups may be helpful. The treatment of patients with chronic cystitis is difficult, and patients may be dissatisfied because the condition is not helped by medication.

Sometimes the bladder becomes so contracted that frequency is intolerable, both by day and night. In this situation, bladder replacement or augmentation, or even urinary diversion may be necessary, but even major surgery correctly done may leave the patient unhappy with the result.

It is very important to exclude any drug interactions that can produce painful contracted bladders, mimicking cancer or interstitial cystitis. If the drug is stopped, the bladder will improve, so a thorough drug history is very important before undertaking major surgery.

Bladder dysfunction may result from neurological problems such as spinal cord trauma and spinal cord compression. Bladder symptoms may develop before motor weakness occurs. The bladder sensation is lost and the patient has difficulty emptying the bladder. However, once the cause is recognised and treated it is already too late to expect improvement in bladder function, although power may return to the lower limbs. The patient may therefore have to resort to long term intermittent self-catheterisation. In men, impotence often occurs as well.

Bladder cancer

A patient who complains of painless passing of blood, or is found to have microscopic haematuria, may be showing the first signs of cancer. The GP should refer, and the Urologist should carry out a cystoscopy. Failure to do so is likely to delay the diagnosis.

One type of bladder cancer, carcinoma-in-situ, affects the surface of the bladder. It may present with frequency and pain passing urine. The urine culture may be negative for bacteria, but red and white cells will be present, and urine cytology may pick up malignant cells. This is a screening test. It is done in certain industrial situations when patients have been exposed to carcinogens which may produce bladder cancer over a 15-20 year period.

At the time of cystoscopy, the bladder wall is carefully inspected, and biopsies taken of abnormal areas. Deep biopsies are safely performed at the base of the bladder, because if extravasation occurs, it is extra-peritoneal and will not cause problems. If a patient is very tender after cystoscopy it is sensible to drain the bladder for 3-4 days.

The bladder wall in a female is very thin. If the patient has had a hysterectomy, the bladder may be perforated if biopsies are taken above the trigone. This will result in intra-peritoneal leakage. If small, this may mend by using catheter drainage for 5 days, but if significant, the patient must be opened and the defect closed. Obviously if this happens, there will be cause for complaint, but defence is possible.

The classical bladder tumour may be small and papillary, but patients quite often present with advanced bladder tumours with few symptoms. Patients often say that their bladder cancer should have been diagnosed earlier. This may well be true, but it is often difficult to estimate what difference earlier diagnosis would have made.

Carcinoma in situ is a special case, because it may advance quite rapidly and change to a deeply infiltrating tumour. It will respond to intra-vesical therapy, and the current favourite is BCG - Bacille Calmette Guerain. Early stage carcinoma in situ may respond in 70% of cases, but of these 30% may relapse.

If cancer is high grade, the surgical choice is between bladder replacement and urinary diversion. Whatever the decision, surgery should be carried out sooner rather than later. There is a vogue for conserving the bladder whenever possible. The functional results are better in men than in women, but not every bladder cancer is suitable for bladder reconstruction. In some situations radiotherapy is the primary treatment, and if this fails, a salvage cystectomy may need to be undertaken. The commonest diversion is to implant the ureters into an isolated segment of small bowel which is brought to the surface as a stoma, over which a bag is worn.

Complications in cystectomy include bleeding, which if severe may require packing of the pelvis. Damage to the rectum may occur, and is not acceptable. Post-operative bowel obstruction is a fairly common but usually non-negligent complication.

It is important to check on renal function post-operatively. An ultrasound or IVP should be done within 4 months, along with blood tests indicating renal function. If obstruction of a ureter develops, it can be treated by interventional radiological means.

COMPARTMENT SYNDROME

Although not strictly a urological problem, this syndrome can occur if a patient is operated on with the legs in the lithotomy position, and the operation lasts for more than 3 hours. The pain that the condition generates may not be felt by the patient, because it is likely that they will have had an epidural anaesthetic.

Whether or not putting the legs down every 3 hours prevents the condition developing is uncertain. If it does occur, one has to question whether it was necessary for the operation to take that long, or whether it was necessary to have the legs in the lithotomy position. The position is necessary for a urethroplasty. In bladder replacement surgery, the position may be necessary when the bladder is removed: it is not necessary for the reconstructive surgery.

RENAL STONES

Patients who develop stones very rarely have to have open operations nowadays due to improvements of endoscopic instrumentation and the use of extra-corporeal shock wave lithotripsy (ESWL) to break up the stones. It is usually not difficult to diagnose the presence of a stone, but a stone may be silent and cause major damage.

Stones in the ureter of under 5 mm can pass spontaneously, but ESWL can speed the passage by breaking the stones up.

Any endoscopic treatment may damage the ureter, and it is therefore sensible to leave in a J-stent to allow oedema or bruising to settle. Any endoscopic treatment should be covered with antibiotics. It is preferable for the results of a urine culture to be available before the procedure.

Urine outside the urinary tract is very irritant, so adequate stenting is mandatory.

Stents will not prevent strictures developing, and may have to be used long term if surgery is not anticipated.

Complications arising from sepsis and urine leakage may be grounds for liability. In such cases it will be important to see if adequate stenting has been performed.

Kidney stones can be treated either by ESWL, percutaneous nephrolithotomy (PCNL), or a combination of the two. Adequate drainage via the ureter with a stent or via a nephrostomy tube is essential in complicated cases.

Damage to the bowel or pleura by the placing of the access tube through which the operation is done is a complication of the radiological technique. When it happens it should be recognised.

If the colon is damaged, a big drainage tube should be placed in the hope that the colon will mend, but if major, a defunctioning colostomy and surgical repair of the damage will be necessary. Failure to diagnose the problem is unacceptable.

PCNL should be covered with antibiotics.

Problems may arise from the influx of too much irrigating fluid, and should be treated in much the same way as a TUR syndrome.

Bleeding is generally a non-negligent complication. It can generally be controlled by the use of a large nephrostomy tube, but if it proves difficult to control, radiological embolisation or even an open operation may be needed. Occasionally a partial nephrectomy or even nephrectomy has to be undertaken.

STENTS

If a stent is left in situ, it is important that a detailed record is left in the notes. If a stent is forgotten, it may encrust and fragment. If this happens, removal can be very difficult. It is therefore important to state when the stents should be removed or changed.

OBSTRUCTION AT THE PELVI-URETERIC JUNCTION

The ureters may become obstructed at the point where the renal pelvis becomes the ureter. This is often congenital. It may be picked up on ante-natal ultrasound, but it may also resolve after birth, and may not need surgical treatment. Any ante-natal abnormalities should be followed up very carefully.

Any child or adult presenting with recurrent bouts of abdominal pain should have an ultrasound performed to exclude an obstructed kidney. It is not acceptable to treat a patient with left sided pain as irritable bowel syndrome, without excluding an obstructed kidney.

Over a period of time, the kidney function will decrease. Surgery to relieve the obstruction should only be contemplated if the kidney has at least 20% of overall function. Medico-legally is often difficult to work out when, in retrospect, the kidney would have had enough function for conservative surgery to be carried out instead of a nephrectomy.

Pyelonephritis secondary to reflux can cause a similar type of obstruction. This is often not diagnosed in children. They often have abdominal pain, diarrhoea and vomiting, rather than renal pain. Because it is often a bilateral disease, they often present with decreased renal function.

Surgery may cure the problem, whether is due to reflux or obstruction, but renal function will often not improve because the damage is irreversible.

KIDNEY TUMOURS

Kidney tumours usually present with frank haematuria. They may, however, grow to a large size and present with an abdominal mass, or present with less specific signs of ill health such as anaemia. Although the diagnosis may be obvious on ultrasound or CT scanning, there may be an unnecessary delay in diagnosis or it may be missed altogether.

If there is a delay, the grade of the tumour will not change, but the stage may advance. It is however very difficult to decide when the tumour may have spread into the renal pelvis, the perinephric fat or the local lymph nodes.

Indefensible complications of nephrectomy include ligation of a major vessel other than the renal artery. If the tumour is very big and on the left side, the spleen may be damaged and require removal. Bowel injury can occur. It will not necessarily be negligent to cause it, but it will always be negligent to fail to recognise the damage.

GYNAECOLOGICAL INJURIES

Many problems may arise during and after gynaecological operations. It is for the gynaecologist to decide whether or not there has been negligence. A urologist is often requested to advise on the management and very often, one finds that the initial management has been far from satisfactory.

Vesico-vaginal fistula (VVF) results from damage to the bladder when it is separated from the cervix. Blood in the urine suggests that the bladder wall has been bruised or damaged. The writer would recommend catheter drainage for at least 5 days after the urine has cleared.

A bladder injury may be associated with a pelvic haematoma. This is likely to discharge per vaginam. It may be very difficult to decide whether or not there is leakage of urine as well. However, a patient developing urinary frequency with leakage may have developed a VVF. Diagnosis is by careful physical examination or a cystogram. It is also important to be certain that there is not an associated ureteric injury as well.

It is very unlikely that catheter drainage per se will allow the fistula to mend. There are urologists who favour early repair once the diagnosis be made, but surgery can be very difficult and the writer favours delayed closure at approximately 3 months. By this time the tissues are more healthy and the size of the defect more easily definable.

Occasionally ureters may be damaged. This will cause backache. Abdominal pain should not be ascribed to gut colic without doing an ultrasound examination. Ultrasound will easily identify whether or not the ureter has been damaged and caused renal obstruction.

A ureteric injury may result in a uretero vaginal fistula (UVF) which causes continual incontinence. The diagnosis is made by doing an X-ray.

The sooner a ureteric injury is mended, the less the damage to the kidney. When a UVF develops and a partial obstruction is present, it may be possible to pass a J-stent cystoscopically, and healing may occur. When significant obstruction is present, a radiologist should place a percutaneous nephrostomy to preserve kidney function. An open operation can then be carried out to re-implant the ureter at a later date.

Although the surgery to repair these gynaecological operations usually gives good anatomical results, patients are very often symptomatic for no good reason. Ureteric reflux in the presence of good bladder emptying should not cause renal pain.

Hysterectomy per se may alter bladder function, due to unavoidable damage to the pelvic autonomic nerves. This may produce urgency and frequency. Occasionally a patient develops an atonic bladder and has to resort to clean intermittent self catheterisation. Patients who develop severe problems are likely to have had some unrecognised bladder dysfunction pre-operatively. Patients who have surgery to repair a VVF often develop bladder symptoms, but it is not possible to say whether it was the hysterectomy or the repair that caused them.

NEPHROLOGY

Martin A. Mansell

INTRODUCTION

Most lawyers and not a few doctors have a worrying lacuna in their knowledge about what nephrologists actually do. The speciality of renal medicine deals with the medical diseases that affect the kidney and the remainder of the urinary tract and has the same slightly edgy relationship to urology as does cardiology to cardiac surgery and rheumatology to orthopaedics. The most important focus of nephrology is on the diseases that cause acute or chronic renal failure and its management by dialysis or renal transplantation. There are important links with common general medical problems such as diabetes and hypertension and patients who are seriously ill, for whatever reason, commonly develop partial or complete renal failure. Paediatric nephrology is even more specialised but many of these children survive into adult life with reduced kidney function so that the adult nephrologist must be familiar with the common childhood problems, which often have a congenital urological origin.

There are about 34,000 patients in the UK with end-stage renal failure being kept alive with dialysis or kidney transplants and spending on these patients represents about 2% of the NHS budget. The numbers are expanding steadily and will approach the current American Health Care budget expenditure of 10%, so that the medico-legal importance of renal medicine will continue to grow. Although patient numbers are relatively small the repeated interventions which they require provide fertile ground for adverse events. Patients are no longer reluctant to seek legal redress, as they were in the past, when they were grateful to be the recipients of a scarce medical resource.

This chapter summarises the relevant medical background required by lawyers and then focus on relevant cases drawn from the writer's experience of about 600 reports over the last 16 years.

SYMPTOMS, SIGNS AND BASIC INVESTIGATIONS

Many potentially serious renal diseases are completely asymptomatic in the initial stages, but an early diagnosis is sometimes established when increased amounts of protein or blood are detected in the urine by "stick" testing. The presence of trace haematuria, not visible to the naked eye, needs to be confirmed by microscopy and a 24hr urine collection is required for accurate measurement of heavy proteinuria. A trace (or 1+) of proteinuria or haematuria may be found in healthy individuals but more pronounced abnormalities need, at least, to be investigated and reviewed.

Symptoms of lower urinary tract infection ("cystitis") such as frequency, dysuria and offensive smell need to be investigated by culture of a mid-stream urine. "Blind" antibiotic treatment of a presumptive urinary infection without bacteriological confirmation can be a risky thing to do.

Many types of serious renal disease cause hypertension so that accurate measurement of the blood pressure with an appropriately sized cuff is an essential part of the clinical assessment of such patients.

Routine urinalysis and blood pressure measurement form part of the screening medical examinations performed on healthy individuals and clinical negligence claims alleging delay in diagnosis of a progressive renal problem are becoming increasingly common. Diseases such as glomerulonephritis and polycystic kidneys which often lead to end-stage renal failure (ESRF) may be picked up in this way but are rarely cured by medication, so that although liability is often easy to demonstrate the chain of causation may be relatively weak. Note that high blood pressure, from whatever cause, will always accelerate progression to renal failure.

Overall renal function is routinely measured by the plasma creatinine (normal range 60-120μmol/l), with an elevated value indicating renal impairment. Interpretation of a particular value is critically dependent on the patient's size. Measurement of the creatinine clearance (70-120ml/min/1.73m^2) is more helpful, although often difficult to achieve in practice because of the need for a 24hr urine collection. Serial plasma creatinine measurements are often expressed as the reciprocal value to give a more easily comprehensible representation of the rate of progression of renal failure. A graphical plot of reciprocal serial creatinine levels is helpful in predicting the likely date for renal replacement therapy and demonstrating the benefit of therapeutic interventions.

It is relatively easy to predict the prognosis of a particular patient from simple observations when they are first seen. If renal function and blood pressure are normal and proteinuria minimal (0.5-1g/24hr) it is likely that serious problems will not develop during follow-up of many years or decades. On the other hand, a patient with a raised blood pressure, proteinuria greater than 2g/24hr and a creatinine over 200μmol/l will probably end up on dialysis within a few years.

Specialist investigations such as ultrasound, intravenous urography (IVU), CT and isotope scanning yield important information about kidney structure and relative function.

Renal biopsy is the gold standard for histological diagnosis and prognosis and is a relatively safe procedure in an uncomplicated patient. It can often be performed as a day case procedure. The major risk of renal biopsy is haemorrhage. This can occur either into or around the kidney. The risk is increased in the presence of uncontrolled hypertension, renal impairment, impaired coagulation, obesity and poor patient co-operation. In straightforward patients macroscopic haematuria requiring a period of bed rest may occur in 3-5%, with about 2-3% of patients requiring a blood transfusion and fewer than 1% requiring arteriography and embolisation to stop the bleeding. The writer knows of 4 fatalities following renal biopsy in the last 4 years, all of which occurred in predictably high risk patients. In such patients adequately informed consent is an important issue. Other relevant medico-legal points include the experience of the operator, the accuracy of ultrasound localisation of the kidney for biopsy, correction of hypertension and impaired coagulation, the adequacy of post biopsy observations and the reaction of the medical staff to serious bleeding. The decision to proceed to renal biopsy should be made by a consultant. Identification of high risk patients helps to prevent many of the serious complications which occur.

GLOMERULONEPHRITIS

This is an immunologically-mediated inflammation affecting both kidneys which can range from the clinically trivial to a fulminant illness causing irreversible renal failure within a few weeks.

Renal biopsy is usually essential, although the simple tests outlined above will often predict the prognosis. Although most cases of glomerulonephritis do not show a dramatic response to treatment a few, such as those associated with systemic vasculitis, will improve and stabilise for many years with intensive and occasionally life-threatening treatment. It is common for patients to develop symptoms of renal failure only when the disease is relatively far advanced. Such patients will often go to law for what they feel must have been a diagnostic delay which has led to the prospect of a transplant or a lifetime of dialysis. Although diagnostic delays are indeed common, the lack of effective therapy often means that causation is weak and quantum is relatively small.

The association between industrial solvent exposure and the development/progression of glomerulonephritis is attracting recent attention and has immense legal potential because of the widespread use of various hydrocarbons in the work place.

NEPHROTIC SYNDROME

This describes the existence of proteinuria which is sufficiently severe to reduce the serum albumin level and cause oedema formation. It is usually caused by glomerulonephritis or diabetes.

Fluid retention may need to be controlled with very large doses of diuretics. It is a prothrombotic state with an increased possibility of venous or arterial thrombosis and pulmonary embolism in, perhaps, 5% of patients. Thromboprophylaxis with either aspirin or warfarin is usually appropriate. Nephrotic syndrome is rare in pregnancy, which is another prothrombotic state, but fatal pulmonary embolism has occurred with sub-optimal anticoagulation.

REFLUX UROPATHY

Vesico-ureteric reflux (VUR) occurs if the normal valve mechanism where the ureter joins the bladder is deficient, so that micturition causes reflux of urine up to one or both kidneys. The combination of high pressure reflux and infected urine causes structural kidney damage and scarring affecting the upper and lower poles of the kidney which is detectable by isotope scanning or radiological techniques.

Maintenance of a sterile urine by long-term antibiotics throughout childhood prevents further scar formation and progression to "reflux nephropathy", in which the development of proteinuria and hypertension presages progression to ESRF in young adulthood.

Scar formation can occur in utero or very early infancy, and urinary infection in a young child, particularly a girl with a positive family history, needs to be taken seriously and actively investigated. General Practitioners are now familiar with the published management guidelines for urinary infection in children, but there is a continuing legacy of cases from 15 or 20 years ago that are only now going into end-stage renal failure. Experts' uncertain recollection of the prevailing standards at the time often causes difficulty.

The radiological changes of VUR were originally described as "chronic pyelonephritis" but this old-fashioned term should now be discarded. Similar changes can result from congenitally abnormal kidneys (renal dysplasia) and from the long-term use of combination pain killers containing phenacetin, (although this is now extremely rare in this country).

Meticulous control of hypertension with the ACE – inhibitor group of drugs may significantly delay or even prevent the otherwise inevitable progression of some of these patients to chronic renal failure.

ADULT POLYCYSTIC KIDNEY DISEASE

APKD is an inherited renal disease characterised by progressive cystic transformation of both kidneys which leads to hypertension, infection and progressive renal failure, typically affecting half the children of an affected parent.

Cyst enlargement can cause serious local complications such as pain or macroscopic haematuria, and about 50-70% of affected patients will require dialysis or transplantation by the time they reach their sixties. About 2% of such patients will suffer potentially fatal subarachnoid haemorrhage from the cerebral aneurysms which are sometimes associated and the sudden onset of severe headache, especially with a positive family history, needs to be actively pursued.

Renal cysts can usually be detected by ultrasound by the age of 30, but their appearance may be delayed and incorrect reassurance of a young patient who subsequently turns out to have the disease is an occasional cause of litigation.

Other causes of litigation include death from uninvestigated subarachnoid haemorrhage and inadequate treatment of the invariably associated hypertension. Most of the underlying chromosome abnormalities can be detected in the children of affected patients, and it is likely that the genetic screening policies which are used in the United States will soon become established in this country.

RENOVASCULAR DISEASE

Progressive arterial narrowing due to atheroma affecting the heart, brain and peripheral circulation is the single major cause of morbidity and mortality in ageing Western populations. It has become clear in the last 20 years that the renal arteries may also be involved.

Renal function declines anyway from the fifth decade onwards so that older patients are more susceptible to acute renal failure occurring as a result of intercurrent surgery or common medication such as ACE-inhibitor drugs for hypertension and non-steroidal analgesics, (with many of the latter available over the counter and consumed in industrial quantities). Renal artery stenosis from atheroma is an important additional cause of chronic renal failure in older patients. Some cases respond to aggressive intervention such as balloon angioplasty, stent insertion or surgical reconstruction. These patients always have significant co-morbidity because of their diffuse arterial problems. Intervention carries significant risks so that conservative management may be appropriate, with the patient being put onto dialysis as and when this becomes necessary. The decision to proceed with interventional treatment requires a very full discussion of the possible risks and benefits. The individual experience of the operator is a crucial factor in determining success or failure.

DIABETES AND KIDNEY DISEASE

Diabetes may progress to chronic renal failure. Diabetic patients account for about 20% of new patients starting dialysis each year in this country. Meticulous control of blood sugar and hypertension has major benefits. The complicated patient requires joint care by the diabetologist and nephrologist. Significant weight reduction is usually important in the common, maturity onset diabetic, although it is often difficult to achieve in practice. Patient compliance with a tight therapeutic regime is often less than ideal.

Diabetic renal failure may worsen dramatically following radiological procedures which use intravenous contrast, and these should not be undertaken without prior renoprotection with fluid loading and N-acetylcysteine.

KIDNEY DAMAGE CAUSED BY HYPERTENSION

Significant renal damage is rarely the result of simple hypertension but may occasionally occur, particularly in Afro-Caribbean patients, and particularly if the hypertension is severe. Poorly treated hypertension can occasionally enter an "accelerated" phase with progression to ESRF in a matter of months. The legal issues usually involve the adequacy of blood pressure control by a General Practitioner and the rather uncertain prediction of the possible benefit from normalisation of the blood pressure.

ACUTE RENAL FAILURE

Any major, life-threatening illness may cause acute renal failure. Common factors include sepsis, emergency surgery, radiological contrast procedures, non-steroidal drugs, ACE-inhibitors and aminoglycoside antibiotics such as gentamicin. Many cases occur in the context of "multiple organ system failure". These patients are usually taken care of by intensivists until their condition stabilises so that they can be treated with intermittent haemodialysis for the days or weeks which are necessary until their kidneys recover. The nephrologist will usually be involved in their care at some time and occasional legal cases involve the missed diagnosis of a treatable renal problem such as vasculitis in a patient with other major pathology.

Mismatched blood transfusion rarely causes acute renal failure. This disaster continues to occur, usually due to errors in blood collection and labelling or transfusion of the wrong blood in an emergency situation.

Many chemotherapeutic agents used for cancer cause renal damage, especially with repeated courses. Careful assessment of renal function pre-treatment with appropriate dose reduction is not always performed adequately. Note that many tumours, such as lymphoma, can also cause renal damage by obstruction to urinary drainage so that causation in these cases may be very difficult to untangle.

UROLOGICAL PROBLEMS

The need for careful pre-operative assessment

Urologists are often called upon to perform major surgery on patients with pre-existing renal damage caused by, for example, renal calculi, tumours or obstruction to urinary drainage. Some urologists are still unaware that a normal plasma creatinine in a malnourished elderly patient is consistent with overall renal function substantially less than 50% of normal, and the nephrologist is often asked to help with the care of unanticipated post-operative renal failure. Such patients need careful pre-operative assessment with control of urinary sepsis, discontinuation of nephrotoxic medication such as ACE-inhibitors and non-steroidal analgesia and avoidance of dehydration. Drainage of an obstructed kidney causes a dramatic diuresis so that acute renal failure from dehydration needs to be anticipated and treated with adequate intravenous fluid replacement.

"TUR syndrome"

Trans-urethral resection of the prostate (TURP) is the commonest urological operation performed in this country and post-operative problems in elderly patients include bleeding and the "TUR syndrome", caused by absorption of the fluid used for irrigation during the surgery. Major complications affecting the heart and brain may result and the legal discussion usually involves the experience and supervision of the surgeon, together with the recognition and appropriate management of the post-operative problems.

Methysergide-induced ureteric obstruction

Methysergide is an old fashioned but effective treatment for intractable migraine and prolonged courses cause the rare complication, in less than 1% of patients, of retroperitoneal fibrosis. This can cause obstruction to one or both ureters with the development of renal failure. The writer has dealt with three such cases in the last 3 years. Methysergide should only be prescribed by a consultant neurologist experienced in its use and a drug "holiday" of a month or two is required every 6 months, although this may be difficult to achieve in patients for whom it is, apparently, the only effective medication.

Complications of urological laparoscopic surgery

Minimally invasive, laparoscopic surgery is making a significant impact in modern urology. The reduced morbidity and inpatient stay with which it is often associated makes it attractive to patients and surgeons alike. Because the patients leave hospital after only a few days, complications such as bleeding or bowel perforation may occur at home. Patients must be warned about this possibility, and told that it is absolutely essential to return to their surgeon if any problems develop. Many general surgeons will have little experience of possible laparoscopic complications and admission to a different hospital for their management may lead to disaster. As urologists come to specialise entirely in laparoscopic surgery it is likely that they will have little experience of traditional "open" procedures and the appropriateness of a decision to continue with a difficult laparoscopic procedure rather than convert to any open procedure may attract legal analysis.

Complications of gynaecological surgery

Ureteric damage seems to be a common complication of gynaecological procedures such as difficult hysterectomy and Caesarian section. The recognition of this injury may be immediately apparent or long delayed, with the potential for complete loss of function of an obstructed kidney. Once recognised, the urologist will be called upon to repair the damage and clinical experience is required to decide if immediate repair or nephrostomy drainage with delayed surgery is appropriate. Legal aspects of these ureteric injuries usually involve the particular experience of the gynaecologist, anticipation of the procedure (which is likely to be complicated) and prompt recognition and management of the ureteric damage which has occurred.

Assessment of condition and prognosis in the patient who has suffered renal damage as a result of surgery should be a matter for the nephrologist rather than the urologist and requires much more than measurement of the plasma creatinine level. Patients with recurring urological problems are likely to have had pre-operative damage to one or both kidneys and the presence of factors such as proteinuria and hypertension may significantly affect prognosis. Specialist tests such as isotope scans may be required to identify continuing obstruction and its likely evolution.

RENAL REPLACEMENT THERAPY

General

There are about 17,000 patients in the United Kingdom with end-stage renal failure being kept alive by dialysis, with about 70% on haemodialysis (HD) and 30% on chronic ambulatory peritoneal dialysis (CAPD). Slightly more patients have a functioning renal transplant of which about 85% are from cadaver donors and about 15% from living related donors. Because only about 1500 kidney transplants are performed every year the current nationwide waiting list of about 2000 patients is steadily increasing. These numbers are very approximate.

The likelihood of ESRF increases with age. Nearly 40% of current patients are more than 65 years old and the 10% annual growth in patient numbers is not predicted to plateau within the foreseeable future. The incidence of ESRF is associated with social deprivation and ethnic minority status and there is significant and worrying regional variation in the provision of dialysis and transplant facilities. Compared to similar European countries there is a significant un-met need for these patients, especially those aged more than 55. Issues of equitable access are likely to be tested in the courts, particularly in view of the recent developments in Europe.

Haemodialysis: General

Maintenance haemodialysis is typically performed for 4-5 hours thrice weekly. Access to the circulation is obviously required which must be capable of supporting a blood flow of 250-300 ml/min through the dialysis machine. Dialysis units may be either hospital-based or stand-alone, satellite facilities which are more conveniently situated. About 20% of all regular haemodialysis places are provided by commercial companies. This number is rapidly increasing so that it will probably soon approach the figure of 80% found in the USA. In effect, NHS Trusts are contracting out the dialysis component of their patients' overall care and there are interesting questions regarding the clinical responsibility for mishaps occurring in these units which have yet to be examined by the courts.

In the United Kingdom and Europe about 10-15% of all dialysis patients die each year, compared to at least 20% in the USA. The reasons for national and local variations in patient survival are complex and poorly understood although some, at least, are explained by differences in case mix, patient selection and clinical practice. As with other areas within the NHS, the last 10 years have seen an increasing focus on the adequacy of dialysis care. The third edition of the National Guidelines was published in 2003. These guidelines combine a mixture of sensible, evidence-based recommendations with well meaning, if unproven, targets of care, many of which seem to have been included to try to help with the continuing battle for increased resources.

The adequacy of the dialysis prescription for a particular patient is an increasingly common issue in litigation because of the serious morbidity and mortality which is associated with maintenance haemodialysis. The current clinical guidelines are sufficiently vague to provide little help for the lawyers. Note that dialysis patients often have notes extending over decades and it is common for the dialysis records, such as they are, to be held in quite different folders from the clinical notes so that the retrieval of all available information can be very difficult indeed. A huge amount of data accumulates in a patient on long-term dialysis which requires complex information technology for its retrieval, and many dialysis units, including the writer's own, do not yet possess this capability.

A UK Renal Registry now exists which has just produced its eighth annual report, but only about half of all Renal Units are able to report their data accurately. Information about the achievement of recommended audit standards is therefore quite thin. Survival statistics may need to be inferred from the more detailed American database and are relatively inaccurate for providing predictions about an individual patient. Morbidity and mortality depends on factors such as age, underlying renal diagnosis and co-morbidity. This information is often simply unobtainable, so that predictions of life expectancy can only be approximate.

Arteriovenous Fistulae

Vascular access for long-term haemodialysis is best provided by the surgical creation of an arteriovenous fistula at wrist or elbow. This allows the insertion of two wide-bore needles for each haemodialysis, which are removed at the end of the procedure. Only about 60% of patients have blood vessels suitable for fistula formation. In the remainder, secondary methods such as central venous catheters or vascular grafts are required, particularly in older or diabetic patients. Unlike an AV fistula which can give trouble-free dialysis access for decades, these alternative techniques carry a significant morbidity and mortality.

Fistula formation is the patient's life-line for dialysis. For optimal results it should be performed by a surgeon experienced in the procedure, with meticulous attention to detail. Such surgeons are in short supply and the operation is often unwisely delegated to a registrar. Delays in the timely formation of a fistula are common for a variety of reasons, so that temporary short-term access often becomes necessary. Only about half of the patients with end-stage renal failure enter dialysis programs in a planned fashion. Serious problems in the remainder who require temporary access are well documented.

AV fistulae may divert a significant proportion of the blood flowing to the hand so that a "steal" syndrome results with the development of ischaemic pain and even gangrene, particularly in patients with pre-existing arterial narrowing such as diabetics. Repeated needling of the fistula may cause thrombosis or haemorrhage which is occasionally fatal. Serious swelling of the arm may result from pre-existing obstruction to venous drainage which needs to be anticipated and appropriately investigated in the high risk patient. Occasionally fistulae will become aneurysmal, particularly with unwise needling in the same place, so that surgical closure of the fistula is required. Despite all these problems a fistula is desirable in all patients and a good fistula is an important predictor of a relatively trouble-free dialysis career.

Central Venous Catheters

These catheters can be inserted percutaneously using local anaesthetic into the great veins such as the internal jugular, subclavian or, occasionally, femoral veins. The technique involves adequately informed consent, appropriate positioning and sedation of the patient and accurate localisation of the vein with an ultrasound probe. The skin and deeper tissues are anaesthetised, a large needle is passed into the vein and a guide wire is passed a further 10 or 15cm so that the tip lies at the entry point to the right atrium. The needle is withdrawn, a dilator is passed over the wire to enlarge the hole in the vein, the catheter is then passed over the wire into the central circulation and the wire is withdrawn. A chest x-ray is performed to confirm satisfactory positioning of the catheter which can then be used for dialysis.

The procedure sounds straightforward but is, in fact, potentially fraught with disaster, including death. The main problem is bleeding which can be due to laceration of the vein, inadvertent puncture of the adjacent carotid artery or damage to the great veins as they enter the chest. Local bleeding will respond to pressure although compression of the trachea occasionally requires intubation and ventilation. Perforation of the distal vein causes bleeding into the chest. Very prompt resuscitation is required if death from exsanguination is to be averted. Cannulation of the subclavian vein carries the additional risks of pneumothorax and subsequent venous stenosis and should be avoided whenever possible. All temporary dialysis catheters are prone to serious problems with thrombosis and infection so that survival of such access for more than a few weeks is unusual.

There are particular problems associated with the use of these catheters in long-term dialysis patients because of ongoing access problems. Repeated procedures cause venous stenosis and distortion of the anatomy, patients are often understandably apprehensive and their co-operation is limited, and the co-existence of renal failure and hypertension increases the risk of bleeding. Wherever possible, written informed consent should be obtained from the patient.

Many Trusts now have written policies for the use of these catheters. Ultrasound localisation should be routine and the skill and experience of the operator is of paramount importance; this is not a procedure to be delegated to a junior SHO who may previously have performed only a small number of relatively easy line insertions. Although access for dialysis is often required promptly it is rarely such an emergency that serious risks cannot be identified and minimised as much as possible. The writer knows of five fatalities in the last 5 years from this cause and, doubtless, there have been many more; it is no surprise that such disasters go unreported and it is very difficult to obtain data on the expected and "acceptable" frequency of this occurrence.

The defence of claims resulting from central venous line insertion often relies on the urgency of clinical need and (in the case of claims asserting inadequate consent) on the implied consent of the reasonable patient. Temporary line insertion is the commonest invasive procedure performed in a renal unit and the frequency of litigation from this cause is likely to increase.

Semi-permanent lines such as Permacaths are often used in patients with a limited prognosis in whom all other possibilities of access have been exhausted. They are usually placed by interventional radiologists or access surgeons with greater experience than the nephrologists who insert temporary lines, so that the risks of immediate bleeding seem to be rather less. About one third of regular dialysis patients in this country use this type of access. It typically lasts for no more than 12-18 months before the inevitable problems of thrombosis and infection occur. Local infection at the exit site will often respond to antibiotics but life-threatening septicaemia is not uncommon and fine clinical judgement is necessary to decide when an infected line needs to be urgently removed and alternative access established. Complications of blood stream infection include endocarditis and metastatic abscess formation and expert microbiological advice is always required both for the management of these patients and for the pursuit of litigation.

Subcutaneous vascular grafts in the arm or leg are used by about 10% of dialysis patients and placement is performed by a vascular surgeon under general anaesthetic. These grafts last no longer than a year or two and usually lead to thrombosis and infection which may necessitate surgical removal of the graft. Interference with peripheral circulation to the limb is common and very careful patient selection is necessary in patients such as diabetics whose arterial supply is already compromised. Aneurysms may form, and these can occasionally be resected surgically. Swelling of the limb due to impaired venous drainage may improve with venoplasty and stent insertion, although these procedures are not without risk and may have only a limited benefit.

Technical problems of haemodialysis

The haemodialysis procedure is complicated and modern machines have a number of fail-safe systems which monitor blood flow, dialysate composition and temperature, membrane integrity and fluid removal. There are national specifications for dialysate sterility and monthly monitoring of the dialysis system is obligatory. Epidemics of Hepatitis B and C have occurred in dialysis units and strict infection control guidelines are essential, although they may not be rigidly enforced because of resource limitations. Progressive liver disease is an occasional result of hospital-acquired hepatitis which will be of increasing interest to clinical negligence lawyers in the future.

Long term medical complications of haemodialysis

Most of the mortality of long-term dialysis is due to cardiac causes and careful attention to control of blood pressure, fluid balance, diabetes and hyperlipidaemia is the cornerstone of these patients' ongoing medical care. They need to consume a vast number of medications and follow fairly tight dietary restrictions. Perfect patient compliance is usually impossible to achieve. The adequacy of the dialysis regime for a particular patient should be monitored on a monthly basis by regular blood tests. Regular outpatient contact with a consultant or other suitably experienced doctor is essential. In the writer's opinion it is unlikely that comparison of survival statistics from an individual unit with the national average will be possible in the foreseeable future because of the huge investment in data retrieval which will be necessary.

Anaemia in patients with renal failure responds to the prescription of erythropoietin with a typical average expenditure of about £3000/yr/patient. Prescription costs are often diverted to the General Practitioner, and this leads to questions about the clinical responsibility for the use of this hormone, particularly when problems occur with under- or overcorrection of anaemia. A recent problem has been the development of aplastic anaemia because of antibody formation. Some of these cases are likely to attract legal attention in the near future.

Chronic Ambulatory Periotoneal Dialysis (CAPD): General

CAPD is performed by running 2 litres of sterile dialysate through a plastic tube placed permanently in the peritoneal cavity. Waste products are absorbed across the peritoneal membrane into the fluid which is then drained out after about 6 hours. The process is performed by the patient away from the hospital and is attractive to British nephrologists because it is easy to initiate, relatively simple and does not require an expensive haemodialysis facility. Although many patients welcome the freedom of a treatment performed at home with only minor dietary restrictions, there are some outstanding questions about patient suitability and selection. In Europe fewer than 10% of all dialysis patients are treated by CAPD, compared to about 40% in this country. Some of this difference, at least, may reflect limitations in resources and service provision. The technique is unlikely to be used in an individual patient for more than 5-7 years - unlike haemodialysis which has been used successfully for decades in some patients. Automated peritoneal dialysis (APD) is used in about 30% of all PD patients and has significantly increased patient acceptability and technique survival.

Catheter insertion in CAPD

The peritoneal catheter can be inserted percutaneously under local anaesthetic and this approach is favoured by many nephrologists, particularly in the uncomplicated patient. Because the procedure is done "blindly" there is significant scope for serious damage to intraperitoneal structures such as bowel, and fatal haemorrhage has resulted from damage to the aorta, iliac vessels or mesenteric vessels. Previous abdominal surgery increases the risk of bowel adherence at the puncture site and adequate analgesia and patient co-operation are essential. Alternatively, the catheter can be inserted by a surgeon under general anaesthetic via a mini-laparotomy. This reduces the risk of intra-abdominal trauma, although delayed recovery from the anaesthetic in the patient with end-stage renal failure should be anticipated. It is sometimes difficult for the tip of the catheter to be placed in the optimal position within the pelvis, so that manipulation or further surgery may be required.

Post-operative pain and constipation usually settle within a few days. After this the patient is trained to perform the dialysis procedure with meticulous attention to aseptic technique and can then be discharged home. Frail, old patients are likely to require a prolonged training period and successful long-term dialysis at home, even with the provision of a thorough care package, is rather unlikely

Complications of CAPD

The main complication of CAPD is peritonitis due to bacterial contamination of the dialysate fluid. This is usually associated with poor technique. Most cases of CAPD peritonitis respond to about a week of antibiotic treatment. This is usually administered intraperitoneally to begin with, and is followed by a short oral course. The initial antibiotic regime often includes gentamicin. Significant systemic absorption can occur from the dialysate despite the use of very low concentrations. Gentamicin damages the auditory nerve and the balance mechanism in the ear is more sensitive to this complication than hearing. Ototoxicity is an invariable result of excessive gentamicin administration and although it is usually sub-clinical, repeated courses have a cumulative effect. Some patients require antibiotic treatment for peritonitis 3 or 4 times a year and the first problems may only become apparent after 2 or 3 years of PD, with the development of dizziness, vertigo and nystagmus. Symptoms often resolve steadily if the gentamicin is discontinued but occasional patients are left with a significant disability and legal action results.

Medico-legal issues include the duration and intensity of therapy, monitoring of blood levels and unwise persistence by the doctors with the technique of CAPD, instead of changing the patient to haemodialysis. Causation may be particularly difficult to establish: a microbiologist with a particular interest in this complication is required, together with an ENT surgeon and nephrologist.

Patients may become seriously ill because of CAPD peritonitis and it is a matter of fine clinical judgement whether to press on with antibiotic treatment or to remove the catheter and change to haemodialysis. Bacterial guidance from the laboratory is important because some infections, such as those due to Staphylococcus aureus, Pseudomonas and Candida are unlikely to respond to antibiotics alone. Prompt removal of the catheter is therefore required if the patient is not to die from overwhelming peritonitis. The patient may refuse to accept a transfer to haemodialysis in some of these cases, but others may be due to the limited availability of haemodialysis places, particularly for older patients. The patient in whom catheter removal has been unwisely delayed is likely to have a very prolonged and stormy hospital course requiring repeated operations and drainage of intra-abdominal abscesses. Death may eventually result.

Sclerosing encapsulating peritonitis (SEP) is an unusual but feared complication of PD in which large segments of the bowel become matted together by dense fibrous tissue leading to progressive intestinal obstruction. Recurrent bacterial peritonitis is the single most important predisposing factor. It is also associated with the duration of PD, so that the frequency of cases is increasing with the recent developments which prolong the survival of the technique. About half of such patients die within the year. The legal issues usually concern the delay in transferring the patient to haemodialysis and the effectiveness of the management of episodes of recurrent peritonitis. Causation may be difficult to establish because there are occasional cases where SEP has first become manifest several months after catheter removal and apparent resolution of peritonitis.

Infection may also occur in the skin where the catheter exits the abdomen. This will often respond to local measures such as antiseptic gel, antibiotics or catheter replacement. If the infection tracks around the tube, a subcutaneous abscess may result which requires surgical exploration and tube removal. A chronic exit-site infection which cannot be cured by simple measures is likely to lead to frank peritonitis, with the occasional severe complications described above. Several types of abdominal herniae are recognised complications of peritoneal dialysis because of the increased intra-abdominal pressure caused by the presence of the dialysate fluid.

Renal transplantation

Although there are about 5000 patients on the waiting list, only about 1900 transplants are performed annually. Delays of many years for a transplant are therefore common and the number waiting is steadily increasing. Not all retrieved cadaver kidneys are allocated nationally and there are significant regional variations in waiting time. Selection of an individual recipient is governed by factors such as tissue match, blood group, age and waiting time spent on dialysis. The majority of patients with ESRF long for the near-normal quality of life provided by a transplant but the reality is that older patients are unlikely ever to receive a kidney because of the limited numbers available. Only about 30% of all kidneys come from living related donors. This number could be doubled, as in Europe, by an appropriate injection of resources. Rewarded living donation, currently unlawful, is now receiving a more objective appraisal than in the past and interesting developments are likely in this area. Living kidney donation has no long-term medical consequences but the surgery required for a nephroureterectomy is substantial and carries an inevitable morbidity and mortality. Potentially fatal complications include bleeding from the renal pedicle, together with venous thrombosis and pulmonary embolism for which thromboprophylaxis with heparin is usually appropriate. Pneumothorax and post-operative chest infection are recognised, minor post-operative problems and it remains to be seen whether the recent increase in popularity of laparoscopic donor nephrectomy is really associated with a lower incidence of problems.

Cadaver kidneys are preserved in ice after retrieval and the aim should be to get them into the recipient in under 24hrs so that immediate renal function occurs: this is associated with a better prognosis. The transplanting surgeon depends on the skill of his colleagues at another centre who have removed the kidney. Occasionally there are problems with the quality of the kidney which are discovered at the time of transplantation, although these cause abandonment of the procedure only very rarely. The surgery may be complicated because of unexpected accessory vessels, a short ureteric stump or very poor recipient vessels, although the latter problem should have been excluded before the patient was put on the waiting list. Selection of the appropriate kidney to remove from a living donor depends on accurate knowledge of the vascular anatomy and occasional disasters have occurred because of unwise reliance on magnetic resonance studies rather than formal bilateral renal arteriography.

The recipient receives powerful drugs to prevent rejection from the time of surgery. These need to be continued for the rest of the patient's life. Thromboprophylaxis is indicated for most of the post-operative period. Preventable disasters at the time of surgery include the use of a blood group-incompatible kidney or flushing of the kidney with water at the time of retrieval. Transplants are usually lost under these circumstances. Irreversible, hyperacute rejection can occur if recipient antibodies are present which have not been detected by the sophisticated tissue typing which is performed on all potential recipients.

An ideal cadaver kidney donor is young and previously fit with no significant previous medical history, infection or malignancy. In reality, because of the shortage of donors, transplant surgeons and nephrologists are under considerable pressure to use kidneys that are less than perfect. This increases the risk of a prolonged post-operative recovery period and reduces chances of long-term survival. A number of centres are currently assessing kidneys retrieved from non-heart beating donors. These carry increased but not necessarily unacceptable problems.. Many patients with a limited prognosis on dialysis are desperate to receive a transplant, however uncertain, so that it may be justifiable to proceed if truly informed consent is given after a very detailed discussion of the possible risks and benefits. Some nephrologists are becoming more cautious about putting up their patients for transplantation because of litigation fears related to the quality of the kidney, the degree of tissue matching, vascular co-morbidity and the long-term effects of immunosuppression.

Living donor transplantation has been described as the only operation with a potential 200% mortality so that it is considered unethical in some transplant units, particularly those in whom a serious problem has previously occurred. However, renal transplantation has become a strikingly successful treatment for ESRF, and half of all transplants are currently surviving for about 15 years. All transplant units should be achieving a 1 year success rate greater than 80% and reliable, comparative data from named units in the United Kingdom is now becoming available. Most of the transplant losses occur in the first year and are usually due to surgical problems or rejection but after this time the attrition rate falls to no more than 2-3%/year. Subsequent losses may result from "chronic allograft nephropathy", cardiovascular death or malignancy and these patients need careful and skilled life-long follow-up. Transplant kidney biopsy is sometimes necessary, with the risk of major complications described above.

Excessive immunosuppression with cyclosporin or Tacrolimus can itself cause graft damage and steroid doses need to be kept as low as possible to minimise complications such as diabetes and osteoporosis. Although the incidence of all cancers is modestly increased in transplant recipients many of these are skin lesions whose management is fairly straightforward. Melanoma and squamous cell carcinoma, however, cause appreciable mortality, especially with excessive exposure to sunlight. Post-transplant lymphoma is a serious problem closely related to the use of monoclonal antibody therapy for prevention of rejection; when it comes to immunosuppression more is definitely not better.

CONCLUSION

The growth in nephrological clinical negligence cases in the last decade has certainly matched that seen in other areas of the NHS and may even be ahead. Patient numbers and expectations are growing, survival is increasing and new opportunities for therapeutic intervention are developing. Diabetes and hypertension are reaching epidemic proportions in the general population and both of these diseases can have significant renal aspects. Surgeons are performing emergency surgery on older patients, and the decline in renal function that occurs with the passage of time means that the development of sometimes irreversible acute renal failure is no surprise. Most renal units carry a heavy work load with inadequate resource provision so that it is not surprising that the courts see a good deal of nephrologists.

CARDIOLOGY

Roger Blackwood

INTRODUCTION

It is hardly surprising that legal claims are quite common in the area of cardiology. Some 30% of all hospital admissions are cardiological. Cardiology, perhaps more than any other specialty, is subject to endless clinical trials and recent advances in cardiological treatment have been very significant. Information on the internet has raised patient expectations enormously. A chest pain patient will often enquire about having angiography at the first meeting with the doctor, even if he is uncertain what it is. Despite technological advantages, it is still the initial interpretation of the symptoms, (classically chest pain) that is so difficult. Every doctor will have sent home a patient with chest pain from the A & E department, and there are occasional disastrous consequences. Every cardiologist is likely to be involved with the law during his career.

This chapter considers the main elements in cardiology which are likely to be legal battlegrounds.

CHEST PAIN

General

Over half the medico-legal actions in cardiology are related to chest pain. This is mainly due to the difficulty of distinguishing between chest pain of cardiac origin and chest pain from other causes. Although there may be a text book history of angina pectoris, the patient presenting in casualty will rarely give such a story. Almost any patient with severe chest pain could be a cardiac case, but as there are so many such patients, it is quite impossible to admit them all or refer them to a cardiologist. Most patients with chest pain do not feel. The history is often vague and unhelpful.

Clinical examination is almost certain to be normal. The situation is not helped by the fact that a resting ECG may well show no abnormalities even in advanced heart disease, and blood tests in casualty are seldom diagnostic. Add to all this the pressure on staff (the doctor only has a few minutes), and the pressure on beds (they are few and far between), and the pressure from relatives, and it is easy to see why mistakes are made.

Causes of Chest Pain

There are many causes of chest pain (see Fig 1) but it is essential that cardiac pain is excluded first. This book cannot deal with the diagnosis of each type of chest pain, but each has its suggestive history, clinical findings and appropriate tests. For cardiac pain the initial investigation would include an ECG and an exercise stress test. Subsequently thallium scanning and a coronary angiogram will be necessary.

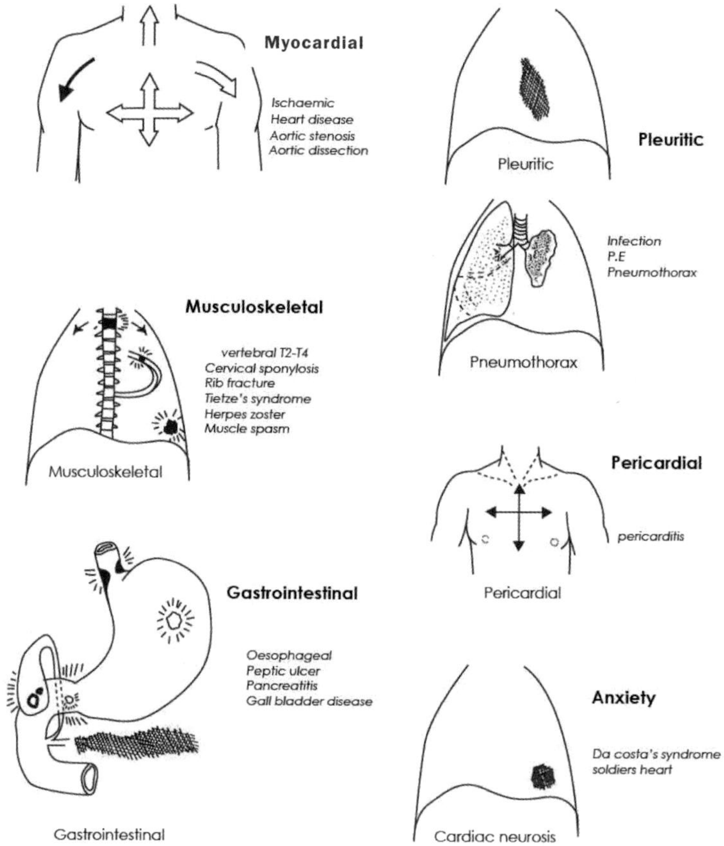

Figure 1. The causes of chest pain

Cardiac Pain

Almost any pain in the chest, especially if severe, could be cardiac. Three types of angina (chest pain of cardiac origin) need to be noted. These are outlined below. The diagnosis is made on the history, not on tests.

Angina is usually due to narrowed coronary arteries (see Fig 2) caused by deposition of cholesterol and cells in the wall of the vessel (atheroma). Significant angina will only exist once the narrowing is greater than 60 – 70%. Most people aged over 60 will have at least 50% narrowing in at least one coronary artery, but this will cause no symptoms. There are other causes of angina- for example aortic stenosis and hypertrophic cardiomyopathy - but these are rare in comparison with atheroma.

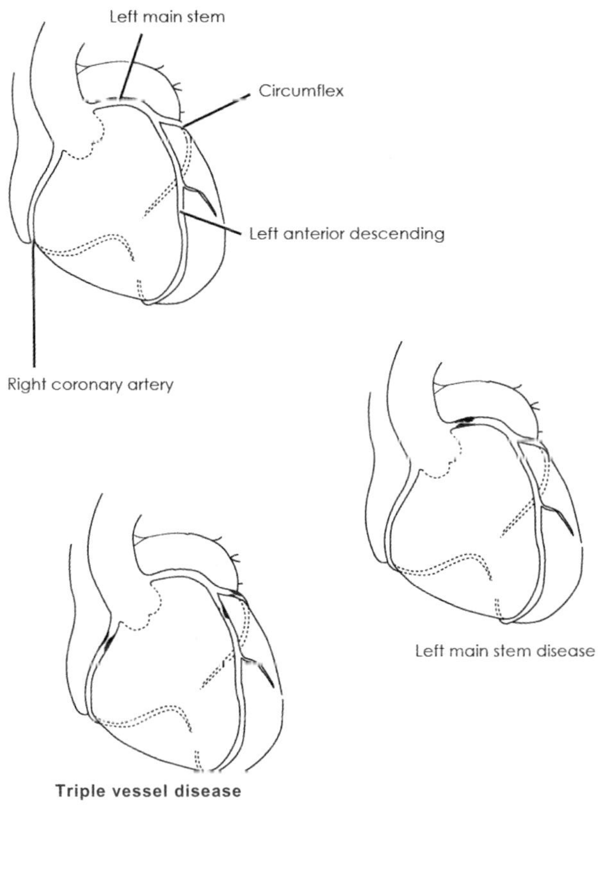

Figure 2. The coronary arteries and atheroma

Stable angina
This is chest pain, which is usually anterior and central, often radiating to the left or right arm and into the neck or throat. It is precipitated by exercise or emotion and disappears within 2 – 3 minutes of relaxing. It is worse if there is cold weather or after eating a meal. It is important to emphasize that the pain is during exercise and not after. Glyceryl trinitrate (GTN – either tablets or a spray) will relieve angina very quickly i.e. within 2 - 3 minutes, but GTN also relieves oesophageal spasm and other muscular conditions and is therefore not of any value as a test for angina.

Unstable angina
This pain is the same as stable angina, but comes on more quickly or at rest without provocation, and lasts for up to 20 minutes. It is a dangerous condition, often leading to a myocardial infarction. Unstable angina occurs because bleeding into the narrowing, the atheroma, will suddenly cause a greater restriction of blood flow. If bleeding continues the artery will block off - i.e. a myocardial infarction will occur.

Myocardial Infarction (MI)
The pain of a myocardial infarction (heart attack) is usually very severe, but of the same type as angina. It is often described as like an elephant sitting on the chest. The pain, if untreated, may last for several hours. The hospital mortality (including elderly patients) is 20% or more.

A higher index of suspicion of chest pain is necessary if the patient has obvious risk factors e.g. diabetes, heavy smoking, family history of heart disease, known high cholesterol, or high blood pressure.

Claims relating to chest pain

Most cases arise because of a failure to diagnose chest pain as cardiac. This failure can be due to several factors.

Taking an inadequate history of the chest pain

Case History:
A man of 55 went to casualty with a classic history of angina. He had woken in the night with unprovoked chest pain lasting 15 minutes. He was seen in A & E by the casualty officer the following morning. The casualty officer only asked about the pain on the night before admission. The casualty officer did an ECG and blood tests, which were normal, diagnosed gastrointestinal pain and referred the patient to the medical registrar on call. The registrar also diagnosed indigestion and sent the patient home. At 3.00 a.m. the following morning the patient was back in casualty with an acute MI. He was treated well after that. The patient started proceedings but withdrew them when he accepted that an earlier admission would not have made much difference to the overall long-term survival or quality of life.

Comment:
In fact the junior doctors would not have had a leg to stand on if the patient had died. There was a clear history of angina with much worse pain just before arriving at A & E. The diagnosis was therefore probable unstable angina. A full medical history is essential. Examination is usually unhelpful and ECG and enzymes are usually normal.

Taking an inadequate history of factors other than chest pain

Case History:
A diabetic man of 58, also a heavy smoker, went to A & E at about midnight. He had mild chest pain which had occurred for about 15 minutes at intervals over the preceding few days. His wife noted that he was sweaty and dyspnoeic when he had chest pain. His father had died of an MI at the age of 62. The casualty officer thought little of the pain and asked no peripheral questions. After a normal ECG the patient was sent home where he died 2 hours later.

Comment:
In this case there was no defence because, although the chest pain was mild, the patient had numerous risk factors and concurrent symptoms of a worrying nature. The patient was working only sporadically because of his diabetes, and the case was settled for a modest sum.

Being confused by previous gastrointestinal symptoms

Case History:
A fit 36 year old girl presented to A & E with unpleasant chest pain which had occurred intermittently for about 4 weeks. She had a long history of indigestion. There was a normal ECG. A diagnosis of possible gastric ulcer was made and the patient was discharged. Later that night she had severe chest pain at home and died. Apart from smoking 20 cigarettes a day, she had no risk factors and no family history of heart disease. At the trial the judge felt that the doctors had not been in error because there was so little indicative history and the patient was both female and young.

Comment:
This case illustrates how easy it is to assume the diagnosis is gastrointestinal just because there was a previous history of indigestion. The casualty doctor emphasized that he had elicited a current history of indigestion as well. Sadly, even if she had been referred to a cardiologist from casualty, it would probably have been too late. Her only hope was to be admitted directly, but this did not seem justified at the time.

Conflict with relatives

Case History:
A man of 80 was seen in A & E. He was brought in by his relatives because of vague chest pains and being unwell. From the time of the initial consultation the daughter was aggressive, insisting the patient was admitted. Eventually the

casualty consultant was involved and could see no obvious reason for admission. After meeting the daughter he became irritated and told her to take her father home. The patient died about 2 days later and the daughter sued the hospital saying he would have lived if he had been admitted.

Comment:
This case was settled, but quite probably would have been avoided altogether if the consultant had not developed such rapid antibodies to the daughter. This is not an uncommon problem and the doctor needs to be very careful not to be inappropriately biased.

Differing histories

Case History:
A 53 year old man had chest pain at work and was sent home. He tried to contact his doctor and eventually saw him 2 days later. He was told he had flu. After a week of returning repeatedly to the doctor he was eventually admitted to hospital with a large anterior MI. He had bypass grafting very shortly after and did not return to work. He brought a large claim against the GP. The problem was that the patient said the doctor refused to see him on the first day but there were no doctors' or practice notes confirming this. There were full notes from the day the patient was seen following the telephone call i.e. on the second day. The solicitors eventually contacted British Telecom who confirmed that there had been no call on day one from the patient.

Comment:
The patient's wife was totally convinced that she had rung the GP as soon as her husband came home on the first day. What the relatives remember after the event is often uncertain, and contemporaneous evidence is vital. This case collapsed when the wife admitted that she probably had not rung on the first day.

Case History:
A 45 year old man was seen in A & E where excellent clerking was done and a full case history of chest pain was recorded. The diagnosis was indigestion. The patient went home and died that night. His wife sued the hospital, saying that he had had chest pain on exertion for weeks before. She made her statement about this some 6 months later. At court it was felt that the contemporaneous evidence was very good and comprehensive enough to suggest a gastrointestinal cause for the pain. As the wife was with her husband in casualty and no mention of previous chest pain was made, the case failed.

Comment:
This case shows the value of good clerking and good contemporaneous notes.

Failure of Follow Up

Case History:
A 60 year old railway worker had moderate angina and was eventually referred for bypass grafting. Six months later he was seen in the outpatient clinic, and the situation was unchanged. He was patiently waiting for his operation. He then did not appear for his following appointment 3 months later. It was then very unclear whether another appointment was sent. Certainly nothing happened until he died 18 months later. His widow took legal action alleging that it was the hospital's responsibility to arrange further appointments. The action was eventually settled for a small sum.

Comment:
This case emphasizes that the hospital is responsible for chasing up patients, but it was agreed that the patient has some responsibility too. As the widow claimed that the patient was getting increasing pain, it was surprising that she did not seek a further appointment for her husband herself. Many hospitals now have a policy of not sending a second follow up appointment if one has been missed - subject to the doctor overruling the policy in individual cases on medical grounds.

Failure to Interpret the ECG Correctly

Case History:
A man of 49 was admitted to an A & E department with chest pain, which was very vague. He had an ECG and his cardiac enzymes were assayed. The ECG and the enzyme results were seen by the A & E SHO and the medical SHO. Both declared he had indigestion. The patient went home. That afternoon he had a cardiac arrest, but was resuscitated by the ambulance crew who arrived very quickly. After 3 weeks in hospital he was discharged to a nursing home with permanent brain damage. His wife sued the health authority for discharging him directly from A & E. The case was indefensible when it became apparent that the ECG in casualty clearly showed an early MI. The health authority is now paying all costs for this poor man's nursing home as well as an income for his wife. As he may live for a long time this will cost the NHS several hundred thousand pounds.

Comment:
Unfortunately both the A & E and medical SHO should have read the ECG correctly. Junior doctors are expected to be able to interpret most of the signs of ischaemia on an ECG from an early stage. Fortunately occurrences like this are rare.

Other medico-legally important issues relating to chest pain

Timing of a myocardial infarction

When exactly an MI begins is very difficult to say. This is important, because medico-legally a lot depends on how quickly treatment can be started. Catching an MI in its first hour means up to a 50% reduction in mortality if thrombolysis is given (see Fig 3). The benefit after 12 hours is, however, only about 12%.

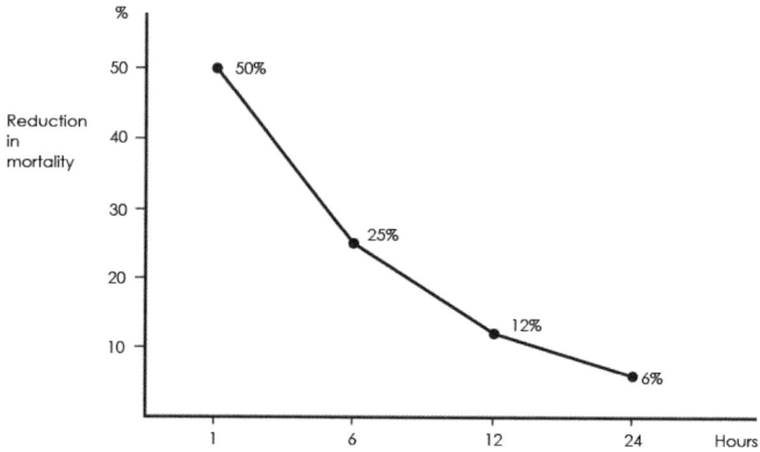

FIGURE 3: APPROXIMATE REDUCTION IN MORTALITY WITH THROMBOLYSIS IN MYOCARDIAL INFARCTION.

There are three ways of timing an MI:

(i) By reference to the chest pain

In some cases the first onset of chest pain heralds the MI. In other cases the pain may stutter on for hours before the MI really sets in. Generally the start of a MI is when the pain is most severe, although there can be many exceptions. A patient who has had pain once a day for 4 or 5 days and presents to casualty with a completed MI could have had the MI at any time during those 4 or 5 days.

(ii) By reference to the ECG

Following an MI the ECG normally goes through an evolutionary series of changes, which may take up to 24 hours. These changes, however, may be complete in 2 – 3 hours. The ECG itself therefore is not very helpful unless there are multiple ECGs tracing the progress of the MI.

(iii) By reference to the cardiac enzymes

The basic point is illustrated in Fig 4. Both troponin and MB creatinine phosphokinase (MBCPK) are enzymes released by the heart muscle when it is damaged. However, they do not appear in the blood stream for about 12 hours, which is one reason why so many patients in casualty have normal enzymes when they go there with chest pain. By looking at consecutive daily enzyme levels it is possible to give a reasonable estimate of when an infarct begins. Unfortunately enzyme results are often missing from the notes, although it is standard for all hospitals to do at least 3 days of consecutive tests following a patient's admission with chest pain.

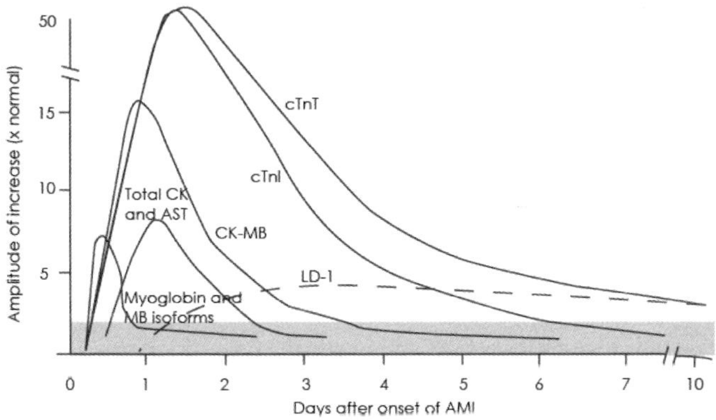

Figure 4. Changes in cardiac enzymes after acute myocardial infarction

cTnT = Troponin T
cTnI = Troponin I
CK = Creatinine Kinase
CK-MB = Myocardial fraction of CK
LD-1 = Lactic dehydrogenase
AST = Aspartate aminotransferase

Should every patient with cardiac chest pain be seen by a cardiologist?

In an ideal world it would be better for all cardiac patients to see a cardiologist. However there simply are not enough cardiologists, and especially in the acute situation all consultants on take will know exactly what to do with an acute MI. The problem arises more significantly after the cardiac event when the patient is being followed up in the outpatient clinic. If, for example, the patient continues to have chest pain, he ought to be referred to a cardiology clinic. In essence a cardiologist will usually refer a cardiac case for further testing or intervention much earlier than the general physician.

Case History:
A man of 56 had an MI and was quite correctly treated. The consultant on call was a GI specialist and at follow up the patient continued to complain of chest pain. A cardiologist would probably have organized an exercise test and other specialist cardiac investigations very quickly, and referred the patient for angiography. The gastroenterologist gave him some additional anti-anginal

therapy and saw him 6 months later. This went on for 3 years. Eventually the patient was sent to the cardiologist and the patient had bypass grafting less than 3 months later. The medico-legal question was whether the operation 3 years earlier would have made a significant difference to the quality of life and prognosis of the patient. These questions are very difficult to answer but in this case it was felt that it would not have made much difference if the patient had been seen earlier. He had been able to return to work soon after the bypass grafting and coped very well.

THE ANGIOGRAM

An angiogram is an x-ray dye test of the coronary arteries. It is performed to see the exact site and degree of narrowing in the arteries in order to see if it can be dealt with by balloon dilatation (angioplasty) or, if necessary, by bypass grafting. The test is invasive. It involves putting a soft plastic tube (the catheter) into the femoral artery and maneuvering it into the coronary arteries by x-ray control. Because it is invasive it carries some risks (see Fig 5). It is important that patients are aware of these when they sign a consent form for the procedure. Almost every patient will end up with bruising in the groin (where the insertion is made) and a lump of scar tissue over the site for 2 – 3 weeks. Despite warnings of side-effects patients often sue if anything goes wrong.

Risk	%
Death	0.14
Embolus/stroke	0.12
Damage to femoral artery	1.70
Heart attack	0.07
Ventricular fibrillation	0.60

FIGURE 5. RISKS OF ANGIOGRAPHY

Case History:
A lady of 67 had an angiogram, and just after the end of the procedure went blind in her right eye. An embolus was thought to be the cause - probably resulting from the catheter rubbing against the internal carotid artery during the procedure. This is a recognized complication even in the best of hands. The claim was not pursued.

Comment:
Angiograms are performed because of atheroma, which can of course be present in other parts of the vascular system e.g. the aorta and carotid arteries. The catheter irritating the surface of the narrowing will cause platelets to aggregate and at some stage fall off in a clump. The clot may go somewhere where it is harmless, but if it ends up in the retinal artery, blindness is likely.

Case History:
A man of 73 who had severe coronary artery disease but who was otherwise well, had acute renal failure following a catheter procedure. He required long-term dialysis and sued the consultant concerned for damaging his kidneys.

Comment:
What happened here was that the catheter had rubbed up and down extensive atheroma in the aorta. Showers of cholesterol laden emboli had then ended up blocking both kidneys. This is a rare but recognized complication of an angiogram. It is not preventable by the operator, who would not have any reason to suspect he is causing problems. The case was abandoned.

Case History:
A man of 70 had an angiogram using the brachial artery (arm approach). This was because he had had previous vascular surgery to the femoral arteries. In exposing the right brachial artery the median nerve was damaged when it was mistaken for the artery itself. The patient had a useless right hand and arm thereafter and successfully sued the doctor. A modest sum was paid out because the patient had already retired.

Comment:
Cutting the median nerve should never happen in these cases. It lies adjacent to the brachial artery and usually great care is taken to avoid it. Damaging it is indefensible.

ANGIOPLASTY

Surprisingly few cases have involved this potentially complex procedure.

Angioplasty is inserting a balloon into the coronary artery, pushing it to the area of narrowing and inflating it with carbon dioxide to many atmospheres pressure: see Fig 6. Once the narrowing is treated it is normal to put in a stent. This is like a cylinder of chicken wire which springs open across the previously narrowed artery and maintains the lumen. It is usually a very successful procedure. It is performed for the relief of chest pain - not simply because the narrowing is there. It is not a very good treatment for the relief of dyspnoea or fatigue, but may help these symptoms to a degree.

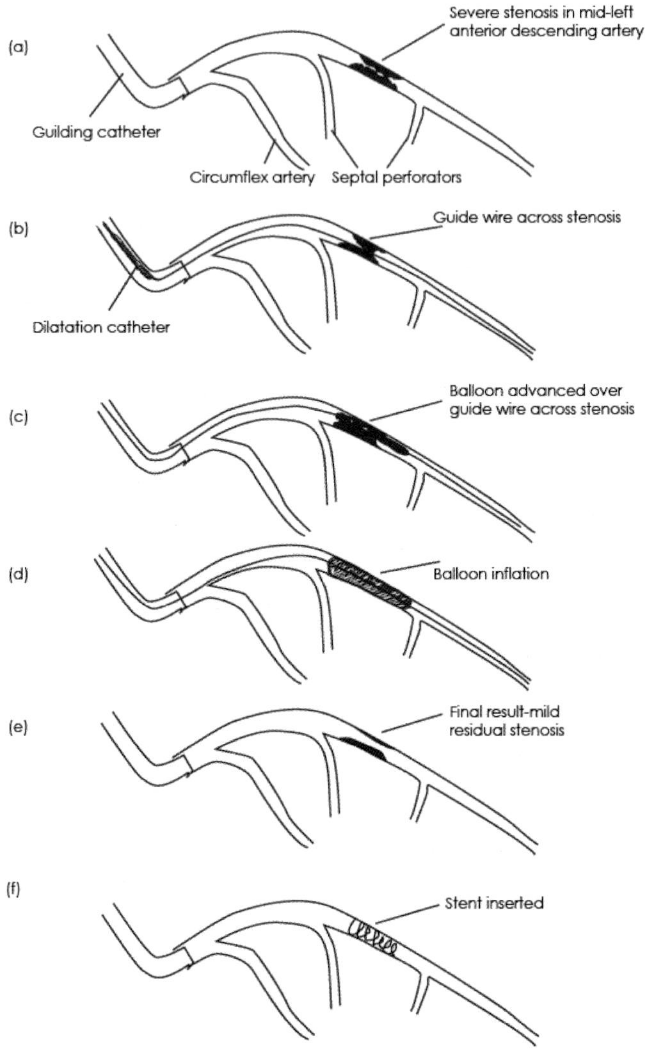

Figure 6. Stages in performing a coronary angioplasty

Case History:
A 52 year old dentist suffered from mild chest pains which were definitely cardiac. The patient was also diabetic. It was decided to do an angiogram because he would be at high risk (being diabetic) and though he had very little pain it was felt that an angioplasty to the left anterior descending coronary artery would be suitable. It was about 70% narrowed. That night, after a successful angioplasty and stent insertion, he had severe chest pain. ECGs were done and the consultant talked to the SHO on call. The consultant did not, however, see the patient, whose pain continued on and off all night. The next day it was clear that the patient had had a large anterior infarction. Unfortunately his blood pressure fell and he went to theatre for bypass grafting. He died at operation.

Comment:
The failure of the consultant to go and see the patient and sort out this problem the previous night meant that it was difficult to defend this claim. The other issue this case brought up was whether any angioplasty was really necessary in the first place as the pain was mild. The health authority eventually settled the case. It was very costly because the dentist's income was considerable.

ROUTINE MEDICAL EXAMINATIONS

The "annual" medical is especially relevant to cardiology. It is designed to check the heart particularly, because so often there are no symptoms until a heart attack occurs. In addition, men in particular ignore their symptoms but the annual medical, with prompting from the doctor concerned, may elicit a history of chest pain and other worrying symptoms. This, plus the ECG, is very important. If there is a suggestion of heart disease from the medical examination it must be vigorously followed up.

Case History:
A man of 45 went for a medical and ticked off chest pain as a symptom. The doctor asked about it and recorded that it was related to exercise. The doctor clearly thought it was possible angina, but the ECG was normal and the patient was not advised about follow up in any way. He went on holiday about one month later and had an extensive heart attack. His chest pain continued and he required a bypass graft. He sued the company responsible for carrying out the annual medical examination for failing to act on the medical information they had. They should, he said, have urged him to see a cardiologist immediately. The case settled.

Comment:
This case was indefensible because the point of such medical examinations is to pick up problems – especially cardiac ones.

Case History:
A business man of 51 had an annual medical at his local private hospital. All was well except for the ECG, which showed minor but definite ischaemic changes. He was assured that all was well, but in Canada about two months later he had a heart attack and subsequent angioplasty. He took up his grievance with the hospital who settled the claim.

Comment:
ECGs at routine medicals are more likely to frighten patients than be of value. Most companies use computer read "ECGs", which over-diagnose considerably. It is not uncommon for a man to be told he has had a heart attack when the ECG is normal. The writer knows of no claims so far which have resulted from this.

VALVE PROBLEMS

With the advent of the echocardiograph, which can assess a valve both diagnostically and prognostically, very few cases of pure valve disease become the subject of claims. The problems usually arise from the timing of valve replacement and infection developing on the valve (endocarditis). Endocarditis is dealt with separately.

Case History:
A young man of 22 with Marfan's syndrome was followed up regularly at a teaching hospital. His aortic valve was known to be leaking but he was a very active individual partaking in many sports and seemingly very healthy. The size of his heart and aorta was measured annually. He was being considered for an aortic valve replacement (AVR) when he developed severe chest pain after a game of soccer and was admitted in extremis to the hospital. An emergency AVR was performed but after over two months in ITU after the operation, he died. He had been "brain dead" for a while. The father argued that the operation should have been done before it became an emergency. The case was eventually dropped. It was accepted that he was very high risk anyway and it would have made very little difference to the outcome if he had had a routine operation.

Comment:
Marfan's syndrome is a congenital abnormality affecting the heart and skeletal system. It is well recognized, and specific measurements of the size of the aortic root determine when an operation is appropriate. All of this had been done correctly, and it was just very sad that this case turned out as it did.

Case History:
A young man of 42 with known, moderately severe but asymptomatic aortic stenosis was followed up regularly at his local cardiac outpatient clinic. He suddenly went blind in his right eye, and the ophthalmologists discovered that this was due to a calcified embolus from the deformed aortic valve. The patient sued the hospital saying that he should have had an aortic valve replacement

(AVR) and that if he had the embolus would have been prevented. All the expert witnesses agreed that there was no case to answer and he dropped the case.

Comment:
A calcified embolus is a very rare event and could not have been predicted by the cardiologist. Furthermore this patient would have been more at risk with a valve replacement. The annual significant bleed rate from Warfarin required after AVR is about 1.7% per annum. This would include strokes. In addition his risk at the operation was probably 2.5% - well above the risk associated with a calcified embolus, which is less than 0.01%.

ENDOCARDITIS

Infection on an already damaged valve is called endocarditis and is a significant problem medico-legally. If a valve is distorted it is much easier for bacteria to grow on it. If this happens the valve distorts more, and bacterial emboli can detach from the valve and end up anywhere in the body. This could be in the brain, causing a stroke. Two particular aspects of endocarditis are medico-legally significant. First, the diagnosis may be too late, and second, the treatment may be inadequate. Patients with endocarditis present initial feeling unwell and having a minor temperature. Unless endocarditis is considered, the condition may remain undiagnosed and untreated for months. Treatment is with high dose intravenous antibiotics, which may need to go on for several weeks. A shorter course may allow the infection to continue.

Case History:
A girl of 22 presented to a teaching hospital pregnant and with hot sweats. She was considered a borderline diabetic. She developed a fever and was in and out of hospital seven times during pregnancy, mostly with a diagnosis of urinary tract infection. There were no problems with delivery, but four weeks afterwards she returned to hospital confused and with a painful right forearm. The orthopaedic surgeons saw her and diagnosed a strain. The forearm became inflamed and a medical registrar was asked to see her. He heard a mitral incompetent murmur. A subsequent echocardiogram showed a virtually destroyed mitral valve with vegetations (lumps of bacteria) on it. She had an immediate mitral valve replacement with high dose antibiotics, but died one week later. At post mortem she was found to have emboli everywhere in the body and profusely throughout the brain. The case was indefensible because the heart murmur had been noted during a previous pregnancy. A heart murmur was also noticed at the initial examination at the start of her last pregnancy. The case was settled for a very substantial sum.

Comment:
In this case the connection between the girl's fever (thought to be recurrent UTIs at the time) and her heart murmur was not made. It was most unfortunate.

Case History:
A GP of 42 presented with breathlessness to a colleague who heard an aortic regurgitant murmur. The GP had been unwell for a couple of months and had a nightly fever. He went to the local hospital but was not seen by the local cardiologist. An echocardiogram showed vegetations, and endocarditis was diagnosed. After two weeks of intravenous antibiotics he went home on a further two week oral course of antibiotics. He improved slowly but relapsed. He was briefly in hospital again, and then went home. His wife subsequently took him to the local cardiologist who admitted him immediately to a teaching hospital where he was found to have an aortic root abscess as well as an almost non-existent valve. An AVR was followed by another because of complications. The GP died after the second AVR. The GPs wife claimed that there had been inadequate treatment. She was considered to be correct, and the hospital had to settle the claim.

Comment:
This case emphasizes that such cases should be under a cardiologist from the outset. This patient should have been referred to the teaching hospital very early on for full assessment including trans-oesophageal echo (TOE). This echo test is performed like an endoscopy and enables the heart to be viewed from behind. The advantage of TOE is that it can view the aortic valve very clearly indeed. In this case it would have demonstrated the abscess very early on. The case also emphasizes that treatment should be in hospital so that the patient's condition can be properly monitored.

Case History:
A patient of 32 developed endocarditis on his aortic valve. After 4 weeks of antibiotic treatment he had a major embolus to the brain, leaving him hemiplegic. He was being considered for an aortic valve replacement because there were signs of cardiac de-compensation due to valve destruction by the infection. He sued, saying that he should have had the operation sooner. Experts on both sides agreed that had the operation been done sooner it would not necessarily have reduced the chance of an embolus. The case was abandoned.

Comment:
Even when treatment is correct problems can occur. Endocarditis is a most unpleasant diagnosis.

ANTICOAGULATION AND THE HEART

Clots forming in the heart can be caused by structural abnormalities e.g. valve lesions, and by arrhythmias – especially atrial fibrillation. Consequently many cardiac patients receive Heparin and Warfarin. This can lead to a number of claims.

Case History:
A lady of 41 developed atrial fibrillation after an operation and was anti-coagulated. She developed intense pain in the left leg and after several days it was finally diagnosed as a retroperitoneal haematoma. The bleeding irritated the sciatic nerve and was located by an abdominal ultra-sound. The pain was unbearable for a while. The patient sued the hospital on the grounds that she had obviously been over anti-coagulated. Although the blood test for Warfarin (the INR) was done somewhat erratically, it was clear that she was not incorrectly dosed and merely had a most unfortunate complication of Warfarin. The case was withdrawn.

Comment:
However careful one is, bleeding can occur with Warfarin and one of the most difficult bleeding areas to locate is the region involving the retroperitoneal space. Blood tests (INRs) are required for the first few days until the desired level is reached – usually between 2 and 3. Thereafter it is not necessary to do tests quite so frequently.

Case History:
A girl of 30 had an aortic valve replacement with tissue valve, which does not require routine anti-coagulation. She had problems with body hair growth and was put onto a female hormone to help this. She noticed an irregular pulse occasionally, but did not report it to the doctor. She then developed a dense hemiplegia and was found to be in atrial fibrillation. She sued the GP concerned for giving her a tablet that increased her clotting risk, and the hospital for failing to anti-coagulate her in the first place for her tissue valve. The case went to the High Court where it was decided that the hormone tablet caused such a small increased risk that it was not likely to add significantly to her heart problems. In addition it was accepted that the hospital would not have expected the heart to fibrillate at this age. Accordingly the claim failed.

Comment:
It is normal to anti-coagulate for atrial fibrillation, but this rhythm rarely happens in women with aortic valve replacements and could not have been foreseen here. However, once AF is established, the risk of clots is reduced by about 70% on Warfarin (5% per annum reduced to 1.5% per annum). Not to anti-coagulate for AF could ground a claim.

Case History:
A man of 57 had atrial flutter and a subsequent electrical cardioversion. Immediately afterwards, he had a left hemiplegia and sued the hospital because they did not anti-coagulate him. The episode had occurred in 1993. The experts for the defence were able to show that in 1993 it was not routine to anti-coagulate for atrial flutter and the case was dropped.

Comment:
If this had happened now the hospital would be liable. Patients must be anti-coagulated for six weeks before cardioversion and for four weeks afterwards to avoid emboli.

OTHER DRUGS

One other cardiological drug, Amiodarone, features often in claims. It is the best anti-arrhythmic agent for many rhythm problems (it is known as the Domestos of arrhythmias) but has a number of side-effects which means that some cardiologists never prescribe it. It can cause the thyroid to be over or under active, cause liver damage, peripheral neuropathy, sun sensitivity, pulmonary fibrosis, slate gray skin, upset sleeping patterns and fatigue. However, if the patient is carefully followed up with blood tests every 6 months or so, problems are rare.

Case History:
A man of 67 was put on Amiodarone to treat a troublesome arrhythmia and it worked very well. Unfortunately he developed a peripheral neuropathy about 2½ years after starting treatment. Otherwise he felt very well. He could not walk any significant distance, was in some pain and could not play golf. He sued his doctors for not warning him about this possibility, saying he never would have had the tablets had he known. The experts on both sides agreed that peripheral neuropathy was a very rare complication and would not normally have been mentioned to the patient. It was also pointed out that he might well have died without the Amiodarone.

Comment:
The problem that arises here is how much a doctor should tell a patient of the complications of a tablet like Amiodarone. Sun sensitivity, a feeling as though one has sun burn after just a few minutes exposure to sun-light, may occur in up to 70% of patients. They must therefore always be warned of this. However the risk of peripheral neuropathy is less than 0.1% and probably can be left unmentioned.

Case History:
A company doctor of 81 had recurrent atrial fibrillation only preventable by Amiodarone. He was warned about various dangers. Before the medication he could not get up to the stand at the football club of which he was a director. The Amiodarone transformed this. After about 4 years on the medication he became increasingly breathless, but said nothing about this to the doctors. He died soon after and was found to have pulmonary fibrosis at the post mortem. His relatives sued the GP and the local cardiologist for not managing the case correctly. The case was withdrawn when it emerged that the patient had been advised to have a chest x-ray if he developed undue breathlessness but had refused, saying that whatever happened he was not going to stop his Amiodarone.

Comment:
At the age of 81 this patient knew what he wanted, and the Amiodarone enabled him to attend his important games. All patients on Amiodarone should have blood tests for thyroid and liver every six months, but they only require a chest x-ray if they become clearly dyspnoeic.

FUTURE MEDICO-LEGAL GROWTH AREAS

Compliance with clinical guidelines

Since the introduction of evidence based medicine most hospitals have guidelines for dealing with problems like myocardial infarction. NICE also recommends treatments. Failure to adhere to such guidelines could attract the lawyers' attention. A case in point here would be the situation after myocardial infarction. Patients are now advised to be on Aspirin, a beta-blocker, an ACE inhibitor and a statin. All of these improve life expectancy by about 25% over and above a group which is not taking the tablets. That is not to say that if the patient is taking all four medications that they would improve their life expectancy by 100%. It is absolutely clear that a patient should be on a statin and aspirin, but side effects mean that it is not absolutely mandatory to be on an ACE inhibitor and a beta-blocker.

Stress and heart disease

Several claims have resulted from alleged connections between stress and cardiac events. Take, for example, a case where a train driver has witnessed a suicide in front of his engine. If the driver drops dead of a myocardial infarction a couple of years later, his relatives may sue saying that he was under stress as a result of the suicide, and that this brought on the heart attack. Causation would presently be difficult to establish, but there is increasing evidence that stress may cause heart disease and it may be possible in some cases to prove a link.

Electrophysiological studies

The inside of the heart can be mapped with electrodes, using a method similar to doing an angiogram, and any inappropriate electrical tissue ablated by an electric shock. This is quite a complicated procedure with a success rate considerably less than 100%. It is likely that the courts will see claims based on patient dissatisfaction with the result.

ONCOLOGY

Elisabeth Macdonald

INTRODUCTION

Oncologists are relatively rarely targets of litigation themselves. They are however very often embroiled in medico-legal disputes where the allegation of negligence is failure by a GP to refer or failure by a clinician in another specialty to diagnose. Hence, oncologists often give crucial evidence about the causal significance of the allegations. For that reason a lot of this chapter is concerned with the natural history of cancer and its response to treatment. This of course underpins all judgments about causation in cancer cases.

Information concerning the proportion of negligence cases that involve oncology has been obtained from the Medical Defence Union (MDU) and the National Health Service Litigation Authority (NHSLA).

The MDU reports that they were notified of 183 claims relating to the primary liability of oncologists (as opposed to claims in which oncology was an element) since the beginning of the 1980s, although only twelve of these claims occurred before 1990.

A large number of claims against general practitioners were recorded between 1990 and 2002 (1224 cases). Of these, some 50% related to delay, failure or incorrect diagnosis. Some 5% relate to delayed or inappropriate referral, or a complete failure to refer. Not all of these cases related to malignancy, but of the settled claims during this period the largest number (19 %) related to malignancy (in comparison with about 16% which related to orthopaedics, 13% to general medicine and 12% to general surgery). The commonest malignant diagnoses involved in these settled claims were breast (21%), cervix (14.5%) and bowel cancer (13.5%)

Data obtained from the National Health Service Litigation Authority (NHSLA) comprise figures taken from claims submitted under their "Clinical Negligence Scheme for Trusts" i.e. claims of clinical negligence relating to incidents which took place on or after 1st April 1995 when the NHSLA was established. Lower value claims handled by Trusts themselves rather than by the NHSLA ("Sub excess claims") are not included. (In fact since April 2002 excesses on clinical claims have been abolished and all clinical negligence claims have been handled by the NHSLA regardless of value.)

As a proportion of all cases recorded, 7.68% concerned patients with a diagnosis of cancer (1839 out of 23932). The most frequent cause of complaint was delay in diagnosis, which amounted to 53% of all cancer claims. Claims concerning failure of communication or improper consent only amounted to 2.5%. Poor communication appears to be a frequent contributor to other complaints but rarely gives rise to a claim of itself. Complaints about breast reconstruction after mastectomy amounted to 1.8% of all cancer cases, but (unsurprisingly) formed an important group among breast cancer cases (9.3%). As in the MDU series, the commonest diagnoses associated with complaints were breast cancer (19.2%), cervical cancer (11.5%) and bowel cancer (7.3%).

THE ONCOLOGICAL LANGUAGE OF CAUSATION

Cancer as a disease process

The causes of cancer are so far incompletely understood. However, recent rapid advances in understanding of the human genome are beginning to unravel some of the factors which lead to failure of the regulatory process which normally controls cell division. The development of cancer is associated with a number of environmental and genetic factors. It is now becoming increasingly clear that changes in the host genome are the final common pathway whatever the initial aetiology (cause).

Malignant change may result from the loss of inhibitory genes which prevent cell proliferation (tumour suppressor genes) or from promotion of growth factors which stimulate cell division (activated oncogenes).

Environmental factors causing chronic irritation at a cellular level have been noted to stimulate the development of malignant disease. These factors may be chemical, physical, viral or endocrine. For example, chronic irritation of the main breathing tubes (bronchi) by carcinogens in cigarette smoke has been observed to correlate strongly with the development of lung cancer. Chronic irritation of the skin by ultraviolet light is associated with the development both of melanoma and of squamous cancers of the skin. The presence of viral particles in soft tissues of the body is thought to provoke malignant change: for example papilloma virus in carcinoma of the cervix and the Epstein-Barr virus in naso-pharyngeal cancer.

Primary Tumours

Most cancers are initiated as a unique focus known as the primary malignant tumour and have, by definition, the ability to invade local tissues and to spread more widely through the body. Cancers starting deep, for example in glandular tissue of the body, may spread and invade more or less spherically and produce a mass or lump, whereas cancers arising on a tissue plane such as the skin or bladder wall may produce an ulcer on the surface with an underlying mass beneath. The extent of a primary tumour is defined by the degree of penetration of surrounding structures by malignant infiltration, by the overall dimensions of the tumour and by the characteristics of the cell type (histology).

Secondary (Metastatic) Spread

As primary tumours grow they tend to infiltrate the channels of both the vascular and lymphatic systems. As they grow, some tumours also produce fragile and primitive blood vessels to supply the tumour. Cells invading blood vessels frequently break off and travel via the blood vasculature to sites in the body far removed from the primary cancer (haematological spread) Highly malignant tumours tend to spread early in their development, when the primary tumour may be quite small. This process is known as metastasisation. Tumour deposits or metastases from different types of tumour tend to produce particular patterns of spread. For example bowel cancer most frequently spreads via the portal blood supply to the liver, whereas prostate cancer, although close to the lower bowel, spreads more often via vertebral veins to the bones of the spine. Many tumours spread at some time via the blood stream to the lungs, liver, bones and brain.

Nodal Spread

The lymphatic system forms part of the body's defences against infection or invasion by "foreign" chemicals or substances. This system is a network of narrow channels leading to "staging posts" at intervals that collect and process foreign matter (lymph nodes). The lymphatic system in the healthy body drains clear protein-laden fluid, which has been transferred into the tissues from the veins. These channels are also used to drain bacteria, viruses or chemicals, such as dust particles, to local lymph nodes before being passed to larger channels and returned to the main vein (superior vena cava) via the thoracic duct. Using the same mechanism, cancer cells spread to local lymph nodes and the degree of penetration of lymph glands, the size of the lymph glands and the number involved form the basis of the "nodal" classification of tumour spread.

Spread via body cavities

Tumours that develop adjacent to a body cavity, such as the pleural space surrounding the lung, or the peritoneal "cavity" in the abdomen, tend to shed cells into the cavity. This is another means of spread. In this way, for example, deposits on the pleural covering of the lung from a breast cancer can spread around the exterior surface of the lung and cause irritation to the pleura. The pleura often react by producing a quantity of fluid or "effusion". Similarly, cancer cells from an ovarian cancer can spread throughout the abdominal cavity and also produce a collection of excess fluid known as "ascites."

Tumour Staging

For the purposes of tumour definition and research, detailed tumour staging classifications have been developed. The UICC (Union International Contre le

Cancer), a branch of the World Health Organisation, regularly issues updated classifications in what is described as a TNM system (Tumour Node Metastases). For some diseases this form of classification is not ideal and other staging classifications have developed in practice. For example, cancer involving the bowel is usually described using the Dukes' classification (named after the surgeon who described what he found at operation and noted how these findings related to the patients' future progress). Experience has shown that in this bowel cancer the degree of penetration by the tumour of the bowel wall and the extent of lymph node involvement nearby are the critical factors that affect survival. Similarly, in the skin tumour melanoma it is the depth of penetration of the layers of the skin by melanoma cells (Clarke's level), which most accurately predicts survival, and these factors are reflected in the specific staging used in each case.

Causes of morbidity and death

Cancer is frequently but not always a fatal condition. Morbidity and death are usually associated with disease progression and metastasisation. Either primary or secondary tumour enlargement may compromise the functioning of normal body organs such as the lungs or liver, or create biochemical abnormalities which compromise normal organ function. For example abnormal "Bence-Jones proteins" produced by myeloma in the bone marrow can "block" and damage the kidneys. High blood calcium levels resulting either from invasion of tumour into bone or from the production of abnormal proteins in a tumour may cause nausea, dehydration, constipation and drowsiness. Cancer deposits in bone, especially weight-bearing bones, may cause weakening and lead to fractures.

Alternatively, morbidity and death may result from the effects of treatment delivered in the attempt to control aggressive disease. High dose intravenous chemotherapy, for instance, may result in the destruction of the white blood cells necessary for protection against infection, and death may result from overwhelming infection (Leukopenic sepsis).

Survival

General

Analysis of patients' survival following the diagnosis of every different form of cancer is essential in order to evaluate each form of treatment. Survival data form a basis for research, so benefiting future patients, and enable doctors to give their patients useful advice about prognosis.

For the purposes of comparison definite time frames are necessary. These usually fall into five year stretches of time, so that survival is quoted in terms of five, ten and fifteen year figures. Some forms of cancer allow the patient to survive for long periods of time with their tumour. In other diseases, any recurrence heralds rapid deterioration in quality of life and imminent death. In this more aggressive type of illness, disease free survival (DFS) is frequently quoted. Some survival figures for common tumours are quoted below (Fig 1) to illustrate the ranges of possible survival depending on tumour type.

FIG 1. – SOME USEFUL BASELINE FIGURES FOR SURVIVAL OF CANCER PATIENTS IN ENGLAND AND WALES (SOURCE CANCER RESEARCH UK 2003)

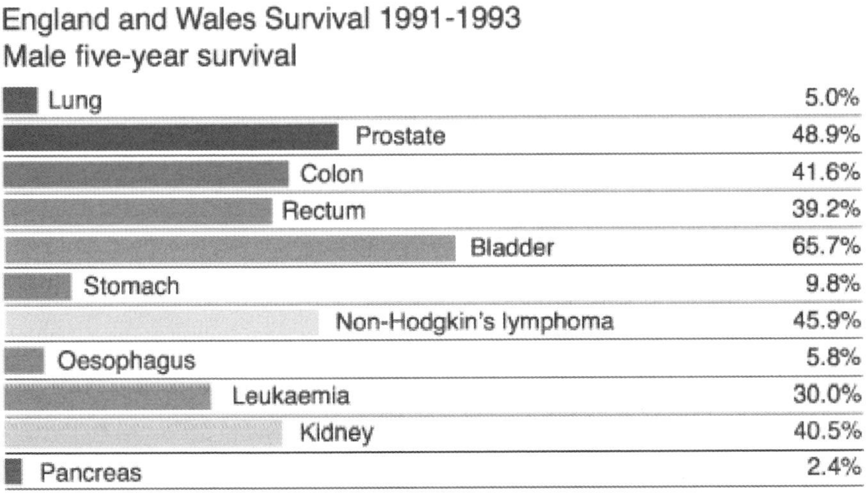

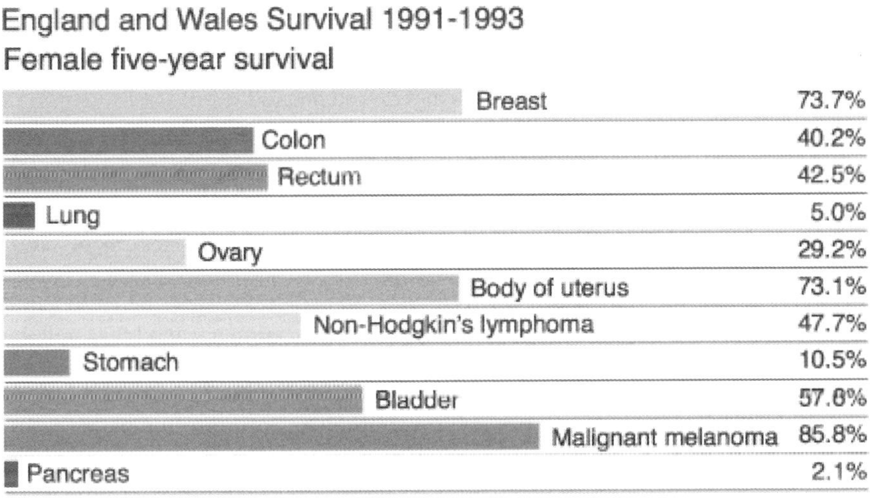

Survival by sex – Male

Of the ten most common cancers in men, bladder cancer has the highest five-year survival rate (over 65 %) and pancreatic cancer the lowest (less than 3%). Lung, oesophageal and stomach cancer all have survival rates of under 10%.

Survival by sex – Female
In women, breast cancer, malignant melanoma and cancer of the uterus have five-year survival rates of over 70%. Of the ten most common cancers in women, only lung and pancreatic cancer have survival rates of less than 10%.

MODES OF TREATMENT

Surgical Oncology

The surgical removal of many tumours is still important in the management of many forms of cancer. In some tumours such as lymphoma the role of surgery is confined to tissue biopsy for the purposes of confirming the diagnosis and establishing the characteristics of the tumour type. These tumours are better managed by either chemotherapy or, possibly, irradiation.

Otherwise, the main aim of surgical oncology is to remove the tumour in its entirety, together with the lymphatic channels and adjacent lymph nodes to which tumour cells may have spread. A second aim is to maintain as far as possible the normal function of the organ involved and by means of good surgical technique to avoid disseminating the tumour further. Surgical removal fulfils an important role in the management of bowel cancer, primary bone tumours, kidney tumours, early lung cancer and breast cancer.

Radiotherapy

Like surgery, radiotherapy is a local treatment, which only treats the tissues which are encompassed in what is known as the tumour volume and its immediate environs. Radiotherapy treatment machines - now mostly Linear Accelerators - use penetrating x-ray beams delivered from a combination of angles to target the tumour, together with any possible microscopic tumour spread within local tissues. Radiotherapy doses are defined in terms of the total dose delivered, the number of treatments given and the overall treatment time. Different tumour types require different doses of radiotherapy. Different tissues in the body have varying sensitivity to irradiation and great care is taken to avoid overdosing sensitive organs such as the spinal cord, the kidneys, the lungs and the heart. The aim of radiation is to destroy tumour cells effectively while causing minimum damage to normal tissue. Both normal and malignant cells are damaged by radiation, but normal tissue generally repairs itself well after moderate doses of radiation damage while malignant cells, once damaged, tend to die.

Damage to normal tissues has been found to occur more often when relatively large daily doses of treatment are delivered over a relatively small number of days. The maximum dose of radiotherapy that can be tolerated by most body tissues is of the order of 60Gy (Gray) in thirty treatments (called fractions) given at the daily dose of 2Gy on five days per week for a six-week course of treatment. This type of radiotherapy course is given to tumours such as breast cancer, primary bone tumours, and prostate or bladder cancer. Other forms of malignant disease such as lymphoma can be cured by lower doses of irradiation such as 40Gy delivered in twenty daily fractions over four weeks. Small volumes such as the prostate can tolerate slightly higher carefully focussed doses.

When radiotherapy is used to treat metastatic cancer, shorter courses of treatment are given to alleviate symptoms such as pain from bone metastases or breathlessness caused by compression of the breathing tubes. In these circumstances, doses of the order of 20Gy in five treatments over five to seven days or 30Gy in ten treatments over two weeks are customary and often effective.

The dose of irradiation needed to kill many cancer cells lies very close to the dose that may cause irrevocable damage to normal tissue. This relationship is described as the "therapeutic ratio". Radiotherapy damage may be acute, occurring during the course of treatment, or long term. Often very marked acute reactions develop into long term or late effects. Damage caused by the effect of irradiation on the lining of blood vessels can lead to narrowing of these vessels and later reduction of blood supply to normal tissues. Tissues starved of oxygen will transform into scar tissue and lose their special functions. For example the bowel wall will lose both its elasticity and the ability to absorb fluids and nutrients. The margin between cure and toxicity in radiotherapy treatment is often quite narrow. In some circumstances a deliberate decision is taken to sacrifice some degree of normal function for the sake of an increased chance of eradicating the tumour altogether and curing the patient. This type of decision needs the full understanding and cooperation of the patient and appropriately informed consent. When such a decision is taken without proper consent and the patient subsequently finds that he or she has been damaged, complaint or legal action may follow.

Examples of radiotherapy toxicity which have led to legal action include damage to the nerves of the arm (brachial plexus) and to the lymphatic drainage of the arm resulting in swelling of the arm (lymphoedema) following radiotherapy for breast cancer, and severe pelvic scarring after irradiation of the cervix (see specific tumours below).

Chemotherapy

Chemotherapy is the use of cytotoxic (cell killing) chemicals, which are usually delivered into an accessible vein and circulate throughout the body in the blood stream. This form of treatment is appropriate when cancer is either known to have the potential for spread or has already spread to sites beyond the primary cancer. The choice of chemotherapeutic agents depends on evidence from research as to which agents are most effective in which disease types. Cytotoxic chemotherapy works by attacking the cancer cells at various stages of the cell cycle. Different agents interfere with cell metabolism at different stages of the cell cycle.

Broadly speaking, chemotherapy attacks dividing cells, and for this reason the side effects of chemotherapy tend to be seen in those tissues of the body which divide most rapidly. The cells of the bone marrow which produce white blood cells and platelets, the cells lining the intestines and mouth, and the cells of the hair follicles normally divide rapidly in the body and therefore manifest toxicity from chemotherapy. Most chemotherapy agents cause delay in the production of those cells which protect the body from infection. This renders the patient more vulnerable to infection during chemotherapy. Damage to the proliferating cells of the bowel wall causes nausea, diarrhoea and mouth ulcers. Damage to hair follicles results in the hair thinning or being temporarily lost altogether.

The risk/benefit ratio of cytotoxic chemotherapy has to be assessed individually for each patient. Typical benefits will be the prolongation of life and reduction of symptoms due to disease. Typical drawbacks will be treatment toxicity, loss of quality of life and disruption of employment and family life during the period of chemotherapy. Many patients, especially young patients and parents of young children, will accept quite severe side effects for a few months for the chance of a likely cure of their disease. However, if there is little potential benefit, side effects will be less acceptable.

Many types of chemotherapy are delivered on a monthly basis for a period of six months, but there are many exceptions to this general rule.

Tumour types which tend to be sensitive to and potentially cured by chemotherapy are for example high grade non Hodgkin's lymphoma, seminoma and some forms of ovarian and breast cancer, together with some juvenile bone tumours and leukaemia. Some tumours that are less sensitive to currently available chemotherapy are non-small cell lung cancer, many bowel cancers, pancreatic cancer and melanoma.

Biological Treatments

Over the last few years new forms of "biological" treatments such as immuno-therapy and targeted antibody therapy have extended the range of therapeutic options. For example, patients with high levels of "HER2 receptors" on the surface of the breast cancer cell may benefit from Herceptin (targeted antibody) infusion into the vein. This antibody treatment is often combined with chemotherapy in patients with recurrent disease. Similarly the antibody treatment "Mabthera" is also combined with chemotherapy in some lymphomas. Many other experimental forms of therapy are on the horizon, emerging from the development of the new specialty of "genomics". (Developments from understanding of our genetic programming).

SPECIFIC CANCERS

Breast cancer

Incidence

Breast cancer is the commonest form of malignant disease affecting women in the western world. It accounts for about 18% of all female cancers. Although mortality rates are declining in some countries, it remains the leading cause of death in the U.K. among women aged 35-55 years. (The incidence of lung cancer among women is climbing and may overtake breast cancer incidence soon as the population of young women who started smoking at a young age reach their middle years.) In the U.K. breast cancer causes about 15,000 deaths each year, and about 25,000 cases are diagnosed annually.

The age-specific incidence of breast cancer increases with age and it is not well understood that this means that the incidence rises steadily in old age. Approximately 50% of breast cancers occur in women aged 50-64 years and a further 30% occur in women over the age of 70 years.

Presentation and diagnosis

Breast cancer can develop in any of the four quarters, or quadrants, of the breast but is slightly more common in the upper outer quadrant of either breast. The commonest findings at presentation are those of a lump or of dimpling in the skin due to retraction of the skin by the tendrils of the underlying tumour. An eczema-like rash appearing adjacent to the nipple can represent the extension of tumour cells through the milk ducts onto the skin surface (known as Paget's disease). Pain is rarely associated with early breast cancer.

Since the advent of breast screening using mammography and breast ultrasound there has been enormous improvement in the early diagnosis of breast cancer. It is worth knowing that breast cancer can be visualised as a characteristic stellate (star-shaped) mass or as clusters of tiny flecks of calcium (microcalcification) with a characteristic malignant pattern seen on mammography. However, some breast cancers are not readily seen on mammography and may be picked up by breast ultrasound. Some more unusual tumours, such as lobular carcinoma, may not appear distinct from surrounding breast tissue and can be difficult to diagnose with either mammography or ultrasound. This illustrates the importance of breast screening combining the examination skills of an experienced health professional with the diagnostic scope of radiography and ultrasound.

Unfortunately some patients undergoing mammography that reveals no abnormality can be falsely reassured when, although a tumour is actually present, it is not detectable by mammogram.

Recently Magnetic Resonance Imaging (MRI) has found a useful place in breast examination especially in the breast containing a cosmetic implant when other examinations have difficulty visualising "behind" the implant.

Treatment Options

Most breast tumours in the United Kingdom are now removed by wide local excision (removal of the lump and surrounding tissue only). However, removal of the entire breast (mastectomy) may still be appropriate in certain circumstances. If, for example, a breast tumour is relatively large, (of the order of 3 to 4 cm), in a very small breast, the cosmetic result of local excision will be very unsatisfactory and mastectomy may be preferable with or without breast reconstruction. Locally advanced tumours, which are nonetheless confined to the breast with a clear margin of normal tissue beneath them, can still most safely be treated by mastectomy.

Following removal of the tumour and a margin of surrounding normal tissue, (which is standard practice) there remains an approximately 30% risk of recurrent tumour developing within the same breast. For this reason post operative radiotherapy is normally carried out. Results for wide local excision with irradiation are identical to the results of mastectomy in terms of overall survival and local recurrence. Postoperative radiotherapy does not totally eradicate the risk of further cancer recurring in the breast, but greatly reduces this possibility.

In the past the main lymphatic channels were removed as far as was surgically feasible, via an incision in the armpit. These channels drain the breast via a chain of lymph nodes extending from the upper outer part of the breast, through the armpit and up to the base of the neck. This procedure was in the past carried out for two reasons: first, to remove any tumour which was present in the lymph nodes; and second, because it gave information about the potential of the individual tumour to spread beyond the breast, which was relevant to the choice of further treatment. Patients who have proven involvement of three or more lymph nodes have been shown to benefit from preventative or "adjuvant" chemotherapy. Chemotherapy given after surgery destroys microscopic tumour cells lurking elsewhere in the body which have already been shed from the primary tumour. This prevents their subsequent development into eventual metastases that may ultimately prove fatal. Until recently adjuvant chemotherapy has been principally offered to the relatively young pre-menopausal patient. However, because of the proven benefit in these patients the use of adjuvant chemotherapy has been extended to treat older patients who favour this approach.

More recently, surgeons have developed a technique known as "sentinel node biopsy", which is proving useful in assessing lymph node involvement without the need to remove all the lymph nodes under the arm. Either blue dye or a small dose of radioactive isotope is injected beneath the skin close to the tumour, and the drainage channel is traced at the time of surgery. The first 2-4 lymph nodes found to drain the dye or radioactive tracer will also be the first stop for cancer cells spreading from the tumour. Removal and analysis of these "sentinel lymph nodes", in experienced surgical and histological hands, permits the risk of axillary lymph node spread to be accurately assessed and full axillary dissection to be carried out only on those patients who do have axillary node involvement. Many patients are spared the more extensive surgery and possible complications of full axillary dissection.

Legally important issues in the management of breast cancer.

The commonest complaints relate to delayed diagnosis of breast cancer and damage caused to the patient by the side-effects of treatment. These are considered in turn.

(i) Delay in diagnosis

- Unnecessary delay in the diagnosis of breast cancer can deprive the patient of an opportunity for cure, or result in the need for other or more aggressive treatments than would otherwise have been necessary. Delay can occur at any level and mistakes can occur at each stage of diagnosis and treatment.
- The General Practitioner who fails to examine patients adequately or to take seriously a woman's anxiety may deprive the patient of the opportunity either of immediate diagnosis or for referral to an appropriate Breast Assessment Centre where the proper diagnosis could be established.
- Radiologically identifiable cancers can be missed on mammography (see the chapter on radiology).

Breast surgeons may accept the evidence of benign cytology and apparently benign mammographic appearances and decide against removal of a single breast lump, which ultimately proves to contain malignant cells.

(ii) Negligent treatment of breast cancer

Surgery

Claims can arise as a result of the inappropriate selection of a surgical procedure (either mastectomy, where more limited surgery was feasible, or inadequate excision of the tumour by limited surgery where mastectomy was preferable). Similarly, inappropriate selection or performance of reconstructive procedures after surgery for breast cancer can result in claims. Inadequate explanation and thus improperly obtained consent may leave the patient angry and disappointed when the cosmetic result is not as good as she anticipated or had been led to expect.

Radiotherapy Toxicity

Damage to normal tissues following irradiation of the breast and lymph node regions can cause gross swelling (lymphoedema) of the arm, and pain and loss of function resulting from nerve damage in the lymph node treatment volume (brachial plexus neuropathy). Following a series of unfortunate and high profile cases of lymphoedema and brachial plexus neuropathy, the use of large fraction sizes, with the danger of increased normal tissue damage, has been discontinued. It was the custom at one time for patients to receive their radiotherapy treatment on five days per fortnight (as opposed to ten treatments per two week period). There was great pressure on radiotherapy treatment machines at that time (as there is today), and this treatment schedule enables two patients to be treated concurrently in place of one.

Claims have arisen as a result of damage to the underlying lung. In order to irradiate breast tissue adequately it is inevitable that some of the ribs and underlying lung will be included in the treatment field and radiation damage will cause scarring and fibrosis in this region. The depth of lung which can be treated without later symptoms is now considered to be of the order of 2 cm. In the past, however, with less accurate planning and less knowledge of radiation effects on normal tissues, depths of 4 cm or more have been irradiated. If such treatment is then followed, as is the custom, by a direct radiotherapy field (boost) to the site of the primary tumour in the breast, the underlying lung may receive unacceptably large doses of irradiation causing scarring and symptoms of breathlessness, cough and fatigue. This damage is irreversible.

Left-sided cancer treatment can also include underlying heart muscle. Narrowing of blood vessels in irradiated heart tissue can lead to later cardiac disease with myocardial infarction and early death. Modern treatment planning now usually enables the heart to be safely excluded from the treatment volume, or permits cardiac protection with lead to be added if necessary.

Cervical cancer

Causation of cervical cancer

The human papilloma virus (HPV), which is transmitted by male sexual partners, has now been clearly established as a critical factor for cervical carcinogenesis (cancer production). Infection of squamous cells in the cervix by the oncogenic HPV sub types (E6 & E7 genes) eventually leads to abnormalities in differentiation and growth. More than 90% of squamous cell cervical cancers contain HPV DNA.

Squamous cell carcinoma of the cervix and its intra-epithelial (premalignant) precursor follow a pattern typical of sexually transmitted disease. The risk of cervical cancer is increased, for example, in prostitutes and in women who have sexual intercourse at a young age. Promiscuous sexual behaviour in male partners is also a risk factor.

Natural history and pattern of spread

Most cervical cancers arise in the mucous membrane overlying the cervical muscle at the junction between the primarily columnar epithelium of the endocervix (cervical canal) and the squamous epithelium of the lower cervix as it protrudes into the upper end of the vagina. This junction is a site of continuous cellular instability and possible pre-malignant change. Virally induced cellular instability developing in this region can progress in time to malignancy. The pre-malignant condition is described as cervical intra-epithelial neoplasia (CIN). The average age of women with CIN is approximately 15 years younger than that of women with invasive cancer, suggesting a slow progression of CIN to invasive carcinoma.

Invasive tumours develop most frequently as a growth protruding from the cervix into the vagina. From the cervix a tumour may extend superiorly to the lower uterus, inferiorly into the vagina or laterally into the broad or utero-sacral ligaments. These are the ligaments by which the uterus is suspended from the pelvic sidewalls in its position in the midline. As the cancer grows the tumour may become fixed to the wall of the pelvis by direct extension or by coalescence of central tumour with adjacent lymph nodes in the pelvis. In late stages the tumour may also extend anteriorly, to involve the bladder, or posteriorly to the rectum.

The cervix has a rich supply of lymphatic channels that drain up to the chain of lymph nodes that follows the large blood vessels from the lower limbs up towards the aorta.

Cervical cancer usually follows a relatively orderly pattern of metastatic progression: initially to primary lymph nodes in the pelvis and then to para-aortic nodes in the abdomen and to distant sites. The most frequent sites of distant spread are the lung, liver and bone.

Classification of premalignant disease

Several systems have been developed for classifying cervical cytological findings (cellular appearances). The commonest used are the dysplasia/CIN system (stages CIN 1, 2 or 3) and the (Papanicolaou system (PAP) class I to IV).

Cervical Screening

The long pre-invasive stage of cervical cancer, the accessibility of the cervix and the sensitivity of cytologic screening, make cervical carcinoma an ideal target for cancer screening. Nations with comprehensive screening programmes have experienced substantial decrease in cervical cancer deaths during the last 60 years.

The incidence of false negative findings on the PAP test is approximately 10-15% in women with invasive cancer, and the accuracy of this test can be improved by ensuring adequate sampling of relevant cells at the squamous columnar junction, described above, as well as the cervical canal. Smears without evidence of both these cell types should be repeated because they may be inaccurate. Patients with abnormal findings on cytologic examination, who do not have obvious cervical lesions should be evaluated by direct inspection (colposcopy) and directed biopsies. Cervical cone biopsy (removal of a circumferential cuff of cervix) is used to diagnose occult (concealed) lesions and is an essential step in the diagnosis and management of micro -invasive carcinoma of the cervix. i.e. the very earliest stages of invasive cancer, thereby preventing the development of established cancer.

Clinical Evaluation of patients with invasive carcinoma

The extent of invasive cervical cancer is evaluated with a detailed history, physical examination, colposcopy and recto-vaginal examination. Many doctors obtain computerised tomography (CT) or magnetic resonance imaging scans to visualise regional lymph nodes, but the accuracy of these studies is compromised by their failure to detect small metastases and because patients with bulky necrotic tumours often have enlarged reactive lymphnodes, i.e. not actually involved by tumour.

Clinical Staging

The most commonly accepted staging system is that of FIGO (International Federation of Gynaecology and Obstetrics staging of carcinoma of the cervix 1994): see Table 1 below.

Prognostic Factors

Although rates of survival and control of pelvic disease in cervical cancer patients reflect FIGO staging, the prognosis is also influenced by a number of tumour characteristics that are not included in the staging system. Tumour diameter is strongly correlated with prognosis for patients treated with radiation or surgery.
Lymph node spread is also an important predictor of prognosis. For example, in patients treated with radical hysterectomy (complete removal of the uterus and surrounding tissues) for stage 1B disease, survival rates are usually reported as 85-95% for patients with negative lymph nodes, and 45 to 55% for those with lymph node metastasis.

TABLE 1 – FIGO STAGING OF CANCER OF THE CERVIX ((AMERICAN CANCER SOCIETY: REVISED 10-21-03)

Stage 0: The tumour is carcinoma in situ. It is very superficial, is found only in the layer of cells lining the cervix, and has not invaded deeper tissues of the cervix.

Stage I: Cancer at this stage has invaded the cervix, but it has not spread anywhere else.
Stage IA: This is the earliest form of stage I. There is a very small amount of cancer, and it is visible only under a microscope.
Stage IB: In this stage, the cancer usually can be seen without a microscope. But this stage also includes cancers that have spread deeper than 5 mm (about 1/5 inch) into connective tissue of the cervix or are wider than 7 mm and can only be detected using a microscope.

Stage II: In this stage, the cancer has spread beyond the cervix to nearby areas, but it is still inside the pelvic area.
Stage IIA: The cancer has spread beyond the cervix to the upper part of the vagina. It is not in the lower third of the vagina.
Stage IIB: The cancer has spread to the tissue next to the cervix, called the parametrial tissue.

Stage III: The cancer has spread to the lower part of the vagina or the pelvic wall. The cancer may be blocking the ureters (tubes that carry urine from the kidneys to the bladder).
Note: In the alternative staging system TNM stage III is defined by the fact that the cancer has spread to lymph nodes in the pelvis.

Stage IV: This is the most advanced stage of cervical cancer. The cancer has spread to nearby organs or other parts of the body.

Treatment

A number of factors may influence the choice of treatment, including tumour size, stage, histological features, evidence of lymph node involvement, risk factors for complications of surgery or radiation, and patient preference. As a rule, however, early (intra epithelial) lesions are treated with superficial removal techniques, and micro- invasive cancers invading less than 3mm (stage 1A1) are managed with conservative surgery.

Early invasive cancers (stages 1A2 and 1B1) and small stage 2A tumours are managed with radical surgery and radiotherapy

Locally advanced cancers, stages 1B2 through to 4A, are managed with radiotherapy alone.

If the tumour recurs, selected patients with centrally recurrent disease (after maximum doses of radiotherapy) may successfully be treated with radical surgery. Pelvic recurrence after hysterectomy can be treated with irradiation.

The results of randomised trials have led to the use of chemotherapy, including the cytotoxic drug Cisplatin, together with radiotherapy for patients whose cancers have a high risk of local or regional recurrence.

The standard surgical treatment for stage 1B and stage 2A cervical cancer is radical hysterectomy and bilateral pelvic lymph node removal. This procedure involves complete removal of the uterus and the cervix, right out to the pelvic side-walls, with removal of as much as the posterior ligaments as possible. For women younger than 40 to 45 years the ovaries are usually not removed since this tumour is not hormonally influenced and it is therefore safe to leave these in place.

Serious complications may occur either during, or immediately after, radical hysterectomy. These may include blood loss, the formation of a fistula (communicating hole) between the bladder and the vagina, small bowel obstruction, postoperative fever with deep vein thrombosis, and pulmonary embolus (blood clot in the lungs). Other possible complications include lung infection, pelvic cellulitis (infection), urinary tract infection or wound infection. Later swelling of the legs can occur as a result of removal of the lymph nodes responsible for drainage of the lower limbs. The risk of such complications may be increased in patients who receive pre-operative or postoperative irradiation.

Although most patients have transient decreased bladder sensation after radical hysterectomy, with appropriate management severe long-term bladder complications are infrequent. However chronic bladder hypotonia (loss of elasticity and muscle tone) occurs in approximately 3-5% of patients despite careful post-operative bladder management. Radical hysterectomy can therefore be complicated later by stress incontinence (leakage of urine when coughing or straining). Some patients also experience long lasting constipation. Five-year survival rates following radical hysterectomy for stage 1B carcinoma of the cervix range between 74 and 91%.

Radiotherapy can also achieve good survival and disease control rates in patients with Stage 1B cervical cancers. The reported five-year survival rate varies between 63 and 91%.

As with radical surgery, the goal of radiation treatment is to eradicate disease in the cervix, the surrounding tissues and the regional lymph nodes in the pelvis. Patients are usually treated with a combination of external beam irradiation to the whole pelvis together with brachytherapy. Brachytherapy, or “intra-cavitary” techniques, use radio-active sources placed inside the body (in this case inside the cervix) to deliver high doses of irradiation to surrounding tissues. Doctors balance external and intra-cavitary treatment in different ways for these patients depending on the clinical findings. However, brachytherapy is a critical element in the curative radiation treatment of all carcinomas of the cervix.

Even relatively small tumours of the cervix are usually treated with total doses of 80 to 85Gy.The combination of external beam and intracavitary irradiation allows tumours to receive safely much higher (and more likely curative) doses than could be safely given by external irradiation alone. (The maximum dose by external radiotherapy is usually of the order of 60Gy in 30 treatments over 6 weeks.) However these high doses of treatment also have the potential to cause serious damage.

Traditionally, cervical brachytherapy has been performed with sources that yield a dose rate of approximately 40 to 50 centigray per hour at what is described as point A (which lies 2cm lateral and superior to the opening of the central cervical canal). These low dose rates permit normal tissues to repair and recover, while cancer cells are destroyed and cannot repair themselves.

In an effort to reduce the 3-4 days of hospitalisation necessary to deliver an appropriate dose of brachytherapy, treatment with an intermediate dose rate was investigated. This increase in dose rate resulted in a significant increase in complications (Haie-Meder et al 1994).

During the past two decades, however, computer technology has made it possible to deliver brachytherapy safely at a very high dose rate using high activity Cobalt or Iridium 192 sources and "remote after loading". Using this technique, empty tubes are placed in the correct position within and adjacent to the cervix and their position checked by x-ray. The empty tubes are subsequently loaded with the radioactive sources by remote control. This technique has the great advantage that patients can attend as outpatients, and do not require admission. Published experience suggests that survival rates are roughly similar to those achieved with traditional low dose rate treatment. The use of high dose rate brachytherapy for cervical cancer continues, however, to be controversial.

Disseminated disease is almost always incurable. The care of patients with such disease centres on the palliation of symptoms with appropriate pain medication and localised radiotherapy. Tumours may respond to chemotherapy but responses are usually short.

The effort to eradicate more advanced stages of cervical cancer from the centre of the pelvis has inevitably led to the delivery of high doses of radiation to surrounding normal tissues. As in other parts of the body, high doses of radiotherapy can lead to the replacement of specialised tissues by scar tissue and narrowing of the blood vessels that supply normal tissues. This in turn leads to further late scarring and loss of function of specialised tissues such as the bladder and bowel. Thus in severe cases the other organs in the pelvis can be severely damaged by radiotherapy. Loops of small bowel occasionally lie behind the uterus and may receive a high dose. This can result in stenosis (narrowing and loss of elasticity) of the bowel. The rectum is positioned immediately behind the cervix and is vulnerable to a very high dose with resulting damage. Occasionally a recto-vaginal fistula (hole between the rectum and vagina) will result from this tissue damage. This complication is more likely when the cancer has invaded the recto vaginal septum (wall) and the tumour is destroyed by the effect of radiation, leaving a hole.

Similarly, scarring of the bladder can lead to loss of elasticity leaving a shrunken, scarred, poorly functioning bladder that causes great distress. The normal pliable pelvic tissues that surround the cervix can also be replaced by profuse scar tissue which is then described as a " wooden" or "frozen" pelvis.

Symptomatically the effects of normal tissue damage can be very unpleasant indeed. The patient may suffer from leakage of bowel contents via the vagina (recto vaginal fistula), obstruction of the small or large bowel, urinary frequency and incontinence with likelihood of bladder infection, vaginal narrowing (stenosis) preventing sexual intercourse, and pelvic inflammatory disease with associated pain and occasionally fever. Unfortunately there is no effective treatment available to reverse the effects of radiation damage.

Legal issues in the management of cervical cancer

The most important issues are delay in diagnosis (especially resulting from the faulty interpretation of cervical smears), and damage resulting from the treatment. These are considered in turn.

(i) Delay in diagnosis

The main issue that has given rise to claims is the faulty interpretation of cervical smears. A number of high profile cases have illustrated the unfortunate consequences of missed diagnosis. False reassurance arising from failure to report abnormal cells can afford the opportunity for disease to develop unrecognised.

However, these cases have also highlighted the intensive nature of the work of cytopathologists who read large numbers of cervical smears. This work is both intensive and repetitive, and the scope for human error is unfortunately considerable. Whether there has been negligence in such cases will obviously depend on the individual facts. No useful general guidance can be given.

(ii) Damage resulting from treatment

A second and important group of cases concerned the long-term effects of irradiation to the pelvis. The late sequelae (effects) of treatment such as the bowel and bladder damage described above have been devastating for some patients, and even though they have been cured of their disease and have achieved long-term survival their quality of life has been very severely reduced as a result of treatment.

Damage is sometimes avoidable without any diminution in the therapeutic benefit of the treatment. Often, though, it is the result of a taking a calculated risk – balancing the potential benefits and risks of aggressive treatment, and the obvious risks of non-treatments. It is not necessarily negligent for the calculation to be wrong.

ISSUES OF COMMUNICATION

Because cancer is known to progress with time, the perceived negligence of doctors in failing to deal correctly and urgently with cancer investigation and referral is a recurring theme in oncology. However, underlying a complaint of delay in diagnosis is often the patient's or the family's inability to come to terms with the diagnosis. This refusal to come to terms with the situation creates a sense of agitation and injustice. The patient may feel "it must be someone's fault" and pursue a claim in negligence as a result.

The public tends to believe that delayed diagnosis always makes a difference. Government guidelines stress the importance of reduced waiting times for cancer referral and treatment. Screening programmes claim to saves lives by early diagnosis. When a case is investigated, however, an expert witness will frequently assert that although delay did occur the impact of this delay on survival was in fact negligible. For the layman this discrepancy between the general and the particular case is difficult to understand. The explanation lies either in the fact that the disease was inherently aggressive and untreatable whenever the diagnosis was made, or that the delay occurred during a stage which was not critical to future prognosis.

Problems of communication arise very frequently in oncology. Most malignant disease carries a serious prognosis, with far reaching implications for work, family, fertility, physical and emotional distress and issues of inheritance. The working environment in busy wards or clinics where time is at a premium is not conducive to the private, gentle, sympathetic communication of bad news which is the ideal. Patients who perceive that the doctor is either uninterested in their welfare, unsympathetic or poorly informed in the subject can become irritated, angry and alienated. The perception that the patient has no control over their situation and no access to information about their disease and its consequences leads to a sense of dissatisfaction and grievance.

Until recently doctors have not been trained in communication skills and patient accounts of rude, sketchy, hasty and unsympathetic consultations are unfortunately all too common.

Also the concepts of treatment options, survival statistics, risks and benefits and randomised clinical trials are difficult to convey in an understandable way to a lay person. Misunderstandings are not uncommon, and if handled unhelpfully can lead on to complaint and the legal process.

Many oncological treatments are both complicated and risky and the possibility of mistakes is considerable. When things go wrong the patient or their family can very quickly feel aggrieved and litigious if an explanation and expression of regret is not speedily forthcoming.

Similarly in the process of obtaining consent the complexities of treatment, and especially the anticipated side effects, need very careful explanation. Patients frequently pursue a complaint when they feel that they were not given adequate information – especially information which might have led them to decline a treatment which subsequently caused damage.

CANCER WRONGLY DIAGNOSED OR WRONGLY COMMUNICATED

Occasionally a diagnosis of cancer is made in error. The circumstances may seem to be an emergency - for example when a serious infection mimics the rapid evolution of cancer and early treatment is considered essential. The unintended sequelae may be devastating for the patient. One case which was widely reported in the press illustrates the point. It concerned a man in whom advanced bladder cancer was diagnosed. As a result this patient was given a very adverse prognosis and decided to sell his property and use his savings to travel around the world in what he thought were the last few weeks of his life. On his return it became evident that his disease was in fact non malignant, and that his life expectancy was much greater than he had been told to expect. The patient sued his professional advisers in negligence on the basis that he would not have spent his savings had he been given the correct information. This case was settled out of court but serves as a timely reminder for practising oncologists to verify the pathological diagnosis of cancer before proceeding to treatment.

In recent years the MDU reports that inappropriate diagnoses among settled hospital claims have totalled 44 of which 14 were false negative and 30 false positive cases. (MDU 2003)

LEGALLY IMPORTANT ISSUES IN CHEMOTHERAPY

Claims involving chemotherapy may arise from inappropriate selection of treatment drugs, over dosage of chemotherapy agents, inadequate information concerning treatment toxicity which would have enabled the patient to decline such treatment, administration of the wrong agent, wrong route of administration and damage caused by faulty intravenous administration with local tissue damage. (extravasation). Some of the issues involving the side effects of chemotherapy given for specific cancers have been discussed above.

Inadequate institution or maintenance of safe procedures are fertile sources of claims. Very often when mistakes occur, they result not from a single error but from a whole series of incidents which although not inherently serious themselves add up eventually to a disaster.

One such case concerned the sequence of events in 1999 that resulted in the mistaken injection of the "corrosive" drug Vincristine into the spinal cord of a 12 year old patient with leukaemia by a specialist registrar in paediatric anaesthesia. This event followed a series of departures from normal practice and it was ultimately realised that "significant systems failures within the hospital administration" were important factors in the boy's death. (Ferner RE 2003) Sadly, despite the report of an expert group chaired by the Chief Medical Officer which was intended to lay down guidelines to prevent such mistakes, the mistake was repeated at the Queen's Medical Centre Nottingham in 2003 (Editorial BMJ 2003) This mistake was the 23rd incident in the UK, and the 14th in 15 years, in which this drug had been mistakenly and fatally injected into the spine.

REFERENCES

Baum, M and Schipper, H, *Breast Cancer: Fast Facts*, 2nd Edition 2003, Health Press, Oxford

Editorial: The criminalisation of fatal medical mistakes, *BMJ*, 327:1118-9

Ferner, RE, 2000 Medication errors that have led to manslaughter charges, *BMJ*, 321: 1212-16

Haie-Meder, C, Kramar, A, Lambin, P *et al*, Analysis of complications in a prospective randomised trial comparing two brachytherapy low dose rates in cervical carcinoma, *Int J Radiat Oncol Biol Phys*, 1994; 29: 1195

Personal Communication, Medical Defence Union, Risk Management Department, 2003

Risk management analyst personal communication, National Health Service Litigation Authority (NHSLA), 2004

DERMATOLOGY

John Cotterill

INTRODUCTION

Doctors are sued for many reasons[1]. Dermatologists are no exception.

This chapter draws on data supplied by the Medical Defence Union relating to 293 of their dermatological cases and on data from the National Health Service Litigation Authority relating to 176 cases from April 1995 until August 2003. It also takes into account 30 legal claims involving Scottish National Health Service dermatology departments from 1989-2001.[2] These data are analysed in Figures 1-5 (see appendix I). The MDU data include actual and potential claims, and for those purposes the potential claims include patient complaints. The cases can be divided into six broad categories: problems related to ultraviolet light, to medication, cryotherapy, (mostly with liquid nitrogen), surgery, failure to diagnose the underlying condition, and a miscellaneous group. There are significant differences between the MDU figures (which of course include a high proportion of claims relating to private work) and the NHS figures. For instance, the number of claims received by the MDU relating to adverse effects following treatment with ultraviolet light is miniscule compared to the number of claims in the NHS sector. Problems following the use of liquid nitrogen accounted for a fifth of Scottish claims, whilst the overall figure was only 3%.

COMMUNICATION

In the MDU series about 5% of cases were related directly to communication problems which included allegations about attitude and rudeness, breaches of confidentiality, problems over obtaining proper consent and delays with appointments.

Good communication is essential and vital to minimising the risk of being sued.[3] It is a stressful experience for some people to consult their doctor and, indeed, it may be a stressful experience for the doctor seeing difficult patients. During the

---

[1] Vincent, C, Young, M and Phillips, A, Why do people sue doctors? A study of patients and relatives taking legal action, *Lancet*, 1994; 343 : 1609-13.

[2] Drummond, A, Kane, D and Bilsland, D, Epidemiology in health services research, Legal claims in Scottish National Health Service Dermatology Departments, 1989 – 2001, *Br J Dermatol*, 2003; 149 : 111 – 114.

[3] Cotterill, JA, Medico-legal aspects of dermatology, In: Rook Wilkinson Ebling, *Textbook of Dermatology*, 7th edition, Ed. Champion, RH, Burton, JL, Burns, DA and Breathnach, SM, 2004, Blackwell Science, Oxford, 71, 19-23.

consultation verbal information is easily forgotten. When communicating with individual patients it is very important to back up verbal communication with good non-verbal communication. Establishing good eye contact with the patient is important.[4] If the patient is not able to sustain good eye contact during the consultation this may indicate psychological or psychiatric problems. The advantages and disadvantages of any proposed medication or procedure must be explained frankly. Data sheets are vital and consent must be adequately informed. It is not appropriate, therefore, to wave a consent form at a patient just before he/she is due to have a general anaesthetic. The patient must be given time to reflect on any therapeutic proposals. It is not good practice, therefore, to see a patient and five minutes later carry out a major cosmetic procedure such as skin resurfacing.

The importance of keeping very good comprehensive, legible and legally complete clinical notes on each patient cannot be stressed too highly.[5]

FAILURE TO DIAGNOSE

This was a problem in almost 22% of cases overall, and in claims involving the National Health Service Litigation Authority (NHSLA) the figure was 26.7% (See Figure 4, Appendix I).

DELAYED DIAGNOSIS

This is most likely in patients with rare disorders but may also occur in patients with more common disorders, such as malignant melanoma, presenting in an atypical way.

MALIGNANT MELANOMA

Delayed diagnosis of malignant melanoma: delays in consultation

There are many pitfalls in the diagnosis of malignant melanoma. The patient may delay in seeking medical advice, particularly if the initial lesion is, to their mind, inconspicuous and occurring on a body area which is not readily visible. It is recognised that men are slower to come forward with malignant melanomas than women. At some stage the patient will consult his/her general practitioner and at this initial consultation a diagnosis of malignant melanoma may or may not be made. Usually a request is sent to the local consultant dermatologist asking for an urgent appointment because of a change in a mole. This change may have been an increase in size, a change in pigment, bleeding, itching or ulceration. Fortunately, most of the pigmented lesions referred to a consultant dermatologist's clinic are absolutely benign lesions, the commonest pathology being a pigmented basal cell

[4] Cotterill, JA, Damage limitation in cosmetic dermatology, *J Cos Dermatol*, 2002, 1, 211-213
[5] See above, footnotes 3 and 4.

papilloma (seborrhoeic wart). In the UK the consultant dermatologist is now expected to see any patient with possible malignant disease within two weeks[6] and many dermatologists have become overwhelmed by the large volume of patients with pigmented lesions referred to them. Nearly 20% of such patients do not attend when given an initial urgent appointment,[7] which is a significant destabilising factor in trying to run this type of clinic. Moreover, general practitioners often wrongly diagnose melanoma and squamous cell carcinoma. Thus, only one patient had a diagnosis of melanoma confirmed out of 26 patients referred urgently with this diagnosis.[8]

The referral letter from the general practitioner is of crucial importance and it is vital that all referral letters are seen and read by the consultant dermatologist. The task should not be delegated to members of the administrative staff as this can lead to significant appointment delays in patients with malignant melanoma. If the general practitioner requests an urgent opinion from a consultant dermatologist about a possible malignant melanoma, the consultant dermatologist should do his/her best to see the patient within two weeks.[9] If, because of sheer volume of work, the consultant dermatologist is unable to see such patients urgently, the dermatologist should bring this problem to the attention of the Chief Executive of the employing Trust in writing as soon as possible, keeping a copy for future reference. If reasonable progress cannot be made because of inadequate staffing, support should be solicited from local and regional colleagues, the British Association of Dermatologists and from the Royal College of Physicians. Advice should also be sought from whichever medical defence organisation the dermatologist is a member of.

Special care should be taken by the administrative staff when sending appointments to potential patients whose first language may not be English. The writer has been involved in one medico-legal case where there was a very significant delay in the patient being seen with a malignant melanoma, because of language difficulties.

Difficulties in the clinical diagnosis of malignant melanoma

Malignant melanoma can be very difficult to diagnose, not only in clinical dermatological practice, but also by pathologists. Clinically, malignant melanoma may mimic, superficially at least, many other commoner conditions. The verrucous malignant melanoma, which mimics almost perfectly a basal cell

[6] Roberts, DLL, Anstey, AV, Barlow, RJ and Cox, NH (on behalf of the British Association of Dermatologists) and Newton Bishop, JA, Corrie, PG, Evans, J, Gore, ME, Hall, PN and Kirkham, N (on behalf of the Melanoma Study Group), UK Guidelines for the Management of Cutaneous Melanoma, *Br J Dermatol*, 2002, 146 : 7-17.
[7] Bottomley, WW and Cotterill, JA, An audit of the factors involved in new patient non-attendance in a dermatology out-patients department, *Clin & Exp Dermatol*, 1994; 19 : 399-400.
[8] Thomson, MA, Lotfeld, A and Marsden, JR, The quality and accuracy of two week skin cancer referrals, *Br J Dermatol*, 2003; 149 (suppl. 64): 28-29.
[9] See above, footnote 6.

papilloma in its clinical appearances, is a pitfall for the unwary. To the inexperienced eye a bleeding malignant melanoma may at times resemble the commoner benign clinical condition, pyogenic granuloma, and even be diagnosed as a vascular tumour, such as an angioma. The fact that a malignant melanoma at times may be amelanotic (non-pigmented) can also cause considerable clinical difficulties. Moreover, a pigmented dermatofibroma, a relatively common lesion on the legs, especially of women, may give rise to diagnostic difficulties. In particular, inappropriate treatment may be given to a malignant melanoma in the mistaken belief that the patient merely has a dermatofibroma.

Currently there is a 7-point check list with major and minor features which underline a history of change in size, shape and colour in an already existing pigmented lesion. These features are listed below.

Major Features
- Change in shape, size or colour

Minor Features
- Diameter > 7 mm
- Redness, bleeding, oozing, itching
- Lesions suspicious of malignant melanoma
- with any one of the major or three of the minor features

The writer considers that the diagnosis of a malignant melanoma cannot always be made clinically. The diagnosis is obvious in a "barn door" case where all the obvious clinical features are present. However, the writer has seen absolutely innocent looking, clinically benign compound naevi, turn out to be malignant melanomas pathologically. This fact underlines the importance of sending any lesion removed from the skin for histology.

Any patient suspected of having a malignant melanoma should be referred urgently to a consultant dermatologist, surgeon or plastic surgeon, choosing whichever local specialist has the shortest out-patient wait.[10] If the lesion has been excised by a general practitioner the patient should be referred urgently to either a consultant dermatologist or plastic surgeon.

As a minimum, the UK Guidelines for the Management of Malignant Melanoma recommend noting and recording the clinical features shown below.

History
Change in size, colour, shape and symptoms of bleeding or itching.

Examination
Site size

---

[10] Mackie, RM, Bray, CA and Hole, DJ, Observational study of type of surgical training and outcome of definitive surgery for primary malignant melanoma, *Br Med J*, 2002; 325 ii : 1276-77.

Lesion characteristics, including margins, ulceration and regularity or irregularity of pigmentation, enlarged lymph glands and liver.

Difficulties in the histological diagnosis of malignant melanoma

The writer has seen several instances of delays in diagnosis of malignant melanoma arising after the specimen has been sent for histology. Specimens can be lost in transit to the laboratory or by the laboratory itself. Reports may also be lost in transit or overlooked in the dermatology department. Ideally, the histopathologist should telephone the consultant dermatologist when the diagnosis of malignant melanoma has been confirmed histologically.

In one instance when an adult male patient with a clinically evident malignant melanoma of the trunk returned for follow up, the pathology department reported a benign lesion, (Spitz naevus), a lesion commonly associated with childhood. The reason for this diagnosis was clear when the data available to the histopathologist was examined. This histology form had been completed incorrectly, indicating that the patient was 8 years old. He was actually 38 years old. This case underlines the importance of dates throughout medical practice.

The histopathological diagnosis of malignant melanoma can also be very difficult, but occasionally pathologists misdiagnose malignant melanoma. In the writer's experience, the most common misdiagnosis is that of a squamous cell carcinoma. Such histopathological misdiagnosis invariably leads to inappropriate management and wrong prognosis. In one instance in the writer's experience the problem was not exposed until many years later when the patient developed a secondary deposit from the initial melanoma. That melanoma had been curetted by a locum in the mistaken belief that the patient had a pyogenic granuloma. It was then misdiagnosed by the histopathologist as a squamous cell carcinoma.

Histopathological recommendations for the reporting of skin lesions removed on the suspicion of being malignant melanoma have been published in an international consensus statement which includes a revised staging system.[11] The Breslaw thickness of the tumour measured from the base of the tumour to the granular layer of the epidermis to the nearest 0.1 mm is an important prognostic indicator. The depth of penetration into the dermis (Clark's level) is also useful, although this is a less reliable indicator of prognosis than the Breslaw thickness in most patients.[12]

UK guidelines have been issued for definitive treatment of the primary lesion[5] including the recommended investigations for patients with melanoma and management of patients with metastatic disease.

---

[11] Association of Directors of Anatomic and Surgical Pathology, Recommendations for the reporting of tissues removed as part of the surgical treatment of cutaneous melanoma, *Pathol Int*, 1998; 48 : 168-70.

[12] See above, footnote 6.

Prognosis in Malignant Melanoma

It is generally agreed that the prognosis in malignant melanoma depends on the initial thickness of the lesion. Early diagnosis is therefore vital. There is no effective cure once the lesion has metastasised. The effect of delay in diagnosis, and treatment on the prognosis is often the central issue in many medico-legal cases involving malignant melanoma. Useful data on prognosis can be obtained from prognostic trees.[13] A recent study of the long term survival rates of patients with malignant melanoma achieved by the end of the 20th Century using a period analysis, gave 20-year relative survival rates of more than 80% for melanomas.[14]

SCABIES

Scabies, a relatively common dermatological problem, can also present considerable diagnostic difficulties. The prevalence of scabies used to follow roughly 30-year cycles. This meant that many practitioners qualified in medicine without having seen a patient with scabies. For instance, the writer only saw one patient with scabies during his medical training. That patient was such a rarity that he was admitted to a hospital ward and left untreated for two weeks so that as many students and other doctors as possible could see the condition. Such medical management would not be tolerated now.

It is always wise to remember the old adage that the commonest cause of the itch (scabies) is indeed scabies. Diagnostic difficulties may be encountered in the very early stages of the disease when the patient may present with itching, but with no clinical signs of any skin disease despite very careful examination. For instance, a teenage boy presented to the writer with generalised pruritus. There was nothing to find either on dermatological or general examination. The patient was seen privately and potentially expensive investigations were undertaken to try and determine why he was so generally itchy. This only became apparent two weeks later when the classical burrows of scabies became readily visible in his finger clefts. The writer received a letter from the patient's father saying that he had no intention of paying my fee because of "negligence"

Scabies may also present difficulties in two other clinical contexts: when presenting with nodules, and in patients with so-called Norwegian or crusted scabies. With regard to the nodules, if these are biopsied and sent to a pathologist without the correct clinical diagnosis being indicated on the pathology form, the pathologist may send a report back indicating that the patient has lymphoma. The writer has seen one patient for medico-legal purposes who went on to be treated with quadruple cytotoxic therapy on two occasions and because of this failed

[13] Aitchison, TC, Sirel, JM, Watt, DC and MacKie, RM, The Scottish Melanoma Group, Prognostic trees to aid diagnosis in patients with cutaneous malignant melanoma, *Br Med J*, 1995; 311 : 1536-1539.
[14] Brenner, H, Long term survival rates of cancer patients achieved by the end of the 20th Century: a period analysis, *Lancet*, 2002; 360: 1131-35.

treatment he eventually agreed to have a bone marrow transplant. The correct diagnosis was made in the nick of time by an experienced ward sister who examined the patient following his admission to the ward for the bone marrow transplant.

Crusted or Norwegian scabies can mimic psoriasis to the untutored eye. Norwegian scabies is relatively common in geriatric institutions where an individual undiagnosed case may be responsible for scores, or even hundreds, of cases of scabies amongst other patients and staff. Individuals with severely compromised immunity, most commonly patients with AIDS, may also present with Norwegian scabies.

The clinical diagnosis of scabies may be difficult in individuals with an African or Afro-Caribbean skin, and also in patients taking steroids.

PYODERMA GANGRENOSUM

Pyoderma gangrenosum is a relatively rare, rapidly evolving ulcerative condition of the skin, sometimes associated with other diseases such as collagen vascular disease and paraproteinaemias. Classically, the patient presents to the Casualty department with what is often thought initially to be an infected insect bite. Antibiotics are prescribed but the area ulcerates. Plastic or even orthopaedic surgeons may be involved in the subsequent management. The patient subsequently undergoes excision and skin grafting but the skin graft breaks down rapidly. The skin grafting procedure may be repeated on or two or more occasions with the same bad result. It is usually only at this stage that a dermatologist is called in to advise. Unfortunately there is no specific histology in this condition so the diagnosis is made clinically and the condition responds relatively rapidly to oral steroids, but there may be delay in diagnosis of many weeks or even months in some patients who may be left with extensive scarring.

FAILURE TO WARN OF THE RISKS OF TREATMENT: THE EXAMPLE OF LIQUID NITROGEN

Overall, there were only 15 cases in the series examined in which there were allegations of adverse effects following liquid nitrogen treatment. In percentage terms this was a much more significant problem in Scotland. It was an issue in only 4 claimants in the MDU (private) series. Liquid nitrogen is used to treat a wide variety of lesions on the skin. It is commonly used to treat warts, and solar keratoses in particular.

Blistering in a treated area, which can become haemorrhagic, can be a worrying complication to patients if not adequately warned about this likely outcome. All patients receiving liquid nitrogen treatment should be informed of this risk and should be given an information sheet informing them to expect this complication and how to deal with it if it arises. Over-aggressive treatment with liquid nitrogen can lead to both peripheral nerve damage and to significant scarring.

In the writer's experience problems have mostly arisen when the liquid nitrogen treatment has been carried out by a general practitioner, who usually claims he/she has been trained to treat an individual lesion for a given number of seconds, whatever the size of the lesion. The correct technique is to freeze the lesion, whatever its size, with liquid nitrogen until a 1 mm rim of normal skin around each lesion is also frozen.[15] At that stage the procedure should be stopped. Two freeze-thaw cycles may be employed for thicker lesions. Three techniques are commonly used in cryosurgery. The simplest is the dipstick technique where liquid nitrogen is applied to the lesion using a cotton-tipped applicator. The spray technique has become more popular, whilst the cryoprobe technique is less extensively used and almost always within dermatological or plastic surgical departments. Treating malignant lesions by cryotherapy is best left to those with special expertise in this area and tissue temperature should be monitored during the procedure. With proper technique there should be no significant problems with liquid nitrogen treatment as long as the patient is informed adequately prior to the procedure of the possible complications, (usually pain and discomfort during the procedure and subsequent blistering), and how to deal with them.

PROBLEMS FOLLOWING ULTRAVIOLET LIGHT TREATMENT

Whilst allegations of problems following ultraviolet light treatment had an overall incidence of 11.6%, the number of claims in the private sector was tiny compared to those in the National Health Service, both North and South of the border. The figures indicate that most ultraviolet light treatment, even for private patients, is carried out in NHS facilities. The high incidence of alleged adverse events following ultraviolet light treatment highlights the need for examination of current practices and comprehensive training in phototherapy.

Traditionally, most dermatology departments have trained their staff very carefully over many years but recent modern management practice has led to the introduction of the concept of "skills mix", where nurses in the whole of an outpatient department may be rotated through the various specialties represented in the outpatient department. This unenlightened management culture has led to very inexperienced nurses supervising phototherapy. In addition to adequate training and resistance to skill mix, it is important that evidence- based protocols are established. It is particularly important that electrical safety and calibration checks are carried out and lamp replacement policies established. Meticulous case documentation is also recommended.[16] National calibration standards of PUVA

---

[15] Kuflik, EG, Cryosurgical treatment of cutaneous lesions. In: *Dermatologic Surgery – Principles and Practice,* Ed. Randall K Roenigk and Henry H Roenigk Jr., 1988, Marcel Dekker Inc., New York, p.222-228.

[16] See above, footnote 2.

and UVB have been produced.[17] Phototherapy should not be delegated to another department such as physiotherapy. Dermatological treatment should be carried out in the dermatological department where well trained nursing staff can be medically supervised and readily seek advice in the event of problems.

LEGALLY IMPORTANT ISSUES INVOLVING MEDICATION

Claims involving medication issues formed 31.7% of the total cases. In the private sector the incidence was 39.6%, whilst in the NHS the percentage varied between 19.3% and 26.7%. In terms of absolute numbers this was the largest claim category, accounting for the 158 out of the 499 cases. The major problems involved allegations about the misuse of topical and parenteral corticosteroids, retinoids, methotrexate and drug allergy.

Topical, Oral and Injected Corticosteroids

Topical steroids can cause a wide variety of local problems, including skin atrophy with striae and purpura, but it is less well recognised that both cataracts and glaucoma can follow use on the face, particularly around the eyes.[18 19] Worsening of acne, hair growth, precipitation of acne rosacea and perioral dermatitis may also follow prolonged topical therapy.[20 21 22]

Systemic effects following the use of topical steroids are less common and more likely to be seen when injected or administered orally. Hypothalamic-pituitary adrenal[23] suppression and aseptic necrosis of the femoral neck, especially in alcoholics has been reported.[24]

---

[17] Moseley, H, Scottish UV dosimetry guidelines, *"ScUViDo" Photodermatol Photoimmunol Photomed*, 2001; 17 : 230-3.

[18] Bevis Cubey, R, Glaucoma following the application of corticosteroid to the skin of the eyelids, *Br J Dermatol*, 1976; 95 : 207-208.

[19] Tani Euchi, H, Ohki, O, Yokozeki, H *et al*, Cataract and retinal detachment in patients with severe atopic dermatitis who have withdrawn from the use of topical steroids, *J Dermat*, 1999; 26 : 658-65.

[20] Dawber, RPR, DeBerker, D and Wojnarowska, F, Disorders of Hair, In: Rook, Wilkinson, *Ebling Textbook of Dermatology*, 6th edn. Vol.IV, Ed. Champion, RH, Burton, JL, Burns, DA and Breathnach, FM, 1998, Blackwell Science, Oxford, p.2894.

[21] Cotterill JA Perioral dermatitis, *Br J Dermatol*, 1979; 101 : 259-62.

[22] Leyden JJ, Thew AM, Kligman AM, Steroid rosacea, *Arch Dermatol*, 1974; 110 : 619-22.

[23] Griffiths WAD, Wilkinson JD, Topical therapy, In: Rook, Wilkinson, Ebling, *Textbook of Dermatology*, 6th edn. Vol IV, Ed. Champion, RH, Burton, JL, Burns, DA and Breathnack, FM, 1998, Blackwell Science, Oxford, 3350.

[24] Cunliffe, WJ, Burton, JL, Holti, G and Wright, V, Hazards of steroid therapy in hepatic failure, *Br J Dermatol*, 1975; 93 : 183-5.

Osteoporosis is a particular concern in patients receiving long term oral corticosteroids therapy and guidelines have been suggested in an attempt to prevent this complication.[25 26 27]

Marked localised skin atrophy following the too superficial injection of triamcinalone (Kenalog), in the writer's experience, is a particular problem in general practice. This steroid is sometimes given for hay fever in a dose of 40 mg and should be injected deeply into gluteal muscle.[28] If it is injected too superficially, skin atrophy can occur, causing dimpling. This can be cosmetically significant, particularly in young females. It is important to avoid the same injection site for any future injection given. The injection should not be given into the deltoid area, where skin atrophy is an almost invariable consequence.

Atopic Eczema and Corticosteroids

Every general practitioner and dermatologist is confronted by patients, often children, with atopic eczema which is severe and difficult to control. In an ideal world only a small quantity of a potent topical steroid should be applied once to three times daily until improvement occurs. Maintenance therapy should always be attempted with a less potent topical steroid and with liberally prescribed emollients. Care should be taken not to prescribe topical steroids for an infective skin condition such as impetigo or herpes simplex infection of the skin. There is a particular risk in babies and children of pituitary adrenal suppression, and long term continuous therapy should be avoided where possible, particularly in infants and children. Potent topical steroids should not be used in the flexures (groins, axillae) as skin atrophy (striae) readily occurs.

It must be accepted that in individual patients with severe eczema there is a very difficult therapeutic situation in that the eczema may not be controlled adequately unless relatively large amounts of oral and/or topical steroids are used, with the inevitable side effects that these agents produce. The dermatologist is "damned if he does, and damned if he doesn't" treat such a patient. Without treatment the life of the patient with severe atopic eczema can be totally miserable. With treatment aimed at totally controlling the problem there may be significant side effects such as skin atrophy and telangiectasia, and, if applied to the face, the ultimate development of cataracts and glaucoma. It may be possible to avoid some of these

---

[25] *Glucocorticoid-induced osteoporosis – Guidelines for prevention and treatment*, Prepared by a Working Group in collaboration with the Royal College of Physicians, The Bone and Tooth Society of Great Britain, and the National Osteoporosis Society, Published by the Royal College of Physicians June 2003.

[26] Wojnarowska, F, Kirtschig, G, Highet, AS, Venning, VA and Khumalo, NP, Guidelines for the management of bullous pemphigoid, *Br J Dermatol*, 2002; 147 : 214-221.

[27] Chave, TA, Mortimer, NJ, Neal, CP, Iqbal, SJ and Hutchinson, PE, Developing guidelines for the prophylaxis of glucocorticoid-induced osteoporosis in patients with bullous pemphigoid, *Br J Dermatol*, 2003; 149 : (suppl. 64), 51-52.

[28] *ABPI Compendium of Data Sheets and Summaries of Product Characteristics 1998-99 with the Code of Practice for the Pharmaceutical Industry*, Data Pharm Publications Ltd, London 1392-1393.

side effects of topical steroids with the judicious use of a recently introduced treatment, Tacrolimus.

If topical steroids, and even a weak topical steroid such as hydrocortisone, have been used on or around the face in the long term the patient, especially if there is a family history of glaucoma, should be referred to an ophthalmic surgeon for regular review because of a real risk of future development of glaucoma.[29] [30]

Glaucoma is thought to be an autosomal recessive disorder. Individuals heterozygous for the gene, (about a third of the U.S.A. population), are much more liable to develop steroid induced glaucoma.

Cataracts are more likely following systemic steroid therapy than topical therapy. Cataracts seen in atopic individuals may resemble those induced by topical or systemic steroids.[31] The eyes of any patient with atopic dermatitis should be examined when PUVA therapy is being considered. Similarly the eyes of patients using topical steroids on the face, and around the eyes in particular, should be examined regularly.[32]

Corticosteroids and Psoriasis

Injected oral and topical steroids should be avoided where possible in patients with psoriasis as this medication may lead to severe rebound relapse, or even generalised pustular psoriasis.[33] [34]

Medico-legal problems have arisen after patients have bought over-the-counter products or used herbal preparations which have illicitly contained potent corticosteroids .

As a general rule, potent and moderately potent topical steroids should not be used on the face unless under consultant dermatological guidance. There may be considerable rebound relapse of rosacea and perioral dermatitis when topical steroids are withdrawn suddenly.

---

[29] Cubey, RB, Glaucoma following an application of corticosteroids to the skin of the eyelids, *Br J Derm*, 1976; 95 : 207-208.

[30] Nielsen, NW and Sorensen, PN, Glaucoma induced by application of corticosteroids to the periorbital region, *Arch Dermatol*, 1978; 114: 953-4.

[31] Holden, CA and Parish, WE, Atopic dermatitis, In: Rook Wilkinson Ebling, *Textbook of Dermatology*, 6th edn. Vol.IV., Ed. Champion, RH, Burton, JL, Burns, DA and Breathnach, FM, 1998, Blackwell Science, Oxford, p. 700-701.

[32] Becker, B and Hahn, KA, Topical steroids and heredity in primary open angled glaucoma, *Am J Ophthalmol*, 1964; 57 : 543-51.

[33] Baker, H, Corticosteroids and pustular psoriasis, *Br J Dermatol*, 1976 l; 94 : (suppl.12) 83-8.

[34] Baker, H and Ryan, TJ, Generalised pustular psoriasis, *Br J Dermatol*, 1968; 80 : 771-93.

The recommended weekly dosage is less than 50 grammes of super potent steroids and 100 grammes of potent steroids. Prolonged usage at this level is best avoided, especially on inflamed skin.[35] Particular care is necessary in children.

TABLE 1 – TOPICAL STEROIDS AVAILABLE IN THE UK AND THEIR POTENCY

Very potent	*Potent*	*Moderately Potent*	*Weak*
Dermovate	Betacap	Alphaderm	Alphosyl HC
Dermovate NN	Bettamousse	Betnovate RD	Canesten HC
Halciderm	Betnovate	Calmurid HC	Cobadex
Nerisone Forte	Betnovate C	Eumovate	Daktacort
	Betnovate N	Modrasone	Dioderm
	Cutivate	Stiedex LP	Econacort
	Diprosalic	Synalar 1:4	Efcortelan
	Diprasone	Trimovate	Eurax hydrocortisone
	Elocon	Ultralanum	Fucidin H
	Fucibet		Mildison Lipocream
	Locoid		Nystaform HC
	Locoid C		Quinocort
	Lotriderm		Synalar 1:10
	Metosyn		Terra-cortril
			Terra-cortril Nystatin
	Nerisone		Timodine
	Propaderm		Vioform hydrocortisone
	Stiedex		
	Synalar		
	Synalar C		
	Synalar N		
	Tri-adcortyl		

Retinoids

The retinoids are important drugs which are used both orally and topically to treat patients with a wide range of dermatological problems. In the UK the commonest retinoids prescribed orally are acitretin (Neotigason), which is used mainly to treat patients with difficult psoriasis, and isotretinoin (Roaccutane), used mainly to treat patients with severe acne and acne unresponsive to antibiotic therapy. In the UK these drugs are only prescribed by hospital dermatological departments - usually by consultant dermatologists. Both drugs are known teratogens and all potential female patients of childbearing age must be warned about the risk of pregnancy whilst taking them. Acitretin has a long half life in the body and contraceptive measures must be taken during and for at least two years after withdrawal of treatment. Blood donation should be avoided for a minimum of one

[35] See above, footnote 23.

year after the last dose. Acitretin has a large number of side effects (table II below):

TABLE 2 – SIDE EFFECTS OF ACITRETIN

Dry skin	Benign intercranial hypertension
Red skin	Visual disturbance
Itching	Liver toxicity
Dry eyes	Elevation of serum lipids
Dry nostrils	Muscle pain
Nose bleeds	Joint pain
Hair thinning (alopecia)	Hyperostosis
Granulomatous lesions	Extra osseous calcification (long term therapy)
Severe headache	

Severe headache and visual disturbance are indications for an urgent neurological examination to exclude the development of benign intracranial hypertension. Effective contraceptive measures must also be taken by women of childbearing age receiving isotretinoin. Pregnancy must be excluded before starting treatment and effective contraceptive measures must be taken in women of childbearing potential for one month before, during and at least four weeks after therapy. The manufacturers advise that liver function tests and fasting blood lipids should be monitored before starting treatment, one month later and thereafter at three-monthly intervals. A careful history should be taken. This should include the psychiatric history. All patients should be monitored for signs of depression and suicidal ideation. Isotretinoin may also produce a wide range of side effects.

TABLE 3 – SIDE EFFECTS OF ISOTRETINOIN

Dry eyes	
Dry mucosae	Increase in serum triglycerides with risk of fatal pancreatitis
Dry nostrils	Headache
Nose bleeds	Mood changes
Thinning of hair	Depression
Abnormal liver function tests	Muscle pain
Hirsutism	Joint pain
Reversible haematuria and proteinuria	
More rarely, allergic vasculitis and diminished platelet count	
Visual disturbances (The patient should be warned about these as they can be sudden.)	
Acne fulminans	
Lymphadenopathy	

In the United States the recommendation is for double contraception and monthly pregnancy tests for all women of childbearing potential receiving this drug. If pregnancy does occur whilst the patient is on this drug the risk of a severely malformed fetus is of the order of 50%.

The main medico-legal problems that have arisen with the retinoids have been because of pregnancy and the development of benign intracranial hypertension. Other problems have arisen because patients have developed a fulminating type of acne (acne fulminans). Exacerbation of existing acne is a well-recognised complication but if a patient is not warned about this side effect, which occurs in about 7.5% of treated cases, litigious thoughts may enter their head. The flare usually occurs within the first few weeks of treatment.[36]

Depression, Suicide and Isotretinoin

There is no general agreement amongst dermatologists about the relationship between isotretinoin therapy, depression and suicide in patients with acne. Whilst anecdotal case reports have suggested a significant relationship between isotretinoin therapy and depression, these cases have to be seen in a setting of possible pre-treatment anxiety and depression in acne patients and a recognised risk of suicide in patients with acne, whether or not they have been treated with isotretinoin. Thus, up to 60% of patients with acne suffer from anxiety and depression, and it has been shown that isotretinoin produces significant improvement in such symptoms in patients with acne.[37] [38] The author believes that a small but significant proportion of patients treated with isotretinoin for acne develop depression, usually during the third month of treatment, and prompt withdrawal of the drug results in prompt resolution of the depression.

The psychiatric reaction to the drug is idiosyncratic and therefore not foreseeable. In the writer's experience it is no more likely to occur in individuals with a past medical history of psychiatric illness, and depression in particular, than in acne patients without a significant previous psychiatric past medical history.

Particular care is needed in the small but important group of dysmorphophobic patients with minimal acne who persuade their consultant dermatologist to prescribe isotretinoin for their problem. Dysmorphophobia is characterised by depression, which is often severe, and is a well-recognised cause of suicide.

Methotrexate

Methotrexate is an antimetabolite inhibiting the enzyme dihydrofolate reductase which leads to an inhibition of cell reproduction.

---

[36] Cunliffe, WJ, *Acne,* Martin Dunitz, London 1989, p.311.

[37] Jacobs, DG, Deusch, NL and Brewer, M, Suicide, depression and isotretinoin: is there a causal link?, *J Am Acad Dermatol*, 2001; 45 : 168-75.

[38] Gupta, MA and Gupta, AK, Depression and suicidal ideation in dermatology patients with acne, *Br Derm*, 1998; 139 : 846-50.

Methotrexate has been used for many years in the UK to manage patients with unstable, difficult and generalised pustular psoriasis. Because there is a real risk of fatal or severe toxic reactions the drug should only be used by physicians (usually consultant dermatologists) experienced in this type of chemotherapy. Comprehensive informed consent is vital. The side effects of methotrexate are listed in Table 4.

TABLE 4 – SIDE EFFECTS OF METHOTREXATE

Bone marrow depression	Cirrhosis
Anaemia	Fatty change
Leucopaenia	Periportal fibrosis
Thrombocytopaenia	Teratogenecity
Bleeding	Adverse effect on gameto genesis (avoid conception during therapy and for at least 6 months thereafter
Liver toxicity	Liver atrophy and necrosis
Drug cross reactions, particularly with non-steroidal anti-inflammatory drugs and diuretics	
Pulmonary fibrosis	
Skin ulceration	

Because methotrexate has a high potential, usually dose-related toxicity, before beginning treatment a full blood count, liver and renal function tests and a chest x-ray should be carried out[39]. Methotrexate is excreted primarily by the kidneys so impaired renal function is a contra-indication to use. A careful drug history should be taken. Methotrexate is, in part, bound to serum albumen and can be displaced from this binding site by drugs such as non-steroidal anti-inflammatories (NSAIs), salicylates, sulphonomides, and diuretics. None of these drugs should be administered concurrently with methotrexate. The drug is contraindicated in pregnant women and breast feeding is contraindicated in women taking the drug. A test dose of 2.5 – 5 mg is usually given. In patients with psoriasis the drug should never be given daily. Effective maintenance treatment in psoriasis usually lies in a dose range of between 7.5 – 30 mg per week.

Serious adverse effects due to methotrexate have occurred when the drug has been taken mistakenly on a daily rather than a weekly basis. Elderly patients may present particular problems, especially if demented. The writer has seen one death due to this drug because it was not appreciated by the dermatologist that his patient was demented and the patient took the drug daily instead of on a weekly basis. It is recognised that patients with psoriasis tend to drink alcohol more heavily than individuals without this skin disease and, indeed, alcohol has been implicated in the pathogenesis of psoriasis. It is very important that patients

[39] Camp, RDR, Psoriasis, In : Rook, Wilkinson, Ebling, *Textbook of Dermatology*, 6th edn. Vol II, Ed. Champion, RH, Burton, JL, Burns, DA and Breathnach, FM, 1998, Blackwell Science, Oxford, p 1622-23.

taking methotrexate refrain from drinking alcohol to try and minimise the toxic effects of the drug, and the toxic effects on the liver in particular. Treatment should always be monitored by the consultant dermatologist in charge of the patient, and not delegated to a general practitioner. Whilst the patient is receiving methotrexate there should be a regular determination of full blood count, liver and renal function tests. The toxic effects on the liver are largely cumulative dose related. A liver biopsy can be delayed until two or three months after commencement of treatment. If at that stage the patient, on balance, is going to require long term methotrexate therapy, a liver biopsy can then be carried out. However, the incidence of cirrhosis remains low for a total cumulative dose of less than 1.5 gm. A liver biopsy should usually be undertaken not less frequently than after every 1.5 gm of cumulative methotrexate dosage.[40] Alternatives to serial liver biopsy have been investigated. These include liver ultrasound screening, dynamic hepatic scintigraphy and assay of the serum levels of amino-terminal propeptide of Type III collagen.[41] In 10 of 11 dermatological centres in Yorkshire routine measurement of serum Type III procollagen aminopeptide is being used as an alternative to routine liver biopsy, greatly reducing the number of liver biopsies performed.[42]

Drug allergy

Whilst a significant number of patients will allege they are allergic to penicillin, the real position is clouded by the fact that an individual patient may develop a rash attributed to one of the penicillins during one course of treatment and receive a further course of penicillin treatment in the future without any apparent problems. However, a small group of patients who have reacted adversely with a drug rash to penicillin may go on to develop severe dermatological complications if given this drug at some stage in the future. These dermatological complications may be life threatening: the patient may develop severe bullous erythema multiforme, merging into life threatening toxic epidermal necrolysis where the skin comes off in sheets (Scalded Skin Syndrome). The writer has advised in two medico-legal cases where the case notes were clearly marked "Allergic to penicillin" and, despite this, the attending doctor went on to prescribe an antibiotic of the penicillin group which led to the development of toxic epidermal necrolysis, with fatal results in one case. Whilst toxic epidermal necrolysis may be drug related and often not foreseeable, it is a recognised complication of Allopurinol therapy when this drug is given in conventional doses for gout to

---

[40] Petrazzuoli, M, Rothe, MJ, Grin-Jorgensen, C *et al*, Monitoring patients taking methotrexate for hepatotoxicity. Does the standard of care match published guidelines?, *J Am Acad Dermatol*, 1994; 31 : 969-77.

[41] Zachariae, H, Heickendorff, L and Søgaard, H, The value of aminoterminal propeptide of Type III procollagen in routine screening for methotrexate-induced liver fibrosis: a 10-year follow up, *Br J Derm* 2001; 144 : 100-3.

[42] Baron, SE and Wilson, CL, A Yorkshire regional audit on methotrexate monitoring, *Br J Derm*, 2003; 149 (suppl. 64) : 19.

hypertensive patients with impaired renal function. In this situation the dose of Allopurinol, if indicated, should always be very much reduced.[43]

Neomicin, Gentamicin and Ototoxicity

The antibiotics neomycin and gentamicin are ototoxic and therefore, if used inappropriately, can damage hearing. The writer has seen two claimants alleging deafness following the prolonged use of gentamicin on a leg ulcer. Whilst gentamicin affects the vestibular (balancing) mechanisms, neomycin affects the auditory branch of the eighth cranial nerve. No more than one gram of neomycin should be used topically and the period of treatment should not exceed seven days. Particular care should be taken in patients with poor renal function.[44]

LEGALLY IMPORTANT SURGICAL ISSUES

General

In total there were 98 allegations (19.6%) following dermatological surgical procedures. Claims involving allegations of an absence of warning of risk of scarring constituted 32 of the 61 private practice MDU claims (52.4%), whilst similar allegations about lack of warning of scarring were made by only 5 patients out of the NHSLA series of surgical cases (15%). In the MDU group, there were also claimants alleging failure to treat, whilst others were disappointed with the results of surgery. A small minority had experienced problems with dermatological laser treatment.

From the data there are clearly problems, particularly in the private sector, about warning patients about the risks of scarring.

There are several different types of scars. Keloid and hypertrophic scars, consisting of hard fibrous tissue, may both develop post-operatively out of proportion to any underlying scar. Keloid scars may occasionally occur spontaneously. Whilst a hypertrophic scar will eventually flatten out, the keloid scar will persist, or even continue to enlarge, and may even become painful and itchy. Stretch or spread scars, which, in contrast to the keloid or hypertrophic scars, are soft and characterised by a thin dermis. This type of scar tends to occur where the skin is thick and under tension, such as on the back, the calves, or the skin over the extensor aspects of joints. Stretch scars are more likely in younger than in older patients and especially in individuals who put tension on the affected area during healing.

---

[43] *ABPI Compendium of Data Sheets and Summaries of Product Characteristics 1998-99 with the Code of Practice for the Pharmaceutical Industry*, Data Farm Publications Ltd., London, p. 1456.

[44] Editorial – Deafness after topical neomycin, *Br Med J*, 1969; 4 : 181-2.

It is important, during the consultation and during the consent process, to make sure that the patient's expectations are realistic. Any skin surgery over the upper chest and upper arms should be avoided unless there is a possibility of a malignant lesion. The patient should be counselled carefully if the lesion is to be removed from the back, calves or over the extensor aspects of joints, when, even with all precautions, including the use of slow dissolving subcutaneous sutures to try and strengthen the wound, there is a definite risk of spread scars.

Other problems with medico-legal implications are wound infection, wound breakdown and bleeding into a wound. One of the writer's patients alleged her wound became infected because the private hospital where her skin surgery was carried out had failed to sterilise the instruments. This allegation was refuted easily when it became apparent that her husband had several boils on his skin at the material time. Bleeding into a wound (haematoma) is largely preventable. It is important to know whether the patient is taking aspirin or anticoagulants, and any previous bleeding problems should be noted. Any dead space in the wound should be closed using a subcutaneous suture.

Wound breakdown may be due to sudden movement or stretching by the patient, or due to excessive tension on the wound at the time of suturing. Infection and haematoma formation can each cause delayed wound breakdown. Poor suturing techniques, such as inverting the wound edges, can also contribute to wound breakdown by reducing dermis to dermis contact.

Cosmetic dermatology and unrealistic expectations

In view of the large increase in cosmetic surgical procedures, especially in the private sector, it is surprising that the MDU figures contain very few cosmetic surgical claims. The specialty of cosmetic dermatology now encompasses a wide variety of procedures. Some are carried out by dermatologists, some by nurses under supervision, and some by plastic surgeons. Whilst the specialty is receiving more attention from dermatologists in the UK, it presently constitutes an enormous proportion of dermatological practice, for instance, in the United States. However, the shortage of consultant dermatologists in the UK has tended to limit the market here.

The media compels many people, and particularly women, to seek ever more youthful skin. Many techniques have been developed to try and satisfy this demand. These include simple and relatively innocuous fruit acid peels, chemical peels (using trichloracetic acid and, more radically, phenol), a variety of skin resurfacing procedures (using the pulsed CO_2 laser and the Erbium YAG laser), extensive use of botulinum toxin (Botox), and skin fillers, temporary and permanent, to abolish wrinkles.

Careful patient selection is very important. The patient with unrealistic expectations is a constant problem. Dissatisfaction with the results of a cosmetic dermatological procedure is likely in patients with depression and dysmorphophobia. Special care should be taken during the history to detect these patients.

Most patients requesting cosmetic dermatological procedures are self referred. They feel embarrassed to burden their busy general practitioner with their cosmetic anxieties, and many patients say that their general practitioner would not be helpful in making an appropriate referral. Further difficulties arise when the patient refuses to allow any letters to be sent to the general practitioner following a consultation in a cosmetic clinic. This can cause problems if complications of the cosmetic dermatological procedure occur, particularly out of hours, when, for instance, the general practitioner or casualty officer is likely to refer to a laser treated area of skin as a "burn", or an "infected burn". Long distance travellers pose particular problems for cosmetic dermatological practitioners. These patients always want their treatment carried out on the same day as the consultation, and follow up is impossible. Communication by telephone with long distance travelling patients is usually unsatisfactory.

Dysmorphophobia (Body Dysmorphic Disorder) and depression

Patients with dysmorphophobia (body dysmorphic disorder) present more often to dermatologists and cosmetic surgeons than to psychiatrists. They typically present because of a distressing preoccupation with an imagined or slight defect in appearance which characteristically involves the skin, hair and nose. Almost 12% of patients in a general dermatological clinic may show features of this disorder[45] and the proportion of patients presenting in a cosmetic dermatological clinic may approach 40%. The condition is characterised by very low self esteem, lack of confidence and poor body image. Depression is the commonest psychiatric illness present.[46] This may be severe, and, together with an obsessional personality, contributes to a very poor quality of life and a high suicide attempt rate.[47] Patients presenting to dermatologists with this disorder may have undergone many other cosmetic procedures such as rhinoplasty, blepharoplasty, breast augmentation and aesthetic dentistry. However, it is best to avoid any cosmetic procedures on dysmorphophobic patients because fewer than 10% are likely to be satisfied with the results of cosmetic surgery.[48] The treatment of choice is a selective serotonin reuptake inhibitor. As there is a definite risk of suicide, it is important to try to involve a psychiatrist in the management at an early stage. Generally speaking, the more ill a patient is from the psychiatric point of view, the more difficult it is to persuade the patient to see a psychiatrist. This generalisation is true in all patients with dysmorphophobia. If the dermatologist has in patient facilities it is

---

[45] Phillips, KA, Dufresne Jnr, RG, Wilkel, C *et al*, Rate of body dysmorphic disorder in dermatology departments, *J Am Acad Dermatol*, 2000; 42 : 436-41.

[46] Cotterill, JA, Dermatological non-disease: a common and potentially fatal disturbance of cutaneous body image, *Br J Dermatol*, 1981; 104 : 611-9.

[47] Phillips, KA and Dufresne Jnr, RG, Body dysmorphic disorder: a guide for dermatologists and cosmetic surgeons, *Am J Clin Dermatol*, 2000; 1 (4) : 235-43.

[48] Veale, D, Boocock, A, Gournay, K *et al*, Body dysmorphic disorder: a survey of 50 cases, *Br J Psych*, 1996; 169 : 169-201.

prudent to admit the patient to the ward where psychiatric help can be requested without any loss of face for the patient. Patients with dysmorphophobia have totally unrealistic expectations about treatment but will go to extreme lengths to persuade an individual dermatologist or plastic surgeon to carry out a procedure which they see as their salvation. The high risk of suicide in this group of patients makes it important to recognise them and manage them appropriately. Table 5 lists the clues which should be explored in the history of a patient with body dysmorphic disorder.

TABLE 5 [49]

(a)	Excessive concern with distress over a minor or non-existent appearance flaw
(b)	Difficulty functioning, e.g. problems at work or social avoidance
(c)	Skin picking
(d)	Camouflaging, e.g. wearing heavy make up or a hat
(e)	Other body dysmorphic disorder related behaviour, such as reassurance seeking or excessive grooming. Constant mirror checking
(f)	Referential thinking, i.e. thinking that others are taking special notice of them because of how they look
(g)	Dissatisfaction with previous dermatological or surgical treatment
(h)	Unusual or excessive requests for cosmetic procedures. Doctor "shopping"
(i)	Belief that the procedure will transform the individual's life or fix all of their problems

Patients with dysmorphophobia are angry. This anger may be vented upon themselves when they try and commit suicide. More rarely the anger may be vented physically on the dermatologist, who may be attacked, or even murdered. Much more commonly, however, the patient vents his/her anger by litigating. This is another reason for refraining from treating this particularly difficult group of patients with cosmetic dermatological procedures.

Depressed patients in the dermatology clinic

Patients with significant depression are commonly seen in a cosmetic dermatological setting. Some depressed patients may go to some lengths to conceal their past psychiatric history, denying, for instance, that they are taking antidepressants, or even self administered antidepressant remedies such as St John's Wort, which can produce a severe phototoxic reaction to laser light.

A depressed patient usually has an impaired or distorted body image and characteristically will not be impressed by the results of cosmetic procedures. The importance of pre and post operative photography in rebutting claims from

[49] See above, footnote 47.

dissatisfied depressed patients cannot be over-emphasised. Besides questions about early morning wakening, appetite etc. in the history, two simple questions have been claimed to detect depression – i) over the past two weeks have you ever felt down, depressed or hopeless? ii) have you ever felt little interest or pleasure in doing things?[50]

In the writer's experience the depressed patient is also more likely to go to litigation than the non depressed patient. In an unpublished assessment of over 600 medico-legal cases a significant history of past or present depression was present in almost two thirds of the claimants.[51]

LASER DERMATOLOGY

Basics

There are now several types of lasers available for dermatological and cosmetic dermatological use (Table 6). Lasers are used most commonly to treat tattoos, obliterate thread veins (telangiectases) of the face and legs, to treat other vascular lesions such as port wine stains, abolish unwanted hair and to rejuvenate the skin. Some of the procedures carried out by lasers can also be carried out using high energy light sources with special filters.

Currently, clinics operating lasers and high energy light sources have to be approved by the National Care Standards Commission[52] and regularly inspected. Safety issues are of paramount importance and are the responsibility of the laser protection advisor (normally a physicist) and the laser protection supervisor (normally a medical practitioner – often the medical director of the unit). Some clinics, especially those operating high energy light sources, are not currently registered with the National Care Standards Commission.

Lasers are classified according to their power output and therefore potential hazards. Most lasers used by dermatologists and in cosmetic dermatology are Class IV lasers, i.e. high power lasers with an output power exceeding 500 mW. Some of these lasers pose hazards, particularly to the eye, and direct and specular reflections can be hazardous to the skin, whilst some Class IV lasers are capable of igniting flammable materials. When a Class IV laser is in use, hazard warning signs should be also be used outside the laser controlled area. Class IV lasers should have a sign on them warning of the need to avoid exposure of the eye or skin to direct or scattered radiation. If the laser emits outside the visible range, the

---

[50] Pignome, MP, Gaynes, BN, Rushton, JL *et al*, Screening for depression in adult: a summary of the evidence for the U.S. Preventative Service Task Force, *Ann Intern Med*, 2002; 136: 765-76.

[51] Cotterill, JA, *High incidence of past or present psychiatric disorder in medico-legal claimants, Unpublished observations.*

[52] From April 2004 the National Care Standards Commission will become part of a larger organisation – The Commission for Health Care Audit and Inspection (CHAI).

warning should mention invisible laser irradiation, and there should be a warning label at the exit beam laser aperture.

TABLE 6

DERMATOLOGICAL AND COSMETIC LASERS CURRENTLY AVAILABLE	COMMENT
Argon - Green/blue light 488-514 nm	Very rarely in current use
Copper vapour - Green/orange light 511-578 nm	Rarely in current use in UK
Krypton ion - Green/Yellow light 530-568 nm	Rarely in current use in UK for treating vascular lesions
Frequency doubled Nd-YAG - Green light 532 nm Invisible near infra red 1064nm	Currently used to treat pigmented and vascular lesions including tattoos
Long pulsed Nd YAG - 1064 nm	Main use/unwanted hair removal
Ruby laser - Red light 694 nm	Black + green areas of tattoos/hair removal
Alexandrite - 755 nm	Hair removal. Pigmented lesions. Tattoos.
Diode - 795-830 nm	Continuous wave output for hair removal
Erbium YAG - Infra red 2940 nm	Wide range of uses from ablation of benign skin tumours to treatment of scars and skin resurfacing
CO_2 - 10600 nm	Continuous wave/main uses vapourising dermatological lesions but leaves scars
Pulsed CO_2	Skin resurfacing procedures
Pulsed dye - 577/585-600 nm	Treatment of vascular lesions including port wine stains
Excimer - 308 nm	Pulsed output for the treatment of psoriasis and vitiligo

The UK Department of Health has issued guidelines on the safe operation of lasers. Guidance on the Safe Use of Lasers in Medical and Dental practice (ISBN 1 858394880) is essential reading in this respect.

The Local Rules, usually drawn up by the laser protection advisor, should designate a register of all authorised users, including nominated key holders and their responsibilities. The nature of the individual laser hazards to patients and staff should be documented. Rules about safe access to the laser unit should be set out.

Safe working methods, together with descriptions of simple pre-use safety checks, and personal protective equipment for both operator and patient, especially eye wear, should be documented. The laser operator's responsibilities should be defined in the Local Rules, which should also aim to prevent unauthorised use of the laser. There should be well defined adverse incident procedures laid down, with clear lines of communication for the laser protection officer and for the laser protection supervisor, whose main role is to make sure that the Local Rules are implemented. Ideally, lasers should be operated in a blame-free culture so that any near misses come to light instead of being concealed. Ideally, there should only be one laser per treatment room. Operating more than one laser in one room significantly increases the hazards of operation, particularly as far as eye protection is concerned.

All staff working in the laser unit should recognise that there is a significant risk of fire and of electrical hazards. Definite risks of fire exist for the pulsed dye laser if this is being operated in a theatre setting in the presence of oxygen enhanced anaesthetic gas mixtures and potentially inflammable material such as gauze and hair.[53] Fire induced by the pulsed dye laser is not readily visible through the appropriate goggles, and first perceptions of the fire may therefore be olfactory and tactile rather than visual. A large bowl of tap water adjacent to operating area is a wise precaution.

Protective gauze placed around the treatment site should be first soaked in sterile saline. Teflon and plastic anaesthetic tubes can ignite readily and should be appropriately protected. Metal equipment and operating equipment such as forceps should have a matt black finish to reduce any possible reflection of the laser beam.

Both the CO_2 and Erbium YAG lasers also have potential for ignition.

Hazards to the Eye

Eye injuries are potentially the most serious hazard in cosmetic dermatological laser use. The operator, patient and any other personnel in the laser controlled area are at risk and it is important to keep the number of people in the laser controlled area to an absolute minimum. The effects on the eye depend on the wavelength of the laser light. For instance, Erbium YAG laser light and CO_2 light are absorbed avidly by water and so any damage to the eye is likely to be located to the anterior eye on either the cornea or sclera. However, visible and near infra red light (780-1400 nm) passes through the cornea and lens and focus on the retina, burning it. If this burn involves the fovea, central vision will be lost irreversibly. Appropriate eye wear must be worn at all times to prevent ocular damage. Laser operators must be aware of the fact that occasionally a laser will fire spontaneously and so eye wear should not be removed until the laser has been placed in standby mode. Particular care must be taken when laser work is undertaken around the eye. Suitable opaque lenses can be inserted under a local anaesthetic for this purpose. When using the Erbium YAG laser or CO_2 laser for a skin resurfacing procedure a metal or acrylic intraocular eye shield is used. The shield must be made of material appropriate for the particular laser in question. It is important not to leave a heavy metal eye shield in contact with the cornea for unduly long periods of time since this will induce hypoxia of the cornea and superficial cornea damage. It is always important to remember to remove any eye

[53] Fretkin, S, Beeson, WH and Hanke, CW, Ignition potential of the 585 nm pulsed-dye laser, *Dermatol Surg*, 1996; 22 : 699-702.

shields after a laser procedure. The writer has known of several instances in young children when an eye shield has been left in situ, sometimes for several days after the laser procedure. The British Standards for suitable protective eye wear are BS EN 207 1994 and BS EN 208 1994.

Possible hazards of the laser plume

Various human viruses, such as the human papilloma virus and HIV, have been demonstrated under experimental conditions in laser smoke plumes.[54 55] Some protection may be afforded by wearing appropriate masks and a high volume smoke extraction is essential when using the CO_2 and Erbium YAG lasers. Tissue splatter is a well marked phenomenon with the Erbium laser and also, to a lesser extent, with some Q-switched lasers, and in this situation a head visor is advised.

Complications of laser treatment

There are many complications of laser treatment, including pain and discomfort during the procedure, blistering, purpura (bruising), infection (bacterial, yeast and viral), scarring (atrophic, hypertrophic and keloid), hyperpigmentation and hypopigmentation, which may be permanent.

Laser treatment of tattoos

Laser treatment of tattoos is a relatively common source of allegations centred around unsatisfactory treatment.

There is no longer any place for the use of intense light source or ablative lasers like the continuous wave CO_2 laser as the initial treatment of choice for tattoos. The CO_2 laser produces very significant scarring and its use has been superseded by more appropriate lasers with fewer side effects.

Tattoos can be classified into two main types: amateur and professional. In the former, Indian ink is injected into the skin at a variable depth. The density of pigment is usually not unduly high. In professional tattoos much larger amounts of pigment of various colours are injected into the skin, often over a wide area, and many patients are extensively tattooed. The solitary amateur tattoo is usually easily removed, using either the Q-switched frequency doubled Nd-YAG laser emitting at 1064 nm or the Q-switched ruby laser at 594 nm. Several treatments are usually necessary and this fact must be stressed to patients. Scarring with these Q-switched lasers is extremely unusual but there may be some permanent hypopigmentation, particularly in individuals who pigment readily (Type IV skin and above) following the use of the Q-switched ruby laser. In these patients the Q-switched Nd-YAG laser is a better treatment option.

---

[54] Garden, JM, O'Banion, K, Shelnitz, LS *et al*, Papilloma virus in the vapor of CO_2 laser-treated verrucae, *JAMA*, 1998; 259 : 1199-1202.

[55] Baggish, MS, Poesz, B, Jorot, D, Williamson, P and Refai, A Presence of human immunodeficiency virus DNA in laser smoke, *Lasers Surg Med*, 1991; 11 : 197-203.

With regard to professional tattoos, not all the colours in an individual tattoo can necessarily be treated by one laser. Some colours are much more difficult to treat than others. It is very difficult, for instance, to remove green pigment completely from individual tattoos, although, in theory, this should react well to red light from the Q-switched ruby laser. Purple and yellow pigment also poses difficulties. Black and red areas of tattoos usually respond best. It is important to warn patients that it may not be possible to eradicate the tattoo completely, and many treatments may be necessary to achieve a satisfied customer.

Some tattoos containing iron pigment may show a phenomenon called "immediate pigment darkening" when exposed to laser light. In this instance immediate blackening of the laser treated tattoo occurs. If this happens, treatment should be suspended and the situation assessed by a dermatologist with a particular interest in laser therapy. In some instances it is possible to abolish the blackened change by further laser treatment, but in other cases the problem does not resolve.

There are anecdotal reports of patients developing anaphylactic shock when the red areas of their tattoo have been treated by lasers. Every laser unit, therefore, should have facilities available for treating anaphylactic shock and patients with red tattoos should be warned about this potential complication. Traumatic tattoos following road traffic accidents, or, in times gone by following mining accidents, respond extremely well to treatment with the Q-switched Nd-YAG laser.

Laser treatment of vascular lesions

Many types of vascular lesion, including port wine stains and facial telangiectasia, respond well to treatment with appropriate vascular lasers such as the pulsed dye laser, or the frequency doubled Nd-YAG laser emitting at 532 nm. In expert hands significant complications are few and the incidence of scarring (textural change) is probably less than 1%. Purpura (bruising) is the main concern of patients undergoing treatment with the pulsed dye laser. This complication can alarm a small proportion of patients, and particularly patients with a tendency to dysmorphophobia, very greatly. Adverse reactions to the vascular lasers are also increased enormously if the patient is taking St John's Wort, a known photo-sensitiser.[56]

Thread veins on the legs respond much less obligingly to laser treatment than thread veins on the face. Patients with leg thread veins should have a full clinical and investigational assessment as many patients have significant major venous reflux which should be dealt with by appropriate surgery prior to any attempts at treating thread veins with lasers.

[56] Cotterill, JA, Severe phototoxic reaction to laser treatment in a patient taking St John's Wort, *J Cosmetic & Laser Ther*, 2001; 3 : 159-160.

Laser treatment of Melasma (Chloasma)

Patients with melasma are characterised by the slow development of a usually symmetrical, brown facial pigmentation. Classically the condition is seen during pregnancy or in patients taking oral contraceptives, but sometimes may be idiopathic. The condition is seen in up to 30% of women taking oral contraceptives. Both ultraviolet light and oestrogen are thought to be important in pathogenesis, together with genetic predisposition. The increased pigment histologically may be predominantly epidermal, confined to the upper layer of skin, or dermal, and in some patients both types occur.

Melasma does not respond well to any treatment and no attempt should be made to treat this condition with lasers. Any laser, whatever its type, is likely to make the condition much worse. Litigation is likely to follow laser treatment of melasma.

Worsening of melasma must be distinguished from post inflammatory hyperpigmentation, which is relatively common after laser treatment, particularly in patients who disregard advice about using broad spectrum sun screens and avoidance of ultraviolet light. In most patients post inflammatory hyperpigmentation gradually settles but this may take two or three years. A test area may predict this complication.

Post-inflammatory hypopigmentation

This complication may be seen in any laser treated patient and is more likely in individuals with a pigmented skin than in individuals with a Type I skin (never tans, always burns). It may that this possible adverse reaction to laser treatment can be predicted by doing a test area . However, persisting hypopigmentation is becoming recognised as a very common late sequela of skin resurfacing using the CO_2 laser. This complication may leave a bizarre-looking tide mark on the jaw/neck border where attempts were made to "feather" a resurfacing procedure, often years before. The condition is not amenable to treatment. Persisting redness, often for several months, is also a worrying complication of CO_2 laser facial skin resurfacing. It is more likely in individuals with a Celtic type of skin, and in a minority of individuals may take up to two years to settle.

Laser test areas

Many, but not all, laser operators will carry out a test patch on appropriate patients in an attempt to predict the outcome of treatment. In the writer's opinion the main advantage of a test patch is to enable the patient to experience and see the changes that occur in the treated area and the duration of these changes. For instance, if the patient has a large port wine stain it is possible for the patient to assess from a small test area the pain and discomfort he/she is likely to experience, whether they would require a local or a general anaesthetic, and how long they may be away from school or work. A test patch will also help the patient reach realistic expectations about the results of treatment.

For the dermatologist a test patch gives some indication of what sort of anaesthetic technique will or will not be necessary, and the possible outcome of treatment. It must, however, be recognised that changes induced by laser treatment in one area may not represent what will happen in other areas. If, for instance, the port wine stain is on the face, it is usual practice to carry out a test in as inconspicuous area of the face as possible, and at a junction of normal skin and birth mark. The test patch should be re-assessed three to six months after treatment. If the results are good, treatment can be continued using the same treatment variables as were used on the test area. If there have been adverse reactions, the energy fluence can be reduced and if there is any evidence of scarring or no beneficial effect from treatment, following further discussion with the patient it may be that further laser treatment is inappropriate.

A test area is not mandatory, but is reassuring for both the doctor and the patient. It may also be helpful to the defence if there are subsequent medico-legal problems.

PHYSICAL ABUSE OF CHILDREN[57]

Dermatologists may see children who have been subject to child abuse. This is one of the most difficult clinical situations a dermatologist is called on to manage. Suspicions of child abuse may be aroused by suggestive physical findings, past medical history, and behavioural abnormalities in the family and by the child in particular.

It has been claimed that in the UK 4% of children under the age of 12 are suspected of being the subject of child abuse, and that about one child in a thousand under the age of 4 suffers severe physical abuse.[58] Most child abuse is inflicted by a family member and it is much more likely if one of the parents was also abused during childhood. Bizarre shaped bruises and burns should arouse suspicion. Marks left by cigarette burns produce multiple rounded, crater-like ulcers or erosions. Immersion burns may be seen with sharply demarcated edges and uniformity of damage. The child may show multiple injuries over many body sites, all in different stages of evolution. Other general signs of abuse include bruising around the eyes, retinal damage, fractures, traumatic hair loss and bite marks.

---

[57] Kennedy, CTC, Mechanical and thermal injury. Skin signs of child abuse, In: Rook, Wilkinson, Ebling, *Textbook of Dermatology*, 6th edn. Vol.I, Ed. Champion, RH, Burton, JL, Burns, DA and Breathnach, FM, 1998, Blackwell Science, Oxford, p 910-914.

[58] Meadow, R, ABC of child abuse: epidemiology, *Br Med J*, 1989; 298 : 727-30.

It should be remembered that up to one fifth of children with Meadow's Syndrome (Munchausen by proxy Syndrome) may have dermatological problems, the majority of which are factitial.

SEXUAL ABUSE OF CHILDREN[59]

Whilst families with children who are physically abused are notoriously difficult to manage, child sexual abuse presents even more serious problems. The dermatologist may see a child with symptoms due to infection or local trauma, such as bleeding, ano-genital pain and vaginal discharge. Dermatologists are less likely to see children presenting with behavioural difficulties such as eneuresis, encopresis and anorexia. A child presenting with perianal warts or molluscum contagiosum in the genital area should always prompt suspicion of sexual abuse. However, sometimes there is a simple explanation and management in these circumstances calls for great tact, skill and diplomacy. If the suspicion of child sexual abuse is strong, further examination should be conducted by a consultant skilled in this area. Most dermatologists practising in the UK would not possess the necessary skills and would need to contact an appropriate paediatric colleague.

Problems constantly arise because some pathological conditions involving the genital area can mimic, at least superficially, child sexual abuse. The most common condition in this respect is lichen sclerosus, which may be characterised by the presence of bleeding just under the surface of the involved skin. However, it should be remembered that lichen sclerosus and child sexual abuse are not mutually exclusive. Rarer conditions which lead to bleeding into the skin, such as Schamberg's disease, idiopathic thrombocytopenia and Ehlers-Danlos Syndrome, may all come into the differential diagnosis. Even dyes on the skin from clothing may cause concern.

TELEDERMATOLOGY

Teledermatology is seen by target-obsessed managers and politicians as a cost effective way of reducing dermatological waiting lists. Presently there are about 350 consultant dermatology posts in the UK and there are plans in the future to expand consultant numbers to over 800. Currently there are about 50 posts unfilled.

Teledermatology raises many legal problems, including issues about confidentiality. Can it be assumed that the medical defence organisations will always back a consultant dermatologist engaged in teledermatology? For instance, what would be the legal situation if a UK consultant dermatologist,

---

[59] Kennedy, CTC, Mechanical and thermal injury. Skin signs of child abuse, In: Rook, Wilkinson, Ebling, *Textbook of Dermatology*, 6th edn. Vol. I, Ed. Champion, RH, Burton, JL, Burns, DA and Breathnach, FM, 1998, Blackwell Science, Oxford, p 914-5.

working from his holiday home in Spain, seriously misdiagnosed a patient resident in Russia? Some of the legal and ethical aspects of telemedicine have been reviewed.[60]

SELLING PRODUCTS AT THE CLINIC[61]

The sale of cosmetic and other products from the clinic raises some fundamental moral issues which affect the doctor/patient relationship. Factors which should influence the dermatologist include whether the patient may have an urgent need for a given product, whether the product is relevant or irrelevant to the patient's skin problems, and whether the products on sale have been properly assessed for efficacy. In a perfect world dermatologists should make full disclosure about their financial interest in selling the product and the patient should be informed about any alternatives. Ideally, charges for products sold through the clinic should be limited to the reasonable costs incurred in making these products available.

CLINICAL TRIALS

Dermatologists are often called upon by the cosmetic and pharmaceutical industry to carry out clinical trials. New regulations on consent in clinical trials will bring into force a European directive (the Medicines for Human Use (Clinical Trials) Regulations 2003). The new regulations underline the importance of giving informed consent to involvement in the trial. Any potential patients entering the trial must have an interview with the authorised health professional responsible for the conduct of the trial or a member of the trial team. During this interview the potential patient must be given an opportunity to understand the objectives, risk and inconveniences of the trial and the conditions under which it is to be conducted. The potential patient must be provided with a contact point to obtain further information about the trial if necessary.

Where proposed clinical trials involve children under 16 years of age, the trial has to be designed to minimise pain, discomfort, fear and other foreseeable risks in relationship to disease and the child's stage of development. The risk of the degree of distress must be specifically defined and constantly monitored, and account taken of the patient's interests. Those interests must prevail over any scientific or societal interests. A parent or someone with parental responsibility must give appropriately informed consent and must have an interview with the health care professional responsible for the trial. That interview will be along the lines described above. A contact point must be available. It must be understood that the child can be withdrawn from the trial at any time. Although the potential child patient may not have the capacity to consent to involvement in the trial, any potential child patient must have received information regarding the trial and its

[60] Stanberry, BA, *The Legal and Ethical Aspects of Telemedicine*, Royal Society of Medicine Press Ltd., London 1998.

[61] Povar, GJ and Snyder, L, For the Ethics and Human Rights Committee, Selling products out of the office, *Ann Intern Med*, 1999; 131 : 863-4.

risks and benefits commensurate with the child's capacity to understand. This information should be given by staff with professional experience of children. If a child indicates an unwillingness to enter the trial those responsible for the trial must consider those wishes. A clinical trial involving a child must relate directly to the clinical condition from which the child suffers and some direct clinical benefit for the children involved in the clinical trial should be obtained from the trial. This may be a difficult condition to satisfy.

These new regulations are such that anyone considering entering a clinical trial would be well be advised to seek legal advice on their effect.

CONCLUSIONS

There are many potential pitfalls in dermatological management. Many of the commoner complaints about doctors, such as inappropriate ultraviolet light treatment or concerns about the risks of surgery, including the appearance of scars, could be very largely avoided by detailed attention to work practices. There will always be patients who present difficulties with diagnosis, particularly when the condition is rare, or presents in an atypical way. Malignant melanoma is a particular problem.

The increasing use of guidelines produced by the dermatological profession (see Appendix II) should lead, together with appropriate postgraduate education, to increasing standards of care, although the guidelines may produce some rigidity and lack of flexibility in individual patient care.

Good communication, together with comprehensive notes, continues to be the bulwark of damage limitation.

APPENDIX I

FIGURE 1

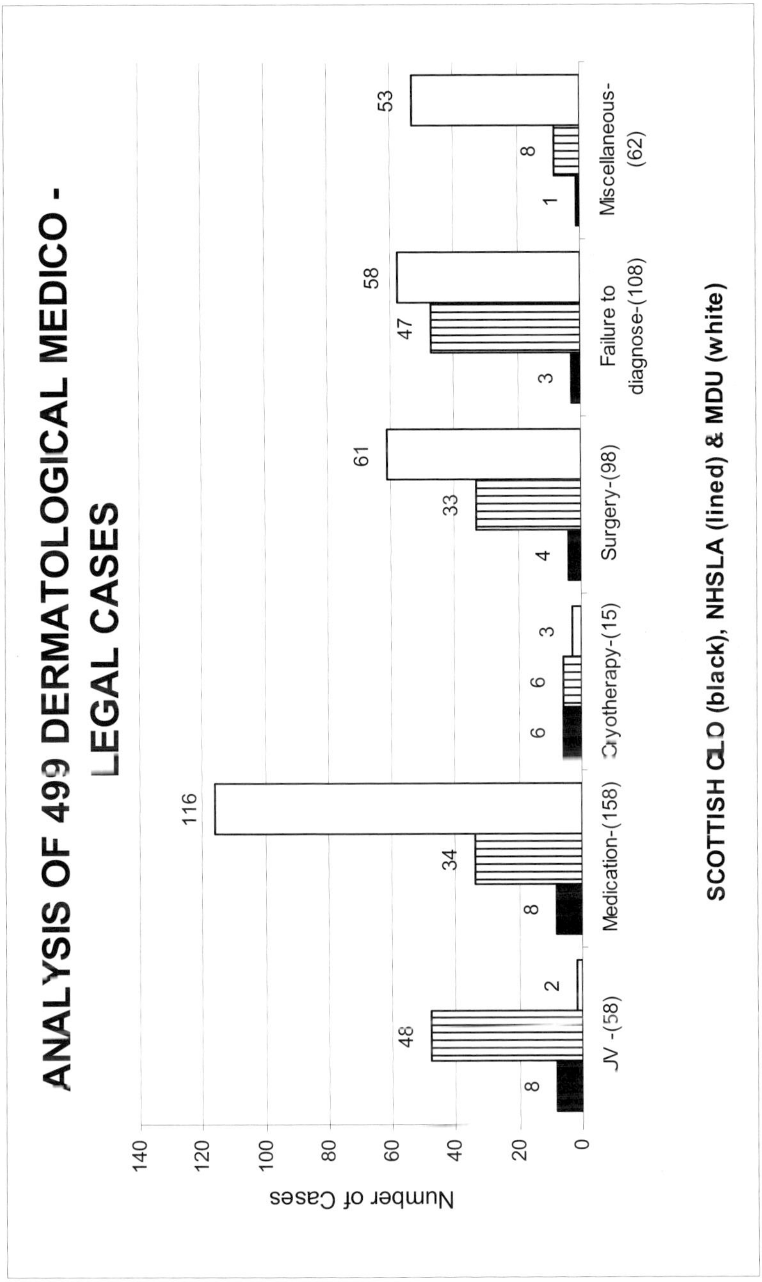

FIGURE 2

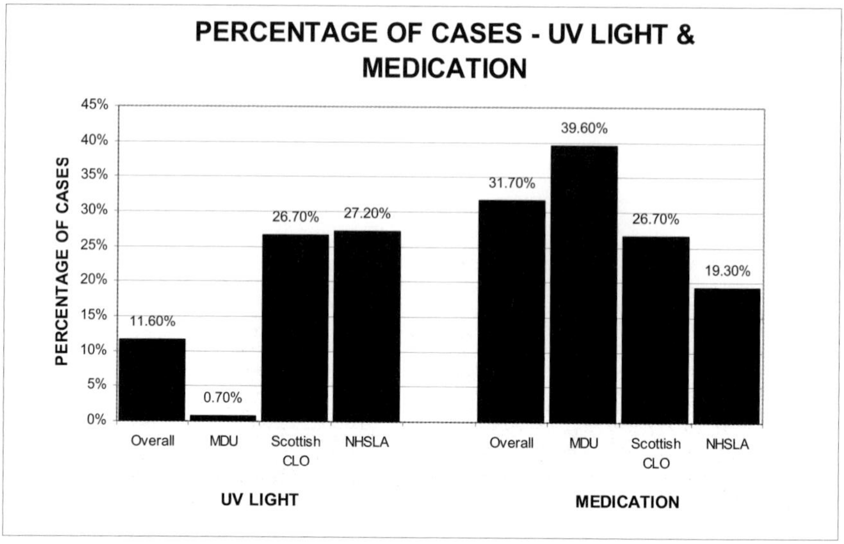

FIGURE 3

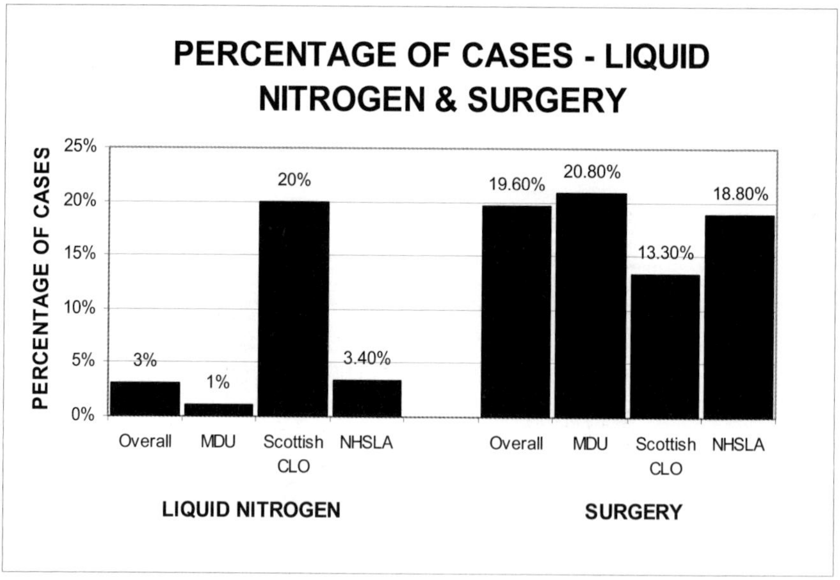

FIGURE 4

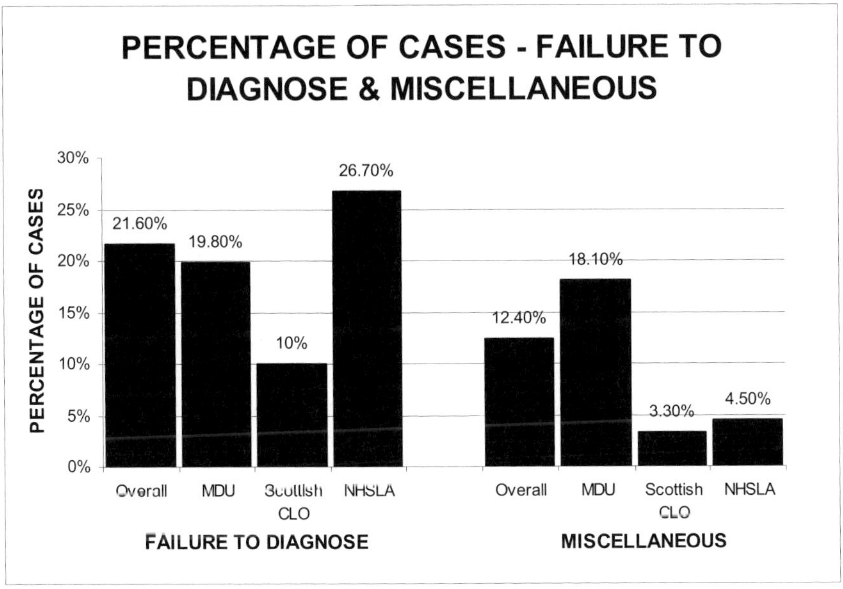

FIGURE 5

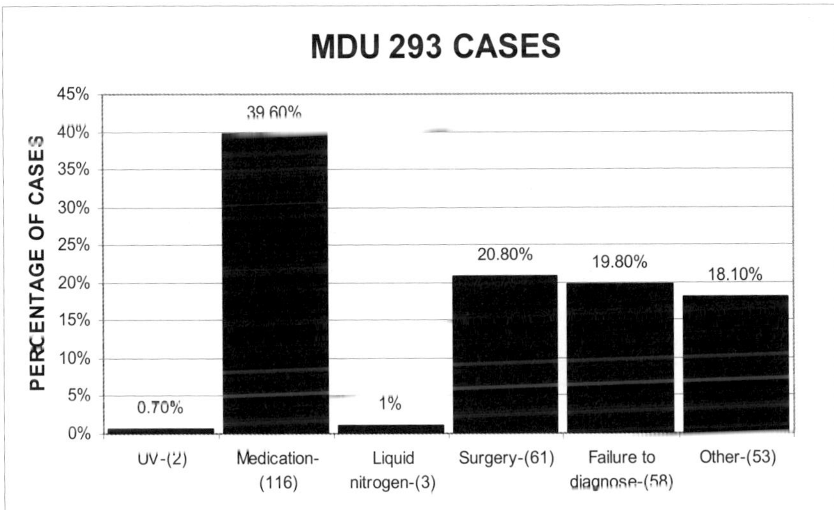

APPENDIX II

UK DERMATOLOGICAL GUIDELINES

(a) Telfer, NR, Colver, GB and Bowers, PW, Guidelines for the management of basal cell carcinoma, *Br J Dermatol*, 1999; 141 : 415-23.

(b) Cox, NH, Eedy, DJ and Morton, CA, Guidelines for the management of Bowen's Disease, *Br J Dermatol*, 1999; 141 : 633-41.

(c) Roberts, DLL, Anstey, AV, Barlow, RJ *et al*, U.K. Guidelines for the management of cutaneous melanoma, *Br J Dermatol*, 2002; 146 : 7-17.

(d) Motley, R, Kersey, P and Lawrence, C, Multiprofessional guidelines for the management of the patient with primary cutaneous squamous cell carcinoma, *Br J Dermatol*, 2002; 146 : 18-25.

(e) Higgins, EM, Fuller, IC and Smith, CH, Guidelines for the management of tinea capitis, *Br J Dermatol*, 2000; 143 : 53-8.

(f) Sterling, JC, Handfield-Jones, F and Hudson, PM, Guidelines for the management of cutaneous warts, *Br J Dermatol*, 2001; 144 : 4-11.

(g) Grattan, C, Powell, S and Humphreys, F, Management and diagnostic guidelines for urticaria and angio-oedema, *Br J Dermatol*, 2001; 144 : 708-14.

(h) Bourke, J, Coulsen, I and English, J, Guidelines for care of contact dermatitis, *Br J Dermatol*, 2001; 145 : 877-85.

(i) Wojnarowska, F, Kirtschig, G, Highet, AS, Venning, VA and Khumalo, NP, Guidelines for the management of bullous pemphigoid, *Br J Dermatol*, 2002; 147: 214-221.

PSYCHIATRY

Trevor Turner

INTRODUCTION

Allegations of negligence against psychiatrists are most commonly allegations of failure to prevent suicide or self-harm. Although there are currently significant legal obstacles to claims based on damage caused to third parties by patients who should have been rendered less harmful by proper treatment, this is an issue which will no doubt be revisited by the courts in the future.

Psychiatry is unique within modern medicine in that it still relies almost entirely on clinical acumen to make an accurate diagnosis. There are no blood tests or X-rays that in themselves can definitively diagnose a psychiatric illness, although such investigations, as well as the standard physical examination, can help eliminate medical conditions causing or mimicking psychiatric symptoms. Psychiatry has also been called 'the other half of medicine', since the psychological consequences of illness, accidents, pain, ageing and bereavement are so pervasive. At least a third of consultations in general practice are to do with psychiatric illnesses, especially anxiety and depression, and as a result some 90% of all psychiatric consultations take place in the General Practitioner's (GP's) surgery. The rising number of prescriptions for tranquillisers and antidepressants, along with the long waiting lists (often up to a year) for specific and popular therapies such as cognitive behaviour therapy (CBT), point to the demand on services

Unfortunately psychiatric diagnoses largely remain at the syndrome rather than the disease level. This means that they are patterns of symptoms which run together, rather than discrete entities. The symptoms often overlap with other disorders (for example there is a category 'mixed anxiety and depression'), and the aetiology, pathology, and course are usually unknown or variable. Contrast this with, for example, the disease of measles. This has a known causal agent (measles virus), a completely standardised course and pattern of symptoms, and there is diagnostic certainty in more than 95% of cases. Nevertheless, and particularly in the more severe mental disorders such as schizophrenia and manic depressive psychosis, operational criteria have been established that are fairly reliable (i.e. most psychiatrists will agree on the diagnosis in most patients), even though the validity (is it really a distinct disease?) remains less certain. Most practitioners will use either the International Classification of Diseases 10th edition (ICD-10), published in 1992 by the World Health Organisation (WHO) and favoured in Europe, or the American Psychiatric Association's fourth revision (1994) of their Diagnostic and Statistical Manual (DSM-IV). Both of these have evolved over time, with new additions expected within the next three years.

Diagnostic certainty is not necessarily required to ensure the right treatment approach. This is because many treatments, for example the use of tranquillisers, are effective to some degree across a number of disorders, and it is well known that the clinical picture can vary over time and depend on a patient's social or personal circumstances. This applies in particular to the commonest category of mental disorders, the Neuroses. Comprising various forms of depression, anxiety (including panic disorder), obsessional compulsive neurosis, phobias (intense, irrational fears), post-traumatic stress disorder (PTSD) and eating disorders such as anorexia nervosa, they are seen as milder than the Psychoses, which comprise conditions in which patients are deemed to be 'out of touch with reality'[1]. Psychoses affect some 2% of the population and comprise schizophrenia (and related disorders), manic depressive psychosis (also known as bipolar affective disorder - BPAD), and a non-specific group of 'organic psychoses', (psychotic reactions where the physical basis, usually some form of brain damage, is known and recognisable). While the psychoses are often more colourful and distinctive, particularly once they have fully evolved (schizophrenia can be quite insidious for a number of months), the greater insight of those with a neurotic disorder alters the doctor/patient relationship. Nevertheless the nature of psychiatric illness in itself (e.g. confused thinking or enhanced anxiety), as well as the stigma associated with it, means that many patients tend to camouflage or entirely deny their symptoms. Some 50% of major depression is missed in general practice, and the notion of 'masked' depression probably underlies many of the suicides that seem to occur out of the blue, not even the closest of friends or families realising anything was wrong.

Finally, in establishing a psychiatric diagnosis, there are some important additions to the standard clinical approach. Thus, taking a proper history from the patient, carrying out a physical examination and performing certain special investigations (e.g. blood tests) are the cornerstones of reaching a clinical diagnosis, whatever the medical/surgical speciality. Management of an illness derives from clarifying the diagnosis and initiating appropriate and accepted treatment (i.e. management = diagnosis + treatment). In the case of psychiatry, however, one also has to carry out a formal mental state examination (MSE) and obtain a corroborative history. This would include talking to a relative or friend (ideally with the patient's permission) and, in the case of more chronic illnesses, obtaining past medical notes, or even occupational health or school records. This approach derives from the difficulties that many psychiatric patients have in providing a clear or coherent account of what has happened to them, particularly in psychotic disorders.

---

[1] Clinical psychiatry avoids the interesting philosophical debate as to what is and is not real by taking an empirical approach. Patients suffering from symptoms such as delusions (false beliefs) or hallucinations (false perceptions, e.g. hearing voices that no one else can hear) are deemed out of touch with reality.

Although the mental state examination is based on a standard pattern of questions (see Table 1), considerable experience is required to identify the nuances of an individual's mood or thinking processes. It relies upon eliciting and critically evaluating the patient's own account of what he feels. Often there are few objective signs of psychiatric illness. An unreliable or inarticulate patient can substantially obscure the diagnosis.

TABLE 1 – OUTLINE OF THE MENTAL STATE EXAMINATION (MSE)

Appearance/Behaviour	Noting how patients dress, their postures and gestures, their facial reactions and their physical reactions to the interview process (i.e. non-verbal communication)
Speech	Noting the form (rather than content) of what people are saying in terms of speed, tone, accent and clarity
Mood/Affect	Outlining a patient's emotional state, in terms of subjective description ("I feel low") as well as objective assessment of the way a patient comes across or even 'affects' the clinician
Thought content/form	Derived from the content of what patients say, in terms of patterns of thinking (e.g. obsession, rumination) as well as the train of thought, which can be 'blocked' or 'tangential' / 'derailed', etc.
Abnormal experiences	Noting descriptions of unusual/false beliefs that comprise delusions (e.g. special powers or persecution) or eliciting hallucinations (perceptions in the absence of a stimulus e.g. voices, visions, smells) that often provide the basis for patients' delusional thinking
Cognition	Assessing a patient's orientation to time, place, or people, their concentration and attention span, and their memory - especially short and medium-term memory.
Insight	Assessing a patient's awareness or lack of awareness of having something wrong with them, their realisation of whether or not they are 'ill', and their willingness to accept treatment and/or their understanding of the treatment approach.

Given the nature of modern psychiatry, it is not surprising that data from the Medical Defence Union (MDU) about the number of claims show that the biggest proportion relates to supervision issues and suicide, followed by medication issues. Failure or delayed diagnosis only accounted for some 4%, but it is important to note that overall numbers are relatively small compared to other specialities. When the MDU data over about ten years are considered more generally in terms of any type of file, claim or otherwise, about half related to the death of a patient. Poor patient outcome is likely to have been a key feature whenever the MDU was contacted. Where there were concerns about diagnosis, there was a fairly even balance between failures to diagnose a physical condition and failure to diagnose a mental health condition. The main mental health conditions involved were depression and schizophrenia. This chapter therefore concentrates on the responsibilities of supervision and suicide avoidance, and the core diagnoses (depression and schizophrenia) which relate to these issues.

DIVISION OF CLINICAL RESPONSIBILITY

All patients in the United Kingdom are registered with a GP. This is part of what is called 'Primary Care'. It is generally accepted that the GP remains the responsible clinician unless a patient is in hospital. It is the GP who initiates the request for involvement of secondary care services, and who makes direct referrals to psychiatric consultants for a second opinion. There are often 'shared care' protocols and guidelines as to the management of patients in a particular geographical area. By and large patients with the more severe forms of mental illness (e.g. schizophrenia) will continue to be supported and treated by psychiatric services (although visiting their GP for prescriptions as well as treatment of physical conditions), while depressive and anxiety disorders tend to be returned to Primary Care after consultation with psychiatric services and treatment and / or advice on treatment from those services. These are not hard and fast rules. Many more stable patients with schizophrenia are only seen by their GP, while many patients with chronic neurotic disorders – a particularly demanding group – will regularly attend psychiatric outpatient clinics, taking the burden off the GP.

A unique feature of psychiatric services is the notion of the 'catchment area'. Each consultant psychiatrist and / or community mental health team will cover a defined geographical locality – for example a particular part of a London Borough – and patients are referred according to their address. This established policy is based upon the need for patients with more chronic conditions to have continuity of care, rather than drifting from hospital to hospital. It also ensures that the more 'difficult' patients are not passed off to someone else, and that a clear pathway of care is established for relapsing conditions. Nevertheless, transient patients are a constant bone of contention. Prolonged debates (and sometimes delays in treatment) occur when hard-pressed services – usually with no available admission beds – try to deflect responsibility for patients deemed 'out of area'.

Most GPs will know their local psychiatric teams, and contact is often strengthened by so called 'liaison clinics' where a community psychiatric nurse (CPN) and / or a consultant psychiatrist visits the GP surgery on a regular basis. Discussion of patients, as well as actually seeing / examining some patients, helps to clarify the diagnosis and to outline a treatment plan for the GP. Many mental health teams have in fact made their catchment area of responsibility coextensive with that of a particular GP or group of GPs. This can, however, be difficult, particularly in the larger conurbations with more transient populations. Also, community mental health teams will provide a filtering mechanism. For example patients referred by GPs for psychotherapy will be screened for suitability before being passed on to specialist resources that are often limited and expensive.

Increasingly community mental health teams are now being linked with social services, providing a single point of entry for all referrals within a particular locality. Such teams will comprise some 15 to 25 individuals, including community psychiatric nurses (CPNs), social workers, occupational therapists, psychologists, support workers and administrative staff. One, or sometimes even two, consultant psychiatrists, as well as junior doctors in training, will be attached to the team. As often as not teams will be associated with a particular hospital ward, but there is considerable national variation in such associations because of the shortage of psychiatric beds. There are also many specialised teams now operating in many parts of the country. Examples include Crisis Response (Home Treatment), Assertive Outreach and Early Intervention. Crisis Response teams see all urgent referrals, briefly. They often treat patients at home in order to try and prevent admission, and pass on those with more severe or chronic illnesses to the regular community teams. Assertive Outreach is aimed at patients who are difficult to engage in services (usually due to lack of insight), and who tend to go in and out of hospital in the so-called 'revolving door' style. Early Intervention Teams are focused on young people developing psychotic illnesses (e.g. in their teens or early twenties), hoping to prevent chronicity. Their effectiveness remains an issue.

All GPs and psychiatric teams should have agreed local guidelines about routine, urgent and emergency referral, in terms of who contacts whom, and where patients will be seen. The routine referral would be where a General Practitioner asks for an outpatient appointment. Waiting times are typically up to three months, although this is very variable. An urgent referral will usually be seen within one or two weeks, while seriously acute requirements are either met by referring the patient directly (on the same day, with an accompanying letter detailing the history and reasons for concern) to the local Accident & Emergency Department (assuming psychiatric involvement is available) or to what are termed 'Psychiatric Emergency Clinics'. These are available in many urban psychiatric departments (often on the same site as general hospitals) during normal working hours. Likewise, routine or urgent home visits (often termed 'domiciliary visits' or DVs for short), for patients reluctant to go to hospital, have to be asked for specifically by the GP. Emergency DVs, for seriously disturbed patients, will involve the on-call ('duty') consultant psychiatrist attending, at any time of the day or night, with the GP, and as often as not with the duty approved social worker[2] and the police.

It is generally accepted that patients admitted to hospital, whether on a voluntary basis or under the 1983 Mental Health Act (MHA) are the responsibility of the consultant psychiatrist. Acute psychiatric wards will generally have one or two

---

[2] The 'Approved Social Worker' (ASW) is required in order to carry out Mental Health Act assessments, the usual basis for emergency home visits.

trainee doctors (at Senior House Officer or Specialist Registrar level) working on them, under the supervision of one or more consultant psychiatrists. Communicating with the GP when patients have been admitted or are discharged, including the provision of a full discharge summary (ideally within two to four weeks of discharge), is standard. Aftercare from hospital admission, particularly for patients with more severe illnesses and who have been treated under the MHA, is based on the Care Programme Approach (CPA). This means that a formal care plan should be written up before discharge, that the patient's needs are fully evaluated, that a Care Co-ordinator (a member of the Community Mental Health Team), takes responsibility for delivering those care needs, and that the patient's aftercare is regularly monitored. The standard documentation on any patient discharged from hospital, or transferred from one district to another, would usually include a full discharge summary (or group of discharge summaries), a CPA form (which should include a crisis plan) and a Risk Assessment (see below). The object is to provide a clear picture of the diagnosis, treatment and any continuing help that an individual patient may need.

In terms of Risk Assessment, there has been some controversy within psychiatry as to whether risk management, (which includes public safety elements), should outweigh the need for a therapeutic doctor-patient alliance and the patient confidentiality which is its corollary. Nevertheless, all patients now seen in psychiatric departments, whether as inpatients, outpatients or in the community, need to be assessed for risk. This involves assessment of the likelihood of self-harm, self-neglect, of exploitation by others and of danger to others. Standard risk assessment forms, of varying length (from one to ten sides of foolscap) have to be filled in, documenting the relevant aspects of a patient's presentation. It is accepted that key factors in assessing risk include the nature of the patient's symptoms, the support available to patients in terms of their home environment (e.g. supportive or exploitative / neglectful family; degree of isolation; quality of housing; available day care) and any previous history of assaultative or self-harming behaviours. These assessments should help to determine the level of support a patient needs and the crisis plan to be adopted if a patient starts to relapse. However, predictions of patient behaviour are most uncertain: even a well-documented history has poor predictive value in the context of the wide range of possible social and family events. There is also no evidence of the effectiveness of such risk management compared to, for example, a trusting therapeutic relationship with one's doctor or a willingness to comply with medication.

A number of patients may be seen both by their General Practitioner and their Community Mental Health Team (including a consultant psychiatrist), because of the complexity of their condition. Individual agreements about division of labour are often tacit rather than written down, but it is routine practice for a psychiatrist seeing a patient in an outpatient department to write a letter to the GP outlining the details of assessment and treatment. It is not routine practice for the GP to write to the secondary care team, updating them on what is happening in primary care, unless further help from the secondary care team is being sought. This can cause problems, eg uncertainty about the medication prescribed, or the monitoring of certain tests (some patients for example require Lithium levels to be assessed by a blood test, in order to ensure that the level is not in the toxic range). Agreement between the GP, the consultant and the community mental health team about who does what should be by express individual arrangement or by agreed local protocols. Copying clinic letters to the patients themselves is becoming increasingly accepted as a means of ensuring that everyone (including the patient) knows the diagnostic and treatment issues.

A particular issue in the primary care / psychiatric team interface, and in terms of the division of responsibility, is concern about confidentiality. It is generally accepted that doctor-to- doctor communications are confidential, but the teamwork approach of psychiatric services means that other healthcare workers will be privy to that information. Some patients may not wish the whole team to be informed. Some may even request that their GP is not informed of their symptom or diagnosis, because of embarrassment or fears of stigma affecting their employment opportunities. Patients may express beliefs or intentions that put them at risk to themselves or others, and clinicians of every type may consider that breaking confidentiality is required to protect public safety. Giving out a patient's details to a third party (e.g. the police, relatives, housing workers), without a patient's documented permission, is a regular bone of contention. It is important to make careful notes about perceived risk and to obtain senior clinical (if not legal) advice as to the confidentiality issue.

The most important clinical mistakes relating to the organisation of psychiatric services are summarised in Table 2.

TABLE 2 – IMPORTANT MISTAKES IN SERVICE ORGANISATION/COMMUNICATION / PRACTICE

- Failure to assess a patient appropriately, in terms of a careful and documented Mental State Examination and obtaining a suitably detailed and corroborated history, and failure in the appropriate communication of the diagnosis and treatment to a relevant professional.

- Failure to prescribe and/or monitor correctly a patient's medication, in terms of dosage, side-effects, interactions with other drugs and assessment of drug levels (e.g. Lithium) when toxicity may occur.

- Failure to communicate clearly between the GP and Consultant (and Community Mental Health Team) about the agreed diagnosis, the care plan, the medication and the level of urgency of any assessment

- Delay in initiating urgent treatment for patients at risk to themselves or others, whether via voluntary or involuntary means (e.g. use of the Mental Health Act), especially when there is an agreed care/crisis plan in place.

- Inappropriate communication to a third party of a patient's details without documented permission, or failure to communicate an at-risk situation when risk to the public is involved.

DEPRESSION

Basics

Depression is a common disorder which affects up to 20% of the population in the course of their lives ('lifetime prevalence'). Its causes remains uncertain, but it tends to run in families. In addition some people are clearly sensitive to untoward life events, (for example bereavements or other losses), in ways that seem to indicate a mixture of innate vulnerability and social stressors. Diagnosis is based upon eliciting a number of typical features. These are outlined in Table 3. Standardised rating scales can be used. These score patients on the basis of their response to a number of set questions. These are generally more useful when assessing the severity of an already diagnosed disorder but scores above a certain cut-off point are also taken as having some diagnostic validity. There is a considerable symptomatic overlap, however, with a number of physical illnesses, in part because of the wide range of symptoms that depressed patients can experience.

TABLE 3 – DEPRESSION: CLINICAL FEATURES

- Depressed mood: "what's the point?"
- Loss of interest and enjoyment in things
- Reduced energy, tiring easily and thus doing less
- Reduced concentration and attention
- Negative view of one's abilities and character
- Sense of guilt and unworthiness
- 'Hopeless' and 'helpless' outlook
- Ideas and / or acts of self-harm or suicide
- Impaired sleep and / or appetite
- Loss of weight, libido and / or excessive sleep

In some cases ('atypical')

- Marked anxiety and agitation; 'histrionic' behaviour
- Enhanced irritability or outbursts of anger
- Increased alcohol or drug usage
- More obsessional, phobic, or hypochondriacal symptoms
- Somatic complaints such as headaches, back pain, constipation, dizzy spells, a sense of pressure on the head

Severe

- Delusions of sin, poverty, imminent disaster, negativity e.g. "unpardonable sins" or "there's no blood in my body"
- Hallucinations – defamatory voices, smelling rotten flesh
- Psychomotor retardation or stupor (inability to move or speak)

Thus, feeling tired, poor sleep, loss of appetite and loss of weight are typical features of a number of physical illnesses (for example cancer and tuberculosis). The natural tendency of medical practitioners is first to explore the possible physical basis of such symptoms, for example by using blood tests and X-rays - a process usually preferred by the patient. The fear of missing something 'organic' – *i.e.* a treatable physical illness posing a risk to life – tends to dominate clinical practice. Depression is seen as a diagnosis of exclusion. Yet the features of depression are in themselves quite striking. This is particularly true of the sense of guilt and self-blame. The *pattern* of symptoms (both psychological and physical) needs to be appreciated. This, together with the absence of any abnormal physical or biochemical / haematological findings, can lead to a confident diagnosis of depression. It is not surprising that there is a high rate of 'masked' depression, especially in general practice, where a lack of time to explore the patient's full history and symptomatology can lead to false reassurances that there is nothing seriously wrong.

Depressed patients may also have elements of a bipolar disorder (manic depressive) with episodes of depression being preceded or followed by episodes of feeling high or manic. This relatively happy stage (although irritability is a common feature), when patients feel energetic, on the go, and can be 'the life and soul of the party', tends to obscure the underlying mood disorder, particularly if it is in the form of hypomania. This is a milder form of mania, in which patients are not obviously disturbed, but just seem to be doing more, talking a bit quicker, needing less sleep, and perhaps taking on more than they can cope with. The classic problems associated with such mood disorders, (whether manic depression or just depression), are suicidal behaviour and actual suicide.

Depression and suicidal behaviour

The typical features of someone at increased risk of suicide are outlined in Table 4. It is generally accepted that at least 70% to 80% of people who commit suicide do have a depressive disorder. This depression is often compounded by personality problems, alcohol or drug dependence, some other chronic or painful illness, personal bereavements or social isolation. Furthermore, the great majority (about 75%) do not attend their GP or even a specialist in the year before suicide, and even those who do attend do not necessarily complain about being depressed. Prevention of suicide, therefore, while certainly enhanced by making the diagnosis of depression and by treating the disorder, tends to rely on broader methods such as making it more physically difficult for the patient to kill himself. The switch from carbon monoxide (coal gas) to North Sea gas in the 1970s led to a significant decline in suicide, and the outlawing of personal handguns, the fitting of catalytic convertors for car exhausts, and better designed bridges and high points (to avoid jumping) can all contribute. Safety audits on inpatient units can also reduce risk by removing ligature points (to avoid hanging) and by checking window / door design (to avoid patients going AWOL).

TABLE 4 – TYPICAL FEATURES OF SOMEONE AT INCREASED RISK OF SUICIDE

- Suicidal/self-blaming attitudes and expressions
- Male – especially if > 50 years and living alone
- Depressive illness of any type
- Alcohol/drug dependence
- Separated/divorced/widowed
- Social and personal isolation ('anomie')
- Serious/painful physical illness
- Recent discharge from psychiatric care
- Job loss/police involvement/prison
- Certain occupations e.g. farmers, doctors, lawyers

Differential diagnosis

In terms of differential diagnosis, the most important disorders are listed in Table 5. Because of the 'organic' bias of most practitioners, it is standard practice to carry out a physical examination and a range of routine blood tests (e.g. thyroid function tests, a full blood count, liver function tests) for any depressed patient, so as to exclude, for example, an underlying cancer or endocrine disorder. Failure to carry out such basic assessments, particularly in middle-aged to elderly people where the prevalence of physical disorders is likely to be higher, should be seen as unacceptable practice. However, the dilemma as to how far to take such investigations is not easily resolved, particularly in patients with atypical features. Should every depressed patient, for example, have a CT brain scan? Repeated cycles of investigation can fuel the illness fears of those of an anxious or hypochondriacal nature, reducing possible compliance with subsequent antidepressant treatment. Nevertheless, every now and then a patient will end up being treated for depression, but will emerge later as having, for example, a brain tumour, that might have responded to earlier intervention. These are generally exceptional and rare cases, but tend to be more widely remembered and documented than the hundreds of routine negative investigations that have created delays in reaching the right diagnosis and treatment (for depression), and which, by reason of that delay, may have increased the likelihood of a suicide attempt.

TABLE 5 – DIFFERENTIAL DIAGNOSIS OF DEPRESSION

PSYCHIATRIC CONDITIONS

- Generalised Anxiety Disorder/Panic Syndrome/Agoraphobia
- Obsessional Compulsive Disorder (OCD)
- Alcohol Dependence
- Drug Dependence (e.g. heroin, cocaine)
- Anorexia / Bulimia Nervosa
- Personality Disorder
- Post-Traumatic Stress Disorder
- Schizophrenia (especially in early stages or as co-morbid condition)
- Dementia (especially in early stages)

PHYSICAL CONDITIONS

- Endocrine disorders e.g. hypothyroidism; Cushing's syndrome, Addison's disease
- Anaemias
- Space-occupying lesion e.g. brain tumour
- Autoimmune disorder e.g. systemic lupus
- Chronic infection e.g. tuberculosis
- Liver disease e.g. hepatitis

While the most dangerous outcome of failing to diagnose depression is suicide, untoward consequences can occur if depression is wrongly diagnosed instead of another psychiatric disorder from which the patient is suffering. Many patients with schizophrenia, particularly in the early stages of the illness, are diagnosed as having depression, do not receive the antipsychotics and other treatment required to minimise both symptoms and the subsequent impact of symptoms, and may indulge in at-risk behaviours including suicide. Some 10% to 15% of schizophrenic patients kill themselves, and many assault others. However, some patients' illnesses do genuinely change over time, so regular assessment is always required.

Likewise, treating patients merely for 'depression' when in fact they are suffering from alcohol dependence, panic attacks (part of panic syndrome with agoraphobia, for example) or features of a personality disorder can deprive people of more appropriate therapy. Again, however, there is a substantial overlap of symptoms, as well as treatments, particularly when patients present with 'agitated depression', and careful review is required. It is particularly difficult in elderly people to differentiate depression from early onset dementia. Both syndromes share a picture of apathy, loss of concentration, impaired memory, impaired orientation (e.g. to time or day) and self-neglect. The unreliability of the diagnosis 'presenile dementia' is such that a trial of treatment (antidepressants or even electroconvulsive therapy – ECT) is accepted as the only safe indicator of the true, underlying diagnosis.

The treatment of depression

While failure to diagnose a treatable organic disorder is one of the most publicized forms of legally important clinical mistake, failure to treat depression with sufficient vigour (and safely) is not uncommon. The standard treatment of depression is antidepressant therapy with or without some form of supportive psychotherapy, and, increasingly, cognitive behaviour therapy (CBT), which aims to change patients' negative views of themselves and their world. Some patients will not accept medication, preferring only a 'talking' therapy, while others wish to avoid what they see as the tiresome and embarrassing exposure of their personalities and lives to strangers, wishing just to take a pill. Documenting patients' attitudes is good practice, as is explaining the nature, side-effects and course of treatment likely to be required. Advice on general lifestyle (sleeping, eating, consumption of drugs or alcohol) and supportive daily activities (e.g. taking exercise) can also be of benefit and should be routine practice.

The mainstay of modern treatment of depression is antidepressant medication. As of March 2003 there were 27 separate antidepressant drugs listed in the British National Formulary (BNF), and there is no evidence that any one drug is more efficacious than another. Between 50% and 80% of patients will improve to some degree on medication, if it is taken for long enough (usually at least four weeks but often up to three months or more) and at the right dosage. Failure to maintain treatment or to provide a full and proper dosage, are the common causes of failure of therapy. Failure may be due to unacceptable side-effects. The popular first-line drugs in the modern era are the so-called SSRIs (specific serotonin reuptake inhibitors). These have fewer troublesome side-effects than the older tricyclic antidepressants, and unlike the tricyclics are also safe in overdose. There is some evidence that their introduction has reduced suicide rates, but prescribing smaller amounts of drug, and giving medication to patients' relatives so that the relatives can supervise administration, can be just as effective. Failure to respond to one SSRI will generally require an alternative type of medication, but many patients are moved from similar drug to similar drug rather than being switched appropriately to another class of drug. Incidentally there will always be higher suicide rates associated with the most heavily prescribed antidepressant, due to their disproportionately higher use for non-responding disorders.

Failure of response to antidepressant treatment should initiate a review of the diagnosis. Alcohol dependence and underlying physical disorder should be checked. Compliance can be assessed by measuring blood levels of the drugs.[3]. The use of combinations of drugs is best left to experienced consultant psychiatrists, and such combinations are generally recommended (often with the addition of the mood stabilizer, Lithium, as a supplement) for what is deemed 'resistant depression'. Unfortunately the evidence base for the most effective

[3] Up to 50% of patients do not take the drugs prescribed to them, some never starting at all, others giving up within a few days or not taking a regular dosage. Unfortunately measurement of drug levels is not routinely available from most NHS laboratories, and such tests can be time-consuming and expensive.

form of treatment for resistant depression remains extremely limited, but the use of ECT, especially in the elderly, can be startlingly effective. Many practitioners would suggest that ECT has fewer side-effects and brings relief more quickly than standard antidepressants, and it is certainly the treatment of choice in those at risk to their health because of stupor (i.e. not eating and drinking) and serious physical and psychological debility (including intense suicidal ideation).

When caring for the seriously depressed patient, and particularly the patient at risk of suicide, both the type and place of treatment must be considered.. Particular risk factors for suicide (see above, Table 4) include age, isolation and severe depressive illness. Hospital admission, possibly under the terms of the Mental Health Act, must always be considered. If necessary, emergency ECT can be given to an unwilling patient under Section 62 of the Mental Health Act, so as to avoid significant risk to health. Management of the suicidal patient on a hospital ward will require close nursing observation (sometimes one to one observation, with a nurse sitting by the patient day and night). The maintenance of physical health is also important.

Despite the greater awareness of depression, and despite most GPs regularly updating themselves on methods of examination and the use of newer treatments (such as the new antidepressants), establishing the diagnosis in a patient unwilling to divulge the way they feel can be extremely difficult. In fact, in the hours or days before a successful suicide a number of patients will seem much better in themselves. They will often be relaxed, will not talk about negative things, and their relatives will judge them to be in a stable state of mind. This may be in contrast to their previous troubled demeanour, the decision to end their life seemingly having taken away the burden of an underlying depressive outlook and their sense of guilt or unworthiness.

Failure to diagnose and / or treat depression will generally be due to lack of time to explore a patient's symptoms, not obtaining a proper corroborative history (e.g. from a wife or husband), inadequate dosages of medication, or persistently hunting for some physical cause, (repeating blood tests endlessly, for example) rather than obtaining a more experienced psychiatric assessment. Depression can sometimes be one element of a mixed picture of presentation, particularly in patients with chronic pain states (e.g. after car accidents) or in patients evolving from states of bereavement or post-traumatic stress disorder (PTSD). In the management of chronic conditions, missing the depressive element can lead to a vicious cycle, with depression-enhancing pain and pain-enhancing depression. The most important clinical mistakes in the management of depression are summarised in Table 6.

TABLE 6 – DEPRESSION – IMPORTANT CLINICAL MISTAKES

- Failure to assess for underlying physical illness, especially in an older patient (e.g. > 50 yrs), either by not performing a standard physical examination or not carrying out appropriate investigations, or both.

- Failure to recognise the severity of a depressive disorder, and the consequent suicidal risk, when a full history and pattern of symptoms has been elicited. (This excludes 'masked' depression, where a patient simply has not informed the clinician of his/her true symptoms).

- Failure to recognise alternative psychiatric diagnoses, especially the symptoms of dementia, schizophrenia or manic depressive psychoses. This is usually due to inadequate history-taking and/or an inadequate MSE.

- Failure to monitor medications closely, especially when prescribing those known to be dangerous in overdosage, such as tricyclic antidepressants, or when potential interactions might occur.

SCHIZOPHRENIA

Basics

Schizophrenia is one of the major psychoses, with a world-wide prevalence of about 1%. Because of the stigma attached to mental illness, and to schizophrenia in particular, the incorrect attribution of schizophrenia tends to be more widely publicised, but failure to diagnose the illness is probably more important in terms of subsequent risk and untoward incident. The term is often used loosely to describe a 'split personality' (e.g. Jekyll and Hyde type), but this does not correctly describe the type of symptoms that patients experience. The typical symptoms are summarised in Table 7, and various combinations of these have been used to outline certain subcategories (e.g. paranoid or hebephrenic schizophrenia). It is also now accepted that there are what seem like partial forms of the condition, such as schizo-typal disorder (rather eccentric, aloof, suspicious personalities with intermittent unusual experiences), or delusional disorder, characterised by the relatively late onset (in middle age) of a set of delusions, usually with no other symptoms whatsoever.

TABLE 7 – THE CORE SYMPTOMS OF SCHIZOPHRENIA

'POSITIVE'	*'NEGATIVE'**
Primary Delusions (incl. delusional perception, akin to a 'brainwave'**)	Loss of insight Poverty of speech
Hallucinations (especially third person, auditory hallucinations ('voices') or a 'running commentary')	Flat / inappropriate affect Loss of drive (apathy) Anhedonia (no interest in pleasurable activities)
Thought disorder (e.g. muddled thoughts, thought block, thought broadcast/insertion/ withdrawal	
Passivity Experience (one's body, ideas, feelings seeming not to be controlled by oneself)	Social Withdrawal

Also: Motor/Postural abnormalities (e.g. waxy flexibility of the limbs) as seen in Catatonic Schizophrenia

* The terms 'positive' and 'negative' are used to outline symptoms that are, apparently, phenomena additional to normal psychological experience (e.g. hallucinations) or deterioration/losses from normal functioning. Antipsychotic medication is primarily effective for positive symptoms, while negative symptoms tend to predict a chronic illness.

** 'Delusional perception' is a term describing the dual process of perceiving something and deriving a false belief from it e.g. "as soon as the lights turned red I realised I was the Angel Gabriel".

As with depression, the diagnosis of schizophrenia is based upon a detailed history. A history from another person is absolutely vital, as is a proper mental state examination. It is not uncommon for insufficient information to be available, or for families to attribute symptoms to drug usage or school pressures. Onset is usually between 15 and 25 years of age, and differentiating a schizophrenic illness from forms of adolescent distress or drug dependence can be very difficult. There are often inherited factors, and dysfunctional families with 'high expressed emotion' (i.e. a tendency to be verbally critical and demanding) can exacerbate relapse. The first-rank symptoms of delusions, hallucinations, thought disorder and passivity experience are central to establishing the diagnosis but may take time and persistence to elicit.

Lack of insight is part of the definition of psychoses such as schizophrenia. This means that many patients will at some time need to be treated against their will, under the terms of the Mental Health Act (MHA). Clinicians are rightly wary of using such powers unless there is clearly a defined mental illness associated with agreed risks to health and / or safety. However, particularly in the acute situation when patients are extremely disturbed and need to be assessed in a safe and therapeutic environment, it is accepted amongst clinicians that what they term 'common law'[4] enables them to treat patients against their will (e.g. by forcibly sedating them), the patient's best health or safety interests being served in that way. There are many causes of acute psychotic presentation (e.g. drug or alcohol abuse and head injury) and inpatient assessment can quickly differentiate these from a true schizophrenia.

TABLE 8 – DIFFERENTIAL DIAGNOSIS OF SCHIZOPHRENIA

- Manic Depressive Psychosis (esp. manic phase)
- Drug-Induced Psychosis e.g. amphetamines; LSD
- Alcohol Dependence / Withdrawal
- Personality Disorder esp. Paranoid or Borderline types
- Temporal Lobe Epilepsy
- Brain Damage from: Trauma e.g. head injury
Tumour esp. Temporal lobe
Infection e.g. encephalitis / meningitis / HIV / GPI
Dementia
- Metabolic disorders (rare) e.g. Systemic Lupus Erythematosus; Wilson's Disease; Porphyria

The most important differential diagnoses to consider in cases of suspected schizophrenia are outlined in Table 8. The most common diagnostic dilemma is distinguishing schizophrenia from some forms of manic depressive psychosis, since they share a number of symptoms (for example delusions and hallucinations). Confusingly there is also an interim condition called schizo-affective disorder, combining elements of both. Sometimes the type of delusion can help to differentiate between the various possibilities: thus grandiose delusions are more likely to be associated with mania, whereas bizarre paranoid delusions (e.g. believing a computer has been transplanted into the brain) are more often of schizophrenic origin. More usefully distinctive are the forms of thought disorder that are particularly linked with schizophrenia: see Table 7. Regular examination of patients and skilled observation by trained nurses, are essential parts of the diagnostic process. A key function of an acute inpatient psychiatric ward is to carry out such assessments. Obtaining the necessary

[4] This term is used widely by doctors in the UK as a means of justifying treatment where the patient is unable (e.g. unconsciousness or gross confusion) to give valid consent, although most doctors probably have no clear idea of the legal issues involved.

collateral information from family and friends is also important. Nevertheless it is accepted that manic depressive and schizophrenic illnesses can change over time. One can transmute into the other. Given the similarity of treatment approaches, outcome often does not depend crucially on a precise diagnosis. Whatever the exact diagnosis, however, failure to treat a psychosis (i.e. with appropriate medication) remains the most important clinical misjudgement.

As with depression, a proper physical examination should be carried out, as should a number of basic special investigations. These generally include a urine drug screen (for all types of illicit drug, especially amphetamines, LSD, and MDMA – 'ecstasy' or 'E'), assessments of renal and liver function (so as to try to exclude alcohol dependence), and for patients with any kind of neurological symptom a CT brain scan and / or an electroencephalogram (EEG) are commonly performed. However, such tests are designed to exclude often quite rare diagnoses, and the typical patterns of schizophrenic symptoms are regarded as reliable indicators of a substantial illness. Even if a test for drugs or some organic abnormality proves positive, the psychotic symptoms will still require antipsychotic treatment. The technical aetiology of psychotic symptoms is often irrelevant to the treatment.

It can be particularly difficult when a patient describes hearing 'voices' (a very common symptom in schizophrenia, affecting over 80% of patients), but the characteristics of that voice-hearing experience do not quite tally with a typical schizophrenic experience. There is evidence that up to 30% of the 'normal' population hear voices at some time (e.g. going off to sleep - so-called hypnagogic hallucinations), without having any particular illness. Some individuals hear voices but otherwise seem quite well. Fleeting or fragmented words or comments can be associated with a number of other psychological conditions, but these may not respond to antipsychotic medication. Likewise, a sense of enhanced self-consciousness, amounting almost to a sense of paranoia, is typically experienced by some patients with agoraphobia and panic disorder (they think people are looking at them) as well as patients with forms of personality disorder, especially when this is combined with heavy alcohol usage. Such paranoid thinking and voice-like experiences, where the voice comes from inside the head (rather than from the TV or through the walls) and is recognised as abnormal by the patient, are termed 'pseudo-hallucinations' and do not indicate schizophrenia.

Delusions can also be a problem. Generally defined as 'false beliefs', and as out of quiltre with a patient's social and cultural background, they by definition tend to dominate a patient's attitudes and thinking, and are held with absolute conviction. When obviously bizarre and complex, (for example a patient believing that the FBI has created a special device that pumps a miasma into his room and communicates with him directly via the television), they are not difficult to diagnose. When more banal, (for example patients complaining of neighbours harassing them through thin tower block walls or adolescents simply complaining of being teased at school), they can be very difficult to unravel.

Interpreting intense religious experiences, (for example hearing the voice of God or feeling the touch of the Holy Ghost), can also be very difficult, especially when family or cultural sensitivities are aroused.

The treatment of schizophrenia

Diagnosing someone as having a schizophrenic illness will almost always mean that antipsychotic drugs will be prescribed, and these can have considerable side-effects. The inappropriate provision of such drugs to individuals not requiring them may lead to significant sedation, endocrine impairment (e.g. amenorrhoea) and forms of movement disorder (e.g. restless or jerky limbs). Great care is therefore required in prescribing and monitoring such treatment. Likewise, maintaining remission in schizophrenia requires long-term medication for the great majority of patients, but using the minimum effective dose, and switching medications if side-effects are intolerable, are all part of good practice. The written care plan should set out the frequency of assessment and what to do if a patient starts to relapse.

Unfortunately up to 80% of patients relapse over the course of the 1 – 2 years after a first admission. This is almost always because they discontinue medication. Failure to monitor such patients regularly, via outpatient or community/ home contact can result in at-risk behaviour in those known to have been assaultative/self-harming in the past. Lack of patient and/or family insight can make it very difficult to maintain contact with some patients and their families. Use of the Mental Health Act, however, has to await some clear symptom of both illness and at-risk behaviour.

Non-pharmacological treatments include the use of day centres to provide social support, help with housing and benefits, and, for some patients the use of cognitive behavioural therapy. This therapy is aimed at challenging delusional beliefs and attempting to help patients develop alternative ideas about the experiences that fuel those beliefs. 'Voices' can be considered as distractions rather than intrusions, and methods of reducing their impact are employed. Failure to provide cognitive behavioural therapy for schizophrenic patients is largely due to lack of trained therapists (usually psychologists or nurses), but the evidence that this therapy 'cures' rather than ameliorates symptomatic distress remains limited. Offering patients some structured psychological support should be seen, nevertheless, as part of routine practice.

Under-diagnosis of schizophrenia, or failure to treat the illness, is unfortunately a significant factor in a number of homicide inquiries and in 'untoward incidents' where patients, having relapsed, have assaulted members of their family or the public. Failure to treat often occurs because a patient is taking illicit drugs and it is wrongly assumed that a psychotic presentation is drug-induced rather than an indication of schizophrenic illness simply associated with drug-taking. Similarly, it is often decided, wrongly, that the dominant problem is a personality disorder, thus shifting responsibility from general psychiatric services. Also, many patients will prefer to see themselves as having something like a depression, and unless the nature of this 'depression' is explored by the clinician, inappropriate treatment may be given. Cultural differences may also be a factor in failure to diagnose, unusual behaviour being attributed to ethnic idiosyncrasy rather than illness. Having said that, there may be real differences in the incidence of schizophrenia between different cultural/racial groups. The higher rates of schizophrenia apparent amongst African-Caribbean people in the UK have not been satisfactorily accounted for.

The most significant clinical mistakes in the management of schizophrenia are summarised in Table 9.

TABLE 9 – CLINICAL MISTAKES IN THE MANAGEMENT OF SCHIZOPHRENIA

- The misdiagnosis of schizophrenia in patients who are not schizophrenic but are suffering from drug or alcohol-related conditions, particularly in association with forms of personality disorder (e.g. paranoid, borderline). This generally results from a failure to assess the mental state on a regular basis, to obtain a proper corroborative history, or to review the patient over a sufficient period of time. Inappropriate treatment with major tranquillisers can lead to significant side-effects including movement disorders (e.g. tardive dyskinesia) or disturbance of endocrine function (e.g. amenorrhoea in women).

- Missing the diagnosis of schizophrenia, by attributing symptoms to drug usage, personality disorder, or another psychiatric diagnosis such as depression. This may be associated with patients presenting with more 'difficult' behaviours (e.g. physical assaults), leading to ward pressures on the clinician to discharge the patient because of difficulties in management. Patients and their families may collude with such approaches, owing to lack of insight and the stigma of mental illness.

- In terms of treatment, prescribing an inadequate or over-large dosage of medication, allowing distressing symptoms to persist, or distressing side-effects to accrue. Regular and documented monitoring of a patient's treatment, discussion with the patient and carers as to the nature of the treatment and possible alternatives, and attempting to ensure compliance, are all part of good practice.

- The formal Homicide Inquiries (about 20 to 30 a year), many of which report on patients with schizophrenia who have been involved in untoward incidents, generally point to poor communication between clinicians, lack of staff resources (especially trained staff), clinicians not taking account of the expressed concerns of family and / or carers, and patients being lost to follow-up because of inadequate monitoring or attempts to make contact. Varying versions of events (e.g. undocumented telephone conversations) tend to make such emotionally charged events quite difficult to clarify.

GENERAL PRACTICE

Gavin Young

INTRODUCTION

General Practice is different - and difficult. Hospitals – with the exception of accident and emergency and genito-urinary medicine departments - only receive patients into secondary care after referral from primary care.

General practice - which makes up much of primary care - has been described by Paul Hodgkin in a brilliant essay[1] as the gatekeeper who allows the wizard (secondary care) to keep his special spells for those who really need it. Without the gatekeeper all would have access to the wizard and he would not cope. This does mean, though, that the gatekeeper can become unpopular when he blocks access to the wizard. Sometimes the gatekeeper gets it wrong and blocks access to someone who really would benefit from the wizard's magic.

Clinical guidelines are increasingly important throughout medicine. General Practice is no exception. There are various compendia of guidelines, and anyone involved in litigation needs to look at the relevant ones.[2]

This chapter begins by looking at three issues which constantly recur in cases of alleged GP negligence (failure to refer/delayed referral, medication errors, and errors in the performance of practical procedures). It then considers the conditions and diseases which most commonly bring GPs into the courts.

FAILURE TO REFER AND DELAYED REFERRAL

General

Most claims against General Practitioners (GPs) involve delay in referral to secondary care. GPs (known also as family physicians) are involved in over 90 % of patient-doctor contacts in the NHS. Only a tiny fraction of such consultations lead to a referral.

---

[1] Mathers, N and Hodgkin, P, The Gatekeeper and the Wizard: a fair tale, *BMJ*, 1989 298: 172-3.

[2] The most useful and up to date compendium is: *Guidelines; summarising clinical guidelines for primary care,* Medendium Group Publishing. Published three times per year (http://www.eguidelines.co.uk). This source includes all relevant guidelines from NICE (the National Institute for Clinical Excellence).

The Medical Defence Union (MDU) and Medical Protection Society (MPS) keep data on cases of litigation against their members. Delays in referral make up about half of all cases. This should be no surprise. GPs have to accept a mass of unfiltered suffering humanity and, unlike hospitals, cannot close their doors when they are busy (albeit some litigation occurs because occasionally receptionists turn patients away or fail to offer timely appointments when the patient's condition merits urgent medical attention). Out of this undifferentiated mass GPs have to select:

- those who will get better without (or maybe, despite!) medical intervention;
- those who need treatment from the GP;
- those who need hospital treatment.

Further decisions need to be taken with this last group: does the patient need urgent admission - now, within the hour or that day, or can treatment await an out-patient appointment and, if so, must this be urgent or can it wait? Sometimes within the NHS such an appointment might be a year away. GPs often have to make these difficult decisions with very poor quality information to guide them because:

- patients are often very poor historians;
- examination findings may be absent or misleading;
- special investigations may take days to come back;
- many tests are unavailable in primary care.

The skill of a good general practitioner is to make a good enough decision given this poor quality information - coping with doubt is a prerequisite for a GP. Many years before Paul Hodgkin wrote *The Gatekeeper and the Wizard* his father, Keith Hodgkin, wrote *Towards Earlier Diagnosis in Primary Care*[3]. Hodgkin wrote: "The GP must use comparatively crude, quick, simple methods to provide the hospital with a suitably refined distillate. The hospital can then apply its own skills and complex techniques of diagnosis." He describes how he had 12 patients over 20 years who developed cerebral tumours. In every case he had initially diagnosed a tension headache. This is hardly surprising, given he saw two hundred patients each year with tension headache. Delay in referral does not equal negligence – though it sometimes can.

There are many reasons for delay in referral or failure to refer. These are considered below.

---

[3] Hodgkin, K, *Towards earlier diagnosis: a family doctor's approach*, 1963, Livingstone, Edinburgh.

Failure to visit or consult with the patient

Although GPs are not obliged to visit patients at home they are required to put themselves in a position to provide appropriate care. If it is not possible to reach a diagnosis and provide management through a telephone consultation, the GP must see the patient, even if that patient only rang for advice. If that patient cannot get to the doctor's surgery or, out of hours, to the emergency treatment centre (ETC), then the doctor will need to visit or arrange transfer to hospital.

Case study

A man complaining of breathlessness and weakness was told to come down to the ETC but said he did not feel up to it. The emergency doctor suggested he see his own GP the next day. The next day the patient was dead from pneumonia. The GP had not gathered enough information over the phone to know it was safe to leave the patient unseen until the next day.

Failure to take a proper history

The history is the cornerstone of proper diagnosis. It is important to probe beyond the patient's own account.

Case study

A GP saw a 35-year-old man who complained of (in the patient's words) "indigestion- like" chest pain and took him at his word without enquiring further. Had he done so the patient would have admitted that antacids did not seem to help the pain very much and that the pain, though worse after meals, was also worse on exertion. Ranitidine was prescribed, but the patient collapsed with a myocardial infarction before he reached the chemist

Failure to examine adequately

It should go without saying that a diligent clinical examination may be crucial.

Case study

A seven-year-old boy complained of lower abdominal pain coming on earlier in the afternoon while playing football. The GP found some lower abdominal tenderness but nothing else and diagnosed a muscle tear. He failed to examine, and therefore failed to find, a very tender left testicle which had twisted. The testicle was not viable the next day when the correct diagnosis was made by another GP.

Failure to consider the correct diagnosis

Even when the history taking and examination have been adequate the GP may fail to consider the correct diagnosis.

Case study

A child was brought between the ages of two and six years to a series of different GPs with a recurrent cough. Asthma was diagnosed but no one doctor followed the child up adequately to see if there was a response to treatment with beta agonists, steroid inhalers or antibiotics. In fact the child had cystic fibrosis. No doctor considered cystic fibrosis until there had been years of lung damage and two more siblings had been born - the last child also being affected.

Considering the correct diagnosis but wrongly discounting it

This often occurs because the patient has no, or few, risk factors for the condition considered. It is important to understand some basic things about risk factors. Take the example of pulmonary embolism (PE). Smoking and obesity are both risk factors for PE. PE is thus commoner in percentage terms in the population of obese women who smoke, than in the general population, but there are far more women who are not obese and do not smoke who can and do get PE than there are obese, smoking women who do get PE. Accordingly PE will occur more regularly in women without the two risk factors than it does in women who do have the factors. Another example: having only one leg makes falling over more likely, yet there are so many more two-legged people around that the great majority of falls occur in patients with two legs. Most heart attacks (myocardial infarctions) will occur in patients with normal cholesterol levels. Most labours with shoulder dystocia will occur in women carrying normal weight babies.

Case study

A forty-year-old woman complained of breathlessness over a period of months. The GP had considered pulmonary embolism (PE) to be a possibility, but had wrongly discounted it because the patient had no risk factors for PE and because chest examination, pulse and blood pressure were normal. He diagnosed asthma despite evidence of lack of response. The woman collapsed in her bathroom and died. Multiple pulmonary emboli were found at post mortem. There are often no abnormal findings on examination in cases of PE.

Failure to manage the condition appropriately, even having made the correct diagnosis

Case study

An 18-month-old girl was seen on a Saturday morning visit by her GP. The doctor correctly diagnosed gastroenteritis and did not feel the child needed to be admitted to hospital as she was not dehydrated. However, the mother was only 17 years old and had little support or experience. She was not given clear instructions as to how to care for the child nor, more importantly, when to seek further medical help. The child was admitted to hospital the next day comatose and suffering from hypernatraemic dehydration and was left with severe cerebral damage.

MEDICATION ERRORS

General

Errors in prescribing make up the second largest group of mistakes in general practice leading to litigation (about one quarter of all claims). The drugs most commonly involved are (in descending order of frequency):

- steroids, e.g. prednisolone
- antibiotics
- contraceptive pills
- opiates
- non-steroidal anti-inflammatory drugs (NSAIDs)
- anticoagulants, e.g. Warfarin
- antipsychotics

An adverse reaction to the drug is the commonest cause for complaint. Death is the second commonest - the ultimate adverse reaction.

Steroids

Oral steroids are potent drugs. They are so widely used in primary care that GPs are apt to forget how powerful they are. If high doses such as 40mg or more are used for longer than one week, follow-up is important. Long-term use of lower doses also needs monitoring (e.g. when used to control a chronic condition such as polymyalgia rheumatica). High doses can cause avascular necrosis of the hip. Suddenly stopping steroids after more than a few weeks treatment can cause severe illness because the steroid suppresses the body's own production of corticosteroids from the adrenal glands.

Corticosteroids suppress the immune system - that is largely why they are used medically - but this is an inherently risky thing to do as the appearance of other diseases, particularly infection, can be suppressed or altered. Ideally, all patients on steroids should be advised of this and told to inform any doctor they may see that they are taking steroids. Again, ideally, all patients on long-term steroids should carry a steroid card on them.

Antibiotics

Antibiotics are overprescribed, as the Department of Health keeps telling GPs, (though UK GPs prescribe far fewer than most of their European colleagues). Much litigation concerns the omission/inadequate/late prescribing of antibiotics. However, there are also many cases of severe adverse reactions where the GP could or should have known that the patient was allergic to that antibiotic.

Unfortunately many patients believe they are allergic to penicillin but:

- half probably are not;
- those who are allergic may well not recognise that the drug they are given is a penicillin - the proprietary name may be Penbritin, Amoxil or Augmentin. Even if prescribed by their proper generic name some penicillins do not reveal themselves: Co-amoxiclav, for example, is a penicillin.

Prescribing by the patient's own GP should be relatively safe as that GP ought to have access to the patient's past records and most computer software in primary care will warn the prescriber about allergies - assuming the previous adverse reaction was originally entered on the patient's record as it should have been.

Most GPs do not now cover their own patients out-of-hours. A variety of services are used in the evenings, through the night and at weekends - a co-operative of local GPs who join together to ease the burden of out-of-hours (OoH) care is the commonest arrangement. Such arrangements have become the norm since GPs have become able to opt out of OoH care following the introduction of the new GP contract[4]. OoH doctors do not usually have access to patients' records and must remember to ask about drugs the patient is taking, and about adverse drug reactions.

Contraceptives

The combined oral contraceptive pill (containing oestrogen and progesterone) is one of the most commonly taken drugs in the UK. It is generally taken by healthy young women. Patients will often forgive their doctors if treatment goes wrong when being treated for a severe illness. They are less likely to be so tolerant when they start off well but the doctor gives them a pill which damages them. The pill can occasionally kill - mainly through thrombo-embolism, and all GPs need to be careful not to prescribe the pill to women in high risk groups.

Women are usually prescribed the pill as a contraceptive and are therefore disappointed or angry when it fails them. Sometimes this can be the prescriber's fault for not giving adequate explanation about when to start the pill, what to do if pills are missed, what to do if the woman has diarrhoea or vomiting, or what to do if given antibiotics (which can reduce serum levels of oestrogen to an level inadequate for effective contraception).

Opiates

Opiates - such as morphine and diamorphine (heroin) - would be voted by most doctors the one drug they would keep in their bag if they were only allowed one drug, because of their dramatic efficacy against severe pain. However, because of

[4] *New GMS Contract 2003*, BMA, London 2003.

their potency they are also highly dangerous, and though a 15mg injection of morphine may bring blessed relief for the severe pain of a fractured tibia or myocardial infarct, 30mg can suppress breathing enough to kill. It would be very unwise for a GP routinely to carry such a high dose ampoule in his bag. Since Shipman it is necessary that any supplies of strong opiates are scrupulously recorded and accounted for. Particular care needs to be taken when prescribing opiates for children and the elderly.

Prescribing for opiate addicts is a difficult area. Addicts are frequently dishonest about the amount they are using and/or may not know the potency of their street supply. Overprescribing for this group with replacement opiates such as methadone has led to deaths.

Non-steroidal anti-inflammatory drugs (NSAIDs)

This group of drugs is very widely prescribed for musculo-skeletal pain in all age groups. One such drug - ibuprofen - is available over the counter (OTC), e.g. as Nurofen, Cuprofen and, less obviously, as Lemsip Power Plus.

NSAIDs are effective pain relievers but have many possible adverse effects and interact with many drugs. Such interactions may not be considered by a prescribing GP. This may be from ignorance of the interactions, or simply because the GP is unaware that the patient is taking an OTC form of NSAID. More commonly the GP prescribes the NSAID which results in an adverse reaction. This of course may come out of the blue and the prescription may have been appropriate. Sometimes it is not. A reasonable GP would be aware of the warnings listed in the British National Formulary (BNF) sent to every GP principal in the UK at least annually - particularly as regards aspirin allergy and asthma.

Anticoagulants

These drugs – particularly warfarin – are increasingly used to prevent blood clots forming within the blood vessels and the heart. Such clots can break loose to become emboli, and lodge in blood vessels. Emboli can cause death (particularly those from clots forming in the leg and pelvic veins – deep vein thrombosis (DVT) which break loose to pass through the right side of the heart to the pulmonary arteries), or stroke (especially associated with atrial fibrillation (AF) where the left atrium does not contract properly and blood can therefore clot on the inner surface to embolise in a cerebral artery). There is now clear evidence that warfarin can save lives and prevent the severe morbidity from stroke (cerebro-vascular accident - CVA).[5]

[5] Aguilar, M and Hart, R, Oral anticoagulants for preventing stroke in patients with non-valvular atrial fibrillation and no previous history of stroke or transient ischaemic attacks (Cochrane review). In: *The Cochrane Library*, Issue 4, 2005, Oxford: Update Software.

However, there is a down side. The body's coagulation system is a fine balance between avoiding clotting within the body's blood vessels and avoiding bleeding to death. Warfarin shifts the balance towards increased bleeding. Internal bleeding can result. This is particularly damaging within the brain.

GPs will often institute warfarin prescribing and, even if not starting such treatment, are almost always responsible for continuing prescriptions. They sometimes have the guidance of a hospital anticoagulant clinic, but increasingly GPs are managing the dose alterations themselves, even using near-patient testing with machines to measure the clotting level (International Normalised Ratio - INR) in their surgeries.

Control of INR is not always easy. Difficulties often arise because of the patient's poor compliance - sometimes because of dietary alterations and sometimes because of alcohol. The most important reason for difficult INR control, so far as the law is concerned, is because of other prescribed drugs. Warfarin unfortunately interacts with many drugs. The patient's INR can be moved outside the therapeutic ideal in both directions by concomitant prescribing. If the INR is low, clots can result. If it is too high, the patient can bleed. Even a one-week prescription of amoxycillin - a very commonly used antibiotic - can raise the INR significantly. Again, out-of-hours doctors are less likely to be aware that the patient is on warfarin and need to ask patients if they are taking other medication.

Monitoring the effect of drugs

Most drugs are given without any need for follow-up. Others are given for chronic conditions in which regular assessment should be provided – e.g. asthma, hypertension, and diabetes. A few have the potential to cause dangerous side effects, and the patient must have regular blood tests to try and pre-empt these. Good examples are azathioprine and salazopyrin, which are given for inflammatory bowel disease and inflammatory forms of arthritis. Although patients are often started on these drugs by hospital specialists, continuing care is commonly in primary care and the responsibility for blood tests lies with the GP. To fail to carry out such supervision would be likely to be considered a breach of duty of care, though sometimes the negligence may be the patient's. Many computer systems in primary care can have an alert set on them to block continuing repeat prescriptions until the patient attends for monitoring.

Some drugs have a narrow therapeutic window. This means that it is easy to give too little or too much, and quite tricky to give just the right amount. Examples are lithium – (given as a mood stabiliser, particularly in bipolar affective disorders (manic depression)), and phenytoin, an anticonvulsant. Patients taking either of these drugs should have blood levels of the drug taken at certain intervals. To fail to do so can cause permanent damage to the patient.

PRACTICAL PROCEDURES IN GENERAL PRACTICE

General

Though most of a GP's work is listening, advising, educating and prescribing, sometimes GPs actually do things to patients. Examples include minor surgery, hormone implants and fitting intra-uterine contraceptive devices - IUCDs -(coils). Claims involving such procedures make up the third commonest category brought against GPs.

No GP has to undertake such procedures. Given the poor, or non-existent, reimbursement for some of them and the level of litigation it is surprising that so much is done. However, it is often much more convenient for the patient to have them done by the GP, and many GPs enjoy using manual skills rather than listening and talking all day.

However, a GP is unlikely to have the same operating skill as a plastic surgeon. Also a GP will probably have less experience fitting IUCDs than a doctor working in a family planning clinic.

There are two main reasons why patients bring claims against GPs after practical procedures. These are considered below.

The procedure was performed negligently

Case study

A GP tried to fit an IUCD. The woman complained of pain at the time of insertion (which is common) but the pain persisted over the next two days (which is much less common). At the six-week post-insertion check the coil threads were not seen coming from the cervical opening. The coil was found at laparoscopy behind the uterus, having penetrated through the cervix. This almost certainly occurred at the time of insertion. Such an occurrence is a recognised complication - occurring in one to two fittings per 1,000. If the correct procedure was followed, liability is unlikely to be established.

The patient was not adequately informed of the possible consequences of the procedure

Case study

A 20-year-old woman saw her GP because of a pigmented mole on her shoulder. This was excised by the GP but the scar became thickened and red (keloid). Such a scar can occur even with the greatest surgical skill but is most common on certain areas of the body - the shoulder being one such. The young woman claimed she would never have agreed to the minor operation had she been informed of the slight chance of keloid. The law recognises doctors have a duty to warn of certain, but not all adverse consequences/side effects. This was one about which the patient should have been warned. Causation in such cases is always difficult to establish. It proved impossible here.

PNEUMONIA

Respiratory diseases are the commonest reason for a patient to consult a GP. Pneumonia is not common in general practice. Hodgkin[6] gives a rate of 4.7 cases per 1,000 patients per year. The figure is probably lower than this now because of more widespread use of antibiotics. This compares with about 1,000 respiratory infections per year. Just on statistical grounds it is easy to see how a GP can miss the one severe infection out of more than 100 other respiratory infections.

Pneumonia is still a killer, and acute lobar pneumonia typically affects, and frequently kills, young adults. Often this severe infection of the lung (or part of it) follows a less severe viral illness, e.g. influenza. This often misleads the GP: the patient often says he has been unwell for a week or two and the urgency of the situation may not be appreciated.

However, pneumonia makes the patient ill and they usually look it. Significant features are a very raised heart rate and high fever. Alarming features are:

- confusion
- respiratory rate > 30/minute
- low diastolic blood pressure < 60 mmHg

Other alarming features, such as a raised blood urea, can only be detected after special tests not immediately available to the GP.

Any unwell patient with a chest infection should have their pulse, blood pressure, temperature and respiratory rate measured. If these are not done the severity of the illness can be overlooked. Surprisingly, the chest, when auscultated, may sound normal. Chest sounds can be difficult to detect. This again may mislead the unwary. A febrile patient with cough and breathlessness needs large doses of broad spectrum antibiotics. If any one of the three alarming features is found, hospital admission should be considered, and if two are present, admission is mandatory. Co-morbidity, e.g. diabetes, worsens the prognosis and should lead to earlier admission.

Breathlessness in a young person at rest is always a very significant complaint unless that person has recurrent episodes of asthma. Even then, it may be significant. Pneumonia is commonly missed because GPs find no chest signs and do not measure the patient's vital signs. The British Thoracic Society has produced very detailed guidelines.[7]

---

[6] See above, footnote 3.
[7] British Thoracic Society: Community Acquired Pneumonia, *Thorax*, 2001:56 (Supplement IV)

PULMONARY EMBOLISM

Data from the USA indicate that about 500,000 patients suffer PE each year. Mortality rate is 30% if untreated. Treatment reduces this to 3% - 8%. The difficulty for the GP is that often the patients he sees in the community who develop PE will not have the classic risk factors (family history of thrombo-embolic disease, obesity, smoking, prescription of the combined oral contraceptive pill, recent immobilization or major pelvic or orthopaedic surgery). Though PE follows deep vein thrombosis (DVT) the diagnosis of this in itself is difficult and there may be no clinical signs to indicate DVT. A swollen ankle and painful calf make the diagnosis of PVT easy, but such helpful signs are usually absent.

Signs of PE itself are rare. Even symptoms may be absent or minimal, especially if the emboli are small and recurrent. The commoner symptoms are breathlessness and pleuritic chest pain (pain with coughing, inspiration and chest movement). Haemoptysis is uncommon. A major acute embolus is usually easy for the GP: the patient suffers acute breathlessness and collapse and needs urgent hospital admission even if the GP is unsure of the diagnosis.

Unfortunately it is common for minor emboli to be overlooked but for the patient then to die from a major one.

The GP needs to have a high threshold of suspicion - even if none of the classic risk factors is present. A unilateral swollen calf may need urgent investigation. Unexplained breathlessness always needs urgent investigation. Many patients with multiple recurrent pulmonary emboli were diagnosed as asthmatics by the GPs who could - or should - have been able to show that the patient's lung function tests had not improved with asthma treatment. Many patients with pulmonary emboli will only complain of breathlessness and physical examination will be normal. The history matters.

SUB-ARACHNOID HAEMORRHAGE (SAH)

This, like pneumonia, is often missed by GPs because the GP has to pick out this very rare cause of headache from the very many headaches he sees. Hodgkin[8] diagnosed tension headache 200 times per year. SAH has an incidence of 8/100,000, i.e. a typical GP is likely to have just one patient suffering SAH in about six years.

Missing SAH can have severe consequences. The next bleed may be bigger and very damaging. A retrospective survey (of patients who survived) found that 6% of patients suffering SAH remembered a previous sentinel headache. However, in general practice only 25% of patients experiencing sudden onset headache will later develop SAH.

---

[8] See above, footnote 3.

Nonetheless a reasonable GP is well used to the apparent mistake of referring patients unnecessarily to hospital – whether with abdominal pain, chest pain or headache. Overworked junior hospital doctors may not welcome the referrals but their older, usually wiser, consultants are more understanding.

A sudden onset headache, described like a kick in the back of the head, must be considered to be SAH until proved otherwise. This proof needs a CT scan and, if the CT scan is normal, lumbar puncture. Neck stiffness takes hours to develop and there may be no physical signs.

CAUDA EQUINA SYNDROME

The cauda equina, or 'horse's tail', is the group of nerves that emerges at the bottom end of the spinal cord after the branches have passed out of the spaces between the lumbar vertebrae. These nerves are particularly important as they serve the sphincters for bowel and bladder control and genital sensation.

Usually a slipped disc prolapses to one side and puts pressure on a nerve root - typically L5 or S1 - causing pain, numbness or pins and needles (paraesthesiae) in the dermatome (skin area) served. In the case of L5 or S1 this will be the foot, ankle and lower calf.

Rarely and more severely, a disc (or a tumour) may protrude centrally and compress the cauda equina. This causes damage to S2, 3 and 4, with altered sphincter control and loss of sensation around the perineum and genitalia (so called saddle anaesthesia). This is a neurosurgical emergency. Unless the pressure on the cauda equina is soon relieved within a matter of hours the nerves may be damaged for ever - as may other higher nerve roots. The patient is left incontinent of urine and faeces, with insensate genitals and possibly weakness or paralysis in both legs - but survives.

Any patient with sciatica must be asked about sphincter control and areas of numbness. As cauda equina syndrome can occur without sciatica, any patient complaining of numbness in the genital area/perineum must be assumed to have cauda equina compression unless this can be excluded by a careful history and examination. Time is crucial.

MENINGOCOCCAL DISEASE IN SMALL CHILDREN

This is a very frightening illness, and an important cause of severe disability and great tragedy. A young child can pass from being well to dead in a matter of hours. It is not only children who are affected. Even when doctors contract meningococcal disease, they simply think they have flu, and their families are surprised to find them dead in bed just hours after reporting sick. Nevertheless, good practice (and luck) can save lives.

Classically, the child develops meningitis with headache, vomiting, neck stiffness and a purpuric rash – a flat, purple rash which does not blanch on pressure. Meningococcal infection does not always lead to meningitis. The child may just be floppy. The combination of lethargy with vomiting is worrying. Even more deceiving is that the meningococcus can cause many lesser kinds of rash.[9]

Lethargy and vomiting are very common features of many childhood illnesses, but a child with this combination of features needs assessment and the mother/father need clear instructions about when to seek further help if hospital admission is not going to take place there and then.

FAILURE TO DIAGNOSE PREGNANCY

Pregnancy is frequently missed, both by the woman herself and her doctor, particularly when it is not expected or hoped for, e.g. after sterilization or when using contraception. Usually this error is made because the woman had a vaginal bleed at the time of the expected period. However, bleeding occurs early on in about a quarter of all pregnancies. If a woman consults her doctor about, for instance, tiredness or breast tenderness, and pregnancy is not considered until it is too late for the woman to contemplate termination of the pregnancy, a claim might result. Though claims for wrongful life are now, usually, financially small, if the baby is born in some way handicapped big sums can be involved. If in any doubt, a pregnancy test should be done.

ECTOPIC PREGNANCY

In about one in 100 pregnancies the fertilized egg fails to move down into the uterus, and so implants in the Fallopian tube (or, in about 3% of ectopics, within the abdominal cavity)

Although nothing can be done to prevent this, delayed diagnosis can result in fatal haemorrhage. One in 3,000 women with an ectopic pregnancy dies. Almost always the affected tube has to be removed. There is now a chance that the tube can be preserved, as a drug, methotrexate, can be given to stop the pregnancy. However, this treatment is new and it is not yet known whether the tube, thus conserved, is any more helpful than no tube. It may possibly be even more of a liability, as, once damaged, it may give rise to further ectopics.

The classical picture of an ectopic pregnancy is a woman of reproductive age who has missed a period and has some slight dark bleeding and unilateral lower abdominal pain. Unfortunately, however, nature is often not so obvious to patient or doctor. An ectopic can occur before a missed period is noticed, and the pain can precede any bleeding. Other features are due to blood within the abdominal cavity. This can result in pain with emptying either bladder or bowel, and

---

[9] See the letter from the Chief Medical Officer - January 1999 PL/CMO/99/1.

shoulder tip pain (referred pain when blood irritates the diaphragm). Often these helpful pointers are missing and the woman can present just feeling faint.

Pregnancy tests, which measure Human Chorionic Gonadotrophin (HCG) in the urine, are now so sensitive that they can be positive within 14 days of conception. Many women will vigorously deny the possibility of pregnancy whilst being pregnant. A urine test can be requested to check for white blood cells (as found in urine infections) - another cause of low abdominal pain. It would be possible to carry out a pregnancy test surreptitiously at the same time, but since this is ethically dubious the doctor should tell the patient that, despite her protestations that pregnancy is impossible, it is important to check.

Pregnancy tests are cheap, quick (two minutes) and very easy to carry in a doctor's bag. The writer is surprised that many doctors do not carry them, given that sometimes the woman will feel too weak to attend surgery and will request a visit.

Doctors should always think of an ectopic in a woman with abdominal pain. Unless the doctor can be sure it is not an ectopic, a pregnancy test should be done. This means carrying pregnancy testing sticks in the doctor's bag.

MISSED CANCERS

General

This is an important category in the group of claims resulting from delayed referral. It can often be successfully argued that earlier diagnosis would have led to a greater chance of survival, or, failing that, that earlier treatment would have been less severe and damaging to the patient. Amongst the commonest malignancies in delayed referral claims are breast, colon and cervical cancer.

Lung cancer is not commonly a cause for a claim despite being the commonest cancer in men – possibly because diagnosis is recognised to be difficult and treatment is usually unsuccessful. Similarly ovarian cancer, though a far commoner cause of death than cervical cancer, is rarely a cause for a claim - again being notoriously difficult to diagnose and to treat - in part because 80% of women present with disease already spread beyond the pelvis.

Cervical cancer

Though a relatively rare cause of death (1,600 women in UK per annum) this is important because in theory almost all could be avoided by good medical care - particularly screening to discover the early stages of cervical intra-epithelial neoplasia (CIN). CIN can be treated. It is important that it is treated before CIN II turns to CIN III (which it may), and CIN III to invasive cancer (which in time it will).

Delay in diagnosis usually occurs because there has been a breakdown in recall. Sometimes the woman rejects the offer of recall. Most health authorities (HAs) and primary care organizations (PCOs) have computerized recall, but this can fail when a woman changes address or GP. The responsibility for ensuring a woman has a smear rests largely with the GP and invitations should be documented in the medical record. It is helpful if the GP explains that the smear is taken to help avoid the development of cancer. It is not a 'cancer' test (unlike mammography - see below). A woman who has smears every three years has approximately 19 times less of a chance of developing cervical cancer than a woman who has never had a smear. (This may be selection bias but probably is a true beneficial effect of screening.)

The other situation leading to delay in diagnosis of cervical cancer is a symptomatic woman - with pelvic pain, discharge or irregular bleeding. The last is a particular problem because many women, and worse still, their doctors, are reluctant to undergo/undertake a vaginal examination in the presence of bleeding. Telling the woman to come back when the bleeding has stopped may be telling her to come back too late. Relying on a normal smear last year may be a false move.

It is important to remember that cervical cytology relies on human beings and is not perfect.

The general message is that doctors need to ensure reliable recall systems. Women with symptoms, -particularly irregular and post-coital bleeding - need investigation and should have their cervices examined at the time of presentation, not later when the bleeding stops: it may not.

Breast Cancer

Breast cancer is the commonest cancer in women. It affects one woman in 11 in the UK and about half of those affected will die of the disease. Survival rates have recently improved, possibly because of screening for early cancer using three-yearly mammograms. But mammography screening does not work in women before the menopause, and so, especially in young women, it is usually the woman herself who finds the lump. This is often true too in older women who will find an interval cancer after an apparently normal mammogram. Although more women die of heart disease than of anything else, women's greatest health fear is probably breast cancer.

Though regular breast self-examination has been shown not to be helpful, it is probably useful for women to know what their breasts feel like so that they can notice any change as a chance finding - when bathing for instance. Often a woman will come to her doctor because she has found a lump, but the GP can find none. What should the reasonable GP do? As a minimum the doctor must record the complaint and the normal examination and ask the woman to return - probably after her next period if she is premenstrual at first examination. If the woman still feels a lump, a reasonable doctor will refer, even if the doctor can find no lump. There is, of course, a risk of swamping hospital breast clinics, but in the writer's experience few women come complaining of breast lumps where ultimately none is found. The question the GP should ask him or herself is: What would you want done if this woman was your wife/sister/daughter/friend?

There are important guidelines for the management of breast disease published by the NHS Breast Screening Programme and the Cancer Research Campaign.[10]

Colo-Rectal Cancer (CRC)

This is the second commonest cause of cancer death in the UK (19,000 per year). The classic symptoms are change in bowel habit – either increased constipation or greater looseness - rectal bleeding, abdominal pain or anaemia.

Unfortunately the last three are very common, and GPs need to develop a filter to avoid surgeons being faced with an impossible number of requests for colonoscopy. Usually if the patient is under 45, follow-up in general practice after first contact may be reasonable unless the patient has two of the above problems or has a first-degree relative who developed bowel cancer before the age of 55 or has two affected relatives. All patients over 45 with alarm symptoms persisting for six weeks – change in bowel habit, rectal bleeding, passing mucus, abdominal pain, faecal incontinence or suffering anaemia and weight loss – should be referred.

Rectal bleeding is common and is usually from haemorrhoids. However, haemorrhoids are so common they often co-exist with bowel cancer, i.e. the piles may not be the only cause of the bleeding.

Some figures:

- 10% of CRC cases present with bleeding alone;
- 21% with change of bowel habit;
- 64% present with both;
- 45% lie within the rectum and nearly half can be felt on rectal examination, hence the ancient instruction to medical students: 'Put your finger in or you'll put your foot in it.'
- 54% of patients with CRC above the rectum have iron deficiency anaemia.

Message: There are guidelines for referral[11]. The combination of altered bowel habit and rectal bleeding needs urgent referral. Iron deficiency anaemia, unless clearly of another cause, needs lower and/or maybe upper gastro-intestinal

[10] *NHS Breast Screening Programme and the Cancer Research Campaign Guidelines for the referral of patients with breast problems*, 1999 ISBN 1 871997 42 9

[11] Primary Care Society for Gastroenterology, *The early detection of colo-rectal cancer in primary care*, Department of Primary Care, Oxford.

endoscopy. Abdominal and rectal examination are obligatory. Piles are common - they do not protect the patient from bowel cancer. Take a family history. Early treatment makes a difference - if CRC is confined to the bowel wall (Duke's A) 83% of patients will be alive five years on.

MYOCARDIAL INFARCTION

Ischaemic heart disease (IHD) is the commonest cause of death in all developed countries. Typically it causes central chest pain on exertion (simple angina), less typically pain even at rest (unstable angina) or, if an artery to the heart becomes blocked, severe pain continuously (myocardial infarction - MI) - when heart muscle is irreparably damaged by anoxia. Often IHD does not present typically. MI itself can be pain-free, (a silent infarct), or the pain may be felt in the neck and jaw rather than the chest or upper arms. If an MI is missed the patient may die or be denied the benefit of thrombolytic (clot-busting) drugs. These are best given as soon as possible: every hour of delay leads to more irreversible damage to the myocardium (heart muscle).

There is no simple clinical test a GP can carry out to diagnose MI. An ECG can be helpful, but can be normal, and therefore misleading, for four to six hours after the event. The situation with angina is even more difficult: the ECG is usually normal and only the hospital investigation of an exercise ECG can define the problem.

Usually, however, the diagnosis is made from the history. Recurring pain related to exertion which eases on resting, felt anywhere from the umbilicus up to the lower jaw, should be assumed to be angina until proved otherwise. A trial of glyceryl trinitrate (GTN) spray or tablets or a trial of beta-blockers may help define the problem. Reflux oesophagitis can cause chest pain but should not give an exertion-related pattern. IHD is not confined to overweight overstressed businessmen. It can occur in premenopausal women. Pain in the upper body relating to exertion must be considered to be angina. Constant pain in the upper body lasting for more than 15 minutes at rest must be considered an MI unless there is an obvious alternative explanation. Minutes matter here.

DEVELOPMENTAL DYSPLASIA OF THE HIP

DDH - previously called congenital dislocation of the hip - affects about one in 100 newborn babies, though true dislocation only occurs in one tenth of these. An unstable hip left untreated can become increasingly unstable and more and more easily dislocatable. Unless the ball fits properly in the socket from birth, neither will develop properly and more drastic treatment will be required to hold the ball of the hip within the acetabulum. Later disability, particularly osteo arthritis, becomes more likely, and the opportunity to have a normal childhood will be lost.

Unfortunately the routine screening test - the combined Ortolani/Barlow test - has both poor sensitivity (it misses cases of DDH) and poor specificity (it suggests a problem where there is none). Nonetheless the test should be carried out on all babies within a day or two of birth, and again at six weeks. Failure to do so is a breach of duty. Failure to detect DDH is not necessarily a breach. No screening test, even if properly performed, has 100% sensitivity. Part of the failure rate of the Ortolani/Barlow test is attributable to the hip being normal at birth and later becoming abnormal. It is therefore crucial that GPs and Health Visitors pay close attention to any mother who later (possibly when the child is one or two years old) says that one leg is different to the other, or that walking is funny or delayed. Asymmetric skin creases can indicate DDH, but as an indicator, lack sensitivity and specificity.

Ultrasonic examination of neonatal hips may soon become a screening test. Sensitivity is excellent, but at the moment specificity is not: the scan often suggests problems where there are none.

SLIPPED UPPER FEMORAL EPIPHYSIS (SUFE)

This occurs when the growing ball of the hip slips away from the shaft through the growth plate. If untreated, the femoral head becomes increasingly damaged, leading to early degenerative arthritis. The classic presentation is of an overweight boy in early adolescence complaining of hip pain and a limp. But as so often, nature does not seem to have read the medical textbooks. The problem can occur in girls - even thin ones - and the pain is often felt in the knee.

A child of between about 10 and 16 years, complaining of pain anywhere from the groin to the knee, may have SUFE. A history of trauma is unhelpful - most adolescents will have injured themselves in the past week. Unless there is full pain-free hip movement within a further week, a lateral hip X-ray of both hips should be arranged: 20% of children have both hips affected.

MISCELLANEOUS CONDITIONS OF MEDICO-LEGAL IMPORTANCE TO GPS

Malaria

Headache and fever, even nine months after a patient has returned to the UK from an affected area, can be malaria. The possibility is often not considered, and the consequences can be severe.

Torsion of the testis

Boys before puberty do not get epididymo-orchitis (except with mumps); they tort.

Splenectomy

Patients are at risk of overwhelming infection for ever after this operation. It is not only pneumococcus that kills them. Patients must be advised to warn any doctor they see of this risk if they become feverish.

Diabetes

This is easily missed unless thought of. Blood sugars are easy to do in surgery. Urine tests can sometimes mislead.

Pre-eclamptic toxaemia

This potential killer can occur from 27 weeks gestation. Though there is no treatment, timely delivery of the baby may save the mother's life. The urine must be tested. Proteinuria must not be considered as due to urine infection unless testing sticks clearly show many pus cells. Proteinuria matters even if the blood pressure is normal.

Depression

This carries a high mortality rate from suicide. All patients with depression must be asked specifically about suicidal and self-harming ideation.

GLOSSARY

This glossary was compiled by the contributors of the various chapters. It is intended to complement those chapters. It is not intended to be a substitute for a medical dictionary.

Abruptio placentae	Bleeding between the placenta and the uterine wall
ACE-inhibitors (ACEI)	Popular, modern group of drugs for control of hypertension with specific benefits to the damaged kidney.
Acetabulum	Socket part of the hip joint
Acidaemia	Acid build up in the blood
Acidosis	Build up of acid in the tissues of the body
Aetiology	Term used to describe the factors causing a specific disease. Depending on our state of knowledge this can be unknown or partly known as well as fully established.
Agoraphobia	An intense fear of crowded places, such as supermarkets (from the Greek *agora* = marketplace). Though irrational, and often seen as such by the sufferer, such fears lead to avoidance, are usually caused by panic attacks, and when severe can lead to people becoming housebound.
Air embolism	Obstruction of blood flow by the presence of air in a vessel
Alcohol dependence	Addictive use of alcohol, such that withdrawal effects (e.g. shaking, sweating, insomnia), occur when alcohol is not available. Morning drinking, tolerance, failed abstinence and the dominance of drinking in terms of day-to-day activities are all part of this state.

Alzheimer's disease	Form of dementia which may be directly inherited in an autosomal dominant manner (see 'inheritance pattern' below). The majority of cases, however, particularly those arising in those over 65, do not fall into this category
Ambient	Background
Ambubag	A self inflating bag attached to a face mask which is used to ventilate a baby in need of resuscitation
Amelia	Absence of a limb or limbs
Amenorrhoea	The term describing loss of menstrual periods. It is thus potential evidence of abnormal hormonal functioning in child-bearing women. The commonest causes are, of course, the natural events of pregnancy and the menopause, but medication such as antipsychotics are well known to have this effect.
Amniocentesis	Removal of amniotic fluid by needle puncture and aspiration
Anaphylaxis	Severe allergic response with rashes, swelling of the throat, abnormal heart rhythms. Potentially fatal
Androgen insensitivity.	A rare genetic disorder, inherited in an X linked manner, (see 'inheritance pattern' below), in which the body cells are unable to respond to the male hormone. This means that despite having a male chromosome make-up and circulating male hormone the baby born appears entirely female
Anencephaly	A congenital malformation in which there is failure of fusion of the top of the neural tube with absence of the brain and skull
Aneuploidy	Abnormal number of chromosomes or parts of chromosomes

Aneurysm	Thin-walled expansion of the blood vessel that may rupture.
Angina Pectoris	Often shortened to angina. Chest pain associated with exertion or emotion.
Angiography	Imaging the blood vessels
Angioplasty	Widening a narrowing in a blood vessel
Anteroposterior	From the front to the back
Anti-arrhythmic drug	Any drug which treats or prevents an abnormal heart rhythm developing
Antidepressants	Medications designed to treat clinical depression, although often having other properties (e.g. anxiety relief). The two major classes are Tricyclics, such as Imipramine and Amitriptyline (available since the 1960s) and specific serotonin reuptake inhibitors (SSRIs), developed in the early '90s. Both types are equally efficacious, but the risks from overdose as well as side-effects are more serious in the Tricyclics. Efficacy rates are between 50 and 70%, assuming compliance and the right dosage. (see also 'SSRIs' and 'Tricyclics')
Anorexia nervosa	A disorder characterised by abnormal eating behaviour, a morbid fear of putting on weight and becoming fat, sustained weight loss (risking one's physical health) and enhanced by a distorted body image (sufferers see themselves as fat).
Aortic stenosis	A closing of the aortic valve so that it causes an obstruction to flow of blood leaving the heart
Apgar score	A composite score of 5 variables noted in the newborn infant at 1, 5 and 10 minutes. It gives an idea of the state of the baby to aid in decisions about resuscitation
Appendicitis	Inflammation of the appendix

Arrhythmia	Any form of heart rhythm other than normal sinus rhythm
Asphyxia	The combination of hypoxia, hypercarbia, reduced perfusion and acidosis
Aspiration	Removal of fluid or cells, usually with a syringe. Inhalation of something other than air e.g. fluid or vomit.
Ataxia	Abnormal control of posture and movement
Atrial fibrillation	A fast irregular rhythm of the heart, often resulting in heart failure
Atrial flutter	A fast regular rhythm of the heart where the top part of the heart flutters rather than contracts regularly
Atrial septal defect	A hole in the wall which divides the atria (or collecting chambers) of the heart. In fetal life, there is a physiological defect in the atrial septum (the foramen ovale) which makes the detection of any other defect extremely difficult
Attenuation	Reduction in the intensity e.g. of an x-ray beam
Autosomal recessive	*see below* 'Inheritance pattern'
Avascular necrosis (AVN)	Death of tissue (often bone) due to interruption of the blood supply
Axial	Transverse anatomical plane
Bacteriuria	Bacteria in urine
Basal ganglia	The deep grey nuclei of the brain
Barlow's test	Test used to detect developmental dysplasia of the hip
Biopsy	The removal of a piece of tissue for analysis
Bolus of fluid	A one off intravenous volume of fluid as opposed to a continuous infusion

Bowel atresia	A condition in which part of the bowel is not fully formed, so that there is a fibrous strip connecting the distal and proximal part of the bowel
Breech birth	Born bottom first either vaginally or by caesarean section
Bronchial	Related to the airways
Bulla	Area of lung damage where the normal anatomy has broken down to leave a large air space
Bypass Grafting	A shortened term for coronary artery bypass grafting –an operation to circumvent narrowings in the arteries and restore flow to normal
C5 – T1	Nerve roots of the Brachial Plexus: 5th Cervical – 1st thoracic.
C- reactive protein (CRP)	An acute phase protein, measured in the blood, usually raised in bacterial infection
Callus	Healing new bone
Cardiomegaly	Enlargement of the heart
Cardioversion	This is either electrical, by shock treatment, or chemical i.e. by drugs, and is the system of converting an abnormal rhythm back to sinus rhythm
Cardiac massage	Manual pumping of the heart. In babies it involves using 2 fingers only over the breast bone
CAT scan	Computerised Axial Tomography
Catheter	The tube inserted into the body in order to obtain a coronary angiogram
Cauda equina	Collection of nerves from the spinal cord running through the lumbar spinal canal
CDH	Congenital Dysplasia of the Hip

Cerebrospinal fluid (CSF)	A clear fluid which is manufactured inside the brain by the choroids plexus. It surrounds the brain and spinal cord thus cushioning them. CSF can be obtained by inserting a fine needle into the spinal canal in the lower back, i.e. a lumbar puncture.
Cervical spine	The seven bones of the neck, i.e. the cervical vertebrae.
Chondral	Of cartilage
Choreo athetoid	A form of movement abnormality revealed as writhing posturing and jerky movements, seen in children with damage to the basal ganglia and thalami
Chorioamnionitis	Inflammation of the membranes (usually bacterial infection) surrounding the fetus
Chorion villus sampling	Obtaining a sample from the developing placenta at about 10 weeks into the pregnancy.
Chromosome	A long strand made up of tightly packed genetic material. The entire genome (see below) is packed into 23 pairs of chromosomes, varying in length, which are present in each cell and can be seen under the microscope. Twenty two pairs, numbered from 1-22 are the same in male and female. The final pair form the sex chromosomes and are labelled X and Y. The X chromosome has many active genes while the Y is small and has only a few. Females have two X chromosomes but only one is active in each cell. Males have one X and a Y.
Chronic Obstructive Airways Disease (COAD)	Lung damage/emphysema, usually due to smoking
Clavicle	Collar bone
Cochlea	Part of the hearing mechanism situated deep within the ear

Cognitive Behaviour Therapy (CBT)	A form of treatment, particularly used for anxiety and depressive disorders, in which therapy is aimed at reframing automatic thoughts into an alternative pattern of thinking. Measurement of its effects and its relative brevity (some 10 to 15 hour long sessions) have enhanced its appeal. The best results usually involve a combined CBT and medication approach.
Colonoscopy	Use of a flexible fibreoptic instrument which allows visualisation of the inside of the colon.
Computed Tomography (CT)	Cross-sectional image taken using x-rays applied in a circular movement around the patient: see also CAT
Comminuted fracture	A comminuted fracture is one in which the bone is shattered into several pieces.
Consultand	The person attending the genetic clinic. They may or may not themselves be affected by the condition causing concern
Contralateral	The other side
Contrast	Agent or drug given to increase soft tissue contrast
Coronal	Side to side anatomical plane
Coronary Angiogram	Putting dye into the coronary arteries and taking x-ray pictures. Shows if arteries are patent or narrowed
Corpus callosum	Extensive communication between two sides of the brain
Cortical	Of bone: Dense outer margin
Creatinine	A naturally occurring substance used as an index of renal function. The normal is 60-120μmol/l. The plasma level increases with worsening renal function.

Creatinine Clearance	Normal 80-120ml/min. A more accurate measurement of overall kidney function than absolute creatinine levels, requiring 24hr urine collection and simultaneous blood test.
Cytokines	Chemicals released by the host in response to infection and other insults
Cytogenetic	Pertaining to the chromosomes
Cytology	The study of the structure and function of cells
Cytotoxic	Toxic to cells
Cytogenetics	The investigation of chromosomes and genes by cell culture techniques.
DDH	Developmental dysplasia of the hip
Debridement	This term relates to the thorough cleaning of wounds, i.e. the removal of debris, together with the trimming away of non-viable skin, fat, subcutaneous tissue, etc.
Delusion	A fixed, generally false belief, impervious to reason and dominating the patient's mind. A core symptom of psychotic illnesses.
Dementia	A progressive loss of global intellectual functioning, due to increasing and irreversible damage to brain cells. It affects to some degree about 10% of over 75s and nearly 50% of the over-85s.
Diaphragm	The flat muscle which separates the abdominal from the thoracic cavity and which is used in respiration.
Diffuse axonal injury	Severe traumatic brain injury which disrupts neural pathways
Dislocation	Movement of one bone relative to another so that a joint becomes disrupted

Displaced fracture	Where the two ends of the fractured bone are separated from each other. Usually occurs in the long bones.
Diplegia	Spasticity or dystonia predominantly affecting the legs
Distal	Further towards the periphery
Diuretic	Medication to increase urine volume and decrease oedema.
Diverticular disease	Disease affecting small diverticulae (pouches) arising from the bowel.
Dominant inheritance	*see below* 'Inheritance pattern'
Dorsal spine	The twelve dorsal or thoracic vertebrae make up the section of the spinal column which forms the back of the chest. Two ribs take origin from each vertebra and form the thoracic cage.
Doppler shift	The change in tone of a sound wave as it moves past the receiver
Down Syndrome	A common genetically determined disorder in which three copies of chromosome 21 are present instead of the usual two, The features include varying degrees of learning difficulty, heart defects, short stature and recognizable facial features.
Drug dependence	A general term to describe addiction to any kind of substance, but generally applied to illicit drugs such as heroin or cocaine (see also alcohol dependence).
Duct dependent	In some congenital heart defects, it is necessary for the ductus arteriosus to remain patent in order to permit the circulation of oxygenated blood. Where this is the case the patient is described as duct dependent.
Dysmorphic	Having distinctive features, often quite subtle, suggesting the possibility that some error of

	development, which may or may not be significant, has occurred.
Dysplasia	Maldevelopment, often congenital
Dyskinesia	Abnormality of action – may be dystonic or choreo athetoid
Dystonia	Stiffness in movement due to co contraction of agonist and antagonist muscles controlling a joint
Echo	Shortened term for echocardiograph i.e. an ultra-sound examination of the heart
Effusion	Excess fluid
EFW	Estimated fetal weight
Enterocolitis	Inflammation of the bowel
Exchange transfusion	Procedure to remove and infuse blood in order to dilute the level of a substance in the blood e.g. bilirubin
Embolus	Particulate matter causing an obstruction in a blood vessel
Electrocardiogram (ECG)	An ECG is a modified galvanometer which records the electrical activity of the heart and is particularly useful in identifying abnormal cardiac rhythms. It also picks up damage to the myocardium or heart muscle, such as would be caused by a heart attack.
Electroconvulsive Therapy (ECT)	A treatment for severe depression involving the passage of an electric shock through the brain, patients being anaesthetised and given muscle relaxant beforehand. It is generally very safe, can be life-saving for those unable (for example) to eat or drink, and has equal if not better efficacy than antidepressant medication.
Electroencephalography (EEG)	A special investigation whereby electrodes are placed around the head to record the electrical activity of the brain. It is painless,

	non-invasive, and particularly used for the diagnosis of forms of epilepsy.
Embolize	To block a blood vessel, often using interventional radiological techniques
Embolus	Small clot or fragment, which breaks off from some part of the vascular system and circulates through the arteries to another area. Emboli can be formed of blood clot, bacteria, calcific deposits, platelets or cholesterol lumps etc
Endotracheal	Positioned within the trachea (windpipe)
Endotracheal tube	Tube used to facilitate breathing passing either through the nose or mouth into the trachea
Enterally	Given into a hollow viscus, or organ (gut, bowel or bladder)
Enzymes	In a cardiological context this refers to cardiac enzymes - substances which are released from dead heart cells following a heart attack
Epiphysis	Growing piece of bone beyond the growth plate that generally forms part of a joint
Episiotomy	A surgical incision in the perineum to enlarge the entrance to the vagina.
Erythropoietin	Hormone produced by the kidneys, now available synthetically, which improves the anaemia associated with renal failure.
Extra-ocular movement	The movements of the eyeball which are controlled by muscles which are outside the globe but attached to its surface. They move the eyeball up, down, sideways, etc.
Exercise Stress Test	A standard walking test on a moving platform. It starts at about 1 mile an hour up a 1 in 10 gradient and ends at the 5th stage as a 5 mile an hour walk up in a 1 in 5 gradient

Ex utero	Outside the womb i.e. born
Extradural	Lying between the Dura and the Skull
Facet joint	Small joint locking the posterior parts of the vertebrae together
Fetal macrosomia	Where the fetus is large - weighing 4500 g or more at birth
Feticide	A procedure performed to cause fetal death prior to the onset of induction of labour in termination of pregnancy
Femur	Upper leg bone
Ferromagnetic	Any object vulnerable to a magnetic field due to the presence of iron
Fluorescent In Situ Hybridisation (FISH)	A technique whereby molecular probes can be used to identify and count specific areas of chromosome.
Fluoroscopy	The use of conventional x-rays to produce a moving image
Foramen magnum	Hole at the base of the skull through which the spinal cord passes
Gamma camera	A measurement device that detects small doses of radiation emitted from a patient
Gene	A string of simple chemicals which gives specific information that then gives rise to a protein or other basic essential of the cell.
Genome	The entire complement of genetic material that makes up an organism. The Human Genome contains 3 thousand million 'bases', the essential components shared with the entire plant and animal kingdoms. Around 10 percent of these are believed to give rise to of the order of 30 thousand active genes.
Germinal mosaicism	A phenomenon whereby, although a person's body cells may be entirely normal when tested genetically, their gonads (testis or

	ovary) may contain many egg or sperm cells which bear a specific genetic error.
Glomerulonephritis	Immunologically-mediated damage to the glomeruli, the filtering units of the kidney, which may cause acute or chronic renal failure.
Glycogen	Form in which glucose (sugar) is stored in the liver
Gonad	Reproductive organ
Grand multipara	A woman who has had five or more children
Haematoma	A collection of blood.
Haemorrhage	Bleeding
Haemoptysis	Coughing up blood
Hallucination	A perception in the absence of a stimulus, the brain seeing or hearing things, for example, that are not in fact there. Hallucinations can occur in any form of sensory modality (sight, hearing, smell, taste, touch) and are a typical symptom of psychotic disorders, commonly in the form of auditory hallucinations (e.g. 'hearing voices').
Hemiplegia	Unilateral spasticity or dystonia or both
Hilum	Part of the lung containing vessels, bronchi and small lymph nodes
Horner's syndrome	Ptosis (drooping) of the eyelid in conjunction with a dilated pupil.
Human Fertilisation and Embryology Authority	The body set up by the Human Fertilisation and Embryology Act 1990 to regulate work done in centres using reproductive technology.
Human Genetics Commission (HGC)	A government body set up to monitor and advise on developments in human genetics
Humerus	Upper arm bone

Huntington's disease	A genetically determined disease, inherited in an autosomal dominant manner (see below), with complete penetrance (see below). Although age of onset is variable, dementia and involuntary movements usually develop in early middle age and progress relentlessly to death 10-15 years later.
Hypoventilation	Reduced ventilation of the lungs
Hydrocephalus	Abnormal accumulation of CSF within the head
Hypertonia	Increased muscle tone (resistance to stretch)
Hypotonia	Low muscle tone
Hypocarbia	Low blood carbon dioxide pressure
Hypoperfusion	Abnormally low blood flow through a tissue
Hypertension	Increased blood pressure
Hypotension	Lowered blood pressure
Hysterosalpingography	A technique for radiological imaging of the uterus and the Fallopian tubes
Idiopathic	Without known cause
Illicit drugs	Those substances currently deemed to be illegal in terms of purchasing or consuming, and consisting largely of opiates (e.g. heroin, morphine, opium) or stimulants, such as cocaine (including the 'crack' form), amphetamines, 'ecstasy' (MDMA) or LSD (lysergic acid diethylamide) and similar hallucinogenics.
Imaging	The use of radiological techniques to produce pictures from which a diagnosis can be made
Incomplete penetrance	See 'penetrance' below

Inferior vena cava — The main vein which drains blood from the lower half of the body and returns it to the right side of the heart.

Inheritance pattern — Depending on the location and mode of action of the gene responsible, different conditions show different patterns within a family: Recessively inherited conditions require the disease (mutated) gene to be present on both of the pair of chromosomes before they manifest themselves. To be affected therefore both parents must carry the mutated gene and, on average, one in four of their children will be affected. Later generations will only be affected if there are further marriages between carriers. Rare recessive conditions occur more frequently in consanguineous marriages and hence in cultures where these are common. Dominantly inherited conditions need the disease (mutated) gene to be present in only one member of the chromosome pair in order to manifest themselves. These conditions are passed through the generations from parent to child. On average half the children of an affected parent will inherit the disease causing gene. X linked genes are those located on the X chromosome. In general (though there are exceptions) X linked 'disease' genes manifest themselves only in males. Females having two X chromosomes are usually protected by their normal X but can pass the genetic error on to their sons. On average half a carrier woman's sons will be affected and half her daughters will be carriers.

INR — International Normalized Ratio. Ratio by which a patient's clotting time differs from the expected time. In patients who are being anticoagulated it is thus a test which indicates their Warfarin requirement.

Intra-articular — Within a joint capsule

Intracerebral — In the brain substance

Intrapartum	During the process of labour and delivery
Intraventricular	Usually used of the brain, where it means in the fluid-filled chambers.
Intracranial pathology	Abnormalities within the brain such as a tumour or bleed
Intracranial pressure	The pressure inside the skull. As the skull of an adult is a closed box, if bleeding occurs inside the skull or if a tumour develops, then the pressure rises and causes such things as headaches, nausea, vomiting, visual disturbances, etc.
In utero	In the womb
In vitro fertilization (IVF)	A technique for fertilizing the egg outside the body.
Ionizing radiation	Radiation that can produce damage in living tissue
Ipsilateral	Same side
IRMER	Ionizing Radiation (Medical Exposure) Regulations 2000
Irritable hip	Tender hip with reduced movement and an effusion but no infection
Isotope study	Image produced by administering a radioactive agent to the patient and measuring the emissions on a gamma camera
IVU (Intravenous Urogram)	X-ray study with radio-contrast which gives hard-copy pictures of kidneys, ureters and bladder.
Karyotype	The chromosome make up of an individual. The normal human karyotype is either 46 XX (female) or 46 XY (male)
Kernig's/Brudzinski's signs	These are two tests which form part of a neurological examination where it is suspected that the patient has an intracranial problem such as meningitis or a subarchnoid

	haemorrhage. If either of these signs are positive, it is felt to indicate irritation of the membranes surrounding the brain, i.e. meningism.
Laparotomy	An exploratory operation of the abdomen
Laparoscope	An instrument for looking inside the abdomen.
Lateral	Side
Lithium	A mood stabilising drug, typically used for people with manic depressive disorder (bipolar affective disorder), as a means of preventing or minimising relapse. Regular blood tests are required in order to ensure the level in the blood is kept within a 'therapeutic' range.
Lipohaemarthrosis	A mixture of blood and fat in a joint
Lumbar	Of the lower back
Lymphoid tissue	Made up of lymph channels and lymph nodes – a filter to prevent the progression of infection.
Magnetic Resonance Imaging (MRI)	Cross-sectional image taken by applying a combination of a strong magnetic field and a radio wave
Mammogram	X-ray of the breast
Mastectomy	Surgical removal of the breast
Meconium	Green stool present in the fetal gut in the womb. Normally passed in the first 24 hours of life in a term infant
Medial	Towards the midline
Mediastinum	Central part of the thorax
Meninges	Layers of tissue surrounding the brain and spinal cord. Divided into 3 layers: Dura, Arachnoid and Pia

Mental Health Act 1983	The Act outlining the basis for detaining patients on an involuntary basis because of mental disorder. Grounds for detention include mental illness, psychopathy and mental subnormality, these being somewhat vague and outdated terms. Illnesses should be of a nature or degree to require treatment in hospital, and associated with risks to the patient's health or to the health and safety of other people. Patients may appeal to a Tribunal and the Act is overseen by the Mental Health Act Commission (MHAC).
Meningitis	Inflammation of the membranes surrounding the brain
Metaphysis	The growing bone proximal to the growth plate
Metastatic	Secondary deposits of cancer
Metformin	Oral drug given to control diabetes
Microcephaly	Where the head is smaller than normal with the implication that the brain also is smaller, so leading to learning difficulty of varying severity
Mitral incompetence	Where the mitral valve does not close properly, so allowing blood backwards in the system from the left ventricle to the left atrium
Mode of inheritance	The way in which a particular condition is known to be inherited (see inheritance pattern above).
Modelling	Change in bone shape through growth
Molecular test	A test using laboratory techniques based on knowledge of the genetic basis of the condition.
MRI	Magnetic Resonance Imaging
Muscular dystrophy	A group of diseases with varying severity and inheritance pattern, in which progressive

	muscular weakness is the predominant feature.
Mutation	A change in the sequence of the genetic material which (in the context of genetic disease) gives rise to incorrect information and resulting disease or malformation
Myeloma	Relatively common primary bone cancer
Myocardial Infarction (MI)	A heart attack. MIs can be divided into anterior or inferior. The anterior infarct is usually when the left anterior descending coronary artery is blocked. The inferior infarct is when the right coronary artery is blocked.
N (Newton)	A SI (system international) unit of force. I Newton is the force that produces an acceleration of 1 metre/sec2 on a mass of 1 Kg.
Natural history	The normal progression of a disease
Neonatal	From birth to the end of the fourth week of life
Neurosis	A form of mental disorder of lesser severity than a psychosis, but often associated with a degree of chronicity or a tendency to relapse. Typical conditions include anxiety, depression, obsessional compulsive disorder (OCD), panic disorders, and phobias.
Necrosis	Death of some or all of the cells in an organ caused by disease or other damage to the blood supply.
Nephrostomy	Tube inserted percutaneously to drain an obstructed kidney.
Nephrotic Syndrome	The triad of heavy proteinuria, reduced serum protein and oedema, often caused by glomerulonephritis or severe diabetes.
Nerve entrapment	Any nerve can become incorporated in healing scar tissue, resulting in nerve

	entrapment syndrome. Sometimes the nerve is incorporated in a suture, again giving rise to an entrapment syndrome.
Neurofibromatosis	A dominantly inherited disease (see above) with variable penetrance (see below). Its features include 'café au lait' patches on the skin, tumours called neurofibromatas which may become malignant and mild learning difficulty.
Non-steroidal anti-inflammatory drugs (NSAIDs)	Popular, over the counter pain killing medication for musculo-skeletal problems which may cause chronic renal failure.
Obsessional Compulsive Disorder (OCD)	A condition dominated by thoughts in the form of obsessions, which constantly recur, but which cannot be put out of one's mind, even though one knows their content is unlikely to be true. Persistent ruminations, and a resort to 'compulsive' rituals (e.g. hand-washing) are characteristic features.
Oesophagus	Gullet or foodpipe
Olfactory groove	Bony channel within the skull above the nose where the olfactory nerves lie
Organic	A term indicating that a particular condition has an established physical basis (e.g. brain damage).
Orthogonal	At perpendicular planes
Ortolani	Test used to detect developmental dysplasia of the hip
Oscillation	Rhythmic molecular vibration
Osteo-arthritis	Degenerative change in a joint
Osteomyelitis	Infected bone
Osteoporosis	Reduction in normal bone density
Osteosarcoma	Form of bone cancer seen particularly in adolescents

PACS	Electronic records system
Oxygen saturation	Measure of the percentage of available oxygen in the blood. The normal measure is 100%
Papilloedema	Swelling of the optic nerve head, usually indicating raised intracranial pressure
Paranoia	A state of mind in which the patient experiences a special relationship with the world or persons around, the coincidental becoming significant. Paranoid delusions can therefore be not only persecutory, but also grandiose, involving morbid jealousy or other attitudes to relationships, or even somatic (related to bodily function or shape).
Paraplegia	Paralysis of the lower limbs
Parenchymal	In the substance of the tissue
Parenterally	Given into the vascular system
Patent ductus arteriosus	The ductus arteriosus is a vessel which links the aorta to the pulmonary artery, necessary in fetal life to permit the circulation of oxygenated blood to the body. In fetal life it is patent, only closing after birth
Pathology	The branch of medicine concerned with the physical abnormalities (often microscopic) associated with disease, i.e. how things go wrong.
Pedicle	Part of the lateral structure in a vertebra
Penetrance	The occurrence of a condition with a basically genetic causation may be influenced by other variables, such as other genes or environmental factors so that the degree to which the gene manifests itself is very variable even within the same family. This is known as variable penetrance. A condition is said to be fully penetrant if the presence of the 'disease' gene always gives rise to the full manifestation of the condition.

Peptic ulcer	An ulcer occurring in the stomach or duodenum.
Perinatal	From the completion of the 24th week of gestation to the end of the first week of life
Peritoneal cavity	The abdominal cavity, which is lined by a fine membrane, the peritoneum.
Periventricular (leucomalacia)	Periventricular refers to the tissue adjacent to the lateral cerebral ventricles. Leucomalacia refers to infarcted tissue
Personality Disorder (PD)	A controversial diagnosis, describing "deeply ingrained maladaptive patterns of behaviour" from adolescence onwards, resulting in a persisting disruption of social relationships, and often associated with low impulse control. Common forms include 'Antisocial' (aka 'Psychopathy') and 'Borderline'.
Perthes Disease	A childhood hip disease due to idiopathic avascular necrosis
Phobia (see also agoraphobia)	An intense fear, outwith the actual threat involved, into which a patient has insight, but which nevertheless leads to avoidance of the feared object. Simple phobias (e.g. of snakes, spiders) rarely intrude significantly on normal social functioning.
Photophobia	Increased sensitivity to light
Physis	Growth plate
Piezo-electric	A crystal that vibrates when an electrical charge is passed through it and vice versa
Pituitary	Hormone producing gland at the base of the brain
Plain film	Image taken using conventional x-rays
Pneumonia	Infection of the lung
Pneumothorax	Air between the lung and the inside of the ribcage, indicating a punctured lung

Posteroanterior	From the back of the patient to the front
Polyuria	Excessive rate of urine flow
Porencephaly	A cyst within the cerebral substance, usually connecting with the ventricular system. Some authorities restrict this term to describe the cleft in the developmental abnormality schizencephaly, though this is not the common usage
Post-Traumatic Stress Disorder (PTSD)	A pattern of symptoms including flashbacks, nightmares, enhanced arousability, depression and social withdrawal deriving from an intense 'traumatising' experience, in which one's life has been endangered, or certainly perceived as at risk. Train or car crashes, or serious assaults, are the common traumatic precursors
Preimplantation genetic diagnosis (PGD)	A diagnostic test done on cell(s) taken from the ball of cells derived from IVF (see above) before implantation.
Prenatal	Prior to birth
Proband	The affected family member who was first identified as having the genetic condition causing concern. (Also sometimes known as 'the propositus').
Probe	A known sequence of genetic material which can be chemically labelled and used to identify other specific sequences.
Prosthesis	Artificial anatomical substitute
Proximal	Closer to the patient's central axis
Psychosis	The term describing forms of serious mental illness, such as schizophrenia or manic depression, which lead to loss of contact with reality due, for example, to delusional beliefs or hallucinations.
Psychotherapy	The term describing all types of treatment that use psychological methods (i.e. 'talking

	treatments'). Specific forms of psychotherapy include psychoanalysis, cognitive behaviour therapy, and variants around these approaches.
Pulmonary artery	The main blood vessel taking de-oxygenated blood to the lungs, where it is re-oxygenated, returned to the left side of the heart and distributed around the body.
Pulmonary embolus	A clot in the pulmonary vessels
Pulmonary hypoplasia	Insufficient growth of the lungs to permit adequate oxygenation after birth
Pulmonary trunk	Main central lung vessels
Pyelonephritis	Infection in the kidney
Radiograph	Image taken using conventional x-rays
Radiographer	A technician trained to acquire images
Radiologist	A doctor trained in acquiring and interpreting diagnostic images
Radiolusent	Lets x-rays through. Appearing dark on an x-ray
Radio-opaque	Does not let x-rays through. Appearing white on an x-ray
Radius	Main forearm bone
Recessive inheritance	*see below* 'Inheritance pattern'
Red reflex	Flash of red reflected from the normal retina looked at with an ophthalmoscope
Resuscitaire	Equipment for the resuscitation of babies with a platform for the baby, a heater, stop watch, oxygen and suction
Retina	Membrane at the back of the eye containing the nervous tissue for sight

Retinoblastoma	A genetically determined tumour of the retina at the back of the eye which arises in infancy and can lead to blindness if not recognized and treated early.
Sagittal	Front to back anatomical plane
Scaphoid	Bone in the wrist situated at the base of the thumb
Sciatica	Sciatica is a symptom found in various back problems such as a prolapsed intravertebral disc (slipped disc). It is caused by pressure upon the nerve supply to the affected leg, the pain appearing to run down the course of the sciatic nerve. The patient complaints of back pain, which radiates down into the buttock and thigh or even right down into the foot.
Sclerotherapy	An injection technique for destroying the lining of a vein, causing it to become completely obliterated.
Seizures	Fits
Septic arthritis	Infected joints
Septicaemia	Bacteria in the blood
Sequela	Any disorder that results from a preceding disease or accident.
Sidmoidoscopy	Use of a rigid or flexible instrument which can be passed through the anus to examine the rectum.
Smith Lemli Opitz syndrome	A rare recessively inherited (see above) condition whose features include cleft palate, microcephaly (see above) extra fingers and learning difficulty.
Somatization	The tendency of some patients to present with and describe physical symptoms, when consulting doctors, rather than express psychological distress. This may reflect the very physical nature of some individuals' experience of psychiatric disorder, as well as

	cultural attitudes and the stigma associated with mental illness.
Spasticity	A characteristic of muscles where there is a velocity dependant increased resistance to passive stretch
SSRIs (Specific Serotonin Uptake Inhibitors)	A group of drugs, acting on serotonin, a neurochemical found in many areas of the brain. Having fewer side-effects than older antidepressants, and being safe in overdose, they have been widely prescribed (see also Antidepressants).
Stenosed	A stenosis is a narrowing. The term is usually applied to blood vessels, which are narrowed by the accumulation of fatty deposits known as atheroma, and to the spinal canal, causing compression of the spinal cord
Steroid	Anti-inflammatory drug
STIR weighting	MRI sequence designed to suppress the signal from fat and enhance pathology
Strangulated hernia	A hernia where the blood supply has been cut off.
Subarachnoid	Lying under the arachnoid membrane covering the brain
Subchondral	Bone immediately below the cartilage layer
Subdural	Lying under the dural membrane covering the brain
SUFE	Slipped upper femoral epiphysis. A condition where the epiphysis moves inferiorly and posteriorly relative to the metaphysis
Supracondylar	Above the condyles (elbow or knee)
Syndrome	A combination of clinical features that add up to a recognised entity.
T1 weighting	MRI sequence designed to make water based structures appear grey

T2 weighting	MRI sequence designed to make pathology and water based structures appear bright
Tachycardia	Abnormally rapid heart rate
Tetraplegia	Total body spasticity or dyskinesia
Thalassaemia	A recessively inherited (see above) form of anaemia occurring in childhood and leading to progressive ill health and premature death.
Thallium Scanning	Isotope test in which thallium is taken up by the heart but disappears under exercise or stress in ischaemic areas of tissue
Therapeutic alliance	The term used to describe the rapport that doctors and patients try to establish, so as to enhance trust, insight and compliance with treatment.
Thorax	Chest
Thrombolytic	A drug which dissolves blood clots, e.g. Streptokinase.
Tibia	Main lower leg bone
Tibial plateau	The weight-bearing part of the tibia at the knee
Tocolysis	Reduction in uterine contraction
Tonic clonic epilepsy	Formerly known as grand mal epilepsy. Generalised fit consisting of a stiff phase (tonic) followed by a jerking phase (clonic)
Trabeculae	Internal bony micro-anatomy
Trachea	Windpipe
Tranquillisers	A group of drugs aimed at sedating patients but often also used for insomnia. Benzodiazepines such as Diazepam (Valium) are the commonest prescribed today, are very effective anti-anxiety agents, but have considerable dependence potential. Cautious prescribing over the short-term is standard.

Tricyclics	The older type of antidepressant such as Amitriptyline or Imipramine, in use since the '60s. Side-effects such as dry mouth and sedation can limit their use (especially in the elderly), and they can be dangerous in overdose (see also Antidepressants and SSRIs).
Tracheo-oesophageal fistula	A congenital malformation in which there is a connection between the trachea (wind-pipe) and oesophagus (gullet). The oesophagus often ends as a blind pouch, failing to join up with the stomach
Transillumination	Lighting from behind
Translocation	A condition in which part of one chromosome is attached to a different chromosome. This may be balanced (where the total chromosome complement is normal) or unbalanced (where there is either excess or missing chromosomal material). Unbalanced translocations are associated with significant defects
Transphenoidal	Surgical approach through the sphenoid bone
Trisomy	The presence of three instead of two chromosomes (see above) of any particular chromosome pair.
Trimester	Stage of pregnancy. There are three trimesters, each of 3 months.
Tuberose sclerosis	A dominantly inherited (see above) condition with very variable penetrance (see above). Features include severe epilepsy, learning difficulty and hyperactivity and unusual pale skin patches.
Tubo-ovarian abscess	A collection of pus involving the fallopian tubes and the ovaries.
Ultrasound	Image taken using sound waves
Variable penetrance	*See above* 'Penetrance'

Varicose veins	Dilated superficial veins.
Vasa praevia	Abnormal presentation of fetal umbilical cord where the fetal blood vessels lie across the membranes before forming the umbilical cord. Vessels are susceptible to rupture causing acute usually severe fetal blood loss
Vasculature	Network of blood vessels
Vascularisation	The development of a blood supply
Vasculitis	Widespread inflammation of arteries which can cause acute or chronic renal failure and a systemic illness which often responds dramatically to treatment with steroids.
Vasospasm	Spasm and consequent narrowing of blood vessels
Venous closure	A technique for closing the long saphenous vein, using either electrical current or a laser.
Ventricles	Fluid chambers in the brain containing cerebral spinal fluid: Heart chambers
Ventricular septal defect (VSD)	A hole in the membrane between the two pumping heart chambers
Vesico-ureteric reflux (VUR)	Congenital abnormality where the ureter enters the bladder so that voiding of urine causes reflux up to the kidney with the possibility of infection and renal damage.
Xanthochromia	Staining of CSF due to the presence of altered blood

INDEX